T0185393

Intel® Galileo and Intel® Galileo Gen 2

API Features and Arduino Projects for Linux Programmers

Manoel Carlos Ramon

Intel® Galileo and Intel® Galileo Gen 2: API Features and Arduino Projects for Linux Programmers

Manoel Carlos Ramon

Copyright © 2014 by Apress Media, LLC, all rights reserved

ApressOpen Rights: You have the right to copy, use and distribute this Work in its entirety, electronically without modification, for non-commercial purposes only. However, you have the additional right to use or alter any source code in this Work for any commercial or non-commercial purpose which must be accompanied by the licenses in (2) and (3) below to distribute the source code for instances of greater than 5 lines of code. Licenses (1), (2) and (3) below and the intervening text must be provided in any use of the text of the Work and fully describes the license granted herein to the Work.

(1) **License for Distribution of the Work:** This Work is copyrighted by Apress Media, LLC, all rights reserved. Use of this Work other than as provided for in this license is prohibited. By exercising any of the rights herein, you are accepting the terms of this license. You have the non-exclusive right to copy, use and distribute this English language Work in its entirety, electronically without modification except for those modifications necessary for formatting on specific devices, for all non-commercial purposes, in all media and formats known now or hereafter. While the advice and information in this Work are believed to be true and accurate at the date of publication, neither the authors nor the editors nor the publisher can accept any legal responsibility for any errors or omissions that may be made. The publisher makes no warranty, express or implied, with respect to the material contained herein.

If your distribution is solely Apress source code or uses Apress source code intact, the following licenses (2) and (3) must accompany the source code. If your use is an adaptation of the source code provided by Apress in this Work, then you must use only license (3).

(2) **License for Direct Reproduction of Apress Source Code:** This source code, from *Intel® Galileo and Intel® Galileo Gen 2: API Features and Arduino Projects for Linux Programmers, ISBN 978-1-4302-6839-0* is copyrighted by Apress Media, LLC, all rights reserved. Any direct reproduction of this Apress source code is permitted but must contain this license. The following license must be provided for any use of the source code from this product of greater than 5 lines wherein the code is adapted or altered from its original Apress form. This Apress code is presented AS IS and Apress makes no claims to, representations or warrantees as to the function, usability, accuracy or usefulness of this code.

(3) **License for Distribution of Adaptation of Apress Source Code:** Portions of the source code provided are used or adapted from *Intel® Galileo and Intel® Galileo Gen 2: API Features and Arduino Projects for Linux Programmers, ISBN 978-1-4302-6839-0* copyright Apress Media LLC. Any use or reuse of this Apress source code must contain this License. This Apress code is made available at Apress.com/9781430268390 as is and Apress makes no claims to, representations or warrantees as to the function, usability, accuracy or usefulness of this code.

ISBN-13 (pbk): 978-1-4302-6839-0

ISBN-13 (electronic): 978-1-4302-6838-3

Trademarked names, logos, and images may appear in this book. Rather than use a trademark symbol with every occurrence of a trademarked name, logo, or image we use the names, logos, and images only in an editorial fashion and to the benefit of the trademark owner, with no intention of infringement of the trademark.

The use in this publication of trade names, trademarks, service marks, and similar terms, even if they are not identified as such, is not to be taken as an expression of opinion as to whether or not they are subject to proprietary rights.

While the advice and information in this book are believed to be true and accurate at the date of publication, neither the authors nor the editors nor the publisher can accept any legal responsibility for any errors or omissions that may be made. The publisher makes no warranty, express or implied, with respect to the material contained herein.

Managing Director: Welmoed Spahr
Associate Publisher: Jeffrey Pepper
Lead Editors: Steve Weiss (Apress); Patrick Hauke (Intel)
Coordinating Editor: Melissa Maldonado
Cover Designer: Anna Ishchenko

Distributed to the book trade worldwide by Springer Science+Business Media New York, 233 Spring Street, 6th Floor, New York, NY 10013. Phone 1-800-SPRINGER, fax (201) 348-4505, e-mail orders-ny@springer-sbm.com, or visit www.springeronline.com.

For information on translations, please e-mail rights@apress.com, or visit www.apress.com.

About ApressOpen

What Is ApressOpen?

- ApressOpen is an open access book program that publishes high-quality technical and business information.

- ApressOpen eBooks are available for global, free, noncommercial use.

- ApressOpen eBooks are available in PDF, ePub, and Mobi formats.

- The user-friendly ApressOpen free eBook license is presented on the copyright page of this book.

This book is dedicated to my children—Mariana, Gabriela, and Matheus—and my lovely wife Najla, for their patience during several late nights and working weekends.

Contents at a Glance

About the Author xix

About the Technical Reviewers xxi

Acknowledgments xxiii

Introduction xxv

■Chapter 1: Intel Galileo and Intel Galileo Gen 2 1

■Chapter 2: Native Development 35

■Chapter 3: Arduino IDE and Wiring Language 93

■Chapter 4: New APIs and Hacks 145

■Chapter 5: Networking and Hacks 217

■Chapter 6: Tweeting with REST API 1.1 289

■Chapter 7: Using OpenCV 319

■Chapter 8: Creating a Soil Moisture Sensor 401

■Chapter 9: Home Automation and Dynamic Web 425

■Chapter 10: Power over Ethernet (PoE) 499

■Chapter 11: Assembling and Controlling a Robotic Arm 509

■Chapter 12: Using an LTE Modem 579

■Appendix A: Intel Galileo I/O and Muxing 605

■Appendix B: Intel Galileo Gen 2 I/O and Muxing 611

■Appendix C: Video Capturing 617

■Appendix D: Picture Grabber 633

Index 643

Contents

About the Author xix

About the Technical Reviewers xxi

Acknowledgments xxiii

Introduction xxv

■Chapter 1: Intel Galileo and Intel Galileo Gen 2 1

The Beginnings.. 1

About this Book 2

Why Use Intel Galileo Boards?.. 3

The Software Advantages... 4

The Hardware Advantages.. 4

Hardware Overview.. 6

The Processor: Intel Quark SoC X1000 6

Introducing Intel Galileo.. 8

Introducing Intel Galileo Gen 2... 17

Preparing Your Cables 23

The Serial Cable for Intel Galileo 24

The Serial Cable for Intel Galileo Gen 2 26

Testing the Serial Cables 27

Exploring the Linux Console 32

Testing the Data Cables.. 33

Summary.. 33

■**Chapter 2: Native Development** **35**

Introduction to the Yocto Build System **35**

Yocto and this Book 36

Creating Your Own Intel Galileo Images **44**

Preparing Your Computer 44

The SPI vs. SD Card Images 46

Building Intel Galileo Images 47

Building and Using the Cross-Compiler Toolchain 52

Creating a Hello World! 56

Debugging Native Applications 59

Booting Intel Galileo with Your Own Images **59**

Booting from SD Card Images 59

Booting from SPI Card Images 64

What to Do If Intel Galileo Bricks **90**

Summary **91**

■**Chapter 3: Arduino IDE and Wiring Language** **93**

A Little Bit of History **93**

The Intel Makers Community **94**

Installing the Arduino IDE for Intel Galileo **94**

Connecting Intel Galileo **96**

Installing the Drivers and the Arduino IDE **97**

Installing the Arduino IDE 97

Installing the IDE on Linux 98

Installing the Drivers 99

Understanding the Arduino IDE **101**

Checking the Port and Board Selected **103**

What Is a Sketch?..105

Compiling and Running the Sketch 106

Persisted and Not Persisted Sketches...107

Persisted Sketches and Long Time to Start..107

Debugging with Serial Console and Serial Communication 108

Serial.begin(int speed)...108

Serial.print(data) 108

Serial.println(data) 108

Serial.available() 109

Serial.read()..109

Printing Debug Messages and Using the Serial Console 109

The Arduino Language Reference and APIs...111

Structure..112

Digital I/O...113

Analog I/O 113

Time...115

Running Some Examples...116

Fade Example 116

Button Example 119

ReadAnalogVoltage Example 122

The Debounce Example 124

Updating the Firmware Using the IDE 127

Updating the Firmware with Different Firmware...129

Troubleshooting the Drivers 130

Serial Communication Issues with IDE on Windows..130

IDE Problems with Virtual Machines and 64-Bit Linux.......................................135

Communicating Sketches with Linux Native Programs 136

   is.Additionalfuture Project Example: Unread Email Alarm with Python
   and POSIX Functions 137

Summary...143

■Chapter 4: New APIs and Hacks 145

Servo API...145

   The Theory versus Practice 145

   The Mistake with Intel Galileo and Servos 150

   What Is New in Servo API? 152

Serial, Serial1, and Serial2 Objects 157

   Testing the Serial, Serial1, and Serial2 Objects.......................................157

Improving the I/O Speed...162

   The New APIs for I/O..163

The Tone API 184

   What's New in the Tone API? 184

The pulseIn API..188

   unsigned long pulseIn(uint8_t pin, uint8_t state, unsigned
   long timeout = 1000000)..188

   What's New with pulseIn()...189

   A Sample Running pulseIn() 189

Hacks 190

   Hacking the Servo Library..190

   Hacking the GPIO Expander for New PWM Frequencies...............................191

   Single Code for Intel Galileo and Intel Galileo Gen 2..................................194

Project: DHT Sensor Library with Fast I/O APIs 195

   Materials List..195

   The DHT Sensor..195

A Workaround Using Tri-State Buffers 198

Creating a New Library for DHT11 Sensor 202

Summary 216

■Chapter 5: Networking and Hacks 217

WiFi Cards 218

Setting Up the WiFi Mini-PCIe Card 218

Checking if the WiFi Card Was Recognized 222

Adding Support to a New WiFi Card 222

The WiFi API 224

Scanning the Wireless Networks 225

Connecting to the WPA or WEB 230

Hacking the WiFi Library 239

Step 1: Setting Up the WiFi Connection 239

Step 2: Restart the Wireless Connection 242

Step 3: Hacking the WiFi Class 243

Ethernet API 247

What's New with Ethernet API and Intel Galileo 248

Ethernet Example: Network Time Protocol (NTP) 248

Dynamic and Static IP Using Ethernet 253

Simplifying the Sketches by Removing the Ethernet Objects 271

Transferring Files Between Intel Galileo and Computers 271

Using ftp 272

Using scp or pscp 273

Using an SD Card 273

Using a USB Pen Drive 274

Hacking the IDE to Improve the Sketch Transfer 276

How the Hacked IDE Works 277

Hacking the Transfers 279

Summary 287

■Chapter 6: Tweeting with REST API 1.1 289

Project Details 289

Material List 290

System and Hardware Clock 290

Assembling the Coin Battery 292

Workaround with 1.5V Batteries 293

Creating a Twitter Application Account 294

Step 1: Creating Your Twitter Account 294

Step 2: Creating the Twitter Application 296

Creating a Script to Post Messages on Twitter 301

Step 1: Identifying the API 301

Step 2: Generating the OAuth Signature with the OAuth Tool 303

Step 3: Creating a Script to Post on Twitter with Intel Galileo 308

Step 4: Creating a Sketch that Tweets 312

Ideas for Improving the Project 315

Flowers and Plants Communicating with You on a Social Network 315

Summary 318

■Chapter 7: Using OpenCV 319

OpenCV Primer 319

Project Details 320

Materials List 321

USB Video Class 322

Preparing the BSP Software Image and Toolchain 323

Using eGlibc for Video4Linux Image 324

Increasing the rootfs Size 324

Disabling GPU Support on OpenCV 324

Building the SD Image and Toolchain 325

Development Library Packages 325

Connecting the Webcam 326

Introduction to Video4Linux 327

Exploring the Webcam Capabilities with V4L2-CTL 327

Changing and Reading Camera Properties 329

Pixel Formats and Resolution 330

Capturing Videos and Images with libv4l2 333

A Program for Capturing Video 333

A Program to Capture Images 347

Working with OpenCV 352

Building Programs with OpenCV 353

Capturing an Image with OpenCV 353

The Same Software Written in Python 359

Processing Images 360

Detecting Edges 361

Face and Eyes Detection 364

Emotions Classification 372

Ideas for Improving the Project 399

Integrating Your Emotions with a Robotic Head 400

Expanding the Classifications 400

Improving the Emotion Classification Using Large Databases 400

Improving the Emotion Classification for Several Faces 400

Summary 400

■**Chapter 8: Creating a Soil Moisture Sensor** **401**

Project Details **401**

Material List **402**

Assembling the Moisture Sensors **403**

Mechanical Assembly 403

Electrical Assembly 404

Assembling the Flower Face **406**

Testing the Flower Face with the Software 410

Reviewing the Code 413

Running the Project **416**

Calibration Procedure 416

Ideas for Improving the Project **421**

Increasing the Number of Sensors 421

Automatic Irrigation 421

Using Appropriate Wires 423

Using a Commercial Sensor 423

Tweeting 424

Summary **424**

■**Chapter 9: Home Automation and Dynamic Web** **425**

Project Details **425**

The Software Architecture 426

Materials List **428**

Integrating the Components Individually **428**

Testing the Keypad 428

Testing the PIR Sensor 438

The PIR Sensor Connection 440

Testing the YwRobot Relay Module 443

Testing the TMP36 Temperature Sensor 447

Creating the Sketch 451

Sending UDP Messages 451

Receiving UDP Messages 452

Joining All Code in a Single Sketch 455

Creating Your Own Web Server with node.js 465

Updating node.js 465

About the npm 467

Installing Cheerio 469

Installing socket.io 469

The Web Page 470

Writing the Web Server Code 474

Running the Home Automation System 486

Ideas for Improving the Project 489

Power of Ethernet (PoE) 489

Using express and node.js 489

Changing the Web Page and Web Server Without Experience with the Web 490

Creating an Analogic Keypad and Having More I/Os Available 495

Adding a Username and Password 497

Using the DHT11 Sensor 497

Summary 497

■Chapter 10: Power over Ethernet (PoE) 499

Project Details 499

Materials List 500

Assembling the PoE Module 500

Powering On with the PoE Injector 504

How It Works 506

Ideas for Improving the Project 506

Summary 507

■Chapter 11: Assembling and Controlling a Robotic Arm 509

An introduction to Robotic Arm Theory 510

Using an Online Tool to Calculate Your Servos.................................... 514

Considerations About This Project 516

The Robotic Arm.. 516

Assembling the Robotic Arm 519

Step 1: Preparing the Servos.. 521

Step 2: Assembling the Base 522

Step 3: Assembling the Shoulder... 526

Step 4: Assembling the Elbow 528

Step 5: Assembling the Wrist.. 531

Step 6: Assembling the Mechanical Gripper... 532

Step 7: Assembling a Base 535

Controlling the Robotic Arm 537

Building a Servo Control Board... 538

The Hardware 538

Assembling the Board 544

The Software 547

A Gripper Based on Coffee and a Balloon... 570

Preparing the Coffee Gripper... 573

A Sketch for the Coffee Gripper.. 575

Ideas for Improving this Project 577

Summary... 577

■Chapter 12: Using an LTE Modem 579

An Introduction to XMM7160 and XMM7260...................................... 580

Project Details 581

Materials List... 581

Considerations Related to Antennas 582

Preparing the Hardware 583

Step 1: Preparing the SIM Card 583

Step 2: The NGFF/mPCIe Adaptor 585

Step 3: Adapting the Modem Card 586

Step 4: Connecting the Antennas.. 587

Step 5: Connecting the Modem to Intel Galileo.......................... 588

Preparing the Software 589

Step 1: Checking the Modem... 589

Step 2: Loading the CDC-ACM Driver... 590

Step 3: Checking if the Modem Responds to AT Commands 591

Step 4: Checking the SIM Card Connection 592

Step 5: Configuring the APN and Attaching it to the Network........... 593

Step 6: Creating an IP Interface with pppd................................. 596

Step 7: Testing the Internet Connection...................................... 600

Testing the Internet Bandwidth 600

Why Aren't the Download/Upload Bandwidths Optimal?................ 601

Ideas for Improving the Project 601

Improving the Chat Script... 601

Loading the cdc-acm Driver Automatically.................................. 603

Summary 604

■Appendix A: Intel Galileo I/O and Muxing 605

■Appendix B: Intel Galileo Gen 2 I/O and Muxing 611

■Appendix C: Video Capturing 617

■Appendix D: Picture Grabber 633

Index.. 643

About the Author

Manoel Carlos Ramon was born in Brazil. He started learning software programming when he was 11 years old, using a TK-85—an 8-bit computer based on a Z80 processor with only 16KB of RAM. His passion for programming and understanding computers started with watching *Bit & Bytes*, a Canadian TV series that aired on TV Cultura, a Brazilian public TV network.

A few years later, Manoel created his first pirate FM transmitter that, instead of music, transmitted programs written in Basic to exchange software saved on cassette tapes with his friends via radio. He created his first commercial software in 1986, at age 13. This was software for storage control, written in DbaseII and running on a CP500/M80 computer. He learned and programmed in Z80 Assembler using his first MSX computer in 1988. Later he bought an IBM PC XT with an Intel 8080 processor, on which he created the first Brazilian software able to compute with precision the lux intensity of irregular surfaces based on photometric curves, written in Turbo C.

Manoel earned a BsSc in electric engineering in 1996, graduating with honors. He has been working in research and development of mobile devices and tablets since graduation. Manoel contributed to porting the first Java virtual machine fully certified by Sun Microsystems in Motorola phones. He has also worked with Linux kernel and device drivers, J2ME, Android NDK/SDK/ADK, audio path, power management, and modem 2G/3G/4G integration, including the first tablet with an LTE modem released in South America.

Manoel has worked on several projects in the Americas, Asia, and Europe. He migrated to the United States in 2011. Manoel is currently part of Intel Corporation's New Devices Group, where he is a member of the team responsible for the development of the Intel Galileo, the Intel Galileo Gen 2, and the Intel Edison Kit for Arduino.

Manoel lives in California with his wife and children. He admires Dr. Steve Mann, who is considered the real father of wearable computers, and David Rolfe, a notable Assembler programmer who created classic arcade games in the 1980s.

About the Technical Reviewers

Krzysztof Sywula joined the Intel Corporation in 2010. He was initially assigned to the LAN Access Division, which provided him a background in UEFI and the Ethernet. He joined the Quark Software team in 2012, where he works on different areas of the chip, gaining an extensive and deep understanding of the workflows of low-level components.

Dino Tinitigan graduated from the University of Nevada Las Vegas (UNLV) with a BS in computer engineering. He is currently a software engineer for Intel, working on maker boards like the Galileo and the Edison. In his spare time he tinkers with robotics, home automation, and wearables.

Acknowledgments

Many people contributed in different ways along the process of writing this book. I hereby express my deepest gratitude to them:

The Apress team, who made this book possible, especially Melissa Maldonado, James Markham, and Steve Weiss.

Patrick Hauke, the Intel Technology Book Program Manager who believed in me and in the idea of this book.

Dino Tinitigan and Krzysztof Sywula for their excellent contributions on this book as technical reviewers, and also as part of the Intel Galileo development team.

Jorgen Ostulan and Dan Nguyen for their support with antenna selections for LTE frequencies and XMM7160 modem information.

Kevin Clarke for his collaboration as tester and developer, going deeply into the Linux signals issues.

Daniel O'Donovan for his amazing collaboration in developing not only the Arduino IDE, but also Linux drivers.

Francis Crowe and Srikanth Vasuki for the fantastic job designing, supporting, and validating the Intel Galileo Gen 2 hardware.

I would especially like to say that I am very thankful to the whole open source community that works continuously on the Linux operation system and on the Arduino IDE. Of course, I could not list all names here, but I would like to express my gratitude in a Linux bash terminal:

```
cd $LINUX_REPOSITORIES; git log --pretty=format:"%an"|sort -u
cd $ARDUINO_REPOSITORIES; git log --pretty=format:"%an"|sort -u
```

Introduction

The Intel Galileo maker development board was announced on October 4, 2013 at the Rome Maker Fair. It was the first for the Intel Corporation. The board was based on the Intel Quark SoC X1000 application processor, powered by Linux OS, and compatible with Arduino reference APIs. The Intel Galileo introduced several extra software and hardware features that exceeded most other Arduino boards available on the market.

Intel received thousands of feedback comments from makers on Intel's Maker forums. Based on this feedback, Intel later unveiled the Intel Galileo Gen 2, a new version with the same Intel Quark SoC application processor but improved hardware.

This book discusses the hardware and the software for the Intel Galileo and the Intel Galileo Gen 2, introducing Arduino reference APIs and APIs created especially for Intel Galileo boards. Practical projects show how to make use of the Linux capabilities and to aggregate this potential in Arduino sketches.

What Is in this Book?

Chapter 1 discusses the hardware design of the Intel Galileo and the Intel Galileo Gen 2, as well as the construction of serial and FTDI cables for debugging using Linux terminal consoles.

Chapter 2 explains how the Yocto build system works and how to generate your custom SPI and SD card images. It also presents how to compile, install, and use the toolchains for native applications development, and discusses procedures to recover bricked Intel Galileo boards.

Chapter 3 shows how to install and use the Arduino IDE, and how to install the drivers needed in the computer or virtual machine used, running real examples of interacting sketches with simple circuits. It also brings a practical project that integrates Python, POSIX calls, and sketches to send an alert when an email is received.

Chapter 4 discusses the new APIs and hacking techniques created especially for the Intel Galileo and Intel Galileo Gen 2 boards. It contains a broad discussion of clusters architecture, and how GPIOs are distributed and their respective speed limits. A practical project demonstrates how to overcome the Intel Galileo's limitations and how to make the DHT11 temperature sensor work.

Chapter 5 presents networking APIs and hackings using an Ethernet adapter and WiFi mPCIe cards. It also explains how to install new WiFi cards and how to share Internet access between the Intel Galileo and computers. This chapter also explains how to hack the Arduino IDE to download sketches using network interfaces instead of a USB.

Chapter 6 offers a practical project on tweeting using Intel Galileo boards with new OAuth authentication and without intermediary computers or servers. The project uses a RTC (real-time clock) with external coin batteries and WiFi mPCIe cards.

Chapter 7 shows techniques using V42L and OpenCV libraries, as well as how to capture images and videos and detect facial expressions and emotions using a webcam. This chapter also explains how to change the Linux BSD to support eglibc instead uClibc and to generate the toolchain to compile C/C++ programs. There are also examples of OpenCV in Python.

Chapter 8 presents a low-cost project to create moisture sensors based in scrap materials and galvanized nails.

Chapter 9 shows a practical home automation project implementing a web server using node.js, interacting with multiple sensors for motion and temperature, and using keypads and switch relays.

Chapter 10 explains how to install and use PoE (Power of Ethernet) modules with the Intel Galileo Gen 2.

Chapter 11 discusses basic principles in robotics and how to design and control a robotic arm using analog controllers. It also presents a practical project using a 6 DOF robotic arm with a mechanical gripper and another one built with ground coffee.

Chapter 12 discusses how to connect a XMM 7160 LTE modem and use data channels in real networks using Intel Galileo boards.

Chapter 13 is a bonus chapter available online. It presents a practical project on how to design and build a low-cost robot head with animatronic eyes and a mouth that expresses emotions. This chapter is available online at http://www.apress.com/9781430268390, under the Source Code/Downloads tab.

■ ■ ■

## CHAPTER 1

Intel Galileo and Intel Galileo Gen 2

Intel is committed to providing the ultimate processors, boards, and tools to its community. The first initiative by Intel is the introduction of Intel Galileo and Intel Galileo Gen 2 boards, which are compatible with the Arduino headers and reference APIs. They also opened the Intel maker forum and created Intel Arduino IDE.

Intel Galileo boards are open source and open hardware; in other words, all the source code and hardware schematics are available online, which you can download, use, and modify.

This chapter describes Intel's focus on the Galileo boards. With those in your toolbox, the only other things you need are passion and creativity.

The Beginnings

There are those who believe the social behavior of mankind is directly connected to the progress of technology.

Walt Disney created his first movie in 1923 in his garage, Steve Jobs and Steve Wozniak developed the first Apple computer in a garage located at 2066 Crist Drive in Los Altos, California, Bill Hewlett and Dave Packard founded HP with $500 in a garage, and the first Harley-Davidson was built in a 10x15-foot wooden garage in 1903. Perhaps the next greatest invention will be created in someone's garage.

All of those inventions have a common factor, which is the convergence of different areas, such as art, mechanics, electronics, and computer science. They involved creativity and passion.

Inventors are makers, and they have existed since the beginning of time when our ancestors started creating tools to fish, to hunt, to make fires, and to draw on cave walls. They created inventions like the wheel and the robot connected to your WiFi that vacuums your carpet.

All of us are makers because we have all created or developed something to make our lives easier and faster. Creativity is intrinsic to human nature.

Nowadays, the makers create robots and drones, automate their houses, make devices to communicate each other, create art that mixes with technology, design and print in 3D their own objects including musical instruments, and more. Figure 1-1 shows a guitar that was 3D printed and developed by ODD guitars (http://www.oddguitars.com/).

Figure 1-1. *A real 3D printed guitar model Atom by ODD guitars*

Intel provides new tiny and powerful processors, low power maker boards, and the tools using the top of technology.

Intel also provides a public Internet forum for makers, not only to support and answer questions but also to help with personal projects and listen to the community. They receive valuable feedback that enables them to create a new generation of products and tools.

Intel Galileo and Intel Galileo Gen 2 are powered by Intel Quark System-on-Chip (SoC) x1000 at 400MHz, with 512MB SRAM built-in. It runs on an embedded Linux kernel v3.8 and supports the Arduino reference API and its hardware headers.

The first board, Intel Galileo, was introduced at Maker Fair Rome in October of 2013.

After the feedback received from the maker fair and from others, Intel created the Intel Galileo Gen 2. It runs on Quark SoC x1000 and has many improvements and features over the first version, most of which are discussed in this chapter.

About this Book

This book covers the hardware and software in the Intel Galileo and Intel Galileo Gen 2 boards, providing information about how to develop in the Arduino environment, how to develop natively using regular Linux libraries and the respective cross-compilers, and how to combine Linux libraries and Arduino code.

This book also explains the Yocto build system, including how to update the board firmware or generate your own images and prepare your cables for debugging.

If you are not interested in the details about the Linux-native development, you can jump directly to Chapter 3.

All the projects in this book were planned using affordable parts and materials. At the end of each project, there is a section entitled, "Ideas for Improving the Project" that discusses other ideas and covers how to integrate other parts and expand on the project's functionalities.

The projects in general are very powerful and include web servers, robot arms, moisture sensors, LTE modems, and interfacing with different sensors. They all describe how everything works in a step-by-step manner, as well as how to debug and run the project.

Each project also includes the source code and the schematics, which can be downloaded from apress.com.

The schematics were created using a tool called DipTrace, which can be downloaded from http://www.diptrace.com/. This tool is freeware when limited to 300 pins and two layers; this limitation is more than enough to support the schematics in the book's projects.

The schematic files created in DipTrace have the .dch extension. However, when you open the schematics in the DipTrace tool, you will see there are some male and female jumper connectors that you don't see in the figures in this book. The reason for these connectors is if you decide to use the DipTrace tool to generate your PCB instead of using the breadboard or a universal board, you will not need to add them by yourself because they are already present. Thus, you have a clear and easy view of the schematics and you can have the complete schematic to generate PCBs if you want.

Some projects, like "Home Automation with Node.js," do not compose a single project with a single code and schematic but instead make up several micro-projects, like the integration of keypads, PIR (Passive Infra-Red) sensors, temperature sensors, switch relays, and a web server that you can use individually. These projects include separate source code and schematics for each part.

Some of the images in this book were created using an open source tool called Fritizing. You can download it at http://fritzing.org/home/.

Why Use Intel Galileo Boards?

Depending on the nature of your project, you can get powerful processing and save a lot of money if you use the regular Arduino boards based on only on microcontrollers.

To get a clear idea why you should use the Intel Galileo boards, assume you need to develop a project with the following requirements:

- Save information to the SD card for logging.

- Connect and transmit the data collected using the Internet.

- Users must be able to transmit log files and monitor logs files on demand. So, a web server must be developed.

- A specific USB peripheral like a webcam will be used and your Arduino board will be a host. The images captured by this webcam will be part of the data to be transmitted.

- The Internet access must be set up using Ethernet or WiFi connections. You must have the correct time and date for the data you are logging in the SD card, even when your board reboots and the system is restored, so a Real Time Clock is needed (RTC).

If you think these requirements are complex, keep in mind that they are common requirements when you want to create a home automation, build a robot that allows you to control remotely, build a surveillance system, or monitor your garden soil, for example. With these requirements in mind, let's compare the cost of using Intel Galileo boards versus a regular Arduino Uno.

The Software Advantages

The default image of Intel Galileo Flash comes with Linux 3.8 and with libraries in the user space for integrating the Arduino wiring platform.

Arduino in the context of the Intel Galileo family runs in the Linux kernel user space and is integrated with IDE, which runs in your personal computer with Windows, Linux or Mac OSX.

Using Linux, developers can build native applications, install device drivers, create their own drivers, change the Linux kernel configuration to accommodate new features, build their own kernel, use the POSIX libraries, and even change and install a new Linux distribution like Debian.

The details about the Linux-embedded image, kernel customization, and toolchain are discussed in Chapter 2. The details regarding the Arduino wiring platform is covered in Chapter 3.

You might wonder why purchase Intel Galileo versus other Arduino boards. The Linux board that supports the Arduino system comes with a microcontroller that executes AVR code and runs the Arduino code called sketches. The microcontroller on these boards is responsible for handling the Arduino headers and only communicates with Linux OS using bridges. This means developers and students have to use specific classes. In other words, in such boards, the microcontroller is responsible for running the sketch, not Linux OS. The communication between the microcontroller and Linux depends on special mechanisms.

With Intel Galileo boards, the Linux OS is responsible for handling all the digital and analogic Arduino headers, thereby avoiding special class and bridges. Therefore, the Arduino code (called sketches) can integrate Arduino APIs with Linux APIs without any problem.

Another important point is that it's possible to run more than one sketch at same time with Intel Galileo. The board with the microcontroller runs only one sketch at a time.

Returning to the idea of this fictitious project, you can use the Linux distribution in the SD card that comes with node.js for the web server. It has WiFi drivers; you can count on Python and bash support if you decide to create scripts in your software, you can use the SD card to store the data until 32GB, and you can easily combine Linux calls and library API with the regular Arduino wiring platform. Regarding the webcam, you just need to make sure you have the appropriate driver installed.

The Hardware Advantages

Consider the common built-in components that are present in both boards that would be used in the fictitious project described in this chapter:

- Ethernet port
- USB host connector
- Micro-SD card capable until 32GB
- Mini-PCIe connector
- RTC maintained by coil battery

All the requirements for this imaginary project are attended by the Intel Galileo boards. If you want to connect to the Internet, you can use a simple Ethernet cable. If you need WiFi you can buy a mini-PCIe Intel Centrino N135 WiFi card, mPCIe card bracket, and antennas. Table 1-1 shows the average costs of these items.

Table 1-1. *Mini-PCIe WiFi Card and Accessories*

Description	Cost in U.S. Dollars(*)
Intel Centrino WiFi N135	$8.00
mPCIe card brackets	$5.00
Antennas with connectors	$7.00
Intel Galileo	$55.70

* *Cost based on the average price on 3/18/2014 from several sites in the United States.*

If you decide to use an Ethernet connection, the only cost is the Intel Galileo board. Otherwise, if you decide you need a WiFi connection, you have an additional of $20.00 to the Intel Galileo board, for a total of $75.70.

Now, suppose you want to compare the total cost of your project if you have an Arduino Uno and decide to buy some shields to meet the project's requirements.

To reach capabilities similar to Intel Galileo family, the shields listed in Table 1-2 are necessary.

Table 1-2. *Average Cost of the Arduino Shields*

Description	Cost in U.S. Dollars(*)
Ethernet	$25.00
SD card/datalogger	$60.00 for 32GB
RTC	$5.00
USB host	$26.00
WiFi	$89.95
Arduino Uno R3	$27.00

* *Cost based on the average price on 3/18/2014, from several sites in United States.*

The total cost using Arduino Uno with Ethernet only is $143.95 and if you decide to use Arduino with the WiFi shield it's $270.95.

As you can evaluate, the same project with Intel Galileo costs $75.70 with WiFi support versus $270.95 with Arduino Uno R3. This same project with Arduino Uno R3 and all shields necessary costs 3.58 times more, besides the fact you will not have access to a powerful Linux-embedded OS, which offers many software resources.

Of course, if your project only requires blinking LEDs, read buttons states, and very simple things, the Arduino R3 is more affordable.

Hardware Overview

Intel Galileo Gen 2 was created to improve on some of the limitations of Intel Galileo. These details will be explained in the following sections, with an overview on the Quark SoC X1000 processor, Intel Galileo, and Intel Galileo Gen 2 boards.

The Processor: Intel Quark SoC X1000

Intel Quark SoC X1000 is a 32-bit processor designed for lower power consumption. It's x86 compatible with Pentium opcode instructions but implements features like ACPI (Advanced Configuration and Power Interface) and includes several interfaces that provide connections with external peripherals. Intel Quark competes directly with ARM A and M class-based products and is the first Intel initiative to merge into the "Internet of Things" (IoT) and the wearable market.

Intel Quark SoC X1000 is code-named Clanton and is shown in Figure 1-2.

Figure 1-2. *The Quark SoC X1000*

Although the package is only 15x15mm, this tiny processor also offers an interface that allows you to connect to several peripherals, including Bluetooth devices, ZigBee, SD/SDIO/eMMC cards, I2C devices, and USB2 host and device ports. It also handles GPIOs interruptible or not by settings, supports temperature ranges that reach industrial, medical, and military applications (not to mention an internal programmable thermal sensor), and can run unmodified Linux kernel v3.8+. Figure 1-3 shows the peripherals supported by Intel Quark SoC.

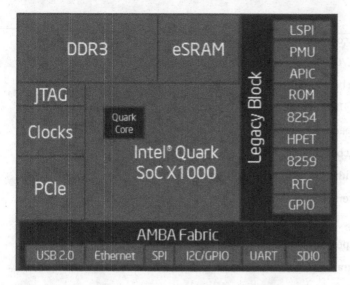

Figure 1-3. Peripheral support of Intel Quark SoC X1000

The following list contains more details regarding the processor:

Processor Core

- Single Quark CPU core, single thread, 32 bits X86, at 400MHz

Processor UnCore

- DDR3 memory controller up to 2GB at 800MTS and ECC-On-Chip

- Embedded 512KB RAM and 16KB cache

- Supports legacy blocks: PC Compatible: IO ports, PCI, ACPI, and so on

- Low-cost 10-pin JTAG

I/O Specifications

- Two 10/100MB Ethernet MACs

- Two USB2 host ports (EHCI and OHCI)

- Two HS UART controllers

- One SPI port for peripherals

- One USB2 HS device port

- One SD/SDIO/EMMC interface

- One I2C/GPIO controller

- Sixteen GPIOs with programmable interrupts (edge)

Software Support

- Pentium ISA compatible (.586 opcodes)

- Standard ICC/GCC/G++ compilers

- Yocto project based on distribution

- Open source UEFI EDK II

- GRUB boot loader support

- Open OCD debugging support

- Compliant with PCIe, USB, and ACPI standards

- Runs Linux kernel v3.8+

Thermals

- External temperature ranges from -40 to 85 degrees Celsius

- Internal programmable thermal sensor

Security

- Supports secure boot technology

- Supervisory mode execution/protection

- Secure recovery for UEFI FW

- Secure remote upgrade with WR IDP 2.0

The next sections explore the Intel Galileo boards in more detail.

Introducing Intel Galileo

Intel Galileo is the first generation and hence has some limitations that are discussed in this section.

The complete set of documents for Intel Galileo—including the board user guide, the IO mappings, the release notes, and the BSP guide—can be found at https://communities.intel.com/community/makers/galileo/documentation/galileodocuments.

The intention of this section is not to duplicate the information present in the documents on this link, but to explain in more detail the most important items that you need to know to start your projects.

If some information is not provided in this chapter, you are encouraged to search the information you need on this link. If this link does not provide what you need, you can contact the Intel Makers community at https://communities.intel.com/community/makers.

Take a look the components on the top of the board, as shown in Figure 1-4 and Table 1-3.

Figure 1-4. *Top view of Intel Galileo*

Table 1-3. *Descriptions of the Main Components*

Number	Component	Description
1	Ethernet port	10/100 Ethernet connector
2	RS-232 serial port	3-pin 3.5mm jack (this is not audio)
3	RS-232	RS-232 transceiver
4	USB 2.0 client	USB client connector: a fully compliant USB 2.0 device controller; typically used for programming
5	USB 2.0 host	USB 2.0 host connector; supports up to 128 USB endpoint devices
6	SPI Flash	8MB Legacy SPI Flash to store the firmware (or bootloader) and the latest sketch
7	SPI Flash program port	7-pin header for Serial Peripheral Interface (SPI) programming
		Defaults to 4MHz to support Arduino Uno shields; programmable up to 25MHz

(continued)

Table 1-3. (*continued*)

Number	Component	Description
8	Arduino headers	Read the section entitled "Arduino Headers on Intel Galileo"
9	ADC	Analog-to-digital converter
10	Intel Quark SoC X1000	See the section entitled "The Processor Intel Quark SoC X1000"
11	ICSP	6-pin in-circuit serial programming (ICSP) header, located appropriately to plug into existing shields. These pins support SPI communication using the SPI library
12	256MB DDR3 RAM	256MB DRAM, enabled by the firmware by default
13	Arduino headers	Read the section entitled "Arduino Headers on Intel Galileo"
14	JTAG debug port	10-pin standard JTAG header for debugging
15	GPIO expander	GPIO pulse width modulation provided by a single I2C I/O expander
16	Micro-SD slot	Supports micro-SD card up to 32GB
17	5V DC power	The board is powered via an AC-to-DC adapter, connected by plugging a 2.1mm center-positive plug into the board's power jack. The recommended output rating of the power adapter is 5V at up to 3A
18	Voltage regulator	Generates a 3.3 volt supply. Maximum current draw to the shield is 800mA
19	Eth PHY	Ethernet physical layer transceiver
20	BATT	3.3V battery terminal used to keep the internal real time clock (RTC); do not power the device through these terminals

The back view of the board is shown in Figure 1-5.

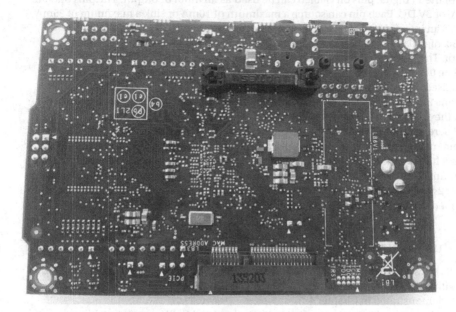

Figure 1-5. *Intel Galileo, bottom view*

From Figure 1-5, you can identify the mini-PCIe connector that allows Intel Galileo to work with full- or half-sized mini-PCIe cards. If you have a half-sized mini-PCIe card, you need an adapter bracket, which costs around $3.00, as demonstrated in Chapter 5 in the section entitled "Setting Up the WiFi Mini-PCI-E Card."

The board dimension is 4.2 inches long and 2.8 inches wide.

Arduino Headers on Intel Galileo

Intel Galileo was the first board developed with Arduino headers compatible to the Arduino Uno revision 3 called Arduino Interface. You can see it in Figure 1-4. There are some software functions on the Arduino reference API that are used to manipulate the digital input and output ports, to generate pulse width modulation (PWM) signals, to read and write analogic values, to communicate with I2C devices, and to establish serial interfaces. It is not the scope of this first chapter to provide details about all these functions. Chapter 3 provides an introduction, but keep in mind that a single pin can be programmed to assume different functions.

Chapter 3 also contains more details about the pins represented by the bubbles 8 and 13 in Figures 3-10 and 3-11, including how to use these pins with basic functions like pinMode(), digitalWrite(), digitalRead(), analogRead(), and analogWrite().

Fourteen Digital Input/Output Pins (IO2 to IO13, TX, and RX)

Each of the 14 digital pins on Galileo can be used as an input or output. The pins operate at 3.3V or 5V DC. Each pin can source a maximum of 10mA or sink a maximum of 25mA and has an internal pull-up resistor (disconnected by default) of 5.6 to 10 KOhms.

Six digital pins can be used as PWM outputs; they are labeled with the tilde (~) symbol. The pins with this capability are 3, 5, 6, 9, 10, and 11.

The 0 and 1 pins can be programmed for the UART interface, such as RX and TX. When used as UART, the serial speed is programmable.

Pins 2 and 3 also can be programmed to be used as the UART interface. However, when they're used as a serial interface, the Linux serial console will be lost.

There is a speed limitation on I/O ports. Due to the limitation of the sysfs implementation on Linux kernel v3.8 and the necessity of sending I2C commands to the Cypress IO expander, there is a delay of 2ms in the ports. This limits the frequency to a maximum of 230Hz when you set the ports as digital output. However, considering that pin header 2 and 3 are connected directly to SoC, it is possible to reach 477KHz to 2.93MHz, as described in Chapter 4 in the section entitled "How to Make Intel Galileo's I/O Faster."

I2C Bus Controlled by the SCL and SDA Pins

The I2C or two-wire interface (TWI) can be controlled by A4 or SDA pin and A5 or SCL pin. Within the Arduino context, the I2C might be programmed easily using the wire library demonstrated in Chapter 4.

An important observation regarding I2C is that Intel Galileo operates only as a master device and the internal I2C expander (Cypress IC) runs only in standard speed (100KHz).

AREF Is Unused

The AD729 A/D is used as internal reference for the analog ports. Thus, external reference voltage for the analog inputs is not supported and it is not possible to change the upper end of the analog input range using the AREF pin and the analogReference() function.

Analog Input Pins (A0-A5)

The six analog ports A0 to A5 have a resolution of 12 bits, which counts until 4096. By default, the analog ports measures from 0V (ground) to 5V.

Power Pins

This bulleted list describes the pins in same order of the headers, from right to left:

- **IOREF:** Some shields on the market work with 3.3V or 5V. In order to select the proper operation voltage level for the Intel Galileo, be sure to use the jumper tagged IOREF. Note that the jumper on the left selects 3.3V and the right operation remains set to 5V.

- **RESET button/pin:** The pin or the Reset button are both used to reset the Arduino sketch, not the board.

- **3.3V output pin:** Provides 3.3V generated by the on-board regulator with a maximum current drain to the shield of 800mA.

- **5V output pin:** This pin outputs 5V from the 5V power supply or the USB connector. However, it is best to keep the power supply connected. Maximum current draw to the shield is 800mA.

- **GND (2 pins):** Only ground pins.

- **VIN:** Instead of using the external and regulated 5V power supply, you can supply voltage through this pin. However, if this pin is used, the power supply must also be regulated at 5V. Otherwise, it might damage the board.

Sink and Source Currents in Outputs

When the pins are set as output, the circuit can provide current (source) or the circuit can receive current (sink), depending on the device or circuit connected to the ports.

Some developers refer to the source current as the "positive" current and to the sink as the "negative" current.

Intel Galileo can be used as source or sink, but it is necessary to be aware of the port's limitations when used as output.

Each individual pin can provide 10mA as source or 25mA as sink. Combined pins can have 40mA as source until 200mA but everything depends on how they are combined.

Table 1-4 explains the limits when used as source and sink in different combinations.

Table 1-4. *Source and Sink Current Limits as Output*

Combination	Source (mA)	Sink (mA)
Each pin	10	25
Digital pins 3, 5, 9, 10, 12, and 13	40	100
Digital pins 0, 1, 2, 4, 5, 6, 7, 8, 11, and analog pins A0 to A5	40	100
Digital pins 0 to 13 and analog pins A0 to A5	80	200

Jumpers and Buttons on Intel Galileo

The board essentially contains three jumpers—IOREF, I2C, and VIN—as shown in Figure 1-6.

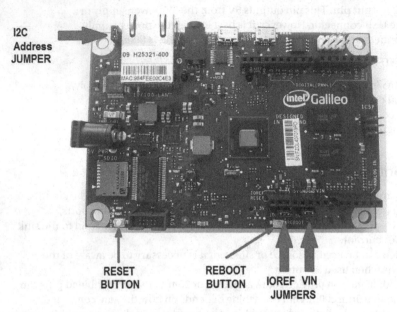

I2C Address JUMPER

RESET BUTTON

REBOOT BUTTON

IOREF VIN JUMPERS

Figure 1-6. *Jumpers' locations and buttons on Intel Galileo*

The following sections summarize the functionality of each jumper.

IOREF Jumper

This jumper needs to be changed when your projects use shields that work with 3.3V or 5V. So, if your shield works with 5V you should connect the jumper in 5V; otherwise, if the shield works with 3.3V, the jumpers must be set to 3.3V.

It's important to note that the IOREF jumper does not affect the voltage reference in the analog input ports. They remain set to 0V (ground) to 5V, regardless of how this jumper is set.

VIN Jumper

If you keep the VIN jumper, Intel Galileo will receive power from the 5V regulated power supply connected to the power jack. However, sometimes there are shields that require more than 5V offered by the power supply. In these cases, it is necessary to remove the VIN jumper and apply the external and regulated voltage to the VIN headers.

Note that the external power must be regulated and the VIN jumper must be removed so that you don't damage your board.

I2C Address Jumper

Considering it is possible to connect external I2C slaves as devices to Intel Galileo, this I2C address jumper was introduced in order to avoid address conflicts between these external devices and the internal I2C devices (the EEPROM and Cypress GPIO expander).

If you keep J2 connected to pin 1, the one marked with a little white triangle, the GPIO expander address will be 0100001 and the 7-bit EEPROM address will be 1010001. If you change the jumper position, the GPIO expander address will be 0100000 and the EEPROM address will be 1010000.

Reset Button

This button resets the currently running sketch, not Linux itself. You can manually kill the sketch process and execute it again.

Reboot Button

This button reboots the whole system, including Linux.

Connection Diagram and Schematics

To understand how all the components are connected, take a good look at Figure 1-7.

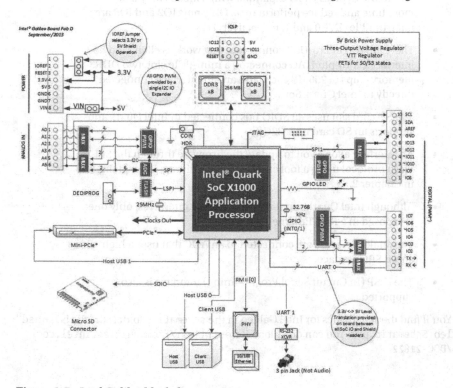

Figure 1-7. *Intel Galileo block diagram*

15

Explanations of Figure 1-7 are detailed here:

- Although Intel Galileo provides a 3-pin 3.5mm jack, this not used for audio and in fact causes confusion at first glance, because this jack is actually used for serial debugging, whereby you can open a Linux shell. Later in this chapter, you learn how to build your own cable and access the Linux shell.

- All pins that support PWM have a tilde (~) in front of their tags. For example, the pin IO3 has a tilde in front of its name, which means it supports PWM.

- The multiplexers (MUX) represented in the diagram are used because pins might assume different functions. For example, the pin IO11 might be used as digital input or output or to generate PWM. The MUX changes the connection of this pin to the appropriate circuit blocks responsible for each function.

- Looking at the headers in Figure 1-7, note that IO2 and IO3 are the only pins connected directly to Intel Quark. All the other IO pins are connected to the Cypress GPIO expander. This means that pins IO2 and IO3 are faster and are managed directly by the SoC. The other IO pins need to be managed through I2C commands sent to the Cypress GPIO expander, which means they take more time and reduce performance. Only pins IO2 and IO3 are interruptible (INT 0 and 1, respectively).

- There are two micro-USB connectors that work as client and host interfaces, a 10-pin JTAG connector, a mini-PCIe slot, two DDR3 memory chips of 256MB each, and an SPI interface connected directly to Intel Quark SoC.

- The SD card slot uses an SDIO bus connected to Intel Quark and supports an SD card until 32GB.

- An interface allows you to update the firmware through the SPI Flash protocol using a tool called SF100 DediProg. It's explained in Chapter 2.

- Although Intel Quark supports two Ethernet interfaces, only one is exposed in a RJ45 Ethernet connector.

- The analog headers are connected to an ADC that uses a high-speed SPI interface.

- The ICSP (In Circuit Serial Programming) interface is also supported.

You'll find the schematics for Intel Galileo in the schematics folder; the file is named Galileo Schematic.pdf. You can download it from https://communities.intel.com/docs/DOC-21822.

From the schematics, you can check the block diagram represented in Figure 1-7. You can also check many other details like the bidirectional TXS0108E voltage-level translators used to convert the header voltage levels, as you can see in Figure 1-8.

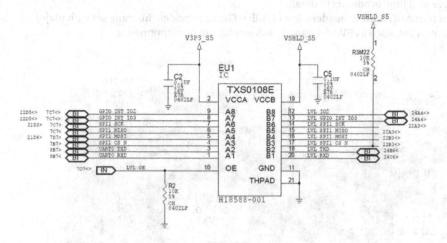

Figure 1-8. *Bidirectional TXS0108E voltage-level translator*

If your intention is to use the board only to connect to external shields and other peripherals, you do not need to worry about the details in these schematics. The block diagrams and details explained here cover your needs.

Intel Galileo GPIO Mappings

The GPIO mappings of Intel Galileo can be found in Appendix A.

Introducing Intel Galileo Gen 2

Intel Galileo Gen 2 came about because of the issues identified by the development team and the feedback received from the makers who contributed to the forums. This is why your participation in this community is extremely important to Intel. You can access the Intel maker's forum at https://communities.intel.com/community/makers.

You can access the complete set of documents for Intel Galileo Gen 2—including the board user guide, IO mappings, release notes, and the BSP guide—at https://communities.intel.com/community/makers/galileo/documentation/intel-galileo-gen-2-development-board-documents.

As discussed in the "Intel Galileo" section, the intention of this section is not to duplicate the information in the documents found on this link, but to explain in more detail the most important items that you need to know to start your projects.

The Intel Quark X1000 SoC was preserved on Intel Galileo Gen 2 as the memory's capacity. It also has the same clock frequency, the same analog and power headers (except for a small improvement in the digital header to allow redirection of UART1 to the pins IO2 and IO3), and the same I2C and SPI speeds. The next section discusses the new changes and improvements in detail.

In terms of Arduino headers, Intel Galileo Gen 2 provides the same set with major improvements, such as PWM. Figure 1-9 shows its major components.

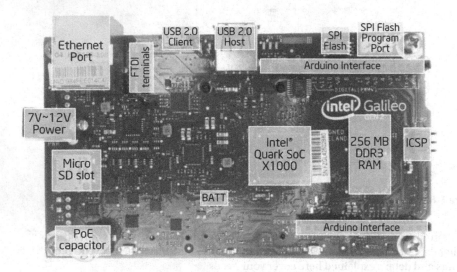

Figure 1-9. *Top view of Intel Galileo Gen 2*

What's New in Intel Galileo Gen 2

Intel Galileo Gen 2 has some significant improvements over the first version. Some components have been removed as well. Consider the following:

- The Cypress GPIO expander was removed and replaced with the PCA 9535 to generate 12-bit PWM with precision. It's not choppy as in Intel Galileo. So, when you create sketches using Servo API, you can move the servos with a precision of 1 degree.

- With the removal of Cypress GPIO expander, the I2C address jumper was also removed. Considering that most of the shields based on the I2C bus allow developers to change their addresses, the only possible conflict is with EEPROM, which still uses the address 0100001.

- Almost all IO headers are connected directly to Quark SoC, which means the pins can achieve 2.97MHz. Chapter 4 discusses the new architecture and all its possible frequencies. With this new port speed, it's possible to run shields and sensors that you couldn't run using the old version.

- The board supports the Power over Ethernet (PoE) module, which wasn't included in the board. It's explained in Chapter 10.

- The client USB connector is still a micro-USB connector but the host USB has changed to a USB-OTG connector.

- The power regulator now supports voltage between 7-15V DC.

- In addition to the IO0 and IO1 pins, which can be used for serial communication as RX and TX respectively, pins IO2 and IO3 can also communicate serially as RX and TX, respectively. The problem with using IO2 and IO3 is that the Linux console is lost.

- The MAX 3232 responsible for converting the RS-232 level to Intel Quark SoC was also removed. Now it is necessary to use FTDI cables that are compatible with TTL-232 3.3 V

- There is no VIN jumper anymore. The VIN is connected directed to the DC jack, as you can see in Figure 1-10. You can check this in the schematics discussed in the section.

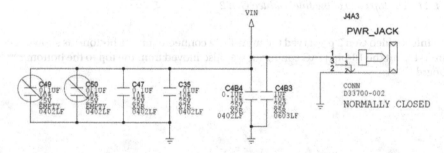

Figure 1-10. *VIN connected directly to power jack DC*

- The board in general is a little bigger compared to Intel Galileo. It is 4.87 inches long and 2.83 inches wide. The reason it's bigger is because some internal voltage regulators on Intel Quark SoC are not being used anymore, and other external voltage regulators were added in order to keep Intel Quark SoC cooler.

Figure 1-11 shows the new form factor of Intel Galileo Gen 2 and the new location of some of the components. Note the buttons have moved and the IOREF jumper is in a totally different position. Note also the presence of the new OTG-USB connector, the FTDI terminals, and the capacitor of 47uF, which supports the PoE module.

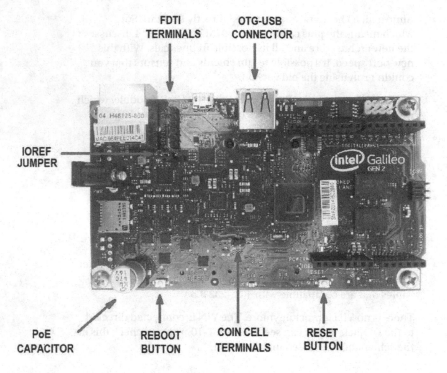

Figure 1-11. The top view of the Intel Galileo Gen 2

The Intel Galileo Gen 2 preserved the mini-PCIe connector on the bottom, as shown in Figure 1-12, but the 10-pin JTAG connector was also moved from the top to the bottom of the board.

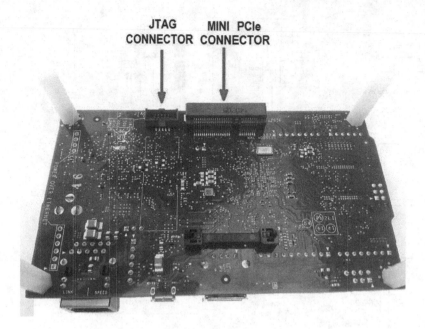

JTAG   MINI PCIe
CONNECTOR   CONNECTOR

Figure 1-12.   *The bottom view of the Intel Galileo Gen 2*

Arduino Headers on Intel Galileo Gen 2

Intel Galileo Gen 2 contains the same headers described in the section entitled "Arduino Headers on Intel Galileo" in this chapter, except for the inclusion of the IO2 and IO3, as explained in the previous section.

Jumpers and Buttons on Intel Galileo Gen 2

Intel Galileo Gen 2 still contains the reset and reboot buttons and the IOREF jumper with the same functionality explained in the section entitled "Jumpers and Buttons on Intel Galileo."

The buttons have swapped locations compared to the first Intel Galileo.

The I2C address and VIN jumpers were removed, as explained in the section "What's New in Intel Galileo Gen 2."

Connection Diagram and Schematics

To understand how all the components are connected, take a good look at Figure 1-13.

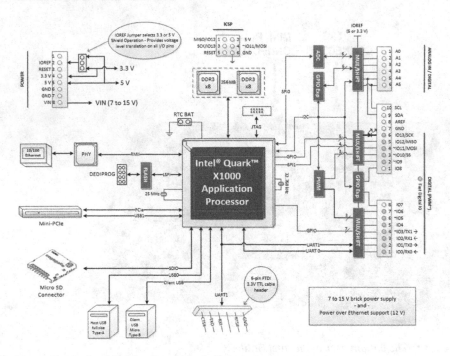

Figure 1-13. *Intel Galileo Gen 2 block diagram*

Consider these issues when you're looking at Figure 1-13:

- Intel Galileo Gen 2 provides a terminal with six pins dedicated to the FTDI cable connection in the TTL level of 3.3V. This terminal provides access to the Linux console. It replaces the previous serial audio jack present on Intel Galileo.

- Like the first Intel Galileo, all pins that support PWM have a tilde (~) in front of their tags. For example, the pin IO3 has a tilde in front of its name, which means it supports PWM.

- The multiplexers (MUX) represented in the diagram are used because the pins might assume different functions. For example, the pin IO11 might be used as digital input or output or to generate PWM, thus the MUX changes the connection of this pin to the appropriate circuit blocks responsible for each function.

- The IO header is completely different compared to the first Intel Galileo. Now, most IO pins are connected directly to Intel Quark SoC with the exception of IO7 and IO8, which are connected to the PCA GPIO expander. Consequently, all pins can achieve 2.97MHz except for pins IO7 and IO8, which will achieve the maximum of 1.8KHz (see Chapter 4 for more details). Note that pins IO2 and IO3 are the only ones that are interruptible

(INT 0 and 1 respectively). Another reason for IO7 and IO8 to be connected to the GPIO expander is because among the 14 IO pins on Intel Quark, they are used to reset the mini-PCIe.

- Note that pins IO2 and IO3 now can be used as serial consoles as well—IO2 as RX and IO3 as TX. If these pins are used as serial, the Linux console through the FTDI cable is lost. Read Chapter 4 for more details.

- The VIN and I2C address jumpers do not exist anymore.

Many other elements haven't changed from the first Intel Galileo, such as:

- There are two micro-USB connectors that work as client and host interfaces—a 10-pin JTAG connector, a mini-PCIe slot, two DDR3 memory chips of 256MB each, and a SPI interface connected directly to Intel Quark SoC.

- The SD card slot uses a SDIO bus connected to Intel Quark and supports the SD card until 32GB.

- There is an interface that allows you to update the firmware through SPI flash protocol using a tool called SF100 DediProg. It's explained in Chapter 2.

- Although Intel Quark supports two Ethernet interfaces only one is exposed in a RJ45 Ethernet connector.

- The analog headers are connected to an ADC that uses a high-speed SPI interface.

- The ICSP (In Circuit Serial Programming) interface is also supported.

You can find the schematics for Intel Galileo Gen 2 in the schematics folder and the file is Galileo_Gen2_Schematic.pdf. You can also download them from https://communities.intel.com/docs/DOC-22895.

Intel Galileo Gen 2 GPIO Mappings

The GPIO mappings of Intel Galileo can be found in the Appendix B.

Preparing Your Cables

Two types of cables are used in this book:

- **A high-speed USB 2.0 male-to-micro USB cable, commonly called a USB data cable**: This cable is used to download, debug, and run sketches via Intel Arduino IDE. This cable is essential; without it, you will not be able to run any of the projects in this book. You can use the same cable on both Intel Galileo and Intel Galileo Gen 2. Figure 1-14 shows this cable. The cost varies between $3.00 and $6.00, depending on the quality of the cable you order.

- **A 3.3V FTDI cable if you have an Intel Galileo Gen 2 or a serial cable with a stereo jack if you have the first Intel Galileo**: As explained, Intel Galileo and Intel Galileo Gen 2 run embedded Linux 3.8 on the official releases. You'll want to access the Linux console for kernel debugging, to install native applications, to write Python programs, and so on. Some chapter of this book utilizes this cable so it is recommended you have it. The details surrounding these cables are discussed in the sections entitled "The Serial Cable for Intel Galileo" and "The Serial Cable for Intel Galileo Gen 2" in this chapter.

There is some confusion between the Arduino serial console, the Arduino serial, and the Arduino debug terminal. All of these terms are commonly used in the community and refer to the debug terminal provided by the Arduino IDE. In other words, this is the first high-speed USB 2.0 A male-to-micro USB cable mentioned earlier.

The next section explains the serial cables you'll need in order to access the Linux console after your connection has more than one cable.

The Serial Cable for Intel Galileo

This section is related to the Linux console. In other words, it assumes you have access to a Linux terminal and can run regular Linux commands directly on your board. In this case, you'll use a serial cable with an audio jack adaptor.

This section also explains how to access the serial cable. Gaining access using WiFi and Ethernet via SSH is explained in Chapter 5.

If your computer contains a RS-232 port, you simply need a serial cable DB9 male connected to a 3.5mm jack, which costs around $4. If your computer only supports USB, you need a second cable converter with a RS-232 male connector to USB, which costs around $9.

Table 1-5 lists the cables and the recommended part numbers.

Table 1-5. *Cables for Serial Debugging on Intel Galileo*

Number	Description
1	Cable with a DB9 male connector to a 3.5mm jack
1	Cable converter RS-232 female connector-to-micro USB 2.0 (only if your computer does not have RS-232 connector)

The DB9 male with stereo 3.5mm jack is shown in Figure 1-14 and the converter RS-232 female connector-to-micro USB 2.0 is shown in Figure 1-15.

Figure 1-14. *Cable with a DB9 male connector to a 3.5mm jack*

Figure 1-15. *Cable converter RS-232 female connector-to-micro USB 2.0*

If your computer does not have the RS-232 port, you can also use a single cable converter with a 3.5mm stereo jack connected to a micro-USB FTDI cable. This cable costs around $17, but if you order a cable converter RS-232 female connector to micro-USB and a simple standard stereo audio jack connector (about $1.00), you can build your own cable with a final cost of $10.

To build your own cable based on a RS-232 to micro-USB converter, remove the female DB9 connector and replace it with the stereo jack 3.5mm. Follow the connections shown in Figure 1-16 to do this.

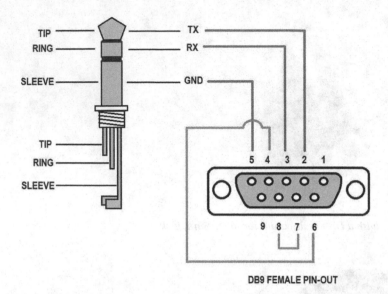

Figure 1-16. *Scheme to build your own 3.5mm stereo serial jack cable*

Note the stereo jack has three contact points—the tip that must be the TX signal is connected to pin 2, the ring that must be the RX signal is connected to pin 3, and the sleeve that must be the ground is connected to pin 5. Optionally, considering the serial communication with Intel Galileo does not require handshaking and parity control, pin 7 (CTS) and pin 8 (RTS) might be used instead as pin 4 (DSR) to pin 6 (DTR).

The next step is to test your cable and access the Linux console.

The Serial Cable for Intel Galileo Gen 2

If you have an Intel Galileo Gen 2, you need a FTDI cable with a 6-pin connector and TTL level of 3.3V IO (serial) to USB.

This cable is necessary because the MAX 3232 on Intel Galileo was removed in Intel Galileo Gen 2, so there is no built-in circuit to convert the TTL levels. On the other hand, the cost was reduced with the removal of this audio jack.

The cable I recommend is sold by SparkFun; see https://www.sparkfun.com/products/9717. It costs $17.95. The cable is shown in Figure 1-17.

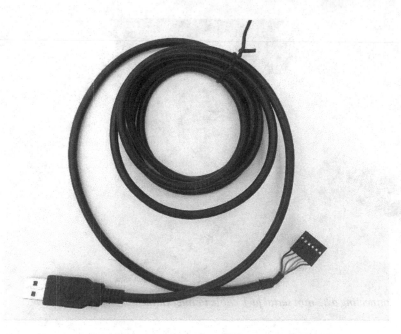

Figure 1-17. FTDI cable 6-pin connector TTL 3.3V IO level to USB

The next step is to test the cables.

Testing the Serial Cables

This section describes how to test your serial cable (if you're using Intel Galileo) or how to test your FTDI cable (if you're using Intel Galileo Gen 2).

To run a Linux console with help of your cables, you need to install the software on your computer in order to be able to open a serial channel with your board. The software you need depends on your operational system and your own preferences.

The software programs mentioned in the following steps are only for reference. They are the most popular. This section explores putty for Windows, minicom for Linux, and screen for Mac OSX. Note that screen is also available on Linux and minicom is also available on Mac OSX.

If you are using Intel Galileo, you simply connect the 3.5mm jack to the jack connector on the board, as shown in Figure 1-18 and then USB or RS-232 to your computer.

Figure 1-18. *Connecting a 3.5mm serial jack cable to Intel Galileo*

If your board is Intel Galileo Gen 2, make sure the inline connector connects pin 1 (usually black) to pin 1 of the FTDI connector on the board. This is represented by a little white triangle shown in Figure 1-19. You'll connect the other end of the cable to your computer.

Figure 1-19. *Connecting the FTDI cable to Intel Galileo Gen 2*

Windows

The following steps explain how to set up the Linux console on Windows:

1. After you insert the cable, wait for a few seconds so that the USB is enumerated. Then open the Windows Device Manager by choosing Start ➤ Control Panel ➤ Hardware and Sound ➤ Device Manager. You can also press the Windows key ![Windows key] and "R" at same time, and then type devmgmt.msc.

2. In the Device Manager, check the COM port available under the Ports section. Figure 1-20 shows an example of a COM port enumerated as COM5.

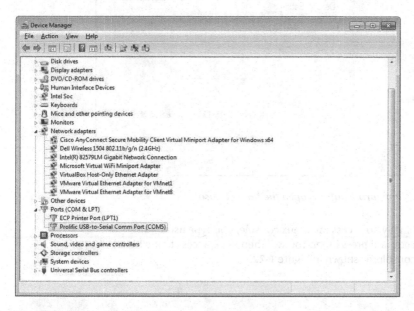

Figure 1-20. Intel Galileo COM port on Windows

3. Download putty and install it on your Windows machine. You can download it from http://www.chiark.greenend. org.uk/~sgtatham/putty/download.html.

4. Execute putty. Select the Serial protocol and enter the COM port number. Then click the Open button, as shown in Figure 1-21.

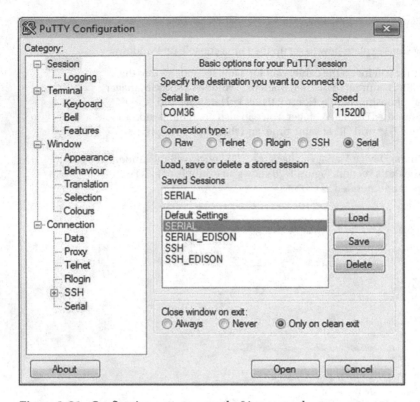

Figure 1-21. *Configuring putty to open the Linux console*

5. Finally, to access the Linux console, you type username root and press Enter. You will then have access to the Linux console, as shown in Figure 1-22.

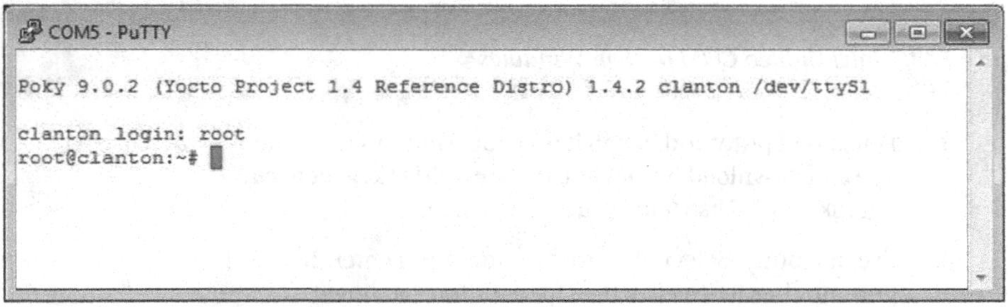

```
COM5 - PuTTY

Poky 9.0.2 (Yocto Project 1.4 Reference Distro) 1.4.2 clanton /dev/ttyS1

clanton login: root
root@clanton:~#
```

Figure 1-22. *The Linux serial console*

Ubuntu Linux

The procedure to set up Intel Galileo's Linux console on a Linux computer is easy. As mentioned, serial communication on Linux computers is based on the minicom software.

The following steps are necessary to get the Linux console working:

1. After you insert the cable, wait for a few seconds for the USB to be enumerated.

2. Open a Linux terminal. You can press Ctrl+T to do this.

3. Check the port by typing the command dmesg|grep tty. For example, Figure 1-23 shows the port enumerated as ttyUSB0.

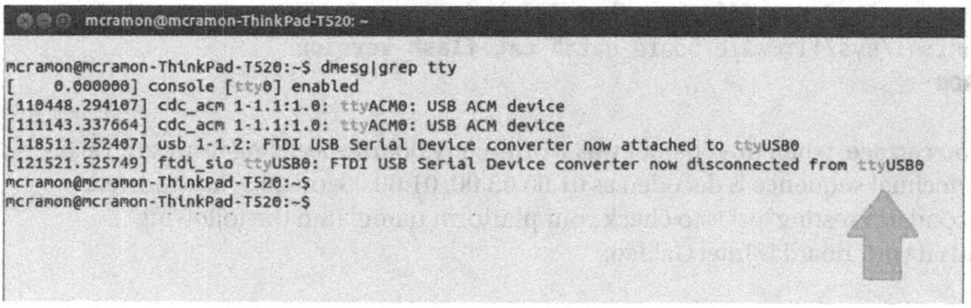

Figure 1-23. *Checking the USB port enumerated on the Ubuntu terminal*

4. Finally, to access the Linux console, you typing the sudo minicom --device /dev/ttyUSB0 command. The terminal will open. You need to use the username root.

Mac OSX

The following steps describe how to set up the Linux console on Mac OSX.

1. After you insert the cable, wait for a few seconds so that the USB is enumerated.

2. Open an OSX terminal. You can press ⌘ and the spacebar at same time to open the Spotlight text box. Then type terminal and press Enter.

3. In the terminal, check what is the serial port enumerated as following command:

    ```
    ~$ ls /dev/tty.usb*
    /dev/tty.usbserial-A603HVUT
    ```

4. Finally, you can access the Linux console by typing
   screen /dev/<YOUR SERIAL HERE> 115200 into the terminal.
   For example

   ~$ screen /dev/tty.usbserial-A603HVUT 115200

5. The console will open. You need to use the username root.

Exploring the Linux Console

Try to run some Linux commands. To check which board you have, you can run the
following command:

root@clanton:~# **cd /sys/firmware/board_data/**
root@clanton:/sys/firmware/board_data# **cat flash_version**
0x01000300

As you can see, when this chapter was written, my board was using firmware 1.0.3.
The hexadecimal sequence is decoded as 01.00.03.00, 01.00.03, or 1.0.3, as expected.

A second interesting test is to check your platform name. Run the following
commands if your board is Intel Galileo:

root@clanton:~# **cd /sys/devices/platform/Galileo**
root@clanton:/sys/devices/platform/Galileo# **cat modalias**
platform:Galileo

If your board is Intel Galileo Gen 2, the following commands work:

root@clanton:~# **cd /sys/devices/platform/GalileoGen2/**
root@clanton:/sys/devices/platform/GalileoGen2# **cat modalias**
platform:GalileoGen2

The releases provided by Intel contain the busybox software utility. It provides about
300 commands that can be executed in the Linux console. If you type busybox and press
Enter, you will be able to see the supported commands.

root@clanton:/sys/devices/platform/GalileoGen2# **busybox**
BusyBox v1.20.2 (2014-08-22 10:41:19 PDT) multi-call binary.
Copyright (C) 1998-2011 Erik Andersen, Rob Landley, Denys Vlasenko
and others. Licensed under GPLv2.
See source distribution for full notice.

Usage: busybox [function] [arguments]...
   or: busybox --list
   or: function [arguments]...

BusyBox is a multi-call binary that combines many common Unix utilities into a single executable. Most people will create a link to busybox for each function they wish to use and BusyBox will act like whatever it was invoked as.

Currently defined functions:
[, [[, acpid, ar, arp, arping, ash, awk, basename, blkid, blockdev, bootchartd, brctl, bunzip2, bzcat, cat, chgrp, chmod, chown, chroot, chrt, clear, cmp, cp, cpio, cttyhack, cut, date, dc, dd, deallocvt, depmod, df, diff, dirname, dmesg, dnsdomainname, du, dumpkmap, echo, egrep, env, expr, false, fdisk, fgrep, find, findfs, flock, free, fsck, fsync, ftpd, ftpget, ftpput, fuser, getty, grep, gunzip, gzip, halt, hd, head, hexdump, hostname, hwclock, id, ifconfig, ifdown, ifup, insmod, ionice, iostat, ip, kill, killall, klogd, less, ln, loadkmap, logger, login, logname, logread, losetup, ls, lsmod, lsof, lspci, lsusb, md5sum, mdev, mkdir, mkfifo, mknod, mktemp, modprobe, more, mount, mv, nc, netstat, nice, nohup, nslookup, od, patch, pidof, ping, ping6, pivot_root, pmap, poweroff, printf, ps, pwd, rdate, readlink, realpath, reboot, renice, reset, resize, rm, rmdir, rmmod, route, run-parts, sed, seq, setconsole, setserial, setsid, sh, sleep, sort, start-stop-daemon, stat, strings, stty, sulogin, switch_root, sync, sysctl, syslogd, tail, tar, tcpsvd, tee, telnet, telnetd, test, tftp, time, timeout, top, touch, tr, traceroute, traceroute6, true, tty, udhcpc, umount, uname, uniq, unzip, uptime, usleep, vconfig, vi, watch, wc, wget, which, who, whoami, xargs, yes, zcat, zcip

If you need to execute one of these commands, you simply type the desired command.

Testing the Data Cables

The high-speed USB 2.0 male-to-micro USB cable, or simply the data cable, is used to transfer and debug the sketches. Testing this cable is covered in Chapter 3 because doing so requires the installation of the IDE.

Summary

This first chapter introduced the importance of the maker community and Intel's commitment to them with Intel Quark X1000 SoC.

You were also introduced to the Intel Galileo boards. You learned about the hardware architecture, the software features, and the advantages of these boards and how powerful they are.

This chapter is more descriptive than practical, but that's not the case for the rest of this book. Enjoy!

CHAPTER 2

■ ■ ■

Native Development

There are projects in this book that require a bit more than the simple usage of Arduino reference APIs. Especially Chapter 7, where the OpenCV and V4L2 are explained, and some examples will not run as simple sketches (Arduino programs). In these cases, you will need to know how to make a new build, how to create the toolchains specifically to your computer and how to use the cross-compilers to compile native applications.

The build system used to create the Intel Galileo images—the Yocto project—is very powerful, but it is not as straightforward as a simple make command. There is some computer preparation that must be done. It is also good to know a little bit about how the build system works and how to compile the SPI and SD card images for Intel Galileo and Intel Quark toolchains in order to have the cross-compilers in hand.

This chapter also shows you how to build a very simple native Hello World application after the installation of the toolchains.

Considering that you will be able to create your own releases, especially the SPI images, there is some instruction on how to recover your board—in case you make a mistake and brick your board.

In the end, this chapter brings you some knowledge that will be necessary in the next chapters. It is not the intention to bring a full understanding of all techniques involved in a native development, especially debugging.

Introduction to the Yocto Build System

Suppose that you are creating a great product that uses Linux as an embedded operating system because is open source and free—reducing the product costs, and brings a great operating system to your users. Does this sound right? The answer is that it depends, because Linux is an amazing operating system, but "reducing the cost" in an embedded development could be a really huge nightmare if you do not have good control of the features required by your product, such as which Linux distribution is able to meet your requirements with minimal effort to join all the pieces together.

In order to create a custom Linux image and bring exactly the features that you need, the Yocto project was created to be a flexible and customizable platform for different hardware architectures and code.

The Yocto project brings a series of tools, methods, and code—allowing you to choose the CPU that your product targets, the software and hardware components, and the footprint size—to build a software release based in the Linux operating system. Among the CPU supported are the Intel Architecture (IA), ARM, PowerPC, and MIPS.

Besides the product releases, Yocto also allows you to build tools like system development kits (SDK) and applications to be used with your product. For example, with Intel Galileo boards, we'll cover how to build your own toolchain that contains cross-compilers for different operating systems.

Once the Yocto project is established with the configuration and components, when new components must be added or removed, or even if a new product must be created based in a legacy one that is supported by Yocto, everything will be easier because your product is reusable.

The Yocto project is maintained by the Linux Foundation, meaning that your product will be independent of any vendor or company. Companies like Intel, Dell, Mindspeed, Wind River, Mentor Graphics, Panasonic, and Texas Instruments, among others, participate in the Yocto project.

Yocto and this Book

To understand all the details regarding the Yocto project, another book dedicated exclusively to Yocto would be necessary, because in the same manner that Yocto is powerful, it is extensive—with a lot of details involved.

In this chapter specifically, some basic concepts regarding Yocto are explained so that you understand the build process in an Intel Galileo and Intel Quark context.

Instead of executing a bunch of commands to have your builds done without any idea of what is going on, this section brings a minimal overview about how the build process works and what the messages on your computer monitor that appear during the build mean.

If you are interested in understanding Yocto more deeply, it is recommended that you access the Yocto's documentation at https://www.yoctoproject.org/ documentation and the manual at http://www.yoctoproject.org/docs/current/ ref-manual/ref-manual.html.

Poky

Poky is the name given to the build system in a Yocto project. Poky depends on a task executor and scheduler called the ***bitbake*** tool.

Bitbake executes all the steps of the build process, based in a group of configuration files and metadata. Basically, bitbake parses and runs several shell scripts and the Python code running all the compilations. If you are a regular C/C++ developer, you usually have dependences of makefiles that were processed having the compilers invoked when you ran the good old make command. Imagine that you have a complex project with different software components and you need to run the make for each of them. Bitbake in a Yocto project context might be considered the "global make command," but you will definitely not use any make commands because bitbake will invoke all of them for you.

The metadata defines which components to build, the components version, and how to build each of them. The metadata can be broken into three individual parts:

- **Configuration files:** Bitbake based in configuration files (.conf) that holds the global definition of variables, the compilation flags, where libraries and applications must be placed, the machine architecture to be used, and so forth.

- **Bitbake classes:** The bitbake classes, is also known as *bbclasses*, are defined in a file with the .bbclass extension. Mostly, the heavy things during the build are done with the definitions in these files, like how the RPM packages are generated, how the root file system is created, and so forth.

- **Recipes:** The recipes are the files with .bb extensions and define the individual pieces of the software to be built, the packages that must be included, where and how to obtain source code and patches, the dependencies, which features and definitions you want to enable in a source, and others.

Perhaps these definitions sound a little complicated for a build system, but they are the magic key to making the system flexible, even if it sounds overengineered. However, in order to better understand how Poky works, and the build system in general, let's build an Intel Galileo image and discuss step by step what's going on during the procedure.

Figure 2-1 was created by a Yocto project team and represents the Yocto build system flow.

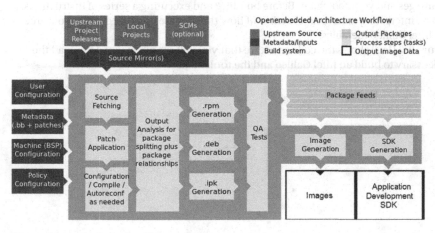

Figure 2-1. *The Yocto build system flow*

Figure 2-1 shows how the Yocto build process works. It warrants a few paragraphs to explain each step.

Along with input files and data, the user **(User Configuration)**, policy **(Policy Configuration)**, and machine configurations **(Machine BSP Configuration)** are loaded and the metadata files are parsed **(Metadata .bb + patches)**.

The build process starts downloading the components from remote repositories, fetching local packages, HTTPS, web sites, FTP sites, and so on, as shown in the **Source Mirror(s)**.

Once all the necessary code is fetched to the working area **(Source Fetching)**, the necessary patches are applied **(Path Application)** and the configurations are applied **(Configuration/Compile/Autoreconf)** based on the information retrieved from the input files and data.

Then thousands of software code starts to compile and the output files goes to a staging area **(output analysis)** until the expected packages are created (`.rpm`, `.deb`, **or** `.ipk`). You will use the **IPK** files in this book.

Some sanity tests are done during the generation of output files **(QA tests)** until all the necessary packages are created and fed **(package feeds)** to generate the final output images **(Image and Application Development SDK)**.

Note that you will need an Internet connection, because lots of code will be downloaded to complete the build process.

The Build System Tree at a Glance

In the next section you will learn how to download metafiles and Poky to build Intel Galileo images and your toolchain. Before building and executing a series of instructions, it would be interesting to have an overview of how the files are organized in the Poky tree and the Intel Galileo metafiles.

Figure 2-2 (left) shows the code structure that you will see when you download the code necessary to build an Intel Galileo and the toolchain.

Figure 2-2. *The Poky and the layers (left) and bitbake tool (right)*

As you can see, there is a folder called poky that contains the basic structure of a Yocto build system. For example, in the poky directory there is a bitbake directory that contains the ***bitbake binary tool*** and other utilities, as shown in Figure 2-2 (right), as well as some directories starting with meta* prefix. Each meta* directory is, in fact, a *layer* containing metadata—in other words, recipes, classes, and configuration files.

On top of the poky directory are other layers, like meta-clanton-bsp, meta-clanton-distro, meta-intel, and meta-oe, which, of course, have their respective recipes, classes, and configuration files, as well as any other metadata.

What defines which layers will in fact be part of compilation is a file called bblayers.conf in the yocto_build/conf directory shown in Listing 2-1.

Listing 2-1. bblayers.conf

```
# LAYER_CONF_VERSION is increased each time build/conf/bblayers.conf
# changes incompatibly
LCONF_VERSION = "6"

BBPATH = "${TOPDIR}"
BBFILES ?= ""
BBLAYERS ?= " \
  /home/mcramon/BSP_1.0.4_T/meta-clanton_v1.0.1/poky/meta \
  /home/mcramon/BSP_1.0.4_T/meta-clanton_v1.0.1/poky/meta-yocto \
  /home/mcramon/BSP_1.0.4_T/meta-clanton_v1.0.1/poky/meta-yocto-bsp \
  /home/mcramon/BSP_1.0.4_T/meta-clanton_v1.0.1/meta-intel \
  /home/mcramon/BSP_1.0.4_T/meta-clanton_v1.0.1/meta-oe/meta-oe \
  /home/mcramon/BSP_1.0.4_T/meta-clanton_v1.0.1/meta-clanton-distro \
  /home/mcramon/BSP_1.0.4_T/meta-clanton_v1.0.1/meta-clanton-bsp \
  "
```

It is time to explore the tree a bit more and check out recipe, configuration, and class files.

An Example of a Recipe (.bb)

Let's look at a recipe file, choose the valid layers, and search for one. For example, let's suppose you chose the meta layer; if you explore this layer a little, you will find very interesting recipes, like the busybox_1.20.2.bb recipe shown in Figure 2-3(a).

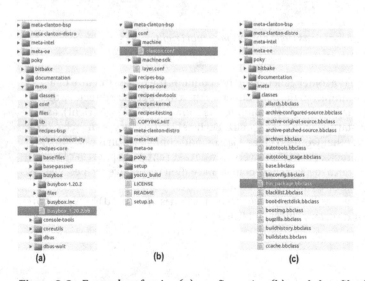

Figure 2-3. *Examples of recipe (a), configuration (b), and class files (c)*

Open the busybox recipe and you will see a code structure similar to the one shown in Listing 2-2.

Listing 2-2. busybox_1.20.2.bb

```
require busybox.inc
PR = "r7"

SRC_URI = "http://www.busybox.net/downloads/busybox-${PV}.tar.
bz2;name=tarball \
           file://B921600.patch \
           file://get_header_tar.patch \
           file://busybox-appletlib-dependency.patch \
           file://run-parts.in.usr-bin.patch \
           file://watch.in.usr-bin.patch \
...
...
...

           file://inetd"

SRC_URI[tarball.md5sum] = "e025414bc6cd79579cc7a32a45d3ae1c"
SRC_URI[tarball.sha256sum] =
"eb13ff01dae5618ead2ef6f92ba879e9e0390f9583bd545d8789d27cf39b6882"

EXTRA_OEMAKE += "V=1 ARCH=${TARGET_ARCH} CROSS_COMPILE=${TARGET_PREFIX}
SKIP_STRIP=y"
```

Note that the recipes contain a SRC_URI variable that defines the URLs to download busybox, and respective md5 and sha256 checksum to make sure that the package downloaded was the one expected. The EXTRA_OEMAKE only adds compilation flags during the build.

Each recipe is parsed and the Yocto build process assumes some functions during the build processing. Some functions are listed next; they can be customized or simply excluded according to the configurations:

- do_fetch

- do_unpack

- do_patch

- do_configure

- do_compile

- do_install

- do_package

Each function is related to the Yocto build flow, as explained earlier, and when you run the build, you will see these functions displayed on your computer, so you will have an idea of what the build process stage is for each package.

The whole list of functions that might be executed during the compilation is specified in Chapter 8 of **the *Yocto Project Reference Manual*** at http://www.yoctoproject.org/docs/1.7/ref-manual/ref-manual.html#ref-tasks.

An Example of a Configuration File (.conf)

At this point, you have a good idea about what a recipe is, so let's look at an example of a configuration file.

Configuration files are usually under a folder called conf in a layer. A good example is the configuration filename clanton.conf that belongs to the meta-clanton-bsp layer under the /conf/machine folder. The content of this file is shown in Listing 2-3 and Figure 2-3(b).

Listing 2-3. clanton.conf

```
#@TYPE: Machine
#@NAME: clanton

#@DESCRIPTION: Machine configuration for clanton systems

PREFERRED_PROVIDER_virtual/kernel ?= "linux-yocto-clanton"
PREFERRED_VERSION_linux-yocto-clanton ?= "3.8%"

require conf/machine/include/ia32-base.inc
include conf/machine/include/tune-i586.inc

#Avoid pulling in GRUB
MACHINE_ESSENTIAL_EXTRA_RDEPENDS = ""

MACHINE_FEATURES = "efi usb pci"

SERIAL_CONSOLE = "115200 ttyS1"
#SERIAL_CONSOLES = "115200;ttyS0 115200;ttyS1"

EXTRA_IMAGEDEPENDS = "grub"
PREFERRED_VERSION_grub = "0.97+git%"
```

In this configuration file, you can see the definitions for clanton machines, such as the serial port speed and the TTY devices to be used as serial console, the kernel name and version, and the drivers supported, like EFI, USB, and PCI.

An Example of a Class File (.bbclass)

The third example of a metadata component is the class file. They keep under a folder called classes with a .bbclass extension. As an example, using the meta layer, search for the class file bin_package.bbclass, as in Listing 2-4 and shown in Figure 2-3(c).

Listing 2-4. bin_package.bbclass

```
#
# ex:ts=4:sw=4:sts=4:et
# -*- tab-width: 4; c-basic-offset: 4; indent-tabs-mode: nil -*-
#
# Common variable and task for the binary package recipe.
# Basic principle:
# * The files have been unpacked to ${S} by base.bbclass
# * Skip do_configure and do_compile
# * Use do_install to install the files to ${D}
#
# Note:
# The "subdir" parameter in the SRC_URI is useful when the input package
# is rpm, ipk, deb and so on, for example:
#
# SRC_URI = "http://foo.com/foo-1.0-r1.i586.rpm;subdir=foo-1.0"
#
# Then the files would be unpacked to ${WORKDIR}/foo-1.0, otherwise
# they would be in ${WORKDIR}.
#

# Skip the unwanted steps
do_configure[noexec] = "1"
do_compile[noexec] = "1"

# Install the files to ${D}
bin_package_do_install () {
    # Do it carefully
    [ -d "${S}" ] || exit 1
    cd ${S} || exit 1
    tar --no-same-owner --exclude='./patches' --exclude='./.pc' -cpf - . \
        | tar --no-same-owner -xpf - -C ${D}
}

FILES_${PN} = "/"

EXPORT_FUNCTIONS do_install
```

This `bbclass` file provides information on what must be done for all meta layers that make usage of binary package recipes, and in this cases **skips** the configure (`do_configure`) and compile (`do_compile`) procedures indexing noexec to 1, but takes action during the package installation (`do_install`).

Creating Your Own Intel Galileo Images

After a small introduction on how the Yocto build system works, it is time to create your own releases using Poky. It is essential to prepare your computer to run the build system, because a series of requirements are necessary to make the build system functional.

Preparing Your Computer

The first thing to do is prepare your computer to be able to build. With Yocto, the system basically runs on Linux, but if you have Windows or Mac OSX, I really recommend that you install a virtual machine, such as VMWare (http://www.vmware.com) or Oracle Virtual Box (https://www.virtualbox.org), and install one of the following Linux distributions:

- Ubuntu 12.04 (LTS)
- Ubuntu 13.10
- Ubuntu 14.04 (LTS)
- Fedora release 19 (Schrödinger's Cat)
- Fedora release 20 (Heisenbug)
- CentOS release 6.4
- CentOS release 6.5
- Debian GNU/Linux 7.0 (Wheezy)
- Debian GNU/Linux 7.1 (Wheezy)
- Debian GNU/Linux 7.2 (Wheezy)
- Debian GNU/Linux 7.3 (Wheezy)
- Debian GNU/Linux 7.4 (Wheezy)
- Debian GNU/Linux 7.5 (Wheezy)
- Debian GNU/Linux 7.6 (Wheezy)
- openSUSE 12.2
- openSUSE 12.3
- openSUSE 13.1

If you have a recent version of a Linux operating system, but it is not listed in the previous distribution list, it is recommended to check that this list is not outdated. To check the most recent distributions supported by Yocto, read the "Supported Linux Distribution" section in the Yocto Reference Project Manual at http://www.yoctoproject.org/docs/1.7/ref-manual/ref-manual.html#detailed-supported-distros.

Some people are able to compile successfully on Mac OSX, but there are so many steps necessary to make this possible that having a virtual machine is the quickest solution.

This book shows a complete build process using Linux **Ubuntu 12.04.04**. If you have a computer or a virtual machine with Ubuntu installed, and you want to check the version, you can run the following command in a terminal shell:

```
mcramon@ubuntu: ~/ $ lsb_release -a
No LSB modules  are available.
Distributor ID: Ubuntu
Description:    Ubuntu 12.04.4 LTS
Release:        12.04
Codename:       precise
```

The next step requires the installation of some packages used by bitbake during the build process. The easiest way to install all the dependences is to run the following command:

```
mcramon@ubuntu:~/$ sudo apt-get install subversion libcurl4-openssl-dev
uuid-dev autoconf texinfo libssl-dev libtool iasl bitbake diffstat gawk
chrpath openjdk-7-jdk connect-proxy autopoint p7zip-full build-essential
gcc-multilib vim-common gawk wget git-core
```

There is an important note regarding the IASL that is a compiler used to support ACPI (Advanced Configuration and Power Interface). When Intel included support to run Windows on Intel Galileo boards, a new power management configuration was created, and, consequently, the IASL compiler had to be updated to attend the ACPI 5.0 specification. Thus, when you install the **IASL** (one of the components) in the previous command, you need to make sure it supports **ACPI revision 5.0** or greater.

If you are using Ubuntu 14, the repositories already point to a version of IASL that supported ACPI 5.0; however, if you have Ubuntu 12, you will probably have problems, because the repositories point to the IASL version that only supports ACPI revision 4.0 and will have problems compiling the UEFI packages. So, if you have Ubuntu 12, the easiest way to install the correct IASL without upgrading your OS or pointing to the repositories of version 14 is to install from a source with the following commands:

```
mcramon@ubuntu:~/tools$ sudo apt-get remove iasl
mcramon@ubuntu:~/tools$ sudo apt-get install libbison-dev  flex
mcramon@ubuntu:~/tools$ mkdir iasl
mcramon@ubuntu:~/tools$ cd iasl/
mcramon@ubuntu:~/tools/iasl$ git clone git://github.com/acpica/acpica.git
mcramon@ubuntu:~/tools/iasl$ cd acpica
mcramon@ubuntu:~/tools/acpica$ make
```

After the make command compiles and links everything, the output files will be in the
.../generate/unix/bin folder.

```
mcramon@ubuntu:~/tools/acpica$ cd ./generate/unix/bin
mcramon@ubuntu:~/tools/iasl/acpica/generate/unix/bin$ ./iasl
Intel ACPI Component Architecture
ASL+ Optimizing Compiler version 20141107-64 [Dec 12 2014]
Copyright (c) 2000 - 2014 Intel Corporation
```

Supports **ACPI Specification Revision 5.1**

The previous command gives you an installation of IASL that supports ACPI 5.1 and,
of course, it is enough to meet the requirements of ACPI 5.0 because it points to the latest
release of IASL repositories in https://github.com/acpica/acpica.
Next, just create a link in /usr/bin/iasl pointing to your IASL, compiled manually:

```
mcramon@ubuntu:~/sudo ln -s <YOUR IASL PATH> /usr/bin/iasl
```

For example:

```
mcramon@ubuntu:~/sudo ln -s /home/mcramon/tools/iasl/acpica/generate/unix/
bin/iasl /usr/bin/iasl
```

After you install all the packages, your machine is able to run the Yocto builds and
you need to follow some steps to create your images, as commented in the next section.

The SPI vs. SD Card Images

The Intel Galileo images are based in Linux 3.8 and there are two possible images
(targets): the SPI image or the SD card image.

The SPI image is an image that fits on Intel Galileo SPI flash memory. It contains the
very basic software, but allows running the sketches (Arduino programs) and contains
some basic utilities, like busybox.

The SD card image must be stored in a micro SD card with a maximum capacity of
32GB and that allows booting Intel Galileo from it. This image contains a powerful variety
of software, such as Python, node.js, and the drivers to support Intel WiFi and Bluetooth
cards, among others.

Both images have the same procedure to build, changing only the target name in the
bitbake command. However, with the SD images, you just need to copy some of the build
output files in the micro SD cards; on the other hand, the SPI images require additional
steps and can be created as capsule files or binary files, which will be discussed later.

The next sections explain how to build Intel Galileo and toolchain images.

Building Intel Galileo Images

There are some steps that must be followed in order to prepare all the metafiles necessary to build such images. The instructions shown in this chapter are related to release 1.0.4. (I can guarantee that the process for 1.0.5 will be simpler because you will not need to worry about downloading and applying patches manually. So, if you are reading this book and a release newer than 1.0.4 is available, you will not need to follow all of these steps, especially the manual application of patches.) The steps are outlined here:

1. **Create a directory where your build will be placed.**

   mcramon@ubuntu:~/$ **mkdir BSP_1.0.4_build**

2. **Download the BSP patches.** Access the download center at https://downloadcenter.intel.com/Detail_Desc. aspx?DwnldID=24355 and read the instructions on how to compile the BSP. With 1.0.4, there are instructions to access the GitHub link at https://github.com/01org/Galileo-Runtime and download the file https://github.com/01org/Galileo-Runtime/archive/1.0.4.tar.gz. Next, decompress the downloaded file:

   mcramon@ubuntu:~/$ **wget https://github.com/01org/Galileo-Runtime/archive/1.0.4.tar.gz**
   mcramon@ubuntu:~/$ **tar -xf Galileo-Runtime-1.0.4.tar.gz**
   mcramon@ubuntu:~/$ **cd Galileo-Runtime-1.0.4**

3. **Decompress the patches.**

   mcramon@ubuntu:~/$ **tar -xvf patches_v1.0.4.tar.gz**
   patches_v1.0.4/
   patches_v1.0.4/.DS_Store
   patches_v1.0.4/meta-clanton.patches/
   patches_v1.0.4/._patch.meta-clanton.sh
   patches_v1.0.4/patch.meta-clanton.sh
   patches_v1.0.4/._patch.Quark_EDKII.sh
   patches_v1.0.4/patch.Quark_EDKII.sh
   patches_v1.0.4/._patch.sysimage.sh
   patches_v1.0.4/patch.sysimage.sh
   patches_v1.0.4/Quark_EDKII.patches/
   patches_v1.0.4/sysimage.patches/
   patches_v1.0.4/sysimage.patches/.DS_Store
   patches_v1.0.4/sysimage.patches/sysimage_v1.0.1+1.0.4.patch
   patches_v1.0.4/Quark_EDKII.patches/.DS_Store
   patches_v1.0.4/Quark_EDKII.patches/Quark_EDKII_v1.0.2+ACPI_for_
   Windows.patch

```
patches_v1.0.4/meta-clanton.patches/.DS_Store
patches_v1.0.4/meta-clanton.patches/meta-clanton.post-patch.init.
patch
patches_v1.0.4/meta-clanton.patches/meta-clanton_v1.0.1+quark-
init.patch
patches_v1.0.4/meta-clanton.patches/post-setup.patches/
patches_v1.0.4/meta-clanton.patches/post-setup.patches/.DS_Store
patches_v1.0.4/meta-clanton.patches/post-setup.patches/1.usb_
improv_patch-1.patch
patches_v1.0.4/meta-clanton.patches/post-setup.patches/2.GAL-193-
clloader-1.patch
patches_v1.0.4/meta-clanton.patches/post-setup.patches/3.GAL-199-
start_spi_upgrade-1.patch
patches_v1.0.4/meta-clanton.patches/post-setup.patches/4.MAKER-
222-Sketch_download_unstable-5.patch
patches_v1.0.4/meta-clanton.patches/post-setup.patches/GAL-118-
USBDeviceResetOnSUSRES-2.patch
patches_v1.0.4/meta-clanton.patches/post-setup.patches/patch.sh
patches_v1.0.4/meta-clanton.patches/post-setup.patches/uart-
1.0.patch
patches_v1.0.4/meta-clanton.patches/post-setup.patches/uart-
reverse-8.patch
```

If you pay attention to the files extracted, you will realize that there are patches for several different repositories, such as meta-clanton, UEFI firmware, and native BSP code. The usage of these patches will be discussed according the steps to build the BSP or to generate the Intel Galileo Images.

4. **Extract the meta-clanton.**

At this point you have some tar.gz files extracted in your directory, such as the directory for SPI flash tools, the firmware based on Intel EDKII, and the sysimage templates; but what really matters at this point is the meta-clanton directory that must be decompressed.

```
mcramon@ubuntu:~/$  tar -zxvf meta-clanton_v1.0.1.tar.gz
Galileo-Runtime-1.0.4/
Galileo-Runtime-1.0.4/Quark_EDKII_v1.0.2.tar.gz
Galileo-Runtime-1.0.4/README.txt
Galileo-Runtime-1.0.4/grub-legacy_5775f32a+v1.0.1.tar.gz
Galileo-Runtime-1.0.4/meta-clanton_v1.0.1.tar.gz
Galileo-Runtime-1.0.4/patches_v1.0.4.tar.gz
Galileo-Runtime-1.0.4/quark_linux_v3.8.7+v1.0.1.tar.gz
Galileo-Runtime-1.0.4/spi-flash-tools_v1.0.1.tar.gz
```

Alternatively, you can decompress all files, if you want, by running the following command:

```
mcramon@ubuntu:~/$ for file in $(ls *.tar.gz); do tar -zxvf
$file;done
```

Enter the decompressed meta-clanton directory, and then observe the files and directories that you have.

```
mcramon@ubuntu:~/$ cd meta-clanton_v1.0.1/
mcramon@ubuntu:~/$ ls
LICENSE  meta-clanton-bsp  meta-clanton-distro  README  setup
setup.sh
```

Note that you have the meta-clanton layer, but the main build processor Poky is not present and you need to fetch it.

5. **Apply the** meta-clanton **patches.** Return to the previous directory and run the meta-clanton patches with following command:

```
mcramon@ubuntu:~/$ cd ..
mcramon@ubuntu:~/$ ./patches_v1.0.4/patch.meta-clanton.sh
```

This patch fetches new metafiles and the Poky, and then applies code patches.

Internally, the patch.meta-clanton.sh script calls a second script named setup.sh that downloads the some new metafiles that are included in the meta-clanton directory. The new metafiles are meta-intel and meta-oe. Also, two new directories were prepared: poky and yocto_build. This might take some time, depending on the speed of your Internet connection.

You can check the new files as follows:

```
mcramon@ubuntu:~/$ cd meta-clanton_v1.0.1/
mcramon@ubuntu:~/$ ls
LICENSE  meta-clanton-bsp  meta-clanton-distro  meta-intel
meta-oe  poky  README  setup  setup.sh  yocto_build
```

At times during the Intel Galileo development, new bugs arise and new fixes are introduced. The Intel Galileo BSP images lays on Intel Clanton BSP baseline but the development of two lines run in parallel with some merges of Intel Galileo fixes sporadically. When new fixes arises before any official Intel Clanton baseline release, then patches are provided and the Intel Galileo BSP continues independently.

For example, this chapter is based on release 1.0.4, but when you downloaded the BSP sources, you have notices such as meta-clanton_v1.0.1.tar.gz that mean baseline **1.0.1**. In this case, Intel provides patches that must be applied on top of 1.0.1, and once applied, you have a legitimate source 1.0.4. It is great if there is no patch to be applied, because the baseline is in sync with previous Intel Galileo fixes.

So, the second action done by patch.meta-clanton.sh is to apply not only code fixes but also possible recipe files that must be correct; for example, patching a new OpenSSL code or applying security fixes.

Intel is doing its best to replace the patches script with efficient .bbappend files provided as a source, so that you will not need to apply any patches manually.

6.   **Set the environment variables.** After applying all the patches, it is necessary to set the environment variables and Poky directly where the build should start. To do this, run the following commands:

```
mcramon@ubuntu:~/$ cd ./meta-clanton_v1.0.1
mcramon@ubuntu:~/$ source poky/oe-init-build-env yocto_build
```

At the end of this command, your prompt in the terminal shell will be automatically moved to the yocto_build directory.

7.   **Enable the cache and set the number of threads.** This step is just a recommendation. It is not necessary to follow because you could start your build; however, these changes will enable the cache and might make your build a little bit faster.

Open the file .../meta-clanton/yocto_build/conf/local.conf with the text editor of your preference.

The change is the variable BB_NUMBER_THREADS that represents the maximum number of threads that your bitbake command will be able to handle. My suggestion is to multiply the numbers of threads on your computer processor by 2; for example, if your computer supports 8 threads, you can change this number to 16. If you are using a free version of virtual machines, check the number of core processors that it allows you to set. For example, the free version of VMware only allows setting a maximum of four cores, and if each core of your processor holds one single thread, then BB_NUMBER_THREADS could be 8.

```
BB_NUMBER_THREADS = "12"
```

Still, in yocto.conf you can make the following changes:

```
SSTATE_DIR ?= "/tmp/yocto_cache-sstate"
SOURCE_MIRROR_URL ?= "file:///tmp/yocto_cache/"
INHERIT += "own-mirrors"
BB_GENERATE_MIRROR_TARBALLS = "1"
```

By enabling the cache, if your build is interrupted for some reason, such as a lapse moment of Internet disconnection, if you re-execute the bitbake command, the build will not start from scratch because the cache is reused and the code that was previously downloaded does not need to be downloaded again.

The next step is the compilation itself.

8. **Compile the images.** It is time to execute the build process using the bitbake tool. At this point, you have two possible images related to Intel Galileo: the **SPI image** and the **SD card image**. To check the name of each target release, type the command bitbake -s, which brings all the targets supported by the current configurations:

```
mcramon@ubuntu:$ bitbake -s |grep galileo
galileo-target                                              :0.1-r0
image-full-galileo                                          :1.0-r0
image-spi-galileo                                           :1.0-r0
```

The target image-full-galileo creates the SD card image; image-spi-galileo creates the SPI image; and galileo-target must be ignored because it is not used anymore.

Then, using bitbake again, you can run the build process for the target you want to work. For example, for SPI you just need to run this:

```
mcramon@ubuntu:$ bitbake image-spi-galileo
```

All the configurations are checked; the download of the sources, packages, and patches that compose the software is started; each component is properly set, enabling and disabling features and software definitions; and finally, everything is compiled and the images are generated.

During the compilation process, you will be able to see the do_ actions in place of different recipes, the number of tasks completed and to be completed, and warnings if the mirrors failed to download the expected code. You do not need to worry about warnings, because they are an indication that the code failed to be fetched and a different mirror will be used. You only need to worry if there are errors reported, and in this case, you need to identify the recipe file and check whether the URL mirrors changed, which would fix the file, or if you have a generic error like an Internet connection loss or insufficient space in the device.

Figure 2-4 shows a snapshot of a full image process given after the command bitbake image-full-galileo is used to create SD card releases. Note that there are 2,924 tasks to be done, but only 190 were executed, which means that this is the beginning of the compilation. You can also observe some actions in place, such as do_configure, do_compile, do_patch, and do_unpack, for different recipes.

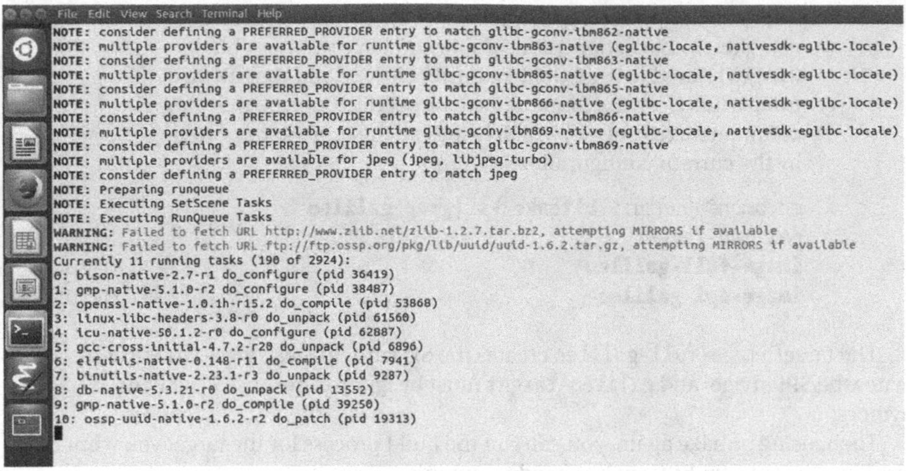

```
File Edit View Search Terminal Help
NOTE: consider defining a PREFERRED_PROVIDER entry to match glibc-gconv-ibm862-native
NOTE: multiple providers are available for runtime glibc-gconv-ibm863-native (eglibc-locale, nativesdk-eglibc-locale)
NOTE: consider defining a PREFERRED_PROVIDER entry to match glibc-gconv-ibm863-native
NOTE: multiple providers are available for runtime glibc-gconv-ibm865-native (eglibc-locale, nativesdk-eglibc-locale)
NOTE: consider defining a PREFERRED_PROVIDER entry to match glibc-gconv-ibm865-native
NOTE: multiple providers are available for runtime glibc-gconv-ibm866-native (eglibc-locale, nativesdk-eglibc-locale)
NOTE: consider defining a PREFERRED_PROVIDER entry to match glibc-gconv-ibm866-native
NOTE: multiple providers are available for runtime glibc-gconv-ibm869-native (eglibc-locale, nativesdk-eglibc-locale)
NOTE: consider defining a PREFERRED_PROVIDER entry to match glibc-gconv-ibm869-native
NOTE: multiple providers are available for jpeg (jpeg, libjpeg-turbo)
NOTE: consider defining a PREFERRED_PROVIDER entry to match jpeg
NOTE: Preparing runqueue
NOTE: Executing SetScene Tasks
NOTE: Executing RunQueue Tasks
WARNING: Failed to fetch URL http://www.zlib.net/zlib-1.2.7.tar.bz2, attempting MIRRORS if available
WARNING: Failed to fetch URL ftp://ftp.ossp.org/pkg/lib/uuid/uuid-1.6.2.tar.gz, attempting MIRRORS if available
Currently 11 running tasks (190 of 2924):
0: bison-native-2.7-r1 do_configure (pid 36419)
1: gmp-native-5.1.0-r2 do_configure (pid 38487)
2: openssl-native-1.0.1h-r15.2 do_compile (pid 53868)
3: linux-libc-headers-3.8-r0 do_unpack (pid 61560)
4: icu-native-56.1.2-r0 do_configure (pid 62887)
5: gcc-cross-initial-4.7.2-r20 do_unpack (pid 6896)
6: elfutils-native-0.148-r11 do_compile (pid 7941)
7: binutils-native-2.23.1-r3 do_unpack (pid 9287)
8: db-native-5.3.21-r0 do_compile (pid 13552)
9: gmp-native-5.1.0-r2 do_compile (pid 39250)
10: ossp-uuid-native-1.6.2-r2 do_patch (pid 19313)
```

Figure 2-4. *bitbake output for full image compilation*

If the compilation is fine, the next step is to check the output files.

9. In the end, if everything downloads and is configured, compiled, and linked, and patches are applied, you should have the images available in the ...meta-clanton/yocto_ build/tmp/deploy/images directory.

If you created SD card images, you just need to copy the files to your SD card; otherwise, some additional steps are necessary with SPI images.

The next section explains how to build the toolchain, but if you are excited to test your release, read the *"Booting Intel Galileo with Your Own Images"* section in this chapter.

Building and Using the Cross-Compiler Toolchain

It is important to understand how to create the ***cross-compilers*** and **IPK** packages because some chapters of this book will make use of them, especially in Chapter 7, and, of course, if you want to create native applications.

The next sections explain how to build the toolchain and how you might generate a toolchain for different operating systems.

Note that if your intention is only to create images to Intel Galileo boards, then this section is not mandatory.

Compiling the Toolchain for Different Architectures

If you are a Windows or Mac OSX user, you are probably running the Yocto build using a virtual machine. At this point, you might be asking if you can create a toolchain for your native operating system, instead of using virtual machines for everything, including the toolchain.

The answer is yes, and it is very simple to create a toolchain for other architectures, even if you have a Linux machine, because it is one of the proposals of the Yocto build system.

To make such a change, it is necessary to open the file .../meta-clanton/yocto_build/conf/local.conf and add the variable SDKMACHINE followed by a string that describes the machine architecture designed to the SDK build.

```
SDKMACHINE = "i386-darwin"

BB_NUMBER_THREADS = "12"

PARALLEL_MAKE = "-j 14"

MACHINE = "clanton"
DISTRO ?= "clanton-tiny"
EXTRA_IMAGE_FEATURES = "debug-tweaks"
USER_CLASSES ?= "buildstats image-mklibs image-prelink"
PATCHRESOLVE = "noop"
CONF_VERSION = "1"
```

Basically, the strings for different operating systems are shown in Table 2-1.

Table 2-1. *Machine Architecture Definition*

String	Target Architecture
i586	Linux, 32-bit
x86_64	Linux, 64-bit
i386-darwin	OSX
i686-mingw32	Windows, 32- and 64-bit

If the SDKMACHINE is not explicitly declared, then the toolchain will assume the computer architecture that runs the Yocto build.

You need to use the text editor of your preference, or simply change the machine using a command line. For example, if you want to specify the target as 32-bit Linux, you can run the following:

```
mcramon@ubuntu:~/$ cd meta-clanton_v1.0.1/yocto_build
mcramon@ubuntu:~/$ echo 'SDKMACHINE = "i586"' >> conf/local.conf
```

The next sections discuss how to build and install the toolchains for different operating systems.

Building the Toolchains

The generations of toolchains require the same steps mentioned in the *"Building Intel Galileo Images"* section; however, the bitbake command is different and additional layers must be downloaded.

Note that it is always recommended to check any possible changes in the process—how the toolchains are generated in case this book becomes outdated. In this case, consult the *Quark BSP Build Guide*, which you can access at http://www.intel.com/content/dam/www/public/us/en/documents/guides/galileo-quark-x1000-bsp-guide.pdf.

The instructions in this section generate the toolchain based on the uclibc library, because it is the default library set in the metafiles. If you are interested in creating the toolchains based in eglibc, you need to read Chapter 7, specifically the "Preparing the BSP Software Image and Toolchain" section.

The generation of toolchains is different for Linux, Windows, and OSX, as you will read in the following instructions.

Linux

The following is the command to generate the toolchain for 32-bit Linux:

```
mcramon@ubuntu:~/$ cd ./meta-clanton_v1.0.1
mcramon@ubuntu:~/$ source poky/oe-init-build-env yocto_build
mcramon@ubuntu:~/$ echo 'SDKMACHINE = "i586"' >> conf/local.conf
mcramon@ubuntu:~/$ bitbake meta-toolchain
```

If you want to generate for 64-bit Linux, you need to change the SDKMACHINE to x86_64. Alternatively, you can replace the command bitbake meta-toolchain with bitbake image_full –c populate_sdk and the result will be the same.

OSX

OSX requires you have a legitimate Mac computer with **OSX 10.8** or later and with **Xcode 5.1.0** or later installed. Initially, using your Mac computer, perform the following steps:

1. Go to the App Store and install **Xcode 5.1.0** or later.

2. Install the command-line development tools using **Preferences ➤ Downloads** and choose command-line tools.

3. Using the terminal shell, create the file OSX-sdk.zip with following commands:

```
$ mkdir ~/Desktop/OSX-sdk
$ cd ~/Desktop/OSX-sdk
$ ditto `xcrun --sdk macosx10.8 --show-sdk-path` .
$ cd ..
$ zip -yr OSX-sdk OSX-sdk
```

4. Copy the OSX-sdk.zip to a directory in your Linux virtual machine. The following are the commands to create the OSX toolchain:

```
mcramon@ubuntu:~/$ cd ./meta-clanton_v1.0.1
mcramon@ubuntu:~/$ sed -i 's|setup/gitsetup.py -c setup/$1.cfg -w
mcramon@ubuntu:~/$ sed -i 's|setup/gitsetup.py -c setup/$1.cfg -w
$1|setup/gitsetup.py -c setup/$1.cfg -w $1 --depth=1|' setup/
gitsetup.py mcramon@ubuntu:~/$ ./setup.sh
mcramon@ubuntu:~/$ git clone git://git.yoctoproject.org/meta-darwin
mcramon@ubuntu:~/$ cd meta-darwin ; git checkout
03b7dd85732838d78e4879332b1cc005dae25754 ; cd ..
mcramon@ubuntu:~/$ (cd poky && patch -p1) < meta-darwin/oecore.patch
mcramon@ubuntu:~/$ mv <YOUR DIRECTORY HERE>/OSX-sdk.zip meta-
darwin/recipes-devtools/osx-runtime/files darwinpath="$(pwd)/
meta-darwin"
mcramon@ubuntu:~/$ echo 'SDKMACHINE = "i386-darwin"' >> yocto_
build/conf/local.conf
mcramon@ubuntu:~/$ echo "BBLAYERS += \"$darwinpath\"" >> yocto_
build/conf/bblayers.conf
mcramon@ubuntu:~/$ source poky/oe-init-build-env yocto_build
mcramon@ubuntu:~/$ bitbake meta-toolchain
```

Windows

For Windows, the commands are the same for Windows, 64 or 32 bits; however, a sequence of two bitbakes is required in addition to the extra metafiles.

```
mcramon@ubuntu:~/$ sed -i 's|setup/gitsetup.py -c setup/$1.cfg -w $1|setup/
gitsetup.py -c setup/$1.cfg -w $1 --depth=1|' setup/gitsetup.py
mcramon@ubuntu:~/$./setup.sh

mcramon@ubuntu:~/$ git clone -b dylan git://git.yoctoproject.org/meta-mingw
mcramon@ubuntu:~/$ (cd poky && patch -p1) < meta-mingw/oecore.patch

mcramon@ubuntu:~/$ mingwpath="$(pwd)/meta-mingw"
mcramon@ubuntu:~/$ echo 'SDKMACHINE = "i686-mingw32"' >> yocto_build/conf/
local.conf
mcramon@ubuntu:~/$ echo "BBLAYERS += \"$mingwpath\"" >> yocto_build/conf/
bblayers.conf

mcramon@ubuntu:~/$ cd $WORKSPACE/meta-clanton_v1.0.1poky
mcramon@ubuntu:~/$ wget http://git.yoctoproject.org/cgit.cgi/poky/patch/
meta/classes/sstate.bbclass?id=4273aa4287ecd36529f2d752c76ab8d09afc33c3 -O
sstate.bbclass.patch
git am sstate.bbclass.patch
```

```
mcramon@ubuntu:~/$ cd $WORKSPACE/meta-clanton_v1.0.1
mcramon@ubuntu:~/$ source poky/oe-init-build-env yocto_build
mcramon@ubuntu:~/$ bitbake gcc-crosssdk-initial -c cleansstate
mcramon@ubuntu:~/$ bitbake meta-toolchain
```

The Output Files

The output files will be in the .../meta-clanton_v1.0.1/yocto_build/tmp/deploy/
sdk directory, while the ipk packages will be in the directory .../meta-clanton_v1.0.1/
yocto_build/tmp/deploy/ipk directory.

The output filename depends on whether your computer is 32 or 64 bits, the
architecture that the toolchain is designated for (we will discuss later), and the uclibc or
eglic library that the image is based on. In the end, you will have just a single script file;
however, it is a big file at around 260MB.

For example, if you compile in a 64-bit Linux machine with an Intel processor, the
output filename is clanton-tiny-uclibc-x86_64-i586-toolchain-1.4.2.sh.

The next sections discuss how to install and test the toolchains.

Installing the Cross-Compilers

The installation of the toolchain just requires you to execute the script created and choose
a destination folder, as shown:

```
mcramon@ubuntu:~/toolchain$ ./clanton-tiny-uclibc-x86_64-i586-toolchain-1.4.2.sh
Enter target directory for SDK (default: /opt/clanton-tiny/1.4.2):
You are about to install the SDK to "/opt/clanton-tiny/1.4.2". Proceed[Y/n]?Y
[sudo] password for mcramon:
Extracting SDK...done
Setting it up...done
SDK has been successfully set up and is ready to be used.
```

The shell script inflates the toolchain in the directory chosen, and all programs that
make part of the toolchain are promptly accommodated.

The **"Creating a Hello World!"** section in this chapter brings a practical usage of the
toolchain.

Creating a Hello World!

This section requires you to have built and properly installed the toolchain in your
computer.

If you enter the toolchain directory chosen during the installation, you will notice
many binary files, including the compilers and directories, but initially what matters is a
file that starts with environment-setup-*; for example, in my setup I have the file named
as environment-setup-i586-poky-linux-uclibc.

This file contains a lot of variables—such as CC, CXX, CPP, AR, and NM—that must be exported to your computer shell. They are used to compile, link, and archive your native programs with the toolchain, so primarily you need to make this variable part of the development environment, sourcing it as follows:

```
mcramon@ubuntu:/opt/clanton-tiny/1.4.2$ source environment-setup-i586-poky-
linux-uclibc
```

For example, you will be able to compile a problem with $(CC) -c $(CFLAGS) $(CPPFLAGS) since CC points to the C compilers, CFLAGS to the C compiler flags, and CPPFLAGS to the C++ compiler flags. If you check some of these variables after sourcing them, you will see something like this:

```
mcramon@ubuntu:/opt/clanton-tiny/1.4.2$ echo $CC
i586-poky-linux-uclibc-gcc -m32 -march=i586 --sysroot=/opt/clanton-
tiny/1.4.2/sysroots/i586-poky-linux-uclibc
mcramon@ubuntu:/opt/clanton-tiny/1.4.2$ echo $CFLAGS
-O2 -pipe -g -feliminate-unused-debug-types
mcramon@ubuntu:/opt/clanton-tiny/1.4.2$ echo $CXXFLAGS
-O2 -pipe -g -feliminate-unused-debug-types -fpermissive
```

Listing 2-5 brings a simple Hello World program written in C, which is present in the code folder of this chapter.

Listing 2-5. HelloWorld.c

```c
#include <stdio.h>
int main(int argc, char const* argv[])
{
    printf("Hello, World! This is Intel Galileo!\n");
    return 0;
}
```

Copy this program to your computer and compile it using the variables you exported.

```
mcramon@ubuntu:/ ${CC} ${CFLAGS} HelloWorld.c -o HelloWorld
```

You should have the executable HelloWorld created using the cross-compiler. Just copy this file to a **micro SD card** formatted using FAT or FAT32. If you do not know how to format the micro SD card, read the *"Boot from SD Card Image"* section of this chapter for instructions.

Insert the micro SD card on your Intel Galileo and boot the board connecting the power supply. Also connect the serial cables, as explained in Chapter 1, and open a Linux terminal shell.

Then locate the micro SD card mounted to the /media/mmcblk0p1 partition, and execute the HelloWorld, as shown:

```
root@clanton:/# cd /media/mmcblk0p1/
root@clanton:/media/mmcblk0p1# ls
HelloWorld
root@clanton:/media/mmcblk0p1# ./HelloWorld
Hello, World! This is Intel Galileo!
```

If you see the output message, it means that your toolchain is functional and generating the binaries correctly. There are multiples ways to transfer your executable to the board, using either WiFi, Ethernet, a pen drive, or a micro SD card. For more information, read the *"Transferring Files Between Intel Galileo and Computers"* section in Chapter 5.

You can also create a simple makefile for this HelloWorld by simply using the variables exported by the environment-setup-i586-poky-linux-uclibc as a base. For example, Listing 2-6 shows a makefile for the HelloWorld program.

Listing 2-6. Makefile

```
SHELL = /bin/bash
TARGET_NAME = i586-poky-linux-uclibc
DIST = clanton-tiny
CC = $(TARGET_NAME)-gcc  -m32 -march=i586 --sysroot=/opt/$(DIST)/1.4.2/sysr
oots/$(TARGET_NAME)
CFLAGS = -O2 -pipe -g -feliminate-unused-debug-types
OUTPUT_FILE = HelloWorld

all: target

target: $(patsubst %.c,%.o,$(wildcard *.c))
        $(CC) $(CFLAGS) $^ -o $(OUTPUT_FILE)

clean:
        rm -f $(TARGET_BIN) *.o $(OUTPUT_FILE)
```

The makefile created is designated to target i586-poky-linux-uClibc, as stored in the variable TARGET_NAME and considers the toolchain installed in the /opt/clanton-tiny directory according the CC variable. So, if you create the toolchain for a different target, or used a different directory installation, it is necessary to adapt this makefile.

The makefile also brings three commands: clean to clean all the object files and the output file named as HelloWorld, because it is the value in the OUTPUT_FILE variable; all and target do the same thing—in other words, compile the C programs, invoking the compiler pointed by CC and CFLAGS.

To create a HelloWorld, all you need to do is type make.

```
mcramon@ubuntu:~/native$ make
i586-poky-linux-uclibc-gcc   -m32 -march=i586 --sysroot=/opt/clanton-
tiny/1.4.2/sysroots/i586-poky-linux-uclibc -O2 -pipe -g -feliminate-unused-
debug-types    -c -o HelloWorld.o HelloWorld.c
i586-poky-linux-uclibc-gcc   -m32 -march=i586 --sysroot=/opt/clanton-
tiny/1.4.2/sysroots/i586-poky-linux-uclibc -O2 -pipe -g -feliminate-unused-
debug-types HelloWorld.o -o HelloWorld
```

The next section talks about debugging native applications.

Debugging Native Applications

It is possible to debug native application and kernel modules using GDB, Eclipse, and JTAG tools. This book focuses on Arduino projects, so all debugging methods are concentrated in the Intel Arduino IDE, and not in native applications or kernel contexts. In the scope of this book, it is important to know how build systems work, how to build and compile native applications, and how to generate the cross-compilers, because these features will be used in the following chapters, especially when you work with OpenCV and V4L2 in Chapter 7.

However, if you are interested in learning how to debug native applications, Intel provides a very good tutorial about how to use Eclipse with Intel Galileo and Intel Edison in the developer zone. This tutorial can be accessed at https://software.intel.com/ en-us/getting-started-for-c-c-plus-plus-eclipse-galileo-and-edison.

For kernel debugging, GDB, and JTAG enabling using openOCD, it is recommended that you read the *Source Level Debugging using OpenOCD/GDB/Eclipse on Intel Quark SoC X1000* manual, present in the manuals folder of this chapter, or you can access it at https://communities.intel.com/docs/DOC-22203.

The next section explains how to make Intel Galileo boot with the images that you created with poky.

Booting Intel Galileo with Your Own Images

As explained earlier, you have two image targets related to Intel Galileo—the SPI card image and the SD card image. The procedures to make Intel Galileo boot using these images differ and must be followed as directed in the following sections.

Booting from SD Card Images

The SD card release only requires that you copy some of the output files to a micro SD card, insert it in Intel Galileo, and then power-on the board.

Preparing the Micro SD Card

Before copying the files, there are important details to know regarding the format of the micro SD card, which must be FAT or FAT32 with a single partition.

First of all, you need to format the SD card in your computer. Nowadays, computers offer SD card slots; if you insert the micro SD card into a SD card adaptor connected to the slot, you are able to read, write, or format your micro SD card, as shown in Figure 2-5. However, if your computer does not provide any kind of access to the micro SD card, then you will need a micro SD card reader that connects to a USB port. Figure 2-6 shows an example of an SD card reader in a laptop and a micro SD card reader device.

Figure 2-5. *An SD card adaptor to be used with a computer*

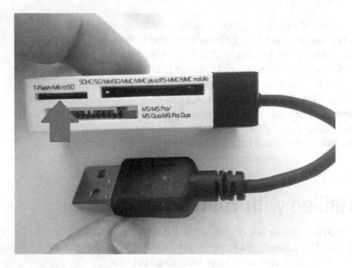

Figure 2-6. *A micro SD card USB adaptor*

With a physical connection between the micro SD card and your computer established, you just need to format the micro SD card according to your OS.

Windows

If you are a Windows user and you are running a virtual machine with Linux to run Yocto builds, you might be excited to use the regular format procedure offered by Windows; in other words, open Explorer, right-click the SD card drive, and select the Format option. In this case, deselect Quick Format and choose the right partition format, as shown in Figure 2-7.

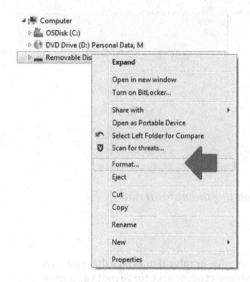

Figure 2-7. *Formatting the micro SD card on Windows*

Mac OSX

Formatting a micro SD card on Mac OSX is quite easy. In Spotlight, type **Disk Utility** and run the **Disk Utility** software. Click the micro SD card in the left panel and then click the Erase tab. Select the format type in the Format combo box and click the Erase button. Figure 2-8 shows the Disk Utility options.

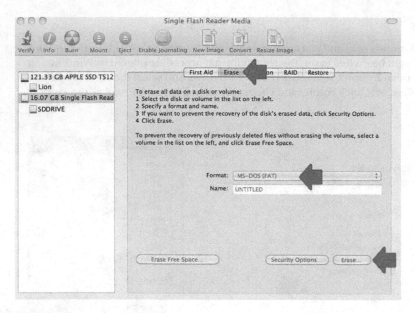

Figure 2-8. *The Disk Utility on Mac OSX formatting the micro SD card*

Ubuntu

On Ubuntu there are several utilities with a very nice graphical interface that can format the micro SD card, including **GParted** (http://gparted.sourceforge.net) and **Disk Utility** for Ubuntu (https://apps.ubuntu.com/cat/applications/precise/gnome-disk-utility/). To avoid any new software installation, however, it is possible to format using simple command-line commands. The steps are as follows:

1. Open a terminal by pressing **Ctrl+Alt+T** at same time.

2. Type the command df to check the partition in your computer, including the micro SD card mounted. Then identify the device name that defines the micro SD card; for example, /dev/sdb1.

3. Unmount the SD card using the umount command followed by the device name. For example:

   umount /dev/sdb1

4. Use the MKDOSFS utility to format the card. For example:

   mkdosfs -F 32 -v /dev/sdb1

With the micro SD card ready, it is time to copy your image into it.

Copying Files to a Micro SD Card

If you successfully create your SD card image, enter ../yocto_build/tmp/deploy/images
in the directory and type the ls -l command:

```
mcramon@ubuntu $ cd ./tmp/deploy/images/
mcramon@ubuntu $ ls -l
total 150576
drwxr-xr-x 3 mcramon mcramon      4096 Nov 18 23:01 boot
-rw-r--r-- 2 mcramon mcramon    373760 Nov 19 00:04 bootia32.efi
lrwxrwxrwx 2 mcramon mcramon        42 Nov 18 23:58 bzImage -> bzImage--3.8-
r0-clanton-20141119062948.bin
-rw-r--r-- 2 mcramon mcramon   1984512 Nov 18 23:58 bzImage--3.8-r0-clanton-
20141119062948.bin
lrwxrwxrwx 2 mcramon mcramon        42 Nov 18 23:58 bzImage-clanton.bin ->
bzImage--3.8-r0-clanton-20141119062948.bin
-rw-r--r-- 1 mcramon mcramon   1689687 Nov 19 00:08 core-image-minimal-
initramfs-clanton-20141119062948.rootfs.cpio.gz
lrwxrwxrwx 1 mcramon mcramon        66 Nov 19 00:08 core-image-minimal-
initramfs-clanton.cpio.gz -> core-image-minimal-initramfs-clanton-
20141119062948.rootfs.cpio.gz
-rw-r--r-- 2 mcramon mcramon    279670 Nov 18 23:59 grub.efi
-rw-r--r-- 1 mcramon mcramon 314572800 Nov 19 00:26 image-full-galileo-
clanton-20141119062948.rootfs.ext3
lrwxrwxrwx 1 mcramon mcramon        53 Nov 19 00:26 image-full-galileo-
clanton.ext3 -> image-full-galileo-clanton-20141119062948.rootfs.ext3
-rw-rw-r-- 2 mcramon mcramon   1556960 Nov 18 23:58 modules--3.8-r0-clanton-
20141119062948.tgz
-rw-rw-r-- 2 mcramon mcramon       294 Nov 19 00:25 README_-_DO_NOT_DELETE_
FILES_IN_THIS_DIRECTORY.txt
```

There is a folder called boot with files and links. The only function of the links is to
make "easy reading" of the files that receive a timestamp in their names. For example,
the bzImage--3.8-r0-clanton-20141119062948.bin, where 20141119062948 is only the
timestamp; thus, if you run the bitbake again without any modification, you will have
another bzImage file with a different timestamp and a link pointing to the newest one.

Thus, you will need to copy to your micro SD card as follows:

1. boot (the whole directory, including subdirectories)

2. bzImage

3. core-image-minimal-initramfs-clanton.cpio.gz

4. grub.efi

5. image-full-galileo-clanton.ext3

Copy these files and directories to your micro SD card, insert it into the micro SD
card slot (see Chapter 1), and power-on your Intel Galileo.

This is everything you need if you are using SD card images. The next section explains this procedure when SPI images are used.

Booting from SPI Card Images

When you build an SPI image, the process results in a single file created to store your image in the SPI flash memory. In this case, two different types of files can be built:

- **Capsule file:** This file contains the system images, the kernel, the file system partition, and the boot loader packages (grub), but it does not contain the platform data. Platform data informs the MAC address of your Ethernet controller and the board model, such as Intel Galileo or Intel Galileo Gen2. This file is very useful in most cases; if you have a board without boot issues and the Ethernet controller is working with a correct MAC address, the file is very handy. Usually, capsule files (or cap files) contain the .cap extension, and you can flash Intel Galileo boards using the Intel Arduino IDE or the UEFI shell, which will be discussed later.

- **Binary file:** This binary file contains everything; in other words, everything in a capsule file, plus the platform data. Usually, these files have the .bin extension and must be flashed with an SPI programmer.

Figure 2-9 shows a flowchart that explains the process to generate both of these files.

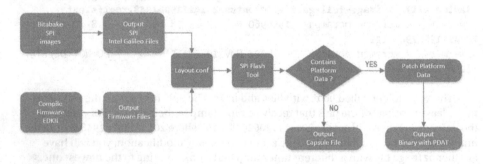

Figure 2-9. *SPI files generation flowchart*

Initially it is necessary to generate the Intel Galileo SPI images that will generate the SPI files as output.

In parallel, it is possible to compile the firmware and generate the files related to firmware as output. Then a template is mounted using a file named layout.conf that contains all the ingredients necessary to build files a single file that will be used to flash the SPI flash memory.

With layout.conf ready, the SPI flash tool is called to generate capsule and binary files without platform data. If the intention is to have files without platform data, at this point the capsule files might be used; otherwise, the platform data must be patched using a Python script, which will be discussed later. A final binary with all the information is created.

Creating the Capsule Files Flash Files

When you downloaded the BSP board support package in the step 2 of the "Creating your Own Intel Galileo Images" section of this chapter, you should have noticed that files in addition to the meta-clanton data were downloaded, among them files called spi-flash-tools_v1.0.1.tar.gz and Quark_EDKII_v1.0.1.tar.gz.

Compiling the UEFI Firmware

To decompress the Linux kernel before your board boots, there is firmware responsible to initialize the board components, including the Intel Quark SoC. It also assumes other activities after the boot.

The Intel Galileo provides firmware compliant with UEFI (Unified Extensible Firmware Interface) standards that consist of boot procedures, runtime services calls, and data tables used for power management methods like ACPI (Advanced Configuration and Power Interface).

EDKII means the environment cross-platform for firmware development.

Of course, to understand the UEFI specification and EDKII development process, it would require a full book dedicated to this subject. In the context of this book, the concept is limited to how to build the EDKII, which is one of the core elements to have a functional SPI image.

The next sections discuss how to prepare your environment and how to compile the firmware.

Preparing the Environment

The following are the dependences to compile the UEFI firmware:

- Python 2.6 or newer

- Any GCC and G++ with versions between 4.3 and 4.7

- Subversion

- uuid-dev

- IASL

If you run the command line proposed in the *"Preparing Your Computer"* section, you should be fine with these dependences, except Python. Check to see if you have Python installed on your Linux by running the following command:

```
mcramon@ubuntu:~$ dpkg --get-selections | grep -v deinstall|grep -i python
```

Or you can run this:

```
mcramon@ubuntu:~$ python --version
Python 2.7.3
```

If you do not have Python installed, you can install it by following the instructions at https://www.python.org/downloads/. If you want a quick try using version 2.7.6, you can run the following commands:

```
mcramon@ubuntu:~/$ wget https://www.python.org/ftp/python/2.7.6/Python-
                       2.7.6.tgz
mcramon@ubuntu:~/$ tar -zxvf Python-2.7.6.tgz
mcramon@ubuntu:~/$ cd Python-2.7.6/
mcramon@ubuntu:~/$ ./configure
mcramon@ubuntu:~/$ make
mcramon@ubuntu:~/$ make install
```

After this, you are ready to compile the firmware by following the steps presented in the next section.

Compiling the Firmware

Once you have downloaded the right package, you need to follow these instructions step by step:

1. **Extract the package.** The first thing to do is go back to the base directory and decompress the file:

   ```
   mcramon@ubuntu $ tar -xvf Quark_EDKII_v1.0.2.tar.gz
   ```

Unfortunately, it is necessary to apply patches manually, but fortunately this can be done with a single command line:

```
mcramon@ubuntu $ ./patches_v1.0.4/patch.Quark_EDKII.sh
```

This patch only fixes some ACPI tables to support Windows, which is not within the scope of this book, but it is recommended to run this patch anyway to keep your firmware updated.

2. **Prepare the SVN project.** The EDKII is maintained using the SVN configuration control release tool.

   ```
   mcramon@ubuntu:~/$ cd Quark_EDKII_v1.0.2/
   mcramon@ubuntu:~/$ ./svn_setup.py
   mcramon@ubuntu:~/$ svn update
   mcramon@ubuntu:~/$ export WORKSPACE=$(pwd)
   ```

The first command, ./svn_setup.py, is a Python script that brings a series of code related to EDKII to your computer. The command svn update makes certain that you have the latest changes in fetched files. This step might take few minutes, depending on your Internet connection speed.

3. **Identify the GCC that you have installed.** There is a *compilation flag* used during the firmware compilation that depends of the GCC compiler installed on your computer. To check which version you have, you can type the following command:

```
mcramon@ubuntu:~/$ gcc --version
gcc (Ubuntu/Linaro 4.6.3-1ubuntu5) 4.6.3
Copyright (C) 2011 Free Software Foundation, Inc.
This is free software; see the source for copying conditions.
There is NO
warranty; not even for MERCHANTABILITY or FITNESS FOR A
PARTICULAR PURPOSE.
```

In the example, GCC informed us that the version is **4.6.3**, which means that the flag to be used in the compilation line of EDKII will be the string GCC46.

The GCC and G++ compilers tested at the time that this book was written was between version 4.3 and 4.7, which means that the flags supported are **GCC43, GCC44, GCC45, GCC46, and GCC47**.

The easiest way to keep the right flag during your compilation is to export a variable in bash with the latest character of the version:

```
mcramon@ubuntu:~/$ export GCCVERSION=$(gcc -dumpversion | cut -c 3)
mcramon@ubuntu:~/$ echo $GCCVERSION
4
```

So, for GCC version 4.6.3, the last character, **6**, is stored in the variable GCCVERSION; if the version was 4.7.x, the character **7** would be stored.

4. **Compile the firmware.** In the folder that you extracted the EDKII, you will notice a file called quarkbuild.sh. This file is a shell script that compiles the firmware for you with the following options:

```
quarkbuild.sh [-r32 | -d32 | -clean] [GCC43 | GCC44 | GCC45 |
GCC46 | GCC47]
[PlatformName] [-DSECURE_LD (optional)] [-DTPM_SUPPORT
(optional)]
```

These can be defined as follows:

- -clean: Delete the build files/folders.

- -d32: Create a DEBUG build.

- -r32: Create a RELEASE build.

- GCC4x: GCC flags used for this build.

- [PlatformName]: Name of the Platform package you want to build.

- [-DSECURE_LD]: Create a Secure Lockdown build (optional).

- [-DTPM_SUPPORT]: Create EDKII build with TPM support (optional).

▪ **Note**   This option has a one-time prerequisite described in CryptoPkg\Library\ OpensslLib\Patch-HOWTO.txt in the EDKII directory that you downloaded and extracted.

So you can type:

mcramon@ubuntu:~/$.**/quarkbuild.sh -r32 GCC46 QuarkPlatform**

Or, if you exported the GCCVERSION variable you can run:

mcramon@ubuntu:~/$.**/quarkbuild.sh -r32 GCC4$GCCVERSION QuarkPlatform**

Several files will be compiled, taking a few minutes to finish.

The files that really matter will be in the output directory at Quark_EDKII_v1.0.2/ Build/QuarkPlatform/RELEASE_GCC46/FV/FlashModules.

```
mcramon@ubuntu:~/BSP_1.0.4_T/Quark_EDKII_v1.0.2/Build/QuarkPlatform/RELEASE_
GCC46/FV/FlashModules$ l -1
EDKII_BOOTROM_OVERRIDE.Fv
EDKII_BOOT_STAGE1_IMAGE1.Fv
EDKII_BOOT_STAGE1_IMAGE2.Fv
EDKII_BOOT_STAGE2_COMPACT.Fv
EDKII_BOOT_STAGE2.Fv
EDKII_BOOT_STAGE2_RECOVERY.Fv
EDKII_NVRAM.bin
EDKII_RECOVERY_IMAGE1.Fv
Flash-EDKII-missingPDAT.bin
RMU2.bin
RMU.bin
```

If you want to see some extra debug messages, especially during the boot, you can generate the debug releases using the -d32 flag, as follows:

```
mcramon@ubuntu:~/$./quarkbuild.sh -d32 GCC4$(GCCVERSION) QuarkPlatform
```

In this case, the output directory is in the DEBUG_GCC4X directory instead of the RELEASE_GCC4X directory with same files.

5. **Create symbolic links.** If you successfully compiled the firmware, you might have the following output:

```
mcramon@ubuntu:~/Quark_EDKII_v1.0.2$ cd Build/QuarkPlatform/
mcramon@ubuntu:~/BSP_1.0.4_T/Quark_EDKII_v1.0.2/Build/QuarkPlatform$ ls
DEBUG_GCC46   RELEASE_GCC46
```

The directories DEBUG_GCC46 and RELEASE_GCC46 are the result of a debug and release compilation using GCC compiler version 4.6. It is necessary to simplify such directories using soft links, naming them DEBUG_GCC and RELEASE_GCC only because these are the names that the system image tools will search for.

```
mcramon@ubuntu:~/$ ln -s DEBUG_GCC46 DEBUG_GCC
mcramon@ubuntu:~/$ ln -s RELEASE_GCC46 RELEASE_GCC
mcramon@ubuntu:~/$ ls -l
total 8
lrwxrwxrwx 1 mcramon mcramon    11 Nov 21 20:21 DEBUG_GCC -> ../DEBUG_GCC46
lrwxrwxrwx 1 mcramon mcramon    13 Nov 21 20:21 RELEASE_GCC -> ../RELEASE_
GCC46
```

If you achieve this step, **congratulations**, you are ready to generate the next step—creating the capsule files.

Troubleshooting Compiling the Firmware

Some problems can show up during the firmware compilation, but all of them are related to your environment settings. The following lists the most common errors and explains how to resolve them.

- *Python does not fetch the code.* In this case, the first thing to do is check whether your Internet connection is working. You can try to test by opening a web browser or via a command line using a wget command like this:

  ```
  mcramon@ubuntu:~/tmp$ wget --spider http://example.com
  Spider mode enabled. Check if remote file exists.
  --2014-11-21 19:53:29--  http://example.com/
  Resolving example.com (example.com)... 93.184.216.119,
  2606:2800:220:6d:26bf:1447:1097:aa7
  Connecting to example.com (example.com)|93.184.216.119|:80...
  connected.
  ```

```
HTTP request sent, awaiting response... 200 OK
Length: 1270 (1.2K) [text/html]
Remote file exists and could contain further links,
but recursion is disabled -- not retrieving.
```

If you are behind a proxy, then you need also to configure the subversion proxy settings, editing the file located in `~/.subversion/servers`. Then search for the section `[global]` and set your proxy configuration as shown in the following lines:

```
[global]
http-proxy-host = <YOUR HOST IP>
http-proxy-port = <YOUR PORT NUMBER>
http-proxy-username = <YOUR USER NAME>
http-proxy-password = <YOUR PASSWORD>
```

- *A GCC compiler not supported.* If you have a GCC compiler that is not supported, you can download and install one of the versions supported and change the link called gcc in the /usr/bin directory to point to the old one. For example:

```
mcramon@ubuntu:~/cd /usr/bin
mcramon@ubuntu:~/sudo ln -s /usr/bin/gcc-4.6 gcc
```

This file contains a tool that is used to create the cap and binary files based in your SPI images.

The procedure for the creation is quite simple, as explained next.

Preparing layout.conf

At this point, you need make the other zipped files that you have downloaded but not used until now. So, move to the base directory and type the following command line to decompress all of them, if you have not done so yet:

```
mcramon@ubuntu:~/BSP_1.0.4_T$ tar -zxvf spi-flash-tools_v1.0.1.tar.gz
mcramon@ubuntu:~/BSP_1.0.4_T$ tar -zxvf sysimage_v1.0.1.tar.gz
mcramon@ubuntu:~/BSP_1.0.4_T$ tar -zxvf grub-legacy_5775f32a+v1.0.1.tar.gz
mcramon@ubuntu:~/BSP_1.0.4_T$ tar -zxvf quark_linux_v3.8.7+v1.0.1.tar.gz
```

Then run a script that will create symbolic links, making the folder names much simpler:

```
mcramon@ubuntu:~/BSP_1.0.4_T$ ./sysimage_v1.0.1/create_symlinks.sh
See if we can: ln -s  ./spi-flash-tools_*  spi-flash-tools
Found spi-flash-tools_v1.0.1
+ ln -s spi-flash-tools_v1.0.1 spi-flash-tools
See if we can: ln -s  ./Quark_EDKII_*  Quark_EDKII
```

```
Found Quark_EDKII_v1.0.2
+ ln -s Quark_EDKII_v1.0.2 Quark_EDKII
See if we can: ln -s ./sysimage_* sysimage
Found sysimage_v1.0.1
+ ln -s sysimage_v1.0.1 sysimage
See if we can: ln -s ./meta-clanton_* meta-clanton
Found meta-clanton_v1.0.1
+ ln -s meta-clanton_v1.0.1 meta-clanton
See if we can: ln -s ./quark_linux_* quark_linux
Found quark_linux_v3.8.7+v1.0.1
+ ln -s quark_linux_v3.8.7+v1.0.1 quark_linux
See if we can: ln -s ./grub-legacy_* grub-legacy
Found grub-legacy_5775f32a+v1.0.1
+ ln -s grub-legacy_5775f32a+v1.0.1 grub-legacy
```

If this script does not work it is because you are executing from the wrong directory. Make sure that you are in the base folder where you download all tar.gz files.

As you can see, the script tried to find each component of the BSP source package and create symbolic links to them using common names. For example, grub-legacy_5775f32a+v1.0.1 turns grub-legacy, and the same process is done to the other directories, as you can see if you type ls -l after the script execution.

```
mcramon@ubuntu:~/BSP_1.0.4_T$ ls -l
total 5292
-rw-r--r-- 1 mcramon mcramon 2657072 Nov 17 23:11 board_support_package_
sources_for_intel_quark_v1.0.1.7z
-rw-r--r-- 1 mcramon mcramon   30720 Nov 17 22:54 BSP-Patches-and-Build_
Instructions.1.0.4.tar
lrwxrwxrwx 1 mcramon mcramon      27 Nov 21 20:32 grub-legacy -> grub-
legacy_5775f32a+v1.0.1
drwxr-xr-x 2 mcramon mcramon    4096 May 22  2014 grub-
legacy_5775f32a+v1.0.1
-rw-rw-r-- 1 mcramon mcramon  192465 May 22  2014 grub-
legacy_5775f32a+v1.0.1.tar.gz
lrwxrwxrwx 1 mcramon mcramon      19 Nov 21 20:32 meta-clanton -> meta-
clanton_v1.0.1
drwxr-xr-x 9 mcramon mcramon    4096 Nov 18 21:58 meta-clanton_v1.0.1
-rw-rw-r-- 1 mcramon mcramon  517412 May 22  2014 meta-clanton_v1.0.1.tar.gz
drwxr-xr-x 2 mcramon mcramon    4096 Oct 20 13:31 patches
lrwxrwxrwx 1 mcramon mcramon      18 Nov 21 20:32 Quark_EDKII -> Quark_
EDKII_v1.0.2
drwxr-x--- 21 mcramon mcramon   4096 Nov 21 18:48 Quark_EDKII_v1.0.2
drwxrwxr-x 6 mcramon mcramon    4096 Nov 21 18:40 Quark_EDKII_v1.0.2-svn_
externals.repo
-rwxr-xr-x 1 mcramon mcramon 1502762 Nov 21 15:20 quark_edkii_v1.0.2.tar.gz
lrwxrwxrwx 1 mcramon mcramon      25 Nov 21 20:32 quark_linux -> quark_
linux_v3.8.7+v1.0.1
```

```
drwxr-xr-x  2 mcramon mcramon    4096 May 22  2014 quark_linux_v3.8.7+v1.0.1
-rw-rw-r--  1 mcramon mcramon  236544 May 22  2014 quark_linux_
v3.8.7+v1.0.1.tar.gz
-rw-rw-r--  1 mcramon mcramon     480 May 22  2014 sha1sum.txt
lrwxrwxrwx  1 mcramon mcramon      22 Nov 21 20:32 spi-flash-tools ->
spi-flash-tools_v1.0.1
drwxr-xr-x  6 mcramon mcramon    4096 May 22  2014 spi-flash-tools_v1.0.1
-rw-rw-r--  1 mcramon mcramon  219559 May 22  2014 spi-flash-tools_
v1.0.1.tar.gz
lrwxrwxrwx  1 mcramon mcramon      15 Nov 21 20:32 sysimage ->
sysimage_v1.0.1
drwxr-xr-x  9 mcramon mcramon    4096 May 22  2014 sysimage_v1.0.1
-rw-rw-r--  1 mcramon mcramon    9876 May 22  2014 sysimage_v1.0.1.tar.gz
-rw-r--r--  1 mcramon mcramon    2938 Nov 18 22:14 uart-reverse-8.patch
```

The reason for this "simplification" is related to the sysimage directory bringing a configuration file that tells the "**ingredients**"—in other words, the files that will be used to compose the flash image and the version of the image.

For example, check the directories that you have in the sysimage file:

```
mcramon@ubuntu:~/BSP_1.0.4_T$ cd sysimage
mcramon@ubuntu:~/BSP_1.0.4_T/sysimage$ ls -l
total 36
drwxr-xr-x 2 mcramon mcramon 4096 May 22  2014 config
-rwxr-xr-x 1 mcramon mcramon 2496 May 22  2014 create_symlinks.sh
drwxr-xr-x 2 mcramon mcramon 4096 May 22  2014 grub
drwxr-xr-x 2 mcramon mcramon 4096 May 22  2014 inf
-rw-r--r-- 1 mcramon mcramon 1488 May 22  2014 LICENSE
drwxr-xr-x 2 mcramon mcramon 4096 May 22  2014 sysimage.CP-8M-debug
drwxr-xr-x 2 mcramon mcramon 4096 May 22  2014 sysimage.CP-8M-debug-secure
drwxr-xr-x 2 mcramon mcramon 4096 May 22  2014 sysimage.CP-8M-release
drwxr-xr-x 2 mcramon mcramon 4096 May 22  2014 sysimage.CP-8M-release-secure
```

Note that there are four directories to generate a flash image with 8MB for debug and release compilation, and for unsecure and secure boots.

In each of these directories, there is a file called layout.conf. This file must be changed to point to the correct "ingredients" of your build and the right version number.

To make your life easier, there is a script that does the changes in all directories automatically for you, even if you do not need to change all of them. Running the script executes the following command in the base directory:

```
mcramon@ubuntu:~/BSP_1.0.4_T$ ./patches_v1.0.4/patch.sysimage.sh
```

You might ask which changes this script really makes. Let's assume one of the directories—sysimage.CP-8M-debug for example—and open the layout.conf file with the text editor of you preference ***before* running** the patch_sysimage.sh script. layout.conf is shown in Listing 2-7.

Listing 2-7. layout.conf

```
# WARNING: this file is indirectly included in a Makefile where it
# defines Make targets and pre-requisites. As a consequence you MUST
# run "make clean" BEFORE making changes to it. Failure to do so may
# result in the make process being unable to clean files it no longer
# has references to.

[main]
size=8388608
type=global

[MFH]
version=0x1
flags=0x0
address=0xfff08000
type=mfh

[Flash Image Version]
type=mfh.version
meta=version
value=0x01000105

[ROM_OVERLAY]
address=0xfffe0000
item_file=../../Quark_EDKII/Build/QuarkPlatform/PLAIN/DEBUG_GCC/FV/
FlashModules/EDKII_BOOTROM_OVERRIDE.Fv
type=some_type

[signed-key-module]
address=0xfffd8000
item_file=config/SvpSignedKeyModule.bin
svn_index=0
type=some_type
in_capsule=no

# On a deployed system, the SVN area holds the last known secure
# version of each signed asset.
# TODO: generate this area by collecting the SVN from the assets
# themselves.
[svn-area]
address=0xfffd0000
item_file=config/SVNArea.bin
type=some_type
```

```
# A capsule upgrade must implement some smart logic to make sure the
# highest Security Version Number always wins (rollback protection)
in_capsule=no

[fixed_recovery_image]
address=0xfff90000
item_file=../../Quark_EDKII/Build/QuarkPlatform/PLAIN/DEBUG_GCC/FV/
FlashModules/EDKII_RECOVERY_IMAGE1.Fv
sign=yes
type=mfh.host_fw_stage1_signed
svn_index=2
# in_capsule=no

[NV_Storage]
address=0xfff30000
item_file=../../Quark_EDKII/Build/QuarkPlatform/PLAIN/DEBUG_GCC/FV/
FlashModules/EDKII_NVRAM.bin
type=some_type

[RMU]
address=0xfff00000
item_file=../../Quark_EDKII/Build/QuarkPlatform/PLAIN/DEBUG_GCC/FV/
FlashModules/RMU.bin
type=none_registered

[boot_stage1_image1]
address=0xffec0000
item_file=../../Quark_EDKII/Build/QuarkPlatform/PLAIN/DEBUG_GCC/FV/
FlashModules/EDKII_BOOT_STAGE1_IMAGE1.Fv
sign=yes
boot_index=0
type=mfh.host_fw_stage1_signed
svn_index=1

[boot_stage1_image2]
address=0xffe80000
item_file=../../Quark_EDKII/Build/QuarkPlatform/PLAIN/DEBUG_GCC/FV/
FlashModules/EDKII_BOOT_STAGE1_IMAGE2.Fv
sign=yes
boot_index=1
type=mfh.host_fw_stage1_signed
svn_index=1
```

```
[boot_stage_2_compact]
address=0xffd00000
item_file=../../Quark_EDKII/Build/QuarkPlatform/PLAIN/DEBUG_GCC/FV/
FlashModules/EDKII_BOOT_STAGE2_COMPACT.Fv
sign=yes
type=mfh.host_fw_stage2_signed
svn_index=3

[Ramdisk]
address=0xffa60000
item_file=../../meta-clanton/yocto_build/tmp/deploy/images/image-spi-
clanton.cpio.lzma
sign=yes
type=mfh.ramdisk_signed
svn_index=7

[LAYOUT.CONF_DUMP]
address=0xffcff000
type=mfh.build_information
meta=layout

[Kernel]
address=0xff852000
item_file=../../meta-clanton/yocto_build/tmp/deploy/images/bzImage
sign=yes
type=mfh.kernel_signed
svn_index=6

[grub.conf]
address=0xff851000
item_file=grub/grub-spi.conf
sign=yes
type=mfh.bootloader_conf_signed
svn_index=5

[grub]
address=0xff800000
item_file=../../meta-clanton/yocto_build/tmp/deploy/images/grub.efi
sign=yes
fvwrap=yes
guid=B43BD3E1-64D1-4744-9394-D0E1C4DE8C87
type=mfh.bootloader_signed
svn_index=4
```

As you can see, this file is has sections like [main], [MFH], [Flash Image Version], [ROM OVERLAY], and so on. Each section contains data fields with respective values, but there are two sections that the script changes:

- **[Flash Image Version]:** It is recommended that you make a simple change in the **[Flash Image Version]** because it brings version 0x01000105 in the value field. This means that when you boot your board, the version read will be 01.00.01.05, or simply 1.0.1, because 05 is omitted; and considering that the release of this example is based on 1.0.4, it is recommended to change to **0x01000400**, which means 1.0.4. If you want to see the correct version number, this change is necessary.

- **[RamDisk]:** This section needs to replace the string image-spi-clanton.cpio.lzma with image-spi-galileo-clanton.cpio.lzma, because if you check the images generated in /meta-clanton/yocto_build/tmp/deploy/images/, the image generated is named image-spi-galileo.cpio.lzma. Thus, this section should be as follows:

```
[Ramdisk]
address=0xffa60000
item_file=../../meta-clanton/yocto_build/tmp/deploy/images/image-spi-galileo-clanton.cpio.lzma
sign=yes
type=mfh.ramdisk_signed
svn_index=7
```

In general, the script also adjusts the path filenames, removing all PLAIN directories and pointing to valid paths.

The sysimage brings the template with the old version because the tool did not require any changes since 1.0.1, and the template comes with the same version number.

The other sections—like [NVM Storage], [RMU], [boot_stage1_image1], [boot_stage1_image2], and [boot_stage_2_compact]—search for the EDKII components that you created in the previous section; but pay attention to **DEBUG**. This explains why you created the soft links in the step 5 of the **"Steps to Compile the Firmware"** section of this chapter.

The sections [Ramdisk], [LAYOUT.CONF_DUMP], [Kernel], [grub.conf], and [grub] try to find the elements that you generated after running the Yocto build, and the directories that you decompressed and created are simple symbolic links in this section with the create_symlinks.sh script.

Thus, when you run the patch_sysimage.sh script, the changes mentioned are automatically done in the layout.conf files of each directory.

Using the SPI Tool

The SPI tool is on the `spi-flash-tool` directory that you decompressed. It is used to create the capsule files and binary files with or without platform data.

In the **same directory as your** `layout.conf` **file,** run the following command:

```
mcramon@ubuntu:~/$ ../../spi-flash-tools/Makefile
```

If everything runs OK, you should have generated three new files in the same directory:

- **Flash-missingPDAT.cap:** This is the expected capsule file, absent of platform data, which you can flash to your Intel Galileo.

- **Flash-missingPDAT.bin:** This is a binary file absent of platform data necessary to generate SPI images, which is discussed in the *"Creating SPI Images with Platform Files"* section.

- **FVMAIN.fv:** This file is used to recover your board if it does not boot anymore. This is discussed in the *"What to Do If Intel Galileo Bricks" section* of this chapter.

Flashing the Capsule Files

After a long procedure and many hours creating your capsule file, it is time to test it by flashing the SPI flash memory. In fact, there are three different ways to flash, as discussed in next sections.

Flashing the Capsule File with the Intel Arduino IDE

This is the easiest way to flash the capsule file with the current software provided at the time this book was published. You just need to copy the `Flash-missingPDAT.cap` file in a specific folder of the IDE, as explained in the *"Updating the Firmware with a Different Firmware"* section of Chapter 3. This procedure only requires usage of the regular USB data cable, which prevents copying the capsule files with a micro SD card or a USB pen driver.

Flashing the Capsule File with a Linux Terminal Shell

The procedure described here is exactly the same thing that Intel Arduino IDE does automatically for you, sending remote commands to Intel Galileo boards. Thus if you do not want to use the IDE, then the procedure to flash your capsule file is as follows:

1. Connect the serial cabled to Intel Galileo and open a Linux terminal, as explained in the *"Preparing Your Cables" section* of Chapter 1.

2. Check which release is being used currently in your board, checking the content of the file /sys/firmware/board_data/flash_version. It possible to check using a Linux terminal shell and typing the following command:

   ```
   root@clanton:~# cat /sys/firmware/board_data/flash_version
   0x01000105
   ```

3. Copy the Flash-missingPDAT.cap that you created in the previous sections to a micro SD card or a pen driver properly formatted with FAT or FAT32 in a single partition, as described in the *"Booting from SD Card"* section of this chapter.

4. If your release is 0.7.5 or 0.8.0, run the following command:

   ```
   # insmod /tmp/0.7.5/efi_capsule_update.ko
   Or
   # insmod /tmp/0.8.0/efi_capsule_update.ko
   ```

5. If your release is 0.9.0 or 1.0.0, run the following:

   ```
   # modprobe efi_capsule_update
   ```

6. With newer releases, run the following:

   ```
   # modprobe sdhci-pci
   # modprobe mmc-block
   # mkdir /lib/firmware
   # cd /media/mmcblk0p1/
   # cp Flash-missingPDAT.cap /lib/firmware/Flash-missingPDAT.cap
   # echo -n Flash-missingPDAT.cap > /sys/firmware/efi_capsule/
   capsule_path
   # echo 1 > /sys/firmware/efi_capsule/capsule_update
   # reboot
   ```

Make sure that you really ran the command reboot; otherwise, the process to update the capsule file will not work.

Flashing the Capsule File with a UEFI Shell

The idea on this procedure is to open a UEFI shell as soon the board boots and then flash your capsule file, but this only works if you have a board with a nonsecure boot; otherwise, the UEFI shell will be locked and this procedure will not work.

This procedure requires that you have the following:

- The Flash-missingPDAT.cap file that must be present in the **same directory of your** layout.conf.

- The CapsuleApp.efi file that was generated when you compiled the EDKII firmware. It must be present in the ./Quark_EDKII/ Build/QuarkPlatform/PLAIN/DEBUG_GCC/FV/Applications/ directory or the ./Quark_EDKII/Build/QuarkPlatform/PLAIN/ RELEASE_GCC/FV/ Applications/ directory, depending whether you compile using release or debug flags as discussed in the "*Compiling the EDKII Firmware*" section of this chapter.

- You will need serial cables to open the terminal shell, as discussed in the "*Preparing Your Cables*" section in Chapter 1. This will allow you to debug the board using a serial audio jack cable for Intel Galileo or a FTDI cable for Intel Galileo Gen 2.

- You need to know how to use some serial terminal software. Read the "*Testing Your Cables*" section in Chapter 1 to understand how to use *putty* for Windows or *minicom* for Linux or Mac OSX. However, you also need to configure the serial software to recognize special characters from your keyboard. For putty, click the left panel, **Terminal ➤ Keyboard**, and select the **SCO box** from **the Functions and Keys and Keypad** tab.

- Finally, you need a micro SD card or a USB pen driver.

Here is the procedure that must be followed:

1. Format the micro SD card or the USB pen drive with FAT or FAT32 in a single partition, as described in the "*Booting from SD Card Images*" section of this chapter.

2. Copy the files CapsuleApp.efi and Flash-missingPDAT.cap to the micro SD card.

3. With the board off, keep the serial cable connected and open the serial terminal software, such as putty or minicom.

4. Power-on the board connecting the power supply.

5. As soon you see the image shown in Figure 2-10, press the **F7 function key**.

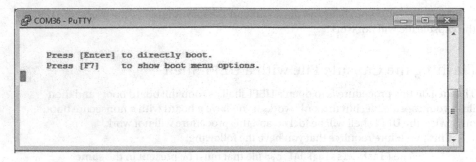

Figure 2-10. *Initial screen just after the boot with the F7 option*

6. In the menu, choose the **UEFI Internal Shell** option by using the arrow keys, as shown in Figure 2-11. Press Enter and then press the ESC key to receive the shell prompt.

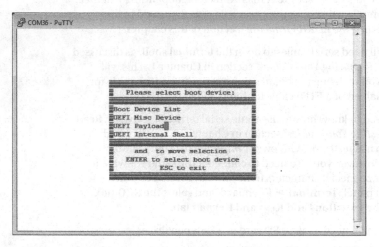

Figure 2-11. *Selecting the UEFI internal shell*

7. You will see the partition mounted on the board. Usually, a micro SD card and a pen drive are **fs0**. Just type **fs0:** and press Enter. Check the content of the micro SD card or the USB pen driver with the command 1s, as shown in Figure 2-12.

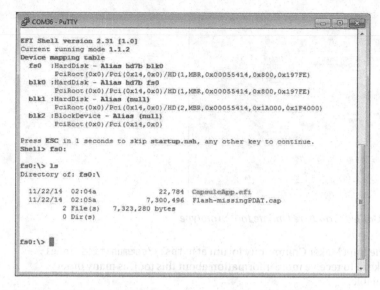

Figure 2-12. Selecting the fs0 partition and checking the files

8. You should be able to see the files you copied to the micro SD card. In this case. just type the following command to start the flashing procedure.

```
fs0:\> CapsuleApp.efi Flash-missingPDAT.cap
CapsuleApp: SecurityAuthenticateImage 0xD504410found.
CapsuleApp: creating capsule descriptors at 0xF0DE510
CapsuleApp: capsule data starts        at 0xD504410 with
size 0x6F6190
CapsuleApp: capsule block/size              0xD504410/0x6F6190
```

Flashing the Capsule File with the Firmware Update Tool

At the end of 2014, Intel provided a new tool called the Intel Firmware Update tool that allows you to select the capsule files that come internally in the application, or to browse your desktop file system to select a custom one. This is a stand-alone application, very simple to use, and it does not require you to have the Arduino IDE installed.

Figure 2-13 shows this application's user interface.

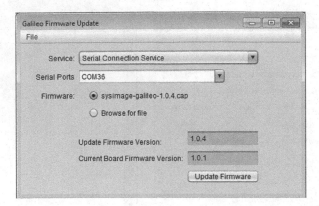

Figure 2-13. *Intel Galileo Firmware Update tool prototype*

Subscribe to the Intel Maker Community forum at `https://communities.intel.com/community/makers` to receive more information about this tool, as many other updates will be available.

Creating SPI Images Flash Files

Imagine this hypothetical situation: due to some mistake, you realized that you bricked your Intel Galileo and it does not boot anymore. Before ordering a new one, you can consider flashing using an SPI flash programmer, but you need to have the binary build patched with platform data files.

In previous sections, I mentioned how to compile using Yocto and how to generate the capsule and binary files that do not contain platform data.

To follow the procedures in this section, you should

1. Have successfully compiled the UEFI firmware (EDKII packages).

2. Identified the Ethernet MAC address of your board.

3. Have a flash programmer, such as DediProg.

As explained before, platform data contains information like the Ethernet MAC address of your board and which board model you have. Thus, each board should contain a unique and exclusive platform file, because each board contains an exclusive MAC address.

To discover the Ethernet MAC address of your board, you just need to take a look at the white label on your board, as shown in Figure 2-14.

Figure 2-14. *The white label with the exclusive Ethernet MAC address*

The tool responsible for generating the binary with platform data is actually a Python script named platform-data-patch.py in the .../spi-flash-tools/platform-data directory. The only thing that this script does is patch the binaries with that platform data configuration file.

In this same directory there is a platform-data template called sample-platform-data. ini, as shown in Listing 2-8.

Listing 2-8. sample-platform-data.ini

```
# Every module contains:
# [unique name]
# id=decimal integer, data type identifier
# desc=string, short description of a data; max 10 characters
# data.value=[ABC | CAFEBEBA | xyz abc | /path/to/file ]
# data.type=[hex.uint[8/16/32/64] | hex.string | utf8.string | file]
# ver=decimal integer, version number; if not specified defaults to 0
```

```
# WARNING: the platform type data.value MUST match the MRC data.value below
[Platform Type]
id=1
desc=PlatformID
data.type=hex.uint16
# ClantonPeak 2, KipsBay 3, CrossHill 4, ClantonHill 5, KipsBay-fabD 6,
GalileoGen2 8
data.value=2

# WARNING: the MRC data.value MUST match the platform type data.value above
[Mrc Params]
id=6
ver=1
desc=MrcParams
data.type=file
data.value=MRC/clantonpeak.v1.bin
#data.value=MRC/kipsbay.v1.bin
#data.value=MRC/crosshill.v1.bin
#data.value=MRC/clantonhill.v1.bin
#data.value=MRC/kipsbay-fabD.v1.bin
#data.value=MRC/GalileoGen2.bin

# If you are developing MRC for a new system you can alternatively
# inline the value like this:

# data.type=hex.string
# data.value=0000000000000001010100030000010001010101017C920000102700001027000000409C000006

# The unique MAC address(es) owned by each device are typically found
# on a sticker.  You must find it(them) and change the bogus values
# below.
[MAC address 0]
id=3
desc=1st MAC
data.type=hex.string
data.value=FFFFFFFFFF00

[MAC address 1]
id=4
desc=2nd MAC
data.type=hex.string
data.value=02FFFFFFFF01
```

Make a copy of this file, saving it using another name—for example,
galileo-platform-data.ini—and open this file in the text editor of your preference.

As you can observe, this file is divided into sections such as [Platform Type], [Mrc Params], [MAC address 0], and [MAC address 1]; but what really matters with Intel Galileo boards are the sections [Platform Type] and [MAC address 0]. On each section there is a field called data.value= that represents the place you will need to modify the platform data.

In the section [Platform Type,] there is the following comment:

**# ClantonPeak 2, KipsBay 3, CrossHill 4, ClantonHill 5, KipsBay-fabD 6,
GalileoGen2 8**

If your board is Intel Galileo Gen 2, the **data.value** must receive the value **8**, and although the Intel Galileo is not mentioned, the value must be **6** and must be considered as KipsBay-fabD.

For example, if your board is Intel Galileo Gen 2, the [Platform Type] must be changed in this way:

```
[Platform Type]
id=1
desc=PlatformID
data.type=hex.uint16
# ClantonPeak 2, KipsBay 3, CrossHill 4, ClantonHill 5, KipsBay-fabD 6,
GalileoGen2 8
data.value=8
```

The other section that you need to modify is the [MAC address 0], again changing the data.value field. For example, suppose your Ethernet MAC address white tag says MAC:984FEE014C6B; then this section must be changed to the following:

```
[MAC address 0]
id=3
desc=1st MAC
data.type=hex.string
data.value=984FEE014C6B
```

Now you need to generate the binary file patching the platform data. First, take a quick look at the option offered by the platform-data-patch.py script:

```
mcramon@ubuntu:~/$ ./platform-data-patch.py --help
Usage: platform-data-patch.py

Options:
  --version             show program's version number and exit
  -h, --help            show this help message and exit
  -i ORIGINAL_IMAGE, --original-image=ORIGINAL_IMAGE
                        input flash image [default: Flash-missingPDAT.bin]
  -p INPUT_FILE, --platform-config=INPUT_FILE
                        configuration (INI) file [default: platform-data.ini]
```

```
-n MODIFIED_IMAGE, --name=MODIFIED_IMAGE
                        output flash image [default: Flash+PlatformData.bin]
-u, --undefined-order
                        By default, items are put in the same order as they
                        come in the config file. However ordering requires
                        python 2.7 or above.
```

The script is very simple: the option -i indicates that the input capsule file, -p, is the platform-data file; -n is the name of your **output file**; and -u must be used *only* if your version of **Python is lower than 2.7**. So, before using this script, check which Python version is installed on your computer by typing python --version on your console to determine if the -u option must be used or not. If you have a recent version of Python, you just need to run the script.

In the next example, the output file was named cool_binary.bin and the input files were the ones created as examples in this chapter.

./platform-data-patch.py -i ../../sysimage/sysimage.CP-8M-debug/Flash-missingPDAT.bin -p galileo-platform-data.ini -n cool_binary.bin

If the script ran smoothly, you should have the output file cool_binary.bin in the same directory. Next it is time to flash your image using the SPI flash programmer described in the next section.

If you make mistakes in the **[Platform Type],** (for example, suppose you specify that the data.value equals 6, which means Intel Galileo, but flash an Intel Galileo Gen 2 board), during the boot, the firmware will recognize the incompatibility and will ask you to select the board type, manually displaying a menu that might be seen using the Linux terminal shell in your board.

```
Type '0' for 'ClantonPeakSVP' [PID 2]
Type '1' for 'KipsBay' [PID 3]
Type '2' for 'CrossHill' [PID 4]
Type '3' for 'ClantonHill' [PID 5]
Type '4' for 'Galileo' [PID 6]
Type '5' for 'GalileoGen2' [PID 8]
```

So, if you see this menu, the platform file on your board was not patched, or it was patched with wrong data.

Flashing Using an SPI Flash Programmer

It is recommended to use the flash programmer called DediProg SF100, which you can order from http://www.dediprog.com/pd/spi-flash-solution/sf100.

Officially, the DediProg SF100 only works on Windows, but the open source community has a program called *flashrom* that supports DediProg SF 100 on Linux and Mac OSX as well.

This section will focus on DediProg for Windows, but if you are a Linux or Mac OSX developer, you can use **flashrom** with DediProg by downloading from http://www.flashrom.org/Flashrom and using the following command line:

```
flashrom -p dediprog -r biosimage.rom
```

The procedure to use the DediProg SF100 using the GUI interface is as follows:

1. Connect the DediProg SF100 to Intel Galileo by using the SPI programmer terminal, as shown in Figure 2-15, but make sure that Intel Galileo is not connected to any power supply and that the DediProg SF100 is connected to your computer via a USB cable. There is no power supply involved in this process, and the DediProg SF100 uses energy from your USB port. Both the board, Intel Galileo, and Intel Galileo Gen 2 offer the SPI flash port, basically in the same position.

Figure 2-15. *DediProg SF100 connected to Intel Galileo Gen 2*

2. After running the installer that comes with DediProg SF100, run the program **DediProg Engineering.** The first thing that this program will ask about is the SPI flash memory present in the board. If you take a quick look in the Intel Galileo schematics (https://communities.intel.com/docs/DOC-21822), you will notice that Intel Galileo and Intel Galileo Gen 2 uses the same type of memory, **W25Q64FV**, as shown in Figure 2-16. Just select the write memory and click the OK button.

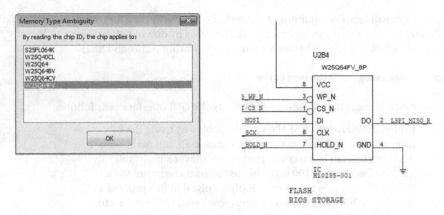

Figure 2-16. *Selecting the right SPI flash memory and Intel Galileo schematics*

3. Click **Configuration** and change the **Vcc** option to **Manual. Select Vcc** and **3.5V**; this will save a lot of problems due to flash error. Click the OK button, as shown in Figure 2-17.

Figure 2-17. *Configuring the DediProg SF100 to Vcc 3.5V*

4. Click the File option and select the binary with the platform you have created, as shown in Figure 2-18. Make sure that the **Raw Binary** option is selected and then click the OK button.

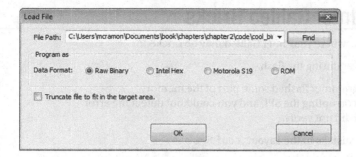

Figure 2-18. *Selecting the binary file to program*

5. Now it is time to program. Click the Erase option to erase the
    SPI flash memory. Then click **Prog** to program the SPI flash
    memory. Finally, click **Verify** to make sure that your binary was
    written correctly in the memory. Figure 2-19 shows the process
    of each step. If the verification fails, repeat this step until you
    have the SPI flash memory properly programmed. This easily
    happens if you did not select the 3.5V mentioned in step 3.

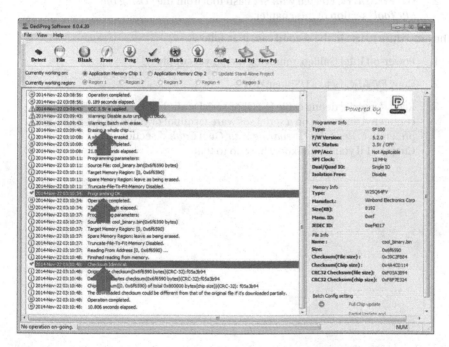

Figure 2-19. *Erasing, programming, and verifying steps in DediProg SF100*

What to Do If Intel Galileo Bricks

There are some situations where your Intel Galileo may be bricked:

- You lost power during the flash.

- The SPI programmer flashed some part of the memory incorrectly, corrupting the SPI, and you could not detect the error because you did not verify.

- You made a mistake in the layout.conf file.

- You patched the binaries, declaring a wrong board model in the platform data. For example, you have an Intel Galileo and you incorrectly modified the platform data to Intel Galileo Gen 2.

There are two procedures that might help solve this situation after you fixed and verified, if you did not make any mistakes with the software you created:

1. Use an SPI flash programmer to reprogram the SPI flash memory. This procedure was mentioned in the "*Flashing Using an SPI Flash Programmer*" section of this chapter.

2. Use FVMAIN.fv, created with SPI flash tool from the "*Using the SPI Tool*" section of this chapter.

The procedure to use in the second case is as follows:

1. Power-off Intel Galileo, removing the power supply.

2. Copy FVMAIN.fv to a USB pen drive.

3. Keep the serial debug cable (FTDI or serial audio) jack connected and open on a serial software terminal of your preference. Read the "*Preparing Your Own Cables*" section in Chapter 1 if you do not know how do to that.

4. Connect the USB pen drive in the USB OTG port on your Intel Galileo Gen 2. If you are using Intel Galileo, you will need an adaptor like the one shown in Figure 5-20 of Chapter 5.

Figure 2-20. *Resistor to ground to enter the recovery mode*

5. Ground the R2B16 resistor, as shown in Figure 2-20.

6. Connect the power supply to Intel Galileo.

7. In the serial shell, a list of platforms will be shown; choose the Galileo model.

8. Remove the resistor from ground.

9. In the serial shell, select the system recovery option. The system recovery will take around 6 minutes to complete.

These are the two methods that you can try. I wish you sincere good luck with them.

Summary

In this chapter, you received an overview of how the Yocto build system works and how to generate SD card and SPI releases for Intel Galileo boards, as well as how to generate the toolchain and IPK packages. You could also tested the cross-compilers present in the toolchain, creating a simple native program, and then run it on Intel Galileo to test it.

The chapter also explained the differences between capsule and binary files with platform data, how to build firmware on EDKII repositories, and how to recover your board if bad firmware was flashed.

■ ■ ■

## CHAPTER 3

Arduino IDE and Wiring Language

This chapter is an introduction to Arduino and its development environment. If you already have your IDE installed, know how to update the firmware using the IDE, understand the wiring libraries, know how to communicate with native Linux programs, and don't have any problem with your development environment, this chapter is not for you and you should move to the next one.

Arduino provides a cross-platform integrated development environment (IDE) based in Java and built to support different Arduino boards. It contains multiple code examples, a debug serial console, and is open source. With the IDE you can create your programs called *sketches*. You can download to Intel Galileo, run the sketches, and debug them using the serial console that's integrated with the IDE.

Intel provides a special Arduino IDE release specific for Galileo boards that includes a firmware update, new APIs, and customization of existing libraries.

This chapter explains how to install Intel Galileo Arduino IDE on Mac, Linux, and Windows OS, covers the new functionalities added in the IDE, and explains how to solve any issues when you run the IDE on virtual machines.

This chapter also discusses how the Arduino framework works on top of embedded Linux OS and includes some basic examples to show how the Arduino libraries can be used for those who have never used Arduino before.

You'll also develop a simple project that integrates POSIX calls and a Python script and create an alarm for unread Gmail emails in your inbox.

A Little Bit of History

You'll often hear terms like "Arduino wiring language" or "Arduino language" and you might think Arduino has a special programming language.

In fact, the language used to program the Intel Galileo using the Arduino IDE is C/C++, so there is no real "wiring language" for Arduino.

In 2003, a student named Hernando Barragan created a hardware thesis describing an IDE and the integration with circuit boards powered by microcontrollers. With contributions from other researches the concept evolved allowing developers to write just a few lines of code in order to reproduce simple connections of hardware components. This allowed interactions such as turning on an LED, receiving events from buttons, emitting sounds, and so on.

Thus, even if the language used in IDE is C/C++, the IDE can provide APIs that enable that wiring, and the code is simple and based on how the electronics components are connected to the circuit.

The Intel Makers Community

If you have questions about Arduino IDE for Intel Galileo, or if you have ideas and projects to discuss, you can count on the maker community created by Intel at https://communities.intel.com/community/makers.

There are several forums that discuss the Arduino wiring libraries and project ideas and one of the best is http://forum.arduino.cc/.

It is very important to be involved with the community, because developers are always helping each other to solve unexpected problems, providing tutorials, and discussing great projects.

Installing the Arduino IDE for Intel Galileo

There are two locations where you can download the Arduino IDE for Intel Galileo:

- The Arduino web site at http://arduino.cc/en/main/software.

  You need to search for "Arduino IDE for Intel Galileo" and click the link provided. You will be redirected to the Intel web site.

- The Intel web site at https://communities.intel.com/docs/DOC-22226.

Choose the best link for you and add the bookmark to your browser so you can easily update the IDE with subsequent releases.

You need to download the "Getting Started Guide" and the correct IDE according to the OS installed on your machine. Intel offers versions for Windows, MacOSX, and 32- and 64-bit Linux. It's best to read the guide before you try to install.

Figure 3-1 shows the link to the "Getting Start Guide."

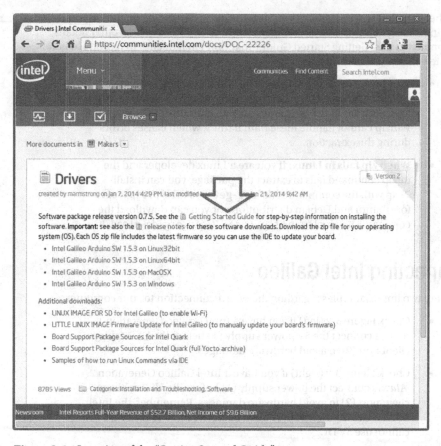

Figure 3-1. *Location of the "Getting Started Guide"*

The installation is usually very straightforward:

- **Windows:** Just unzip the zip file using 7-zip, preferably to C:\. Open the folder that's extracted and execute the arduino.exe file.

- **Linux 32/64 bits:** Extract the tarball zipped file to a new directory and execute the ./arduino. Use the following command with the appropriate file name:

  tgz file: tar -xvzf <filename>.tgz

- **MacOSX:** Drag and drop the file into the /Applications folder to install the IDE. Launch it by double-clicking Arduino in the Applications folder.

There are different procedures you should check, depending on the OS you're using, including if the gadget driver was properly installed, as well as several other details documented in the "Getting Started Guide" that don't make sense to reproduce here.

A few things you need to know:

- **Windows: Never use Winzip!** You should use the 7-zip tools (see http://www.7-zip.org/) because the cross-compiler used for Quark has long path names and several sub-directories. Winzip cannot handle these path names, which causes errors during the extraction.

- **When zip fails in Linux:** If you are a Linux developer and the unzip command fails to extract the package, you can install 7-zip with the command sudo apt-get install p7zip-full for Ubuntu and Debian distributions or you can download the command-line tool from http://www.7-zip.org/download.html.

Connecting Intel Galileo

There are two important rules regarding the board connection to your computer:

- Check Figure 3-2 (left) if you have a Intel Galileo Generation 1. *Always* connect the 5V power supply (1) before the USB cable on client port (2) to avoid hardware damages.

- Check Figure 3-2 (right) if you have a Intel Galileo Generation 2. *Always* connect the power supply (1) before the USB cable on client port (2) to avoid hardware damages. Remember, the Intel Galileo Gen 2 power supply must be between 7V and 12V DC. You cannot use 5V DC.

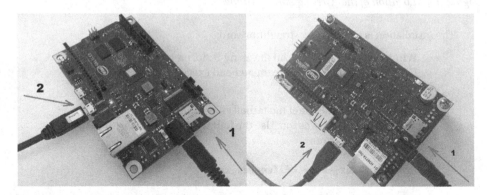

Figure 3-2. Intel Galileo Generation 1 (left) and Intel Galileo Generation 2 (right)

- *Always* keep the power supply connected to Intel Galileo when transferring sketches or updating the firmware of your board. Developers are tempted to use the USB Client Port because it can boot the board and run the sketches but the 5V power supply is really recommended to keep connected in all occasions and to avoid hardware instability.

Wait about 35 seconds and the Gadget Serial driver should be available.

Installing the Drivers and the Arduino IDE

Refer to the "Getting Started Guide" (https://communities.intel.com/docs/DOC-22226) for the latest instructions on how to install the serial driver and Arduino IDE. For your convenience, a version of the steps is provided here as well.

Installing the Arduino IDE

For most OSs, the installation process is very simple. For Windows, though, there is a small detail regarding the installation.

Installing the IDE on Windows

When you download the files for Windows you will see that, according to the version of IDE you are using, the extension is either .7z or .zip.

Never use the WinZip tool because the toolchain that contains the cross-compiler, has files with long path names and WinZip is not able to decompress them.

Thus, for Windows it's better to use a free tool called 7-zip, which you can download from http://www.7-zip.org. This web site contains the installers for downloading. It is very simple to install; just follow the recommendations on the site. You then simply extract the zip file on any directory using the 7-zip tool.

The current "Getting Started" guide (released December 23, 2013) says that it is necessary to extract the files to C:\, but this is wrong. You are free to install anywhere.

Installing the IDE on Linux

To install the IDE on Linux machines, follow the steps:

1. Open a terminal shell of your preference. If you are using Ubuntu, you can press Ctrl+Shift+T to open a terminal shell.

2. In your home directory, extract the package with the appropriate command:

    ```
    tar -zxvf arduino-1.5.3-linux32.tar.gz
    ```

    or

    ```
    tar -zxvf arduino-1.5.3-linux64.tar.gz
    ```

    for 32 or 64 bits, respectively.

3. Some Linux distributions include a package called "modem manager" that can affect the serial port communication. You should remove this package from your distribution. If you are using Ubuntu or Debian, you can remove this package by typing this command in the terminal shell:

    ```
    sudo apt-get remove modemmanager
    ```

4. In the same directory where the package was downloaded, launch the Arduino IDE by executing the following:

    ```
    ./arduino
    ```

If you execute the IDE and you can't select the serial ports (see the section entitled "Checking the Port and Board Selected"), you did not execute the program with the appropriate access. If you are using Debian or Ubuntu, you have two ways to resolve the problem. You can use the following commands:

```
sudo arduino
```

or

```
sudo chmod 755 /dev/ttACM[X]
```

where [X] is the number of port enumerated in your machine, such as /dev/ttyACM0.

Installing the IDE on MacOS

To install the IDE on MacOS, follow these steps:

1. Download the zip file on the Mac hard drive and unzip it.

2. Drag and drop the Arduino application into the `Applications` folder on your Mac.

Installing the Drivers

The Intel Galileo boards use the gadget serial drivers called "Galileo" only.

The most problematic installation process with this serial gadget driver is in Windows. If you are a Windows user and you have problems communicating with the serial interface on your IDE, read the section entitled "Serial Communication Issues with IDE on Windows."

The Common Step to Install the Driver

Before starting the driver installation, follow the steps recommended in the section entitled "Installing the Arduino IDE," power on your Intel Galileo board, and then connect the USB cables as described in the "Connecting the Intel Galileo" section. This is the first and common step with all operation systems. You can then jump to the section that represents the operation system you are using.

Installing the Driver on Windows

1. Once the power and USB cables are connected, wait a few seconds and open the Device Manager by clicking on the Start menu. Open the Control Panel and then click on System. Once the System window is open, open the Device Manager.

2. Look under Ports (COM & LPT). You should see an open port named "Gadget Serial V2.4" if you using an old release like 0.7.5 or simply "Galileo" in newer releases. Figure 3-3 shows the serial driver.

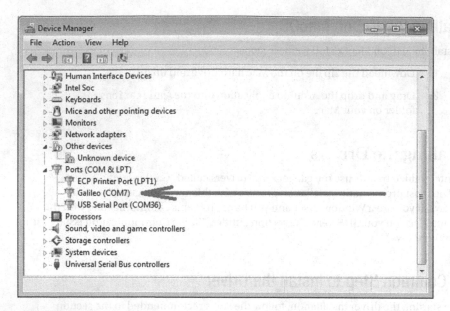

Figure 3-3. Galileo serial driver in Windows the Control Panel

If you do not see this open port, read the section called "Serial Communication Issues with IDE on Windows."

3. Right-click on the Gadget Serial V2.4 port and choose the Update Driver Software option.

4. Choose the Browse My Computer for Driver Software Option.

5. Based in the location you extracted your IDE, navigate to the hardware/arduino/x86/tools directory. This allows the proper driver file called linux-cdc-acm.inf to be installed.

6. Once the driver is successfully installed, Device Manager will show a Galileo (COMx) device under Ports (COM & LPT). Note the COMx port number, as it will be needed in the IDE later. The example in this chapter shows COM5.

Installing the Driver on Linux

1. Check if an ACM port is available. If you are using Ubuntu, you can press Ctrl+Shift+T to open a terminal shell. Then type the following in the terminal:

```
ls /dev/ttyACM*
```

2. You should be able to see at least one serial port like `ttyACM0` or any other `ttyACM[X]`, where `[X]` represents an integer number. If you cannot see a serial port, follow these steps:

    a. Create a file called **/etc/udev/rules.d/50-arduino.rules** and add the following:

        KERNEL=="ttyACM[0-9]*", MODE="0666"

    b. Restart the udev service with the following command:

        sudo service udev restart

3. If you are using a virtual machine (VM), you may need to reboot Linux within the VM.

Installing the Driver on MacOS

Check the System Profiler ➤ USB setting to be sure that Gadget Serial is selected. If you are installing a new version of the IDE, you may need to re-select this setting.

Understanding the Arduino IDE

Once Intel Galileo is connected to your computer and you have the drivers properly set up, execute the IDE to access the window shown in Figure 3-4. Table 3-1 provides a description of each numbered item.

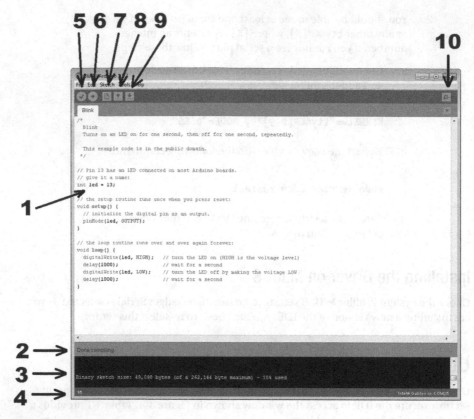

Figure 3-4. *Arduino IDE graphical interface*

Table 3-1. *Descriptions of Callouts in Figure 3-4*

Number	Description
1	Area code where you develop the code.
2	Notification bar informing you if the code was saved and whether the compilation was successful.
3	Console message with details of compilation, file transfer messages, and error messages.
4	Informs the line number of the cursor in the editor.
5	Verify icon: compile the code.
6	Transfer icon: compile the code and transfer to Intel Galileo.
7	Open a new sketch.
8	Open a sketch.
9	Save the edited sketch.
10	Open the serial debug console.

Explore the IDE a little bit by opening the example discussed at the beginning of this chapter and then selecting File ➤ Examples ➤ 01.Basic ➤ Blink.

Checking the Port and Board Selected

Before you run the sketch, you need to check a couple of things in the IDE. First of all, make sure you selected the right board by choosing Tools ➤ Board, as shown in Figure 3-5.

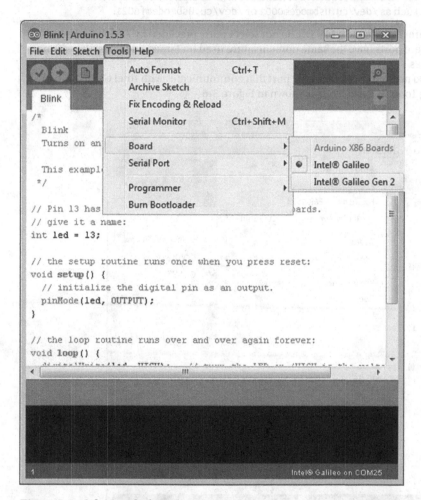

Figure 3-5. *Selecting the board*

Note that the port name varies according to the operational system:

- **Windows**: The ports are named with the COM prefix, followed by an integer number, such as COM5.

- **Linux**: The ports are named with the ttyACM prefix, followed by an integer number, such as ttyACM0.

- **MacOS**: The ports are named with the /dev/cu.usbmodem prefix, followed by a sequence of numbers and/or alphabetic characters, such as /dev/cu.usbmodem0001 or /dev/cu.usbmodemfd021.

If you are installing to a MacOS, do not select ports preceded by /dev/tty, because although these ports have the same nomenclature used on Linux machines, they are not the right ones.

You also need to check the serial port that communicates with Intel Galileo. Do this by selecting Tools ➤ Serial Port, as shown in Figure 3-6.

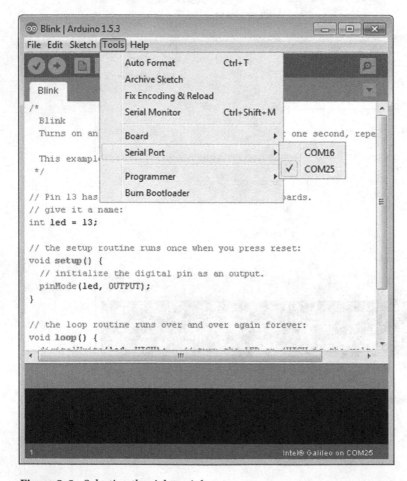

Figure 3-6. *Selecting the right serial port*

What Is a Sketch?

Before you run the first code, you need to know the meaning of the word "sketch" that's regularly used in the Arduino development. When you develop code using the Arduino reference API and its libraries, you've created a sketch.

In order to understand how a sketch works, consider the Blink example mentioned in the previous section.

```
/*
  Blink
  Turns on an LED on for one second, then off for one second, repeatedly.

  This example code is in the public domain.
 */

// Pin 13 has an LED connected on most Arduino boards.
// give it a name:
int led = 13;

// the setup routine runs once when you press reset:
void setup() {
  // initialize the digital pin as an output.
  pinMode(led, OUTPUT);
}

// the loop routine runs over and over again forever:
void loop() {
  digitalWrite(led, HIGH);   // turn the LED on (HIGH is the voltage level)
  delay(1000);               // wait for a second
  digitalWrite(led, LOW);    // turn the LED off by making the voltage LOW
  delay(1000);               // wait for a second
}
```

The sketch is composed by two main functions: setup() and loop().

The setup() function is executed one time, and this function establishes the initial setup of your hardware, including the pin directions, the speed of the serial ports, device initializations, and so on.

The loop() function is cyclic, which means it works like an infinite loop. It is on this function that you control your hardware.

As mentioned, the code is very close to how the hardware components are connected. For example, the previous code shows that:

- There is an LED connected to pin number 13.

- In the setup() function, the pin is configured as OUTPUT by the pinMode() function.

- In the loop() function, the LED will be turned ON for one second and then turned OFF for one second again. The LED is turned on and off when the digitalWrite() function sets the pin to HIGH and LOW, respectively and the delay of one second is set by the delay() function, which received the number of milliseconds as an argument.

Looking to the code you can imagine there is an LED on pin 13 and you also can easily understand what the code does. Note that there is no assembler language involved and even with the code being compiled in C++, there are no complex function calls to access the GPIO, which makes the development easier.

The next section discusses how to run this sketch.

Compiling and Running the Sketch

Click the icon represented by the number 5 in Figure 3-4, select Sketch ➤ Verify/Compile from the menu bar, or press Control+R.

The concept of "verify" on Arduino IDE really means compile the code. That should report "Done compiling" in the area represented by the number 2 in Figure 3-3.

Do not be worried if the compilation takes a long time—the first compilation is always slow. The cross-compilers are installed during the first compilation in order to provide a transparent mechanism to the developers. After the install, the cross-compiler is related to the compilation of the wiring API to generate the object files. After the first compilation, all subsequent compilations will be faster.

Click the icon represented by the number 6 shown in Figure 3-4 to upload the file. If the transfer is successful, you should see the "Done uploading" message in the notification bar and the "Transfer complete" message in the console message area. These messages are represented by the numbers 2 and 3, respectively, in Figure 3-4.

You should see an LED blinking on Intel Galileo. This LED is connected internally to pin number 13, thus proving your system is properly configured and you are ready to explore the IDE. If you are using the first Intel Galileo release, this LED is close to the BATT terminal, as shown in Figure 3-7.

Figure 3-7. *Built-in LED connected to pin 13 on Intel Galileo*

The blink example is similar to the "*HELLO WORLD!*" example you see in other programming environments, which is used to test if the development environment is working properly.

Persisted and Not Persisted Sketches

Intel Galileo can boot from SPI flash (SPI releases) or from an SD card. You can download both releases from the same web page where you downloaded the IDE.

Due to SPI flash part being very small (8MB), SPI flash releases contain only the very basic features. In order to take advantage of more advanced software, such as Python, WiFi capability, Node.js, OpenCV, V4L2, and other features, you have to use the SD card release.

The SD card releases contain all those features, plus the capability to persist the sketches.

If you have plans to keep your sketches after the system reboots, you need to use the SD card releases. Otherwise, when Intel Galileo reboots, the sketch will not run because it was not persisted.

Persisted Sketches and Long Time to Start

Intel Galileo is different from other Arduino boards because everything is controlled by the Quark SoC that runs Linux instead of by a simple microcontroller like the Atmel processors used in Arduino Uno, Due, Nano, and other boards.

Those microcontrollers do not have an OS, but they access a memory segment and execute specific opcodes to run the program.

Thus, the persisted sketches on Intel Galileo are executed only when Linux boots, all modules are loaded, and the user space is ready. This process takes around 50 seconds. The next section explains how to debug the sketches.

Debugging with Serial Console and Serial Communication

The Arduino reference API contains a serial terminal that's used to print debug messages from the sketches. This causes the Arduino boards to transmit messages to your computer using the Arduino IDE serial console.

The communication occurs using a static class called Serial; however, if you need to communicate with external devices like XBee shields, you should use the 0 and 1 pins to connect to such devices. The communication in this case is done by a different object but with same class methods, called Serial1. Arduino Uno uses the Serial object to establish communication with the 0 and 1 pins, so if you are porting some sketch code created for Arduino Uno as the serial interface, you need to change the object from Serial to Serial1.

There are five Serial object methods used to establish a communication and transmit messages: begin(), print(), println(), available(), and read().

Serial.begin(int speed)

The speed argument indicates baud rate. The values typically are 300, 600, 1200, 2400, 4800, 9600, 14400, 19200, and 115200.

If you are using the Serial object for debugging messages, this argument is irrelevant because the communication with Serial object is always 115200 bauds. If you set it to a different speed like 9600 bauds, the communication will still be 115200.

There is no impact on the development cycle. This was done because most of the Arduino examples were created for Atmel microcontrollers, and they have the sketches with the speed set to 9600 bauds by default. Trying to reduce the code changes and make the developer's life easier, it is not necessary to change the baud rate to 115200 on each example provided by IDE.

But with other objects like Serial1, which uses pins 0 and 1, speed really does have an effect in the communication because this object was created to communicate with external devices.

Note that this method must be called before any serial method—before you transmit or receive data, you must call this method.

Serial.print(data)

This method transmits the data argument through the serial port. The data argument might be a string, an integer, a char, a byte, a long, or any other standard type supported in the Arduino reference.

Serial.println(data)

This has the same functionality of Serial.print() method except a carrier and return is added to the end of the data message.

Serial.available( )

Informs you if there is any data in the receiver buffer. It returns an integer representing the quantity of bytes in the receiving buffer that are ready to be read.

Serial.read( )

Reads from the receiver buffer any available data. It's best to use this method only after you check for data using the available( ) method.

The data read might be a simple integer, a single character, an array of characters, a string, or any serialized object.

The next example shows you how to use such Serial objects and how to invoke the serial console terminal.

Printing Debug Messages and Using the Serial Console

This section sketches the print messages on the serial console and transmits messages from IDE to Intel Galileo, as shown in Listing 3-1.

Listing 3-1. serialtest.ino

```
String inputString = "";          // a string to hold incoming data
boolean stringComplete = false;  // whether the string is complete

void setup() {
  // put your setup code here, to run once:
  Serial.begin(9600);  // does not matter for this object
  delay(3000);
}

void loop() {
  // transmitting something from Galileo to IDE
  Serial.println("Hi there!! type something and press SEND button!!! ");
  delay(1000);

  // if the developer sent something from IDE to Galileo
  while (Serial.available()) {
    // get the new byte:
    char inChar = (char)Serial.read();

    // add it to the inputString:
    inputString += inChar;

    if (inChar == '\n') {
      stringComplete = true;

    }
  }
```

```
if (stringComplete == true) {

    Serial.print("\nCOOL!! RECEIVED YOUR MESSAGE: ");
    Serial.println(inputString);
    inputString = "";
    stringComplete=false;

  }

}
```

Upload the board with this sketch and access the serial console.

The Serial console can be accessed if you click Tools ➤ Serial Monitor, press Ctrl+Shift+M, or click the #10 icon highlighted in Figure 3-4.

You'll then see something similar to Figure 3-8.

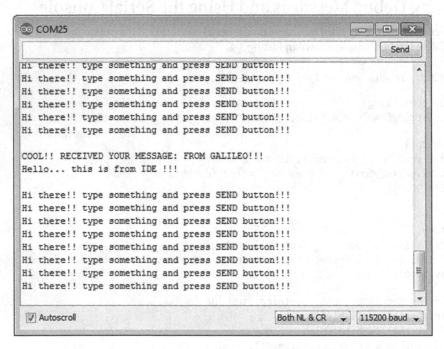

Figure 3-8. *Arduino IDE serial monitor console*

Note in the right-bottom corner there is the baud rate used in the communication (115200). You can also see the messages being displayed. At the top of the screen, there's a text box followed by a Send button. This is used to transmit data from your computer to the Intel Galileo board.

Also in Figure 3-8, considering the code is detecting the newline "\n" character, it is necessary to change the list box in the right-bottom corner to Both NL & CR. That means both newline and carriage return characters.

Just type some text using the text box on the left of Send button and press this button or click the Enter key at the end of your message.

Intel Galileo will receive the message you typed and display it in the serial console for you. To understand how this "magic" happens, read the next section.

Understanding the serialtest.ino Code

In the setup() function, the serial object is initiated with 9600 bauds by Serial.begin(). This is irrelevant as explained before because the communication is always 115200 bauds for Serial.

Also in setup(), there is a delay of three seconds to give you time to access the serial monitor. For Intel Galileo, if you are creating sketches that immediately print something, it is recommended that you add a small delay; otherwise, you can miss some messages (Galileo is faster than you).

In the loop() function, there is a message being printed by Serial.println() followed by Serial.available() that will always return false if you do not type anything in the text box and press the Send button in the serial console.

If you send a message to the board, the Serial.available() will return true. Each character of your message will be read by Serial.read() and accumulated in the variable inputString until the newline character (\n) is encountered (this character is automatically added when you press the Send button or press Enter).

If the message is completed after it detects the newline feed character, the message that's received is transmitted back using Serial.print() in the while loop block contained by Serial.available().

A message printed by Serial.print() and Serial.println() that asks to the user to transmit something is added to the end of the loop() function. There is a delay of 1000ms (1 second) initiated by the delay() function to avoid multiples messages running in the serial console.

The Arduino Language Reference and APIs

If you read this chapter from the beginning, you are already familiar with some references, including:

- **Structure:** loop() and setup()
- **Digital I/O:** pinMode() and digitalWrite()
- **Time:** delay()
- **Communication:** Serial.begin(), Serial.print(), Serial.println(), Serial.available(), and Serial.read()

These are only a small part of Arduino reference API. You can find the complete Arduino reference at http://arduino.cc/en/Reference/HomePage, as shown in Figure 3-9.

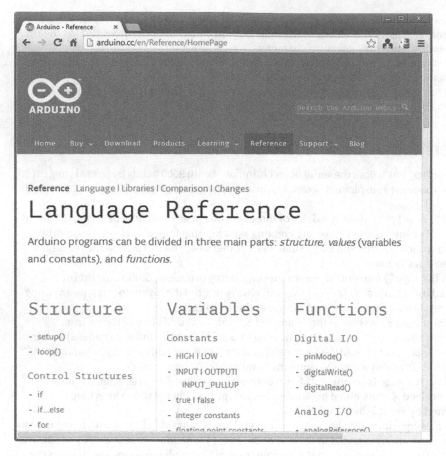

Figure 3-9. *Arduino reference page*

Let's organize the most important and most commonly used functions by category: Structure, Digital I/O, Analog I/O, and Time.

Remember that there are several functions and data types in the Arduino reference web page and the functions mentioned on this chapter are just the most common ones. An entire book could be devoted just to the Arduino reference, which is not the intention of this book.

Structure

Each sketch has two mandatory functions—setup() and loop(). Even if your sketch doesn't need these functions, you should at least keep them empty in your sketch to avoid compilations. Each of these items is discussed next.

setup()

As mentioned, this function is called just once. It is the first function called during sketch execution and it is used to set up the pins manually as well as initialize the serial ports and external devices.

loop()

This function was also discussed before. This function is called like a infinite loop while the sketch is executed and is basically responsible for the main state machine of the hardware.

Digital I/O

The digital I/O are related to pins 0 to 13 in the Intel Galileo headers, as explained in the section called "Arduino Headers on Intel Galileo" in Chapter 1. The following functions manage the digital I/Os.

pinMode(int pin, int mode)

This function is normally used in the setup() function and sets the "pin" that means the pin number to a specific "mode," which can be INPUT, OUTPUT, or INPUT_PULLUP.

If mode is INPUT, the pin is used as INPUT; for example, to read the state of a button.

If mode is OUTPUT, the pin is used as OUTPUT; for example, to turn on/off an LED.

Note that if mode is set to INPUT_PULLUP and the pullup resistor is around 20k ohms, that means if you use a pulldown resistor the logic will be inverted. If no pulldown resistor is used, the reading still will be 1 if you have 5 to 3.3V or 0 if it's connected to the ground.

digitalWrite(int pin, int state)

This function sets the pin state according to the state argument that's passed, which can be HIGH or LOW. It works only if pin was set as OUTPUT by the pinMode() function.

int digitalRead(int pin)

This reads the state of the pin number and returns HIGH or LOW (both are integers).

Analog I/O

The analog I/O are related to pins A0 to A5 in the Intel Galileo headers, as explained in the section called "Arduino Headers on Intel Galileo" in Chapter 1. Remember that the AREF is unused on Intel Galileo boards so external references for analog input are not supported.

The following functions are used to manage the analog I/Os.

int analogRead(int pin)

This function reads the analog specified by pin that can assume the values A0 to A5, according to the six analog ports supported by Intel Galileo. The value returned is an integer between 0 and 1023 and refers to the scale of 0 to 5V, respectively. Intel Galileo has 12-bit maximum resolution in the ADC. Figure 3-10 shows the analog ports on the Intel Galileo board.

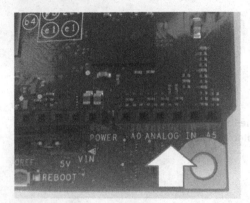

Figure 3-10. Analog port A0 to A5

analogWrite(int pin, int value)—PWM

This function generates pulse width modulation (PWM) to control servos, create fading effects on LEDS, control DC motors, and so on.

The pin argument specifies which PIN must generate the PWM with a duty cycle set by value.

The PINs that can be set to use PWN on Intel Galileo are 3, 5, 6, 9, 10, and 11. You also can easily identify such pins because there is a small tilde (~) in front of the pins that support PWM, as shown in Figure 3-11.

Figure 3-11. *The tilde (~) identifies which pins support PWM*

The value must be an integer between 0 and 255, and this range is proportional to the percentage of 0% to 100% of the duty cycle to be generated. Thus, if the value is 0, the duty cycle is zero. 127 will generate a PWM with 50% of duty cycle and 255 a duty cycle with 100%.

This function does not return anything.

Time

The following functions enable you to insert delays into sketch and obtain uptime—the amount of time the board was booted for.

long millis( )

This function returns the number of milliseconds from the time Intel Galileo was booted.

long micros( )

This function returns the number of microseconds from the time Intel Galileo was booted.

delay(int milliseconds)

Delay pauses sketch execution for the amount of time specified by `milliseconds`.

delayMicroseconds(int microseconds)

This function pauses the sketch during the time specified in the `microseconds` argument.

Running Some Examples

The next examples demonstrate the Arduino IDE and the intention is to cover the most common functions discussed previously. Note the code used in each example and compare it to the circuit. If you understood the reference functions discussed thus far, you will realize that it was not necessary to show the example's schematics because the reference functions used are simple. Looking just at the code, you can imagine the circuit and make this circuit interact with the exterior LEDs and buttons. This is the main purpose of the wiring platform.

Fade Example

Load the example in the IDE by accessing Files ➤ 01.Basics ➤ Fade and checking the materials list in Table 3-2.

Table 3-2. *Materials List for the Fade Example*

Number	Description
1	LED
1	220 ohm resistor
1	Breadboard
n	Hook-up wires (assorted)

This example demonstrates using the `pinMode()` function to set pin 9 to `OUTPUT`. It also shows how to generate a PWM to simulate a fading effect. The code varies the duty cycle applied in a pin port connect to an LED, which changes the intensity of the LED.

Fade Materials list

Table 3-2 provides the materials list for this example.

Fade Schematics

Connect the LED's cathode to the ground and the LED's anode to the 220 ohm resistor, as shown in Figure 3-11. The resistor is connected directly to pin 9.

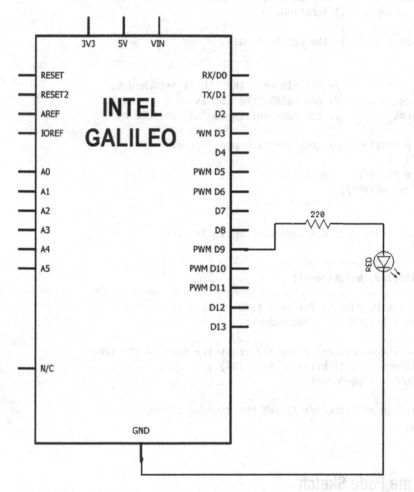

Figure 3-12. *Schematic used in the Fade example*

Fade Code

Listing 3-2 provides the code for the Fade example.

Listing 3-2. Fade.ino

```
/*
 Fade

 This example shows how to fade an LED on pin 9
 using the analogWrite() function.

 This example code is in the public domain.
 */

int led = 9;           // the pin that the LED is attached to
int brightness = 0;    // how bright the LED is
int fadeAmount = 5;    // how many points to fade the LED by

// the setup routine runs once when you press reset:
void setup() {
  // declare pin 9 to be an output:
  pinMode(led, OUTPUT);
}

// the loop routine runs over and over again forever:
void loop() {
  // set the brightness of pin 9:
  analogWrite(led, brightness);

  // change the brightness for next time through the loop:
  brightness = brightness + fadeAmount;

  // reverse the direction of the fading at the ends of the fade:
  if (brightness == 0 || brightness == 255) {
    fadeAmount = -fadeAmount ;
  }
  // wait for 30 milliseconds to see the dimming effect
  delay(30);
}
```

Running the Fade Sketch

As soon the sketch runs, setup() is executed only once. It sets pin 9 to OUTPUT through the pinMode() function. In the loop() function, analogWrite() generates a PWM with a duty cycle of 0 stored in the brightness variable. The duty cycle increases by five, as defined by the variable `fadeAmount`, until it reaches 255. At this point, the duty cycle reduces by five again until it reaches 0. The logic then starts increasing the duty cycle again. This logic will create a PWM varying the duty cycle, causing a diming effect.

There is a 30-millisecond delay to allow you to see the dimming effect; otherwise, the code would run so fast you would think the LED is only turning `ON` and `OFF`.

Button Example

Load the example in the IDE by accessing Files ➤ 02.Digital ➤ Button and checking the materials needed in Table 3-3.

Table 3-3. *Materials List for the Button Example*

Number	Description
1	10k ohm resistor
1	Pushbutton or switch
1	Breadboard
n	Hook-up wires (assorted)

This example focuses on how to use the `digitalRead()` function to read the state of a working input method. It uses `digitalWrite()` to turn on an LED. Note that this example uses an LED on pin 13, which means you do not need to connect an LED to pin 13 because pin 13 is connected to the LED built in to the Intel Galileo, as shown in Figure 3-7. However, if you connect an LED to pin 13 similar as you connected on pin 2 in the fade example , you will see two LEDs working at same time you push the button or switch. In other words, you will see the built-in and the external LED having the same effect. The 10k ohm resistor is used to limit the current and then the button is opened. This prevents a short circuit between the 5V and the GND in the board.

The `pinMode()` function is used to set the pins to `OUTPUT` and `INPUT`.

Button Materials List

Table 3-3 provides the materials list for this example.

Button Schematics

Use the pushbutton or switch connect to the 10k ohm and pin number 2, as shown in Figure 3-13.

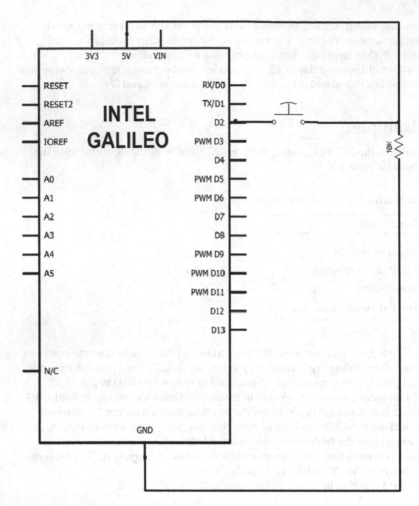

Figure 3-13. *Schematic used in the Button example*

Button Code

Listing 3-3 provides the code for the Button example.

Listing 3-3. Button.ino

```
/*
  Button

  Turns on and off a light emitting diode(LED) connected to digital
  pin 13, when pressing a pushbutton attached to pin 2.
```

```
* LED attached from pin 13 to ground
* pushbutton attached to pin 2 from +5V
* 10K resistor attached to pin 2 from ground

* Note: on most Arduinos there is already an LED on the board
attached to pin 13.

created 2005
by DojoDave <http://www.0j0.org>
modified 30 Aug 2011
by Tom Igoe

This example code is in the public domain.

http://www.arduino.cc/en/Tutorial/Button
*/

// constants won't change. They're used here to
// set pin numbers:
const int buttonPin = 2;      // the number of the pushbutton pin
const int ledPin =   13;      // the number of the LED pin

// variables will change:
int buttonState = 0;          // variable for reading the pushbutton status

void setup() {
  // initialize the LED pin as an output:
  pinMode(ledPin, OUTPUT);
  // initialize the pushbutton pin as an input:
  pinMode(buttonPin, INPUT);
}

void loop(){
  // read the state of the pushbutton value:
  buttonState = digitalRead(buttonPin);

  // check if the pushbutton is pressed.
  // if it is, the buttonState is HIGH:
  if (buttonState == HIGH) {
    // turn LED on:
    digitalWrite(ledPin, HIGH);
  }
  else {
    // turn LED off:
    digitalWrite(ledPin, LOW);
  }
}
```

Running the Button Sketch

The setup() function is called once you've set pin 13 to OUTPUT and pin 2 to INPUT through pinMode().

In the loop() function, the variable buttonState receives the current state of the switch or pushbutton. When you press the button, digitalRead() returns HIGH and buttonState saves this value and the digitalWrite() function sets pin 13 (LED) to HIGH, thus turning ON the built-in LED.

Otherwise, if the pushbutton or switch is not pressed, digitalRead() returns LOW and the buttonState variable saves this value. Then the digitalWrite() function sets pin 13 (LED) to LOW, turning OFF the built-in LED.

ReadAnalogVoltage Example

Load the example in the IDE by accessing Files ➤ 01.Basics ➤ ReadAnalogVoltage and checking the materials list in Table 3-4.

Table 3-4. Materials List for ReadAnalogVoltage Example

Number	Description
1	Potentiometer (any!)
1	Breadboard
n	Hook-up wires (assorted)

This example uses the analogRead()function to convert the voltage over a potentiometer to a digital reading.

This example also uses the Serial object discussed previously to print the value read in the serial console terminal.

ReadAnalogVoltage Materials List

Table 3-4 provides the materials list for this example.

ReadAnalogVoltage Schematics

Connect the potentiometer only to the 5V and the ground, and then connect the variable terminal to the A0 port, as shown in Figure 3-14.

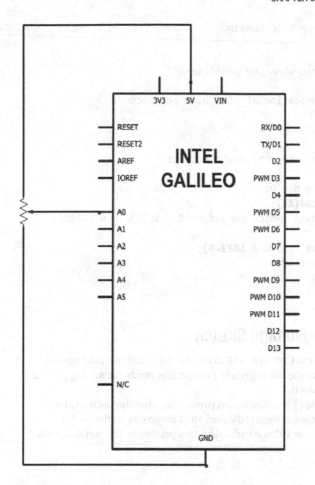

Figure 3-14. *Schematic used in the ReadAnalogVoltage example*

The ReadAnalogVoltage Code

Listing 3-4 provides the code for the ReadAnalogVoltage example.

Listing 3-4. ReadAnalogVoltage.ino

```
/*
  ReadAnalogVoltage
  Reads an analog input on pin 0, converts it to voltage, and prints the
result to the serial monitor.
  Attach the center pin of a potentiometer to pin A0, and the outside pins
to +5V and ground.
```

```
This example code is in the public domain.
*/

// the setup routine runs once when you press reset:
void setup() {
  // initialize serial communication at 9600 bits per second:
  Serial.begin(9600);
}

// the loop routine runs over and over again forever:
void loop() {
  // read the input on analog pin 0:
  int sensorValue = analogRead(A0);
  // Convert the analog reading (which goes from 0 - 1023) to a voltage
(0 - 5V):
  float voltage = sensorValue * (5.0 / 1023.0);
  // print out the value you read:
  Serial.println(voltage);
}
```

Running the ReadAnalogVoltage Sketch

As soon as you run the sketch, press Ctrl+Shift+M to invoke the serial monitor console. Notice in the loop() function that the analogRead() command reads the analog port A0 and the variable sensor value saves it.

Remember when analogRead() was discussed previously, that the return value was between 0 and 1023. In this case, 0 means 0V and 1023 means 5V in the port A. This conversion is being done by the voltage variable that's printed in the serial console terminal by Serial.println().

The Debounce Example

Load the example in the IDE by accessing Files ➤ 02.Digital ➤ Debounce. Check the materials list used in Table 3-3.

This example demonstrates the use of the millis() function to add logic based on time. It determines whether a button was pressed after a period of time, in order to avoid interpreting multiples presses. This is called *debounce*.

The example uses the same material and circuit used in the example button previously discussed in this chapter.

Debounce Materials List

You can use the same material from Table 3-3 from the Button example.

Debounce Schematics

Use the same circuit shown in Figure 3-12 from the Button example.

Debounce Code

Listing 3-5 provides the code for the Debounce example.

Listing 3-5. Debounce.ino

```
/* Listing 3-5 Debounce.ino.

Debounce

Each time the input pin goes from LOW to HIGH (e.g. because of a push-button
press), the output pin is toggled from LOW to HIGH or HIGH to LOW. There's
a minimum delay between toggles to debounce the circuit (i.e. to ignore
noise).

The circuit:
* LED attached from pin 13 to ground
* pushbutton attached from pin 2 to +5V
* 10K resistor attached from pin 2 to ground

* Note: On most Arduino boards, there is already an LED on the board
connected to pin 13, so you don't need any extra components for this
example.

created 21 November 2006
by David A. Mellis
modified 30 Aug 2011
by Limor Fried
modified 28 Dec 2012
by Mike Walters

This example code is in the public domain.

http://www.arduino.cc/en/Tutorial/Debounce
*/
```

```
// constants won't change. They're used here to
// set pin numbers:
const int buttonPin = 2;    // the number of the pushbutton pin
const int ledPin = 13;      // the number of the LED pin

// Variables will change:
int ledState = HIGH;        // the current state of the output pin
int buttonState;            // the current reading from the input pin
int lastButtonState = LOW   // the previous reading from the input pin

// the following variables are long's because the time, measured in
miliseconds,
// will quickly become a bigger number than can be stored in an int.
long lastDebounceTime = 0   // the last time the output pin was toggled
long debounceDelay = 50;    // the debounce time; increase if the output flickers

void setup() {
  pinMode(buttonPin, INPUT);
  pinMode(ledPin, OUTPUT);

  // set initial LED state
  digitalWrite(ledPin, ledState);
}

void loop() {
  // read the state of the switch into a local variable:
  int reading = digitalRead(buttonPin);

  // check to see if you just pressed the button
  // (i.e. the input went from LOW to HIGH),  and you've waited
  // long enough since the last press to ignore any noise:

  // If the switch changed, due to noise or pressing:
  if (reading != lastButtonState) {
    // reset the debouncing timer
    lastDebounceTime = millis();
  }

  if ((millis() - lastDebounceTime) > debounceDelay) {
    // whatever the reading is at, it's been there for longer
    // than the debounce delay, so take it as the actual current state:

    // if the button state has changed:
    if (reading != buttonState) {
      buttonState = reading;
```

```
    // only toggle the LED if the new button state is HIGH
    if (buttonState == HIGH) {
      ledState = !ledState;
    }
  }
}

  // set the LED:
  digitalWrite(ledPin, ledState);

  // save the reading.  Next time through the loop,
  // it'll be the lastButtonState:
  lastButtonState = reading;
}
```

Running the Debounce Sketch

In this example, the setup() function sets pin 2 to INPUT because the button or switch should be connected to this pin. Pin 13 (the internal built-in LED) is set to OUTPUT.

The loop() function reads the button state through digitalRead() and the variable reading assumes the value. If the button state differs from the last read, the lastDebounceTime variable assumes the current millis(). Then the loop function keeps running and reading the button states, but when the debounceDelay interval is reached after the first button pressing, the state is checked again. If the code detects that the user was still pressing the button, the LED state is changed.

In the next section, you learn how to update the firmware.

Updating the Firmware Using the IDE

Besides the dediprog and the manual procedure to upload the firmware to the board, which was discussed in the Chapter 2, there is a third option involving IDE and it is much simpler.

Every time Intel releases a new IDE, it typically comes with a new firmware for Intel Galileo. It's recommended that you update it for the bug fixes and the new APIs.

The update process in the IDE is very simple:

1. Remove the USB cable and 5V power supply.

2. Remove the SD card or USB stick if you are using one.

3. Insert the 5V power supply.

4. Insert the USB cable.

5. Start the IDE and make sure the Intel Board and serial port is properly configured, as explained in the section entitled "Checking the Port and Board Selected" in this chapter.

6. Select Help ➤ Firmware Update, as shown in Figure 3-15.

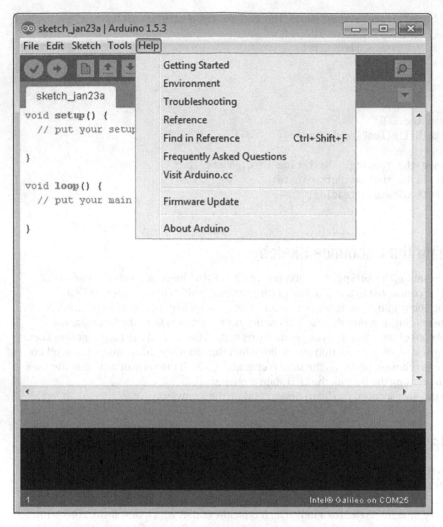

Figure 3-15. Firmware Update option in the Help menu

7. A warning dialog will show up to warn you that the 5V power supply must be connected. See Figure 3-16.

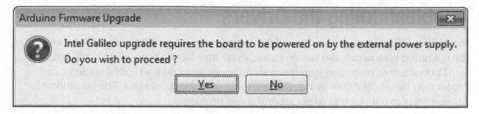

Figure 3-16. *5V power supply warning during the firmware update*

8. Another dialog will ask you if you want to update the firmware. Just click Yes. You'll then need to wait around six minutes.

If the firmware version in the Intel Galileo is newer than the IDE, you will be informed of this. But if you click yes, the firmware will be downgraded, as shown in Figure 3-17.

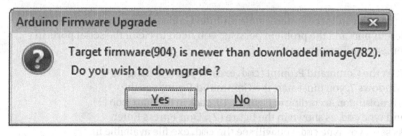

Figure 3-17. *You do have the option to downgrade*

Updating the Firmware with Different Firmware

Sometimes Intel provides new firmware releases before a new IDE release comes out. In this case, you do not need to wait for a new IDE to upgrade your firmware. Just download the firmware provided using the same link you used before (https://communities. intel.com/docs/DOC-22226) and then download the file with the .cap extension to the following locations:

Windows: .../Arduino<IDE VERSION>/hardware/tools/x86/bin/

Linux: .../Arduino<IDE VERSION>/hardware/tools/

MacOS: Arduino.app/Contents/Resources/Java/hardware/tools/x86/bin/

After you copy the .cap file to one of these locations, make sure you delete or change the extension of the old .cap file because only one cap file can be present in this location.

Troubleshooting the Drivers

The Arduino IDE is designed to run in different operational systems with different versions. The operation system can also run on virtual machines like VMware and Virtual Box.

This variety of operation systems, with different versions and configurations, can impact how the serial driver works. There are some known problems. The intention of this section is to tell you how to get around those problems.

Serial Communication Issues with IDE on Windows

Sometimes after you plug the serial cable in several times or reboot your computer, the serial communication fails. This happens sometimes even when the COM port is present in the device manager and you have selected the right serial port and board in the IDE.

In the IDE console message (see Figure 3-4), the following error might appear:

```
C:\galileo-arduino-1.5.3/hardware/arduino/x86/tools/izmir/clupload_win.sh:
line 40: /dev/ttyS8: No such file or directory
```

It means the IDE cannot communicate with Intel Galileo. If you connect the USB cable to a different port and the problem persists, you need to clean the serial ports in your computer using following steps:

1. Start the Command Prompt (cmd.exe). If you are using Windows 7, you must start the Command Prompt as the administrator. According to Figure 3-18, click in the Start icon (1) and type cmd, as shown in the figure (2). Don't press Enter. As soon you type cmd, you will see the cmd.exe file available in Programs, as shown in Figure 3-18 (3).

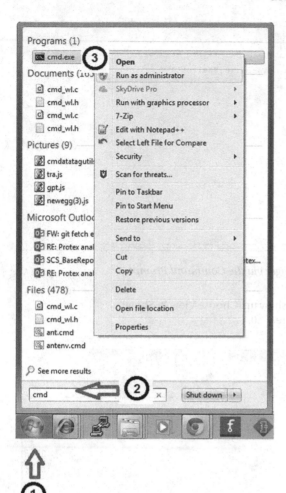

Figure 3-18. Starting the Command Prompt as an administrator on Windows 7

2. The Command Prompt will be shown. Type the following commands: `set devmgr_show_nonpresent_devices=1` and `start devmgmt.msc`. See Figure 3-19.

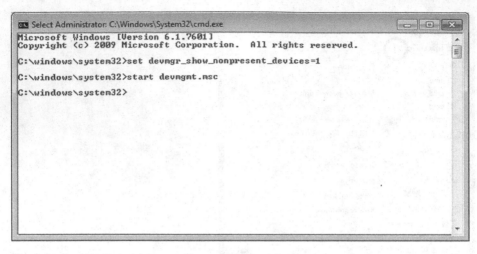

Figure 3-19. *Starting the Device Manager via the Command Prompt*

3. The Device Manager will show up. Choose View ➤ Show Hidden Devices. See Figure 3-20.

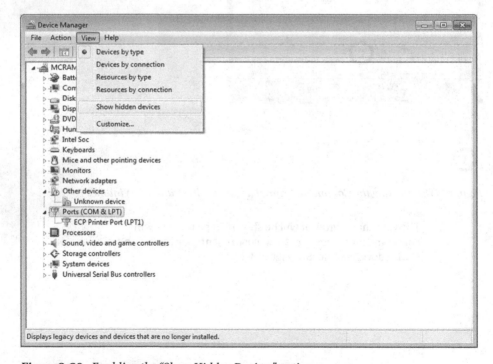

Figure 3-20. *Enabling the "Show Hidden Devices" option*

After you enable the option to see the hidden devices, the Ports (COM & LPT) node will show all the hidden devices as faded icons, as shown in Figure 3-21.

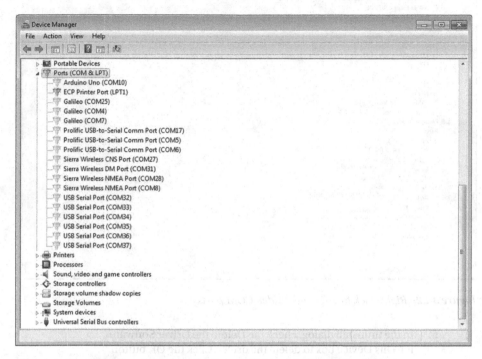

Figure 3-21. All hidden devices under Ports (COM & LPT) are grayed out

4. Select the COM port to be uninstalled. Right-click it and select Uninstall. See Figure 3-22.

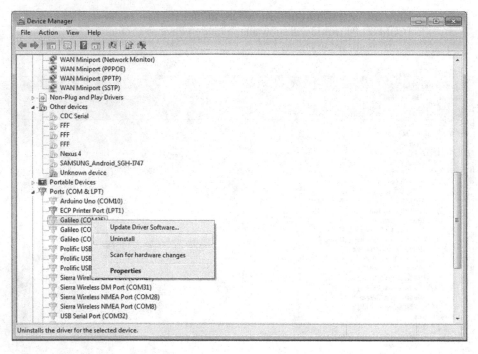

Figure 3-22. *Right-click to uninstall hidden COM ports*

5. In the uninstall dialog, check the Delete the Driver Software for This Device box to delete the driver. Click the OK button, as shown in Figure 3-23.

Figure 3-23. *Deleting the hidden COM port and driver*

6. After deleting all the hidden COM ports, repeat the installation process mentioned in the "Installing the Drivers" section of this chapter.

IDE Problems with Virtual Machines and 64-Bit Linux

If you are using the Arduino IDE for Intel Galileo in a virtual machine or in a 64-bit Linux OS, there are some errors you'll encounter that aren't covered in the "Getting Started Guide."

These errors are possible to resolve but they require some tricks. The following sections describe a few of them.

Warning Messages with 64-Bit Linux

If you see a warning message like /ibus/bus is not root, try starting the IDE using gksudo ./arduino instead of sudo ./arduino. To install the gksudo, use the sudo apt-get install gksu command.

Problems with VMware

If you installed the IDE into VMware, you might have issues detecting the /dev/ttySx where x is the port number. There is a bug in VMware if the comm port is automatically recognized and selected without any manual intervention. If that happens, disconnect the port as shown in Figure 3-24 and then reconnect it.

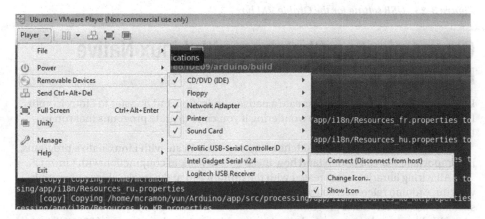

Figure 3-24. Option to disconnect serial port

135

Problems with Oracle Virtual Box

If you encounter communication issues, make sure you have the Enable USB 2.0 (EHCI) Controller enabled by selecting Settings ➤ USB, as shown in Figure 3-25.

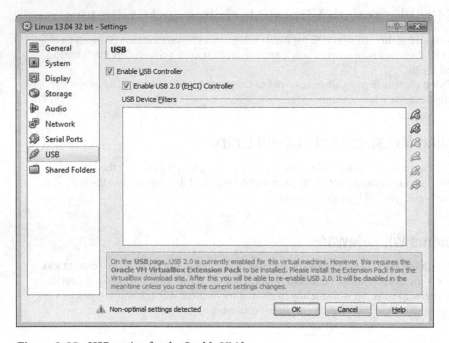

Figure 3-25. *USB setting for the Orable VM box*

Communicating Sketches with Linux Native Programs

In Chapter 2 you learned how to create a native application and transfer to Linux in your Intel Galileo board. You might be wondering if you can integrate programs that run in Linux with sketches.

Before we discuss how the sketches might communicate with Linux-native programs, it is important that you understand how the sketches work in conjunction with Linux OS.

All wiring libraries were created with the initiative to make Intel Galileo compatible with the Arduino reference, so they run in the Linux user space. In other words, the sketches are like any other program.

APIs like shared memory, sockets, signaling libraries, and a vastness of POSIX libraries can be used to establish communication as any other regular program in Linux OS.

It possible also to call direct programs like Python, curl, OpenSSL, bash scripts, start services, and so on.

The example provided in the next section integrates the unread email alarm with Python and POSIX. Considering Python is being used you should have an SD card image because SPI images are very tiny and do not contain additional software like Python. Additional examples are covered in future chapters.

is.Additionalfuture Project Example: Unread Email Alarm with Python and POSIX Functions

This project explains how to use regular Linux POSIX APIs to create a timer that asynchronously calls a function handler every 10 seconds. When this function handler is executed, it calls a Python script that counts the number of emails unread in a Gmail account. If the number of emails increased, an LED is ON, which informs you that there is new email in the inbox.

The connection to Gmail is made using WiFi or an Ethernet cable.

Materials List

Table 3-5 provides the materials list for this example. Table 3-6 provides an optional list.

Table 3-5. Materials List for Fade Example

Number	Description
1	LED
1	220 ohm resistor
1	Breadboard
n	Hook-up wires (assorted)

Table 3-6. Optional Materials

Quantity	Components
1	Intel Centrino Wireless-N 135 or Ethernet cable
2	Dual band antennas 350mm cable 2118060-1 TE Connectivity (only if WiFi)
1	LED
1	220 ohm resistor
n	Hook-up wires (assorted)
1	Breadboard

The Schematics

Use the same schematic in Figure 3-12. Note the WiFi card or Ethernet setup, and then follow the instructions in Chapter 5.

The PythonP Code

The Python script is called emailCounter.py and it accepts two arguments wherein the first argument is your Gmail's username or email and the second argument is your password.

You can execute this script manually to test the terminal serial:

python email.counter <your username or email> <your password>

The Python code is provided in Listing 3-6.

Listing 3-6. gmail.py

```
# based in the discussion in:
# http://stackoverflow.com/questions/953561/check-unread-count-of-gmail-
  messages-with-python
# by manoel.c.ramon@intel.com

import imaplib
import sys

obj = imaplib.IMAP4_SSL('imap.gmail.com','993')
obj.login(sys.argv[1],sys.argv[2])
obj.select()
obj.search(None,'UnSeen')
print len(obj.search(None,'UnSeen')[1][0].split())
```

The sketch code is provided in Listing 3-7.

Listing 3-7. gmailAlarm.ino

```
#include <signal.h>
#include <stdio.h>
#include <string.h>
#include <sys/time.h>

// the led
int led = 2;  // the built-in LED

// emails counters
int current_emails_counter = -1;
int last_emails_counter = -1;
```

```
// add here your credentials
String gmailUserName="";  // email or password
String gmailPassword="";  // your password

String script_name = "python /home/root/emailCounter.py ";

// this function calls a Python script to read the number of emails not read
int processEmailCounter()
{

    char cmd_rsp[8];  // This buffer will containg the script response

    FILE *fpipe;

    String command = script_name;

    command += gmailUserName;
    command += " ";

    command += gmailPassword;

     // buffer to be used with popen
    char cmd_char[300];

    // clear message buffer
    memset((void *)cmd_char, sizeof(cmd_char), 0);

    // convert the message to char array
    command.toCharArray(cmd_char, sizeof(cmd_char), 0);

    if ( !(fpipe = (FILE*)popen((char *)cmd_char,"r")) )
        {  // If fpipe is NULL
        Serial.println("Problems with pipe");
    }
    else
    {

        while ( fgets( cmd_rsp, sizeof(cmd_rsp), fpipe)) {}

        pclose(fpipe);

        // let's print the serial result
        Serial.println(cmd_rsp);

        return atoi(cmd_rsp);
    }

    return -1;
}
```

```
// this is my time handler...
void timerHandler (int signum)
{
    current_emails_counter = processEmailCounter();
    if (last_emails_counter == -1)
    {
        last_emails_counter = current_emails_counter;
        Serial.println("I am ready to check now... ");
    }

    if (current_emails_counter != last_emails_counter)
    {
        // turn on the LED
        digitalWrite(led, HIGH);
    }
}

int setAlarm ()
{
  struct sigaction sa;
  struct itimerval timer;

  /* Install timer_handler as the signal handler for SIGVTALRM.   */
  memset (&sa, 0, sizeof (sa));
  sa.sa_handler = &timerHandler;
  sigaction (SIGVTALRM, &sa, NULL);

  // Configure the timer to expire after 1 seconds
  timer.it_value.tv_sec = 1;
  timer.it_value.tv_usec = 0;
  // ... and every 10 seconds after that
  timer.it_interval.tv_sec = 10;
  timer.it_interval.tv_usec = 0;

  // Start a virtual timer. Counter while sketch runs
  setitimer (ITIMER_VIRTUAL, &timer, NULL);

}

void setup() {
    // only a small delay to allow you press CTRL+SHIT+M
    // and see the Serial Monitor
    delay(3000);
```

```
    // set the alarm
    setAlarm();
    pinMode(led, OUTPUT);
    digitalWrite(led, LOW);
}

void loop() {
    // put your main code here, to run repeatedly:

}
```

Preparing the Project to Run

The first thing to do is transfer the Python script to the Intel Galileo board using FTP, as described in the Chapter 2, or any other method you prefer. Make sure you transferred to the correct path because the sketch searches for /home/root/emailCounter.py. Otherwise, you have to change the sketch code to the path you want.

Make sure that you have the WiFi or Ethernet working properly, as explained in the Chapter 2. Note that Sketch does not use a client for connection. You can use any connection since the board has an IP address and Internet connection available.

Before you run the sketch, you need to add your credentials to the beginning of the code:

```
// add your credentials here
String gmailUserName="";  // email or password
String gmailPassword="";  // your password
```

If your Python script is copied to the right path, your Internet connection is working, and your credentials are in the sketch's code, you are ready to run.

Running the Code

If everything is prepared, run the sketch. As soon it runs, press Ctrl+Shift+M to see the debug messages in the serial console.

If you are fast enough, you will see the following message:

I am ready to check now...

This means the code read the quantity of emails unread and is waiting for new ones. Using your browser, open your Gmail and send an email to yourself.

In a maximum of 10 seconds you should see the LED ON.

Reviewing the Code

The setup() function has a delay of three seconds in order to allow you to start the serial console and catch the first debug messages printed by Serial.print() and Serial.println(). The setup() function also initializes the timer setting by calling the setAlarm() function. It sets pin 2 to OUTPUT through pinMode() because the LED must be connected to this pin and then turns off the LED by having digitalWrite() pass LOW.

The setAlarm() function creates a timer using setitimer(), which in turn calls a function handler called timerHandler() in one second, as soon the sketch runs, and then every 10 seconds after that. With the regular Arduino reference you could control the seconds passed in the **loop()** function using **millis()**; however, using the POSIX functions is much easier. The timer that's created is the ITIMER_VIRTUAL type, which means the function handler is called only while the sketch is running.

For more information on how setitimer() works, visit this link: http://unixhelp.ed.ac.uk/CGI/man-cgi?setitimer+2.

When timerHandler() is called, it calls the processEmailCounter() function, which is responsible for executing the emailCounter.py Python script. This script receives your credentials and returns the number of unread emails in your Gmail inbox. The sketch receives the response using the popen() function (ANSI C) and receives the number of emails in a char array, which is converted to an integer format using atoi().

In sequence, timerHandler() uses two variables called current_emails_counter and last_emails_counter. They determine if the number of unread email increased according to the processEmailCounter() function. If there was an increase, the LED connected to pin 2 is set to HIGH by digitalWire().

The project requires an Internet connection, so it is recommended that you use a WiFi card or Ethernet cable and set up the board as explained in the Chapter 2.

When the Internet connection is established before the sketch is executed, you can avoid using WiFi or Ethernet libraries. This is discussed in Chapter 4.

FINAL THOUGHTS ON THIS PROJECT . . .

Check the function loop():

```
void loop() {
  // put your main code here, to run repeatedly:


}
```

It is empty! Most of the code was developed using Python and POSIX calls provided by the Linux libraries. Note that a few functions from the Arduino reference were used: pinMode() and digitalWrite().

You can see how powerful Intel Galileo is and how easy it is to integrate the Arduino reference APIs into the Linux libraries.

Summary

At this point you are able to install and run the Arduino IDE, install the drives in different operational systems, and load, compile, and download sketches.

You were introduced to the wiring platform concept and to the most common functions used in the Arduino reference library in order to manage the digital and analog headers of Intel Galileo. With such headers, you were able to interface with LEDs and buttons, generate PWM signals, and debug the sketches using serial communication.

At the end of this chapter, you learned how to make the sketches communicate with the native Linux applications using POSIX functions and how to interface with Python scripts.

This chapter is very simple but one of most important because it provides basic concepts that will be used in the remainder of the book.

CHAPTER 4

■ ■ ■

New APIs and Hacks

The challenge when Intel Galileo was designed was to create a board that would be compatible with Arduino headers and reference language using only the Quark microprocessor, and to have the same capabilities running Linux and making any needed bridges with microcontrollers.

The competitor's boards that run Linux do in fact use microcontrollers to interface with pin headers and all have decent performance.

Intel Galileo and Intel Galileo Gen 2 do not use a microcontroller, which makes sketch implementations easier because there is no bridge between the microprocessor and microcontroller. On other hand, the implementation of Linux drivers and the Arduino reference API on the Linux userspace context without a microcontroller to guarantee performance in real-time is a huge challenge.

This chapter describes the new APIs as well as some of the design workarounds introduced in the first Intel Galileo version. The chapter also discusses some hacks that you can make if the regular Arduino reference API does not meet the needs of your project.

Some APIs work exclusively with Intel Galileo, some only with Intel Galileo Gen 2, and others with both. Thus, each section on APIs hacks includes a note explaining which version it works with.

Servo API

Servo motors are widely used in robots and devices controlled remotely, such as RC planes. At the same time, they are confusing because the practice is a little different than the theory. Let's take a look at the theory and the practice.

The Theory versus Practice

In theory, the servo rotates between 0 to 180 degrees using PWM pulses that vary between 1 to 2 milliseconds in a period of 20 milliseconds (50Hz) and operating between 4.5 to 6 VDC. Figure 4-1 shows the servo movement according to the pulses to 0, 90, and 180 degrees.

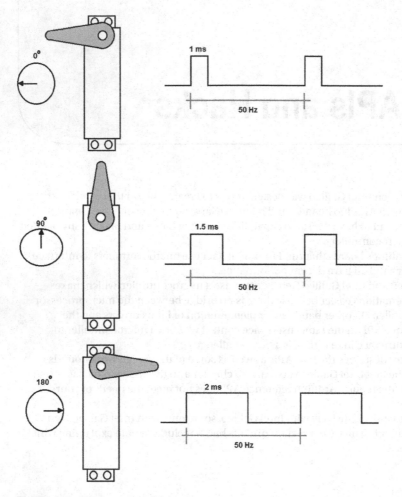

Figure 4-1. *How servos work in theory*

With only three wires, the VCC wire is usually red, the ground is usually black, and the pulse signal wire comes in different colors depending on the manufacterer. It's possible to move the servo to a specific position between 0 to 180 degrees.

To exercise the servos and understand how they really work with the new APIs, connect a servo to an Intel Galileo header. See the materials list in Table 4-1.

Table 4-1. *Materials List for Servo Exercises*

Number	Description
2	Servo Futaba S3003 or equivalent

This servo can be found online for around $7 to $15 US.

Schematic for Servo: One Servo

Connect the VCC to 5V, the ground to a ground, and the pulse to pin 9, as the schematic shows in Figure 4-2.

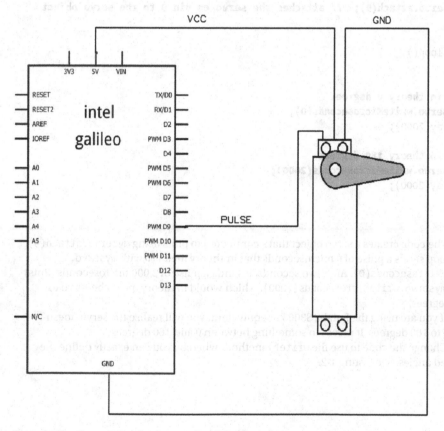

Figure 4-2. *Connecting the servo to Intel Galileo*

   With this theory in mind if you decide to buy a servo online, you will see quite a variety of servos with prices ranging between $5 and $15 US.

   Choose a servo, such as the servo Futaba S3003 mentioned in the material list Table 4-1.

   Then write the code shown in Listing 4-1.

Listing 4-1. servotheory.ino

```
#include <Servo.h>

Servo myservo;

void setup()
{
  myservo.attach(9);  // attaches the servo on pin 9 to the servo object
}

void loop()
{

  // in theory 0 degrees
  myservo.writeMicroseconds(0);
  delay(2000);

  // in theory 180 degrees
  myservo.writeMicroseconds(2000);
  delay(2000);

}
```

   The code creates a servo object that's connected to pin 9 using myservo.attach(9). The loop sends a pulse of 0 microseconds that in theory means 0 with myservo. writeMicroseconds(0). After two seconds, it sends a pulse of 2,000 microseconds (2ms) with myservo.writeMicroseconds(2000), which would in theory move the servo to 180 degrees.

   If you are using the Futaba S3003 or equivalent, you will realize the servo doesn't move to 180 degrees. It moves to something between 0 and 160 degrees.

   Change the code to use the write() method, whereby you can exactly define the desired angles. See Listing 4-2.

Listing 4-2. servo_write_angles.ino

```
#include <Servo.h>

Servo myservo;

void setup()
{
  myservo.attach(9);  // attaches the servo on pin 9 to the servo object
}

void loop()
{

  // move to 0 degrees
  myservo.write(0);
  delay(2000);

  // move to 180 degrees
  myservo.write(180);
  delay(2000);

}
```

This servo specifically does not move to 0 degrees with a pulse of 1 millisecond nor to 180 degrees with a pulse of 2,000 milliseconds. What the IDE is doing differently when angles are passed to the write() method?

If you run the code in Listing 4-2 you will realize the servo really moves from 0 to 180 degrees without problems.

After you install the IDE, open the file Servo.h in the directory ...\arduino-1.5.3\ hardware\arduino\x86\libraries\Servo. Take a look at the definition of this file:

```
#define MIN_PULSE_WIDTH       544     // the shortest pulse sent to a servo
#define MAX_PULSE_WIDTH      2400     // the longest pulse sent to a servo
```

When 0 degrees is specified in the write() method, the servo library uses 544 microseconds (0.544ms) and when 180 degrees is specified, it uses 2400 microseconds (2.4ms). The servo used in this experiment actually works with these values, not the theoretical values.

This range between 544 and 2400 microseconds is the most common range that attends the servos you can buy online. You can also change the maximum and minimum if you attach the servos specifying the maximum and minimum according to the specification of the servo. For example, suppose you got a servo where 0 degrees requires a pulse of 800 microseconds and 180 degrees requires a pulse of 2200 microseconds. In this case, it is possible to specify boundaries like so:

```
myservo.attach(9, 800, 2200);  // attaches the servo on pin 9 to the servo
object
```

But this method only accepts maximum and minimum pulses according to the range specified by MIN_PULSE_WIDTH and MAX_PULSE_WIDTH (544 and 2400 microseconds, respectively).

One last observation regarding the write() method. If an angle bigger than 180 degrees is passed to this function, it will be considered microseconds and write() will behave the same way as the writeMicroseconds() method. For example, both methods do the same thing:

```
// move to 180 degrees
myservo.writeMicroseconds(2000);

// the value is > 180, so it means microseconds
myservo.write(2000);
```

The Mistake with Intel Galileo and Servos

If you're using the Intel Galileo Gen 2 board, this section is irrelevant because Intel Galileo Gen 2 uses an expander PCA95555 that works perfectly.

The first Intel Galileo version in the market uses a GPIO expander called CY8C9540A and manufactured by Cypress. It communicates with Intel Galileo through the I2C protocol and unfortunately does not offer high enough precision to have a granularity of 1 degree at a frequency of 50Hz. In other words, the PWM generated by this IC can't provide pulses in one-to-one microsecond increments and you can't move the servo in one-to-one degree increments in a frequency close to 50Hz.

This expander does not work at 50Hz but does work at 48Hz, which is acceptable for working with servos because the tolerance of the servos to the frequencies is around 5 to 10 percent (47.5Hz to 55Hz) and that's acceptable for the domain of 50Hz.

The Cypress CY8C9540A datasheet is in the folder code/datasheets of this chapter in the file named CY8C95x0A.pdf or you can access it at http://www.cypress.com/?rID=3354.

However, some servos might work in higher frequencies and CY8C9540A offers a better angular granularity if the frequency is increased. The duty cycle of this expander is programmed using I2C and only accepts eight bits, which is the source of the problem. Table 4-2 provides a small sample that explains the issues.

Table 4-2. *CY8C9540A Angle Granularity Min Pulse 0.544ms and Max 2.4ms*

Angle	Pulse Needed	Duty Cycle Byte @ 188Hz [0-255]	Duty Cycle Byte @ 48Hz [0-255]
1	0.554311111	26	6
2	0.564622222	27	6
3	0.574933333	27	6
4	0.585244444	28	7
5	0.595555556	28	7
6	0.605866667	29	7
7	0.616177778	29	7
8	0.626488889	30	7
9999	0.636800000	30	7
10	0.647111111	31	7
11	0.657422222	31	7
12	0.667733333	32	8

In the first column of Table 4-2 represents the angle to move, the second column is the ideal pulse for the respective angle considering the minimum pulse of 544 microseconds and maximum pulse of 2400 microseconds (the standard used by the Arduino reference implementation). The third and fourth columns represent the byte necessary to send to the controller to achieve the desired pulse.

As you can see, when the CY8C9540A expander is working at 48Hz the same byte 7 appears to the angles 4 to 11 degrees. If you try to move the servo between 4 and 11 degrees the servo will not move because the byte is the same. When the angle becomes 12 degrees, the byte changes to 8. The servo movements will be choppy and will only move from 4 to 8 degrees drastically, with horrible precision.

However, if you work with a frequency of 188Hz and move 4 to 11 degrees, the servo will move a more smoothly because the granularity is better. For example, when the servo moves from 4 to 6 degrees, it will not move at 5 degrees, because 4 and 5 degrees share the same byte (28). At 6 degrees, the byte is 29, so the servo moves.

So, when you're working with servos at 188Hz, it's still not possible to move in one-to-one degree increments, but the granularity is much better compared to working with the expander at 48Hz.

Table 4-2 contains just a small angle set from 1 to 12 degrees. In the folder called code of this chapter, there is a spreadsheet named frequence_versus_resolution.xls that contains all angles from 0 to 180 and the resolution offered by CY8C9540A.

What Is New in Servo API?

This section is applicable to Intel Galileo only.

In order to attenuate the problem of servo granularity introduced by the expander CY8C9540A, the software team added an optional argument to the attach() method and included two new methods in Intel Galileo—set48hz() and set188hz(). Keep in mind that the frequency control is not independent per servo and once it's set for one servo, all the other servos must use the same frequency. Otherwise, the servos will not work properly.

void Servo::set48hz()

Forces CY8C9540A to work at 48Hz. As explained, the resolution is very bad and it is useful only if your application does not require precision.

void Servo::set188hz()

Forces CY8C9540A to work at 188Hz and offers a resolution of 2 to 2 degrees. It is not perfect, but for simple robots and RC controllers it is enough. On Intel Galileo, this is the initial frequency used when a servo is created. Thus, if your servo does not support 188Hz, you can force the attach() method to set 48Hz in the servo initialization to avoid servo burns.

uint8_t Servo::attach(int16_t pin, bool force48hz = false)

The only difference with this method compared to the traditional Arduino reference servo API is the inclusion of the argument force48hz. If this argument is set to true, the initial frequency in the servo will be 48Hz; otherwise the default of 188Hz is assumed.

The other argument, called pin, only specifies the PWM pin to be used to emit the pulse signals to the servo.

uint8_t Servo::attach(int pin, int min, int max, bool force48hz = false)

Again, the only difference with this method compared to the traditional Arduino reference servo API is the inclusion of argument force48hz. If this argument is set to true, the initial frequency in the servo will be 48Hz; otherwise, the default of 188Hz is assumed.

The pin argument specifies the PWM pin to be used to emit the pulse signals to the servo. The and min and max arguments specify the minimum and maximum frequency in microseconds, respectively.

Schematic for Servo: Two Servos

In order to create some practical tests with these new methods, let's assemble a circuit using two servos. Connect both VCC to 5V and both grounds to ground. Connect one of the servos' pulse to pin 9 and the another one to pin 3, as the schematic shown in Figure 4-3 shows.

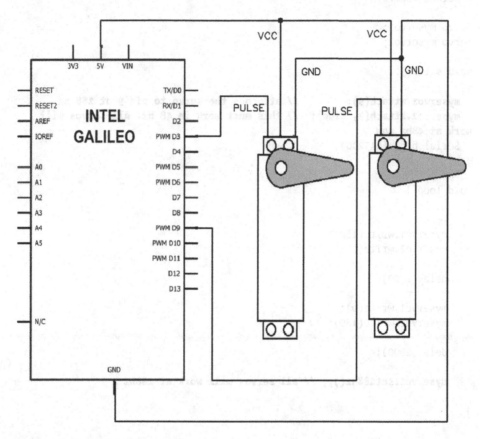

Figure 4-3. *Two servos connected*

Testing the New Servo APIs

Listing 4-3 shows a program to be used with the schematics of Figure 4-3.

Listing 4-3. servo_set_freq.ino

```
#include <Servo.h>

Servo myservo1;
Servo myservo2;

void setup()
{
  myservo1.attach(9);        // attaches the servo to pin 9 at 188 hz
  myservo2.attach(3, true);  // this must work in 48 hz. All servos will
work at 48hz now
  Serial.begin(115200);
}

void loop()
{

    myservo1.write(180);
    myservo2.write(0);

    delay(2000);

    myservo1.write(0);
    myservo2.write(180);

    delay(2000);

    myservo1.set188hz();;; // all servos will work at 188hz

}
```

Reviewing servo_set_freq.ino

In the setup() function, two servos are added to the system, one in pin 9 at 188Hz (the default frequency). The second servo object is created specifying a servo on pin 3 at 48Hz.

However, as soon the myservo2.attach(3, true) method is called, both servos begin operating at 48Hz.

Then in the loop() function, the first servo moves 180 degrees and the second moves to 0 degrees. After two seconds, they invert the order to 0 and 180, respectively.

```
myservo1.write(180);
myservo2.write(0);

delay(2000);

myservo1.write(0);
myservo2.write(180);

delay(2000);
```

Thus, in the first interaction of loop(), both servos are initially working in 48Hz. After two seconds, all the servos will be working at 188Hz because one of the servos selected this frequency with myservo1.set188hz(). The rest of the loop() interactions the servos will remain in 188Hz.

Challenges with Servos

The biggest challenge when working with servos is the lack of standardization and the huge variety of servos available in the market, many with different specifications.

For example, there are servo that reach 0 degrees in 1ms and 180 degrees in 2.2ms. This movement is proportional to the pulse length in one single direction.

However, there are servos limited to 120 degrees, so 1.5ms represents 0 degrees, 1ms represents -60 degrees, and 2ms represents +60 degrees. These are totally different than the example in this chapter and the servo API will not have the expected results. Figure 4-4 represents how these kinds of servos work.

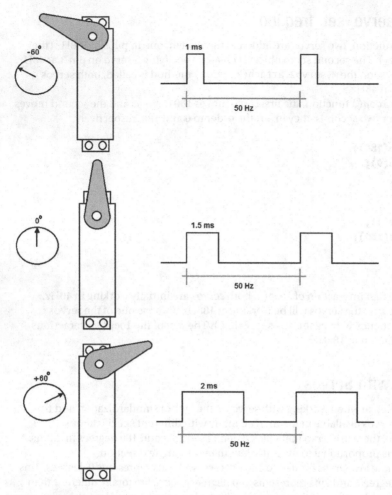

Figure 4-4. *Example of a servo with 0 degrees in 1.5ms*

This does not mean that the servo API is useless in these cases. You simply need to understand your servo specifications and use the API to apply the right pulses at the right time so that the servo moves to the correct angles.

Another common mistake is using servos that do not reach more than 160 degrees. Such servos have an internal mechanical delimiter that prevents them from moving more than 160 degrees.

Some developers remove this mechanical delimiter and make a couple of changes in the servo inputs to make them to have a continuous rotation. In this case, continuous servos do not control the position but the rotation speed.

Another problem is the Arduino reference API. Intel created the servo API according to the reference provided by Arduino, but in practical ways some boards have different behaviors. For example, if you use the Arduino UNO, the initial angle (for most servos) is

90 degrees due to an initial pulse of 1.5ms; however Intel Galileo tries to put your servo initially in 0 degrees. In both implementations, the reference is respected and there is no error in terms of implementation because there is no mandatory requirement that says the initial position must be 0 or 90 degrees.

Serial, Serial1, and Serial2 Objects

This section is applicable to Intel Galileo and Intel Galileo Gen 2.

In Chapter 3, in the section entitled "Debugging with Serial Consoles and Serial Communication," you learned a bit about the usage of Serial to print debug messages from the IDE serial debug console and about the Serial1 object.

In fact Intel Galileo and Intel Galileo Gen 2 count to Serial as any other regular Arduino board, but also include the new Serial1 and Serial2 objects for serial communications.

Serial1 uses pin 0 as its RX port and pin 1 as TX for both Intel Galileo and Intel Galileo Gen 2.

Serial2 uses pin 2 as RX and pin 3 as TX on Intel Galileo Gen 2 and you will use the audio jack on Intel Galileo.

There is a limitation when using Serial2 and a Linux console shell. If Serial2 is used in the sketch, the Linux console is lost because the mux are set to redirect the ports used on Linux console to provide the Serial2 functionality.

The baud rates accepted for such objects are 300, 600, 1200, 2400, 4800, 9600, 14400, 19200, 38400, 57600, 115200, 230400, and 460800.

The usage is very simple and very similar to the regular Serial object used to debug the sketches. So all methods used to communicate with Serial1 and Serial2 are the same ones explained in Chapter 3 with the Serial object. This section's focus is therefore the few and new details related to Serial1 and Serial2. It includes a simple example for how to use all three objects in the same sketch.

Testing the Serial, Serial1, and Serial2 Objects

This example was created to run on Intel Galileo Gen 2 due to the simplicity of dealing with Serial2 in the I/O headers instead of having to prepare a cable exclusively for the audio jack on Intel Galileo. The idea is to create a sketch that makes a loop between Serial1 and Serial2 using only two wires. Serial1 will transmit a message that will be read by Serial2, and then Serial 2 will read the message and send another message to Serial 1. The process is repeated.

Table 4-3 provides a list of the materials necessary to run this example.

Materials List

Table 4-3. *Materials List for the Serial Object Example*

Number	Description
2	Simple wires for hookup

Schematic for the Serial Example

Figure 4-5 shows how the wires must be hooked up to create a serial loopback.

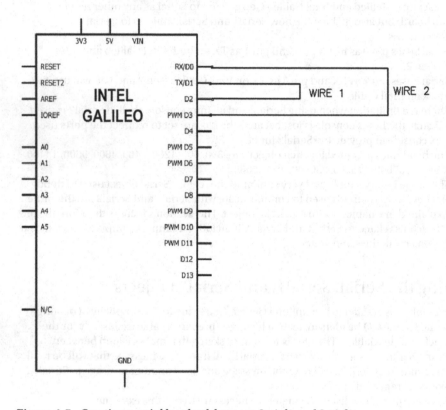

Figure 4-5. *Creating a serial loopback between Serial1 and Serial2*

Serial1 RX (pin 0) is connected to Serial2 TX (pin 3) and Serial1 TX (pin 1) is connected to Serial2 RX (pin 2). This creates a loop between Serial1 and Serial2.

The code for testing is shown in Listing 4-4.

Listing 4-4. all_serials.ino

```
String inputString = "";          // a string to hold incoming data

void setup() {
  // put your setup code here, to run once:
    Serial.begin(115200);     // Serial console debugger
    Serial1.begin(115200);    // PIN 0->RX and 1->TX
    Serial2.begin(115200);    // PIN 2->RX and 3->TX

}

void loop() {

    Serial.println("Transmitting from Serial 1 to Serial 2");
    Serial1.println("Intel"); // this will transmitt using PIN 1
    inputString="";

  // Serial2 will wait for something
  while (Serial2.available()) {
    // get the new byte:
    char inChar = (char)Serial2.read();  // receiving by Serial2 on pin 2

    // add it to the inputString:
    inputString += inChar;

  }

  // Serial 2 receive the word "Intel"
  // let's send the word "Galileo" back to Serial 1

    Serial.print("Message received from Serial 1:");
    Serial.println(inputString);
    inputString = "";

  // transmitting another word to Serial2
    Serial.println("Transmitting from Serial 2 to Serial 1");
    Serial2.println("Galileo");  // transmitting by Serial2 using pin 3

  // Serial1 will wait for something
  while (Serial1.available()) {
    // get the new byte:
    char inChar = (char)Serial1.read();  // receiving by Serial1 using pin 0
```

```
  // add it to the inputString:
  inputString += inChar;

}

Serial.print("Message received from Serial 2:");
Serial.println(inputString);
inputString = "";

delay(2000);
}
```

Reviewing all_serials.ino

In the setup() function, all three objects are initiated with a 115200 baud rate.

```
Serial.begin(115200);    // Serial console debugger
Serial1.begin(115200);   // PIN 0->RX and 1->TX
Serial2.begin(115200);   // PIN 2->RX and 3->TX
```

In the loop() method, the Serial object is used only for debugging purposes. Serial1 object starts transmitting the word "Intel" to Serial2 using the println() method.

```
Serial1.println("Intel"); // this will transmitt using PIN 1
```

Then Serial2 receives the message from Serial1 and reads the whole buffer using the available() method. The available() method will keep returning the number of bytes available in the buffer and the loop will remain until available() returns zero bytes (when there are no more bytes to be read). The read() method reads the byte and casts it to a char byte using the inChar variable. Once the byte is read the number of bytes reported by the available() method is decreased and the byte is accumulated in the string buffer called inputString.

```
// Serial2 will wait for something
  while (Serial2.available()) {
    // get the new byte:
    char inChar = (char)Serial2.read();  // receiving by Serial2 on pin 2

    // add it to the inputString:
    inputString += inChar;

  }
```

Once Serial2 reads the "Intel" message from Serial1, the word "Galileo" is sent back to Serial1. Again, the println() method is used for this purpose.

```
// transmitting another word to Serial 2
...
...
...
Serial2.println("Galileo");  // transmitting by Serial2 using pin 3
```

After Serial2 sends back the word "Galileo", Serial1 must receive it. The code has the same logic as was used for Serial2, using the available() and read() methods.

```
// Serial1 will wait for something
while (Serial1.available()) {
  // get the new byte:
  char inChar = (char)Serial1.read();  // receiving by Serial1 using pin 0

  // add it to the inputString:
  inputString += inChar;

}
```

■ **Note**   To write in the serial port, the println() method is used because it deals with strings more easily. However, if you're transmitting raw bytes or integers, you could use the write() method instead.

As soon as you run the sketch, open the IDE serial console by choosing Tools ➤ Serial Monitor or pressing CTRL+SHIFT+M. You should see something similar to the following messages in the debug serial console:

```
Transmitting from Serial 1 to Serial 2
Message received from Serial 1:Intel

Transmitting from Serial 2 to Serial 1
Message received from Serial 2:Galileo

Transmitting from Serial 1 to Serial 2
Message received from Serial 1:Intel
```

This happens every two seconds due to the delay(2000) command that's used at the end of the loop() function.

Improving the I/O Speed

This section is applicable to Intel Galileo and Intel Galileo Gen 2.

In Chapter 3, you learned how to use basic functions like `digitalWrite()`, `digitalRead()`, and `pinMode()` to manage the I/O header.

If you tried to use the I/O ports when creating a project that requires high-speed performance, you would probably face some problems due to a latency of the ports limited to 230Hz with Intel Galileo and or a maximum of 470KHz with Intel Galileo Gen 2 (except pin 7, which achieved 1.8KHz). This happens when the regular Arduino functions mentioned in the previous paragraph are used.

If you aren't familiar with this limitation, take a look at Listing 4-5.

Listing 4-5. running_at_230hz_or_max_470KHz.ino

```
/*
 * This program tests the digital port speed
 * using regular Arduino functions
 *
 * Intel Galileo: the max speed is 230Hz
 * Intel Galileo Gen 2: the speed is 470KHz to all pins except
 *                      pin 7, which achieves 1.8KHz
 *
 */
int pin = 2;  // this is pin header 2
void setup() {
  // put your setup code here, to run once:

  pinMode(pin, OUTPUT);
}

void loop() {
    // put your main code here, to run repeatedly:
    int state = LOW;
    while(1){
        digitalWrite(pin, state);
        state =!state;   // if as HIGH it will be LOW and vice-versa
    }
}
```

The `setup()` function sets pin 2 as `OUTPUT`. In the `loop()` function, the variable `"state"` is used in an infinite loop. It switches between LOW (0) and HIGH (1) and the pin state changes according to this variable through `digitalWrite()`.

If you probe an oscilloscope on this pin, the oscilloscope will state a frequency around 230Hz. Try to change the variable `pin` to other pins and see if the same frequency is achieved.

The process of inverting the pins' state in an infinite loop to generate a square wave with a certain frequency will be used in the rest of this chapter. Thus, every time the word "frequency" is used, in all situations this simple algorithm must be considered.

The following factors were responsible for this limitation in the first generation of Intel Galileo:

- When the first Intel Galileo was designed with the GPIO expander CY8C9540A, manufactured by Cypress, some limitations were introduced. All header ports with the exception of pins 2 and 3 were connected to the GPIO expander, which made the management of these pins flow only through I2C commands at 100KHz. This limited the port's speed to 230Hz. Also, the resolution of 8 bits to set the PWM duty cycle on this GPIO expander significantly impacted the performance of the servo motors, as explained in the section entitled "What's New in the Servo API" in this chapter.

- As explained in the beginning of this chapter, Intel Galileo runs Linux OS. The Arduino API is present in the userspace context, where the tasks run in a lower priority compared to the kernel. This makes it more difficult to have precision not only in terms of GPIOs, but also in terms of timer and interruptions controls. Also, Intel Galileo does not create bridges between the processor and the microcontroller. It allows you to run more than one application (or sketch) in Arduino API instead of only one instance. Quark can provide an I/O port speed superior to Arduino Uno if the new API that is discussed later is used.

To improve the I/O performance, some macros were created that allow some Intel Galileo pins to achieve 2.94MHz. They are discussed in the next section.

The New APIs for I/O

Before you learn about the new API, you need to consider a simple concept about how the I/O ports are connected. It's important to understand because there are some limitations.

On Intel Galileo, there are paths that connected the pins 2 and 3 directly to Quark SoC, not with the Cypress GPIO expander, and with these connections the pins can get close to 2.94MHz. With the other pins, there is a software optimization that makes them achieve 470KHz. 470KHz is a good improvement compared to the weak 230Hz, but it's still not enough to make some sensors like the temperature sensor DHT11 work, since this sensor requires the pins to work in higher frequencies.

When Intel Galileo Gen 2 was designed, all pins were connected directly to Quark SoC, except for pins 7 and 8, which are shared with a new GPIO expander PCAL9555 that runs around 357KHz (the kernel stated 400KHz but it is not right) and it is used to reset the mini PCIe card.

In other words, while Intel Galileo has all pins set to "slow" with exception of pins 2 and 3, Intel Galileo Gen 2 has all pins set to "fast" with the exception of pins 7 and 8.

The original Arduino functions called `digitalWrite()` and `digitalRead()` offer 230Hz only and they use `sysfs` to manage the pins. They manage the pins through a Linux character driver that accesses the file system and consequently is very slow.

The idea for improving performance is to create an API that allow you to read and write the pins states and directly access Quark's port-mapped and memory-mapped I/O. Accessing these pins directly from these registers significantly reduces latency.

Access to these registers never conflicts with access done by kernel, thus even the I/O ports being accessed directly through Quark is safe, even in a userspace context.

Memory-Mapped and Port-Mapped I/O

As the developer/maker, you do not need to worry about all the details of the Quark processor in order to use the new API created to improve the I/O performance.

However, some basic concepts regarding the I/O interface and how the pin headers are connected to Quark SoC are important to understand in order to make API calls and obtain the best performance when your software requires more than one pin in high frequencies.

For example, when you're using memory-mapped I/O, one single function call can handle more than one pin; otherwise, if you simply try to make two functions calls and declare the pins as isolated, the performance will be divided into two.

Memory-Mapped I/O

When the I/O interface is memory-mapped, the I/O states, configurations, and reading and writing operations are done in the memory context. Thus, the pin headers connected to the memory-mapped I/O offer the best performance because it is simple memory access. In the case of Quark SoC X1000, such pins are part of the south-cluster and the Linux kernel is configured to support UIO (see `http://www.hep.by/gnu/kernel/uio-howto/` for more info).

Port-Mapped I/O

When the I/O interface is port-mapped, the processor needs to execute some instructions to manage the I/O interface instead of a simple memory access. These I/O offer a slower interface compared to memory-mapped I/O. In the case of Quark SoC X1000, such pins are part of the north-cluster.

If you want to understand how Intel Arduino IDE maps the I/O, you must read sections 19.5.2 and 21.6.5 of the Intel Quark SoC X1000 datasheet at `https://communities.intel.com/docs/DOC-21828` or access a copy of this datasheet from the `code/datasheet` folder.

The I/O Distribution

Intel Galileo and Intel Galileo Gen 2 have the I/O distributed according to Table 4-4.

Table 4-4. I/O distrubutions

Pins	Intel Galileo Gen 2	Intel Galileo
0	South-cluster	Expander
1	South-cluster	Expander
2	South-cluster	South-cluster
3	South-cluster	South-cluster
4	North-cluster	Expander
5	North-Cluster	Expander
6	North-Cluster	Expander
7	Expander	Expander
8	Expander	Expander
9	South-cluster	Expander
10	South-cluster	Expander
11	North-cluster	Expander
12	South-cluster	Expander
13	North-cluster	Expander

The rows with "Expander" means that the pin is connected to the GPIO Expander instead. This provide a direct path to Quark SoC; it's not possible to improve the frequency of these pins.

Note that Intel Galileo is the worst case with only pins 2 and 3 available. Intel Galileo Gen 2 uses all pins except 7 and 8, as explained.

At the moment, this table might not seem to be very useful, but it will be later in this chapter.

OUTPUT_FAST and INPUT_FAST

Intel created two modes to be used in conjunction with the pinMode() function as the first attempt to improve the read and writing performance of the pins by abolishing the access using the regular sysfs. The next sections discusses these two modes and some metrics.

OUTPUT_FAST - 470KHz

It is possible to improve the performance of the digitalWrite() and digitalRead() functions with a small trick when the pins are configured with pinMode().

In Chapter 3, you learned that pinMode() is used to configure the pin direction using the OUTPUT and INPUT defines.

However, as you can see in Listing 4-5, the frequency reached was 230KHz, but replacing OUTPUT with OUTPUT_FAST in the pinMode() function changes the frequency achieved to 470KHz.

Make this change in Listing 4-6 or simply load running_at_470hz.ino using the IDE.

Listing 4-6. running_at_470KHz.ino

```
int pin = 2;  // this is pin header 2
void setup() {
  // put your setup code here, to run once:

  pinMode(pin, OUTPUT_FAST);
}

void loop() {
    // put your main code here, to run repeatedly:
    int state = LOW;
    while(1){
        digitalWrite(pin, state);
        state =!state;   // if as HIGH it will be LOW and vice-versa
    }
}
```

Reviewing the Code

OUTPUT_FAST, when used with digitalWrite(), works only with pins 2 and 3 on Intel Galileo and all pins on Intel Galileo Gen 2.Recall that pins 7 and 8 reach a maximum of 1.7KHz instead of 470KHz.

INPUT_FAST

In the same manner that OUTPUT_FAST replaces the OUTPUT when the pin is configured with pinMode(), INPUT_FAST replaces INPUT.

Listing 4-7 compares the performance of digitalRead() using INPUT and INPUT_FAST.

Listing 4-7. INPUT_FAST_example.ino

```
/*
    This program is only a demonstration of INPUT_FAST
*/
#define MAX_COUNTER 200000

void setup() {

  Serial.begin(115200);

  pinMode(2, INPUT_FAST);  // using the pin 2
  pinMode(3, INPUT);       // using the pin 3

  delay(3000); // only to give you time to open the serial debugger terminal

  Serial.print("Number of interactions under test:");
  Serial.println(MAX_COUNTER);

  unsigned long t0,t;
  unsigned int counter = 0;

  t0 = micros(); // number of microseconds since booted
  for (counter = 0; counter < MAX_COUNTER; counter++)
  {
       digitalRead(2);   // this is the fast reading !!!!
  }

  t=micros()-t0; // delta time
  Serial.print("digitalRead() configured with INPUT_FAST took: ");
  Serial.print(t);
  Serial.println(" microseconds");

  t0 = micros(); // resetting to new initial time
  for (counter = 0; counter < MAX_COUNTER; counter++)
  {
     digitalRead(3);   // this is the lazy reading !!!!
  }

  t=micros()-t0; // delta time
  Serial.print("digitalRead() configured with INPUT took:");
  Serial.print(t);
  Serial.println(" microseconds");

}

void loop() {
}
```

167

Reviewing the Code

The sketch globally defines the maximum number of cycles.

#define MAX_COUNTER 200000

In the setup() function, pinMode() sets pin 2 as INPUT_FAST and pin 3 as INPUT. This works for Intel Galileo and Intel Galileo Gen 2. A small delay of three seconds was introduced to give you a chance to open the IDE serial console.

The t0 variable is created and receives the number of microseconds passed since the board was booted.

t0 = micros(); // number of microseconds since booted

Then a for loop calls the digitalRead() macro, which reads the state of pin 2 during MAX_COUNTER for the number of interactions (200000).

```
t0 = micros(); // number microseconds since booted
for (counter = 0; counter < MAX_COUNTER; counter++)
{
    digitalRead(2);   // this is the fast reading !!!!
}
```

When the for loop is finished, the t variable evaluates how many microseconds the digitalRead() took for pin 2:

t=micros()-t0; // delta time

The same procedure is done using digitalRead() for pin 3, which uses INPUT mode.

Along the program the Serial object is only used to print some debug messages with the time performance.

If you run this code and check the IDE serial console using Tools ➤ Serial Monitor or by pressing CTRL+SHIFT+M, you will see output similar to the following.

Using Intel Galileo Gen 2:

```
Number of interactions under test:200000
digitalRead() configured with INPUT_FAST took: 233937 microseconds
digitalRead() configured with INPUT took:233716 microseconds
```

Using Intel Galileo Gen:

```
Number of interactions under test:200000
digitalRead() configured with INPUT_FAST took: 231954 microseconds
digitalRead() configured with INPUT took:437786889 microseconds
```

As you can see, Intel Galileo took 437786889 microseconds (more than seven minutes) using INPUT and only 231954 microseconds (0.23 seconds) to read 200.000 times pin 3 with INPUT_FAST. Thus, INPUT_FAST is 1,888 times faster than INPUT when you are using Intel Galileo.

On other hand, if your board is Intel Galileo Gen 2, INPUT_FAST and INPUT have the same performance because they share the same implementation. Therefore, if digitalRead() is being used to read a port in Intel Galileo Gen 2, it doesn't matter if INPUT or INPUT_FAST are used. They are both equally fast.

The Fast I/O Macros

Chapter 3 explained how to select the Intel Galileo and Intel Galileo Gen 2 boards using the IDE.

When a board is selected in the IDE, a series of files corresponding to the board are exclusively selected to be part of the sketch compilation. These files bring configurations specific to the hardware (board) selected, such as the mux scheme, the I/O mappings, the SPI settings, and how the pins are connected.

Among these files one of most important is variant.h because it determines the I/O mappings and which pins are connected directly to the Quark SoC.

When you select the Intel Galileo Gen 2 board, the IDE loads the hardware/arduino/x86/variants/galileo_fab_g/variant.h file and contains the following macros:

```
#define GPIO_FAST_IO0    GPIO_FAST_ID_QUARK_SC(0x08)
#define GPIO_FAST_IO1    GPIO_FAST_ID_QUARK_SC(0x10)
#define GPIO_FAST_IO2    GPIO_FAST_ID_QUARK_SC(0x20)
#define GPIO_FAST_IO3    GPIO_FAST_ID_QUARK_SC(0x40)
#define GPIO_FAST_IO4    GPIO_FAST_ID_QUARK_NC_RW(0x10)
#define GPIO_FAST_IO5    GPIO_FAST_ID_QUARK_NC_CW(0x01)
#define GPIO_FAST_IO6    GPIO_FAST_ID_QUARK_NC_CW(0x02)
#define GPIO_FAST_IO9    GPIO_FAST_ID_QUARK_NC_RW(0x04)
#define GPIO_FAST_IO10   GPIO_FAST_ID_QUARK_SC(0x04)
#define GPIO_FAST_IO11   GPIO_FAST_ID_QUARK_NC_RW(0x08)
#define GPIO_FAST_IO12   GPIO_FAST_ID_QUARK_SC(0x80)
#define GPIO_FAST_IO13   GPIO_FAST_ID_QUARK_NC_RW(0x20)
```

When you select the Intel Galileo Gen board, the IDE loads the hardware/arduino/x86/variants/galileo_fab_d/variant.h file and contains the following macros:

```
#define GPIO_FAST_IO2    GPIO_FAST_ID_QUARK_SC(0x40)
#define GPIO_FAST_IO3    GPIO_FAST_ID_QUARK_SC(0x80)
```

When Intel Galileo Gen 2 is selected, the "fast IO" macros exist for all pins except for pins 7 and 8 because they are not connected directly to Quark. When Intel Galileo is selected, only pins 2 and 3 use the respective macro because they are the only pins connected directly to Quark.

If you do not use the right macros, you might see compilation errors. For example, if your board is Intel Galileo and you try to create a sketch to make pin 4 faster, the compilation will fail because there is no GPIO_FAST_IO4 available. The same problem will occur with Intel Galileo Gen 2 if you try to use the GPIO_FAST_IO7 or GPIO_FAST_IO8 macros because they are not defined.

Each macro calls other macros that access the I/O memory mapped through GPIO_FAST_ID_QUARK_SC, where _SC means south-cluster or through port-mapped registers with the macro GPGIO_FAST_ID_QUARK_NC_RW macro, where _NC means north-cluster.

These GPIO_FAST_IOx macros (x refers to the pin number) are used to create the I/O descriptors using 32 bits for each pin. A description is a sequence of bits in memory that describes the ports directions, the state bitmask, and the reading and writing offset of each pin. This explains why each pin contains its own descriptor.

The hexadecimal value in the macro is the bitmask in the I/O register that's used to represent which bit in the register contains each individual the pin state, HIGH or LOW (1 and 0) respectively, and this bitmask is called mask in the IDE code.

These descriptions use other information besides the mask, such as if the type of pin is present in the north-cluster or south cluster and whether the offsets for reading and writing operation are in the register.

The composition of 32 bits can be verified in the hardware/arduino/x86/cores/ arduino/fast_gpio_common.h file, as shown the code in bold:

```
// Macros to (de-)construct GPIO_FAST_* register descriptors
#define GPIO_FAST_TYPE_NONE                     0x00
#define GPIO_FAST_TYPE_QUARK_SC                 0x01
#define GPIO_FAST_TYPE_QUARK_NC                 0x02
#define GPIO_FAST_ID(type, rd_reg, wr_reg, mask) \
        (0UL | ((type) << 24) | ((rd_reg) << 16) | ((wr_reg) << 8) | (mask))
#define GPIO_FAST_ID_TYPE(id)    (((id) >> 24) & 0xFF)
#define GPIO_FAST_ID_RD_REG(id)  (((id) >> 16) & 0xFF)
#define GPIO_FAST_ID_WR_REG(id)  (((id) >> 8) & 0xFF)
#define GPIO_FAST_ID_MASK(id)    ((id) & 0xFF)
```

Note the bitmask that defines each pin mask in the descriptor is the last 8 less significant bits (LSB). This is a detail you need to keep in mind because once a pin is configured you usually just want to use the mask to locate the pin state in the register.

fastGpioDigitalWrite(GPIO_FAST_IOx, unsigned int value) - 652KHz to 684KHz

This macro allows you to write to an I/O port and achieve a frequency between 652KHz to 684KHz.

The first parameter, called GPGIO_FAST_IOx, is a fast I/O macro used to identify the pin of interest.

The second parameter, called value, is the value of the pin that might be LOW or HIGH.

If Intel Galileo is used, the pinMode() function must receive the OUTPUT_FAST configuration and only pins 2 and 3 work.

If Intel Galileo Gen 2 is used, the pinMode() function must receive the OUTPUT or OUTPUT_FAST configuration because, unlike Intel Galileo, they provide the same effect. And all pins work except for pins 7 and 8, which achieve 684KHz. Pin 13 reaches 657KHz because it's also connected to a built-in LED and there is a small loss when triggering this LED.

Listing 4-8 shows how to reach 687KHz using pin 2.

Listing 4-8. Running_at_684khz.ino

```
/*
  This program makes the I/O speed to achieve 684KHz.
  If you are using Intel Galileo: Only pins 2 and 3 work
  If you are using Intel Galileo Gen 2: ALL pins work

  Note: if you are using Intel Galileo Gen 2 and change
  this software to support pin 13, the frequency will be
  close to 657KHz and not 687KHz.
*/
void setup() {
  // put your setup code here, to run once:
  unsigned int pin = 2;  // this is pin header 2
  pinMode(pin, OUTPUT_FAST);
}

void loop() {
    // put your main code here, to run repeatedly:
    int state = LOW;
    while(1){
        fastGpioDigitalWrite(GPIO_FAST_IO2, state);
        state =!state;   // if as HIGH it will be LOW and vice versa
    }

}
```

Reviewing 684khz.ino

In the setup() function, the pin variable is created to represent the pin 2 and pinMode() sets this pin to OUTPUT_FAST. This works for Intel Galileo and Intel Galileo Gen 2.

Then in the loop() function, the state variable is initiated with state LOW which creates an infinity loop. In this infinity loop, the fastGpioDigitalWrite() macro identifies the GPGIO_FAST_IO2 macro and the state variable. Finally, the state variable has its stated inverted on each loop interaction, switching between LOW (0) and HIGH (1).

Try to change the variable pin and the corresponding fast I/O macro used in fastGpioDigitalWrite() to explore more other pins.

Frequency Reduction with fastGpioDigitalWrite()

The problem with fastGpioDigitalWrite() is the reduction of performance when fastGpioDigitalWrite() is called multiple times in a single loop cycle.

It does not matter if fastGpioDigitalWrite() is handling different pins; the maximum frequency is divided by the number of fastGpioDigitalWrite() methods in one loop interaction.

The code in Listing 4-9 is one example. Considering that fastGpioDigitalWrite() is called twice, the end frequency will be 340KHz.

Listing 4-9. fastGpioDigitalWrite_340khz_two_pins.ino

```
/*
   This program makes the I/O speed achieve 340KHz.
   If you are using Intel Galileo: Only pins 2 and 3 work
   If you are using Intel Galileo Gen 2: ALL pins work

*/

void setup() {
  // put your setup code here, to run once:

  pinMode(2, OUTPUT_FAST);
  pinMode(3, OUTPUT_FAST);
}

void loop() {
    // put your main code here, to run repeatedly:
    int state = LOW;
    while(1){
        fastGpioDigitalWrite(GPIO_FAST_IO2, state);
        fastGpioDigitalWrite(GPIO_FAST_IO3, state);

        state =!state;   // if as HIGH it will be LOW and vice versa
    }

}
```

To resolve this problem, a new macro was created called fastGpioDigitalRegWriteUnsafe(). It's explained later in this chapter.

int fastGpioDigitalRead(GPIO_FAST_IOx)

This macro allows you to read to an I/O port and achieve much faster performance than the regular digitalRead().

The GPGIO_FAST_IOx parameter is a fast I/O macro used to identify the pin of interest.

As a result, the macro might return 0 for LOW or any other value representing HIGH, because the value returned is the current value in the register mask according to the register offset.

If Intel Galileo is used, the pinMode() function must receive the INPUT_FAST configuration and only pins 2 and 3 work.

If Intel Galileo Gen 2 is used, the pinMode() function must receive the INPUT or INPUT_FAST confuguration because, unlike Intel Galileo, they provide the same effect and all pins work except pins 7 and 8.

Listing 4-10 shows a sketch that compares the performance between digitalRead() and fastGpioDigitalRead() and detects when a state changes in a pin. If you are interested only in checking the performance, it is not necessary to assemble any circuit. In this case, you can just run the sketch. Otherwise, if you want to detect when the pin state is changed, it is necessary to assemble the same circuit and materials mentioned in the section entitled "The Button Example" in Chapter 3.

Listing 4-10. fastGpioDigitalRead_example.ino

```
/*
   This program is only a demonstration of fastGpioDigitalRead()
*/
int pin = 2;

#define MAX_COUNTER 200000

void setup() {

  Serial.begin(115200);

  pinMode(pin, INPUT_FAST);  // using pin 2

  delay(3000); // only to give you time to open the serial debugger terminal

  Serial.print("Number of interactions under test:");
  Serial.println(MAX_COUNTER);

  unsigned long t0,t;
  unsigned int counter = 0;

  t0 = micros(); // number of microseconds since booted
  for (counter = 0; counter < MAX_COUNTER; counter++)
  {
      if (fastGpioDigitalRead(GPIO_FAST_IO2)) // using the fast I/O macro related
                                        // to pin 2
      {
          // the pin is HIGH
          Serial.println("HIGH detected by fastGpioDigitalRead()");
      }

  }
```

```
t=micros()-t0; // delta time
Serial.print("fastGpioDigitalRead() took: ");
Serial.print(t);
Serial.println(" microseconds");

t0 = micros(); // reseting to new initial time
for (counter = 0; counter < MAX_COUNTER; counter++)
{
    if (digitalRead(pin)) // using the fast I/O macro related
                          // to pin 2
    {
        // the pin is HIGH
        Serial.println("HIGH detected by digitalRead()");
    }

}

t=micros()-t0; // delta time
Serial.print("digitalRead() took: ");
Serial.print(t);
Serial.println(" microseconds");

}

void loop() {

}
```

Execute the sketch and open the IDE serial console with Tools ➤ Serial Monitor or by pressing CTRL+SHIFT+M. In the first test, do not press the button even if you assembled the recommended circuit. Simply run it and you will be able to see this output in the serial console:

```
Number of interactions under test:200000
fastGpioDigitalRead() took: 123207 microseconds
digitalRead() took: 239766 microseconds
```

The output indicates that the fastGpioDigitalRead() executed 200000 readings in 123302 microseconds, while digitalRead() took 239766 microseconds for the same amount of cycles. In other words:

239766/123207 = 1.94

The fastGpioDigitalRead() method was almost twice as fast as the regular digitalRead() method using the INPUT_FAST mode.

If you assembled the circuit recommended for this test, run the sketch again and press the button to check in the serial console output. Check if the HIGH state is being detected by fastGpioDigitalRead() and digitalRead() in INPUT_FAST mode.

Reviewing fastGpioDigitalRead_example.ino

The sketch globally defines a variable to specify pin 2 and to define to the maximum number of cycles.

```
int pin = 2;
#define MAX_COUNTER 200000
```

In the setup() function, pinMode() sets pin 2 to INPUT_FAST, which works for Intel Galileo and Intel Galileo Gen 2. A delay of three seconds was introduced only to give you a chance to open the IDE serial console.

The variable t0 is created and receives the number of microseconds passed since the board was booted.

```
t0 = micros(); // number microseconds since booted
```

Then a for loop is created by calling the macro fastGpioDigitalRead(), which reads the state of pin 2 and passes the fast I/O macro GPIO_FAST_IO2 as the parameter during **MAX_COUNTER** number of interactions (200000).

```
t0 = micros(); // number of microseconds since booted
for (counter = 0; counter < MAX_COUNTER; counter++)
{
    if (fastGpioDigitalRead(GPIO_FAST_IO2)) // using the fast I/O macro
related
                                            // to pin 2
    {
        // the pin is HIGH
        Serial.println("HIGH detected by fastGpioDigitalRead()");
    }
}
```

If you assembled the recommended circuit, you still have the option to press the button and check the detection (HIGH state) because the Serial object prints a message reporting the HIGH state.

When the for loop is finished, the t variable evaluates how many microseconds the fastGpioDigitalRead() took and again, using the Serial object, prints the information to the serial console.

```
t=micros()-t0; // delta time
```

The same procedure is done using digitalRead() instead of fastGpioDigitalRead(), allowing you to compare the performance between both functions when INPUT_FAST mode is used.

fastGpioDigitalRegSnapshot(GPIO_FAST_IOx)

This macro latches the current register values specified by the macro in the first parameter, called GPGIO_FAST_IOx. It's a fast I/O macro used to identify the pin of interest.

An example is shown in Listing 4-11.

Listing 4-11. latch_example.ino

```
/*
    This program is only a demonstration of fastGpioDigitalRegSnapshot()
    and the importance of the bitmask fields.
*/

void setup() {

    unsigned int latchValue;

    Serial.begin(115200);

    delay(3000); // only to give you time to open the serial debugger terminal

    // latches the current value
    latchValue = fastGpioDigitalRegSnapshot(GPIO_FAST_IO3);

    // identifies the bit corresponding to pin 3 in the bitmask
    unsigned int mask = 0x000000ff & GPIO_FAST_IO3;

    if (latchValue & mask)
    {
        // the register indicated the pin is HIGH
        Serial.println("HIGH");
    }
    else
    {
        // the register indicated the pin is LOW
        Serial.println("LOW");
    }

}

void loop() {

}
```

Reviewing latch_example.ino

The setup() method starts with a delay of three seconds to give you a chance to open the IDE serial console with Tools ➤ Serial Monitor or with CTRL+SHIFT+M.

Then fastGpioDigitalRegSnapshot() is called to retrieve the I/O latch regarding pin 3, using the descriptor constructed by the macro GPIO_FAST_IO3.

```
latchValue = fastGpioDigitalRegSnapshot(GPIO_FAST_IO3);
```

As explained in the section called "The Fast I/O" in this chapter, a variable called mask is created by retrieving only the bitmask used an AND operation with 8 fewer significant bits than the description created for pin 3.

```
unsigned int mask = 0x000000ff & GPIO_FAST_IO3;
```

Then the value retrieved by the latchValue variable is compared to the mask variable to determine whether pin 3 is doing another simple AND operation.

```
if (latchValue & mask)
```

This program always prints out LOW because it is the initial state of the pins and the logic in this case is merely illustrative. This same logic is used in the next section with the macro fastGpioDigitalRegWriteUnsafe().

The Serial object is only used to debug messages along the code.

fastGpioDigitalRegWriteUnsafe (GPIO_FAST_IOx, unsigned int value) - 2.94MHz

This macro allows you to write to an I/O port and achieving a frequency up to 2.94MHz.

The first parameter, called GPGIO_FAST_IOx, is a fast I/O macro used to identify the pin of interest.

The second parameter, called value, corresponds to the descriptors and all current pin states.

If Intel Galileo is used, the pinMode() function must receive the OUTPUT_FAST configuration and only pins 2 and 3 work.

If Intel Galileo Gen 2 is used, the pinMode() function must receive the OUTPUT or OUTPUT_FAST configurations because, unlike Intel Galileo, they provide the same effect. All the pins work. Pins 7 and 8 can achieve 2.93MHz whereas pin 13 reaches 1.16MHz, because it's also connected to a built-in LED and there is a small loss when triggering this LED.

This function has the word Unsafe on its name because you must preserve the I/O descriptor and not mess with other I/Os masks when a particular I/O is being used. If you mess with the description and pin states' bitmask, unexpected results will be observed in the pin headers.

The code shown in Listing 4-12 shows how to make pin 2 reach 2.93MHz.

Listing 4-12. running_at_2_93Mh.ino

```
/*
    This program makes the I/O speed achieve 2.93MHz.
    If you are using Intel Galileo: Only pins 2 and 3 work
    If you are using Intel Galileo Gen 2: ALL pins work
    except pins 7 and 8

    Note: if you are using Intel Galileo Gen 2 and change
    this software to support pin 13, the frequency will be
    close to 1.16MHz.
*/

unsigned int latchValue;
unsigned int bmask;

void setup() {
  // put your setup code here, to run once:

  pinMode(2, OUTPUT_FAST);

  // latches the current value
  latchValue = fastGpioDigitalRegSnapshot(GPIO_FAST_IO2);

  // extract the mask that identifies pin 2 in the
  // descriptor
  bmask = 0x000000ff & GPIO_FAST_IO2;

}

void loop() {

  while(1)
  {

    if (latchValue & bmask)
    {
      // state is HIGH
      latchValue = GPIO_FAST_IO2 & !bmask;
    }
    else
    {
      // state is LOW
      latchValue = GPIO_FAST_IO2 | bmask;
    }

    fastGpioDigitalRegWriteUnsafe (GPIO_FAST_IO2, latchValue);

  }

}
```

Reviewing running_at_2_93Mh.ino

The setup() function configures pin 2 as OUTPUT_FAST for Intel Galileo and Intel Galileo Gen 2. Then the variable latchValue reads the latest I/O states according to the GPIO_FAST_IO2 descriptor using fastGpioDigitalRegSnapshot().

```
pinMode(2, OUTPUT_FAST);

// latches the current value
latchValue = fastGpioDigitalRegSnapshot(GPIO_FAST_IO2);
```

At the end of setup(), the variable bmask extracts only the I/O bitmask for pin 2, disregarding the rest of I/O descriptor. Remember this mask occupies only the 8 LSB among the total of 32 bits that compose the I/O descriptor, as explained in the section entitled "The Fast I/O Macros" in this chapter.

```
bmask = 0x000000ff & GPIO_FAST_IO2;
```

In the loop() function, an infinity while is introduced and latchValue is tested to check if the state is HIGH.

If the latched value contains the pin bitmask on its 8 LSB, it means the state is HIGH, because the bit mask will have the bit 1 in the respective pin state; otherwise, the latchValue state is LOW. This operation can be checked with a simple AND:

```
if (latchValue & bmask)
```

If the state is HIGH, it is necessary to change it to LOW. For this, you just need to invert the bitmask bits and create an AND operation again:

```
latchValue = GPIO_FAST_IO2 & !bmask;
```

Otherwise, if the state is LOW, it is necessary to change it to **HIGH**. For this, you must add an OR using the bitmask:

```
latchValue = GPIO_FAST_IO2 | bmask;
```

Finally, fastGpioDigitalRegWriteUnsafe() is called, informing the fast I/O descriptor for pin 2 (GPIO_FAST_IO2) and the current value of latchValue to be changed.

An important point—the bitmask bmask" was retrieved and used with the AND and OR operation, which will preserve the other bits in the I/O descriptor. With this type of logic, you can handle more than one bit safely.

North-Cluster (1.12MHz) versus South-Cluster (2.93MHz)

The previous example in Listing 4-12 uses pin 2. If you take a look in Table 4-4, you will realize this pin belongs to the south-cluster.

Based on this table, you can change the code and replace it with a pin that belongs to the north-cluster, such as pin 4.

With this change, pinMode() must be modified and all GPIO_FAST_IO2 calls must be replaced with GPIO_FAST_IO4. You could also just open the code running_at_1_12MHz.ino, which contains these changes.

If you run the sketch again, you will see that pin 4 can achieve only 1.12MHz because it is a port-mapped I/O. That means it's slower than the memory-mapped I/O that pin 2 uses.

Keeping the Same Frequency on All Pins

If you create a sketch that works with pins that belong to the same cluster, it's possible to keep the same frequency on all of them using fastGpioDigitalRegWriteUnsafe(). This provides a good alternative to fastGpioDigitalWrite(), which cannot do this.

Listing 4-13 is an example that runs only on Intel Galileo Gen 2 and shows how to run three pins from the south-cluster, ensuring the speed of 2.93MHz on all of them. You can run this example in the first board Intel Galileo if you remove the code related to pin 12 from this listing.

Listing 4-13. running_at_2_93Mhz_three_pins.ino

```
/*
   This program makes the I/O speed to achieve 2.93MHz.
   If you are using Intel Galileo: Only pins 2 and 3 work
   If you are using Intel Galileo Gen 2: ALL pins work
   except pins 7 and 8

*/

unsigned int latchValue;
unsigned int bmask_pin2;
unsigned int bmask_pin3;
unsigned int bmask_pin12;

void setup() {
  // put your setup code here, to run once:

  pinMode(2, OUTPUT_FAST);
  pinMode(3, OUTPUT_FAST);
  pinMode(12, OUTPUT_FAST);

  // latches the current value
  latchValue = fastGpioDigitalRegSnapshot(GPIO_FAST_IO2);
```

```
  // retrieving bitmasks from descriptors
  bmask_pin2 = 0x000000ff & GPIO_FAST_IO2;        //south-cluster
  bmask_pin3 = 0x000000ff & GPIO_FAST_IO3;        //south-cluster
  bmask_pin12 = 0x000000ff & GPIO_FAST_IO12;      //south-cluster

}

void loop() {

  while(1)
  {
    if (latchValue & bmask_pin12)
    {
      // state is HIGH
      latchValue = GPIO_FAST_IO2 & !bmask_pin2;
      latchValue |= GPIO_FAST_IO3 & !bmask_pin3;
      latchValue |= GPIO_FAST_IO12 & !bmask_pin12;

    }
    else
    {
      // state is LOW
      latchValue = GPIO_FAST_IO2 | bmask_pin2;
      latchValue |= GPIO_FAST_IO3 | bmask_pin3;
      latchValue |= GPIO_FAST_IO12 | bmask_pin12;

    }

    // considering all pins in this example belong to the south-cluster
    // they share the same register in memory-mapped I/O. Only one
    // fastGpioDigitalRegWriteUnsafe() must be called ensuring 2.93MHz
    // to ALL pins
    fastGpioDigitalRegWriteUnsafe (GPIO_FAST_IO2, latchValue);

  }

}
```

Reviewing running_at_2_93Mhz_three_pins.ino

This code has the same logic as Listing 4-12; the difference is that now there are three pins
(2, 3, and 12) that belong to the same cluster.

In the setup() function, all pins are set to OUTPUT_FAST as expected. The bitmask for
each descriptor is captured and the latchValue latches the current GPGIO_FAST_IO2 state.
The latchValue will contain the state of all pins in the south-cluster because all the pins
share the same register in the memory (memory-mapped I/O) and it does not matter if
the fast macro I/O is used.

In the loop() function, the logic is the same. One of the pin states is checked and the latchValue changes the state of each pin, inverting the original state.

But the most important point in this code is the fact that only one fastGpioDigitalRegWriteUnsafe() is called. The explanation is quite simple—all pins belong to the same cluster and share the same memory registers, so only one call ensures 2.93MHz to all the pins used in the code (pins 2, 3, and 12).

If you change to pins that belong to the north-cluster, the effect will be the same as explained in the previous section. In other words, the maximum frequency will be 1.12MHz.

When Pins from North-Cluster and South-Cluster Are Used in Same Sketch

To achieve best performance, it is recommended that you keep using the pins of same cluster, but in practice this is not always possible. When pins from the north-cluster and south-cluster must be used in a same sketch, you must call fastGpioDigitalRegWriteUnsafe() twice in order to configure the I/O pins for both clusters.

When this situation occurs, the maximum frequency for each pin is not respected and you'll get a maximum of 980KHz in this case.

Listing 4-14 shows an example that runs using Intel Galileo Gen 2. It uses two pins from the south-cluster (pins 2 and 3) and one from the north-cluster (pin 4).

Listing 4-14. mixing_north_and_south_clusters.ino

```
/*
    This program is an example of how to mix pins from the
    north-cluster and south-cluster
    If you are using Intel Galileo: Only pins 2 and 3 work
    If you are using Intel Galileo Gen 2: ALL pins work
    except pins 7 and 8

*/

unsigned int latchValue;
unsigned int bmask_pin2;
unsigned int bmask_pin3;
unsigned int bmask_pin4;

void setup() {
  // put your setup code here, to run once:

  pinMode(2, OUTPUT_FAST);
  pinMode(3, OUTPUT_FAST);
  pinMode(4, OUTPUT_FAST);

  // latches the current value
  latchValue = fastGpioDigitalRegSnapshot(GPIO_FAST_IO2);
```

```
    // retrieving bitmasks from descriptors
    bmask_pin2 = 0x000000ff & GPIO_FAST_IO2;    //south-cluster
    bmask_pin3 = 0x000000ff & GPIO_FAST_IO3;    //south-cluster
    bmask_pin4 = 0x000000ff & GPIO_FAST_IO4;    //north-cluster !!!!

}

void loop() {

    while(1)
    {

        if (latchValue & bmask_pin4)
        {
            // state is HIGH
            latchValue = GPIO_FAST_IO2 & !bmask_pin2;
            latchValue |= GPIO_FAST_IO3 & !bmask_pin3;
            latchValue |= GPIO_FAST_IO4 & !bmask_pin4;

        }
        else
        {
            // state is LOW
            latchValue = GPIO_FAST_IO2 | bmask_pin2;
            latchValue |= GPIO_FAST_IO3 | bmask_pin3;
            latchValue |= GPIO_FAST_IO4 | bmask_pin4;

        }

        // pins from cluster different used, so it is necessary
        // to make a couple call using pins from south-cluster and north-cluster
        fastGpioDigitalRegWriteUnsafe (GPIO_FAST_IO2, latchValue);
        fastGpioDigitalRegWriteUnsafe (GPIO_FAST_IO4, latchValue);

    }

}
```

Reviewing mixing_north_and_south_clusters.ino

The code has the same logic as commented in the Listing 4-12 except that there are two pins from the south-cluster (pins 2 and 3) and one from the north-cluster.

As explained, this scenario requires two fastGpioDigitalRegWriteUnsafe() calls, one for each cluster.

If you probe each pin, you can verify that the maximum frequency reached is 980KHz.

When Port Speed Is Not Enough - pinMode() Limitations

Until now, you could read methods that help to improve the speed in the digital I/O headers. Sometimes speed is not enough. There is a limitation when pinMode() is used to change the pin direction that introduces a three-millisecond delay due to the need to send the I2C command to set the mux in the boards.

Thus, if you are working with devices that require communication in one single pin (when a single pin is used to send commands), you need to consider this delay every time the pin direction is changed.

There are methods for working around this problem, as explained in the section entitled "Practical Project - DHT Sensor Library with Fast I/O APIs" in this chapter.

The Tone API

This section is applicable to Intel Galileo Gen2 only.

The Tone API is part of the Arduino reference and it was created to generate square waves in specific frequencies (tones) with a duty cycle close to 50 percent. The original Arduino reference for the Tone API is discussed at http://arduino.cc/en/reference/tone.

Due to the latencies in the I/O ports on Intel Galileo, the Tone API cannot work with pins 2 and 3 when using OUTPUT_FAST and INPUT_FAST because the frequencies required are not achieved with such modes in other pins. There is no PWM involved.

With Intel Galileo Gen 2, you cannot provide direct connection between Quark SoC I/O with I/O headers.

So, if you are connecting a speaker or a buzzer and want to use this API, make sure that pins 7 and 8 are not being used for this purpose.

What's New in the Tone API?

In the regular Arduino implementation, the Tone API is a blocking call that prevents the use of more than one tone at the same time. In the implementation created for Intel Galileo Gen 2, there are blocking and non-blocking calls, which provides more flexibility to the effect desired when a sketch is created. The next pages discuss these new features.

void tone(unsigned int pin, unsigned int frequency, unsigned long duration = 0)

The first parameter, called pin, specifies the pin to be used. Note that if you are using this pin as PWM, the PWM will be disabled automatically.

The second parameter is the frequency in hertz desired.

The third parameter is the duration of the tone in milliseconds to be generated and it is optional. If it's not specified in the function call, the default value is 0. In this case, the tone will be generated continuously until the noTone() function is called. Note when a duration is not specified, the continuous generation of this tone makes the tone() function call non-blocking.

With tone() called as a non-blocking call, multiple tones can be generated in multiples pins. However, the accuracy goes down as the number of tones increases because each tone called as non-blocking is implemented with POSIX threads called mutually exclusively.

If the duration parameter is specified, the function will generate the tone until the duration is attended; the function call in this case is blocking. In these cases, multiples tones cannot be generated; the accuracy is better when compared to non-blocking calls.

void noTone(uint8_t pin)

This function will stop the generation of the tone in the pin that's specified as the function parameter.

A Sample Running Non-Blocking Tone Calls

To run this example, the components listed in Table 4-5 are necessary.

Table 4-5. *Materials List for the Non-Blocking Tone Example*

Number	Description
2	Resistor 100 Ohms
2	Speaker 8 Ohms

The schematics are represented in Figure 4-6.

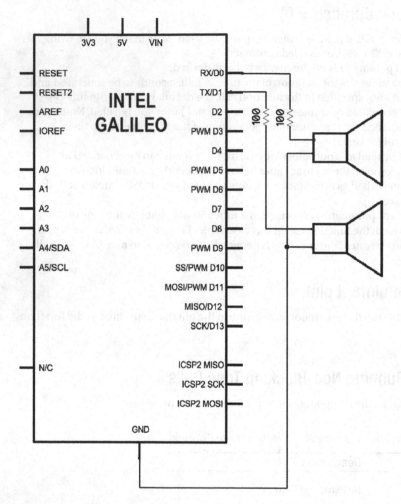

Figure 4-6. *Two speakers connected to Intel Galileo*

Listing 4-15 shows a sketch to be tested.

Listing 4-15. Tone.ino

```
// some tones in hertz
#define NOTE_C4  262
#define NOTE_G3  196
#define NOTE_A3  220
#define NOTE_B3  247

// melody on pin 0:
int melody_pin0[] = {
   NOTE_C4, NOTE_G3,NOTE_G3, NOTE_A3, NOTE_G3,0, NOTE_B3, NOTE_C4};

// melody on pin 1:
int melody_pin1[] = {
   NOTE_G3, NOTE_C4,NOTE_G3, NOTE_G3, NOTE_A3,0, NOTE_C4, NOTE_B3};

void setup() {
  // iterate over the notes of the melody:
  for (int thisNote = 0; thisNote < sizeof(melody_pin0)/sizeof(int);
thisNote++) {

    //the duration is not specified to make a non-blocking call.
    tone(0, melody_pin0[thisNote]);
    tone(1, melody_pin1[thisNote]);

    // small delay
    delay(500);

    // stop the tone playing:
    noTone(0);
    noTone(1);
  }
}

void loop() {
  // no need to repeat the melody.
}
```

When you run the code, you will hear some tones coming out from the speakers connected to pins 0 and 1 in intervals of 500 milliseconds.

Reviewing Tone.ino

The code starts globally defining the tones C4, G3, A3, and B3 in hertz. The melody_pin0 and melody_pin1 arrays, which contain the sequence of tones to be played, are created for pins 0 and 1, respectively.

Then in the setup() function, a for loop scans the tone arrays and plays the arrays on pin 0 and 1 using the tone() function. This is done without defining a duration, which means the call is non-blocking.

```
tone(0, melody_pin0[thisNote]);
tone(1, melody_pin1[thisNote]);
```

A small delay of 500ms is added with the delay() function. It's used only to allow the perception of tones in the speakers. Finally the tones are stopped by the noTone() function call.

```
// stop the tone playing:
noTone(0);
noTone(1);
```

If you are interested in testing the tone() function in a blocking scenario, check out http://arduino.cc/en/Tutorial/tone and run the simple sketch.

The pulseIn API

This section is applicable to Intel Galileo and Intel Galileo Gen2.

The pulseIn() API is used to measure a pulse length in some specified pin.

unsigned long pulseIn(uint8_t pin, uint8_t state, unsigned long timeout = 1000000)

The first parameter called pin specifies the pin to be used. Note if you are using this pin as PWM, the PWM will be disabled automatically.

The second parameter is the state. If HIGH is specified, pulseIn() will start timing when the pin changes from LOW to HIGH, and stop timing when it moves to the LOW state again. If the state parameter is LOW, the inverse order will be used to measure the pulse from HIGH to LOW, and LOW to HIGH again.

The third parameter called timeout is in microseconds and is optional. It imposes the maximum timeout that pulseIn() needs to wait for the pin state transition. If it is not specified, the default value is 1.000.000 microseconds (1 second).

If pulseIn() measures the pulse length, the length in microseconds is returned. Otherwise, if some timeout occurred, the value returned is 0.

For example, if you use the following code in your sketch:

```
duration = pulseIn(3, HIGH);
```

The pulseIn() method will wait for pin 3 to reach the HIGH state and then start timing until the state becomes LOW. The pulseIn() function returns the pulse length in microseconds (duration).

The pulseIn API created for Intel Galileo boards follows the same proposal as the Arduino reference; see http://arduino.cc/en/Reference/pulseIn. However, it is crucial to understand its limitations if your sketch intends to use this API.

There is a limitation of the Tone API related to pins that work on Intel Galileo. This API works only if pins 2 and 3 are used; Intel Galileo Gen 2 works in all pins except 7 and 8.

What's New with pulseIn()

The implementation created for Intel Galileo boards has as timeout parameter that's an unsigned long that occupies 32 bits. It has certain advantages compared to a board with 16 bits because the timeout can be set to measure pulses from 3 microseconds to 2^{32} microseconds (71.58 minutes).

The accuracy is around 2 microseconds.

A Sample Running pulseIn()

The idea of this sample is to have a button connection to one of the digital I/O headers and, using this button, you can generate a pulse. The pulseIn() function will then read how long the pulse was present.

The pin chosen is pin 2 because it works with Intel Galileo and Intel Galileo Gen 2.

The material and schematics used in this example are the same as explained in the section entitled "The Button Example" in Chapter 3. This circuit allows you to inject 5V into pin 2 when the button is pressed; pulseIn() will measure how long the pulse is generated by the button and will remain in the HIGH state during this time.

Listing 4-16 shows an example of how to use the pulseIn API.

Listing 4-16. pulseIn.ino

```
int pin = 2;
unsigned long duration;

void setup()
{
  Serial.begin(115200);
  pinMode(pin, INPUT);
}

void loop()
{
  // measuring the pulse lengh during 20 seconds
  duration = pulseIn(pin, HIGH,20000000);
  Serial.println(duration);
}
```

189

Run the sketch and open the IDE serial console by choosing Tools ➤ Serial Monitor or pressing CTRL+SHIFT+M. Then, try to press the button during intervals of 20 seconds. The IDE serial console will display 0 if the pulse could not be read; otherwise, the reading is displayed in microseconds.

Reviewing pulseIn.ino

The code starts globally defining the variable pin, which is used to indicate that pin 2 is used to receive the pulse event. Another variable duration is used to receive the metric returned by the pulseIn() function.

In the setup() function, pinMode() is used only to set the pin to the INPUT mode. The Serial object is initiated for debugging purposes.

In the loop() function, pulseIn() is set to read pin 2 and measure the transition from LOW to HIGH using 20 seconds as the timeout.

When read with success, the duration variable receives the measurement during a HIGH state; otherwise, it receives 0. The Serial object prints the results in microseconds.

Hacks

Sometimes there are requirements that the regular Arduino reference API cannot address. For example, when you need a different PWM frequency and duty cycle than provided by the regular analogWrite(), or need a servo motor that works with pules out of regular Arduino reference range, or want to create a single sketch that works in both Intel Galileo and Intel Galileo Gen 2.

The next sections provide a few hacks that you might find useful.

Hacking the Servo Library

This hack is applicable to Intel Galileo and Intel Galileo Gen 2.

Suppose you acquired a new servo motor and the specification of this servo is a pulse of 500ms to 0 degrees and 2600ms to 180 degrees. This servo will not work correctly if you use the Arduino IDE with any changes in the library. This is not specific to Intel Galileo; the reference implementation of Arduino IDE really uses 544 (MIN_PULSE_WIDTH) and 2400 (MAX_PULSE_WIDTH) microseconds.

To resolve such a problem, you must change these defines. In the case of the servo mentioned, the hack would be to change the ...\arduino-1.5.3\hardware\arduino\ x86\libraries\Servo.h file:

```
#define MIN_PULSE_WIDTH       500    // the shortest pulse sent to a servo
#define MAX_PULSE_WIDTH       2600   // the longest pulse sent to a servo
```

Then the servo can receive the pulses that attend its specification.

Hacking the GPIO Expander for New PWM Frequencies

This hack is applicable to Intel Galileo only.

The first generation of Intel Galileo uses the expander CY8C9540A from Cypress. It is a PWM generator that can be commanded using I2C commands and the base PWM frequency can be changed by changing the clock sources and the divider in the IC.

Before reading this section, it's best to have the datasheet on hand. The Cypress CY8C9540A datasheet is in the code/datasheets folder of this chapter in the file named CY8C95x0A.pdf. You can also access it at http://www.cypress.com/?rID=3354.

In case of Intel Galileo, the CY8C9540A can be reached by I2C commands through the address 0x20.

Four simple I2C commands must be sent to generate your custom PWM, discussed in the following sections.

Changing the Frequency

It is necessary to use the divider register 0x2C.

The formula to specify the frequency is:

Freq = Clock Source/Divider

The divider is 8 bits—something from 1 to 255 (0 is not a valid divider).

Selecting the Clock Source

The clock source must be selected using the register 0x29. Check Table 11 in the datasheet, named "PWM Clock Sources," for all the available PWM clock sources.

Selecting the Duty Cycle

The duty cycle is set using the command 0x2B and must be represented for 8 bits. It follows the regular theory, in other words:

Duty cyle = Pulse Width/Period

Setting the Period Register

Sets the period of thePWM counter; only two values are accepted—0 for falling pulse edge and 255 (0xff) for rising pulse edge.

Changing the PWM

Suppose you want to generate a PWM with 123Hz, with a minimum duty cycle possible with a rising edge period.

Looking at the datasheet, the clock source closest to this frequency is 367.6Hz (see Table 11 of the datasheet). So the divisor that must be used to get close to 123Hz is 3 because 367.6/3 = 122.533Hz.

Thus the clock source register 0x29 is 4 and the divisor 0x2C is 3.

The duty cycle register 0x2b can be set 1 to 255. Dividing the maximum period of 122.533Hz by 255 gives you the minimum granularity of a duty cycle. In this case you have:

```
122.533 hz = 8.16ms
Minimum granularity is: 8.16 / 255 = 32 microseconds
```

So the minimum duty cycle is 32 microseconds and must be represented by 1 in the 0x2b register. Figure 4-7 shows this logic graphically.

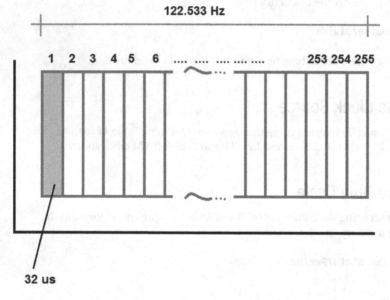

Figure 4-7. Minimum granularity for duty cycle in 255 possibilites

Thus, if a duty cycle of 64 microseconds is desired, the 0x2b register will receive the value of 2; if the duty cycle desired is 94 microseconds, the value received is 3, and so on.

Knowing all registers that must be used and the respective values that each one must receive, it is time to create the sketch. The Arduino reference has a library called Wire API that is created to send I2C commands.

Basically to send an I2C command using Wire API, you use three methods— beginTransmission(), write(), and endTransmisstion().

The basic sequence to use these commands is as follows:

```
Wire.beginTransmission(DEVICE_ADRESS_HERE);
Wire.write(BYTE1);
Wire.write(BYTE2);
Wire.write(BYTE3);
...
...

Wire.endTransmission();
```

It's simple to create the sketch in order to send such commands using I2C and pin 9. This process is demonstrated in Listing 4-17.

Listing 4-17. custom_pwm.ino

```
#include "Wire.h"

int PIN = 9;

void setup()
{

    // Set divider to get 122.533Hz freq.
    Wire.beginTransmission(0x20);
    Wire.write(0x2C);
    Wire.write(0x03);
    Wire.endTransmission();

    // Select PWM source clock
    Wire.beginTransmission(0x20);
    Wire.write(0x29);
    Wire.write(0x04);
    Wire.endTransmission();

    // Set period register
    Wire.beginTransmission(0x20);
    Wire.write(0x2a);
    Wire.write(0xff);
    Wire.endTransmission();

    // Duty cycle of 32us @ 122.533hz
    Wire.beginTransmission(0x20);
    Wire.write(0x2b);
    Wire.write(0x01);  // 1 is the minimum granularity
    Wire.endTransmission();

}

void loop()
{
}
```

Run the code using the IDE. If you have an oscilloscope, you will be able to see the PWM on pin 9.

Single Code for Intel Galileo and Intel Galileo Gen 2

This chapter covers some particularities that are supported by Intel Galileo Gen 2 but are not supported or only partially supported by Intel Galileo.

How do you guarantee compatibility when it is necessary to create a sketch that must run in these different boards? Or how do you port libraries and ensure they have code that deals with these particularities?

One way is to use preprocessing by adding a directive that differentiates one board from other. This directive is present only in Intel Galileo core libraries and is defined as PLATFORM_ID representing the value 0x06.

Thus, during compilation time it is possible to implement the following checking logic:

```
#if PLATFORM_ID == 0x06
// this is Intel Galileo
#else
// this is Intel Galileo Gen 2
#endif
```

It is also possible to check the board used during run-time using the PLATFORM_NAME directive, which is represented by the string "GalileoGen2" for Intel Galileo Gen 2 and "Galileo" for Intel Galileo. For example, the following code snippet shows how to check the board during run-time:

```
if(PLATFORM_NAME == "GalileoGen2")
{
    // this is Intel Galileo Gen 2
...
...
...

} else if (PLATFORM_NAME == "Galileo")
{
    // this is Intel Galileo
...
...
...
}
```

Project: DHT Sensor Library with Fast I/O APIs

The idea is to create a project that provides environmental temperature and humidity control using sensors called DHT. This project runs on Intel Galileo and Intel Galileo Gen 2. You'll do the following with this project:

1. Introduce a simple project that explores fast I/O APIs.

2. Provide a workaround to solve the impact caused by pinMode() when the pin direction changes.

3. Create a library especially for Intel Galileo to communicate with DHT sensors.

Materials List

This project requires the materials listed in Table 4-6.

Table 4-6. Materials List for the DHT Sensor Library Project

Number	Description
1	DHT11 sensor
1	1/4W 5K Ohm resistor
1	Low enable tri-state buffer NTE74HC125 or equivalent

The cost of this project is estimated at about $6.00 US, not including the Intel Galileo board.

The DHT Sensor

The DHT sensor is a humidity and temperature sensor that communicates using one single wire connected to one of the digital ports on the microcontrollers. This connection is called a single-wire two-way.

The basic connection of the DHT is shown in Figure 4-8.

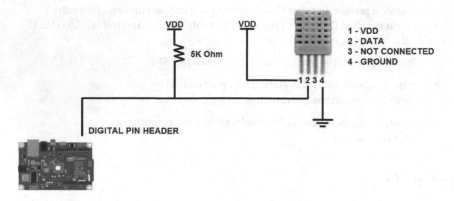

Figure 4-8. *Connecting DHT11 to Intel Galileo*

To communicate with this sensor, you need a simple yet fast protocol, so the fast I/O API discussed in this chapter will be used. Basically, the protocol sends a command to the sensor and waits for a response that contains the local temperature and humidity.

Figure 4-9 shows how the protocol works when a command is sent and data is received.

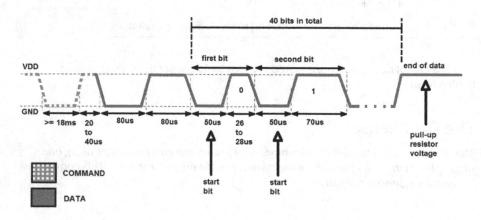

Figure 4-9. *DHT11 protocol*

Initially Intel Galileo must pull down the digital port at at least 18ms. The sensor's interpreter will intepret that as a command and start to transmit the data response after 20 to 40 microseconds.

The sensor pulls down and pulls up the voltage level during 80 microseconds on each state.

Then the transmission of bits that will report the temperature and humidity starts. Each bit is composed of a start bit and the bit value in general; in other words, a signal will tell if the bit value is 0 or 1. The start bit is always identified by a pull down voltage of 50 microseconds. When the bit is a pull up voltage that remains between 26 to 28 microseconds, the bit value is 0. If the voltage remains at 70 microseconds, the bit value is 1. It is expected to receive 40 bits that will be used to fill five bytes (5 bytes = 8 bits * 5 = 40 bits).

These five bits will be parsed as follows:

- **Byte 0** -> Contains the humidity

- **Byte 1** -> Always 0

- **Byte 2** -> Contains the temperature

- **Byte 3** -> Always 0

- **Byte 4** -> The checksum that must match the sum of other four bytes

If you understand how the protocol works, it is time to learn what must be done that make it work using Intel Galileo's digital I/O headers.

In a single wire, commands and responses move between the sensor and the Intel Galileo based on the transition of pin states (high and low) during a specific short period of time. This protocol is based on the voltage transition in a short period of time. This is possible because Intel Galileo is supposed to change the port direction all the time. In other words, when a command must be sent to the sensor, the port I/O is configured as OUTPUT. The pin state changes during short periods and the sensor detects it, interpreting as a command.

The next step is to be ready to receive the response. For this, Intel Galileo must configure to port direction to INPUT. With the command received by the sensor, a response is sent back to Intel Galileo. It reads the state transition during a short period of time, thereby converting it to a sequence of bits that will be used to "read" the sensor's values.

In case of the DHT sensor, this transition between OUTPUT and INPUT that sends the commands and receives the responses is done in the order of microseconds (20 to 40 microseconds). This is impossible to do using pinMode() with Intel Galileo because it takes around 3 milliseconds (see the section entitled "When Port Speed Is Not Enough - pinMode() Limitations" in this chapter).

Figure 4-10 shows the catastrophic result with the addition of the DC level while the pinMode() is still processing the change of pin direction. Pay attention to the numbered arrows. The number 1 arrow points to the oscilloscope channel that's set to 5ms per time division. The number 2 arrow shows how pinMode() takes almost 3ms (less than one division of 5ms) and applies a DC level in the port.

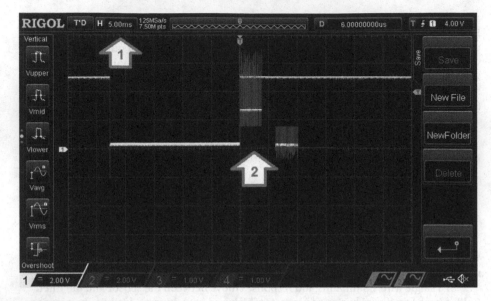

Figure 4-10. When pinMode() *takes 3ms to change the port direction*

A Workaround Using Tri-State Buffers

If pinMode() does not have enough performance for this sensor; however, it is possible to create a workaround and separate commands from responses using two different pins even if the sensor uses a single wire to communicate.

One of the techniques used to make such an isolation is to use a low-enabled tri-state buffer, as shown in Figure 4-11.

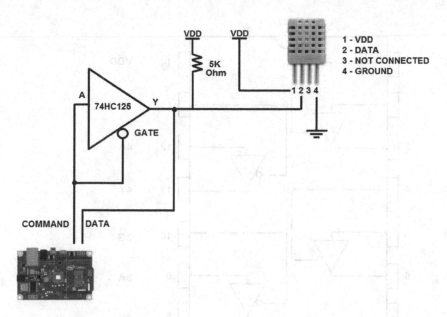

Figure 4-11. *Transforming a one-wire to a two-wires connection*

The NTE74HC125 is a low-enabled tri-state buffer that internally contains four gates. Figure 4-12 shows the gates disposition internally in the NTE74HC125. The letter G is used to represent the gate, Y is the output, and A is the input. The numbers in front of each letter represent the gate number. You need only one gate for this project.

74HC125

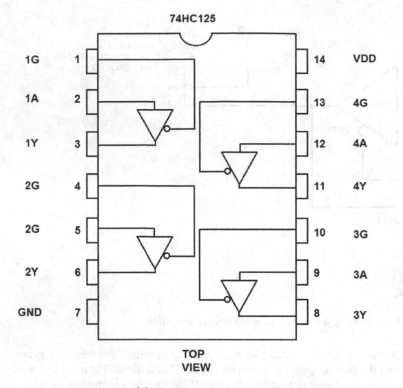

1G	1		14	VDD	
1A	2		13	4G	
1Y	3		12	4A	
2G	4		11	4Y	
2G	5		10	3G	
2Y	6		9	3A	
GND	7		8	3Y	

**TOP
VIEW**

Figure 4-12. Top view of the 74HC125 and pin-out disposition

To understand how this is possible, it is necessary to understand some basic concepts related to tri-state buffers.

The tri-state provides three logic states: LOW (0), HIGH (1), and Z (high impedance), as shown in Table 4-7.

Table 4-7. Logic Table of a Low-Enabled Tri-State Buffer

INPUT	GATE	OUTPUT
0	0	0
1	0	1
0	1	Z (High impedance)
1	1	Z (High impedance)

In a low-enabled tri-state buffer, the gate enables the input to the output only when the gate has a low state (0). When the gate is high (1), the output is high impedance, in other words, it's floating.

Floating means that the current never will pass over there due to the high impedance, so the circuit is totally isolated. Figure 4-13 shows a representation of the low-enabled gate operation in a tri-state buffer.

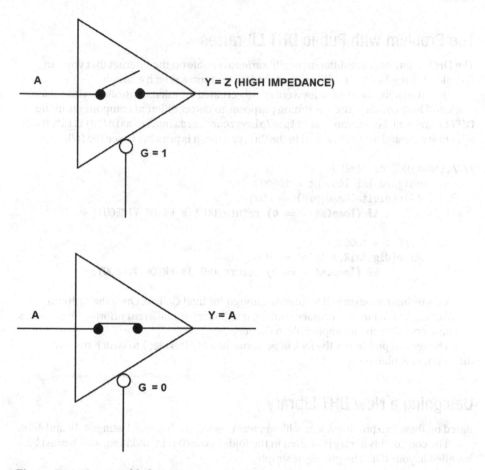

Figure 4-13. *Low-enabled tri-state gate operation*

The idea for resolving the pinMode() issue is very simple. As soon as the command is sent, the gate will be opened, which will isolate the input pin. The current will flow exclusively to the output pin, which will receives the response.

In that way, it is possible to isolate commands from responses even when the sensor uses a single wire to communicate and there are not concerns regarding voltage level.

Creating a New Library for DHT11 Sensor

This section explains how to create a functional DHT sensor library for Intel Galileo boards.

The Problem with Public DHT Libraries

The DHT11 sensors have different free libraries available on the Internet that you can download to the libraries directory of the IDE and run a sketch example.

Unfortunately, these libraries were mostly created for microcontrollers with a fixed clock and loop counters used as timing purposes to detect different components in the DHT11 protocol. For example, at http://playground.arduino.cc/main/DHT11Lib, there is a library created for DHT11, and in the DHT.cpp file, it is possible to see the following:

```
// ACKNOWLEDGE or TIMEOUT
        unsigned int loopCnt = 10000;
        while(digitalRead(pin) == LOW)
                if (loopCnt-- == 0) return DHTLIB_ERROR_TIMEOUT;

        loopCnt = 10000;
        while(digitalRead(pin) == HIGH)
                if (loopCnt-- == 0) return DHTLIB_ERROR_TIMEOUT;
```

This technique never will be precise enough for Intel Galileo. Once the Arduino libraries run in the Linux userspace context, it will receive a different priority. Fixed clocks and loop counting are not applicable to Galileo.

The second problem is the lack of performance of pinMode() to switch the pin direction, as explained.

Designing a New DHT Library

Based on these two problems, a new library was created, as shown in Listings 4-18 and 4-19.

The code of this library is located in the folder code/DHT11_Galileo, which must be installed in your IDE. The process is simple:

1. Close all IDEs running.

2. Move the folder called DHT11_Galileo within the directory called arduino-1.5.3/libraries of your IDE installation.

3. Open the IDE again and select Sketch➤Import Library from the menu. Check if DHT11_Galileo is listed. If it is, open the sketch called DHT_4_Galileo.ino in the examples folder of the library. You can also select Files➤Examples➤ DHT11_Galileo➤ DHT11_4_Galileo using the menu. If the library is not present, check if the library is properly installed as recommended. You can also learn more about the libraries installed at http://arduino.cc/en/Guide/Libraries.

Listing 4-18. DHT_4_Galileo.h

```
#ifndef DHT_4_GALILEO
#define DHT_4_GALILEO
#include <Arduino.h>
#include <stdint.h>

class DHT_4_Galileo
{

public:

    // to report ACK status
    static const int DHT_ACK_OK = 0;
    static const int DHT_ACK_ERROR = -1;

    // to report reading status
    static const int DHT_READ_SUCCESS = 0;
    static const int DHT_READ_TIMEOUT_ERROR = -1;
    static const int DHT_READ_CHECKSUM_ERROR = -2;

    int humidity;
    int temperature;

    /*
     * The class constructor must receive the pins
     * used as gate/command and the pin to read
     * the data from the sensor
     */
    DHT_4_Galileo(uint8_t p_gate, uint8_t p_read);

    /*
     *  sendCommand():
     *  sends the commands and wait for the acknowledgement from the sensor
     *
     */
    int sendCommand();  // end of send_command()

    /*
     *  read():
     *  Reads the 40 bits of data, parse the data in
     *  temperature and humidity
     */
    int read ();
```

```
private:
   int pin_gate;
   int pin_read;

   /*
    * getFastIOMacro(int pin)
    * only an utility function to return
    * the right macro according to the pin
    */
   static int getFastIOMacro(int pin);

}; // end of class
#endif
```

The idea is to create a very simple class thay sends a command to the sensor and read its response. That's exactly what the class DHT_4_Galileo does with the sendCommand() and read() methods.

Note that the class constructor asks for two pins—p_gate is the pin that is connected to the gate of one of the tri-state gates (G) of 74HC125 and p_read is for the pin that will receive the data (Y).

Some constants were created to check if acknowledgement signals were received or if an error happened during the data readings:

```
// to report ACK status
static const int DHT_ACK_OK = 0;
static const int DHT_ACK_ERROR = -1;

// to report reading status
static const int DHT_READ_SUCCESS = 0;
static const int DHT_READ_TIMEOUT_ERROR = -1;
static const int DHT_READ_CHECKSUM_ERROR = -2;
```

Listing 4-19 shows the DHT_4_Galileo implementation.

Listing 4-19. DHT_4_Galileo.cpp

```
#include "DHT_4_Galileo.h"

#define DEBUG 1  // change to 0 if you do not want debug messages

   /*
    * The class constructor must receive the pins
    * used as gate/command and the pin to read
    * the data from the sensor
    */
```

```
DHT_4_Galileo::DHT_4_Galileo(uint8_t p_gate, uint8_t p_read)
{
    pin_gate = p_gate;
    pin_read = p_read;

    pinMode(pin_gate, OUTPUT_FAST);
    pinMode(pin_read, INPUT_FAST);
};

/*
 * sendCommand():
 * sends the commands and wait for the acknowledgement from the sensor
 *
 */
int DHT_4_Galileo::sendCommand()
{

    // pull down during 18 microseconds.. this is our command!
    fastGpioDigitalWrite(getFastIOMacro(pin_gate), LOW);
    delay(18);
    fastGpioDigitalWrite(getFastIOMacro(pin_gate), HIGH);  // High
impedance
    delayMicroseconds(40);

    // now let's check if some ACK was received
    unsigned long t0,ti;

    int state = fastGpioDigitalRead(getFastIOMacro(pin_read));
    int new_state = state;

    boolean ack = false;
    t0 = micros(); // number microseconds since booted
    while (micros()-t0<80)
    {
        new_state = fastGpioDigitalRead(getFastIOMacro(pin_read));
        if (new_state==0)
        {
            // cool!!! first ACK received during 80 microseconds
            ack = true;
            break;
        }
    }
```

```
        if (!ack)
        {
#if (DEBUG)
        Serial.println("problem in FIRST PART OF ACK");
#endif
        return DHT_ACK_ERROR;
        }

        ack=false;
        t0 = micros(); // number microseconds since booted
        while (micros()-t0 < 80)
        {
            // waiting for HIGH
            new_state = fastGpioDigitalRead(getFastIOMacro(pin_read));
            if (new_state!=0)
            {
                // the second ACK received!!! let's wait for the data!!!
                ack = true;
                break;
            }
        }

        if (!ack)
        {
#if (DEBUG)
        Serial.println("problem in SECOND PART ACK");
#endif
        return DHT_ACK_ERROR;
        }

        return DHT_ACK_OK;
    } // end of send_command()

    /*
     * read():
     * Reads the 40 bits of data, parse the data in
     * temperature and humidity
     */
    int DHT_4_Galileo::read () {

        unsigned long t0;

            // BUFFER TO RECEIVE
        uint8_t bits[5];
        uint8_t cnt = 7;
        uint8_t idx = 0;
```

```
int start_bit[40];
int reading_bit[40];

// cleaning arrays
for (int i=0; i<40; i++)
{
  start_bit[i] = 0;
  reading_bit[i] = 0;
}

for (int i=0; i<5; i++)
{
  bits[i] = 0;
}

 // READ OUTPUT - 40 BITS => 5 BYTES or TIMEOUT
for (int i=0; i<40; i++)
{

        //start bit
        // will stay low for 50us

        t0 = micros(); // number microseconds since booted
        while(fastGpioDigitalRead(getFastIOMacro(pin_read)) == 0)
        {
            // using 70 instead 50 us due to the remaining
            // state of last ack
            if ((micros() - t0) > 70) {
                return DHT_READ_TIMEOUT_ERROR;
            }
        }

        start_bit[i] = micros() -t0;

        t0 = micros(); // number microseconds since booted

        //reading bit
        // 26 to 28us  -> 0
        // up tp 70 us -> 1
        //int c = 0;
        while( fastGpioDigitalRead(getFastIOMacro(pin_read)) != 0) {
                if ((micros() - t0) > 77) {
                        return DHT_READ_TIMEOUT_ERROR;
                }
        };
```

```
                    unsigned long delta_time =  micros() - t0;
                    reading_bit[i] = delta_time;

                    if (delta_time > 50) bits[idx] |= (1 << cnt);
                    if (cnt == 0)        // next byte?
                    {
                            cnt = 7;     // restart at MSB
                            idx++;       // next byte!
                    }
                    else cnt--;
        }

        // dump
#if (DEBUG)
        Serial.println();
        for (int i=0; i<40; i++)
        {
          Serial.print(i);
          Serial.print("   ");
          Serial.print(start_bit[i]);
          Serial.print("   ");
          Serial.print(reading_bit[i]);
          Serial.print("   ");
          if (reading_bit[i] > 40)
             Serial.println("1");
          else
             Serial.println("0");
        }

        Serial.println();
        Serial.println("BYTES PARSED:");
        Serial.println("------------");

        for (int i=0; i<5; i++)
        {
          Serial.print(i);
          Serial.print(": ");
          Serial.println(bits[i]);
        }
                Serial.println();
#endif
        // parsing the bits
        humidity    = bits[0];
        temperature = bits[2];
        uint8_t sum = (bits[0] +  bits[1] + bits[2] +  bits[3]) & 0xff;
```

```
        if (bits[4] != sum)
        {
          return DHT_READ_CHECKSUM_ERROR;
        } else {
                   return DHT_READ_SUCCESS;
        }

}


    /*
     * getFastIOMacro(int pin)
     * only an utility function to return
     * the right macro according to the pin
     */
    int DHT_4_Galileo::getFastIOMacro(int pin)
    {
        int macro;
        switch (pin)
        {
#if PLATFORM_ID != 0x06
            // this is Galileo Gen 2
            case 0: macro = GPIO_FAST_IO0;
                break;
            case 1: macro = GPIO_FAST_IO1;
                break;
#endif
            case 2: macro = GPIO_FAST_IO2;
                break;
            case 3: macro = GPIO_FAST_IO3;
                break;
#if PLATFORM_ID != 0x06
            // this is Galileo Gen 2 - no fast I/O for pins 7 and 8
            case 4: macro = GPIO_FAST_IO4;
                break;
            case 5: macro = GPIO_FAST_IO5;
                break;
            case 6: macro = GPIO_FAST_IO6;
                break;
            case 9: macro = GPIO_FAST_IO9;
                break;
            case 10: macro = GPIO_FAST_IO10;
                break;
            case 11: macro = GPIO_FAST_IO11;
                break;
```

```
            case 12: macro = GPIO_FAST_IO12;
                break;
            case 13: macro = GPIO_FAST_IO13;
                break;
#endif
            default:
                    macro = 0;
                break;

        }

    return macro;
} // end of getFastIOMacro()
```

Reviewing the DHT_4_Galileo.cpp Library

The constructor of this class receives the pin connected to the gate and the pin connected to the data, as explained. In the constructor, the pins are set as INPUT_FAST and OUTPUT_FAST through the pinMode() function. It defines the possibility for using the new fast I/O functions.

The second method implemented is sendCommand(). It pulls the pin connected to the tri-state gate up and down during the 18 milliseconds, which immediately keeps the acknowledgement waiting. The sensors pull the voltage levels down and up during the 80 microseconds on each state. If the acknowledgement is not received, sendCommand() reports this by returning DHT_ACK_ERROR; otherwise, DHT_ACK_OK is returned. Note that this method uses fastGpioDigitalWrite() and fastGpioDigitalRead() fast I/Os. The static function getFastIOMacro() is used only to convert the regular pin to the specific fast I/O macros.

Finally, the read() method tries to read the 40 bits transmitted by the sensors containing the data to be parsed. The fast I/O fastGpioDigitalRead() function reads the start and data bits. In the first code sequence, the code waits for the start bit:

```
t0 = micros(); // number microseconds since booted
while(fastGpioDigitalRead(getFastIOMacro(pin_read)) == 0)
 {
            // using 70 instead 50 us due to the remaining
            // state of last ack
            if ((micros() - t0) > 70) {
                return DHT_READ_TIMEOUT_ERROR;
            }
 }

start_bit[i] = micros() -t0;

t0 = micros(); // number microseconds since booted
```

```
//reading bit
// 26 to 28us  -> 0
// up tp 70 us -> 1
 while( fastGpioDigitalRead(getFastIOMacro(pin_read)) != 0) {
         if ((micros() - t0) > 77) {
             return DHT_READ_TIMEOUT_ERROR;
      }
 };
unsigned long delta_time =  micros() - t0;
reading_bit[i] = delta_time;
```

Note that the reading_bit[] array saves how long each data bit took in microseconds. Thus to decide if the bit received was a 0 or a 1, you use this simple code:

```
if (delta_time > 50) bits[idx] |= (1 << cnt);
   if (cnt == 0)    // next byte?
   {
           cnt = 7; // restart at MSB
           idx++;   // next byte!
   }
else cnt--;
```

The bits[] array is responsible for saving the five bytes expected from the sensor after parsing the 40 bits received. The code checks if the time that the bit was received is bigger than 50us. If it is, it's considered bit 1; otherwise, it is 0 and each bit is shifted properly until eight bits are received. When the total of eight bits are received, the index in the array is incremented and the logic continues by saving the next eight bits in the next element of bits[] array.

With the bits[] array properly filled, the humidity and temperature classes members are loaded and the checksum is checked to make sure the data received is correct:

```
// parsing the bits
humidity    = bits[0];
temperature = bits[2];
uint8_t sum = (bits[0] +  bits[1] + bits[2] +  bits[3]) & 0xff;

if (bits[4] != sum)
{
    return DHT_READ_CHECKSUM_ERROR;
} else {
    return DHT_READ_SUCCESS;
}
```

Creating the Sketch for DHT Sensor

Listing 4-20 shows the sketch itself. Note that the sketch is still simple but now two pins are defined in the contructor of the DHT_4_Galileo class.

Listing 4-20. DHT11_4_Galileo.ino

```
#include <DHT_4_Galileo.h>

void setup() {
  // put your setup code here, to run once:
  Serial.begin(115200);
  Serial.println("start......");
  delay(3000);
}

void loop() {
  // put your main code here, to run repeatedly:

  Serial.println("send command..");
  Serial.println();

  DHT_4_Galileo dht(3, 2);

  dht.sendCommand();

  int response = dht.read();
  if (response == DHT_4_Galileo::DHT_READ_SUCCESS)
  {
      Serial.println("RESULTS:");
      Serial.println("----------------");
      Serial.print("Humidity:");
      Serial.print(dht.humidity,1);
      Serial.print(",\t");
      Serial.print("Temperature (C):");
      Serial.println(dht.temperature,1);
  }
  else
  {
      Serial.print("there is an error:");
      Serial.println(response);
  }
  delay(5000);

}
```

With the class, the sketch is very simple. In loop(), a dht object is created using pin 3 as the gate and pin 2 as the data. The methods sendCommand() and read() are used.

Running the Code

As soon you run the sketch, open the IDE serial console by chooseing Tools ➤ Serial Monitor or pressing the keys CTRL+SHIFT+M.

With the debug enabled, you will be able to see the index of the bit received, the respective start time, the bit time duration, and whether the bit is considered a 0 or a 1 in the last column for all 40 bits. You will also see these 40 bits parsed in five bytes and, if the checksum matches, the humidity and temperature.

0	2	19	0
1	53	23	0
2	54	70	1
3	53	25	0
4	53	22	0
5	54	69	1
6	54	23	0
7	53	69	1
8	54	22	0
9	54	23	0
10	53	24	0
11	53	23	0
12	54	23	0
13	54	23	0
14	53	24	0
15	53	25	0
16	53	23	0
17	54	23	0
18	54	23	0
19	53	71	1
20	53	70	1
21	54	23	0
22	54	23	0
23	53	24	0
24	53	23	0
25	54	23	0
26	54	23	0
27	53	24	0
28	53	23	0
29	54	22	0
30	54	22	0
31	53	26	0
32	53	24	0
33	53	23	0
34	54	70	1
35	53	71	1
36	53	70	1
37	54	70	1
38	54	23	0
39	53	67	1

```
BYTES PARSED:
------------
0: 37
1: 0
2: 24
3: 0
4: 61
```

```
RESULTS:
-----------------
Humidity:37,    Temperature (C):24
```

If you probe pins 2 and 3 in the oscilloscope, you will see signals similar to the ones in Figure 4-14.

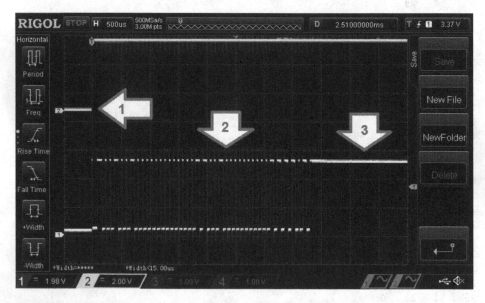

Figure 4-14. *The correct signals when operating a DHT11 sensor*

As you can see in Figure 4-14, the arrow 1 pointing to the signal is the command, the arrow 2 is pointing to the acknowledgements and the sequence of 40 bits received from the sensor, and the arrow 3 is the end of transmission with the tension in the pull-up 5K Ohms resistor.

Replacing the Tri-State Buffer with a Diode

Suppose you are very excited to have your DHT sensor working with Intel Galileo but you don't have a tri-state buffer. You can't wait for the electronic store near you to open and did not yet order a buffer online.

A simple, but not perfect, solution is to replace the tri-state buffer with a diode, as shown in Figure 4-15.

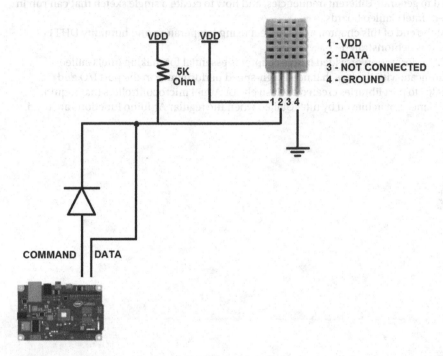

Figure 4-15. *Replacing the tri-state buffer with a diode*

It's best to use a 1N4148, 1N4448, 1N916A, or 1N916B diode, as they are the fastest.

The diode offers a voltage level reduction in the digital port input on Galileo but does not compromise the detection of the level state (HIGH or LOW).

This is not a perfect solution, but if you have a diode in hand, you can make the test.

Summary

This chapter discussed the new APIs created specially for Intel Galileo boards, including the differences when the APIs are used on Intel Galileo and Intel Galileo Gen 2, the best way to optimize the pins' performance, choosing the right clusters, and what's new with tone and pulsein APIs.

You also learned about techniques for hacking the servo API, the GPIO expander needed to generate different frequencies, and how to create a single sketch that can run in different Intel Galileo boards.

At the end of this chapter, a real project using temperature and humidity DHT11 sensor was demonstrated.

The information provided in this chapter is essential for making Intel Galileo communicate with devices that need high-speed performance in the port I/O and also helps to port libraries created exclusively for Atmel microcontrollers that require performance not achieved by Intel Galileo when the regular Arduino functions are used.

CHAPTER 5

■ ■ ■

Networking and Hacks

Computers, mobile devices, surveillance systems, robots, cameras, smart TVs, thermostats, and many other devices can communicate each other using wired or wireless interfaces.

The scope of such communication can be a simple intranet or external access using the Internet, making these devices accessible in any part of the world.

Intel Galileo boards are not only an Arduino board micro-controlled but are real microcomputers operated by Linux OS whose boards contain an Ethernet interface and a mini-PCIe slot that can receive mini-PCIe cards, including WiFi cards. This combination of software and hardware enables Intel Galileo to communicate with other devices in an intranet network or through the Internet using wired or wireless adapters, just like a regular computer.

This chapter provides information about how to:

- Install WiFi cards and antennas

- Add firmware for new WiFi mini-PCIe cards

- Use the Arduino WiFi API

- Hack the WiFi API and simplify the sketches

- Create dynamic and static IPs via an Ethernet adapter

- Use Internet access shared by your computer via Ethernet

- Run samples of the Arduino Ethernet API

- Simplify Ethernet sketches

- Transfer files between Intel Galileo and other computers

- Hack the IDE to transfer sketches via TCP/IP

Throughout the chapter, you'll see several commands using the Linux terminal shell of Intel Galileo, so keep your serial cables in hand, as described in Chapter 1.

WiFi Cards

Intel Galileo and Intel Galileo Gen 2 contain a mini-PCIe slot at the bottom of the board that allows you to connect WiFi, Bluetooth, video cards, and other modules using the mini-PCIe form factor.

With the availability of this resource, the cost of integrating a WiFi card to the board is reduced because the WiFi mini-PCIe cards are usually cheaper than the regular WiFi shields design for Arduino. However, using a mini-PCIe card does not prevent you from using a regular Arduino API created specifically for WiFi shields. For example, if you are using the mini-PCIe slot for a video card but you need a WiFi, you need a WiFi shield.

The only requirement for using WiFi cards in terms of software is the SD image releases. This is because the SPI releases do not have enough space to hold the Linux WiFi drivers and the cards' firmware.

With the Intel Galileo SD releases provided by Intel, the Intel N135 Centrino is supported by default, but in this chapter you learn how to add other cards using Intel 6236A.

■ **Note**   If your WiFi card is not manufactured by Intel and is not supported by an `iwlwifi` driver, this procedure will not work. In this case, it is necessary to search for your driver and integrate it into the Yocto builds, as explained in Chapter 2.

Setting Up the WiFi Mini-PCIe Card

In addition to the mini-PCIe card, you need the items listed in Table 5-1.

Table 5-1. *Materials List for WiFi Exercises*

Number	Description
1	Intel WiFi mini-PCIe Intel Centrino model N135 or 6235A
2	Dual-band antennas 350mm cable 2118060-1 TE connectivity
1	Half to full height mini-PCIe card bracket
1	Micro SD card (minimum of 4GB)

The procedure for installing these cards on Galileo is quite simple, as explained in the following steps:

1. Power off Intel Galileo. Remove the USB and power supply before starting.

2. Install the half to full height bracket. Connect the brackets using the little screws, as shown in Figure 5-1.

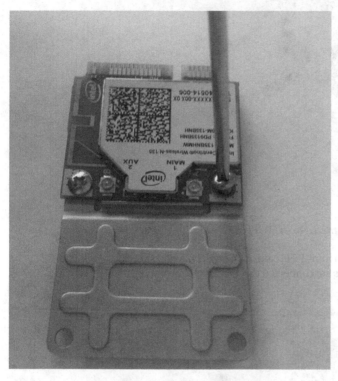

Figure 5-1. *Connecting the bracket to the WiFi card*

3. Connect the dual-band antennas in the card connector by pressing them down until you feel a small "click" in the connector. Check Figure 5-2 for reference.

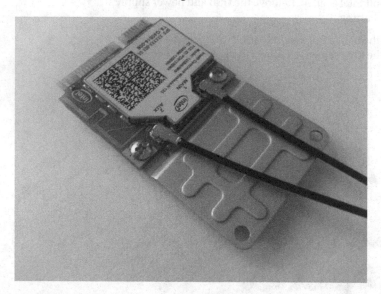

Figure 5-2. *Antennas connected to the WiFi card*

4. Insert the WiFi mini-PCIe card at an angle, making sure the card's contacts are connected to the slot, as shown in Figure 5-3.

Figure 5-3. *Connecting the WiFi card and bracket at an angle*

5. Press the bracket down and connect the bracket's holes to the slot's plastic clips until you feel a click. Figure 5-4 shows the WiFi card properly connected.

Figure 5-4. WiFi card properly installed

6. Download the BSP SD card image from the Intel Galileo web site at https://communities.intel.com/docs/DOC-22226.

7. Transfer the downloaded images to a micro SD card formatted as FAT32 or FAT and insert the SD card into Intel's Galileo SD card slot.

8. Connect the power supply and then the USB cable (exactly in this order, as explained in the section entitled "Connecting Intel Galileo" in Chapter 3.

Checking if the WiFi Card Was Recognized

If the card was inserted as expected using a Linux terminal shell, you can type ifconfig
-a or ifconfig wlan0. You'll see the following output:

```
root@clanton:~# ifconfig -a
eth0      Link encap:Ethernet HWaddr 98:4F:EE:01:4C:71
          UP BROADCAST MULTICAST MTU:1500 Metric:1
          RX packets:0 errors:0 dropped:0 overruns:0 frame:0
          TX packets:1 errors:0 dropped:0 overruns:0 carrier:0
          collisions:0 txqueuelen:1000
          RX bytes:0 (0.0 B) TX bytes:322 (322.0 B)
          Interrupt:40 Base address:0x8000

lo        Link encap:Local Loopback
          inet addr:127.0.0.1 Mask:255.0.0.0
          inet6 addr: ::1/128 Scope:Host
          UP LOOPBACK RUNNING MTU:65536 Metric:1
          RX packets:0 errors:0 dropped:0 overruns:0 frame:0
          TX packets:0 errors:0 dropped:0 overruns:0 carrier:0
          collisions:0 txqueuelen:0
          RX bytes:0 (0.0 B) TX bytes:0 (0.0 B)

wlan0     Link encap:Ethernet HWaddr 0C:D2:92:58:F8:27
          BROADCAST MULTICAST MTU:1500 Metric:1
          RX packets:0 errors:0 dropped:0 overruns:0 frame:0
          TX packets:0 errors:0 dropped:0 overruns:0 carrier:0
          collisions:0 txqueuelen:1000
          RX bytes:0 (0.0 B) TX bytes:0 (0.0 B)
```

You should be able to see the wlan0 interface. If this interface is not shown it means
the SD image was not recognized by your card due to missing firmware or improper card
installation. To resolve this problem, read the section entitled "Adding a New WiFi Card"
in this chapter.

If the wlan0 interface is shown, at this point there is no IP associated with
the interface. You need to scan the WiFi routers and use the right credentials and
authentication methods to connect Intel Galileo.

Adding Support to a New WiFi Card

This section is useful only if you have a mini-PCIe WiFi card that hasn't been recognized.
Otherwise, you can move on to the next section.

If you have a mini-PCIe WiFi card that's not recognized and you are sure you
connected the card to the mini-PCIe slot correctly, it's likely that the SD card image
does not contain the firmware required for your card and you need to add it. The other
possibility is that your card is damaged.

If your card is fine, you simply need to transfer the WiFi card's firmware to the /lib/firmware folder and reboot the system.

For example, if your mini-PCIe WiFi card is Intel, use the following steps to upgrade your SD image to support the new card:

1. Access the site http://wireless.kernel.org/en/users/Drivers/iwlwifi.

2. On this web site, search for the Firmware section and download the firmware corresponding to your card. Figure 5-5 shows a list of the newest cards available from the web site.

Device	Kernels	Firmware
Intel® Wireless WiFi 5150AGN	2.6.29+	iwlwifi-5150-ucode-8.24.2.2.tgz
Intel® Wireless WiFi 5100AGN,	2.6.27+	iwlwifi-5000-ucode-5.4.A.11.tar.gz
Intel® Wireless WiFi 5300AGN,	2.6.30+	iwlwifi-5000-ucode-8.24.2.12.tgz
Intel® Wireless WiFi 5350AGN	2.6.38+	iwlwifi-5000-ucode-8.83.5.1-1.tgz
Intel® Centrino® Advanced-N 6230,	2.6.36+	iwlwifi-6000g2b-ucode-17.168.5.1.tgz
Intel® Centrino® Wireless-N 1030,	2.6.36+	iwlwifi-6000g2b-ucode-17.168.5.2.tgz
Intel® Centrino® Wireless-N 130,		
Intel® Centrino® Advanced-N 6235	3.2+	iwlwifi-6000g2b-ucode-18.168.6.1.tgz
Intel® Centrino® Advanced-N 6205	2.6.35+	iwlwifi-6000g2a-ucode-17.168.5.1.tgz
	2.6.35+	iwlwifi-6000g2a-ucode-17.168.5.2.tgz
	2.6.35+	iwlwifi-6000g2a-ucode-17.168.5.3.tgz
	3.2+	iwlwifi-6000g2a-ucode-18.168.6.1.tgz
Intel® Centrino® Wireless-N + WiMAX 6150,	2.6.30+	iwlwifi-6050-ucode-9.201.4.1.tgz
Intel® Centrino® Advanced-N + WiMAX 6250	2.6.37+	iwlwifi-6050-ucode-41.28.5.1.tgz
Intel® Centrino® Ultimate-N 6300,	2.6.30+	iwlwifi-6000-ucode-9.176.4.1.tgz
Intel® Centrino® Advanced-N 6200	2.6.30+	iwlwifi-6000-ucode-9.193.4.1.tgz
	2.6.30+	iwlwifi-6000-ucode-9.221.4.1.tgz
Intel® Centrino® Wireless-N 1000	2.6.30+	iwlwifi-1000-ucode-128.50.3.1.tgz
	3.2+	iwlwifi-1000-ucode-39.31.5.1.tgz
Intel® Centrino® Wireless-N 100	2.6.37+	iwlwifi-100-ucode-39.31.5.1.tgz
Intel® Centrino® Wireless-N 135	3.2+	iwlwifi-135-ucode-18.168.6.1.tgz
Intel® Centrino® Wireless-N 105	3.2+	iwlwifi-105-ucode-18.168.6.1.tgz
Intel® Centrino® Wireless-N 2200	3.2+	iwlwifi-2000-ucode-18.168.6.1.tgz
Intel® Centrino® Wireless-N 2230	3.2+	iwlwifi-2030-ucode-18.168.6.1.tgz
Intel® Wireless 7260	3.10+	iwlwifi-7260-ucode-22.1.7.0.tgz
	3.13+	iwlwifi-7260-ucode-22.24.8.0.tgz
	3.14+	iwlwifi-7260-ucode-23.214.9.0.tgz
Intel® Wireless 3160	3.10+	iwlwifi-3160-ucode-22.1.7.0.tgz
	3.13+	iwlwifi-3160-ucode-22.24.8.0.tgz
	3.14+	iwlwifi-3160-ucode-23.214.9.0.tgz
Intel® Wireless 7265	3.13+	iwlwifi-7265-ucode-22.24.8.0.tgz
	3.14+	iwlwifi-7265-ucode-23.214.9.0.tgz

Figure 5-5. Intel WiFi cards

3. Transfer the file to Intel Galileo. You can transfer using scp or ftp, or simply copy the file to your SD card or connect a USB drive to Intel Galileo. Read the section entitled "Transferring Files Between Intel Galileo and Computers" in this chapter for the details. You can copy the downloaded file to a temporary file in your /root/home directory, for example.

4. Extract the zipped tar file. For example:

```
root@clanton:~/tmp# tar -zxvf iwlwifi-6000g2b-ucode-18.168.6.1.tgz
iwlwifi-6000g2b-ucode-18.168.6.1/
iwlwifi-6000g2b-ucode-18.168.6.1/iwlwifi-6000g2b-6.ucode
iwlwifi-6000g2b-ucode-18.168.6.1/README.iwlwifi-6000g2b-ucode
iwlwifi-6000g2b-ucode-18.168.6.1/LICENSE.iwlwifi-6000g2b-ucode
```

5. The file that you really need has a .ucode extension. Move this file to the /lib/firmware folder.

```
mv iwlwifi-6000g2b-6.ucode /lib/firmware/.
```

6. Reboot the system using the reboot command.

7. After the reboot, log in again and check if the wlan0 interface is available using the ifconfig wlan0 command.

```
root@clanton:~# ifconfig wlan0
wlan0     Link encap:Ethernet HWaddr C8:F7:33:A4:56:1E
          BROADCAST MULTICAST MTU:1500 Metric:1
          RX packets:0 errors:0 dropped:0 overruns:0 frame:0
          TX packets:0 errors:0 dropped:0 overruns:0 carrier:0
          collisions:0 txqueuelen:1000
          RX bytes:0 (0.0 B) TX bytes:0 (0.0 B)
```

Your SD image should now support the new WiFi card without problems.

The WiFi API

If the card and the firmware were properly installed and recognized, it is possible to create some sketches using the WiFi adapter.

This section provides an introduction to this API by showing a couple of sketches in several examples present in the IDE. These examples also explain how these sketches can be optimized to run on Intel Galileo.

There are several examples related to the WiFi API in File ➤ Examples ➤ WiFi in the IDE. As an introduction, two sketches specifically are discussed—one that scans the wireless networks and the other that connects to one of the networks using WPA or WEP.

The full reference with details of the WiFi API for Arduino can be found at http://arduino.cc/en/Reference/WiFi.

Scanning the Wireless Networks

The first example scans the wireless networks and checks if your WiFi card is working.

Using the Intel Galileo IDE, open the example by choosing File ➤ Examples ➤ WiFi ➤ ScanNetworks.

Note that this code is not in the code folder of this chapter because this example is part of your IDE.

Listing 5-1 shows the code related to this scanning example.

Listing 5-1. ScanNetworks.ino

```
/*

This example prints the WiFi shield's MAC address and
scans for available WiFi networks using the WiFi shield.
Every ten seconds, it scans again. It doesn't actually
connect to any network, so no encryption scheme is specified.

Circuit:
* WiFi shield attached

created 13 July 2010
by dlf (Metodo2 srl)
modified 21 Junn 2012
by Tom Igoe and Jaymes Dec
*/

#include <SPI.h>
#include <WiFi.h>

void setup() {
  //Initialize serial and wait for port to open:
  Serial.begin(9600);
  while (!Serial) {
    ; // wait for serial port to connect. Needed for Leonardo only
  }

  // check for the presence of the shield:
  if (WiFi.status() == WL_NO_SHIELD) {
    Serial.println("WiFi shield not present");
    // don't continue:
    while(true);
  }

  String fv = WiFi.firmwareVersion();
  if( fv != "1.1.0" )
    Serial.println("Please upgrade the firmware");
```

```
  // Print WiFi MAC address:
  printMacAddress();

  // scan for existing networks:
  Serial.println("Scanning available networks...");
  listNetworks();
}

void loop() {
  delay(10000);
  // scan for existing networks:
  Serial.println("Scanning available networks...");
  listNetworks();
}

void printMacAddress() {
  // the MAC address of your WiFi shield
  byte mac[6];

  // print your MAC address:
  WiFi.macAddress(mac);
  Serial.print("MAC: ");
  Serial.print(mac[5],HEX);
  Serial.print(":");
  Serial.print(mac[4],HEX);
  Serial.print(":");
  Serial.print(mac[3],HEX);
  Serial.print(":");
  Serial.print(mac[2],HEX);
  Serial.print(":");
  Serial.print(mac[1],HEX);
  Serial.print(":");
  Serial.println(mac[0],HEX);
}

void listNetworks() {
  // scan for nearby networks:
  Serial.println("** Scan Networks **");
  int numSsid = WiFi.scanNetworks();
  if (numSsid == -1)
  {
    Serial.println("Couldn't get a wifi connection");
    while(true);
  }

  // print the list of networks seen:
  Serial.print("number of available networks:");
  Serial.println(numSsid);
```

```
// print the network number and name for each network found:
for (int thisNet = 0; thisNet<numSsid; thisNet++) {
  Serial.print(thisNet);
  Serial.print(") ");
  Serial.print(WiFi.SSID(thisNet));
  Serial.print("\tSignal: ");
  Serial.print(WiFi.RSSI(thisNet));
  Serial.print(" dBm");
  Serial.print("\tEncryption: ");
  printEncryptionType(WiFi.encryptionType(thisNet));
}
}

void printEncryptionType(int thisType) {
  // read the encryption type and print out the name:
  switch (thisType) {
  case ENC_TYPE_WEP:
    Serial.println("WEP");
    break;
  case ENC_TYPE_TKIP:
    Serial.println("WPA");
    break;
  case ENC_TYPE_CCMP:
    Serial.println("WPA2");
    break;
  case ENC_TYPE_NONE:
    Serial.println("None");
    break;
  case ENC_TYPE_AUTO:
    Serial.println("Auto");
    break;
  }
}
```

Run the sketch and then open the IDE serial console by choosing Tools ➤ Serial Monitor or pressing CTRL+SHIFT+M.

In few seconds, you will be able to see your WiFi MAC address as the output, along with the wireless networks scanned around Intel Galileo with their respective power level and encryption method. For example:

```
MAC: 1E:56:A4:33:F7:C8
Scanning available networks...
** Scan Networks **
number of available networks:3
0) 55JW5      Signal: -89 dBm Encryption: None
1) PXDP6      Signal: -79 dBm Encryption: WPA2
2) WDJ36      Signal: -84 dBm Encryption: None
```

Reviewing ScanNetworks.ino

The inclusion of the WiFi.h header gives you access to WiFi classes and functions. There are some static methods excluded from the sketch regarding object instantiations.

```
#include <WiFi.h>
```

Using the WiFi object, the program checks if the WiFi card is in place:

if (WiFi.status() == WL_NO_SHIELD)

If the card is not installed, WL_NO_SHIELD is returned and the program is aborted. Then next section of the code checks the firmware version:

```
String fv = WiFi.firmwareVersion();
  if( fv != "1.1.0" )
    Serial.println("Please upgrade the firmware");
```

This line checks the firmware version and prints a warning message if the firmware does not match the latest version.

The sketches prints the MAC address by calling WiFi.macAddress() and passing a byte array as the reference. This call is done by the local function printMacAddress().

```
void printMacAddress() {
  // the MAC address of your WiFi shield
  byte mac[6];

  // print your MAC address:
  WiFi.macAddress(mac);
  Serial.print("MAC: ");
  Serial.print(mac[5],HEX);
  Serial.print(":");
  Serial.print(mac[4],HEX);
  Serial.print(":");
  Serial.print(mac[3],HEX);
  Serial.print(":");
  Serial.print(mac[2],HEX);
  Serial.print(":");
  Serial.print(mac[1],HEX);
  Serial.print(":");
  Serial.println(mac[0],HEX);
}
```

The setup() function ends the call to the local function listNetworks(), which is where the magic happens.

The listNetworks() function calls the method WiFi.scanNetworks(), which returns the total number of WiFi networks found during scanning. At this moment, an internal array is created, starting from 0 to the number of wireless networks found minus one. Each element of this array contains information related to each network scanned.

```
void listNetworks() {
  // scan for nearby networks:
  Serial.println("** Scan Networks **");
  int numSsid = WiFi.scanNetworks();
  if (numSsid == -1)
  {
    Serial.println("Couldn't get a wifi connection");
    while(true);
  }
...
...
...
}
```

To retrieve information about each network scanned, the methods WiFi.SSID(), WiFi.RSSI(), and WiFi.encryptionType() are called and passed to the network index as references.

The sketch implements a for loop that prints the information about each network using the methods mentioned with the appropriate index.

```
void listNetworks() {
...
...
...
  // print the network number and name for each network found:
  for (int thisNet = 0; thisNet<numSsid; thisNet++) {
    Serial.print(thisNet);
    Serial.print(") ");
    Serial.print(WiFi.SSID(thisNet));
    Serial.print("\tSignal: ");
    Serial.print(WiFi.RSSI(thisNet));
    Serial.print(" dBm");
    Serial.print("\tEncryption: ");
    printEncryptionType(WiFi.encryptionType(thisNet));
  }
}
```

Note that the method WiFi.encryptionType() returns integers that specify the encryption used and are parsed properly by the local function printEncryptionType().

```
void printEncryptionType(int thisType) {
  // read the encryption type and print out the name:
  switch (thisType) {
  case ENC_TYPE_WEP:
    Serial.println("WEP");
    break;
  case ENC_TYPE_TKIP:
    Serial.println("WPA");
    break;
  case ENC_TYPE_CCMP:
    Serial.println("WPA2");
    break;
  case ENC_TYPE_NONE:
    Serial.println("None");
    break;
  case ENC_TYPE_AUTO:
    Serial.println("Auto");
    break;
  }
}
```

If you can list the WiFi networks that are available. The next step is to connect to some of these networks, as explained in the next sections.

Connecting to the WPA or WEB

Choose a WiFi network you have access to and determine whether the network requires WPA (WiFi Protected Access) or WEP (Wired Equivalent Privacy). Using the Intel Galileo IDE, open one of the following examples:

1. If the WiFi network requests WPA, open the example File ➤ Examples ➤ WiFi ➤ ConnectWithWPA. See Listing 5-2.

2. If the WiFi network requests WEP, open the example File ➤ Examples ➤ WiFi ➤ ConnectWithWEP. See Listing 5-3.

Listing 5-2. ConnectWithWPA.ino

```
/*

This example connects to an unencrypted WiFi network.
Then it prints the MAC address of the WiFi shield,
the IP address obtained, and other network details.

Circuit:
* WiFi shield attached
```

```
  created 13 July 2010
  by dlf (Metodo2 srl)
  modified 31 May 2012
  by Tom Igoe
  */
  #include <WiFi.h>

  char ssid[] = "yournetwork";      //  your network SSID (name)
  char pass[] = "secretPassword";  // your network password
  int status = WL_IDLE_STATUS;     // the WiFi radio's status

  void setup() {
    //Initialize serial and wait for port to open:
    Serial.begin(9600);
    while (!Serial) {
      ; // wait for serial port to connect. Needed for Leonardo only
    }

    // check for the presence of the shield:
    if (WiFi.status() == WL_NO_SHIELD) {
      Serial.println("WiFi shield not present");
      // don't continue:
      while(true);
    }

    String fv = WiFi.firmwareVersion();
    if( fv != "1.1.0" )
      Serial.println("Please upgrade the firmware");

    // attempt to connect to WiFi network:
    while ( status != WL_CONNECTED) {
      Serial.print("Attempting to connect to WPA SSID: ");
      Serial.println(ssid);
      // Connect to WPA/WPA2 network:
      status = WiFi.begin(ssid, pass);

      // wait 10 seconds for connection:
      delay(10000);
    }

    // you're connected now, so print out the data:
    Serial.print("You're connected to the network");
    printCurrentNet();
    printWifiData();

  }
```

```
void loop() {
  // check the network connection once every 10 seconds:
  delay(10000);
  printCurrentNet();
}

void printWifiData() {
  // print your WiFi shield's IP address:
  IPAddress ip = WiFi.localIP();
    Serial.print("IP Address: ");
  Serial.println(ip);
  Serial.println(ip);

  // print your MAC address:
  byte mac[6];
  WiFi.macAddress(mac);
  Serial.print("MAC address: ");
  Serial.print(mac[5],HEX);
  Serial.print(":");
  Serial.print(mac[4],HEX);
  Serial.print(":");
  Serial.print(mac[3],HEX);
  Serial.print(":");
  Serial.print(mac[2],HEX);
  Serial.print(":");
  Serial.print(mac[1],HEX);
  Serial.print(":");
  Serial.println(mac[0],HEX);

}

void printCurrentNet() {
  // print the SSID of the network you're attached to:
  Serial.print("SSID: ");
  Serial.println(WiFi.SSID());

  // print the MAC address of the router you're attached to:
  byte bssid[6];
  WiFi.BSSID(bssid);
  Serial.print("BSSID: ");
  Serial.print(bssid[5],HEX);
  Serial.print(":");
  Serial.print(bssid[4],HEX);
  Serial.print(":");
  Serial.print(bssid[3],HEX);
  Serial.print(":");
  Serial.print(bssid[2],HEX);
```

```
    Serial.print(":");
    Serial.print(bssid[1],HEX);
    Serial.print(":");
    Serial.println(bssid[0],HEX);

    // print the received signal strength:
    long rssi = WiFi.RSSI();
    Serial.print("signal strength (RSSI):");
    Serial.println(rssi);

    // print the encryption type:
    byte encryption = WiFi.encryptionType();
    Serial.print("Encryption Type:");
    Serial.println(encryption,HEX);
    Serial.println();
}
```

Listing 5-3. ConnectWithWEP.ino

```
/*

This example connects to a WEP-encrypted WiFi network.
Then it prints the MAC address of the WiFi shield,
the IP address obtained, and other network details.

If you use 40-bit WEP, you need a key that is 10 characters long,
and the characters must be hexadecimal (0-9 or A-F).
e.g.  for 40-bit, ABBADEAF01 will work, but ABBADEAF won't work
(too short) and ABBAISDEAF won't work (I and S are not
hexadecimal characters).

For 128-bit, you need a string that is 26 characters long.
DODODEADF00DABBADEAFBEADED will work because it's 26 characters,
all in the 0-9, A-F range.

Circuit:
* WiFi shield attached

created 13 July 2010
by dlf (Metodo2 srl)
modified 31 May 2012
by Tom Igoe
*/
#include <WiFi.h>
```

```
char ssid[] = "yourNetwork";              // your network SSID (name)
char key[] = "DODODEADFOODABBADEAFBEADED"; // your network key
int keyIndex = 0;                         // your network key Index number
int status = WL_IDLE_STATUS;              // the WiFi radio's status

void setup() {
  //Initialize serial and wait for port to open:
  Serial.begin(9600);
  while (!Serial) {
    ; // wait for serial port to connect. Needed for Leonardo only
  }

  // check for the presence of the shield:
  if (WiFi.status() == WL_NO_SHIELD) {
    Serial.println("WiFi shield not present");
    // don't continue:
    while(true);
  }

  String fv = WiFi.firmwareVersion();
  if( fv != "1.1.0" )
    Serial.println("Please upgrade the firmware");

  // attempt to connect to Wifi network:
  while ( status != WL_CONNECTED) {
    Serial.print("Attempting to connect to WEP network, SSID: ");
    Serial.println(ssid);
    status = WiFi.begin(ssid, keyIndex, key);

    // wait 10 seconds for connection:
    delay(10000);
  }

  // once you are connected :
  Serial.print("You're connected to the network");
  printCurrentNet();
  printWifiData();
}

void loop() {
  // check the network connection once every 10 seconds:
  delay(10000);
  printCurrentNet();
}
```

```
void printWifiData() {
  // print your WiFi shield's IP address:
  IPAddress ip = WiFi.localIP();
  Serial.print("IP Address: ");
  Serial.println(ip);
  Serial.println(ip);

  // print your MAC address:
  byte mac[6];
  WiFi.macAddress(mac);
  Serial.print("MAC address: ");
  Serial.print(mac[5],HEX);
  Serial.print(":");
  Serial.print(mac[4],HEX);
  Serial.print(":");
  Serial.print(mac[3],HEX);
  Serial.print(":");
  Serial.print(mac[2],HEX);
  Serial.print(":");
  Serial.print(mac[1],HEX);
  Serial.print(":");
  Serial.println(mac[0],HEX);
}

void printCurrentNet() {
  // print the SSID of the network you're attached to:
  Serial.print("SSID: ");
  Serial.println(WiFi.SSID());

  // print the MAC address of the router you're attached to:
  byte bssid[6];
  WiFi.BSSID(bssid);
  Serial.print("BSSID: ");
  Serial.print(bssid[5],HEX);
  Serial.print(":");
  Serial.print(bssid[4],HEX);
  Serial.print(":");
  Serial.print(bssid[3],HEX);
  Serial.print(":");
  Serial.print(bssid[2],HEX);
  Serial.print(":");
  Serial.print(bssid[1],HEX);
  Serial.print(":");
  Serial.println(bssid[0],HEX);
```

```
// print the received signal strength:
long rssi = WiFi.RSSI();
Serial.print("signal strength (RSSI):");
Serial.println(rssi);

// print the encryption type:
byte encryption = WiFi.encryptionType();
Serial.print("Encryption Type:");
Serial.println(encryption,HEX);
Serial.println();
}
```

Both examples have the same goal, which is to provide access to your WiFi network. There are minor changes between two programs that will be reviewed later. In order to make the examples work, it is necessary to provide your credentials. If you are using the WPA example, the only lines that must be changed are in the beginning of sketch:

```
#include <WiFi.h>

char ssid[] = "yourNetwork";     // your network SSID (name)
char pass[] = "secretPassword";  // your network password
int status = WL_IDLE_STATUS;     // the Wifi radio's status
```

If you are using WEP examples, you need to provide the username and the network's key and key index. The key should be 10 characters long if WEP uses 40 bits or 26 bits long if WEP uses 128 bits.

```
#include <WiFi.h>

char ssid[] = "yourNetwork";                      // your network SSID (name)
char key[] = "D0D0DEADF00DABBADEAFBEADED";         // your network key
int keyIndex = 0;                                  // your network key Index number
```

Edit these lines with your credentials and run the sketch. As soon as it runs, open the IDE serial console by using Tools ➤ Serial Monitor or pressing CTRL+SHIFT+M.

After a few seconds, you will see similar messages in your IDE serial console:

```
Attempting to connect to WPA SSID: S6KFF
You're connected to the networkSSID: S6KFF
BSSID: C6:0:7B:28:7F:0
signal strength (RSSI):-58
Encryption Type:4
```

```
IP Address: 192.168. 1. 7
192.168. 1. 7
MAC address: 27:F8:58:92:D2:C
SSID: S6KFF
BSSID: C6:0:7B:28:7F:0
signal strength (RSSI):-58
Encryption Type:4
```

This example used WPA. The network name is S6KFF (my personal one) and the IP was acquired as expected (192.168.1.7). The MAC address of the WiFi card in the example is 0x27f85892d20c.

If you have a USB cable attached and a terminal shell opened, in parallel to the Linux terminal shell, you will see messages like these:

```
[  736.741664] wlan0: deauthenticating from 00:7f:28:7b:00:c6 by local
choice (reason=3)
[  736.762909] cfg80211: Calling CRDA to update world regulatory domain
[  741.827223] iwlwifi 0000:01:00.0: L1 Disabled; Enabling L0S
[  741.841249] iwlwifi 0000:01:00.0: Radio type=0x0-0x0-0x0
[  742.111928] IPv6: ADDRCONF(NETDEV_UP): wlan0: link is not ready
[  742.598315] wlan0: authenticate with 00:7f:28:7b:00:c6
[  742.643220] wlan0: send auth to 00:7f:28:7b:00:c6 (try 1/3)
[  742.650993] wlan0: authenticated
[  742.660676] wlan0: associate with 00:7f:28:7b:00:c6 (try 1/3)
[  742.670682] wlan0: RX AssocResp from 00:7f:28:7b:00:c6 (capab=0x431
status=0 aid=1)
[  742.682587] wlan0: associated
[  742.685652] IPv6: ADDRCONF(NETDEV_CHANGE): wlan0: link becomes ready
```

These messages appear while the IP is being acquired with WPA. Note the message "wlan0: link becomes ready", which indicates that the wlan0 is ready to be used.

If the WiFi router is connected to the Internet, try to ping Intel using the terminal shell:

```
root@clanton:~# ping www.intel.com
PING www.intel.com (63.80.4.74): 56 data bytes
64 bytes from 63.80.4.74: seq=0 ttl=60 time=26.506 ms
64 bytes from 63.80.4.74: seq=1 ttl=60 time=26.525 ms
64 bytes from 63.80.4.74: seq=2 ttl=60 time=28.880 ms
64 bytes from 63.80.4.74: seq=3 ttl=60 time=27.931 ms
```

Reviewing ConnectWithWPA.ino and ConnectWithWEP.ino

The code used in the example is very simple and there are minor changes between the WPA and WEP examples. The whole connection process starts with the setup() function.

Initially, it is necessary to provide the credentials as explained in the previous section. The program then determines if the card is in place:

```
if (WiFi.status() == WL_NO_SHIELD)
```

If the card is not installed, WL_NO_SHIELD is returned and the program is aborted. Then next section of the code checks the firmware version:

```
String fv = WiFi.firmwareVersion();
  if( fv != "1.1.0" )
    Serial.println("Please upgrade the firmware");
```

This line checks the firmware version and prints a warning message if the firmware does not match the latest version. Don't worry about this method because BSP always returns 1.1.0. This method is useless with Intel Galileo.

The connection is established using the WiFi.begin() call. If you are using the WPA example, the following code snippet describes the process for connecting:

```
// attempt to connect to Wifi network:
while ( status != WL_CONNECTED) {
  Serial.print("Attempting to connect to WPA SSID: ");
  Serial.println(ssid);
  // Connect to WPA/WPA2 network:
  status = WiFi.begin(ssid, pass);

  // wait 10 seconds for connection:
  delay(10000);
}
```

If you are using WEP, this code snippet establishes the connection:

```
while ( status != WL_CONNECTED) {
    Serial.print("Attempting to connect to WEP network, SSID: ");
    Serial.println(ssid);
    status = WiFi.begin(ssid, keyIndex, key);

    // wait 10 seconds for connection:
    delay(10000);
}
```

In both examples, the program will try to connect through the WiFi.begin() functional call every 10 seconds, which is calculated by delay() function, and will keep trying in the while loop until the status returned by WiFi.begin() is WL_CONNECTED.

The only difference is in the begin() method. For WPA, the user credentials are passed in WiFi.begin(ssid, pass), whereas with WEP, the keys are used with WiFi.begin(ssid, keyIndex, key).

The rest of program is identical for both WPA and WEP. The loop() function calls printCurrentNet(), which prints some info regarding the connection. For example, WiFi.BSSID() connects the MAC address of the router, WiFi.RSSI() reports the signal strengths, and WiFi.encryptionType() reports the type of encryption.

Hacking the WiFi Library

This hack is applicable to Intel Galileo and Intel Galileo Gen 2.

If you played with the sketches mentioned in the section "Testing the WiFi Mini-PCIe" in this chapter or if you played with any other sketches running other WiFi examples from the IDE, you should have noticed that every time you run the sketches the connection to the WiFi routers is redone. This takes time. If you are developing a project that requires WiFi, this will be considered a huge annoyance for sure.

However, considering that the Intel Galileo boards use Linux as the operating system, it is possible to set the WiFi connection in the board to be persisted. With a few changes in the sketches, the development process will become very fast.

In other words, Intel Galileo will try to establish the connection as soon as the board boots or as soon as the network interfaces restart, without any sketch or native code for it.

With the WiFi connection handled by the Linux kernel, the sketches will not need to find the SSID. Instead, the sketches will use the connection that's present, which will drastically improve the sketch development cycle.

To do this, follow these steps:

1. Set up your connection using the terminal shell on Linux OS.

2. Restart the wireless interface.

3. Perform a small hack in the WiFi library class.

Step 1: Setting Up the WiFi Connection

In the context of Linux for Intel Galileo, the WiFi card is enumerated with the interface called wlan0. This interface will be mentioned several times in the terminal shell command lines.

The following sections explain how to create such a setup for the WPA and WEP connections.

Persisted Connection with WPA

You can use the command-line tool wpa_passphrase to generate the PSK (Pre-Shared Key) for the WPA connection. You pass the network name (SSID) and password for connecting to this command. It's then possible to create a configuration file as shown here:

```
root@clanton:~# wpa_passphrase YOUR_SSID YOUR_PASSWORD_HERE >
/etc/wpa_supplicant.conf
```

You can then set Intel Galileo to connect to the WiFi router automatically by editing the /etc/network/interfaces file. You can edit this file directly in the command shell using the vi editor.

```
root@clanton:~# vi /etc/network/interfaces
```

The auto wlan0 directive is added to the beginning of iface wlan0, as shown here:

```
# /etc/network/interfaces -- configuration file for ifup(8), ifdown(8)

# The loopback interface
auto lo
iface lo inet loopback

# Wireless interfaces
auto wlan0
iface wlan0 inet dhcp
        wireless_mode managed
        wireless_essid any
        wpa-driver wext
        wpa-conf /etc/wpa_supplicant.conf

iface atml0 inet dhcp

# Wired or wireless interfaces
auto eth0
iface eth0 inet dhcp
iface eth1 inet dhcp

# Ethernet/RNDIS gadget (g_ether)
# ... or on host side, usbnet and random hwaddr
iface usb0 inet static
        address 192.168.7.2
        netmask 255.255.255.0
        network 192.168.7.0
        gateway 192.168.7.1

# Bluetooth networking
iface bnep0 inet dhcp
```

Note that the WPA searches for the file /etc/wpa_supplicant.conf, which you created with wpa_passphrase, observing the wpa-conf /etc/wpa_supplicant.conf field.

Persisted Connection with WEP

The WEP procedure is similar to the WPA one.

Edit the /etc/network/interfaces file and add the line auto wlan0 to the top of iface wlan0, following the same procedure used in the WPA configuration discussed in the previous section.

It's necessary to include the SSID and the key to be used as well. See the following example:

```
# /etc/network/interfaces -- configuration file for ifup(8), ifdown(8)

# The loopback interface
auto lo
iface lo inet loopback

# Wireless interfaces
auto wlan0
iface wlan0 inet dhcp
        wireless_mode managed
        wireless-essid your_network_ssid
        wireless-key 0123456789ABCDEF0123456789
        wpa-driver wext

iface atml0 inet dhcp

# Wired or wireless interfaces
auto eth0
iface eth0 inet dhcp
iface eth1 inet dhcp

# Ethernet/RNDIS gadget (g_ether)
# ... or on host side, usbnet and random hwaddr
iface usb0 inet static
        address 192.168.7.2
        netmask 255.255.255.0
        network 192.168.7.0
        gateway 192.168.7.1

# Bluetooth networking
iface bnep0 inet dhcp
```

Step 2: Restart the Wireless Connection

Restart the connection by typing the following command:

```
root@clanton:~# /etc/init.d/networking restart
```

If the WiFi router was identified and the connection is accepted, something similar to the following output will appear:

```
Running /etc/init.d/networking restart is deprecated because it may not
enable again some interfaces
Reconfiguring network interfaces...
[ 5786.598692] wlan0: deauthenticating from 00:7f:28:7b:00:c6 by local
choice (reason=3)
[ 5786.630939] cfg80211: Calling CRDA to update world regulatory domain
ifdown: interface eth0 not configured
Successfully initialized wpa_sup[ 5786.932111] iwlwifi 0000:01:00.0: L1
Disabled; Enabling L0S
plicant
[ 5786.946981] iwlwifi 0000:01:00.0: Radio type=0x0-0x0-0x0
[ 5787.228184] IPv6: ADDRCONF(NETDEV_UP): wlan0: link is not ready
udhcpc (v1.20.2) started
Sending discover...
[ 5787.881882] wlan0: authenticate with 00:7f:28:7b:00:c6
[ 5787.925896] wlan0: send auth to 00:7f:28:7b:00:c6 (try 1/3)
[ 5787.933589] wlan0: authenticated
[ 5787.940668] wlan0: associate with 00:7f:28:7b:00:c6 (try 1/3)
[ 5787.950731] wlan0: RX AssocResp from 00:7f:28:7b:00:c6 (capab=0x431
status=0 aid=3)
[ 5787.962655] wlan0: associated
[ 5787.965719] IPv6: ADDRCONF(NETDEV_CHANGE): wlan0: link becomes ready
Sending discover...
Sending select for 192.168.1.10...
Lease of 192.168.1.10 obtained, lease time 86400
/etc/udhcpc.d/50default: Adding DNS 192.168.1.1
udhcpc (v1.20.2) started
Sending discover...
Sending discover...
Sending discover...
No lease, failing
```

In this case, wlan0 is available and the connection to WiFi router is completed, so the IP is received and the DNS is set with success. If you reboot the board, the WiFi connection will automatically be re-established.

It is possible also to disable and enable the interface using the ifdown and ifup commands, respectively. Just type the command followed by the "wlan0" string to specify the wireless interface. See the following examples:

```
root@clanton:/etc/network# ifdown wlan0
[  717.113913] wlan0: deauthenticating from 00:7f:28:7b:00:c6 by local
choice (reason=3)
[  717.150903] cfg80211: Calling CRDA for country: US

root@clanton:/etc/network# ifup wlan0
Successfully initialized wpa_sup[  722.047319] iwlwifi 0000:01:00.0: L1
Disabled; Enabling LOS
plicant
[  722.062243] iwlwifi 0000:01:00.0: Radio type=0x0-0x0-0x0
[  722.347953] IPv6: ADDRCONF(NETDEV_UP): wlan0: link is not ready
udhcpc (v1.20.2) started
Sending discover...
[  723.026324] wlan0: authenticate with 00:7f:28:7b:00:c6
[  723.080172] wlan0: send auth to 00:7f:28:7b:00:c6 (try 1/3)
[  723.087765] wlan0: authenticated
[  723.100140] wlan0: associate with 00:7f:28:7b:00:c6 (try 1/3)
[  723.110014] wlan0: RX AssocResp from 00:7f:28:7b:00:c6 (capab=0x431
status=0 aid=3)
[  723.122344] wlan0: associated
[  723.125408] IPv6: ADDRCONF(NETDEV_CHANGE): wlan0: link becomes ready
Sending discover...
Sending select for 192.168.1.7...
Lease of 192.168.1.7 obtained, lease time 86400
/etc/udhcpc.d/50default: Adding DNS 192.168.1.1
```

Step 3: Hacking the WiFi Class

At this point the Intel Galileo WPA or WEP connection process is persisted and functional, so you need to make a small change in the WiFi class to allow sketch to use this Linux connection instead of having to pass through the whole process again very quickly.

To understand how this is possible, take a look at the begin() methods implemented in the WiFi library class. Open the ./hardware/arduino/x86/libraries/WiFi/WiFi.cpp file and search for the two begin() methods:

```
int WiFiClass::begin(char* ssid, uint8_t key_idx, const char *key)
{
        char cmd[256];
        trace_debug("begin ssid=%s,key_idx=%d,key=%s",ssid,key_idx,key);
        /*
        iwconfig [interface] mode managed key [WEP key]
        (128 bit WEP use 26 hex characters, 64 bit WEP uses 10)
        */
```

```
        if(ssid == NULL)
                return WL_NO_SSID_AVAIL;
        if(key == NULL)
                return WL_CONNECT_FAILED;
        sprintf(cmd, "iwconfig wlan0 mode managed key %s", key);
        system(cmd);
        sprintf(cmd, "iwconfig wlan0 essid %s", ssid);
        system(cmd);
        sprintf(cmd, "ifup %s", ARDUINO_WLAN);
        system(cmd);
        delay(5000);
        _local_ip = getLocalIP();
        if(_local_ip._sin.sin_addr.s_addr == 0) {
                trace_debug("didnt get an IP address, cant connect");
                sprintf(cmd, "ifdown %s", ARDUINO_WLAN);
                _status = WL_IDLE_STATUS;
                return _status;
        }
        _subnet = getSubnet();
        strcpy(_ssid, ssid);
        _status = WL_CONNECTED;
        return _status;
}

int WiFiClass::begin(char* ssid, const char *passphrase)
{
        char cmd[256];
        trace_debug("begin ssid=%s,passphrase=%s",ssid,passphrase);
        if(ssid == NULL)
                return WL_NO_SSID_AVAIL;
        if(passphrase == NULL)
                return WL_CONNECT_FAILED;
        sprintf(cmd, "iwconfig wlan0 mode managed");
        system(cmd);
        sprintf(cmd, "iwconfig wlan0 essid %s", ssid);
        system(cmd);
        sprintf(cmd, "wpa_passphrase %s %s  > /etc/wpa_supplicant.conf",
                        ssid, passphrase);
        system(cmd);
        sprintf(cmd, "ifup %s", ARDUINO_WLAN);
        system(cmd);
        delay(5000);
        _local_ip = getLocalIP();
        if(_local_ip._sin.sin_addr.s_addr == 0) {
                trace_debug("didnt get an IP address, cant connect");
                sprintf(cmd, "ifdown %s", ARDUINO_WLAN);
                _status = WL_IDLE_STATUS;
                return _status;
        }
```

```
    _subnet = getSubnet();
    strcpy(_ssid, ssid);
    _status = WL_CONNECTED;
    return _status;
}
```

The first begin() method is used with a WEP connection and the second is with a WPA connection. If you take a look at the bold code in both methods, the sketches try to do the same procedure you have done manually, but instead of using the configuration for wlan0 present in the /etc/network/interfaces. file, the sketches use the iwconfig, wpa_passphrase, and ifup commands. In other words, the system calls send the commands to Linux in same way they would be typed into the terminal shell.

The iwconfig command tool sets up the wireless interface. In the begin() method that's used for WPA and WEP, the iwconfig wlan0 mode managed and iwconfig wlan0 mode managed key %s commands are used, respectively. These commands set the wlan0 interface to be managed by the access point called mode managed. In other words, the access point will determine the channel frequency that Intel Galileo might camp. Note that, in WEP, the key is included at the end of the command line and %s will receive the char pointer key passed to the begin() method. This makes the key part of the command. This key might be represented by a 10-hexadecimal string if WEP used encryption with 40 bits or a 26-hexadecimal string if the WEP encryption is 128 bits.

The next usage of iwconfig and is to set the SSID name with iwconfig wlan0 essid %s, where %s receives the char pointer SSID with the network SSID name.

In the WPA, there is also a wpa_passphrase command being used in the same way it was used in the "Persisted Connection with WPA" section of this chapter. In this case, it simply generates a configuration file for the WPA connection.

Both methods call ifup wlan0 (since ARDUINO_WLAN is the string "wlan0") to make the wlan0 interface available. To make everything worse, there is a five-second delay implemented by the delay() function on this process.

Finally, the original code in both methods checks if the IP is available through getLocalIP(). If it is, the status WL_CONNECTED is returned; otherwise, WL_IDLE_STATUS is used.

When the WiFi connection is manually configured and persisted in Intel Galileo, the system simply has to determine if there is an IP available for the wlan0 interface once Linux can handle the connection.

Thus, if you are developing a project that uses WiFi and you want to speed up the sketch execution by avoiding this process, make the following simple changes to the code:

```
int WiFiClass::begin(char* ssid, uint8_t key_idx, const char *key)
{
    char cmd[256];

    local_ip = getLocalIP();
    if(_local_ip._sin.sin_addr.s_addr == 0) {
```

```
            trace_debug("begin ssid=%s,key_idx=%d,key=%s",ssid,key_idx,key);
            /*
            iwconfig [interface] mode managed key [WEP key]
            (128 bit WEP use 26 hex characters, 64 bit WEP uses 10)
            */
            if(ssid == NULL)
                return WL_NO_SSID_AVAIL;
            if(key == NULL)
                return WL_CONNECT_FAILED;
            sprintf(cmd, "iwconfig wlan0 mode managed key %s", key);
            system(cmd);
            sprintf(cmd, "iwconfig wlan0 essid %s", ssid);
            system(cmd);
            sprintf(cmd, "ifup %s", ARDUINO_WLAN);
            system(cmd);
            delay(5000);
            _local_ip = getLocalIP();
            if(_local_ip._sin.sin_addr.s_addr == 0) {
                trace_debug("didnt get an IP address, cant connect");
                    sprintf(cmd, "ifdown %s", ARDUINO_WLAN);
                    _status = WL_IDLE_STATUS;
                    return _status;
            }
        }
    _subnet = getSubnet();
    strcpy(_ssid, ssid);
    _status = WL_CONNECTED;
    return _status;
}

int WiFiClass::begin(char* ssid, const char *passphrase)
{
        char cmd[256];

        local_ip = getLocalIP();
        if(_local_ip._sin.sin_addr.s_addr == 0) {

            trace_debug("begin ssid=%s,passphrase=%s",ssid,passphrase);
            if(ssid == NULL)
                    return WL_NO_SSID_AVAIL;
            if(passphrase == NULL)
                    return WL_CONNECT_FAILED;
            sprintf(cmd, "iwconfig wlan0 mode managed");
            system(cmd);
            sprintf(cmd, "iwconfig wlan0 essid %s", ssid);
            system(cmd);
            sprintf(cmd, "wpa_passphrase %s %s  > /etc/wpa_supplicant.
            conf",
                        ssid, passphrase);
```

```
                system(cmd);
                sprintf(cmd, "ifup %s", ARDUINO_WLAN);
                system(cmd);
                delay(5000);
                _local_ip = getLocalIP();
                if(_local_ip._sin.sin_addr.s_addr == 0) {
                        trace_debug("didnt get an IP address, cant connect");
                        sprintf(cmd, "ifdown %s", ARDUINO_WLAN);
                        _status = WL_IDLE_STATUS;
                        return _status;
                }

        }
        _subnet = getSubnet();
        strcpy(_ssid, ssid);
        _status = WL_CONNECTED;
        return _status;
}
```

First off, the code determines whether there is a valid IP for the interface wlan0 through the function getLocalIP(). If there is, the authentication process is avoided. That means there is no needed to specify the SSID, a password, or the keys in the sketches once these fields are already configured (as demonstrated in the first step).

You can run the sketches from Listings 5-1 and 5-2 again without changing the SSID, key, or passwords. The programs will run very fast and work perfectly.

Ethernet API

One advantage to having Intel Galileo boards is the presence of Ethernet connector, which eliminates the need of an external shield. The Quark SoC supports two Ethernet interfaces but only one is available on the Intel Galileo boards.

In terms of Ethernet API, Intel Galileo complies with the Arduino reference. There are several classes implemented on this API: Ethernet, EthernetClient, EthernetUDP, IPAddress, and Server. For details, visit http://arduino.cc/en/reference/ethernet.

When this API was created, the purpose was to support Ethernet shields and Ethernet is the primary class used to configure the Ethernet adapter.

For example, to configure the Ethernet interface using the DHCP connection, you must determine the board MAC address and call the proper begin() method of this class. The following code snippet shows this process:

```
#include <Ethernet.h>
byte mac[] = { 0xDE, 0xAD, 0xBE, 0xEF, 0xFE, 0xED };
  if (Ethernet.begin(mac) == 0) {
    Serial.println("Failed to configure Ethernet using DHCP");
    // no point in carrying on, so do nothing forevermore:
    for(;;)
      ;
  }
```

The mac[] array must be changed according to the MAC address of your Intel Galileo. It's usually shown on a white label on the top of the Ethernet connector or on the bottom of the board.

What's New with Ethernet API and Intel Galileo

In the case of Intel Galileo, considering we have a real operational system running with Quark SoC that supports Ethernet interfaces, the Ethernet class is because the interface might be configured directly on the Linux context.

This brings a performance improvement, especially when a DHCP connection is being used. Otherwise, every time the sketch runs, the Ethernet class checks if the interface is configured. If it's not, the DHCP negotiation process is restarted, which takes time.

Nothing blocks you from using the Ethernet class, but in case of Intel Galileo boards, once the Ethernet interface is already configured on the Linux scope, this class becomes irrelevant.

It's also not necessary to hard code the MAC address in the sketches, which makes your sketches more flexible on different boards.

Ethernet Example: Network Time Protocol (NTP)

The IDE includes several sketches that use the Ethernet API. They can be accessed by choosing File ➤ Examples ➤ Ethernet.

The examples are from regular Arduino IDE and several sketches have comments in the code referring to Ethernet as a shield that must be ignored. One sketch example in particular, TwitterClient, will not work because Twitter changed the API with the OAuth methods discussed and resolved in Chapter 6.

Among the sketches presented, there is a sketch (choose File ➤ Examples ➤ Ethernet ➤ UdpNtpClient) that implements a simple UDP client that displays the Network Time Protocol (NTP) in the IDE serial console.

Listing 5-4 shows the source code.

Listing 5-4. WiFiUdpNtpClient.ino

```
/*
  Udp NTP Client

  Get the time from a Network Time Protocol (NTP) time server
  Demonstrates use of UDP sendPacket and ReceivePacket
  For more on NTP time servers and the messages needed to communicate with them,
  see http://en.wikipedia.org/wiki/Network_Time_Protocol

  Warning: NTP Servers are subject to temporary failure or IP address change.
  Plese check

    http://tf.nist.gov/tf-cgi/servers.cgi
```

if the time server used in the example didn't work.

created 4 Sep 2010
by Michael Margolis
modified 9 Apr 2012
by Tom Igoe

This code is in the public domain.

*/

```
#include <SPI.h>
#include <Ethernet.h>
#include <EthernetUdp.h>

// Enter a MAC address for your controller below.
// Newer Ethernet shields have a MAC address printed on a sticker on the shield
byte mac[] = {
  0x98, 0x4f, 0xee, 0x01, 0x4c, 0x44 };

unsigned int localPort = 8888;        // local port to listen for UDP packets

IPAddress timeServer(132, 163, 4, 101); // time-a.timefreq.bldrdoc.gov NTP
server
// IPAddress timeServer(132, 163, 4, 102); // time-b.timefreq.bldrdoc.gov
NTP server
// IPAddress timeServer(132, 163, 4, 103); // time-c.timefreq.bldrdoc.gov
NTP server

const int NTP_PACKET_SIZE= 48; // NTP time stamp is in the first 48 bytes of
the message

byte packetBuffer[ NTP_PACKET_SIZE]; //buffer to hold incoming and outgoing
packets

// A UDP instance to let us send and receive packets over UDP
EthernetUDP Udp;

void setup()
{
  // Open serial communications and wait for port to open:
  Serial.begin(9600);
   while (!Serial) {
    ; // wait for serial port to connect. Needed for Leonardo only
  }
```

```
  // start Ethernet and UDP
  if (Ethernet.begin(mac) == 0) {
    Serial.println("Failed to configure Ethernet using DHCP");
    // no point in carrying on, so do nothing forevermore:
    for(;;)
      ;
  }
  Udp.begin(localPort);
}

void loop()
{
  sendNTPpacket(timeServer); // send an NTP packet to a time server

  // wait to see if a reply is available
  delay(1000);
  if ( Udp.parsePacket() ) {
    // We've received a packet, read the data from it
    Udp.read(packetBuffer,NTP_PACKET_SIZE);  // read the packet into the buffer

    //the timestamp starts at byte 40 of the received packet and is four bytes,
    // or two words, long. First, esxtract the two words:

    unsigned long highWord = word(packetBuffer[40], packetBuffer[41]);
    unsigned long lowWord = word(packetBuffer[42], packetBuffer[43]);
    // combine the four bytes (two words) into a long integer
    // this is NTP time (seconds since Jan 1 1900):
    unsigned long secsSince1900 = highWord << 16 | lowWord;
    Serial.print("Seconds since Jan 1 1900 = " );
    Serial.println(secsSince1900);

    // now convert NTP time into everyday time:
    Serial.print("Unix time = ");
    // Unix time starts on Jan 1 1970. In seconds, that's 2208988800:
    const unsigned long seventyYears = 2208988800UL;
    // subtract seventy years:
    unsigned long epoch = secsSince1900 - seventyYears;
    // print Unix time:
    Serial.println(epoch);

    // print the hour, minute and second:
    Serial.print("The UTC time is ");        // UTC is the time at Greenwich
    Meridian (GMT)
    Serial.print((epoch  % 86400L) / 3600); // print the hour (86400 equals
    secs per day)
```

```
    Serial.print(':');
    if ( ((epoch % 3600) / 60) < 10 ) {
      // In the first 10 minutes of each hour, we'll want a leading '0'
      Serial.print('0');
    }
    Serial.print((epoch % 3600) / 60); // print the minute (3600 equals
    secs per minute)
    Serial.print(':');
    if ( (epoch % 60) < 10 ) {
      // In the first 10 seconds of each minute, we'll want a leading '0'
      Serial.print('0');
    }
    Serial.println(epoch %60); // print the second
  }
  // wait ten seconds before asking for the time again
  delay(10000);
}


// send an NTP request to the time server at the given address
unsigned long sendNTPpacket(IPAddress& address)
{
  // set all bytes in the buffer to 0
  memset(packetBuffer, 0, NTP_PACKET_SIZE);
  // Initialize values needed to form NTP request
  // (see URL above for details on the packets)
  packetBuffer[0] = 0b11100011;   // LI, Version, Mode
  packetBuffer[1] = 0;       // Stratum, or type of clock
  packetBuffer[2] = 6;       // Polling Interval
  packetBuffer[3] = 0xEC;  // Peer Clock Precision
  // 8 bytes of zero for Root Delay & Root Dispersion
  packetBuffer[12]  = 49;
  packetBuffer[13]  = 0x4E;
  packetBuffer[14]  = 49;
  packetBuffer[15]  = 52;

  // all NTP fields have been given values, now
  // you can send a packet requesting a timestamp:
  Udp.beginPacket(address, 123); //NTP requests are to port 123
  Udp.write(packetBuffer,NTP_PACKET_SIZE);
  Udp.endPacket();
}
```

Connect your Intel Galileo board using the Ethernet cable to the router in a port that can establish a DHCP connection, or to a computer that shares the Internet connection.

Change the mac[] array with the MAC address of your Intel Galileo board. Observe the white tag at the top of the Ethernet connector or at the bottom of your board.

With the cable properly connected, run the sketch and open the IDE serial console by using Tools ➤ Serial Monitor or pressing CTRL+SHIFT+M.

Reviewing WiFiUdpNtpClient.ino

This section simply provides a general explanation as to how the Ethernet API is used.

If you are interested in how NTP works and how to implement a client using UDP, visit http://www.ietf.org/rfc/rfc958.txt and http://en.wikipedia.org/wiki/Network_Time_Protocol.

The code initially includes two headers, which are necessary to establish the Ethernet setting and use the UDP datagrams:

```
#include <Ethernet.h>
#include <EthernetUdp.h>
```

The mac[] array defines the MAC address that must match the MAC address of your board.

The timerServer and Udp instances are created to point to the NTP server and provide access to UDP datagrams' functions, respectively:

```
IPAddress timeServer(132, 163, 4, 101); // time-a.timefreq.bldrdoc.gov NTP
server

// A UDP instance to let us send and receive packets over UDP
EthernetUDP Udp;
```

In the setup() function, the Ethernet interface is configured with Ethernet object and the Udp instance is initialized with localport (8888).

```
unsigned int localPort = 8888;        // local port to listen for UDP packets

...
...
...
  // start Ethernet and UDP
  if (Ethernet.begin(mac) == 0) {
    Serial.println("Failed to configure Ethernet using DHCP");
    // no point in carrying on, so do nothing forevermore:
    for(;;)
      ;
  }
  Udp.begin(localPort);
```

In the loop() function, the function sendNTPpacket() is called and passes the server address through the timeServer object. The sendNTPpacket() function is implemented by the sketch and it is not part of the Ethernet API.

In the sendNTPpacket(),Udp sends a datagram to timeServer using port 123 and an NTP request. Note that the mechanism is similar to how Wire API sends I2C commands. beginPacket() initiates to the server and port, write() stacks packages to be sent, and endPacket() transmits the outgoing data. The write() method must always be wrapped between beginPacket() and endPacket().

```
// all NTP fields have been given values, now
// you can send a packet requesting a timestamp:
Udp.beginPacket(address, 123); //NTP requests are to port 123
Udp.write(packetBuffer,NTP_PACKET_SIZE);
Udp.endPacket();
```

After sendNTPpacket() is called, the response is received by the parsePacket() method of the Udp instance.

```
Udp.read(packetBuffer,NTP_PACKET_SIZE);  // read the packet into the buffer
```

The rest of the code parses the response and, using the Serial object, displays the results every 10 seconds provided by the delay() function at the end of loop() function.

You should see something like this in the output:

```
Seconds since Jan 1 1900 = 3614060697
Unix time = 1405071897
The UTC time is 9:44:57
Seconds since Jan 1 1900 = 3614060708
Unix time = 1405071908
The UTC time is 9:45:08
Seconds since Jan 1 1900 = 3614060719
Unix time = 1405071919
The UTC time is 9:45:19
```

Dynamic and Static IP Using Ethernet

This section describes the process for connecting Intel Galileo to a router or computer. One important point regarding connecting Intel Galileo to a personal computer is that most people use this kind of connection only to transfer files via scp or ftp, but in this section, you will learn how to use it for Internet access as well.

The connection to your router or computer depends on the network configuration you use. Both offer ways to reach the boards and access the Internet and computers.

As mentioned, you can configure the Ethernet interface using Linux and the Ethernet.begin() method can be removed from the sketches without any problems. The interface can be configured manually, using the Linux serial console, persisted in the configuration of the network, or even through sketches.

The Ethernet adapter present in the Intel Galileo boards is identified in Linux as interface eth0. The next sections explain how to configure the IP on Linux for dynamic and static connections.

However, it is necessary to know how your router is configured in order to understand the range of IPs used as dynamic IPs, the range for the static IPs, the IP mask, and the gateway used.

Your routers can be accessed by typing 192.168.1.1 in the address box of a browser. A password and username are required; the username and password are usually admin. If that does not work, you can try to reset your router to the default settings (check your router manual).

From the router settings, you will be able to see which IP range is configured for DHCP and which range is set for static IPs.

Most routers use the 192.168.1.X range for dynamic IPs, where X is a number above 100 (static IPs use numbers below 100). There are also reserved addresses. For example, 192.168.1.1 is often used to provide the configuration for the web interface and 192.168.1.2 and 192.168.1.15 usually provide the Ethernet connection through a USB if your router contains a USB port. Again, these addresses depend on your router.

There are thousands of network configurations that affect how your Intel Galileo must be configured, so this section assumes you have a laptop connected to a router using WiFi and you have an Ethernet adapter.

Dynamic IP (DHCP)

It is possible to connect Intel Galileo with a dynamic IP to a router or computer, but it is necessary to create two configurations—one for Intel Galileo and the other for the computer or router. The next sections explain how to create such configurations.

Configuring Intel Galileo for Dynamic IP

By default, the Intel Galileo software supports dynamic IPs obtained by the DHCP (Dynamic Host Configuration protocol). You can check this configuration in the /etc/network/interfaces file in the following lines:

```
# Wired or wireless interfaces
auto eth0
iface eth0 inet dhcp
iface eth1 inet dhcp
```

The eth1 is totally irrelevant because Intel Galileo supports only one Ethernet adapter.

With this configuration set, you simply connect your cable to your router or to a computer that shares the Internet connection.

You can bring the interface down by using the terminal console and typing ifdown eth0 and bring it back up by typing ifup eth0.

Testing Intel Galileo with a Router Using DHCP

If /etc/network/interfaces is configured for DHCP as mentioned, you just need to connect Intel Galileo and your router using the Ethernet cable.

If you have a Linux serial console, you might be a message like this when you connect the cable:

```
[10737.520194] libphy: stmmac-1:01 - Link is Up - 100/Full
[10737.525495] IPv6: ADDRCONF(NETDEV_CHANGE): eth0: link becomes ready
```

You can then try to ping your computer IP or ping some valid server on the Internet. For example:

```
root@clanton:/etc# ping www.google.com
PING www.google.com (74.125.224.52): 56 data bytes
64 bytes from 74.125.224.52: seq=0 ttl=57 time=17.777 ms
64 bytes from 74.125.224.52: seq=1 ttl=57 time=18.588 ms
```

Static IPs

Sometimes the router is far from Intel Galileo and extending a cable to your router is not an option. If your computer is closer and provides an Ethernet port to connect Intel Galileo, this is a good solution.

You can specify a static IP to Intel Galileo using the local connection in your computer to transfer files. You can even go a little bit beyond by allowing your computer to share its Internet connection with Intel Galileo.

If you choose to make your computer share its Internet connection, you need to determine which adapter will be used to connect to Intel Galileo and identify the adapter that will share the connection. For example, suppose you have a local connection in your computer that's used to connect Intel Galileo via the Ethernet cable and you have a wireless adapter that connects your computer to a router that gives you access to the Internet. What you need to do is tell your computer that this wireless adapter will share the Internet connection with the local connector, which indirectly tells Intel Galileo to use the Internet as well.

The only problem is that this configuration must be done in your computer and the process varies according to the operation system. The following sections use the most common operation systems—Windows 7, Ubuntu 12.04, and MACOSX 10.06—as examples.

Configuring on Windows 7

The configuration on Windows is a little bit odd. You have to change or create a local connection and configure IPv4 as the static IP. Then, using the adapter that provides the Internet connection, you tell this adapter that the "local connection" will use its Internet access. The procedure is as follows:

1. Access the Control Panel by choosing Control Panel ➤ Network and Internet ➤ Network and Sharing Center.

2. Click on Change Adapter Settings and right-click on Local Area Connection. The Local Area Connection Properties will be shown, as shown in Figure 5-6.

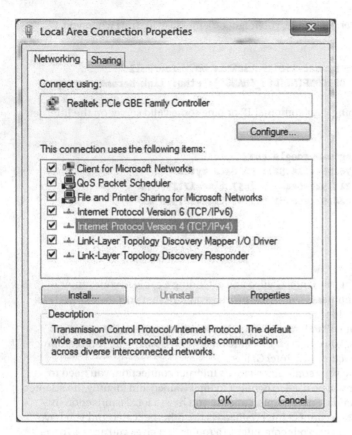

Figure 5-6. Local area connection properties

3. Select Internet Protocol Version 4 (TCP/IPv4) and click the
    Properties button. The IPv4 setting will be shown, as shown
    in Figure 5-7. Add a valid static IP, subnet mask, and gateway
    (usually your router IP).

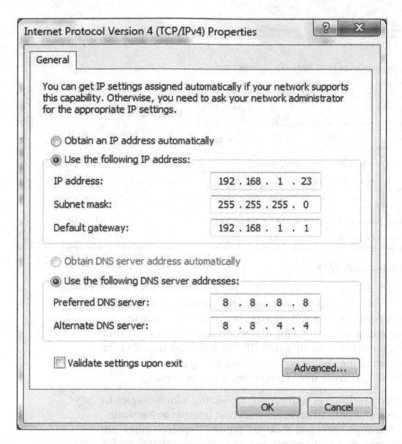

Figure 5-7. IPv4 properties on Windows 7

4. In this case, IPv4 was set to the Google DNS servers 8.8.8.8
    and 8.8.4.4, but you can change this to the servers of your
    preference.

5. The subnet mask must be the same as your router, otherwise
    this connection will be out of the common network. If you do
    not know the subnet mask your Internet adapter is using, you
    can access it using the ipconfig command in the Windows
    commands shell. For this, click the Start icon or press the
    Windows key ■, and then type cmd and press Enter to open
    the Windows command shell. In the shell, type ipconfig and
    press Enter. Figure 5-8 shows the output of the ipconfig
    command on my computer.

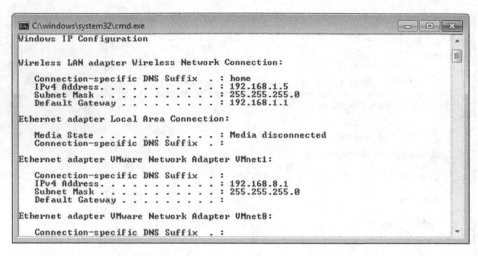

Figure 5-8. *Output of* `ipconfig`

6. In this case, the adapter that shares the Internet is the Wireless Lan Adapter and the subnet mask is `255.255.255.0`. You need to determine the right adapter on your computer. If your intention is to have only a static IP, this is the last step. You can move on to the section entitled "Configuring Intel Galileo for Static IP" in this chapter. Otherwise, continue reading!

7. To share the Internet connection, access your adapters again by choosing Control Panel ➤ Network and Internet ➤ Network and Sharing Center and clicking Change Adapter Settings. But now, right-click in the adapter of your computer that provides Internet access to you and select `Properties.` Then click in the Sharing tab and check the option to share the Internet in the listbox. Figure 5-9 shows an example that uses a wireless adapter to access the Internet and a Local Area Connection for Intel Galileo.

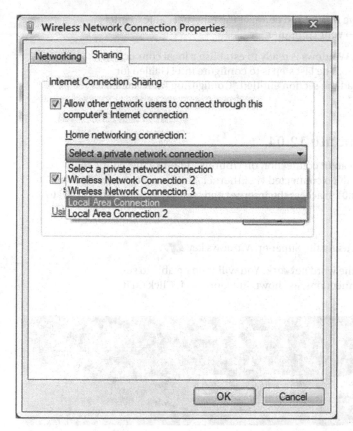

Figure 5-9. *Sharing the Internet connection*

Windows might show you a message saying that some other static IP will be associated with your local connection. This happens because Windows reserved some IPs for sharing, as shown in Figure 5-10.

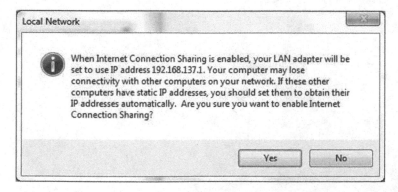

Figure 5-10. *Windows provides a specific IP for Internet sharing*

Just accept the new IP and connect the Ethernet cable to Intel Galileo and to your computer.

8. At this point, Windows is ready to establish a local connection to Intel Galileo. The last step is to configure Intel Galileo for static IPs. Read the section entitled "Configuring Intel Galileo for Static IPs."

Configuring on Ubuntu 12.04

It's quite easy to establish an IP connection on Ubuntu and make this connection offer Internet access to Intel Galileo connected via Ethernet. The following steps illustrate an example using WiFi (wlan0) to access the Internet and an Ethernet interface (eth0) to connect to Intel Galileo.

The procedure is:

1. Access Dash using the Super or Windows key [⊞].

2. Start typing the word network. You will soon be able to see Network Connections, as shown in Figure 5-11. Click on it.

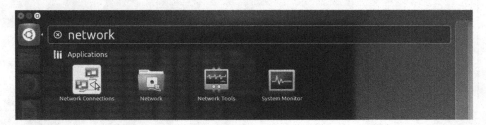

Figure 5-11. *Network connections in Ubuntu Dash*

3. From the Wired tab, select the wired connection and click the Edit button, as shown in Figure 5-12.

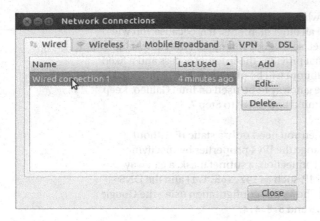

Figure 5-12. Selecting the wired connection

4. At this point, you need to determine whether you want a static IP only or a static IP with Internet access. If you need Internet access, go to Step 5. Otherwise, move to Step 7. Ubuntu is a little bit tricky in how it deals with IPv4 settings.

5. Change the IPv4 settings as follows: change Method to Shared to Other Computers and check the Available to All Users checkbox. Save the changes by clicking Save. Figure 5-13 shows how these settings must be made.

Figure 5-13. IPv4 Settings sharing the Internet

You might wonder why you did not specify the IP, subnet mask, gateway, and all other elements. It is because you will use a shared Internet, so Ubuntu will update the route table with the resource that provides the Internet access and a fixed IP determined by Ubuntu will be provided. The IP provided by Ubuntu must be the gateway to be used on Intel Galileo. Keep this information in mind and move to Step 7.

6. This step is used when you need only a static IP without Internet access. Change the IPv4 properties by specifying an IP for your local connection, a subnet mask, a gateway (usually your router IP, such as 192.168.1.1) and the DNS servers. Figure 5-14 shows this configuration using the Google DNS servers 8.8.8.8 and 8.8.4.4.

Figure 5-14. IPv4 properties with static IP only

7. Power on Intel Galileo and connect to the computer using the Ethernet cable. In few seconds, the wired connection will be ready.

8. Open a Linux terminal shell on Ubuntu by pressing CTRL+ALT+T and typing ifconfig eth0 to check the configuration that Ubuntu gave to your eth0.

   If you selected a shared Internet connection, you probably will see the static IP that Ubuntu provided. Otherwise you will see the IP that you configured in Step 6.

```
mcramon@mcramon-ThinkPad-T520:/media/F42E-D989$ ifconfig eth0
eth0      Link encap:Ethernet HWaddr 3c:97:0e:15:67:91
          inet addr:10.42.0.1 Bcast:10.42.0.255 Mask:255.255.255.0
          inet6 addr: fe80::3e97:eff:fe15:6791/64 Scope:Link
          UP BROADCAST RUNNING MULTICAST MTU:1500 Metric:1
          RX packets:38 errors:0 dropped:0 overruns:0 frame:0
          TX packets:208 errors:0 dropped:0 overruns:0 carrier:0
          collisions:0 txqueuelen:1000
          RX bytes:7616 (7.6 KB) TX bytes:36586 (36.5 KB)
          Interrupt:20 Memory:f2500000-f2520000
```

9. At this point, your Ubuntu is ready to establish a local connection with Intel Galileo. The last step is to configure Intel Galileo for a static IP. Read the section "Configuring Intel Galileo for Static IPs" to learn how to do so.

A Common Problem with Ubuntu and Multiple Adapters

If you are losing your Internet connection on Ubuntu when the Ethernet cable is connected to Intel Galileo and its properly powered on, it means you have a masquerading problem with your IP route (MASQ). To fix this issue, open a Ubuntu command shell and type the following (this code assumes wlan0 is the adapter that gives you access to the Internet and the local adapter used to connect Intel Galileo is eth0):

```
sudo -i
echo 1 > /proc/sys/net/ipv4/ip_forward
/sbin/iptables -t nat -A POSTROUTING -o wlan0 -j MASQUERADE
/sbin/iptables -A FORWARD -i wlan0 -o eth0 -m state --state
RELATED,ESTABLISHED -j ACCEPT
/sbin/iptables -A FORWARD -i eth0 -o wlan0 -j ACCEPT
```

Then remove your Ethernet cable and reconnect. After a few seconds, when the local connection is re-established, try to ping Intel with the ping www.intel.com command to test whether your Internet is working.

263

Configuring on MacOSX 10.0

It's quite easy to set up an IP connection on a Mac and make this connection offer Internet access to Intel Galileo connected via Ethernet. The first thing you need to do is determine if your Mac has an Ethernet adaptor. If it doesn't, you need to order one. One example of such an adapter is the Thunderbolt to Gigabit Ethernet adapter, which costs around $30 and is shown in Figure 5-15.

Figure 5-15. *Thunderbolt to gigabit Ethernet*

There are other more affordable adapters in the market that use the USB interface, but considering the limited number of USB ports on the Mac and the stability offered by this product, it is the best choice in my opinion.

The steps to set a static IP with an Internet connection are as follows:

1. Disconnect the Ethernet cable.

2. Click on System Preferences and then on Network.

3. Change the Configure IPv4 listbox to Manually and then add the IP address, the subnet mask, and the gateway. Note that the gateway is named Router. Figure 5-16 shows an example.

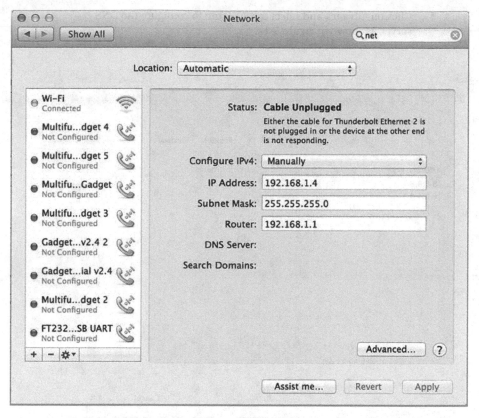

Figure 5-16. *Configuring the IP statically on MacOSX*

4. Click on Advance and select the DNS tab to configure the DNS server, as shown in Figure 5-17.

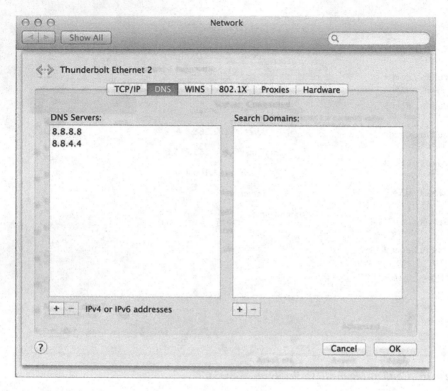

Figure 5-17. *Configuring the DNS servers on MacOSX*

5. Connect Intel Galileo to your Mac using the Ethernet cable. You should be able to see the cable with its Status changed to Connected, as shown in Figure 5-18.

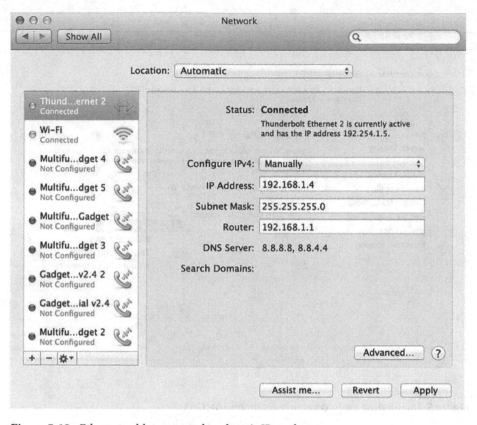

Figure 5-18. *Ethernet cable connected and static IP ready*

At this point, the setting needed to transfer files between Intel Galileo and the Mac is ready. If you do not want to share the Internet connection, you can move to the "Configuring Intel Galileo for Static IP" section. Otherwise, if you want Internet access on Intel Galileo through your Mac, continue to Step 6.

6. It's easy to share the Internet connection between different adapters on a Mac. Using the Apple menu, choose System Preferences and select Internet Sharing. Then select the adapter that will share the Internet connection and the adapter that will receive the sharing. For example, Figure 5-19 shows the WiFi adapter on MacOSX sharing the Internet connection with the Ethernet adaptor, wherein Intel Galileo is connected.

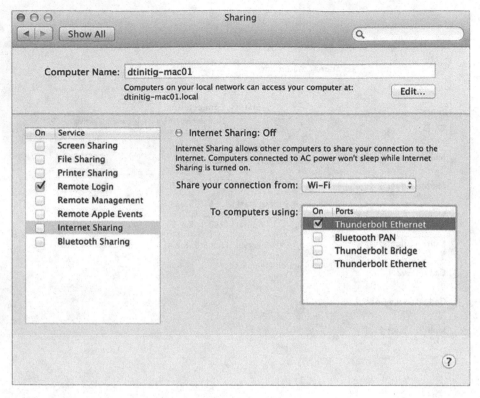

Figure 5-19. *Sharing an Internet connection on MacOSX*

Configuring Intel Galileo for Static IP

If you read the previous section, your computer is ready to connect Intel Galileo as a local connection via an Ethernet cable.

The static IP can be set manually using the command line. It is possible to persist the configuration after booting up and it can be configured using sketch. In the same way that the /etc/network/interfaces file is used to configure the DHCP connection, it is also used to configure the static IP.

It is recommended that you test the configuration using the command line before you persist the /etc/network/interfaces.

The next sections describe these methods.

Programming the IP with Intel Galileo's Linux Console

Using the ifconfig command, type the valid IP address to be configured in your network and enter the right subnet mask.

```
root@clanton:~# ifconfig eth0 192.168.1.27 netmask 255.255.255.0 up
```

Note if you use Ubuntu with a shared Internet, it is necessary to specify a static IP in the same network group of the IP that's automatically provided. For example, in Step 8 of the "Ubuntu 12.04" section, the IP was 10.42.0.1, so try to provide an IP close to this, such as 10.42.0.2.

Try to ping your computer using the static IP that your computer is using. If the ping fails, see if you need to include the gateway also.

For example, suppose your gateway is 192.168.1.1. Try the following procedure:

1. Check your route using the route command:

```
root@clanton:~# route
Kernel IP routing table
Destination     Gateway     Genmask         Flags  Metric Ref  Use Iface
192.168.1.0     *           255.255.255.0   U      0      0    0   eth0
```

2. If the gateway is not specified, add a default route to it. Use the route command again:

```
root@clanton:~# route add default gw 192.168.1.1 netmask 255.255.255.0
```

3. Check if the route was added successfully:

```
root@clanton:~# route
Kernel IP routing table
Destination     Gateway       Genmask         Flags  Metric Ref  Use Iface
default         192.168.1.1   255.255.255.0   UG     0      0    0   eth0
192.168.1.0     *             255.255.255.0   U      0      0    0   eth0
```

4. Try to ping your computer. Suppose your computer uses the IP 192.168.1.22 for the local connection:

```
root@clanton:~# ping 192.168.1.22
PING 192.168.1.22 (192.168.1.22): 56 data bytes
64 bytes from 192.168.1.22: seq=0 ttl=128 time=3.018 ms
64 bytes from 192.168.1.22: seq=1 ttl=128 time=1.795 ms
64 bytes from 192.168.1.22: seq=2 ttl=128 time=1.879 ms
```

If you are able to ping your computer, your configuration is fine and you can persist this configuration in /etc/network/interfaces.

Persisting the Static Configuration

The static IP configuration can be done in the file /etc/network/interfaces.

Using the Linux command console, open this file (you can use vi) and replace the following lines:

```
auto eth0
iface eth0 inet dhcp
iface eth1 inet dhcp
```

Replace the IPs with the IP of your interest:

```
auto eth0
iface eth0 inet static
address 192.168.1.27
netmask 255.255.255.0
gateway 192.168.1.1
```

You can restart the network configuration using the following command:

```
root@clanton:~# /etc/init.d/networking restart
```

Or you can reboot Intel Galileo using the reboot command. Try to ping your computer or router. If it does not work, try to configure the connection manually, as explained in the previous section, in order to understand what's wrong with the configuration.

Configuring the IP via Sketch

The configuration of IP using sketch it is quite simple. Since Intel Galileo is powered by a Linux OS, it is possible to use functions that make system calls, for example, system and popen.

Listing 5-5 shows an example of how to configure the IP statically using system calls.

Listing 5-5. configure_static_ip.ino

```
void setup() {
  // put your setup code here, to run once:

system("ifconfig eth0 192.168.1.28 netmask 255.255.255.0 up");
system("route add default gw 192.168.1.1 netmask 255.255.255.0");

}

void loop() {
  // put your main code here, to run repeatedly:

}
```

This code is so simple that does not need a review section. The system call exactly the same commands explained in the section "Programming the IP with Intel Galileo's Linux console".

Simplifying the Sketches by Removing the Ethernet Objects

As mentioned, the Ethernet API was created for Ethernet shields. In Intel Galileo, if the interface eth0 is configured on a Linux context, the Ethernet object becomes useless.

For example, suppose you have you IP configured on Intel Galileo Linux and your computer is also sharing the Internet access to Intel Galileo. Then you decide to run the example in Listing 5-4 and remove or comment out the Ethernet object from the code. In this case, the setup() function will look like this:

```
void setup()
{
  // Open serial communications and wait for port to open:
  Serial.begin(9600);
   while (!Serial) {
    ; // wait for serial port to connect. Needed for Leonardo only
  }

/* THIS CODE IS COMMENTED!!! REMOVED FROM THE LOGIC!!!!
   Ethernet object is not being used!!!!

  // start Ethernet and UDP
  if (Ethernet.begin(mac) == 0) {
    Serial.println("Failed to configure Ethernet using DHCP");
    // no point in carrying on, so do nothing forevermore:
    for(;;)
      ;
  }
*/

  Udp.begin(localPort);
}
```

You can compile the example again, and with the Internet working on Intel Galileo, the example runs without problems. Thus, the Ethernet object is useless when the IP is already configured on Linux.

The sketch will work not with the Ethernet object.

Transferring Files Between Intel Galileo and Computers

This section describes how to transfer files between an Intel Galileo board and your computers through a TCP/IP connection, SD card, or USB pen drive.

If you have an IP configured using the procedures mentioned in this chapter, you will be able to transfer files using secure copy (scp) or ftp. It doesn't matter if the adaptor is a mini-PCIe WiFi card or simply an Ethernet cable, you simply need to provide the IP on Intel Galileo and determine if this IP is achievable on your computer.

If you are using WiFi, check the IP using the Linux terminal shell and typing ifconfig wlan0. If you are using an Ethernet cable, you can check it by typing ifconfig eth0. The previous sections in this chapter explain the procedures you need to follow to have a functional IP using WiFi or Ethernet.

Using ftp

After you set the IP on your Intel Galileo it is necessary to start the ftpd deamon. To use the ftp with a standard port, type the following command into the Linux terminal shell: tcpsvd 0 ftp ftpd -w &. For example, suppose you want to establish a static IP and start the ftp deamon:

```
root@clanton:~# ifconfig eth0 192.168.1.27 netmask 255.255.255.0 up
root@clanton:~# tcpsvd 0 ftp ftpd -w &
```

On your computer using a terminal shell, you can use the ftp and pass the Intel Galileo IP using root as the username:

```
C:\Users\mcramon>ftp 192.168.1.27
Connected to 192.168.1.27.
220 Operation successful
User (192.168.1.27:(none)): root
230 Operation successful
```

After this, you can transfer files between your computer and Intel Galileo using the regular ftp commands. For example, suppose you want to extract a binary file called a.bin, which is located in /home/root on Intel Galileo:

```
ftp> bin
200 Operation successful
ftp> get a.bin
200 Operation successful
150 Opening BINARY connection for a.bin (3 bytes)
226 Operation successful
```

If, for some reason, you want to change the ftp deamon port to something, you just need to change the standard port (called port in the command) to the specific port you want. For example, if you want to start the ftpd deamon using the port 1080, but you already have a ftp deamon running, you can kill the deamon and start a new one by specifying the new port:

```
root@clanton:~# kill -9 $(pidof tcpsvd)
root@clanton:~# tcpsvd 0 1080 ftpd -w &
```

Note that ftp, which represents the standard port number 21, is replaced by 1080.

Using scp or pscp

If you are a Linux or MacOSX user, you can transfer files using scp tool.

If you are a Windows user, you can install a free software program called pscp.exe, which is similar to the scp tool. The installation of pscp.exe on Windows is described in the section "Tools to Be Used (Needed on Windows Only)" when an example of hacking involving the IDE is discussed. Follow the procedure to download and copy the pscp.exe file to your preferable directory.

By default, once you have an IP established on your Intel Galileo and the IP is reachable by your computer (test it using the ping command), you simply use scp or pscp. For example, imagine you have a static IP of 192.168.1.27 set on your board and you want to transfer a file named test.txt to the /home/root directory on your Intel Galileo. The commands to be used on the Linux command shell are as follows.

- On Linux or MacOSX:

```
mcramon@mcramon-ThinkPad-T520:$ scp test.txt root@192.168.1.27:/home/root/.
```

- On Windows with pscp.exe installed:

```
C:\Users\mcramon\tools>pscp -scp test.txt root@192.168.1.27:/home/root/.
test.txt | 0 kB | 0.0 kB/s | ETA: 00:00:00 | 100%
```

Note that there is a slight difference in the command syntax between pscp and scp. On Windows, pscp.exe requires that the protocol be specified. That's why -scp is the first argument when the tool is invoked.

Using an SD Card

It's possible to transfer files using an SD card even if you are running an SD image.

Your SD card must be formatted as FAT or FAT32. Accessing the files in the SD card depends on if you are using an SPI image or an SD card image on Intel Galileo.

SPI Images with SD Card Inserted on Demand

If you are using an SPI image instead of an SD card image, as soon you connect your SD card, the device will be mounted and it will be accessible from /media/mmcblk0p1.

You can confirm this by typing fdisk -l into the Linux terminal shell:

```
root@clanton:/media/mmcblk0p1# fdisk -l

Disk /dev/mmcblk0: 3965 MB, 3965190144 bytes
49 heads, 48 sectors/track, 3292 cylinders
Units = cylinders of 2352 * 512 = 1204224 bytes
```

```
Device Boot      Start      End    Blocks   Id System
/dev/mmcblk0p1       4      3293   3868160   b  Win95 FAT32
```

If you enter the /media/mmcblk0p1 folder, the files from your SD card will be there. For example:

```
root@clanton:/media# cd /media/mmcblk0p1/
root@clanton:/media/mmcblk0p1# ls
test.txt
```

SD Card Image

If you are using an SD card image, you can include on the SD card the kernel, sysimage, grub, and all files needed to make your Intel Galileo boot from the SD card.

In this case, you need to access the /media/realroot folder.

For example, suppose you have a file called HI_I_AM_NEW_FILE.txt in the root of the SD card that you will use as the SD image. If you access /media/realroot, you will see something like this:

```
root@clanton:/ # cd /media/realroot/
root@clanton:/media/realroot# ls
HI_I_AM_NEW_FILE.txt
boot
bzImage
core-image-minimal-initramfs-clanton.cpio.gz
grub.efi
image-full-galileo-clanton.ext3
```

With all the files accessible, you can copy them to any other folder using the regular cp command.

Using a USB Pen Drive

If you have an Intel Galileo Gen 2, you can connect a USB pen drive directly to the OTG USB port. However, if you have the first generation of Intel Galileo, you need to use a micro USB to USB 2.0 OTG adapter, as shown in Figure 5-20.

Figure 5-20. *Micro USB to USB 2.0 OTG adapter*

If you need such an adapter, do not buy one in an "L" shape because, if you are using the serial audio jack cable, the adapter will press against the audio jack and might damage your board.

With the adapter in place, you can connect the USB pen drive and see messages like these from the Linux terminal shell:

```
root@clanton:~# [ 3691.870165] usb 2-1: new high-speed USB device number 2
using ehci-pci
[ 3692.043645] scsi0 : usb-storage 2-1:1.0
[ 3693.128613] scsi 0:0:0:0: Direct-Access     Kingston DataTraveler 109
PMAP PQ : 0 ANSI: 0 CCS
[ 3693.171753] sd 0:0:0:0: Attached scsi generic sg0 type 0
[ 3694.815187] sd 0:0:0:0: [sda] 15240576 512-byte logical blocks: (7.80
GB/7.26 GiB)
[ 3694.827134] sd 0:0:0:0: [sda] Write Protect is off
[ 3694.834139] sd 0:0:0:0: [sda] No Caching mode page present
[ 3694.839721] sd 0:0:0:0: [sda] Assuming drive cache: write through
[ 3694.855254] sd 0:0:0:0: [sda] No Caching mode page present
[ 3694.860912] sd 0:0:0:0: [sda] Assuming drive cache: write through
[ 3694.891920]  sda: sda1
[ 3694.906548] sd 0:0:0:0: [sda] No Caching mode page present
[ 3694.912207] sd 0:0:0:0: [sda] Assuming drive cache: write through
[ 3694.918365] sd 0:0:0:0: [sda] Attached SCSI removable disk
```

You can also check with fdisk -1, as follows:

```
root@clanton:/media/realroot# fdisk -1

Disk /dev/mmcblk0: 3965 MB, 3965190144 bytes
49 heads, 48 sectors/track, 3292 cylinders
Units = cylinders of 2352 * 512 = 1204224 bytes

Device Boot      Start      End     Blocks  Id   System
/dev/mmcblk0p1       4     3293    3868160   b   Win95 FAT32

Disk /dev/sda: 7803 MB, 7803174912 bytes
122 heads, 58 sectors/track, 2153 cylinders
Units = cylinders of 7076 * 512 = 3622912 bytes

Device  Boot    Start      End    Blocks  Id   System
/dev/sda1 *          2     2154   7616256   b   Win95 FAT32
```

This code indicates that Intel Galileo recognized your USB pen drive and the content can be accessed in the /media/sda1 folder. For example:

```
root@clanton:~# cd /media/sda1/
root@clanton:/media/sda1# ls
NewFile1.jpg
NewFile1.png
NewFile2.jpg
NewFile2.png
NewFile3.png
NewFile4.png
NewFile5.png
NewFile6.png
NewFile7.png
poky-edison-eglibc-i686-edison-image-core2-32-toolchain-1.6
```

With all the files accessible, you can copy them to any other folder using the regular cp command.

Hacking the IDE to Improve the Sketch Transfer

Chapter 3 contains a section called "Troubleshoot with Drivers" that describes several workarounds and procedures for minimizing the problems with the Gadget serial driver, especially on Windows.

Besides the problem with drivers, Intel Galileo and Intel Galileo Gen 2 use an old protocol to transfer files called ZMODEM. So the IDE and the Intel Galileo boards talk to each other over a serial Gadget driver using the ZMODEM protocol.

This ZMODEM protocol is managed by two applications: lrz runs in the Intel Galileo boards and is used to received files with ZMODEM (the "r" on this case stands for "receive") and lsz runs in the IDE and is used to send files with the ZMODEM protocol (the "s" stands for "send").

These two software protocols are based on command lines and certain problems might occur during the file transfer. In order to manage the corner cases, an application called clloader runs like a deamon in the Intel board and manages the lrz tool. The same process happens on the IDE but there is only a script responsible for sending the file to the Intel Galileo board and for invoking the lsz.

Figure 5-21 shows a simplified stack of how these software protocols interact with other using the Gadget serial driver.

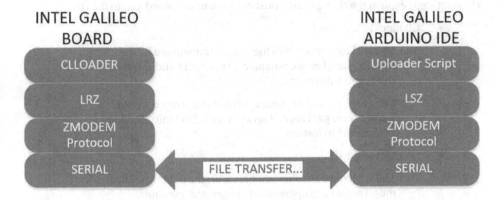

Figure 5-21. *The regular file transfer mechanism*

The problem is, even with the clloader application, the architecture that transfers the files is still poor because there is no real state machine implemented between the clloader and the script responsible for transferring from the IDE. When something fails, the serial hangs. This can force the IDE to close and reboot the computer.

How the Hacked IDE Works

If your Intel Galileo board has an IP that's reachable from your computer, it is possible to make some changes to the IDE and program to transfer the files using TCP/IP. This brings a significant improvement in terms of stability because it reduces significantly the serials handling during the sketch transfer. The serial objects are still available without problems.

It does not matter if Intel Galileo is using a WiFi card or an Ethernet cable connected to the router or computer. If there is an IP available, it is possible to hack the IDE and improve the file transfer.

Before implementing these changes, you need to understand some details about how the IDE and Intel Galileo boards work. Take a look at the new mechanism proposed in Figure 5-22.

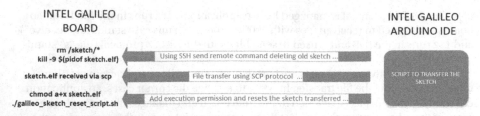

Figure 5-22. *The hacked file transfer mechanism via TCP/IP*

Configuring the Sketch Transfer

The next steps explain the changes that must be done to the board and to the IDE.

- Changes to the board:

  1. When clloader receives the sketch transmitted by the IDE, the sketches are renamed sketch.elf and saved in the /sketch directory.

  2. The galileo_sketch_reset_script.sh script is located in /opt/cln/galileo/. It sends a signal to Linux, forcing sketch.elf to restart.

- Changes to the IDE:

  1. The IDE contains some text files with the platform*.txt moniker for each operational system that contains information as to which software protocol is responsible for uploading the sketch to the board, the compiler to be used and the directives used in the compilation. They are located in the ...\arduino-1.5.3\hardware\arduino\x86 directory relative to your IDE installation. The files are as follows:

     platform.linux.txt is used with Linux 32 OS bits.

     platform.linux64.txt is used with Linux 64 OS bits.

     platform.osx.txt is used with MacOSX.

     platform.win.txt is used with Windows OS.

Among compilation directives and compilers to be used, these files tell the IDE which tool or script must be used to upload the files, as well as the pattern (arguments) passed to this tool.

Thus, when the IDE is started, the file that corresponds to the operational system is opened and the IDE is properly configured.

When the user asks the IDE to upload the sketch in the board, the scripts in this file will be responsible for the transfer; they call the lsz tool as explained.

Hacking the Transfers

Now that you understood the files you must change in the IDE and what the board does when the sketches are received, the changes are quite simple. However, it's necessary to prepare your desktop with the tools required to make this hack possible.

If you are a MacOSX or Linux user, you do not need to download any tool. If you are a Windows user, you need to download some free tools.

After you have all the tools you need, you must make changes to the platform files, as explained next.

Tools to Be Used (Needed for Windows Only)

As you can see in Figure 5-22, the files will be transferred using the SCP protocol. Remote commands are sent to the boards using ssl.

The SCP protocol can be used with the scp command-line tool on Linux and MacOSX. Unfortunately, it's not available on Windows. However, there is a free tool called pscp.exe that works like the scp command-line tool.

The remote commands are sent using the SSL protocol, which can be used with the ssl command-line tool on Linux and MacOSX. Again, there is a free tool for Windows called plink.exe.

Both of these Windows tools can be downloaded from http://www.chiark. greenend.org.uk/~sgtatham/putty/download.html. You need to place the pscp.exe and plink.exe files in the ...\ arduino-1.5.3\hardware\tools\x86\bin directory, relative to your IDE installation directory. Both tools do not require any installation; just download and move them to the right folder.

This folder is where most external tools are installed for the IDE. Figure 5-23 shows this directory on a Windows system, with all the other tools including lsz and some cygwin-related files present.

Name	Date modified	Type	Size
bash.exe	6/20/2014 3:09 PM	Application	524 KB
cyggcc_s-1.dll	6/20/2014 3:09 PM	Application extens...	104 KB
cygiconv-2.dll	6/20/2014 3:09 PM	Application extens...	986 KB
cygintl-8.dll	6/20/2014 3:09 PM	Application extens...	35 KB
cygncurses++w-10.dll	6/20/2014 3:09 PM	Application extens...	52 KB
cygncursesw-10.dll	6/20/2014 3:09 PM	Application extens...	245 KB
cygreadline7.dll	6/20/2014 3:09 PM	Application extens...	163 KB
cygwin1.dll	6/20/2014 3:09 PM	Application extens...	3,043 KB
grep.exe	6/20/2014 3:09 PM	Application	190 KB
lsz.exe	6/20/2014 3:09 PM	Application	301 KB
md5sum.exe	6/20/2014 3:09 PM	Application	33 KB
plink.exe	7/13/2014 4:16 PM	Application	304 KB
pscp.exe	7/13/2014 1:43 PM	Application	316 KB
Readme	6/20/2014 3:09 PM	File	1 KB
strings.exe	6/20/2014 3:09 PM	Application	819 KB
sysimage-galileo-1.0.2.cap	6/20/2014 3:09 PM	CAP File	7,126 KB
upgrade.sh	6/20/2014 3:09 PM	SH File	1 KB

Figure 5-23. *The command IDE tool directory on Windows*

Recall that if you are a Linux or MacOSX user, you do not need to download an external tool.

Changes to the Platform Files

Open the platform file related to the operational system using your favorite test editor. For example, if you are a Windows user, you open the platform.win.txt file.

All platform files are similar because they contain the same configuration fields. The section that really matters is X86 Uploader/Programmers tools. The following lines are an example of the platform.win.txt file.

```
# X86 Uploader/Programmers tools
# -------------------
tools.izmirdl.cmd.path={runtime.ide.path}/hardware/arduino/x86/tools/
izmir/clupload_win.sh

#todo: pass extra args to shell script
tools.izmirdl.upload.params.verbose=-vvvvvv
tools.izmirdl.upload.params.quiet=-q

tools.izmirdl.upload.pattern={runtime.ide.path}/hardware/tools/x86/bin/bash
--verbose  --noprofile {cmd.path} {runtime.ide.path}/hardware/tools/x86/bin
{build.path}/{build.project_name}.elf {serial.port}
```

The tools.izmirdl.cmd.path field specifies the tool or scripts that will be used to upload the sketch. In Windows, a script called clupload_win.sh is used.

The tools.izmirdl.upload.pattern field specifies the pattern of command calls. In other words, it determines the arguments to be passed to the tool specified in tools.izmirdl.cmd.path and how they must be called.

Basically these two fields are critical for making this hack work.

If you open other platform files, you will see that these fields have minimal changes. For example, for Linux 64 bits the platform file is platform.linux64.txt, the script used to upload is clupload_linux.sh (same for Linux 32 bits), and it's clupload_osx.sh for MacOSX.

The process for changing the platform files is the same for Linux 64 and 32 bits and MacOSX. It's shown in the following lines:

```
# X86 Uploader/Programmers tools
# --------------------

tools.izmirdl.cmd.path="{runtime.ide.path}/hardware/arduino/x86/tools/
izmir/clupload_linux_and_osx_hacked.sh"

tools.izmirdl.upload.params.verbose=-vvvvvv
tools.izmirdl.upload.params.quiet=-q

tools.izmirdl.upload.pattern=/bin/bash --verbose  --noprofile {cmd.path}
{build.path}/{build.project_name}.elf
```

The script used with Linux and MacOSX is the same (clupload_linux_and_osx_hacked.sh) and only one argument is used ({build.path}/{build.project_name}.elf), because there is no needed to indicate the path of an external tool, since ssh and scp are part of the Linux and MacOSX distributions.

With only one argument used, the script for Linux and MacOSX is simpler than for Windows:

```
#!/bin/bash

echo "starting download script"
echo "Args to shell:" $*

# ARG 1: Path of tools used to transfer and send remote commands
# ARG 2: Elf File to download

# ATTENTION: ADD HERE YOU IP
galileo_ip="10.42.0.2"

# cleaning the sketch in /sketch folder
ssh root@$galileo_ip 'rm /sketch/*;kill -9 $(pidof sketch.elf)'

#transfer using scp protocol
scp $1 root@$galileo_ip:/sketch/sketch.elf
```

```
#giving permission to be executed and reseting to start the sketch
 ssh root@$galileo_ip 'chmod a+x /sketch/sketch.elf;/opt/cln/galileo/
galileo_sketch_reset_script.sh'
```

```
#END!!
```

The changes name the platform files. In other words, a new script is created to transfer the files and the scripts use the respective command-line tools to transfer the files (scp or pscp.exe) and send remote commands (ssl or plink.exe).

The platform files are available in the code/hacked_platforms_files folder of this book. However, you need to change to the right IP address presented in the transfer scripts.

All hacked files can be found in the code/hacked_platforms_files folder of this chapter, including the platform files and upload scripts for Windows, Linux 32 and 64 bits, and MacOSX.

Practical Example of a Hack

The following hack uses Windows, which is basically the same as Linux and Mac.

Step 1: Changing the Platform File

The first step is to create a new script to replace the clupload_win.sh file with something else, such as with clupload_win_hacked.sh.

tools.izmirdl.cmd.path="{runtime.ide.path}/hardware/arduino/x86/tools/
izmir/**clupload_win_hacked.sh"**

Imagine this script will receive two arguments—the path you have the tools installed and the sketch's filename. The instruction you received a couple pages ago was to download them to the folder.

Changing the pattern field based on this, you have:

tools.izmirdl.upload.pattern={runtime.ide.path}/hardware/tools/x86/bin/bash
--verbose --noprofile {cmd.path} **{runtime.ide.path}\hardware\tools\x86\bin
{build.path}/{build.project_name}.elf**

Stripping this line, you have:

- {runtime.ide.path}/hardware/tools/x86/bin/bash: No changes here. This line is kept because it is the bash that will call the script.

- --verbose --noprofile: No changes here either. This line is kept to keep verbose when bash invokes the script.

- {cmd.path}: No changes. This is the path and script to be called. Basically, it's a call to the path and script programmed by tools.izmirdl.cmd.path.

- {runtime.ide.path}\hardware\tools\x86\bin: This is the first parameter in the script and basically is where the tools are installed (pscp.exe and plink.exe).

- {build.path}/{build.project_name}.elf: This is the second parameter in the script and contains the sketch name with the .elf extension created by the IDE. This is the sketch that will be transmitted to the board.

If you still don't understand, basically this line is doing something like the following pseudo-code:

bash <VERBOSE_OPTIONS> <SCRIPT_NAME> <WHERE_THE_TOOLS_ARE> <THE_SKETCH_TO_BE_TRANSMITTED>

For Linux and MacOSX, the changes are simple because they assume that the scp and ssh tools are already on the operational system, so it's not necessary to specify the directory of an external tool. For example, the change to Linux 64-bit (file platform_linux64.txt) is:

```
# X86 Uploader/Programmers tools
# -------------------

tools.izmirdl.cmd.path="{runtime.ide.path}/hardware/arduino/x86/tools/
izmir/clupload_linux_and_osx_hacked.sh"

tools.izmirdl.upload.params.verbose=-vvvvvv
tools.izmirdl.upload.params.quiet=-q

tools.izmirdl.upload.pattern=/bin/bash --verbose  --noprofile {cmd.path}
{build.path}/{build.project_name}.elf
```

As you can see, only the path to the sketch .elf file is passed to the script that will be uploaded.

Step 2: Creating the Hacked Script

The script will do exactly what Figure 5-22 shows. Listing 5-6 is an example of the clupload_win_hacked.sh file created for Windows.

Listing 5-6. clupload_win_hacked.sh

```
#!/bin/sh

echo "starting download script"
echo "Args to shell:" $*

# ARG 1: Path of tools used to transfer and send remote commands
# ARG 2: Elf File to download

# ATTENTION: ADD HERE YOU IP
galileo_ip="192.168.1.27"

# cleaning the sketch in /sketch folder
$1/plink root@$galileo_ip 'rm /sketch/*;kill -9 $(pidof sketch.elf)'

#transfer using scp protocol
$1/pscp -scp $2 root@$galileo_ip:/sketch/sketch.elf

#giving permission to be executed and reseting to start the sketch
$1/plink root@$galileo_ip 'chmod a+x /sketch/sketch.elf;/opt/cln/galileo/
galileo_sketch_reset_script.sh'

#END!!
```

For Linux and MacOSX, the upload script is simpler because ssh and scp are called directly. The same script can be used for both operational systems, as you can see in Listing 5-7.

Listing 5-7. clupload_linux_and_osx_hacked.sh

```
#!/bin/bash

echo "starting download script"
echo "Args to shell:" $*

# ARG 1: Path of tools used to transfer and send remote commands
# ARG 2: Elf File to download

# ATTENTION: ADD HERE YOU IP
galileo_ip="10.42.0.2"

# cleaning the sketch in /sketch folder
ssh root@$galileo_ip 'rm /sketch/*;kill -9 $(pidof sketch.elf)'
```

```
#transfer using scp protocol
scp $1 root@$galileo_ip:/sketch/sketch.elf

#giving permission to be executed and reseting to start the sketch
 ssh root@$galileo_ip 'chmod a+x /sketch/sketch.elf;/opt/cln/galileo/
galileo_sketch_reset_script.sh'

#END!!
```

Step 3: Reviewing the Script

As programmed by the pattern field in the platform file, the first parameter is where the transfer and remote commands tools are installed and the second is the sketch with the full path.

You need to change the galileo_ip variable to your Intel Galileo IP address.

The current sketch is then removed and the sketch process is stopped from the board through remote commands. The rm command is used to remove the sketch.elf file and the kill command is used to kill the current sketch.elf process. The process ID is returned by the pidof command:

```
# cleaning the sketch in /sketch folder
$1/plink root@$galileo_ip 'rm /sketch/*;kill -9 $(pidof sketch.elf)'
```

The sketch is then transferred to the board:

```
#transfer using scp protocol
$1/pscp -scp $2 root@$galileo_ip:/sketch/sketch.elf
```

Finally, the sketch receives permission to be executed and is restarted:

```
#giving permission to be executed and reseting to start the sketch
$1/plink root@$galileo_ip 'chmod a+x /sketch/sketch.elf;/opt/cln/galileo/
galileo_sketch_reset_script.sh'
```

Step 4: Running the Hacked IDE

First of all, if you have an IDE running, close it. The IDE reads the platform file changes only when they initially run, so do not expect the changes to the platform files and the new script created to be read dynamically.

Make sure you replace the platform file to the directory ...\arduino-1.5.3\ hardware\arduino\x86.

Also make sure you set your Intel Galileo IP in the script and copy the script to the right directory. In this example, the script must be moved to the .../arduino-1.5.3\ hardware\arduino\x86\tools\izmir directory.

Before you run the IDE, make sure the public keys were informed during an ssh (or plink.exe for Windows) connection. There is no way to accept the ssh connection from the IDE since it is necessary to confirm by pressing the Y key on the keyboard. For Linux and MacOSX, run ssh root@<INTEL GALILEO'S IP>. For Windows, run plink. exe root@<INTEL GALILEO'S IP>. If you are using Linux or MacOSX, you can modify the script and add the ssh call:

```
ssh -o "StrictHostKeyChecking no" root@<INTEL GALILEO'S IP>
```

With this command, the ssh connection will be accepted without prompting.

Run the IDE and select a sketch from the examples or choose some of your own sketches. Transfer to the board as you usually do with the IDE.

If everything was okay, you should see the output of bash script execution in the IDE, as shown in Figure 5-24.

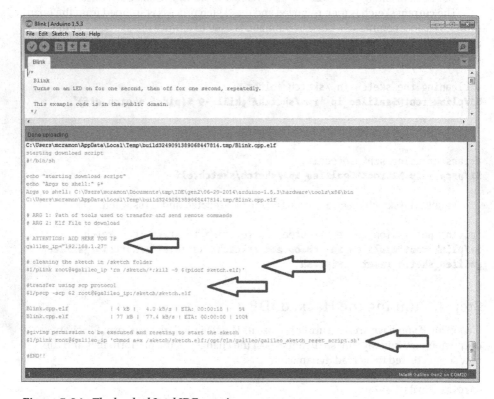

Figure 5-24. *The hacked Intel IDE running*

Note that each arrow in the figure represents the execution of the hacked script.

Summary

This chapter is very important because it explained how to connect Intel Galileo with the computer and the Internet and increase the possibilities for creating projects that require external commands. It also explained how to send information to remote computers and devices, which helps Intel Galileo connect to the world.

You also learned how to use the WiFi and Ethernet API and how these APIs can be improved. You can simplify their usage with Intel Galileo when a static or dynamic IP is configured in the board.

This chapter also explained how to transfer files using ftp and scp. You learned about an alternative for transferring sketches. You can hack the IDE in order to transfer files using the secure copy protocol instead of using the old z-modem protocol handled by the clloader application, which is present in the BSP images. This significantly improves the stability of the IDE and the Intel Galileo boards.

CHAPTER 6

■ ■ ■

Tweeting with REST API 1.1

This chapter explains the procedure involved in posting messages using Twitter with REST API 1.1 and OAuth authentication directly from Intel Galileo boards, thereby enabling you to avoid intermediary web services. This chapter also explains how to integrate Linux scripts with sketch, the advantages of using Linux to post on Twitter, including the commands involved and the hardware required. It also explains why the examples provided by Intel Galileo IDE 1.5.3 do not work with Arduino boards.

Project Details

If you tried to post on Twitter using the code in `Examples->Ethernet->TwitterClient`, which is offered by IDE 1.5.3, you probably became frustrated. These examples don't work with Intel Galileo or on any board compatible with Arduino APIs.

The main reason for the failure is related to the new REST API 1.1. Twitter now requires a new authentication method and the messages have a new format as well. The old functions based on API 1.0 do not work anymore, which means thousands of applications around the world, including the examples in the Arduino IDE, don't work anymore either.

The authentication is based in `OAuth`, so the procedure involves processing the `sha1` algorithm. There are secret and token codes, encoded in base64, which is special format required by the API that forces string manipulations. The board must be able to provide timestamps according to the current real world time, which is independent of time zones or daylight savings time.

Some developers created web services that bridge between the Arduino boards and the Twitter servers. These web services compute the `sha1`, the encodes, and all the string manipulation, but require the developers to host the service in some server and have a public IP available. This complication increases the cost of your project and might affect its performance and stability.

The idea here is to explore the power offered by Linux OS and integrate with sketches, thereby avoiding a massive quantity of code. This will make the project efficient and simple.

The Linux shell script:

- Computes the `sha1` (secure hash algorithm based on a 160-bit hash value) and encodes to different bases using `openssl`.

- Manipulates the strings using `sed` and other tools.

- Posts messages using proper authorization, headers, and message using `curl`.

In the sketch, the code will interact with the script. It will show, in a few lines, its ability to post to a Twitter account.

Using the Linux capabilities offered by Intel Galileo, in few lines of code and scripting, you will be able to communicate with the Twitter server. You can therefore avoid a massive quantity of code and be free of licensing issues, huge code development, and debugging.

However, you must be able to create a Twitter account, get the secret code and token, understand how the software works, and understand the hardware requirements to make this project functional.

This chapter describes how to make posts, but if you understand how the software was created and the concept of Twitter APIs, you can change this software to accommodate the best API for your project.

Material List

Although you can do everything in this project using just the Ethernet interface already present on your board, it is recommended that you have the coin battery plugged into the board to persist the hardware clock (this is explained in more detail later in this chapter).

You can make the connection using the Ethernet, a WiFi, a modem, or any other kind of interface that gives you access to the Internet. The code and script involved does not require any special kind of client. This project uses the WiFi listed in Table 6-1.

Table 6-1. Optional Material

Quantity	Components
1	Intel Centrino Wireless-N 135
2	Dual band antennas 350mm cable 2118060-1 TE connectivity
1	3V coin battery
1	Coin battery holder case
2	Wires jumper 10cm long 1/4w female-male

System and Hardware Clock

Maybe you are wondering why I am discussing the system and hardware clock if all you have to do is simply post on Twitter? One of the key elements for computing the string base and getting authorization to post on Twitter is a timestamp.

This timestamp must be in sync with the rest of world, in other words, your board must have a valid and actual time and date. If you type date in the terminal shell as soon you log in, you will see something like this:

```
clanton login: root
root@clanton:~# date
Mon Jan  1 00:19:31 UTC 2001
```

This date represents the system time in UTC maintained by the kernel software. To check the hardware clock, use the hwclock command:

```
root@clanton:~# hwclock
Mon Jan  1 00:19:56 2001  0.000000 seconds
```

If you try to get the timestamp based on one of these dates, Twitter will not authorize because they are not synchronized with the real time.

There are several ways to fix the date and time according to the busybox help manual:

```
date
date [OPTIONS] [+FMT] [TIME]
Display time (using +FMT), or set time
Options:
        [-s] TIME       Set time to TIME
        -u              Work in UTC (don't convert to local time)
        -R              Output RFC-822 compliant date string
        -I[SPEC]        Output ISO-8601 compliant date string
                        SPEC='date' (default) for date only,
                        'hours', 'minutes', or 'seconds' for date and
                        time to the indicated precision
        -r FILE         Display last modification time of FILE
        -d TIME         Display TIME, not 'now'
        -D FMT          Use FMT for -d TIME conversion
Recognized TIME formats:
        hh:mm[:ss]
        [YYYY.]MM.DD-hh:mm[:ss]
        YYYY-MM-DD hh:mm[:ss]
        [[[[[YY]YY]MM]DD]hh]mm[.ss]
```

One format not documented here is MMDDhhmmYYYY. Change the date and clock using your preferable format. The following command uses YYYY-MM-DD hh:mm[:ss]:

```
root@clanton:~# date 2014.01.08-11:14:20
Wed Jan  8 11:14:20 UTC 2014
```

To synchronize the hardware clock, you can use the following command:

```
root@clanton:~# hwclock -w
```

Check the hardware and system clock again:

```
root@clanton:~# hwclock
Wed Jan  8 11:19:38 2014  0.000000 seconds
root@clanton:~# date
Wed Jan  8 11:19:42 UTC 2014
```

Updating the time clock might be irrelevant because if you decide do not use a coin battery attached to the BATT pins on Intel Galileo and if your system reboots, the clock will be reset and you will have the wrong date and clock again (Mon Jan 1 UTC 2001). This will cause an error if your sketches try to post messages again when they're restarted.

Several factors might force you to reboot your system, such as high temperatures if your board is not cooling properly, some instability in the firmware, some new driver or native application installed, and so on. Thus, it is recommended that you include the coin battery in your project if you want to run for several hours.

If you are interested in adding a coin battery to your system, read the next section. Otherwise, jump to the section entitled "Workaround with 1.5V Batteries" later in the chapter.

Assembling the Coin Battery

Connect two female connectors of the jumper wires to the BATT terminal on the Intel Galileo board, as shown in Figure 6-1.

Figure 6-1. Battery terminals location

Then weld the other end of jumper cable to the battery holder terminals according to the polarity provided by your case, as shown in Figure 6-2. Strip the end of the wires and then weld directly to the battery case's terminals.

Figure 6-2. *Coin battery 2032 in the case and the polarity*

Note that there are different coin battery cases and the polarity in the terminal varies depending on the model. Insert the coin battery in the case and use a voltmeter to check the right polarity before you weld the wires.

With the battery in the case and the case properly connected to the BATT terminals, Intel Galileo will be able to keep the date and time even when the system reboots.

Workaround with 1.5V Batteries

If you want test your project and preserve the hardware clock after the boot but you do not have a coin battery, it is possible to make a simple workaround using two AA or AAA batteries connected in a series. These are the same batteries you find in your TV remote control. Keep in mind that this is a temporary and dirty workaround. Table 6-2 lists the materials you need.

Table 6-2. *Materials for Temporary Battery Workaround*

Quantity	Components
2	AA or AAA 1.5 batteries
1	Tape
1	Wire plier or equivalent to strip wires
1	Voltmeter
2	Wires jumper 10cm long 1/4w female-male

Connect two 1.5 batteries in a series and tape them, strongly pushing one battery against the other. Using a voltmeter, make sure you have 3V in the battery terminals.

Then connect the two wire jumpers (female connectors) to the BATT terminals, as shown in Figure 6-1.

You should have something very ugly but temporarily functional, as shown in Figure 6-3.

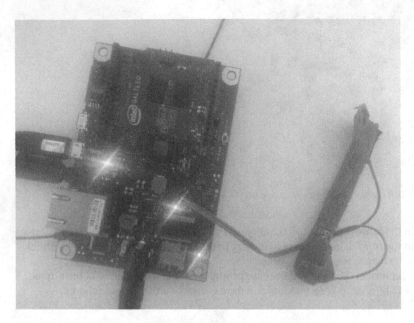

Figure 6-3. *Temporary workaround to keep hardware clock*

Creating a Twitter Application Account

The new Twitter API requires some elements like secret code and tokens. Such elements are automatically generated when you create an application account. You'll see how to do that in the next two sections.

The next steps describe how to create your account and how to avoid a potential bug in the Twitter server present as of the writing of this chapter.

Step 1: Creating Your Twitter Account

The first thing you need to have is an email. You can create an email account using the provider of your preference, including Gmail, Yahoo, or any other.

If you already have a Twitter account and you want to use it for your tests, you can skip to Step 2.

Otherwise, access the `https://twitter.com/signup` link (see Figure 6-4).

Figure 6-4. *Creating a Twitter account*

■ **Tip**　This step looks simple but you need to know a very important tip. After you create your Twitter account, you will be able to log in and use Twitter normally. However, in parallel you will receive a confirmation email. If you do not confirm it, in the next step, the Twitter application will fail.

You might feel lost because in fact you have a Twitter account, but you received a warning that it's not valid. As soon you create your Twitter account, check your email and confirm it. If you did not receive the confirmation email, you will be able to click the Resend Confirmation button at the top of screen as soon you log in, as indicated by the arrow in Figure 6-5.

Figure 6-5. *The Resend Confirmation button after you log in*

The next step is to create your Twitter application.

Step 2: Creating the Twitter Application

From this application you will receive the secret code and authentication token that you need to incorporate your C++ code.

Access the https://dev.twitter.com/apps/new link and using your confirmed Twitter account to log in (see Figure 6-6).

Figure 6-6. *Signing in to create the Twitter application*

The next screen will ask for some data related to your application. One of mandatory details is a website, as shown in Figure 6-7. Because you will not use it, feel free to add any website, like http://www.intel.com.

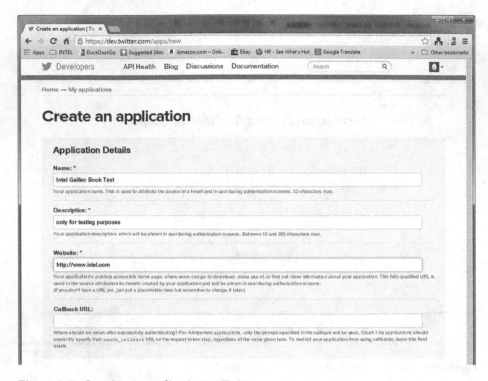

Figure 6-7. *Creating an application on Twitter*

After you fill all the required data, you will be able to see a screen with the data you entered. This screen also includes the OAuth settings data such as the consumer secret string and URL token access. See Figure 6-8.

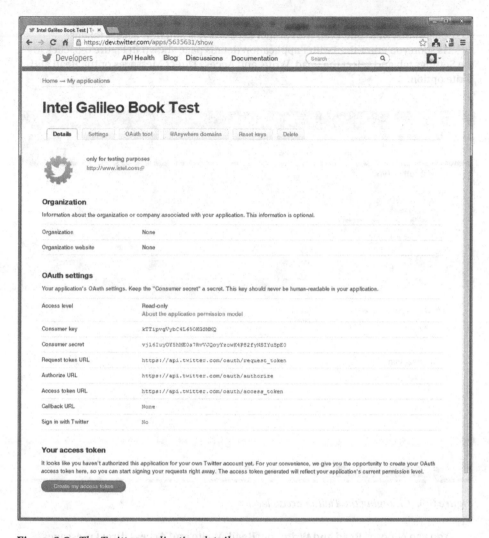

Figure 6-8. *The Twitter application details page*

At the bottom of this page is a button called Create My Access Token. You will need access tokens in order to make the software work; however, *do not* click on this button! You still need to change the access level.

Check on this same page the Access Level in the OAuth settings. Initially, it is Read-Only but considering you will post messages on Twitter, you need to change this access level in order to support write operations.

As of January, 2014, Twitter has a bug that's initiated when you create tokens by clicking the Create My Access Token button. If you create the tokens with read-only access, even if you change the access to read/write access and reset the tokens, your tokens still will have read-only access.

It took me several hours to figure out why the GET operations were working but the POST operations were not, even with proper access levels and new access tokens.

As soon you enter the Twitter application details page shown in Figure 6-9, click in the Settings tab and select the Read, Write, and Access Direct Messages or the Read and Write option.

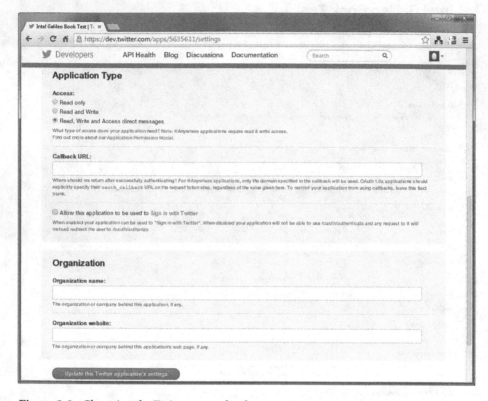

Figure 6-9. *Changing the Twitter access level*

You can choose **"Read and Write"** or **"Read, Write and Access direct messages"**. Then click in the Update this Twitter Application's Settings button on the bottom of the page.

Click again in the Details tab and wait a few seconds. Then reload the page by pressing F5. You will see that the access level was properly changed and you can click in the Create My Access Token button.

Wait a few seconds and then press the F5 key again. You will be able to see your access token, secret token, consumer key, and secret consumer key, as shown in Figure 6-10.

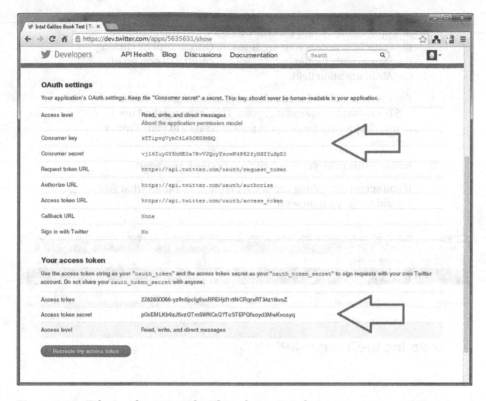

Figure 6-10. *Token and consumer keys have been created*

Creating a Script to Post Messages on Twitter

Once you have created a Twitter account and the application's tokens, you can initiate a creation of your software. The method in this chapter was used to POST messages on Twitter but you can create a different one if you understand the process. That means you can create a method to get data, create other types of POST methods, and any other functions provided by the Twitter API.

Step 1: Identifying the API

First of all, you must identify the structure of the POST API. To do so, follow the steps:

1. Open the developer console and access
   https://dev.twitter.com/console.

2. For the service, select https://api.twitter.com/1.1.

3. For the authentication, select OAuth1. When you're selecting this option, the Twitter console will ask you if you authorize the console to access your application. Only accept by clicking the Sign In with Twitter option. Your account will pop up in the Authentication field.

4. For the Select an API method option, select the API Tweet -> POST -> /statuses/update.json. This is the method used in this chapter. It allows you to post messages to your Twitter account.

5. In the Status field, you can write a message if you want.

    If you set up everything correctly, Figure 6-11 shows what you should see in your browser.

Figure 6-11. *Using the developer console to POST messages*

6. Click the Send button and you should have your status posted in your Twitter page. You should see the server response HTTP/1.1 200 OK. See Figure 6-12.

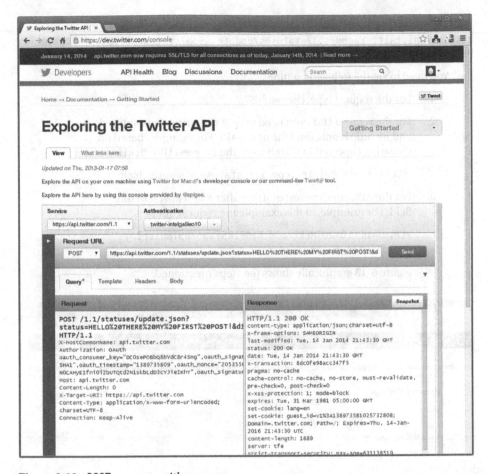

***Figure 6-12.** POST response with success*

7. After you send your post, copy the string generated in your POST to the clipboard. For example:

```
https://api.twitter.com/1.1/statuses/update.
json?status=HELLO%20THERE%20MY%20FIRST%20
POST&display_coordinates=false
```

Step 2: Generating the OAuth Signature with the OAuth Tool

Access your Twitter application again, as shown in Figure 6-8. You will see a tab called OAuth Tool.

On this tab there is a section called Request Settings. Based on the string captured previously, you should be able to fill these fields properly.

Suppose the string you captured is as follows:

```
https://api.twitter.com/1.1/statuses/update.json?status=HELLO%20THERE%20
MY%20FIRST%20POST&display_coordinates=false
```

You need to set the following settings:

1. For the request type, choose POST.

2. For the request URL, you need to split the string you captured and include it only until the name API. For example, based on the string captured in this chapter, the Request URL field is:

    ```
    https://api.twitter.com/1.1/statuses/update.json
    ```

3. For the API, copy the rest of string after & and post it in this field. For example, in this example the request query is:

    ```
    status=HELLO%20THERE%20MY%20FIRST%20POST&display_
    coordinates=false
    ```

Figure 6-13 graphically shows the steps mentioned.

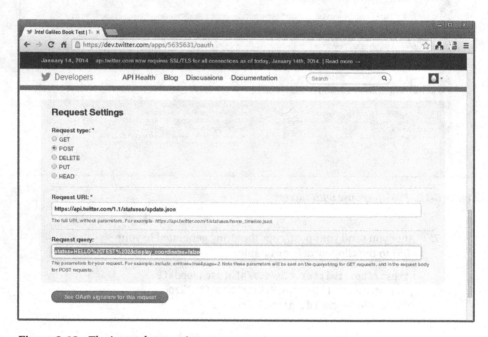

Figure 6-13. *The input data session*

4. Click the See OAuth Signature for this Request button.

If everything was okay, you will be able to see the OAuth signing result in the same tab. Data such as the signature base string and authorization header help you program your script and keep the `curl` command informed to test using the terminal. Figure 6-14 shows the OAuth signing for your reference.

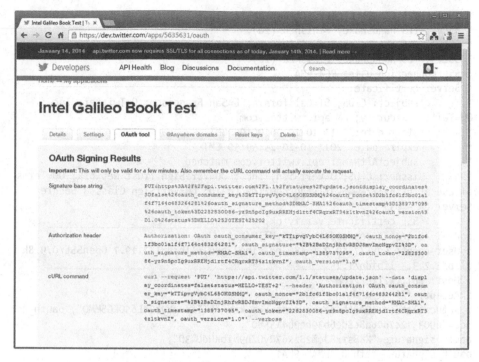

Figure 6-14. *OAuth signing results*

Ensure that there a curl command is generated. If you are using Linux or Mac, or if you have Windows with a Cygwin terminal, try to copy and paste this curl command into a Terminal shell. You will be able to tweet using this command if you get a HTTP 2000K response.

```
mcramon@ubuntu:~$ curl --request 'POST' 'https://api.twitter.com/1.1/
statuses/update.json' --data 'display_coordinates=false&status=%2
2HELLO+TEST+2%22' --header 'Authorization: OAuth oauth_consumer_
key="kTTipvgVybC4L65OKGSMMQ", oauth_nonce="690331247b06d8c8de6b39be9b415580",
oauth_signature="XBBsrxFJq%2Bzx67RyOZn9NibKHdU%3D", oauth_signature_
method="HMAC-SHA1", oauth_timestamp="1390173936", oauth_token="2282830086-yz9
n5pcIg9uxRREHjd1rtf4CRqrxRT34z1tkvnZ", oauth_version="1.0"' --verbose
* About to connect() to api.twitter.com port 443 (#0)
*   Trying 199.59.148.20... connected
* Connected to api.twitter.com (199.59.148.20) port 443 (#0)
* successfully set certificate verify locations:
*   CAfile: none
  CApath: /etc/ssl/certs
* SSLv3, TLS handshake, Client hello (1):
* SSLv3, TLS handshake, Server hello (2):
* SSLv3, TLS handshake, CERT (11):
* SSLv3, TLS handshake, Server finished (14):
* SSLv3, TLS handshake, Client key exchange (16):
```

```
* SSLv3, TLS change cipher, Client hello (1):
* SSLv3, TLS handshake, Finished (20):
* SSLv3, TLS change cipher, Client hello (1):
* SSLv3, TLS handshake, Finished (20):
* SSL connection using RC4-SHA
* Server certificate:
*        subject: C=US; ST=California; L=San Francisco; O=Twitter, Inc.;
OU=Twitter Security; CN=api.twitter.com
*        start date: 2013-10-10 00:00:00 GMT
*        expire date: 2014-10-10 23:59:59 GMT
*        subjectAltName: api.twitter.com matched
*        issuer: C=US; O=VeriSign, Inc.; OU=VeriSign Trust Network; OU=Terms
of use at https://www.verisign.com/rpa (c)10; CN=VeriSign Class 3 Secure
Server CA - G3
*        SSL certificate verify ok.
> POST /1.1/statuses/update.json HTTP/1.1
> User-Agent: curl/7.19.7 (i486-pc-Linux-gnu) libcurl/7.19.7 OpenSSL/0.9.8k
zlib/1.2.3.3 libidn/1.15
> Host: api.twitter.com
> Accept: */*
> Authorization: OAuth oauth_consumer_key="kTTipvgVybC4L65OKGSMMQ", oauth_no
nce="690331247b06d8c8de6b39be9b415580",
oauth_signature="XBBsrxFJq%2Bzx67RyOZn9NibKHdU%3D",
oauth_signature_method="HMAC-SHA1",
oauth_timestamp="1390173936",
oauth_token="2282830086-yz9n5pcIg9uxRREHjd1rtf4CRqrxRT34z1tkvnZ",
oauth_version="1.0"
> Content-Length: 51
> Content-Type: application/x-www-form-urlencoded
>
< HTTP/1.1 200 OK
< cache-control: no-cache, no-store, must-revalidate, pre-check=0, post-check=0
< content-length: 1866
< content-type: application/json;charset=utf-8
< date: Sun, 19 Jan 2014 23:26:57 GMT
< expires: Tue, 31 Mar 1981 05:00:00 GMT
< last-modified: Sun, 19 Jan 2014 23:26:57 GMT
< pragma: no-cache
< server: tfe
< set-cookie: lang=en
< set-cookie: guest_id=v1%3A139017401726629941; Domain=.twitter.com; Path=/;
Expires=Tue, 19-Jan-2016 23:26:57 UTC
< status: 200 OK
< strict-transport-security: max-age=631138519
< x-access-level: read-write-directmessages
< x-frame-options: SAMEORIGIN
< x-transaction: 093eea24eede2302
< x-xss-protection: 1; mode=block
```

{"created_at":"Sun Jan 19 23:26:57 +0000 2014","id":425046751838355456,"
id_str":"425046751838355456","text":"\"HELLO TEST 2\"","source":"\u003ca
href=\"http:\/\/www.intel.com\" rel=\"nofollow\"\u003eIntel Galileo Book
Test\u003c\/a\u003e","truncated":false,"in_reply_to_status_id":null,"in_
reply_to_status_id_str":null,"in_reply_to_user_id":null,"in_reply_to_user_
id_str":null,"in_reply_to_screen_name":null,"user":{"id":2282830086,"id_s
tr":"2282830086","name":"intelgalileo","screen_name":"intelgalileo10","l
ocation":"","description":"","url":null,"entities":{"description":{"url
s":[]}},"protected":false,"followers_count":0,"friends_count":0,"listed_
count":0,"created_at":"Thu Jan 09 01:05:45 +0000 2014","favourites_
count":0,"utc_offset":null,"time_zone":null,"geo_enabled":false,"verifie
d":false,"statuses_count":2,"lang":"en","contributors_enabled":false,"is_
translator":false,"profile_background_color":"C0DEED","profile_
background_image_url":"http:\/\/abs.twimg.com\/images\/themes\/theme1\/
bg.png","profile_backgroun* Connection #0 to host api.twitter.com left
intact
* Closing connection #0
* SSLv3, TLS alert, Client hello (1):
d_image_url_https":"https:\/\/abs.twimg.com\/images\/themes\/theme1\/
bg.png","profile_background_tile":false,"profile_image_url":"http:\/\/
abs.twimg.com\/sticky\/default_profile_images\/default_profile_5_normal.
png","profile_image_url_https":"https:\/\/abs.twimg.com\/sticky\/
default_profile_images\/default_profile_5_normal.png","profile_link_
color":"0084B4","profile_sidebar_border_color":"C0DEED","profile_sidebar_
fill_color":"DDEEF6","profile_text_color":"333333","profile_use_background_
image":true,"default_profile":true,"default_profile_image":true,"following":
false,"follow_request_sent":false,"notifications":false},"geo":null,"coordin
ates":null,"place":null,"contributors":null,"retweet_count":0,"favorite_coun
t":0,"entities":{"hashtags":[],"symbols":[],"urls":[],"user_mentions":[]},"f
avorited":false,"retweeted":false,"lang":"en"}mcramon@ubuntu:~$

You might be thinking that you should do the same using your Intel Galileo terminal shell. If you posted the curl command using your desktop terminal, be sure to change the text message. Otherwise, Twitter might respond with "duplicate status".

You will see the following error:

```
* About to connect() to api.twitter.com port 443 (#0)
*   Trying 199.59.149.199...
* Connected to api.twitter.com (199.59.149.199) port 443 (#0)
* error reading ca cert file /etc/ssl/certs/ca-certificates.crt (Error while
reading file.)
* Closing connection 0
curl: (77) Problem with the SSL CA cert (path? access rights?)
```

There is no CA certification installed on your Intel Galileo. Twitter requires your code to trust in G2 and G3 root certificated provided by VeriSign. For more information, check out `https://dev.twitter.com/docs/security/using-ssl`.

To follow all the procedures to have the certificates in your Intel Galileo board, you instead must include the `-k` option in the `curl` command generated by the OAuth tool. This makes the `curl` command process insecure SSL connections, thereby allowing you to execute `curl` and avoid any certificates.

After you install the certificates or use `-k` in the `curl` command, you'll be able to tweet directly from your Intel Galileo terminal shell.

Step 3: Creating a Script to Post on Twitter with Intel Galileo

If you read the "Important" information provided after you compute the OAuth signing results as shown in Figure 6-14, you will see the following phrase: `"This is only valid for few minutes..."`.

It means the `curl` commands generated by this tool will not work indefinitely because they are based on the timestamp provided. In few minutes, the Twitter server will consider the command generated with `"time out of bounds"`. This is the same error message presented when Intel Galileo uses the wrong time and date.

Therefore, before you run the scripts, make sure you have the date and time of your Intel Galileo board properly set, as explained in the section entitled "System and Hardware Clock".

Once you have a Twitter account and the application's tokens created, you can initiate a creation of your software. The method used in this chapter posted messages on Twitter, but you can create different methods if you understand the process.

Each step presented in the sequence might seem a little "hacking," but they work and were developed after reading the documentation on `https://dev.twitter.com/docs` and participating in some of the Twitter discussions.

In order to understand the details, take a look Listing 6-1.

Listing 6-1. twitter.sh

```bash
#!/bin/bash
#
# POST MESSAGES ON TWITTER
#
# part of this code was based in the discussion:
# https://dev.twitter.com/discussions/14460, info provided by
# https://dev.twitter.com/docs and small hacking observing
# the OAuth Signing Results provied by OAuth tool.
#

debug=1 # set 1 to debug messages

internet_ok=0
# checking for all internet connection except the loopback (lo)
for interface in $(ls /sys/class/net/ | grep -vi lo);
```

```
do
  #if there is any, the carrier must be "1"
  if [[ $(cat /sys/class/net/$interface/carrier 2>/dev/null) = 1 ]]; then
      internet_ok=1;
      break;
  fi
done

if [ $internet_ok = 0 ]; then
      echo "ERROR: No internet connection"
      exit 1
fi

consumer_key=$1
consumer_secret=$2
oauth_token=$3
oauth_secret=$4

message=$(echo -n $5|sed -e "s: :+:g"| sed -e s':!:%21:g')
message_special_space_cases=$(echo -n $5|sed -e "s: :%2520:g"|sed -e
"s:!:%2521:g")

#nonce evaluation
timestamp=`date +%s`
nonce=`date +%s%T555555555 | openssl base64 | sed -e s'/[+=/]//g'`

#POST regular format
signature_base_string="POST&https%3A%2F%2Fapi.twitter.
com%2F1.1%2Fstatuses%2Fupdate.json&display_coordinates%3Dfalse%26oauth_
consumer_key%3D${consumer_key}%26oauth_nonce%3D${nonce}%26oauth_signature_
method%3DHMAC-SHA1%26oauth_timestamp%3D${timestamp}%26oauth_token%3D${oauth_
token}%26oauth_version%3D1.0%26status%3D${message_special_space_cases}"

#only add both
signature_key="${consumer_secret}&${oauth_secret}"

#oauth_signature
oauth_signature=`echo -n ${signature_base_string} | openssl dgst -sha1
-binary -hmac ${signature_key} | openssl base64 | sed -e s':+:%2B:' -e
s':\/:%2F:' -e s':=:%3D:'`

#the message header
header="Authorization: OAuth oauth_consumer_key=\"${consumer_key}\",
oauth_nonce=\"${nonce}\", oauth_signature=\"${oauth_signature}\", oauth_
signature_method=\"HMAC-SHA1\", oauth_timestamp=\"${timestamp}\", oauth_
token=\"${oauth_token}\", oauth_version=\"1.0\""
```

```
if [ $debug = 1 ] ; then

  echo -e "\nmessage:"$message
  echo -e "\nmessage spaces:"$message_special_space_cases
  echo -e "\nonce:"$nonce
  echo -e "\nsignature_base_string:"$signature_base_string
  echo -e "\noauth_signature:"$oauth_signature

fi

curl --request "POST" "https://api.twitter.com/1.1/statuses/update.json"
--data "display_coordinates=false&status=${message}" --header "${header}" -k
```

The first part of the script checks if there is an Internet connection available. This chapter is using a WiFi mPCIe module, but the system could use any other interface like Ethernet.

Thus, it is necessary to check if there is an Internet connection present, independent of interface used. The following snippet of bash code is responsible for this task:

```
internet_ok=0
# checking for all internet connection except the loopback (lo)
for interface in $(ls /sys/class/net/ | grep -vi lo);
do
  #if there is any, the carrier must be "1"
  if [[ $(cat /sys/class/net/$interface/carrier 2>/dev/null) = 1 ]]; then
      internet_ok=1;
      break;
  fi
done

if [ $internet_ok = 0 ]; then
      echo "ERROR: No internet connection"
      exit 1
fi
```

So basically, this code searches all the interface drivers, looking if at least one interface has a connection available (it checks for the number 1 in the carrier file). Note the loopback interface lo is not considered. It is eliminated from the search by grep -vi lo because it is the only loopback interface for the 127.0.0.1 address.

Depending on the kernel version used, when the cat command is used to check the carrier file, it might return an error like cat: read error: Invalid argument if the interface is down. In order to make the code reusable in a different Linux kernel version and patches, if the interface is down and cat returns an error during the reading, the stdout redirects this error to a null device (/dev/null).

The next part formats the timestamp according to the Twitter server, evaluates the nonce, changes some specific characters in the text message, assembles the signature base and signature key, assembles the header, and finally sends the request to the Twitter server.

The consumer key, consumer secret, OAuth token, and OAuth secret code are passed as arguments to the script:

```
consumer_key=$1
consumer_secret=$2
oauth_token=$3
oauth_secret=$4
```

Some characters used in the text message must be converted. The signature base string and the messages used in the curl command receive different conversions. Two variables were created to hold each of them—message and message_special_space_cases.

```
message=$(echo -n $5|sed -e "s: :+:g"| sed -e s':!:%21:g')
message_special_space_cases=$(echo -n $5|sed -e "s: :%2520:g"|sed -e
"s:!:%2521:g")
```

If you tweet text messages with space characters, these must be replaced by the + character in the curl command and by %2520 in the signature base string. Other characters must be considered as well. For example, the character ! must be replaced by %21 in the curl command and by %2521 in the signature base string. The character : must be replaced by %3A and %253A.

You might wonder where you get these conversions. The simple answer is using the OAuth tool! You can see how each character used in the text messages was replaced in the signature base string and curl command in Figure 6-14. This script supported alphabetic characters, spaces, !, and :, covering most common characters used to tweet simple text messages. However, if you need special characters, you need to change the script as explained.

To determine how characters are converted, use the OAuth tool and observe how each character was replaced by comparing the new string to your original text message.

The timestamp must be the number of seconds since 00:00:00 1970-01-01 UTC and to do this, the command date with the %s argument is used. The OAuth nonce is the timestamp with hours, minutes, seconds, and nanoseconds. However, in base64 the +, =, and / characters are removed from the string.

```
timestamp=`date +%s`
nonce=`date +%s%T555555555 | openssl base64 | sed -e s'/[+=/]//g'`
```

The signature base string is only a copy of string generated by the OAuth tool.

The next step is the generation of signature_key. This is only a junction of the consumer secret code with the OAuth secret code. However, this variable is used to generate the OAuth signature using sha1 algorithm, converting to base64, and replacing some characters like + with %2B, \ with %2F, and = with %3D.

```
signature_key="${consumer_secret}&${oauth_secret}"

#oauth_signature
oauth_signature=`echo -n ${signature_base_string} | openssl dgst -sha1
-binary -hmac ${signature_key} | openssl base64 | sed -e s':+:%2B:' -e
s':\/:%2F:' -e s':=:%3D:'`
```

At this point you have all the elements you need to assemble the message header and to assemble the curl command. Note that the curl command used in the script removed the option called --verbose and added -k so that Intel Galileo didn't need the CA certificate to be installed.

```
#the message header
header="Authorization: OAuth oauth_consumer_key=\"${consumer_key}\",
oauth_nonce=\"${nonce}\", oauth_signature=\"${oauth_signature}\",
oauth_signature_method=\"HMAC-SHA1\", oauth_timestamp=\"${timestamp}\",
oauth_token=\"${oauth_token}\", oauth_version=\"1.0\""

curl --request "POST" "https://api.twitter.com/1.1/statuses/update.json"
--data "display_coordinates=false&status=${message}" --header "${header}" -k
```

If you have the certificates installed in your board and you want to connect to Twitter securely, remove the -k option of the curl command from the script.

Step 4: Creating a Sketch that Tweets

Finally, you need to create a sketch that interacts with the script. Take a look Listing 6-2.

Listing 6-2. twitter_sketch.ino

```
#include <unistd.h>
#include <stdio.h>
#include <stdlib.h>
#include <sys/wait.h>

char cmd_rsp[256];

/* Add your consumer and OAuth string codes here */
String consumer_key="";
String consumer_secret="";
String oauth_token="";
String oauth_secret="";

/* this is the name of the script in the target
   you need to push this script to the target before you run this software */
String script_name = ". /home/root/twitter.sh ";
```

```
/* prototype */
boolean post(String message);

void setup() {

  Serial.begin(115200);

  delay(3000);  // just a delay to allow you to see the serial monitor messages
                // you can remove this delay

  String message="TWEETING!!!";
  post(message);

}

void loop() {
  delay(100);
}

boolean post(String message)
{

  boolean result = true;

  String command = script_name;

  command += consumer_key;
  command += " ";

  command += consumer_secret;
  command += " ";

  command += oauth_token;
  command += " ";

  command += oauth_secret;
  command += " ";

  command += "'";
  command += message;
  command += "'";

    // buffer to be used with popen
    char cmd_char[1024];

    // clear message buffer
    memset((void *)cmd_char, sizeof(cmd_char), 0);
```

```
// convert the message to char array
command.toCharArray(cmd_char, sizeof(cmd_char), 0);

Serial.println(cmd_char);

FILE *fpipe;

if ( !(fpipe = (FILE*)popen((char *)cmd_char,"r")) )
    {  // If fpipe is NULL
    Serial.println("Problems with pipe");
    result = false;

}
else
{

    while ( fgets( cmd_rsp, sizeof(cmd_rsp), fpipe)) {}

    pclose(fpipe);

    // checking for errors
    if ((strstr(cmd_rsp, "{\"errors\":[{\"message\"") != NULL) ||
        (strstr(cmd_rsp, "ERROR: No internet connection") != NULL))
    {
        Serial.println("OPS!!! ERROR!!");
        Serial.println(cmd_rsp);
        result = false;
    }
    else
    {
        Serial.println("POSTED WITH SUCCESS!");
        Serial.println(cmd_rsp);
    }
}

return result;
}
```

The code is pretty simple. You just need to define your consumer key, consumer secret, OAuth token, and OAuth secret, represented in Figure 6-10, and include them at the beginning of the code:

```
/* Add your consumer and OAuth string codes here */
String consumer_key="";
String consumer_secret="";
String oauth_token="";
String oauth_secret="";
```

Define your text message and call the post() function. Note that the post() function calls the script using popen(), which is responsible for calling the scripts passing the consumer, OAuth string codes, and the text message. It opens a *pipe* between the sketch and the script, therefore allowing you to read the curl command string responses using fgets().

The fact curl command returns a string or explains why the system() function was not called once this system() function returns only integers.

If you want to see the command response as the command executed by the sketch, you can open the serial console (Ctrl+Shift+M) because you have some debug messages in the sketch, as shown in Figure 6-15.

Figure 6-15. *Debug messages from the serial console after a tweet*

Ideas for Improving the Project

This chapter described how to post messages on Twitter and also explained how to create your Twitter application and successfully communicate with the Twitter server.

The next sections explains how to improve the code presented and include some ideas for how to integrate this code into other projects.

Flowers and Plants Communicating with You on a Social Network

One example is to integrate this chapter's code with the code used in Chapter 8. The idea is, if each sensor corresponds to a plant and the sensor detects when the plants need water, each plant can tweet messages asking for water.

You can find the example by searching for soil_moisture_with_twitter.ino.

The integration is very simple. There is a function called should_post_today() that determines, using regular C functions, whether the day has changed. If the day has changed, that means the system must tweet for each sensor if the plants need water.

```
boolean should_post_today(int * day)
{

  boolean mustTweet = false;
  time_t rawtime;
  struct tm *timeinfo;
```

```
time ( &rawtime );
timeinfo = localtime ( &rawtime );

if (old_day[current_sensor] == 0) old_day[current_sensor] = timeinfo->tm_mday;

if (old_day[current_sensor] != timeinfo->tm_mday)
{
    old_day[current_sensor] = timeinfo->tm_mday;
    mustTweet = true;
}

if (day != NULL) *day = timeinfo->tm_mday;

return mustTweet;
}
```

The code changes required in the loop() function are also very simple, as you can see in Listing 6-3.

Listing 6-3. soil_moisture_with_twitter.ino

```
void loop() {

    int day;

    // reading the button state
    checkButtonState();

    if( button_state != lastButtonState)
    {
        // button pressed
        current_sensor++;
        if (current_sensor > 1) current_sensor = 0;
    }


    // reading the sensor
    switch (current_sensor)
    {
        case 0:
            sensor_value = analogRead(ANALOG_MOISTURE_SENSOR_1);

            // first sensor - one LED ON
            digitalWrite(PIN_RIGHT_EYE, HIGH);
            digitalWrite(PIN_LEFT_EYE, LOW);

        break;
```

```
      case 1:
          sensor_value = analogRead(ANALOG_MOISTURE_SENSOR_2);

          // second sensor - two LEDs ON
          digitalWrite(PIN_RIGHT_EYE, HIGH);
          digitalWrite(PIN_LEFT_EYE, HIGH);

      break;
}

switch (current_sensor)
{
  case 0: plant_name = "orquidea";
  break;

  case 1: plant_name = "sunflower";
  break;

  default:
      Serial.println("There is an error in your logic!");
  break;
}

if (DEBUG)
{
    Serial.print("current_sensor:");
    Serial.println(current_sensor);

    Serial.print("   sensor_value:");
    Serial.println(sensor_value);
}

if (sensor_value >=SOIL_IS_GOOD)
{
    drawMatrix(array_happy_face);
    if (should_post_today(&day))
    {
       char strDay[2];
       sprintf(strDay, "%d", day);

       message = "This is ";
       message += plant_name;
       message += " I am ok thanks! Day:";
       message += strDay;
       post(message);
    }
}
```

```
else
{
    drawMatrix(array_sad_face);
    if (should_post_today(&day))
    {
        char strDay[2];
        sprintf(strDay, "%d", day);

        message = "This is ";
        message += plant_name;
        message += " HEY! I NEED WATER! Day:";
        message += strDay;
        post(message);
    }

}
}
```

Summary

This chapter walked step-by-step through how to create a Twitter application and how to integrate with Intel Galileo in order to tweet messages using simple sketches.

It also discussed the integration of bash scripts and how to use the popen instructions to parse string responses from the web, along with how to avoid using simple and poor system call instructions. You also read about how RTC (Real Time Clock) works, how to set up the time, and how to connect a battery coin to your Intel Galileo boards.

CHAPTER 7

■ ■ ■

Using OpenCV

Open source Computer Vision (OpenCV) is a set of cross-platform libraries containing functions that provide computer vision in real time.

OpenCV is huge framework and there are some basic functions needed to capture and process videos and images V so that they can communicate with input devices, such as a webcams. This chapter introduces the basic concepts needed to build powerful applications with your Intel Galileo board. The project will focus on how to connect a webcam to Intel Galileo, how the webcam works in Linux, how to capture pictures and videos, how to change the pictures with OpenCV algorithms, and how to detect and recognize faces and emotions.

BSP (board support package) SD card images of the Intel Galileo board support OpenCV and allow projects like the one in this chapter to be developed.

Several programs and tasks will be executed in this project. They are divided into Video4Linux and OpenCV categories as follows:

1. Identify the capabilities of webcam with V4L2.

2. Capture pictures using V4L2.

3. Capture videos using V4L2.

4. Capture and process images with OpenCV.

5. Incorporate edge detection in your pictures with OpenCV.

6. Incorporate face and eye detection with OpenCV.

7. Detect emotions with OpenCV.

Note that the V4L2 examples use C and the OpenCV examples are written in C++ and Python. This is done to illustrate the performance of OpenCV in different languages and its cross-platform capabilities.

OpenCV Primer

OpenCV was developed by Intel research and is now supported by Willow Garage under the open source BSD license.

But what is computer vision and what is used for? Computer vision is the ability to provide methods and algorithms that help computers interpret the environment around them. Human eyes are able to capture the environment around us stereographically.

They send the images to our brains, which interpret the images with a sense of depth, format, and dimension to all the components that compose an image.

For example, when you look at a dog in a park, you can tell how far the dog is from you, where exactly the dog is, whether you know the dog and his name, the format of the objects in the park such as sandboxes, trees, and parked cars, if it is going to rain or not, and so on.

A three-month old baby can identify objects and faces in a process that looks so natural for human beings.

What about computers? How do we program computers to use the same kind of analysis and come to the same conclusions when analyzing a simple picture of the park?

Several mathematic models, static data, and machine learned methodologies have being developed hat allow computers to "see" the world and understand the environment around them.

Robots use computer vision to assemble cars, recognize people, help patients in hospitals, and replace astronauts in dangerous missions in the space. In the future they will be able to replace soldiers in the battlefield, perform surgeries with precision, and more.

The OpenCV libraries offer a powerful infrastructure that enables developers to create sophisticated computer vision applications, abstracting all mathematic, static, and machine learning models out of the application context.

It is important to understand how V4L2 works because sometimes OpenCV throws some "mysterious" messages related to issues with V4L2. If you focus exclusively in OpenCV, it will be difficult to understand what is going on and how to fix these issues. These "mysterious" messages are related to V4L2 and not to OpenCV, which can be confusing.

If you need more details about how the algorithms works, visit the OpenCV website (opencv.org) and improve your knowledge with books dedicated exclusively to OpenCV and image processing.

Project Details

This project requires a webcam to serve as Intel Galileo's "eyes" to capture pictures and videos and apply algorithms using OpenCV. If you are using Intel Galileo, you will also need an OTG-USB adapter in order to connect the webcam because, unlike Intel Galileo Gen2, Intel Galileo does not have an OTG-USB connector.

You'll need to generate a custom BSP image that contains all the tools and software packages that will be used. You can also download the BSP image from the code folder and copy it to the micro SD card, which will save you hours building with Yocto. The tools and *ipks* packages used in this chapter require more space than the SPI images can support, thus a micro SD card is necessary.

To focus directly on the OpenCV examples, it is necessary to understand the capabilities of your webcam, like the resolution, encodes, and frames per second that are supported. Understanding these capabilities using V4L2 will prevent you from wasting hours trying to decipher errors that in fact do not come from OpenCV but from V4L2.

Materials List

If you are using the Intel Galileo Gen 2, you need a webcam that's compatible with the UVC standard. Intel Galileo Gen 2 has an OTG USB connector and you can connect the camera directly to the board.

Table 7-1 lists this project's materials. If you are using the Intel Galileo only (first generation), you need to buy an OTG USB 2.0 adaptor similar to the one shown in Figure 7-1.

Table 7-1. *Materials List*

Quantity	Components
1	Webcam Logitech C270
1	OTG-USB 2.0 adaptor with Micro-USB male to USB A Female (only for Intel Galileo)
1	Micro SD card, 4GB to a maximum of 32GB

Figure 7-1. *OTG-USB 2.0 adaptor with micro-USB male to USB A female*

The Logitech webcam C270 is the best bet for this project because it is an affordable camera (US$ 26.00), complies with the USB Video Class (UVC), and works with the programs presented in this chapter. The Logitech webcam C270 is shown in Figure 7-2.

Figure 7-2. Logitech webcam C270

Avoid using the OTG-USB adaptor with an L connector due to space constraints with other connectors in the board.

For more details about UVC, read the next section.

USB Video Class

UVC is a standard that defines how the device streams video and pictures through a USB port. It uses a driver named uvcvideo, which is supported by the BSP SD card software releases. In this case, the device is a simple webcam, but there are other types of devices that support UVC, such as transcoders, video recorders, camcorders, and so on.

If you have a different webcam and you want to use it with this project, just check if the webcam is UVC compliant on the website http://www.ideasonboard.org/uvc/ and check the Supported Devices section, as shown in Figure 7-3.

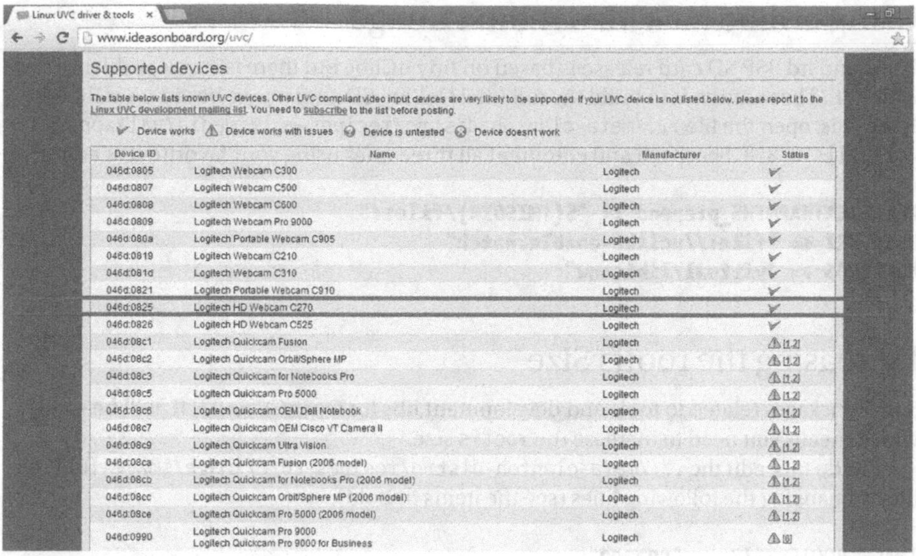

Figure 7-3. *Checking if the webcam supports the UVC standard*

This website will tell you if the webcam works with the uvcvideo driver. If it does, it will be classified as "Device Works" or "Device Works with Issues."

However, even when the device is classified as working, that does not mean you can trust that information completely. Developers often end up setting the camera to a lower resolution or decreasing the frames per second in order to make the code work, even when the webcam is reported as one that works.

Preparing the BSP Software Image and Toolchain

As mentioned, it is necessary to prepare a custom BSP image and save the deployed files in a micro SD card in order to run the examples in this chapter. The toolchain is also necessary to align with eGlibc enabled in the build.

The procedure to create a BSP image and toolchain based on the Yocto project was discussed in Chapter 2, so if you have not read Chapter 2 yet, now is a good time to do so.

Alternatively, if you do not want to learn how to generate the image you can download all files into the **/code/SDcard** folder of this chapter and copy it to your micro SD card. Doing so will save you hours.

Once you have copied the files to the micro SD card, insert in the micro SD card slot (review Chapter 1) and boot the board.

Using eGlibc for Video4Linux Image

The standard BSP SD card release is based on tiny uClibc but there is some problem with V4L. The solution is to build the full Intel Galileo SD card image based on eGlibc. To do this, open the file .../meta-clanton-distro/recipes-multimedia/v4l2apps/ v4l-utils_0.8.8.bbappend and comment all three lines using your favorite text editor:

```
#FILESEXTRAPATHS_prepend := "${THISDIR}/files:"
#SRC_URI += "file://uclibc-enable.patch"
#DEPENDS += "virtual/libiconv"
```

Increasing the rootfs Size

Some packages related to tools and development libs for OpenCV and V4L will be used, which means you need to increase the rootfs size.

To do this, edit the .../meta-clanton-distro/recipes-core/image/image-full.bb file by changing the following lines (see the items in bold):

```
IMAGE_ROOTFS_SIZE = "507200"
IMAGE_FEATURES += "package-management dev-pkgs"
IMAGE_INSTALL += "autoconf automake binutils binutils-symlinks cpp
cpp-symlinks gcc gcc-symlinks g++ g++-symlinks gettext make libstdc++
libstdc++-dev file coreutils"
```

In the first line, rootfs (IMAGE_ROOTFS_SIZE) is increased to 5GB. A new image feature (IMAGE_FEATURES) is enhanced with the integration of the development packages (dev-pkgs). If IMAGE_INSTALL is added, a series of development tools will be part of the image (g++, make, and so on).

Disabling GPU Support on OpenCV

The Quark SoC used on Intel Galileo does not contain any GPUs (Graphics Processing Units). OpenCV can be compiled so that it enables or disables GPU through a definition called CUDA. For Intel Galileo, GPU must be disabled.

To disable GPU, you need to edit two files: .../meta-oe/meta-oe/recipes-support/ opencv/opencv_2.4.3.bb and .../meta-clanton-distro/recipes-support/opencv/ opencv_2.4.3.bbappend. Make the same changes to both of the lines in EXTRA_OECMAKE (see the items in bold):

```
EXTRA_OECMAKE = "-DPYTHON_NUMPY_INCLUDE_DIR:PATH=${STAGING_LIBDIR}/
${PYTHON_DIR}/site-packages/numpy/core/include \
                -DBUILD_PYTHON_SUPPORT=ON \
                -DWITH_FFMPEG=ON \
                -DWITH_CUDA=OFF \
                -DBUILD_opencv_gpu=OFF \
                -DWITH_GSTREAMER=OFF \
```

```
                    -DWITH_V4L=ON \
                    -DWITH_GTK=ON \
                    -DCMAKE_SKIP_RPATH=ON \
                    ${@bb.utils.contains("TARGET_CC_ARCH", "-msse3",
"-DENABLE_SSE=1 -DENABLE_SSE2=1 -DENABLE_SSE3=1 -DENABLE_SSSE3=1", "", d)} \"
```

Building the SD Image and Toolchain

You use the same procedure explained in Chapter 2 to build the image here. For your quick reference, the build process commands are:

```
cd meta-clanton*
./setup.sh
source poky/oe-init-build-env yocto_build
```

To build the full SD image, the bitbake is:

```
bitbake image-full-galileo
```

To create the toolchain, use this command:

```
bitbake image-full-galileo -c populate_sdk
```

Development Library Packages

You might encounter the following message when running OpenCV programs on Intel Galileo:

```
error while loading shared libraries: libopencv_gpu.so.2.4: cannot open
shared object file: No such file or directory
```

If you do, it means some libraries are not properly installed on Intel Galileo. You can install the packages (the ipk files) individually as well.

The code folder contains a tarball named ipk.tar.gz with all the ipk files needed for OpenCV and V4L. Copy that file to Intel Galileo and install the libraries using opkg. To decompress and install the ipk files for OpenCV and V4L, you use the following command:

```
root@clanton:#tar -zxvf ipk.tar.gz
root@clanton:#cd ipk
root@clanton:#opkg install libopencv-gpu2.4_2.4.3-r2_i586.ipk
libopencv-stitching2.4_2.4.3-r2_i586.ipk libopencv-ts2.4_2.4.3-r2_i586.ipk
libopencv-videostab2.4_2.4.3-r2_i586.ipk libv4l-dev_0.8.8-r2_i586.ipk
libv4l-dbg_0.8.8-r2_i586
```

Connecting the Webcam

After inserting the micro SD card and booting the board, you need to load the uvcvideo driver and connect your webcam.

Open a terminal shell and type the following command to load the driver:

```
root@clanton:~# modprobe uvcvideo
[31372.589998] Linux video capture interface: v2.00
[31372.701722] usbcore: registered new interface driver uvcvideo
[31372.707513] USB Video Class driver (1.1.1)
```

If you cannot load the uvcvideo module driver, it means you have a problem with the custom BSP image. Review the build process or use the micro SD card files provided with this chapter.

The driver must be loaded with success. Then, connect your webcam and you should see messages similar to these:

```
root@clanton:~# [31372.707513] USB Video Class driver (1.1.1)[31474.420165]
usb 2-1: new high-speed USB device number 3 using ehci-pci
[31474.801403] uvcvideo: Found UVC 1.00 device <unnamed> (046d:0825)
[31474.930869] input: UVC Camera (046d:0825) as /devices/
pci0000:00/0000:00:14.3/usb2/2-1/2-1:1.0/input/input2
```

The kernel message input:UVC Camera confirms the webcam is in compliance with UVC.

To determine on which device the camera was installed, type the following command:

```
root@clanton:~# ls /dev/video*
/dev/video0
```

In this case the device was properly installed and it is mapped as /dev/video0. The last number (0 in this case) won't always be 0. When you connect the webcam the driver can assign any integer number. For example, if you have a USB host and connect two cameras, one might be /dev/video0 and the other might be /dev/video1. If you keep connecting more and more webcams to the USB host, each one is mapped and then integer will increase, such as /dev/video2, /dev/video3, and so on.

If you have a single webcam currently mapped as /dev/video0 and for some reason the webcam crashes and was not released properly, the next time you connect, it might be mapped as /dev/video1.

This information sounds irrelevant, but keep it in your mind because it will be useful when working with OpenCV later.

Introduction to Video4Linux

Video4Linux, also called V4L, is a set of API and drivers developed to allow Linux to communicate with devices that receive and transmit audio and video. With V4L it is possible to communicate with video cameras, TVs and radio cards, codecs converters, streaming devices, and remote controllers.

This chapter focuses exclusively on the C270 webcam using the second version of this API called Video4Linux 2 (V4L2).

V4L2 includes several bug fixes and new API functions that were not covered in the first release, V4L.

The code samples regarding V4L2 in this chapter come from the official V4L2 website with minor changes to adapt to the C270 webcam. For more detail regarding the API, visit http://linuxtv.org/downloads/v4l-dvb-apis.

Before discussing the technical details about how the API works, let's explore the C270 webcam using a tool based on V4L2, called v4l2-ctl.

It is important to use your camera with this tool before writing your own code or using OpenCV. It will help to understand the settings necessary to make this API work. If you are using a different camera, You will be able to exercise your camera to understand the adaptations that will be necessary for the code examples in this chapter.

Exploring the Webcam Capabilities with V4L2-CTL

Before you start using OpenCV it is important to understand the following aspects of your camera:

- The encode/pixel formats supported

- The resolutions supported to capture images

- The resolutions supported to capture video

- The frames per second (fps) supported in different encode modes

- The resolutions that really work

If these packages were properly installed you should have a command-line tool called v4l2-ctl. This tool not only informs the capabilities of your camera but is able to set/change some properties.

For example, with Logitech C270, you should connect the uvcvideo driver properly. You can type v4l2-ctl --all to check the current capabilities.

```
root@clanton:~# v4l2-ctl --all
Driver Info (not using libv4l2):
        Driver name   : uvcvideo
        Card type    : UVC Camera (046d:0825)
        Bus info     : usb-0000:00:14.3-1
        Driver version: 3.8.7
```

```
        Capabilities  : 0x84000001
                Video Capture
                Streaming
                Device Capabilities
        Device Caps   : 0x04000001
                Video Capture
                Streaming
Priority: 2
Video input : 0 (Camera 1: ok)
Format Video Capture:
        Width/Height  : 640/480
        Pixel Format  : 'MJPG'
        Field         : None
        Bytes per Line: 0
        Size Image    : 341333
        Colorspace    : SRGB
Crop Capability Video Capture:
        Bounds     : Left 0, Top 0, Width 640, Height 480
        Default    : Left 0, Top 0, Width 640, Height 480
        Pixel Aspect: 1/1
Streaming Parameters Video Capture:
        Capabilities    : timeperframe
        Frames per second: 30.000 (30/1)
        Read buffers    : 0
                     brightness (int)  : min=0 max=255 step=1 default=128
                                         value=128
                       contrast (int)  : min=0 max=255 step=1 default=32
                                         value=32
                     saturation (int)  : min=0 max=255 step=1 default=32
                                         value=32
 white_balance_temperature_auto (bool) : default=1 value=1
                           gain (int)  : min=0 max=255 step=1 default=64
                                         value=192
            power_line_frequency (menu) : min=0 max=2 default=2 value=2
       white_balance_temperature (int)  : min=0 max=10000 step=10 default=4000
                                          value=1070 flags=inactive
                       sharpness (int)  : min=0 max=255 step=1 default=24
                                          value=24
           backlight_compensation (int)  : min=0 max=1 step=1 default=0 value=0
                    exposure_auto (menu) : min=0 max=3 default=3 value=3
                exposure_absolute (int)  : min=1 max=10000 step=1 default=166
                                           value=667 flags=inactive
           exposure_auto_priority (bool) : default=0 value=1
```

The current encode is set to MJPG, which is a motion JPEG streamer, and the resolution is 640/480 pixels. The current frame per seconds (fps) is 30 and video cropping is set to the actual video resolution of 640/480, as informed by Crop Capability Video Capture.

Even if you are using the same webcam model, you might see different settings. These are the current settings of my webcam and considering this webcam supports other resolutions and encodes, yours might use different settings.

Changing and Reading Camera Properties

In the previous command, other properties like brightness, contrast, and saturation are used. You can change a property using the --set-ctrl argument with v4l2-ctl tool. Suppose you want to change the contrast attribute from 32 to 40. To do so, type the following in your terminal:

```
root@clanton:~# v4l2-ctl --set-ctrl=contrast=40
```

You can instead use the delimiter =:

```
root@clanton:~# v4l2-ctl --set-ctrl contrast=40
```

To read an individual property, use --get-ctrl rather than --all, which lists all the properties. For example:

```
root@clanton:~# v4l2-ctl --get-ctrl contrast
contrast: 40
```

You can also use the -L argument to get the list of controls. See the following example:

```
root@clanton:~# v4l2-ctl -L
                        brightness (int)  : min=0 max=255 step=1 default=128
                                            value=128
                          contrast (int)  : min=0 max=255 step=1 default=32
                                            value=40
                        saturation (int)  : min=0 max=255 step=1 default=32
                                            value=32
     white_balance_temperature_auto (bool) : default=1 value=1
                              gain (int)  : min=0 max=255 step=1 default=64
                                            value=64
               power_line_frequency (menu) : min=0 max=2 default=2 value=2
                                        0 : Disabled
                                        1 : 50 Hz
                                        2 : 60 Hz
          white_balance_temperature (int)  : min=0 max=10000 step=10 default=4000
                                            value=4000 flags=inactive
                         sharpness (int)  : min=0 max=255 step=1 default=24
                                            value=24
             backlight_compensation (int)  : min=0 max=1 step=1 default=0 value=0
```

329

```
     exposure_auto (menu) : min=0 max=3 default=3 value=3
                        1 : Manual Mode
                        3 : Aperture Priority Mode
  exposure_absolute (int) : min=1 max=10000 step=1 default=166
                            value=166 flags=inactive
exposure_auto_priority (bool) : default=0 value=1
```

Pixel Formats and Resolution

To check the encodes that your webcam supports with v4l2-ctl, use v4l2-ctl --list-formats.

```
root@clanton:~# v4l2-ctl --list-formats
ioctl: VIDIOC_ENUM_FMT
        Index        : 0
        Type         : Video Capture
        Pixel Format: 'YUYV'
        Name         : YUV 4:2:2 (YUYV)

        Index        : 1
        Type         : Video Capture
        Pixel Format: 'MJPG' (compressed)
        Name         : MJPEG
```

As you can see, the webcam supports two types of encodes in this case: YUYV (index 0) and Motion JPEG (index 1) can both capture video as shown by the field Type.

When the v4l2-ctl --all command was previously executed, the current settings were pointing to MJPG.

The webcam C270 supports 1280x720 resolution. Use the following command to change the current 640x480:

```
root@clanton:~# v4l2-ctl --set-fmt-video width=1920,height=780,pixelformat=0
```

The resolution needs to be changed to 1920x720 and the pixel format with index 0 represents YUYV, as demonstrated by the byte command --list-formats.

To determine the current pixel format and resolution, you can run the following command (alternative to --all), which is used before in order to have summarized information:

```
root@clanton:~# v4l2-ctl --get-fmt-video
Format Video Capture:
        Width/Height  : 1280/720
        Pixel Format  : 'YUYV'
        Field         : None
        Bytes per Line: 2560
        Size Image    : 1843200
        Colorspace    : SRGB
```

To check all the resolutions supported by the webcam on each encode as the frame per seconds supported, you must run the v4l2-ctl --list-formats-ext command.

```
root@clanton:~# v4l2-ctl --list-formats-ext
ioctl: VIDIOC_ENUM_FMT
        Index      : 0
        Type       : Video Capture
        Pixel Format: 'YUYV'
        Name       : YUV 4:2:2 (YUYV)
                Size: Discrete 640x480
                        Interval: Discrete 0.033 s (30.000 fps)
                        Interval: Discrete 0.040 s (25.000 fps)
                        Interval: Discrete 0.050 s (20.000 fps)
                        Interval: Discrete 0.067 s (15.000 fps)
                        Interval: Discrete 0.100 s (10.000 fps)
                        Interval: Discrete 0.200 s (5.000 fps)
                Size: Discrete 160x120
                        Interval: Discrete 0.033 s (30.000 fps)
                        Interval: Discrete 0.040 s (25.000 fps)
                        Interval: Discrete 0.050 s (20.000 fps)
                        Interval: Discrete 0.067 s (15.000 fps)
                        Interval: Discrete 0.100 s (10.000 fps)
                        Interval: Discrete 0.200 s (5.000 fps)
...
...
...
                Size: Discrete 1184x656
                        Interval: Discrete 0.100 s (10.000 fps)
                        Interval: Discrete 0.200 s (5.000 fps)
                Size: Discrete 1280x720
                        Interval: Discrete 0.133 s (7.500 fps)
                        Interval: Discrete 0.200 s (5.000 fps)
                Size: Discrete 1280x960
                        Interval: Discrete 0.133 s (7.500 fps)
                        Interval: Discrete 0.200 s (5.000 fps)
        Index      : 1
        Type       : Video Capture
        Pixel Format: 'MJPG' (compressed)
        Name       : MJPEG
                Size: Discrete 640x480
                        Interval: Discrete 0.033 s (30.000 fps)
                        Interval: Discrete 0.040 s (25.000 fps)
                        Interval: Discrete 0.050 s (20.000 fps)
                        Interval: Discrete 0.067 s (15.000 fps)
                        Interval: Discrete 0.100 s (10.000 fps)
                        Interval: Discrete 0.200 s (5.000 fps)
```

```
Size: Discrete 160x120
        Interval: Discrete 0.033 s (30.000 fps)
        Interval: Discrete 0.040 s (25.000 fps)
        Interval: Discrete 0.050 s (20.000 fps)
        Interval: Discrete 0.067 s (15.000 fps)
        Interval: Discrete 0.100 s (10.000 fps)
        Interval: Discrete 0.200 s (5.000 fps)
...
...
...
Size: Discrete 1184x656
        Interval: Discrete 0.033 s (30.000 fps)
        Interval: Discrete 0.040 s (25.000 fps)
        Interval: Discrete 0.050 s (20.000 fps)
        Interval: Discrete 0.067 s (15.000 fps)
        Interval: Discrete 0.100 s (10.000 fps)
        Interval: Discrete 0.200 s (5.000 fps)
Size: Discrete 1280x720
        Interval: Discrete 0.033 s (30.000 fps)
        Interval: Discrete 0.040 s (25.000 fps)
        Interval: Discrete 0.050 s (20.000 fps)
        Interval: Discrete 0.067 s (15.000 fps)
        Interval: Discrete 0.100 s (10.000 fps)
        Interval: Discrete 0.200 s (5.000 fps)
Size: Discrete 1280x960
        Interval: Discrete 0.033 s (30.000 fps)
        Interval: Discrete 0.040 s (25.000 fps)
        Interval: Discrete 0.050 s (20.000 fps)
        Interval: Discrete 0.067 s (15.000 fps)
        Interval: Discrete 0.100 s (10.000 fps)
        Interval: Discrete 0.200 s (5.000 fps)
```

This command provides a long list for webcam C270 with several resolutions supported for each pixel format. Note that each resolution has a list of frames per second supported in case you capture video. At a glance, it looks like the table contains the same resolutions and frames per second, but in fact there are a few differences. For example, the resolution 1184x656 with pixel format YUYV only supports capturing video in 10 and 5 fps, whereas the same resolution in MJPG supports 30, 25, 20, 15, 10, and 5 fps.

If these kinds of details are unnoticed and the wrong settings are made, the video or picture capture will fail and cause problems when working with OpenCV.

To change the frames per second using v4l2-ctl, use the set-parm argument. For example, you can set 30 fps using the following:

```
root@clanton:~# v4l2-ctl --set-parm=30
Frame rate set to 30.000 fps
```

Capturing Videos and Images with libv4l2

The process for capturing video and images using V4L2 is quite similar because it involves the same IOCTL calls and the same sequence. When the webcam is single-planar that means one single video frame has a single buffer address as a starting point. Some devices are multi-planar, which means a single video frame requires more than one start address.

The sequence for capturing the video is quite the same, but the difference is in how the software saves the frames—individually or as an entire stream.

Copy the images between the kernel and the userspace. Remember that the applications run in the userspace context There are three I/O operations supported in V4L2 API:

- **Memory mapped buffers (mmap):** The buffers are allocated in the kernel space. The device determines the number of buffers that can be allocated as the size of the buffers. Usually the mmap() function and the application must inform this method using V4L2_MEMORY_MMAP before it queries the buffers. This is the method used with the webcam C270.

- **Userspace pointers:** The buffers are allocated to the userspace context using the regular malloc() or calloc() functions. In this case, the V4L2_MEMORY_USERPTR is used to query the buffer.

- **Direct Read/Write:** The application in this case can read/write the buffer directly. Thus, no mapped memory (mmap) or userspace memory allocation is necessary (malloc/calloc).

In all three methods, the device determines which ones are supported. You must also set the resolution, the pixel format, and the frames per second.

A Program for Capturing Video

The code used in this section is from "Appendix D: Video Capture Example" of the *Linux Media Infrastructure API* documentation at http://linuxtv.org/downloads/v4l-dvb-apis/capture-example.html (with a few changes to support the C270 motion JPEG stream).

All communication between the userspace and the kernel driver is made through IOCTL calls. Therefore, it's a good idea to have a function to do that.

```
static int xioctl(int fh, int request, void *arg)
{
        int r;

        do {
                r = ioctl(fh, request, arg);
        } while (-1 == r && EINTR == errno);

        return r;
}
```

This function will be used several times in all IOCTL calls that send IOCTL to the kernel using the **ioctl( )** function.

Figure 7-4 represents the sequence for video and images.

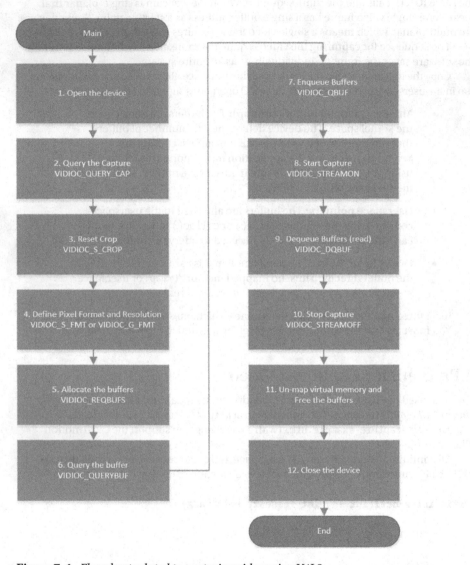

***Figure 7-4.** Flowchart related to capturing video using V4L2*

Each step in the flowchart is explained with the respective snippet:

1. **Open the device:** You use a file descriptor to open the device. In this case, a string representing the device is used. The string contains the proper device name in /dev. For example, the string might be "/dev/video0". The O_NONBLOCK option prevents the software from remaining blocked when the buffers are read (this is explained in more detail in the dequeue process in Step 9).

```
static void open_device(void)
{
...
...
...


        fd = open(dev_name, O_RDWR /* required */ | O_NONBLOCK, 0);

        if (-1 == fd) {
                fprintf(stderr, "Cannot open '%s': %d, %s\n",
                        dev_name, errno, strerror(errno));
                exit(EXIT_FAILURE);
        }

}
```

2. **Initiate the device:** If the device opens properly, you need to ask the device about its capabilities using VIDIOC_QUERYCAP.

```
struct v4l2_capability cap;
    ...
...
...
...

if (-1 == xioctl(fd, VIDIOC_QUERYCAP, &cap)) {
        if (EINVAL == errno) {
                fprintf(stderr, "%s is no V4L2 device\n",
                        dev_name);
                exit(EXIT_FAILURE);
        } else {
                errno_exit("VIDIOC_QUERYCAP");
        }
}
```

3. **Reset any image cropping set:** Use VIDIOC_S_CROP set to its default values. If the devices do not support cropping, you can ignore the errors because the image will always have the same resolution.

```
struct v4l2_crop crop;
struct v4l2_cropcap cropcap;
...
...
...


cropcap.type = V4L2_BUF_TYPE_VIDEO_CAPTURE;

if (0 == xioctl(fd, VIDIOC_CROPCAP, &cropcap)) {
                crop.type = V4L2_BUF_TYPE_VIDEO_CAPTURE;
                crop.c = cropcap.defrect; /* reset to default */

                if (-1 == xioctl(fd, VIDIOC_S_CROP, &crop)) {
                        switch (errno) {
                        case EINVAL:
                                /* Cropping not supported. */
                                break;
                        default:
                                /* Errors ignored. */
                                break;
                        }
                }
}
```

4. **Set pixel format and resolution:** If VIDIOC_S_FMT is used, the device will assume the setting passed to IOCTL with the structure v4l2_format. Otherwise, if VIDIOC_G_FMT is used, the current programmed settings are used. In this case you can use the v4l2-ctl tool as explained before. This is the only part of the code that changed from the original code on the V4L2 website. The force_format variable, when set to true, forces the format to motion JPEG stream with 1280x720 resolution. Otherwise, use the current setting of your camera, which can be changed using the v4ctl tool.

```
fmt.type = V4L2_BUF_TYPE_VIDEO_CAPTURE;
    if (force_format) {
                fmt.fmt.pix.width       = 1280;
                fmt.fmt.pix.height      = 720;
                fmt.fmt.pix.pixelformat = V4L2_PIX_FMT_MJPEG;
                fmt.fmt.pix.field       = V4L2_FIELD_NONE;
```

```
        if (-1 == xioctl(fd, VIDIOC_S_FMT, &fmt))
                errno_exit("VIDIOC_S_FMT");

        /* Note VIDIOC_S_FMT may change width and height. */
} else {
        /* Preserve original settings as set by v4l2-ctl for example */
        if (-1 == xioctl(fd, VIDIOC_G_FMT, &fmt))
                errno_exit("VIDIOC_G_FMT");
}
```

5. **Allocate buffers:** With the v4l2_requestbuffers structure
   and more precisely using the count field, it is passed to
   the device using IOCTL VIDIOC_REQBUFS, which requires a
   certain number of buffers to be used by the device to store the
   images. In the case of webcam C270, the maximum number of
   buffers is five. More than five and the webcam will report
   "out of memory" and VIDIOC_REQBUFS will fail. It's best to set
   at least two buffers. If the device accepts the number of buffers
   asked, due to the VIDIOC_REQBUFS call, the size of the buffer
   is reported. Then you allocate the buffers in the userspace
   context to allow the device to fill them. The allocation might
   be done using regular functions like calloc() and malloc().

```
struct v4l2_requestbuffers req;

CLEAR(req);

req.count = 5;
req.type = V4L2_BUF_TYPE_VIDEO_CAPTURE;
req.memory = V4L2_MEMORY_MMAP;

if (-1 == xioctl(fd, VIDIOC_REQBUFS, &req)) {
        if (EINVAL == errno) {
                fprintf(stderr, "%s does not support "
                        "memory mapping\n", dev_name);
                exit(EXIT_FAILURE);
        } else {
                errno_exit("VIDIOC_REQBUFS");
        }
}

if (req.count < 2) {
        fprintf(stderr, "Insufficient buffer memory on %s\n",
                dev_name);
        exit(EXIT_FAILURE);
}
```

```
            buffers = calloc(req.count, sizeof(*buffers));

    if (!buffers) {
            fprintf(stderr, "Out of memory\n");
            exit(EXIT_FAILURE);
    }
```

6. **Query buffers' statuses and map the memory for each:**
   For each buffer allocated, it is necessary to query their status
   using VIDIOC_QUERYBUF. In response to VIDIOC_QUERYBUF, the
   offset of the buffer from the start device as the length of each
   buffer is reported. With this information, the function mmap()
   must be called to map the virtual memory that will be shared
   between the userspace and the device.

```
for (n_buffers = 0; n_buffers < req.count; ++n_buffers) {
            struct v4l2_buffer buf;

            CLEAR(buf);

            buf.type        = V4L2_BUF_TYPE_VIDEO_CAPTURE;
            buf.memory      = V4L2_MEMORY_MMAP;
            buf.index       = n_buffers;

            if (-1 == xioctl(fd, VIDIOC_QUERYBUF, &buf))
                    errno_exit("VIDIOC_QUERYBUF");

            buffers[n_buffers].length = buf.length;
            buffers[n_buffers].start =
                    mmap(NULL /* start anywhere */,
                            buf.length,
                            PROT_READ | PROT_WRITE /* required */,
                            MAP_SHARED /* recommended */,
                            fd, buf.m.offset);

            if (MAP_FAILED == buffers[n_buffers].start)
                    errno_exit("mmap");
    }
```

7. **Enqueue the buffers:** Considering that the C270 webcam
   operated with the mmap method, it is necessary to exchange
   each buffer obtained with VIDIOC_REQBUFS, with the driver
   using VIDIOC_QBUF. The VIDIOC_QBUF enqueues each buffer.

```
case IO_METHOD_MMAP:
            for (i = 0; i < n_buffers; ++i) {
                    struct v4l2_buffer buf;
```

```
        CLEAR(buf);
        buf.type = V4L2_BUF_TYPE_VIDEO_CAPTURE;
        buf.memory = V4L2_MEMORY_MMAP;
        buf.index = i;

        if (-1 == xioctl(fd, VIDIOC_QBUF, &buf))
                errno_exit("VIDIOC_QBUF");
}
```

8. **Start the capture:** With all buffers ready, it is necessary to start the streaming with VIDIOC_STREAMON.

```
if (-1 == xioctl(fd, VIDIOC_STREAMON, &type))
        errno_exit("VIDIOC_STREAMON");
```

9. **Dequeue the buffers to read the frames:** By calling VIDIOC_DQBUF, the buffers are dequeued and the frames can be read in case of success. Note that there is no specific order for the buffers, so as result beside the data, the buffer index is informed. It is necessary to keep waiting for all the buffers to be dequeued and a while loop can be implemented for this purpose. However, to avoid the blocking operation in context of the userspace, the select() function is used. Note that if you try to read a specific buffer that's not available in memory and if the device was opened with O_NONBLOCK, the error EAGAIN is thrown during the VIDIOC_DQBUF call. Otherwise it remains blocked until the buffer is ready.

```
static void mainloop(void)
{
        unsigned int count;

        count = frame_count;

        while (count-- > 0) {
                for (;;) {
                        fd_set fds;
                        struct timeval tv;
                        int r;

                        FD_ZERO(&fds);
                        FD_SET(fd, &fds);

                        /* Timeout. */
                        tv.tv_sec = 2;
                        tv.tv_usec = 0;

                        r = select(fd + 1, &fds, NULL, NULL, &tv);
```

```
                        if (-1 == r) {
                                if (EINTR == errno)
                                        continue;
                                errno_exit("select");
                        }

                        if (0 == r) {
                                fprintf(stderr, "select timeout\n");
                                exit(EXIT_FAILURE);
                        }

                        if (read_frame())
                                break;
                        /* EAGAIN - continue select loop. */
                }
        }
}
...
...
...

static int read_frame(void)
{
        struct v4l2_buffer buf;
        unsigned int i;
...
...
...

                if (-1 == xioctl(fd, VIDIOC_DQBUF, &buf)) {
                        switch (errno) {
                        case EAGAIN:
                          printf("EAGAIN\n");
                                return 0;

                        case EIO:
                          printf("EIO\n");
                                /* Could ignore EIO, see spec. */

                                /* fall through */

                        default:
                          printf("default\n");
                                errno_exit("VIDIOC_DQBUF");
                        }

                }

}
```

10. **Stop the stream**: Simply call `VIDIOC_STREAMOFF`.

```
type = V4L2_BUF_TYPE_VIDEO_CAPTURE;
if (-1 == xioctl(fd, VIDIOC_STREAMOFF, &type))
        errno_exit("VIDIOC_STREAMOFF");
```

11. **Free the buffers and unmap the memory**: The memory virtually mapped with `mmap()` must be unmapped with the `munmap()` function and the memory allocated to the buffer must be freed with the `free()` function.

```
static void uninit_device(void)
{
        unsigned int i;

        switch (io) {
...
...
...

        case IO_METHOD_MMAP:
                for (i = 0; i < n_buffers; ++i)
                        if (-1 == munmap(buffers[i].start, buffers[i].length))
                                errno_exit("munmap");
                break;
...
...
...

        free(buffers);
}
```

12. **Close the device**: The device file descriptor is closed.

```
static void close_device(void)
{
        if (-1 == close(fd))
                errno_exit("close");

        fd = -1;
}
```

The code excerpts used in this section are from "Appendix D: Video Capture Example" of the Linux Media Infrastructure API documentation at http://linuxtv.org/downloads/v4l-dvb-apis/capture-example.html (with a few changes to support the C270 motion JPEG stream). The complete program highlighting the changes is provided in Appendix C "Video Capturing," Listing C-1.

Building and Transferring the Video Capture Program

With the toolchain properly installed on your computer, open a terminal shell and type the following:

```
mcramon@ubuntu:~/ $ cd <YOUR BASE TOOLCHAIN PATH>
mcramon@ubuntu:~/xcompiler$ source environment-setup-*
```

This command will set all the variables of the environment in your system to the current installation of your toolchain.

To test if it is working, considering the programs created in this book to understand how V4L is written in C, run the following command in your computer shell:

```
mcramon@ubuntu:~/xcompiler$ ${CC} --version
i586-poky-linux-gcc (GCC) 4.7.2
Copyright (C) 2012 Free Software Foundation, Inc.
This is free software; see the source for copying conditions.  There is NO
warranty; not even for MERCHANTABILITY or FITNESS FOR A PARTICULAR PURPOSE.
```

The GCC compiler represented by ${CC} was properly set and you are ready to build the program.

To build the program, you need to run the following:

```
${CC} -O2 -Wall 'pkg-config --cflags --libs libv4l2'
galileo_video_capture.c -o galileo_video_capture
```

Note that pkg-config is being used to inform the libv4l2 what will be used in the compilation.

Now you can transfer the galileo_video_capture program using your favorite program, as explained in Chapter 5. For example, if you are using an Ethernet cable or a WiFi card in Intel Galileo and your operation system is Linux/MacOSX, you can use scp. If your computer is Windows, you can use WinSCP. Here's an example using scp.

On the Intel Galileo terminal shell, create a direct connection like the following:

```
root@clanton:~# ifconfig eth0 192.254.1.1 netmask 255.255.255.0 up
```

Then on your Linux/MacOSX, transfer the file:

```
mcramon@ubuntu:~/scp galileo_capture root@192.254.1.1:/home/root/.
```

If you are using a customized BSP image with the development tools present on your SD card image, it is easier because you can compile directly through Intel Galileo's terminal shell. There is no needed to transfer files once the executable is already in the file system.

Running the Program and Capturing Videos

The program is executed in the command line and must run using the Intel Galileo terminal shell. The program accepts some arguments that are used to configure the capture type and redirect the content capture.

Among the arguments supported, this code supports all three IO methods and the method to be used during the capture is passed as a simple argument during the program execution. The arguments are as follows:

- -m: Memory mapped; used for the C270 webcam

- -u: Userspace pointers

- -r: Direct read/write

Another important argument is -f. If this argument is not set, the current camera settings are used to capture the video. This means you can change them using the v4l2-ctl tool, as explained.

If -f is used, the capture is forced to use a width of 1280, a height of 720, and the pixel format that supports the Motion JPEG stream (MJPEG). This is the only change from the original code, which supports a different format.

You also can define the number of frames you want to be part of your video with the argument -c. You need to use -c <NUMBER OF FRAMES>.

Finally, the -o argument redirects the content captured to an output that can be redirected to a file.

With all these arguments in mind, suppose you want to capture a video with 100 frames, force the resolution to 1280X720 using Motion JPEG encode, and create an output file named video.mjpeg. For this, you can execute the program with the following arguments using the Intel Galileo terminal shell:

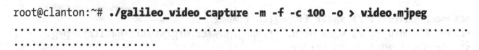

```
root@clanton:~# ./galileo_video_capture -m -f -c 100 -o > video.mjpeg
................................................................................
.....................
```

Each dot "." represents a frame captured in the output.

Now use a different setting using the v4l2-ctl command tool and run the same command line as before, but omit the -f. Let's reduce the video resolution.

```
root@clanton:~# v4l2-ctl --set-fmt-video width=320,height=176,pixelformat=1
```

Then run the command to accept this configuration, by omitting the -f option.

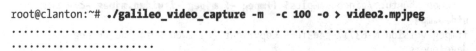

```
root@clanton:~# ./galileo_video_capture -m  -c 100 -o > video2.mjpeg
................................................................................
.....................
```

You will have a new video but with a different resolution.

If your device is not enumerated as /dev/video0, it is necessary to use the -d </dev/video*> option. For example, suppose your device is enumerated as /dev/video1. Your command line must then be:

```
root@clanton:~# ./galileo_video_capture -d /dev/video1 -m  -c 100 -o >
video2.mpjpeg
```

Converting and Playing Videos

If you read and worked through the previous section, you have two videos collected with the Motion JPEG encode and with different resolutions. If you transfer these files to your computer and try to play them you, will have a very sad surprise. They cannot be played because they are created for streaming, which means some specific headers in the files are missing.

To include the headers in the files, you must use an external tool. The recommended tools is ffmpeg, for three reasons:

- It's vastly maintained by the open source community

- It can run directly on Intel Galileo SD image or on your computer

- It supports different encoders

In case you prefer to run it on your computer, the instructions for downloading and installing ffmpeg in different operational systems are found at http://www.ffmpeg.org/download.html. If your computer runs Linux, the easier way is to install it from static releases present at http://ffmpeg.gusari.org/static/ and then run the following commands:

```
mcramon@ubuntu~$:~/$ mkdir ffmpeg;cd ffmpeg
mcramon@ubuntu~$:~/$ wget http://ffmpeg.gusari.org/static/64bit/ffmpeg.
static.64bit.2014-03-02.tar.gz

mcramon@ubuntu:~/$ tar -zxvf ffmpeg.static.64bit.2014-03-02.tar.gz
```

ffmpeg will be available in the same directory you extracted the files.

On your personal computer or in Intel Galileo, you need to execute ffmpeg to convert the videos to a "playable" format in most systems. For example, to convert the first and second videos captured, you can run the following:

```
mcramon@ubuntu:~/video_samples$ ffmpeg -f mjpeg -i video.mjpeg -c:v copy
video.mp4
ffmpeg version N-63717-g4e3fe65 Copyright (c) 2000-2014 the FFmpeg
developers
  built on Jun 3 2014 01:10:16 with gcc 4.4.7 (Ubuntu/Linaro 4.4.7-1ubuntu2)
  configuration: --disable-yasm --enable-cross-compile --arch=x86
--target-os=linux
```

```
  libavutil       52. 89.100 / 52. 89.100
  libavcodec      55. 66.100 / 55. 66.100
  libavformat     55. 42.100 / 55. 42.100
  libavdevice     55. 13.101 / 55. 13.101
  libavfilter      4.  5.100 /  4.  5.100
  libswscale       2.  6.100 /  2.  6.100
  libswresample    0. 19.100 /  0. 19.100
Input #0, mjpeg, from 'video.mjpeg':
  Duration: N/A, bitrate: N/A
    Stream #0:0: Video: mjpeg, yuvj422p(pc), 1280x720, 25 fps, 25 tbr,
1200k tbn, 25 tbc
Output #0, mp4, to 'video.mp4':
  Metadata:
    encoder        : Lavf55.42.100
    Stream #0:0: Video: mjpeg (l[0][0][0] / 0x006C), yuvj422p, 1280x720,
q=2-31, 25 fps, 1200k tbn, 1200k tbc
Stream mapping:
    Stream #0:0 -> #0:0 (copy)
Press [q] to stop, [?] for help
frame=  100 fps=0.0 q=-1.0 Lsize=     2871kB time=00:00:03.96
bitrate=5939.9kbits/s
video:2870kB audio:0kB subtitle:0kB other streams:0kB global headers:0kB
muxing overhead: 0.041544%
mcramon@ubuntu:~/video_samples$ ffmpeg -f mjpeg -i video2.mjpeg -vcodec
copy video2.mp4
ffmpeg version N-63717-g4e3fe65 Copyright (c) 2000-2014 the FFmpeg
developers
  built on Jun 3 2014 01:10:16 with gcc 4.4.7 (Ubuntu/Linaro 4.4.7-1ubuntu2)
  configuration: --disable-yasm --enable-cross-compile --arch=x86
--target-os=linux
  libavutil       52. 89.100 / 52. 89.100
  libavcodec      55. 66.100 / 55. 66.100
  libavformat     55. 42.100 / 55. 42.100
  libavdevice     55. 13.101 / 55. 13.101
  libavfilter      4.  5.100 /  4.  5.100
  libswscale       2.  6.100 /  2.  6.100
  libswresample    0. 19.100 /  0. 19.100
Input #0, mjpeg, from 'video2.mjpeg':
  Duration: N/A, bitrate: N/A
    Stream #0:0: Video: mjpeg, yuvj422p(pc), 320x176, 25 fps, 25 tbr,
1200k tbn, 25 tbc
Output #0, mp4, to 'video2.mp4':
  Metadata:
    encoder        : Lavf55.42.100
    Stream #0:0: Video: mjpeg (l[0][0][0] / 0x006C), yuvj422p, 320x176,
q=2-31, 25 fps, 1200k tbn, 1200k tbc
```

```
Stream mapping:
  Stream #0:0 -> #0:0 (copy)
Press [q] to stop, [?] for help
frame=  100 fps=0.0 q=-1.0 Lsize=      843kB time=00:00:03.96
bitrate=1743.1kbits/s
video:841kB audio:0kB subtitle:0kB other streams:0kB global headers:0kB
muxing overhead: 0.137993%
```

Basically, -f indicates that the file is encoded as the Motion JPEG pixel format; the -i indicates an input file, and -vcodec copy maintains the same encode and quality, but adds the frames to a MP4 container.

All videos with the extensions of MJPEG and MP4 used in this section are present in the code/video_samples folder of this chapter. Thus you can exercise this conversion independently, with or without a webcam.

Videos with MP4 extensions can be played on your computer. If you are using Ubuntu, you can play them directly using the Movie Player. If you are using Windows or MacOSX, you can play them with the VLC player or using QuickTime (see Figure 7-5).

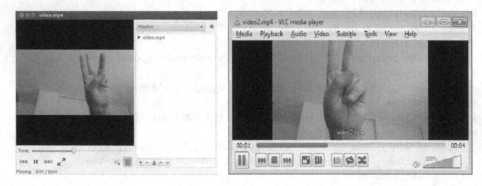

Figure 7-5. *Videos captured by Intel Galileo reproduced in VLC and Movie Player*

By comparing the files before and after the inclusion of headers by ffmpeg, you can see that the frames in general were maintained in the same content and only the headers were added to the end of MP4 file and a few bytes in the beginning. Figure 7-6 shows the header added to the end of the original MJPEG file.

Figure 7-6. *The frames have not changed, only the headers have been added to the MP4 file*

A Program to Capture Images

The process for capturing images using V4L2 is the same as with videos except that frame-by-frame images should be saved in the file system.

The code used in this section is based on the software presented in "Appendix E. Video Grabber Example Using libv4l" of the *Linux Media Infrastructure API* documentation, with some changes to accommodate the webcam C270 and to choose different encodes. The complete program can be found at http://linuxtv.org/downloads/v4l-dvb-apis/v4l2grab-example.html.

The software has some requirements that must be explained before you review the code:

- It is also a command-line program similar to the software used to capture videos that runs in the Intel Galileo's terminal shell.

- It only supports the mapped memory IO method, and it is a simplified version of the software used to capture videos. Remember that the software used to capture video was created to cover the whole scenario necessary to communicate with different types of devices. Limiting the software to memory mapped IO devices enables the code to be incredibly simplified. No argument in the command line is necessary because it is hard coded.

- It accepts different resolutions related to width and height. It accepts the -W or --width arguments for the image's width and the -H or --height arguments for the image's height. If the options are omitted, the default resolution is 1280x720 (width and height, respectively). If some resolution not supported by the webcam is defined through these arguments, the closest resolution is automatically selected. libv4l2 compares the ones supported by the camera and a warning message is displayed to the user in the terminal shell.

- It can select two different encodes, YUYV or RGB24. If the -y or --yuyv arguments are used, the YUYV encode is used; otherwise if this argument is omitted, the RGB24 encode is used by default.

- It is possible to set the number of images that will be stored in the files using the -c or --count argument, followed by the number of images desired. If this option is omitted, the number of images stored in the file system will be 10 by default. The image's names will have the prefix out, followed by three decimals formatting the image order with the extension .ppm. For example, out000.ppm, out001.ppm, and so on.

You might wonder how it is possible to set the pixel format to RGB24 if it was demonstrated using v4l2-ctl --list-formats that the webcam C270 only supports MJPEG and YUYV? Actually, RGB24 is not supported by the webcam C270, but libv4l2 supports to conversion from YUYV to RGB24 and BGR24. In other words, even when you set the pixel format to RGB24 or BGR24, more precisely V4L2_PIX_FMT_RGB24 and V4L2_PIX_FMT_BGR24, if your camera does not offer such formats natively, YUYV is considered and the V4L2 library makes the conversion from YUYV to RGB24 or BGR24 for you.

The following snippet demonstrates the selection of pixel format controlled by the variable isYUYV.

```
CLEAR(fmt);
fmt.type = V4L2_BUF_TYPE_VIDEO_CAPTURE;
fmt.fmt.pix.width        = width;
fmt.fmt.pix.height       = height;

if (!isYUYV)
   {
       printf("Encode RGB24\n");
       fmt.fmt.pix.pixelformat = V4L2_PIX_FMT_RGB24;
   }
else
   {
       printf("Encode YUYV\n");
       fmt.fmt.pix.pixelformat = V4L2_PIX_FMT_YUYV;
   }
```

```
        fmt.fmt.pix.field        = V4L2_FIELD_INTERLACED;
        xioctl(fd, VIDIOC_S_FMT, &fmt);
        if (fmt.fmt.pix.pixelformat != V4L2_PIX_FMT_RGB24 &&
            fmt.fmt.pix.pixelformat != V4L2_PIX_FMT_YUYV) {
                printf("Libv4l didn't accept RGB24 or YUYV format. Can't
proceed.\n");
                exit(EXIT_FAILURE);
        }
        if ((fmt.fmt.pix.width != width) || (fmt.fmt.pix.height != height))
                printf("Warning: driver is sending image at %dx%d\n",
                        fmt.fmt.pix.width, fmt.fmt.pix.height);
```

If YUYV or RGB24 is selected, the image will have the same extension, .ppm. The PPM file extension means "portable pixmap" and consists of a file with an ASCII header following by a sequence of raw bytes.

A valid example of a PPM header file is:

P6

1280 720 255

The string P6 is called the "magic identifier" and it can be P3 as well. Then the next line contains the image width and height, represented by 1280 and 720 in this example.

The number 255 is the maximum value of the color component RGB, so it might vary between 0 to 255. Thus it's used to delimit the maximum color range in the image.

The following code lines can be used to create the file with fopen() and write this string sequence in this file using fprintf().

```
fout = fopen(out_name, "w");
...
...
...
fprintf(fout, "P6\n%d %d 255\n", fmt.fmt.pix.width, fmt.fmt.pix.height);
```

The maximum color component in the header is retried by the image returned by the webcam and that's why it is not part of fprintf() function.

If you selected the RGB24 and the image provided by libv4l2 is already converted from YUYV to RGB24, you simply need to write the header text for the PPM image and attach the binary data received when the buffers were "dequeued" through VIDIOC_DQBUF.

```
        xioctl(fd, VIDIOC_STREAMON, &type);

        for (i = 0; i < images_count; i++) {
                do {
...
...
...
                        CLEAR(buf);
                        buf.type = V4L2_BUF_TYPE_VIDEO_CAPTURE;
                        buf.memory = V4L2_MEMORY_MMAP;
                        xioctl(fd, VIDIOC_DQBUF, &buf);
```

```
                    sprintf(out_name, "out%03d.ppm", i);
                    printf("Creating image: %s\n", out_name);
                    fout = fopen(out_name, "w");
                    if (!fout) {
                            perror("Cannot open image");
                            exit(EXIT_FAILURE);
                    }
                    fprintf(fout, "P6\n%d %d 255\n", fmt.fmt.pix.width,
fmt.fmt.pix.height);

...
...
...
                    fwrite(buffers[buf.index].start, buf.bytesused, 1, fout);
...
...
...


                    fclose(fout);

                    xioctl(fd, VIDIOC_QBUF, &buf);
            }
```

If YUYV is selected, you must convert from YUYV to RGB24 in order to create
the .ppm file.

In the case of webcam C270, the YUYV is 4:2:2, which means 4 bytes per 2 pixels;
or 1 pixel per 2 bytes. RGB24 represents 24 bits per pixel or 3 bytes per pixel. Thus, to
convert YUYV 4:2:2 to RGB24 each 2 bytes (1 pixel) from YUYV 4:2:2 originates to 3 bytes
(pixel) to RGB24.

It means the function that converts the image needs to allocate a buffer because the
resultant image in RGB24 is 1.5 times bigger than the YUYV 4:2:2 image.

So, if in RGB24 each pixel is represented by three bytes, the buffer that will receive
the image allocated must be evaluated. You get the total number of pixels and multiply
that by three bytes each. The following code represents this logic:

```
// each pixel 3 bytes in RGB 24
int size = fmt.fmt.pix.width * fmt.fmt.pix.height * sizeof(char) * 3;
unsigned char * data = (unsigned char *) malloc(size);
```

To make this conversion, the code example uses a function extracted from OpenCV,
copied without any changes under Intel licenses. The function is called yuyv_to_rgb24()
and it is from the file cvcap_v4l.cpp. For reference, you can see the whole file at
https://code.ros.org/trac/opencv/browser/trunk/opencv/src/highgui/
cvcap_v4l.cpp?rev=284.

The following snippet makes the conversion function call by passing the image's
dimensions (fmt.fmt.pix.width and fmt.fmt.pix.height), the initial buffer address
(buffers[buf.index].start) to the current frame returned, and the destination buffer
allocated (data).

```
yuyv_to_rgb24(fmt.fmt.pix.width,
              fmt.fmt.pix.height,
              (unsigned char*)(buffers[buf.index].start),
              data);

fwrite(data, size, 1, fout);
free (data);
...
...
...
fclose(fout);
```

The software is shown in Listing D-1. The portions of the code relevant to this section are in bold.

The code excerpts used in this section are based on the software presented in "Appendix E. Video Grabber Example Using libv4l" of the Linux Media Infrastructure API documentation, with some changes to accommodate the webcam C270 and to choose different encodes (http://linuxtv.org/downloads/v4l-dvb-apis/v4l2grab-example.html). The complete program highlighting the changes discussed in this section are provided in Appendix D "Picture Grabber," Listing D-1.

Building and Transferring the Picture Grabber

The procedure for building and transferring the file is the same as the one used in the section "Building and Transferring the Video Capture Program" of this chapter, except for the command line used to compile the picture grabber program.

Type the following into the command line with the toolchain properly set.

```
${CC} -O2 -Wall 'pkg-config --cflags --libs libv4l2'
picture_grabber.c -o picture_grabber
```

Then transfer the file to your Intel Galileo board.

Running the Program and Capturing Images

The program is executed in the command line and can be used with Intel Galileo terminal shell. The program accepts some arguments explained in the previous section.

The first step is to capture five images in RGB24 format with a resolution of 352x288.

```
root@clanton:~# ./picture_grabber -W 352 -H 288 -c 5
Encode RGB24
Creating image: out000.ppm
Creating image: out001.ppm
Creating image: out002.ppm
Creating image: out003.ppm
Creating image: out004.ppm
```

As a result, five images with the prefix out and extension ppm are created. Copy these images to your computer and open them using an image viewer.

If you try to use a resolution not supported by the webcam, the V4L2 library will adjust to the closest one supported by the camera and a warning message will appear informing you of the real resolution used. For example, 300x200 is not supported:

```
root@clanton:~# ./picture_grabber -W 300 -H 200 -c 5
Encode RGB24
Warning: driver is sending image at 176x144
Creating image: out000.ppm
Creating image: out001.ppm
Creating image: out002.ppm
Creating image: out003.ppm
Creating image: out004.ppm
```

If you try to run the problem using YUYV encode, just add the -y or --yuyv argument to it:

```
root@clanton:~# ./picture_grabber -W 352 -H 288 -c 5 -y
Encode YUYV
Creating image: out000.ppm
Creating image: out001.ppm
Creating image: out002.ppm
Creating image: out003.ppm
Creating image: out004.ppm
```

Working with OpenCV

At this moment you have explored your webcam, you understand how to load the drivers, adjust the resolutions and other settings on your camera, you are aware of the type of formats (encodes) that are supported, and you have idea how Video4Linux works.

Now it is time to start exercising some applications created using OpenCV.

As mentioned in the beginning of this chapter, the topic of OpenCV is worthy of a whole book, and there are several books available with this purpose. The idea here is to learn what is possible with Intel Galileo and OpenCV, to compare performance between C++ and Python, and to identify when a problem is related to OpenCV or if it is related to the wrong settings in Video4Linux.

■ **Note** The examples demonstrated in this chapter are in C++ and Python. OpenCV also supports C, which is not explored here. This is because the C++ interface created for OpenCV is simpler than the C language interface, which requires you to manage memory allocations.

Building Programs with OpenCV

To build programs that run OpenCV, you must follow the same process you followed when compiling the program for Video4Linux in the previous sections. In order words, it is necessary to set the toolchain and run the proper command line.

The procedure is the same as the one outlined in the "Building and Transferring the Video Capture Program" section of this chapter, except the command line changes a little bit because the programs are written in C++ instead C, and it is necessary to invoke the OpenCV libs instead of the V4L2.

For example, to build the program used in the next section listed as Listing 7-1 and named opencv_capimage.cpp, use the following line:

```
${CXX} -O2 'pkg-config --cflags --libs opencv' opencv_capimage.cpp -o
opencv_capimage
```

${CXX} invokes the C++ compiler (g++) of the toolchain and pkg-config invokes the opencv libs.

Once this compiles, you just transfer the program to Intel Galileo if the toolchain is not installed directly on your Intel Galileo.

Capturing an Image with OpenCV

Capturing an image using OpenCV is very simple because all the complexity is abstracted by OpenCV, which uses V4L2 as a baseline.

Figure 7-7 shows the flowchart used to capture images and videos and process the images.

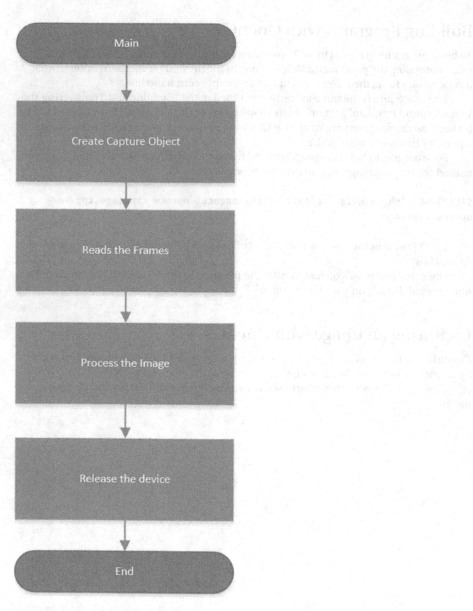

Figure 7-7. *OpenCV flowchart to capture a frame*

Listing 7-1 shows an example of how to capture an image and store it in the file system as a JPEG file.

Listing 7-1. opencv_capimage.cpp

```
#include <opencv2/opencv.hpp>
using namespace cv;
using namespace std;

int main()
{

    VideoCapture cap(-1);

    //check if the file was opened properly
    if(!cap.isOpened())
    {
        cout << "Webcam could not be opened succesfully" << endl;
        exit(-1);
    }
    else
    {
        cout << "p n" << endl;
    }

    int w = 960;
    int h = 544;
    cap.set(CV_CAP_PROP_FRAME_WIDTH, w);
    cap.set(CV_CAP_PROP_FRAME_HEIGHT, h);

    Mat frame;
    cap >>frame;
    imwrite("opencv.jpg", frame);

    cap.release();

    return 0;
}
```

Reviewing opencv_capimage.cpp

This first example uses a few objects based in the following classes. VideoCapture is used to create the capture objects that open and configure the devices, capture images and videos, and release the devices when they are not in use any more. Mat receives frames read and works with some algorithms to process the images. It can apply filters, change colors, and transform the images according to mathematical and statistical algorithms. In the next example, Mat is used only to read the image. However, in the next couple of examples, Mat will be used to process images as well.

To understand the code in Listing 7-1, you need a quick overview of each class used.

355

VideoCapture:: VideoCapture

The first thing to do is to use the VideoCapture class to create a video capture object and open the device or some video stored in the files system.

For more information regarding the VideoCapture class, see http://docs.opencv.org/modules/highgui/doc/reading_and_writing_images_and_video.html.

In the case of the webcam, you will create the object with the parameter -1 in the constructor, as follows:

```
VideoCapture cap(-1);
```

The value -1 means, "open the current device enumerated in the system," so if you have the camera enumerated as /dev/video0 or /dev/video1, the webcam will be opened anyway. Otherwise, if you want to be specific regarding which device to open, you have to pass to the constructor the index of the enumerated device. For example, to open the device /dev/video0, you must pass the number 0 to the constructor like this:

```
VideoCapture cap(0);
```

If you're using Intel Galileo and one camera, I recommend you use -1 to avoid problems with camera enumeration indexes versus the hardcoded number you use in the constructor.

VideoCapture::isOpened()

You can check if the webcam was opened and initiated with success by invoking the isOpened() method. It returns a Boolean as true if the webcam was opened and false if not.

VideoCapture::set(const int prop, int value)

This method sets a property (prop) to a specific value (value). You can set the image's width, height, frames per second, and several other properties. In the code example, the video width and height are set to 960x544:

```
int w = 960;
int h = 544;
cap.set(CV_CAP_PROP_FRAME_WIDTH, w);
cap.set(CV_CAP_PROP_FRAME_HEIGHT, h);
```

For more information about the properties supported, visit http://nullege.com/codes/search/opencv.highgui.CV_CAP_PROP_FPS.

VideoCapture::read(Mat & image) or operator >> (Mat & image)

This method reads the image from the device. It grabs the image in one single call. The return is a Mat object that is explained shortly.

This example uses the operator >>:

```
Mat frame;
cap >>frame;
```

VideoCapture::release()

Once the video is captured, if the destructor of the object is not called, you must release the camera by invoking the release() method.

```
cap.release();
```

At a glance, you can see how simple this is, compared to the software used when we were focusing on Video4Linux.

cv::Mat::Mat

Mat is an awesome class used for matrix operations and it is constantly used in OpenCV applications. Mat is used to organize images in the format of matrixes responsible for saving details of each pixel, including color intensity, position in the image, image dimension, and so on.

The Mat class is organized into two parts—one part contains the image headers with generic information about the image and the second part contains the sequence of bytes representing the image.

In the code example, Mat is called only as Mat instead of as cv::Mat because the namespace was defined in the beginning of the code:

```
using namespace cv;
```

Also, in the code example, there is a Mat object created with the simple constructors available in the class:

```
Mat frame;
```

In the next examples, other methods will be used and properly discussed. For now, keep in mind what the Mat class is for and this simple constructor.

For more details regarding the Mat class, visit http://docs.opencv.org/modules/core/doc/basic_structures.html#mat-mat. The tutorial maintained by docs.opencv.org is also recommended at http://docs.opencv.org/doc/tutorials/core/mat_the_basic_image_container/mat_the_basic_image_container.html.

cv::imwrite(const string& filename, InputArray img, const vector<int>& params=vector<int>())

This method saves an image to the file system. In the code example, the file is opencv.jpg, the input array is intrinsically casted as my Mat class with the object frame, and the optional vector of the params argument is omitted.

```
Mat frame;
cap >>frame;
imwrite("opencv.jpg", frame);
```

In this case, with the omission of the vector of the params argument, the encode used to capture the image is based on the file extension .jpg. Remember that the camera does not support capturing images in the JPEG format. It captures streaming in Motion JPEG but JPEG is not extracted from Motion JPEG because there is segment called DHT that's not present in this stream (check out http://www.digitalpreservation.gov/formats/fdd/fdd000063.shtml). You can extract a series of JPEG images using ffmpeg from a Motion JPEG streaming file, but they will not be viewable in any image software due to the DHT segment missing.

In other words, when the file extension is specified and not supported by the webcam, the OpenCV framework converts the file.

The extensions supported besides JPEG are PNG, PPM, PGM, and PBM.

The docs.opencv.org site maintains a nice tutorial about how to load, modify, and save an image at http://docs.opencv.org/doc/tutorials/introduction/load_save_image/load_save_image.html.

Running opencv_capimage.cpp

Compile the code and transfer the file to Intel Galileo. Make sure the uvcvideo driver is loaded and the webcam is connected to the USB port (read the section called "Connecting the Webcam" in this chapter). Finally, smile at your webcam and run the software:

```
root@clanton:~# ./opencv_capimage
VIDIOC_QUERYMENU: Invalid argument
VIDIOC_QUERYMENU: Invalid argument
VIDIOC_QUERYMENU: Invalid argument
VIDIOC_QUERYMENU: Invalid argument
VIDIOC_QUERYMENU: Invalid argument
VIDIOC_QUERYMENU: Invalid argument
VIDIOC_QUERYMENU: Invalid argument
Webcam is OK! I found it!

VIDIOC_QUERYMENU: Invalid argument
VIDIOC_QUERYMENU: Invalid argument
VIDIOC_QUERYMENU: Invalid argument
VIDIOC_QUERYMENU: Invalid argument
```

```
VIDIOC_QUERYMENU: Invalid argument
VIDIOC_QUERYMENU: Invalid argument
VIDIOC_QUERYMENU: Invalid argument
```

You should have a file named opencv.jpg in the same folder. Now, you might asking what the VIDIOC_QUERYMENU: Invalid argument message mean. Such messages are not related to OpenCV and there is nothing wrong with the code. It is simply OpenCV using the Video4Linux framework to understand the capabilities and controls offered by the webcam. When some control or capability is not offered, V4L informs you with these warning messages.

If you do not want to see these messages, you can redirect them using a stderr stream to a null device. For example:

```
root@clanton:~# ./opencv_capimage 2> /dev/null
Webcam is OK! I found it!
```

The Same Software Written in Python

You can use Python with OpenCV because the Python Opencv development packages are part of the BSP SD card images introduced in this chapter.

The program in Listing 7-1 can easily be converted to Python, as demonstrated by Listing 7-2.

Listing 7-2. opencv_capimage.py

```
import cv2
import cv
import sys

cap = cv2.VideoCapture(-1)

w, h = 960, 544
cap.set(cv.CV_CAP_PROP_FRAME_WIDTH, w)
cap.set(cv.CV_CAP_PROP_FRAME_HEIGHT, h)

if not cap.isOpened():
    print "Webcam could not be opened successfully"
    sys.exit(-1)
else:
    print "Webcam is OK! I found it!"

ret, frame = cap.read()
cv2.imwrite('pythontest.jpg', frame)

cap.release()
```

As you can see, the objects are quite the same. To run the software, transfer to Intel Galileo board and run the following in the terminal shell:

```
root@clanton:~# python opencv_capimage.py  2> /dev/null
Webcam is OK! I found it!
```

However, the examples in this chapter are written in C++. This is because code written in C++ runs significantly faster than the same code written in Python.

Performance of OpenCV C++ versus OpenCV Python

To check for performance issues, suppose you have the Python program shown in Listing 7-2 and the C++ program shown in Listing 7-1 properly installed on Intel Galileo. You can measure performance using the bash terminal with the command date +%s, which returns the number of seconds passed since 00:00:00 1970-01-01 UTC. Execute the program and evaluate the time difference.

First, run the Python program with the following command:

```
root@clanton:~# s=$(date +%s);python opencv_capimage.py; echo $(expr
'date +%s' - $s)
Webcam is OK! I found it!
8
```

Python took eight seconds to take the picture. Do the same thing with the C++ program:

```
root@clanton:~# s=$(date +%s);./opencv_capimage 2> /dev/null; echo
$(expr 'date +%s' - $s)
Webcam is OK! I found it!
4
```

The same program written in C++ took only four seconds. Even the programs running in the userspace context suffer some time execution variation because it's not a real-time system. The OpenCV applications created in C++ are much faster than the same applications running in Python.

Processing Images

In the previous section, you captured images from the webcam and saved them into the files system, but no image processing was done. The next examples explore some of the infinite possibilities of image processing using OpenCV. Some of them use a huge algorithm in the background and it is not in the scope of this book to discuss the details of each one. However, references are included for more information.

Detecting Edges

For the first example of image processing, you'll learn about how to detect images using the Canny edge algorithm developed by John F. Canny in 1986.

OpenCV has a function called Canny() that implements such an algorithm. For details about this algorithm, see http://docs.opencv.org/doc/tutorials/imgproc/imgtrans/canny_detector/canny_detector.html.

With a few changes to Listing 7-1, the Canny algorithm is shown in Listing 7-3.

Listing 7-3. opencv_capimage_canny.cpp

```cpp
#include <opencv2/opencv.hpp>
using namespace cv;
using namespace std;

int main()
{

  VideoCapture cap(-1);

  //check if the file was opened properly
  if(!cap.isOpened())
  {
      cout << "Webcam could not be opened succesfully" << endl;
      exit(-1);
  }
  else
  {
      cout << "Webcam is OK! I found it!\n" << endl;
  }

  int w = 960;
  int h = 544;
  cap.set(CV_CAP_PROP_FRAME_WIDTH, w);
  cap.set(CV_CAP_PROP_FRAME_HEIGHT, h);

  Mat frame;
  cap >>frame;

  // converts the image to grayscale
  Mat frame_in_gray;
  cvtColor(frame, frame_in_gray, CV_BGR2GRAY);

  // process the Canny algorithm
  cout << "processing image with Canny..." << endl;
  int threshold1 = 0;
  int threshold2 = 28;
  Canny(frame_in_gray, frame_in_gray, threshold1, threshold1);
```

361

```
// saving the images in the files system

cout << "Saving the images..." << endl;
imwrite("captured.jpg", frame);
imwrite("captured_with_edges.jpg", frame_in_gray);

// release the camera
cap.release();

return 0;
}
```

Reviewing opencv_capimage_canny.cpp

In this example the following is changed in Listing 7-3:

1.   A new static method called cvtColor() is added.

2.   The Canny() function is used for image processing.

The image originally captured by the camera and the image processed with Canny algorithm are both stored in the file system as captured.jpg and captured_with_edges.jpg using the imwrite() function explained previously.

void cv::cvtColor(InputArray src, OutputArray dst, int code, int dstCn=0)

Converts the image space color to another one. In the following code example:

```
Mat frame_in_gray;
cvtColor(frame, frame_in_gray, CV_BGR2GRAY);
```

The input image was the one captured by the webcam and stored in the Mat object frame. The frame_in_gray object was created to receive the image converted in gray space color as requested by code CV_BGR2GRAY.

For more detail about the cvtColor() function and color in general, visit http://docs.opencv.org/modules/imgproc/doc/miscellaneous_transformations.html#cvtcolor.

void cv::Canny(InputArray image, OutputArray edges, double threshold1, double threshold2, int apertureSize=3, bool L2gradient=false)

The Canny function takes the image input array as a source image and transforms the edges into sharp ones. It stores the output array in edges. The input and output image in the example is the same object (frame_in_gray); for best effect, a grayscale image is used.

The apertureSize argument is the size of the Sobel operator used in the algorithm (see http://en.wikipedia.org/wiki/Sobel_operator for more details) and the code keeps the default value of 3.

The L2gradient argument is a Boolean; when it's true, the image gradient magnitude is used and when it's false, only the normative equation is considered. This example used the default value of false.

Two hysteresis thresholds are represented by the arguments threshold1 and threshold2 and the values 0 and 28 were used, respectively. These values are based on my experiments with changing these values until I got results I considered good. You can change these values and check the effects you get.

```
int threshold1 = 0;
int threshold2 = 28;
Canny(frame_in_gray, frame_in_gray, threshold1, threshold1);
```

The official documentation about Canvas function is found on this link "*http://docs.opencv.org/modules/imgproc/doc/feature_detection.html?highlight=canny#canny.*"

Running opencv_capimage_canny.cpp

Compile the code and transfer the file to Intel Galileo. Make sure the uvcvideo driver is loaded and the webcam is connected to the USB port (read the section entitled "Connecting the Webcam" in this chapter). Point your webcam to some object rich in edges, like the image shown in Figures 7-8 and 7-9.

```
root@clanton:~# ./opencv_capimage_canny 2> /dev/null
Webcam is OK! I found it!

processing image with Canny...
Saving the images...
```

Figure 7-8. Original image before the Canny effect

Figure 7-9. *Image after the Canny effect*

You should have two images stored in the file system as *captured.jpg* and *captured_with_edges.jpg*.

Face and Eyes Detection

This next example detects multiples faces and eyes in a picture captured using the webcam. The class used to detect the faces and eyes is named CascadeClassifier.

The basic concept is that this class loads some XML files that use the *classifier model*. In the code, two files are loaded—called haarcascade_frontalface_alt.xml and haarcascade_eye.xml—during the creation of the CascadeClassifier objects. Each file brings a series of models that defines how specific objects are represented in the image based on the sum of intensity of pixels in a series of rectangles. The difference of these sums is evaluated in the image. Both files have characteristics about faces and eyes from an image and the class CascadeClassifier can determine the detections when the method detectMultiScale() is invoked.

For more information related to CascadeClassifier(), visit http://docs.opencv.org/modules/objdetect/doc/cascade_classification.html?highlight=cascadeclassifier#cascadeclassifier.

Also read "Global Haar-Like Features: A New Extension of Classic Haar Features for Efficient Face Detection in Noisy Images," 6th Pacific-Rim. Symposium on Image and Video Technology, PSIVT 2013," by Mahdi Rezaei, Hossein Ziaei Nafchi, and Sandino Morales.

When a face is detected a rectangle will be drawn around the face and when the eyes are detected circles will be drawn around the eyes. These drawing are done using very basic draw functions in OpenCV called rectangle() and circle().

Listing 7-4 shows the code for this example.

Listing 7-4. opencv_face_and_eyes_detection.cpp

```cpp
#include <opencv2/opencv.hpp>
#include "opencv2/core/core.hpp"

using namespace cv;
using namespace std;

String face_cascade_name = "haarcascade_frontalface_alt.xml";
String eye_cascade_name = "haarcascade_eye.xml";

void faceDetect(Mat img);
CascadeClassifier face_cascade;
CascadeClassifier eyes_cascade;

using namespace cv;
using namespace std;

int main(int argc, const char *argv[])
{

  if( !face_cascade.load( face_cascade_name ) )
  {
    cout << face_cascade_name << " not found!! aborting..." << endl;
    exit(-1);
  };

  if( !eyes_cascade.load( eye_cascade_name ) )
  {
    cout << eye_cascade_name << " not found!! aborting..." << endl;
    exit(-1);
  };

  // 0 is the ID of the built-in laptop camera, change if you want to use
other camera
  VideoCapture cap(-1);

  //check if the file was opened properly
  if(!cap.isOpened())
  {
    cout << "Capture could not be opened succesfully" << endl;
    return -1;
  }
```

```
    else
    {
        cout << "camera is ok\n" << endl;
    }

    int w = 432;
    int h = 240;
    cap.set(CV_CAP_PROP_FRAME_WIDTH, w);
    cap.set(CV_CAP_PROP_FRAME_HEIGHT, h);

    Mat frame;
    cap >>frame;

    cout << "processing the image...." << endl;

    faceDetect(frame);
    imwrite("face_and_eyes.jpg", frame);

    // release the camera
    cap.release();

    cout << "done!" << endl;
    return 0;
}

void faceDetect(Mat img)
{
    std::vector<Rect> faces;
    std::vector<Rect> eyes;
    bool two_eyes = false;
    bool any_eye_detected = false;

    //detecting faces
    face_cascade.detectMultiScale( img, faces, 1.1, 2, 0|CV_HAAR_SCALE_IMAGE,
Size(30, 30) );

    if (faces.size() == 0)
    {
        cout << "Try again.. I did not dectected any faces..." << endl;
        return;
    }

    // it is possible to face more than one human face in the image
    for( size_t i = 0; i < faces.size(); i++ )
    {
```

```
    // rectangle in the face
    rectangle( img, faces[i], Scalar( 255, 100, 0 ), 4, 8, 0 );

    Mat frame_gray;
    cvtColor( img, frame_gray, CV_BGR2GRAY );

    // croping only the face in region defined by faces[i]
    std::vector<Rect> eyes;
    Mat faceROI = frame_gray( faces[i] );

    // In each face, detect eyes
    eyes_cascade.detectMultiScale( faceROI, eyes, 1.1, 2, 0
|CV_HAAR_SCALE_IMAGE, Size(30, 30) );

    for( size_t j = 0; j < eyes.size(); j++ )
    {
        Point center( faces[i].x + eyes[j].x + eyes[j].width*0.5,
faces[i].y + eyes[j].y + eyes[j].height*0.5 );
        int radius = cvRound( (eyes[j].width + eyes[j].height)*0.25 );
        circle( img, center, radius, Scalar( 255, 0, 0 ), 4, 8, 0 );

    }

    }

}
```

Reviewing opencv_face_and_eyes_detection.cpp

In this example there are a few new components:

- Introduction of the CascadeClassifier class.

- Usage of the Point class

- The cvRound() function

- Usage of the rectangle() and circle() functions

- The Rect class and vectors

The following sections provide an explanation of each item used in the code.

cv::CascadeClassifier::CascadeClassifier()

Creates the CascadeClassifier object. In the example code, two objects are created, one to detect the face and the other to detect the eyes.

```
CascadeClassifier face_cascade;
CascadeClassifier eyes_cascade;
```

cv::CascadeClassifier::load(const string & filename)

Loads the file with the classifier to the object. In the code, two classifiers were used, one to detect the face and the other to detect the eyes.

```
if( !face_cascade.load( face_cascade_name ) )
{
  cout << face_cascade_name << " not found!! aborting..." << endl;
  exit(-1);
};

if( !eyes_cascade.load( eye_cascade_name ) )
{
  cout << eye_cascade_name << " not found!! aborting..." << endl;
  exit(-1);
};
```

void cv::CascadeClassifier::detectMultiScale(const Mat& image, vector<Rect>& objects, double scaleFactor=1.1, int minNeighbors=3, int flags=0, SizeminSize=Size(), Size maxSize=Size())

The detectMultiScale() method is where the magic happens in terms of detections. A description of each argument follows:

- image is the image source.

- vector<Rect>& objects is a vector of rectangles and is where the object detects are in the image.

- scaleFactor is a factor that determine if the image is reduced.

- minNeighbors determines how many neighbors each candidate rectangle has. If 0 is passed, there is a risk of other objects in the image being detected incorrectly, which results in false positives in the detection. For example, if you have a clock on your wall it might be detected as a face (a false positive). During my practical experiments, specifying 2 or 3 is good. More than 3 and there is a risk of losing true positives and faces not being detected properly.

- Flags is related to the type of optimization. CV_HAAR_SCALE_IMAGE tells the algorithm to be in charge of the scaled image. This flags accepts CV_HAAR_DO_CANNY_PRUNNING, which skips flat regions, CV_HAAR_FIND_BIGGEST_OBJECT if there is interest in finding the biggest object in the image, and CV_HAAR_DO_ROUGH_SEARCH, which must be used only with CV_HAAR_FIND_BIGGEST_OBJECT lile "0|CV_HAAR_DO_ROUGH_SEARCH |CV_HAAR_FIND_BIGGEST_OBJECT".

- SizeminSize defines the minimum object size and objects smaller than this are ignored. If it's not defined this argument is not considered.

- maxSize defines the maximum object size and objects bigger than this are ignored. If it's not defined this argument is not considered.

```
//detecting faces
face_cascade.detectMultiScale( img, faces, 1.1, 2, 0|CV_HAAR_SCALE_IMAGE,
Size(30, 30) );
```

```
...
...
...
```

```
//In each face, detect eyes
eyes_cascade.detectMultiScale( faceROI, eyes, 1.1, 2, 0
|CV_HAAR_SCALE_IMAGE, Size(30, 30)
```

In this code, the scaling factor used is 1.1, minNeighbors is 2 (a kind of hint), the flags are optimized for performance using CV_HAAR_SCALE_IMAGE, and the minimum size of the object to detect is 30x30 pixels. No maximum size is defined, so you can put your face very close to the webcam.

The code detected the faces in the image. For each face that's detected, a rectangle is drawn delimiting the region.

```
// rectangle in the face
rectangle( img, faces[i], Scalar( 255, 100, 0 ), 4, 8, 0 );
```

The resulting regions containing the faces detected are stored in vector<Rect> faces. For example, faces[0] is the first face in the picture. If there is more than one person, you will have face[1], face[2], and so on. The object type Rect means rectangle so the faces vector is a group of rectangles without graphical objects. They are objects that store the initial coordinates (upper-left points) in (Rec.x,Rec.y) and the width (Rec.w) and height (Rec.h) of the rectangle in the object class.

For each region detected, a new image is created with the image content delimited by the rectangle, which forms a small area. This small area is called the *ROI* (Region of Interest). For best performance and to normalize the image in the eye, detection is converted to grayscale using the cvColor() function.

```
Mat frame_gray;
cvtColor( img, frame_gray, CV_BGR2GRAY );
// croping only the face in region defined by faces[i]
std::vector<Rect> eyes;
Mat faceROI = frame_gray( faces[i] );
```

In this small area that contains only the face, the cascade classifier tries to identify the eyes. For each eye detected, a circle is drawn. So the while the face uses the whole image to be detected, the eyes are detected only in the face regions. This optimizes the algorithm.

```
// In each face, detect eyes
eyes_cascade.detectMultiScale( faceROI, eyes, 1.1, 2, 0
|CV_HAAR_SCALE_IMAGE, Size(30, 30) );
```

The resultant regions containing the eyes is stored in vector<Rect> eyes.
This process is done with the for loops in this code:

```
for( size_t i = 0; i < faces.size(); i++ )
{

...
...
...

    for( size_t j = 0; j < eyes.size(); j++ )
    {
...
...
...     }

}
```

To draw the circles around the eyes, the Point class was used. It extracts information from vector<Rect> eyes and stores the exact center of the eyes (the central coordinates):

```
Point center( faces[i].x + eyes[j].x + eyes[j].width*0.5, faces[i].y +
eyes[j].y + eyes[j].height*0.5 );
int radius = cvRound( (eyes[j].width + eyes[j].height)*0.25 );
circle( img, center, radius, Scalar( 255, 0, 0 ), 4, 8, 0 );
```

Thus, the Point center object is based on the rectangle's dimension of the current face, identified by the center point of the eye and the variable radius. Using the function cvRound(), it determines the radius to be drawn around the eyes.

With those two information, it is possible to draw a circle using the function circle().

Figure 7-10 shows this code's sequence.

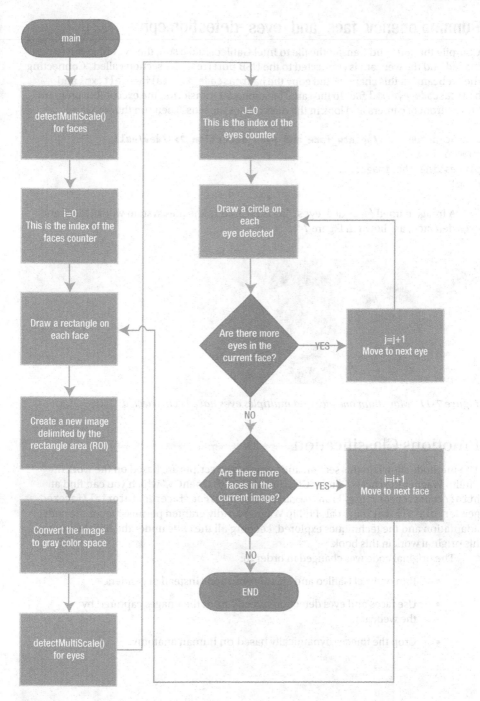

Figure 7-10. Flowchart for detecting faces and eyes

Running opencv_face_and_eyes_detection.cpp

Compile the code and transfer the file to Intel Galileo. Make sure the uvcvideo driver was loaded and the webcam is connected to the USB port (read the section called "Connecting the Webcam" in this chapter) and copy the haarcascade_frontalface_alt.xml and haarcascade_eye.xml files to the same location you transferred the executable program. Stay in front of camera and look in the direction of the lens. Then run the software:

```
root@clanton:~# ./opencv_face_and_eyes_detection 2> /dev/null
camera is ok
processing the image....
done!
```

A image named face_and_eyes.jpg is created in the files system wilt all faces and eyes detected, as shown in Figure 7-11.

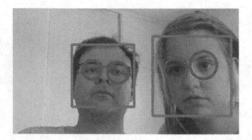

Figure 7-11. *More than one face and multiples eyes have been detected*

Emotions Classification

The methods shown in this section and some of the scripts are based on the work of Phillip Wagner in article "Gender Classification with OpenCV," which you can find at http://docs.opencv.org/trunk/modules/contrib/doc/facerec/tutorial/facerec_gender_classification.html. Phillip Wagner kindly granted permission for the code adaptation and the techniques explored, keeping all the code under the BSD licenses as his original work in this book.

The original code was changed in order to:

- Run on Intel Galileo and classify emotions instead of genders.

- Use faces and eyes detection directly from the images captured by the webcam.

- Crop the images dynamically based on human anatomy.

The emotions classifications in this example are divided into three categories:

- Happy
- Sad
- Curious

The idea is that you take pictures with the webcam, and Intel Galileo will try to describe your emotional state.

You need to create a database with images of you showing each emotional state. This database will contain images that use specific algorithms explained later. These images are used as references to allow Intel Galileo to determine your emotions while you look at the webcam through a model named fisherface.

The database in this chapter is based on my face, but there are instructions for recreating the database based on your face. If you run the program using this section, there is a remote chance that it will recognize your emotions (if you are lucky enough to look like me). Okay, if you look like me, you are not necessarily lucky (ha ha).

Preparing the Desktop

You need to create a database with a few pictures of you. The process for generating this database is explained in detail in conjunction with some scripts that run in Python.

It's necessary to have Python installed on your computer, with the pillow and setuptools modules installed.

Pillow is used to treat images using Python scripts and setuptools is a dependence that pillow requests. You should install the setuptools module first.

Pillow can be downloaded from https://pypi.python.org/pypi/Pillow and the setuptools module can be downloaded from https://pypi.python.org/pypi/setuptools. Both sites include information on how to install these modules on Linux, Windows, and MacOSX.

You will also need an image editor because it's necessary to take some pictures of your face with different emotions and identify the coordinates of the center of each of your eyes. You can use Paint in Windows, Gimp on Linux/OSX and Windows, or any other software that allows you to move the mouse cursor in the image and obtain the coordinates.

You can download Gimp from http://www.gimp.org/.

Creating the Database

Follow these steps to create the database:

1. Obtain the initial images.

2. Crop the images.

3. Organize the images in directories.

4. Create the CSV file.

Let's look at each step in more detail.

Obtaining the Initial Images

This example uses three emotions—happy, sad, and surprised. That means the database must contain at least three pictures of you of each state.

Such pictures must be obtained using your webcam. It doesn't matter if you obtain the images with Intel Galileo using the code examples described previously, or if you connect the webcam to your computer and take the pictures using other software. The most important thing is to take at least three pictures of each emotion—sad, surprised, and happy—totalizing nine pictures. I recommend you take these pictures at a resolution of 1280x1024 or 1280x720. The images will be cropped and reduced and it is important to maintain the images with good definition after these changes.

In the initial_pictures subfolder of the code folder of this chapter, there are some pictures of me of each emotion. For each picture the pixel coordinates of the center of my eyes were taken—see Table 7-2.

Table 7-2. *Central Coordinate of Each Eye on Each Emotional State*

Picture	Left Eye Center (x,y)	Right Eye Center (x,y)
serious_01.jpg	528, 423	770, 431
serious_02.jpg	522,412	758, 415
serious_03.jpg	518, 423	754, 425
smile_01.jpg	516, 377	753, 379
smile_02.jpg	533, 374	763, 380
smile_03.jpg	518, 379	749, 381
surprised_01.jpg	516,356	754,355
surprised_02.jpg	548, 364	793, 364
surprised_03.jpg	528, 377	770, 378

Be expressive when you take the pictures. Otherwise, it will be more difficult for the program to guess your emotional states.

Cropping the Images

The next step is to crop the images, removing the ears and hair, and try to generate 20x20 images with only the faces showing. The Python script that was initially created for gender classification was adapted to emotion classification, as shown in Listing 7-5.

Listing 7-5. align_faces.py

```python
#!/usr/bin/env python
# Software License Agreement (BSD License)
#
# Copyright (c) 2012, Philipp Wagner
# All rights reserved.
#
# Redistribution and use in source and binary forms, with or without
# modification, are permitted provided that the following conditions
# are met:
#
#  * Redistributions of source code must retain the above copyright
#    notice, this list of conditions and the following disclaimer.
#  * Redistributions in binary form must reproduce the above
#    copyright notice, this list of conditions and the following
#    disclaimer in the documentation and/or other materials provided
#    with the distribution.
#  * Neither the name of the author nor the names of its
#    contributors may be used to endorse or promote products derived
#    from this software without specific prior written permission.
#
# THIS SOFTWARE IS PROVIDED BY THE COPYRIGHT HOLDERS AND CONTRIBUTORS
# "AS IS" AND ANY EXPRESS OR IMPLIED WARRANTIES, INCLUDING, BUT NOT
# LIMITED TO, THE IMPLIED WARRANTIES OF MERCHANTABILITY AND FITNESS
# FOR A PARTICULAR PURPOSE ARE DISCLAIMED. IN NO EVENT SHALL THE
# COPYRIGHT OWNER OR CONTRIBUTORS BE LIABLE FOR ANY DIRECT, INDIRECT,
# INCIDENTAL, SPECIAL, EXEMPLARY, OR CONSEQUENTIAL DAMAGES (INCLUDING,
# BUT NOT LIMITED TO, PROCUREMENT OF SUBSTITUTE GOODS OR SERVICES;
# LOSS OF USE, DATA, OR PROFITS; OR BUSINESS INTERRUPTION) HOWEVER
# CAUSED AND ON ANY THEORY OF LIABILITY, WHETHER IN CONTRACT, STRICT
# LIABILITY, OR TORT (INCLUDING NEGLIGENCE OR OTHERWISE) ARISING IN
# ANY WAY OUT OF THE USE OF THIS SOFTWARE, EVEN IF ADVISED OF THE
# POSSIBILITY OF SUCH DAMAGE.
#
# Manoel Ramon 06/11/2014- changed the code to support images used
#                          as example of emotion classification
#
import sys, math, Image

def Distance(p1,p2):
    dx = p2[0] - p1[0]
    dy = p2[1] - p1[1]
    return math.sqrt(dx*dx+dy*dy)
```

375

```
def ScaleRotateTranslate(image, angle, center = None, new_center = None,
scale = None, resample=Image.BICUBIC):
  if (scale is None) and (center is None):
    return image.rotate(angle=angle, resample=resample)
  nx,ny = x,y = center
  sx=sy=1.0
  if new_center:
    (nx,ny) = new_center
  if scale:
    (sx,sy) = (scale, scale)
  cosine = math.cos(angle)
  sine = math.sin(angle)
  a = cosine/sx
  b = sine/sx
  c = x-nx*a-ny*b
  d = -sine/sy
  e = cosine/sy
  f = y-nx*d-ny*e
  return image.transform(image.size, Image.AFFINE, (a,b,c,d,e,f),
resample=resample)

def CropFace(image, eye_left=(0,0), eye_right=(0,0), offset_pct=(0.2,0.2),
dest_sz = (70,70)):
  # calculate offsets in original image
  offset_h = math.floor(float(offset_pct[0])*dest_sz[0])
  offset_v = math.floor(float(offset_pct[1])*dest_sz[1])
  # get the direction
  eye_direction = (eye_right[0] - eye_left[0], eye_right[1] - eye_left[1])
  # calc rotation angle in radians
  rotation = -math.atan2(float(eye_direction[1]),float(eye_direction[0]))
  # distance between them
  dist = Distance(eye_left, eye_right)
  # calculate the reference eye-width
  reference = dest_sz[0] - 2.0*offset_h
  # scale factor
  scale = float(dist)/float(reference)
  # rotate original around the left eye
  image = ScaleRotateTranslate(image, center=eye_left, angle=rotation)
  # crop the rotated image
  crop_xy = (eye_left[0] - scale*offset_h, eye_left[1] - scale*offset_v)
  crop_size = (dest_sz[0]*scale, dest_sz[1]*scale)
  image = image.crop((int(crop_xy[0]), int(crop_xy[1]),
int(crop_xy[0]+crop_size[0]), int(crop_xy[1]+crop_size[1])))
  # resize it
  image = image.resize(dest_sz, Image.ANTIALIAS)
  return image
```

```python
if __name__ == "__main__":

#Serious_01.jpg
#left -> 528, 423
#right -> 770, 431

  image =  Image.open("serious_01.jpg")
  CropFace(image, eye_left=(528,423), eye_right=(770,431),
offset_pct=(0.2,0.2)).save("serious01_20_20_70_70.jpg")

#Serious_02.jpg
#left  -> 522,412
#right -> 758, 415

  image =  Image.open("serious_02.jpg")
  CropFace(image, eye_left=(522,412), eye_right=(758,415),
offset_pct=(0.2,0.2)).save("serious02_20_20_70_70.jpg")

#Serious_03.jpg
#left  -> 518, 423
#right -> 754, 425

  image =  Image.open("serious_03.jpg")
  CropFace(image, eye_left=(518,423), eye_right=(754,425),
offset_pct=(0.2,0.2)).save("serious03_20_20_70_70.jpg")

#Smile_01.jpg
#left  -> 516, 377
#right -> 753, 379

  image =  Image.open("smile_01.jpg")
  CropFace(image, eye_left=(516,377), eye_right=(753,379),
offset_pct=(0.2,0.2)).save("smile01_20_20_70_70.jpg")

#Smile_02.jpg
#left  -> 533, 374
#right -> 763, 380

  image =  Image.open("smile_02.jpg")
  CropFace(image, eye_left=(533,374), eye_right=(763,380),
offset_pct=(0.2,0.2)).save("smile02_20_20_70_70.jpg")

#Smile_03.jpg
#left  -> 518, 379
#right -> 749, 381
```

```
  image =  Image.open("smile_03.jpg")
  CropFace(image, eye_left=(518,379), eye_right=(749,381),
offset_pct=(0.2,0.2)).save("smile03_20_20_70_70.jpg")


#surprised_01.jpg
#left -> 516,356
#right -> 754,355

  image =  Image.open("surprised_01.jpg")
  CropFace(image, eye_left=(516,356), eye_right=(754,355),
offset_pct=(0.2,0.2)).save("surprised01_20_20_70_70.jpg")


#surprised_02.jpg
#left -> 548, 364
#right -> 793, 364

  image =  Image.open("surprised_02.jpg")
  CropFace(image, eye_left=(548,364), eye_right=(793,364),
offset_pct=(0.2,0.2)).save("surprised02_20_20_70_70.jpg")

#surprised_03.jpg
#left -> 528, 377
#right -> 770, 378

  image =  Image.open("surprised_03.jpg")
  CropFace(image, eye_left=(528,377), eye_right=(770,378),
offset_pct=(0.2,0.2)).save("surprised03_20_20_70_70.jpg")
```

If you use the same filenames in your pictures, the only thing that you must change are the coordinates of your eyes for each picture. Then you copy the script into the same folder your pictures are in and run this in the computer shell:

```
mcramon@ubuntu:~/tmp/opencv/emotion/mypics$ python align_faces.py
```

A series of images with the suffix _20_20_70_70 is created:

```
mcramon@ubuntu:~/tmp/opencv/emotion/mypics$ ls *20*
serious01_20_20_70_70.jpg  smile01_20_20_70_70.jpg  surprised01_20_20_70_70.jpg
serious02_20_20_70_70.jpg  smile02_20_20_70_70.jpg  surprised02_20_20_70_70.jpg
serious03_20_20_70_70.jpg  smile03_20_20_70_70.jpg  surprised03_20_20_70_70.jpg
```

If you use different filenames and a different number of pictures, you need to change the script accordingly.

Do not worry about the details of this code; only keep in mind that this script uses the `pillow` module to create an image object that, using the `CropFace()` function, crops the image according to the scale reduction. For example, to crop the image file `surprised_02.jpg` to a scale of 20% x 20%, the following line of code is necessary:

```
image = Image.open("surprised_02.jpg")
CropFace(image, eye_left=(548,364), eye_right=(793,364),
offset_pct=(0.2,0.2)).save("surprised02_20_20_70_70.jpg")
```

As a result, all the images will contain only your face, as shown in Figure 7-12.

Figure 7-12. *Emotion pictures cropped*

The next step is to transfer these cropped images to Intel Galileo. A quick way to do that if you are using Linux, MacOSX, or Windows Cygwin and have Intel Galileo with a valid IP address on your network is to use `scp`. Run the following in the command line in the directory containing your images:

```
mcramon@ubuntu:~/tmp/opencv/emotion/mypics$ for i in $(ls *20*);do scp $i
root@192.254.1.1:/home/root/. ;done
```

All the images are transferred to the /home/root directory.

Organizing the Images in Directories

With the images transferred to Intel Galileo, organize the images by creating a directory for each type of emotion and transfer the pictures to the corresponding directory. For example, use the `mkdir` command to create the `serious`, `smile`, and `surprised`

379

directories. Move each picture with the mv command to the corresponding directory.
The result is something like this:

```
.
├── serious
│   ├── serious01_20_20_70_70.jpg
│   ├── serious02_20_20_70_70.jpg
│   └── serious03_20_20_70_70.jpg
├── smile
│   ├── smile01_20_20_70_70.jpg
│   ├── smile02_20_20_70_70.jpg
│   └── smile03_20_20_70_70.jpg
└── surprised
    ├── surprised01_20_20_70_70.jpg
    ├── surprised02_20_20_70_70.jpg
    └── surprised03_20_20_70_70.jpg
```

Creating the CSV File

The last step in creating the database is to create a CSV (comma-separated values) file.
This is a simple text file that describes the exact location of each image and categorizes
each image by emotion based on the directory.

An example of a CV file is shown in Listing 7-6.

Listing 7-6. my_csv.csv

```
/home/root/emotion/pics/smile/smile01_20_20_70_70.jpg;0
/home/root/emotion/pics/smile/smile02_20_20_70_70.jpg;0
/home/root/emotion/pics/smile/smile03_20_20_70_70.jpg;0
/home/root/emotion/pics/surprised/surprised01_20_20_70_70.jpg;1
/home/root/emotion/pics/surprised/surprised02_20_20_70_70.jpg;1
/home/root/emotion/pics/surprised/surprised03_20_20_70_70.jpg;1
/home/root/emotion/pics/serious/serious01_20_20_70_70.jpg;2
/home/root/emotion/pics/serious/serious02_20_20_70_70.jpg;2
/home/root/emotion/pics/serious/serious03_20_20_70_70.jpg;2
```

Note that each image is delimited by ; with an index that represents the emotional
state of the picture. In Listing 7-6, 0 represents smiling, 1 represents surprise, and 2
represents seriousness.

The script that helps create CSV files is shown in Listing 7-7.

Listing 7-7. create_csv.py

```
#!/usr/bin/env python
# Software License Agreement (BSD License)
#
# Copyright (c) 2012, Philipp Wagner
# All rights reserved.
#
```

```
# Redistribution and use in source and binary forms, with or without
# modification, are permitted provided that the following conditions
# are met:
#
# * Redistributions of source code must retain the above copyright
#   notice, this list of conditions and the following disclaimer.
# * Redistributions in binary form must reproduce the above
#   copyright notice, this list of conditions and the following
#   disclaimer in the documentation and/or other materials provided
#   with the distribution.
# * Neither the name of the author nor the names of its
#   contributors may be used to endorse or promote products derived
#   from this software without specific prior written permission.
#
# THIS SOFTWARE IS PROVIDED BY THE COPYRIGHT HOLDERS AND CONTRIBUTORS
# "AS IS" AND ANY EXPRESS OR IMPLIED WARRANTIES, INCLUDING, BUT NOT
# LIMITED TO, THE IMPLIED WARRANTIES OF MERCHANTABILITY AND FITNESS
# FOR A PARTICULAR PURPOSE ARE DISCLAIMED. IN NO EVENT SHALL THE
# COPYRIGHT OWNER OR CONTRIBUTORS BE LIABLE FOR ANY DIRECT, INDIRECT,
# INCIDENTAL, SPECIAL, EXEMPLARY, OR CONSEQUENTIAL DAMAGES (INCLUDING,
# BUT NOT LIMITED TO, PROCUREMENT OF SUBSTITUTE GOODS OR SERVICES;
# LOSS OF USE, DATA, OR PROFITS; OR BUSINESS INTERRUPTION) HOWEVER
# CAUSED AND ON ANY THEORY OF LIABILITY, WHETHER IN CONTRACT, STRICT
# LIABILITY, OR TORT (INCLUDING NEGLIGENCE OR OTHERWISE) ARISING IN
# ANY WAY OUT OF THE USE OF THIS SOFTWARE, EVEN IF ADVISED OF THE
# POSSIBILITY OF SUCH DAMAGE.

import sys
import os.path

# This is a tiny script to help you creating a CSV file from a face
# database with a similar hierarchie:
#
#   philipp@mango:~/facerec/data/at$ tree
#   .
#   |-- README
#   |-- s1
#   |   |-- 1.pgm
#   |   |-- ...
#   |   |-- 10.pgm
#   |-- s2
#   |   |-- 1.pgm
#   |   |-- ...
#   |   |-- 10.pgm
#   ...
```

```
# |-- s40
# |    |-- 1.pgm
# |    |-- ...
# |    |-- 10.pgm
#

if __name__ == "__main__":

    if len(sys.argv) != 2:
        print "usage: create_csv <base_path>"
        sys.exit(1)

    BASE_PATH=sys.argv[1]
    SEPARATOR=";"

    label = 0
    for dirname, dirnames, filenames in os.walk(BASE_PATH):
        for subdirname in dirnames:
            subject_path = os.path.join(dirname, subdirname)
            for filename in os.listdir(subject_path):
                abs_path = "%s/%s" % (subject_path, filename)
                print "%s%s%d" % (abs_path, SEPARATOR, label)
            label = label + 1
```

Transfer this file to Intel Galileo and run the following command line:

```
python create_csv.py <the ABSOLUTE directory path> > <your file name>
```

For example:

root@clanton:~/emotion# python create_csv.py $(pwd)/pics/ > my_csv.csv

And check the file:

root@clanton:~/emotion# cat my_csv.csv
```
/home/root/emotion/pics/smile/smile01_20_20_70_70.jpg;0
/home/root/emotion/pics/smile/smile02_20_20_70_70.jpg;0
/home/root/emotion/pics/smile/smile03_20_20_70_70.jpg;0
/home/root/emotion/pics/surprised/surprised01_20_20_70_70.jpg;1
/home/root/emotion/pics/surprised/surprised02_20_20_70_70.jpg;1
/home/root/emotion/pics/surprised/surprised03_20_20_70_70.jpg;1
/home/root/emotion/pics/serious/serious01_20_20_70_70.jpg;2
/home/root/emotion/pics/serious/serious02_20_20_70_70.jpg;2
/home/root/emotion/pics/serious/serious03_20_20_70_70.jpg;2
```

The Code for Emotion Classification

The code for emotion classification uses a class called FaceRecognizer, which is responsible for reading your models. In other words, it reads the pictures and each state index in the database and, using a model called fisherface, feeds (or trains) the model in order to be able to predict emotions.

The code in this section is based on the code presented in Listing 7-7. Listing 7-8 shows the code with the new parts in bold.

Listing 7-8. opencv_emotion_classification.cpp

```
/*
 * Copyright (c) 2011. Philipp Wagner <bytefish[at]gmx[dot]de>.
 * Released to public domain under terms of the BSD Simplified license.
 *
 * Redistribution and use in source and binary forms, with or without
 * modification, are permitted provided that the following conditions are met:
 *    * Redistributions of source code must retain the above copyright
 *      notice, this list of conditions and the following disclaimer.
 *    * Redistributions in binary form must reproduce the above copyright
 *      notice, this list of conditions and the following disclaimer in the
 *      documentation and/or other materials provided with the distribution.
 *    * Neither the name of the organization nor the names of its contributors
 *      may be used to endorse or promote products derived from this software
 *      without specific prior written permission.
 *
 *   See <http://www.opensource.org/licenses/bsd-license>
 *
 *   Manoel Ramon - 06/15/2014
 *   manoel.ramon@gmail.com
 *                 code changed from original facerec_fisherface.cpp
 *                 added:
 *                 - adaption to emotions detection instead gender
 *                 - picture took from the default video device
 *                 - added face and eyes recognition
 *                 - crop images based in human anatomy
 *                 - prediction based in face recognized
 *
 */

#include <opencv2/opencv.hpp>
#include <stdio.h>
#include "opencv2/imgproc/imgproc.hpp"
#include "opencv2/core/core.hpp"
#include "opencv2/contrib/contrib.hpp"
#include "opencv2/highgui/highgui.hpp"
```

```cpp
#include <iostream>
#include <fstream>
#include <sstream>

using namespace cv;
using namespace std;

String face_cascade_name = "haarcascade_frontalface_alt.xml";
String eye_cascade_name = "haarcascade_eye.xml";

Mat faceDetect(Mat img);
CascadeClassifier face_cascade;
CascadeClassifier eyes_cascade;

using namespace cv;
using namespace std;

enum EmotionState_t {
    SMILE      =0,   // 0
    SURPRISED,       // 1
    SERIOUS,         // 2
};

static void read_csv(const string& filename, vector<Mat>& images,
vector<int>& labels, char separator = ';') {
    std::ifstream file(filename.c_str(), ifstream::in);
    if (!file) {
        string error_message = "No valid input file was given, please check
the given filename.";
        CV_Error(CV_StsBadArg, error_message);
    }
    string line, path, classlabel;
    while (getline(file, line)) {
        stringstream liness(line);
        getline(liness, path, separator);
        getline(liness, classlabel);
        if(!path.empty() && !classlabel.empty()) {
            images.push_back(imread(path, 0));
            labels.push_back(atoi(classlabel.c_str()));
        }
    }
}
```

```
int main(int argc, const char *argv[])
{

  EmotionState_t emotion;

  // Check for valid command line arguments, print usage
  // if no arguments were given.
  if (argc < 2) {
    cout << "usage: " << argv[0] << " <csv.ext> <output_folder> " << endl;
    exit(1);
  }

  if( !face_cascade.load( face_cascade_name ) ){ printf("--(!)Error
loading\n"); return -1; };
  if( !eyes_cascade.load( eye_cascade_name ) ){ printf("--(!)Error
loading\n"); return -1; };

  // 0 is the ID of the built-in laptop camera, change if you want to use
other camera
  VideoCapture cap(-1);

  //check if the file was opened properly
  if(!cap.isOpened())
  {
      cout << "Capture could not be opened succesfully" << endl;
      return -1;
  }
  else
  {
      cout << "camera is ok.. Stay 2 ft away from your camera\n" << endl;
  }

  int w = 432;
  int h = 240;
  cap.set(CV_CAP_PROP_FRAME_WIDTH, w);
  cap.set(CV_CAP_PROP_FRAME_HEIGHT, h);

  Mat frame;
  cap >>frame;

  cout << "processing the image...." << endl;

  Mat testSample = faceDetect(frame);
```

```
// Get the path to your CSV.
string fn_csv = string(argv[1]);
// These vectors hold the images and corresponding labels.
vector<Mat> images;
vector<int> labels;
// Read in the data. This can fail if no valid
// input filename is given.
try
{
  read_csv(fn_csv, images, labels);
} catch (cv::Exception& e) {
  cerr << "Error opening file \"" << fn_csv << "\". Reason: "
<< e.msg << endl;
  // nothing more we can do
  exit(1);
}
// Quit if there are not enough images for this demo.
if(images.size() <= 1)
{
  string error_message = "This demo needs at least 2 images to
work. Please add more images to your data set!";
  CV_Error(CV_StsError, error_message);
}
// Get the height from the first image. We'll need this
// later in code to reshape the images to their original
// size:
int height = images[0].rows;

// The following lines create an Fisherfaces model for
// face recognition and train it with the images and
// labels read from the given CSV file.
// If you just want to keep 10 Fisherfaces, then call
// the factory method like this:
//
//      cv::createFisherFaceRecognizer(10);
//
// However it is not useful to discard Fisherfaces! Please
// always try to use _all_ available Fisherfaces for
// classification.
//
// If you want to create a FaceRecognizer with a
// confidence threshold (e.g. 123.0) and use _all_
// Fisherfaces, then call it with:
//
//      cv::createFisherFaceRecognizer(0, 123.0);
//
```

```
Ptr<FaceRecognizer> model = createFisherFaceRecognizer();
model->train(images, labels);

// The following line predicts the label of a given
// test image:
int predictedLabel = model->predict(testSample);

// To get the confidence of a prediction call the model with:
//
//      int predictedLabel = -1;
//      double confidence = 0.0;
//      model->predict(testSample, predictedLabel, confidence);
//
string result_message = format("Predicted class = %d", predictedLabel);
cout << result_message << endl;

// giving the result
switch (predictedLabel)
{
  case SMILE:
    cout << "You are happy!" << endl;
    break;
  case SURPRISED:
    cout << "You are surprised!" << endl;
    break;
  case SERIOUS:
    cout << "You are serious!" << endl;
    break;
}

  return 0;

  cap.release();

  return 0;
}

Mat faceDetect(Mat img)
{
  std::vector<Rect> faces;
  std::vector<Rect> eyes;
  bool two_eyes = false;
  bool any_eye_detected = false;
```

```
//detecting faces
face_cascade.detectMultiScale( img, faces, 1.1, 2, 0|CV_HAAR_SCALE_IMAGE,
Size(30, 30) );


if (faces.size() == 0)
{
     cout << "Try again.. I did not dectected any faces..." << endl;
     exit(-1);  // abort everything
}

Point p1 = Point(0,0);
for( size_t i = 0; i < faces.size(); i++ )
{

  // we cannot draw in the image !!! otherwise will mess with the prediction
  // rectangle( img, faces[i], Scalar( 255, 100, 0 ), 4, 8, 0 );


    Mat frame_gray;
    cvtColor( img, frame_gray, CV_BGR2GRAY );

    // croping only the face in region defined by faces[i]
    std::vector<Rect> eyes;
    Mat faceROI = frame_gray( faces[i] );

    //In each face, detect eyes
    eyes_cascade.detectMultiScale( faceROI, eyes, 1.1, 3, 0
|CV_HAAR_SCALE_IMAGE, Size(30, 30) );

     for( size_t j = 0; j < eyes.size(); j++ )
     {
        Point center( faces[i].x + eyes[j].x + eyes[j].width*0.5,
        faces[i].y + eyes[j].y + eyes[j].height*0.5 );
        // we cannot draw in the image !!! otherwise will mess with the
           prediction
        // int radius = cvRound( (eyes[j].width + eyes[j].height)*0.25 );
        // circle( img, center, radius, Scalar( 255, 0, 0 ), 4, 8, 0 );

        if (j==0)
          {
             p1 = center;
             any_eye_detected = true;
          }
```

```
      else
      {
          two_eyes = true;
      }
    }

  }

cout << "SOME DEBUG" << endl;
cout << "------------------------" << endl;
cout << "faces detected:" << faces.size() << endl;
cout << "x: " << faces[0].x << endl;
cout << "y: " << faces[0].y << endl;
cout << "w: " << faces[0].width << endl;
cout << "h: " << faces[0].height << endl << endl;

Mat imageInRectangle;
imageInRectangle =  img(faces[0]);
Size recFaceSize = imageInRectangle.size();

cout << recFaceSize << endl;

// for debug
imwrite("imageInRectangle.jpg", imageInRectangle);

int rec_w = 0;
int rec_h = faces[0].height * 0.64;


// checking the (x,y) for cropped rectangle
// based in human anatomy
int px = 0;
int py = 2 * 0.125 * faces[0].height;

Mat cropImage;


cout << "faces[0].x:" << faces[0].x << endl;
p1.x = p1.x - faces[0].x;
cout << "p1.x:" << p1.x << endl;
```

389

```cpp
if (any_eye_detected)
{
    if (two_eyes)
    {
        cout << "two eyes detected" << endl;
        // we have detected two eyes
        // we have p1 and p2
        // left eye
        px = p1.x /  1.35;

    }
    else
    {
        // only one eye was found.. need to check if the
        // left or right eye
        // we have only p1
        if (p1.x > recFaceSize.width/2)
        {
            // right eye
          cout << "only right eye detected" << endl;
          px = p1.x / 1.75;

        }
        else
        {
            // left eye
          cout << "only left eye detected" << endl;
          px = p1.x /  1.35;
        }
    }

}
else
{

    // no eyes detected but we have a face
    px = 25;
    py = 25;
    rec_w = recFaceSize.width-50;
    rec_h = recFaceSize.height-30;

}

rec_w = (faces[0].width - px) * 0.75;
cout << "px   :" << px << endl;
cout << "py   :" << py << endl;
cout << "rec_w:" << rec_w << endl;
cout << "rec_h:" << rec_h << endl;
```

```
cropImage = imageInRectangle(Rect(px, py, rec_w, rec_h));

Size dstImgSize(70,70); // same image size of db
Mat finalSizeImg;
resize(cropImage, finalSizeImg, dstImgSize);

// for debug
imwrite("onlyface.jpg", finalSizeImg);

cvtColor( finalSizeImg, finalSizeImg, CV_BGR2GRAY );

return finalSizeImg;

}
```

Reviewing opencv_emotion_classification.cpp

In the beginning of the code, there is an enumerator created to define the emotional state. Note the value of each element on this enum matches the emotion index in the CSV file.

```
enum EmotionState_t {
  SMILE    =0,  // 0
  SURPRISED,    // 1
  SERIOUS,      // 2
};
```

In the main() function, a variable of type EmotionState_t is created and it is expected to receive the name of the CSV file as an argument.

```
int main(int argc, const char *argv[])
{

  EmotionState_t emotion;

  // Check for valid command line arguments, print usage
  // if no arguments were given.
  if (argc < 2) {
    cout << "usage: " << argv[0] << " <csv.ext> <output_folder> " << endl;
    exit(1);
  }
```

When the webcam is opened, the picture is collected as before. The faceDetect() method changes, compared to the faceDetect() method shown earlier:

```
Mat testSample = faceDetect(frame);
```

This new object stored in testSample contains the cropped face. This cropped image is the same size as the images in the database. This image returned is in grayscale and is cropped like the images shown in Figure 7-12.

The frame contains an 432x240 image and the testSample image is 70x70. For now, let's continue with the main() function. faceDetect() will be discussed in more detail later.

With the image prepared to be analyzed, new components are used to predict the emotional state:

```
Ptr<FaceRecognizer> model = createFisherFaceRecognizer();
model->train(images, labels);

// The following line predicts the label of a given
// test image:
int predictedLabel = model->predict(testSample);
```

class FaceRecognizer : public Algorithm

At a glance, FaceRecognizer looks very simple, but in fact it's very powerful and complex. This class allows you to set different algorithms, including your own, to perform different kinds of image recognitions.

The model used in the code is fisherface and it's created by the line:

```
Ptr<FaceRecognizer> model = createFisherFaceRecognizer();
```

void FaceRecognizer::train(InputArrayOfArrays src, InputArray labels)

This method trains the model based on your database. The code passes the images and index (or labels):

```
model->train(images, labels);
```

int FaceRecognizer::predict(InputArray src) const = 0

This method predicts the classification index (label) based on the image casted as the input array src.

For example, if the emotion "happy" is labeled as 0 in the CSV file and the FaceRecognizer was trained, the prediction will return 0 if the image src is a picture of you smiling.

This is represented by the following snippet:

```
int predictedLabel = model->predict(testSample);
```

...
...
...

```
// giving the result
switch (predictedLabel)
{
  case SMILE:
    cout << "You are happy!" << endl;
    break;
  case SURPRISED:
    cout << "You are surprised!" << endl;
    break;
  case SERIOUS:
    cout << "You are serious!" << endl;
    break;
}
```

If the image returned by faceDetect()is cropped properly and your expression is similar to the expression in the database, the algorithm will predict accurately.

The faceDetect() method basically does what was done before, as explained in the flowchart in Figure 7-10. In other words, it detects the face and eyes.

After this example detects the face and eyes, an algorithm containing a few simple concepts about human anatomy was introduced that crops the image to the face area.

It tries to crop the image captured by the webcam dynamically and do the same thing that was done manually by the script in Listing 7-7, but instead crop the image exclusively in the area the face is detected.

To understand how the logic works, see Figure 7-13.

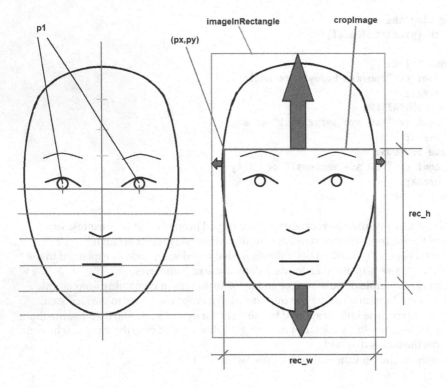

Figure 7-13. *Human anatomy and the variables used to crop the face*

Take a look at Figure 7-13 and follow this logic. When a face is recognized the whole face is typically captured, including the ears, head or hat, part of the neck, and part of the background image (imageRectangle). However, these elements are not interesting to the emotion classifier and must be removed (the red arrows area) and only the portion containing eyes, nose, and mouth are cropped (cropImage).

The cropped image has the initial px and py coordinates with the extensions rec_w and rec_h, which forms a triangle with perfect dimensions for cropping the area. Such a rectangle corresponds to the ROI (Region of Interest) area.

To reach the ROI area, the eyes are detected and then the human proportions are found using the px, px, rec_w, and rec_h values in the image and crop the image.

When the eyes are detected, it is possible to define a point object p1 that corresponds to the center of the eye. The point object p1 has two members x and y that represent the distance in pixels to the original image. There are a couple of problems, however. Sometimes only one eye is detected and the algorithm must determine if it's the right or the left. Other times, no eye is detected.

```
//detecting faces
face_cascade.detectMultiScale( img, faces, 1.1, 2, 0|CV_HAAR_SCALE_IMAGE,
Size(30, 30) );
Point p1 = Point(0,0);
for( size_t i = 0; i < faces.size(); i++ )
{

...
...
...

    //In each face, detect eyes
    eyes_cascade.detectMultiScale( faceROI, eyes, 1.1, 3, 0
|CV_HAAR_SCALE_IMAGE, Size(30, 30) );

    for( size_t j = 0; j < eyes.size(); j++ )
    {
        Point center( faces[i].x + eyes[j].x + eyes[j].width*0.5,
faces[i].y + eyes[j].y + eyes[j].height*0.5 );

...
...
...

        if (j==0)
          {
            p1 = center;
            any_eye_detected = true;
          }
        else
        {
            two_eyes = true;
        }
    }
}

}
```

At the moment, you might have the center of one of the eyes and it is known if one, two, or none eyes were detected. Now it is necessary to find the px and py coordinates, as well as the ROI dimensions, rec_w and rec_h.

In human anatomy, the eyes are located at the top of the horizontal red line that splits the human face in half. If you split the middle horizontal line equally in four parts, the eyes are separated by each other by half of the largest horizontal proportion and one-fourth from the laterals.

The nose and mouth are centralized in the middle of the face, with the inferior proportional divided in five equal parts. The eyebrows are 12.5% above the lines of the eyes because they are 50%/4 of the superior part of the face.

If no eye is detected then it is not possible to crop using a simple algorithm. With these proportions in mind, the following lines were created:

```
int rec_w = 0;
int rec_h = faces[0].height * 0.64;

// checking the (x,y) for cropped rectangle
// based in human anatomy
int px = 0;
int py = 2 * 0.125 * faces[0].height;

Mat cropImage;

cout << "faces[0].x:" << faces[0].x << endl;
p1.x = p1.x - faces[0].x;
cout << "p1.x:" << p1.x << endl;
if (any_eye_detected)
{
    if (two_eyes)
    {
        cout << "two eyes detected" << endl;
        // we have detected two eyes
        // we have p1 and p2
        // left eye
        px = p1.x /  1.35;

    }
    else
    {
        // only one eye was found.. need to check if the
        // left or right eye
        // we have only p1
        if (p1.x > recFaceSize.width/2)
        {
            // right eye
          cout << "only right eye detected" << endl;
          px = p1.x / 1.75;

        }
        else
        {
            // left eye
          cout << "only left eye detected" << endl;
          px = p1.x /  1.35;
        }
    }

}
```

```
else
{

    // no eyes detected but we have a face
    px = 25;
    py = 25;
    rec_w = recFaceSize.width-50;
    rec_h = recFaceSize.height-30;

}

rec_w = (faces[0].width - px) * 0.75;
cout << "px    :" << px << endl;
cout << "py    :" << py << endl;
cout << "rec_w:" << rec_w << endl;
cout << "rec_h:" << rec_h << endl;

cropImage = imageInRectangle(Rect(px, py, rec_w, rec_h));
```

For debugging purposes, the faceDetect() method saves two images in the file system every time the software runs. One is called onlyface.jpg and it contains the cropped image. The other is called imageInRectangle.jpg and it contains the detected image.

```
Mat imageInRectangle;
imageInRectangle =  img(faces[0]);
...
...
...
 // for debug
 imwrite("imageInRectangle.jpg", imageInRectangle);
 cropImage = imageInRectangle(Rect(px, py, rec_w, rec_h));
...
...
...
  Size dstImgSize(70,70); // same image size of db
  Mat finalSizeImg;
  resize(cropImage, finalSizeImg, dstImgSize);
```

Running opencv_emotion_classification.cpp

Compile the code and transfer the file to Intel Galileo. Make sure the uvcvideo driver is loaded and the webcam is connected to the USB port (read the "Connecting the Webcam" section in this chapter), and transfer the program to the same location of your CSV file. Stay in front your camera, preferably two feet away, make some emotional expressions, and then run the following command:

```
root@clanton:~/emotion# ./opencv_emotion_classification my_csv.csv 2> /dev/null
camera is ok.. Stay 2 ft away from your camera
```

```
processing the image....
SOME DEBUG
-------------------------
faces detected:1
x: 172
y: 25
w: 132
h: 132

[132 x 132]
faces[0].x:172
p1.x:-172
px   :25
py   :25
rec_w:80
rec_h:102
Predicted class = 0
```
You are happy!

The software classifies the image as happy. Extracting the debug images onlyface.jpg and imageInRectangle.jpg from the file system, it is possible to observe my expression in the cropped image, shown in Figure 7-14.

Figure 7-14. *The happy face is detected and the image is cropped automatically*

Note in Figure 7-14 the areas that are cropped out, including the background, the hair, and the ears.

root@clanton:~/emotion# **./opencv_emotion_classification my_csv.csv 2> /dev/null**
camera is ok.. Stay 2 ft away from your camera

processing the image....
SOME DEBUG
----
faces detected:1

```
x: 178
y: 3
w: 143
h: 143

[143 x 143]
faces[0].x:178
p1.x:43
two eyes detected
px   :31
py   :35
rec_w:84
rec_h:91
Predicted class = 1
```
You are surprised!

The software classifies this image as surprised. Extracting the debug images only face.jpg and imageInRectangle.jpg from the file system, it observes my expression and crops the image, as shown in Figure 7-15.

Figure 7-15. *The surprised face is detected and the image is cropped automatically*

Keep varying the expression and checking the efficiency of the captured images.

Ideas for Improving the Project

At this point you should see the potential that OpenCV and Intel Galileo have. However, all projects have room for improvement. Let's discuss some of the ways you can improve this project.

Integrating Your Emotions with a Robotic Head

Chapter 13 demonstrated a robotic head that expressed emotion. The idea here is to integrate the emotion classification in this chapter and make the robot to imitate emotions. Thus, if you smile the robot will smile; if you are sad, the robot will be sad, and so on.

Expanding the Classifications

The fisherface model was used to classify emotions but the same technique can be used to classify gender or recognize your family and friends.

You need to create databases for gender and for the faces of people you know.

An example of gender classification can be found at this link http://docs.opencv.org/ trunk/modules/contrib/doc/facerec/tutorial/facerec_gender_classification.html.

Improving the Emotion Classification Using Large Databases

There are several databases on the Internet containing thousands of images showing emotions (some with more than 4,000 faces). To learn about these different database and download the images, visit http://face-rec.org/databases/.

Improving the Emotion Classification for Several Faces

On the example of Listing 7-8, I created a database using my own pictures and the software is prepared to classify only me using the first face detected in the code, in other words, the object **faces[0]**. Add more people in the database and improve the code to classify all faces detected instead only one.

Summary

This chapter explained many principles needed to explore OpenCV: The creation of SD releases based on eGlibc, the suppression of GPU support in OpenCV development packages, the generation of the right toolchain to support V4L and OpenCV, the study of UVC devices, and the exploration of the webcam capabilities using Video4Linux. These principles serve as a study of OpenCV.

You learned how to capture and process images in OpenCV, including complex tasks like edge detection with the Canny algorithm, face and eyes detection based on Haar techniques, and the emotion classification based on the fisherface model.

This is only the beginning in terms of OpenCV and its possibilities. There are several articles on the Internet and specialized books if you want to explore more features.

CHAPTER 8

■ ■ ■

Creating a Soil Moisture Sensor

The project in this chapter explains how to use the analog and digital ports of Intel Galileo to create a very low-cost system that measures the moisture levels in the soil for home applications. This project was demonstrated in a Maker Faire in October 2013 in Rome, Italy and the purpose was to create a project with only $4.00, excluding the cost of Intel Galileo board.

Project Details

To measure moisture in the soil, you simply measure the quantity of water in it. There are different kinds of sensors available in the market, including neutron moisture gauge sensors, frequency domain sensors, capacity sensors, and simple electrodes. These are all used in home applications and each type uses different techniques.

The electrodes are one of the most affordable solutions, and for simple applications like monitoring the plants in your home, they are good solutions.

The challenge is to create a very affordable system whereby you can use material that you usually dispose in the trash or have in your garage.

You can build your own electrode sensor using galvanized nails, such as roofing nails that are used to hold the interlocked concrete tiles.

Considering that the electrodes will be in constant contact with moisture, galvanized nails are highly recommended to avoid rusting. Rust can cause poor analog readings, forcing you to adjust the system frequently.

Each sensor consists of two electrodes, in this case, two nails separated by about two inches. The first electrode receives a voltage and the other one is connected to an analog port.

Soil has conductive properties that are affected proportionally by the amount of moisture present. If there is a good quantity of water in the soil, the electrical current propagation is good; dry soil means the propagation is bad. Of course, other factors affect soil conductivity, including the degree of salts and nutrients in the soil.

This project is very simple and its purpose is only to indicate whether the soil has enough water for the houseplants. It doesn't measure any details about soil type, water type, or mineral concentrations. This project can be applied to *any* kind of soil or water.

For practical purposes, this project will follow the same demonstration as performed at Maker Faire in Italy. The project includes two sensors, so you will be able to monitor two plants. You will have visual feedback about the sensors' readings through a group of LEDs forming a flower face, with eyes and a mouth. The mouth is used to represent emotions such as happiness and sadness, according to the level of moisture in the soil. In other words, a "happy face" will tell you if your plant has enough water; when the soil is dried out, the face will be sad. The eyes indicate which sensor is currently selected. One eye is related to sensor number 1 and the other eye relates to sensor number 2. You can switch between the sensors by pressing a push button.

You are free to change this project; for one, you could increase the number of sensors and use all six possible analog ports (A0 to A5) on the Intel Galileo instead of only two sensors.

The section called "Ideas for Improving the Project" at the end of the chapter explains how to increase the number of sensors how to use solenoid and pumps for automatic irrigation, among other ideas.

Material List

To build this project you need the components listed in Table 8-1.

Table 8-1. Mandatory Components

Quantity	Components
2	Green 5mm LED
8	Red 5mm LED
1	Push button
10	220 ohms 1/4 w
2	12K ohms 1/4 w
4	Galvanized nails
1	Universal board
2	Pieces of foam 3x3 inches
3 ft	Wires (at least 1/4 w)
1	Scissors

The list in Table 8-2 is not mandatory; these materials are used for aesthetic purposes during the development of the flower face, which is discussed in detail in this chapter.

Table 8-2. *Optional Materials*

Quantity	Components
1	White prime spray
1	Assorted colored papers or free paint paper samples
1	3/4 transparent tape
1	Black gel pen

Assembling the Moisture Sensors

To assemble the sensors, there are mechanical and electrical procedures you must follow. They are explained in the following sections.

Mechanical Assembly

Each sensor needs two galvanized nails and a piece of non-conductive foam in order to keep the nails separated.

For the foam, you can use the kind used to protect electronic devices packed into boxes. You might have some in your house, in the recycling, or in your office. You can also use pieces of Styrofoam.

Once you have the nails and the foam, simply insert the nails 1.5 to 2 inches apart. Figure 8-1 shows you an example of the final build.

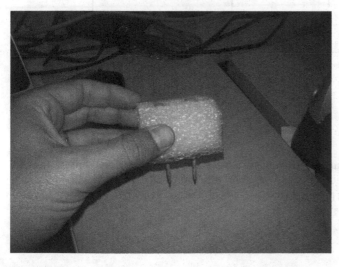

Figure 8-1. *The soil moisture sensor using nails and foam*

Once the nails are inserted into the foam, make sure they can penetrate the soil at least 1.5 inches. You will not bury the foam; you simply use it to keep the nails separated and connected to the soil.

If you do not have enough nail area at the bottom, cut the foam or use bigger nails.

Electrical Assembly

The next step is to understand how the nails are connected electrically. Therefore, remove the nails from the foam and review the image in Figure 8-2.

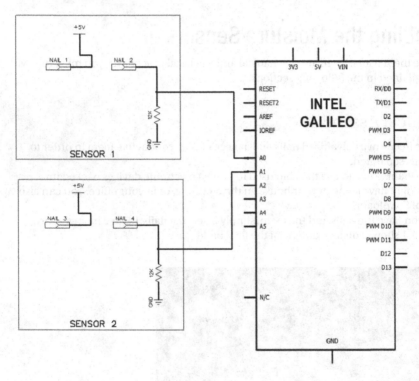

Figure 8-2. *Sensor electric connection*

As you can see in Figure 8-2, two nails are necessary to assemble one sensor. One of the nails is connected directly to the 5V port and other must be connected with the 12K Ohm resistor to an analog port. In Figure 8-2, sensor 1 is connected to A0 and sensor 2 is connected to A1.

The nails can be connected using wire wrapped around the nail's head, as demonstrated in Figures 8-3 and 8-4, or they can be soldered.

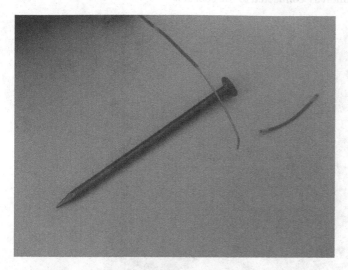

Figure 8-3. *The wire being prepared*

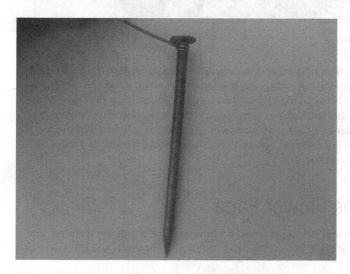

Figure 8-4. *Wrapping the wire around the nail's head*

Wrap the wires around each nail and place the sensors in the foam again.

The resistors work as a voltage divisor with 5V. To assemble the 5V and the resistor, connections are arranged using a universal board represented in Figure 8-2. This board will be used to assemble the flower face, which is explained later in this chapter.

Figure 8-5 shows the sensor components solder into the verse of the board (the surface without copper layer) containing a single ground (GND), the sensors cables (S1 and S2), and the common 5V connected to the sensors.

Figure 8-5. *Sensors circuits*

Using the verse of universal board and soldering the components to the backside is not normally a good approach, but in this case it is used to emulate the demo created in Italy. You will understand better in the sub-session entitled "Assembling the Flower Face" in the following pages of this chapter. You can mount your sensor circuit in a different board or create a particular PCB for each sensor, or use any other solution that you feel is appropriate for your case. For example, you can use a breadboard instead of a universal board to avoid the soldering process.

Assembling the Flower Face

The flower face will represent emotions based on how well the plants are watered. For a better user interface, the LEDs in the eyes are a different color than the LEDs used in the mouth.

Figure 8-6 shows the schematics for the flower face, where "D" means digital and "A" means analog.

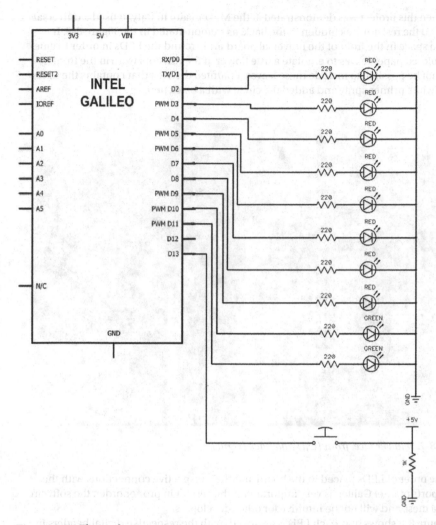

Figure 8-6. *Flower face connection*

The D10 and D11 ports are used to control the green LEDs, which inform which sensor is selected. The other ports D2 to D10 are the red LEDs and they represent the mouth. They should be aligned horizontally containing four LEDs. The push button B1 is used to select the sensor.

When this project was demonstrated at the Maker Faire in Italy, it used a universal board and the resistor was hidden in the back, as demonstrated in the Figure 8-7. It reserved space in the front of the universal board and around the LEDs in order to glue some colored paper leaves to emulate a true flower. If the resistors were in the front, it would not be possible to include these leaves. I painted the area that contains the LEDs using a white primer spray and added the circle with a black pen.

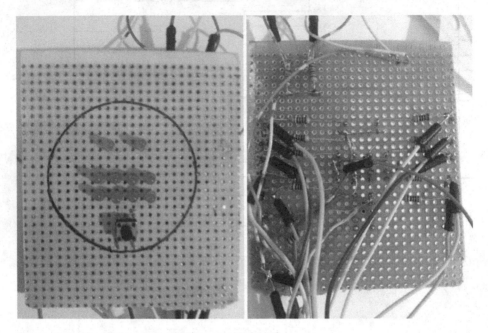

Figure 8-7. *Flower face, front (left) and back (right)*

The order of LEDs placed in the board and their respective connections with the digital ports of Intel Galileo is very important. If they aren't in proper order, the software will be a mess and will not be intuitive for other developers.

Figure 8-8 shows how each LED is arranged, with the respective digital headers in Intel Galileo boards.

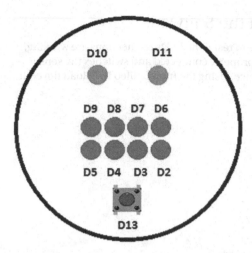

Figure 8-8. *Physical connection to Intel Galileo ports (front view)*

It is recommended that you mark each wire with the corresponding port number to avoid confusion with connections and to save time. You can do that using regular tape and paper, as shown in Figure 8-9.

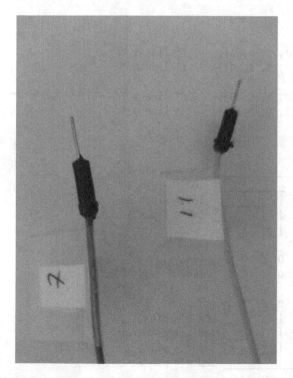

Figure 8-9. *Marking the wires with their port numbers*

Testing the Flower Face with the Software

After you have built the flower face, it is time to test if the LEDs connections are working, if they are in the right order, if the button is properly connected and switches the sensor when pressed, and adjust the button debounce. Using the Intel Galileo IDE, load the code from Listing 8-1.

Listing 8-1. flower_face_test.ino

```
// Author: Manoel Carlos Ramon
// email: manoel.c.ramon@intel.com

#define DEBUG                    0

/* Pins that define if system is ON */
#define PIN_LEFT_EYE             10
#define PIN_RIGHT_EYE            11

/* Sensor switch button */
#define PIN_SWITCH_SYSTEM        13

void clear();
int current_sensor = 0;
int button_state = 0;

int array_happy_face[2][4] = {{1, 0, 0, 1},    /* line 1 */
                              {0, 1, 1, 0}};    /* line 0 */

int array_sad_face[2][4]   = {{0, 1, 1, 0},    /* line 1 */
                              {1, 0, 0, 1}};    /* line 0 */


/*  THE MOUTH - back view
            _____        led 0 - pin 6
           |   _____         led 1 = pin 7
           |  |   ____           led 2 = pin 8
           |  |  |  _____        led 3 = pin 9
           |  |  |  |

         0  0  0  0      line 1
         0  0  0  0      line 0

         ^  ^  ^  ^
         |  |  |  |__    led 3 = pin 5
         |  |  |_____    led 2 = pin 4
         |  |_____    led 1 = pin 3
         |_____    led 0 = pin 2
*/
```

```
int lastButtonState = LOW;    // the previous reading from the input pin
long lastDebounceTime = 0;    // the last time the output pin was toggled
long debounceDelay = 500;     // adjust this value if necessary to avoid
flickering

void clear()
{
   int pin = 0;
   for (pin = 0; pin < 12; pin++)
   {
     digitalWrite(pin, LOW);
   }

}

void drawMatrix(int array[2][4])
{
  int line = 0;
  int pin = 2;
  int c = 0;
  int level = LOW;

  while (line < 2)
  {
     digitalWrite(line, LOW);

     while (c <= 3)
     {

        level = array[line][c];

        digitalWrite(pin, level);
        c++;pin++;
     }
     c=0;
     line++;
     delay(10);
  }

}

void setup() {

  if (DEBUG) Serial.begin(9600);
  // put your setup code here, to run once:
   int pin = 0;
```

```
    for (pin = 0; pin < 12; pin++)
    {
      pinMode(pin, OUTPUT);
      delay(10);
    }

    // switch button
    pinMode(PIN_SWITCH_SYSTEM, INPUT);

    // turn off all leds
    clear();

}

void checkButtonState()
{

  // read the state of the switch into a local variable:
  int reading = digitalRead(PIN_SWITCH_SYSTEM);

  // check to see if you just pressed the button
  // (i.e. the input went from LOW to HIGH),  and you've waited
  // long enough since the last press to ignore any noise:

  // If the switch changed, due to noise or pressing:
  if (reading != lastButtonState) {
    // reset the debouncing timer
    lastDebounceTime = millis();
  }

  if ((millis() - lastDebounceTime) > debounceDelay) {
    // whatever the reading is at, it's been there for longer

    // if the button state has changed:
    if (reading != button_state) {
      button_state = reading;

    }
  }

  lastButtonState = reading;

  return;
}
```

```
void loop() {

  // reading the button state
  checkButtonState();

  if( button_state != lastButtonState)
  {
      // button pressed
      current_sensor++;
      if (current_sensor > 1) current_sensor = 0;
  }

  if (DEBUG) Serial.println(current_sensor);
  if (current_sensor == 0)
  {
    //sensor 1 - only one LED on
    digitalWrite(PIN_RIGHT_EYE, HIGH);
    digitalWrite(PIN_LEFT_EYE, LOW);

    drawMatrix(array_sad_face);
  }
  else
  {
    // sensor 2 - two LEDs ON
    digitalWrite(PIN_RIGHT_EYE, HIGH);
    digitalWrite(PIN_LEFT_EYE, HIGH);

    //sad face
    drawMatrix(array_happy_face);
  }
}
```

Reviewing the Code

Before you test the circuit, review the code by checking the different functions discussed in the following sections.

setup() function

In the setup() function, you set the ports 2 to 9 (the mouth) and the ports defined by PIN_LEFT_EYE and PIN_RIGHT_EYE (the eyes) as output because they are the LEDs connections. PIN_LEFT_EYE and PIN_RIGHT_EYE are defined by the following code:

```
#define PIN_LEFT_EYE            10
#define PIN_RIGHT_EYE           11
```

The only port defined as input in the setup() function is the port that determines which button is connected. Its represented by the definition PIN_SWITCH_SYSTEM with port 13 by default.

```
/* Sensor switch button */
#define PIN_SWITCH_SYSTEM        13
```

loop() function

The loop() function checks the button state. If it is different from the previous state, that means the user pressed the button and the sensor selection must be changed.

Thus, if sensor 1 is the selected sensor, the variable current_sensor is zero (0) and a sad face will be displayed using the LEDs. Note that only one eye, represented by the green LED connected to PIN_RIGHT_EYE, is ON, which means that when there is only one eye ON, it's sensor 1.

Otherwise, if the user selected sensor 2, a happy face will be displayed and both "eyes," represented by the green LEDs, will be ON. In this case, the current_sensor variable value is one (1).

drawMatrix() function

The drawMatrix() function is responsible for drawing the mouth according to the matrix passed as its argument.

Each expression is defined by a double dimension matrix, represented by the array_happy_face[][] and array_sad_face[][] integer arrays.

```
int array_happy_face[2][4] = {{1, 0, 0, 1},    /* line 1 */
                              {0, 1, 1, 0}};    /* line 0 */
int array_sad_face[2][4]   = {{0, 1, 1, 0},    /* line 1 */
                              {1, 0, 0, 1}};    /* line 0 */
```

In the matrixes, the value 1 means the LED must be turned ON and 0 means OFF. Considering this, you can see that the 1s in array_happy_face[][] form a smiling mouth and that they form a sad mouth in the array_sad_face[][].

checkButtonState() function

The checkButtonState() function is responsible for determining whether the user pressed the button. For this, the checkButtonState() implements the same logic used by the debounce example in the IDE (see Examples->02.Digital->Debounce).

In the global scope, the variable called debounceDelay adjusts the button's debounce interval. If, during your tests, you think the button is flickering, you can increase this interval.

```
long debounceDelay = 500;    // adjust this value if necessary to avoid
flickering
```

Testing the Flower Face

This test is quite easy and fun. Just make all the connections according to the schematics. If everything is working okay, the first thing you will see is a sad face with only one eye ON, as shown in Figure 8-10.

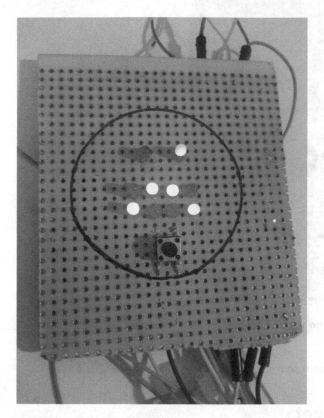

Figure 8-10. *The sad face and sensor 1 selected*

Then press the button. If the button connection and its debounce interval are working properly, you will see a happy face with two eyes ON, as shown in Figure 8-11.

Figure 8-11. *The happy face and sensor 2 selected*

Remember, one eye ON means sensor 1 and two eyes ON means sensor 2.

Running the Project

Now it's time to run the project. You'll make a few changes to the code shown in Listing 8-1.

Calibration Procedure

If you tested the flower face and assembled the sensor correctly, the project is ready to go. You now need to integrate the logic with the sensors in the code and make some final adjustments.

The final code that joins the flower face and the sensors is called soil_moisture.ino. Just a few simply changes need to be made to the code.

Defining the Connections

The first change is to define where the sensors are connected and define a variable to set the initial value.

```
/* Moisture sensor - Analog Input */
#define  ANALOG_MOISTURE_SENSOR_1        A0
#define  ANALOG_MOISTURE_SENSOR_2        A1
int sensor_value = 0;
```

Setting the Boundary Values

The next change is to create a definition that will set a boundary value for when soil is wet enough. You can initiate your test using good soil; in other words, soil that contains the quantity of water that you judge good for your plants. The first thing to do is to enable to debug messages by setting the DEBUG defitition to "1".

```
#define DEBUG                   1
```

As soon as you upload the problem using the IDE, you should start the serial monitor by pressing Ctrl+Shift+M or by selecting Tools ➤ Serial-Monitor, as explained in Chapter 3. You will see a message in the serial terminal that reads "sensor value:" with the appropriate value. Make sure you are selecting the right sensor during this calibration.

Next, set SOIL_ID_GOOD to the appropriate value. In Listing 8-1, it was set to 350, which determined if the soil is completely dried out or had enough moisture. The 350 value was tested in three different locations in the United States and in one location in Italy and worked very well for this demo. However, you should test and determine the best value for your soil and moisture level.

```
/* The analog reading boundary when soil is good */
#define  SOIL_IS_GOOD           350
```

The loop function is changed so that it reads the current analog port selected by the push button, compares the value, and displays the right emotion in the flower face circuit, as shown in the following excerpt from Listing 8-1.

```
void loop() {

  // reading the button state
  checkButtonState();

  if( button_state != lastButtonState)
  {
    // button pressed
    current_sensor++;
    if (current_sensor > 1) current_sensor = 0;
  }
```

```
// reading the sensor
switch (current_sensor)
{
    case 0:
        sensor_value = analogRead(ANALOG_MOISTURE_SENSOR_1);

        // first sensor - one LED ON
        digitalWrite(PIN_RIGHT_EYE, HIGH);
        digitalWrite(PIN_LEFT_EYE, LOW);

    break;

    case 1:
        sensor_value = analogRead(ANALOG_MOISTURE_SENSOR_2);

        // second sensor - two LEDs ON
        digitalWrite(PIN_RIGHT_EYE, HIGH);
        digitalWrite(PIN_LEFT_EYE, HIGH);

    break;
}

if (DEBUG)
{
    Serial.print("current_sensor:");
    Serial.println(current_sensor);

    Serial.print("    sensor_value:");
    Serial.println(sensor_value);
}

if (sensor_value >=SOIL_IS_GOOD)
{
    drawMatrix(array_happy_face);
}
else
{
    drawMatrix(array_sad_face);
}

}
```

The code is very simple and everything is done using the digital and analog headers. In the loop() function will call the function checkButtonState(), which updates the variable button_state. If button_state is different than the previous state saved in the lastButtonState variable, the current_sensor variable changes and can assume two values—0 or 1. The value 0 represents the first sensor and the value 1 represents the second one.

The switch instruction will determine which sensor the user selected and call the analogRead() function, which will read the analog port that corresponds to the connected sensor and load the value to the sensor_value variable.

If the first sensor (case 0) is selected, digitalWrite() will turn ON just one flower eye, because only one LED will be HIGH, as shown here:

```
digitalWrite(PIN_RIGHT_EYE, HIGH);
digitalWrite(PIN_LEFT_EYE, LOW
```

In case 1, two eyes will be ON because both LEDs will be HIGH:

```
digitalWrite(PIN_RIGHT_EYE, HIGH);
digitalWrite(PIN_LEFT_EYE, HIGH);
```

After this there is a debug message section, which will be displayed in the serial monitor if DEBUG is defined as 1, as explained previously.

Finally, if the sensor_value variable reports moist soil, the drawMatrix() function will draw a smile in the flower face. Otherwise, a sad face is shown, as explained in the section called "Testing the Flower Face with Software" of this chapter.

Showing This Project in a Fair

When this project was used as a demo at the Maker Faire, two soil samples were used, one dried and the other one with a good quantity of moisture. The soil was in two disposable cups with sensors connected. The flower face included some colored leaves that were added using free painting paper samples you can find in construction stores like Lowes and Home Depot.

Figure 8-12 shows how the sensors were arranged in the cups and Figure 8-13 shows the flower face with the leaves when sensor 1 measured dry soil.

Figure 8-12. *The sensors in the cups*

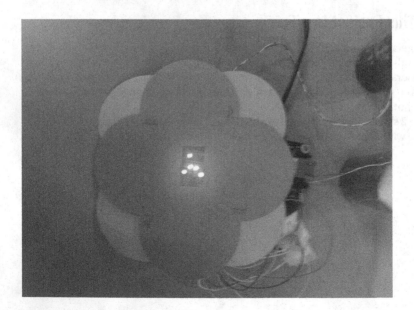

Figure 8-13. *The flower face with leaves*

Ideas for Improving the Project

This project was created knowing that it would be used as a demo in a fair or classroom. But how could you change the project to attend to your real needs? For example, sprinkler systems usually irrigate plants periodically, regardless of moisture level, which can be wasteful. The next sections discuss ideas for adjusting this project to meet real-life scenarios.

Increasing the Number of Sensors

This project uses only two sensors, but the Intel Galileo pin-out includes six analog ports. That means you can expand the number of sensors with minimal changes to the software and hardware.

If you want to have more than two sensors, instead of the flower face, you can build a simple board with multiple LEDS with each LED representing a sensor. When the LED is ON, the respective sensor indicates the plant needs water. When the LED is OFF, the soil has water enough.

Automatic Irrigation

It's possible to use this project to make an automatic irrigation system, but there are small differences when you need to irrigate a small plant or a large area.

Such differences are related to what type of device will be used in the irrigation: a pump or a solenoid valve.

When the quantity of water required is small, such as with indoor plants, you can use low voltage water pumps that operate between 3V to 9V, and you need a recepticle that collects water and distributes it to the plants. The recepticle might be a bottle, a bucket, a basin, or anything that can hold the water to be used by your plants.

When you're irrigating a large area, you'll need 12V or 24V solenoid valves that control the water that comes from a hose or pipe. These values work as a switch on and switch off. In other words, they either enables or do not enable the water flow.

In both cases, the pumps and solenoid valves work with different voltage levels and require higher levels of current than your board is able to control. Therefore, it's better to isolate the Intel Galileo and use a mechanical or solid state relay.

Figure 8-14 represents a practical circuit using a mechanical relay.

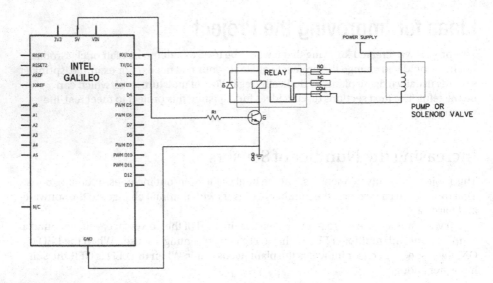

Figure 8-14. *Drive relay connected to a pump or solenoid*

The circuit shown in Figure 8-14 can be assembled using the material listed in Table 8-3.

Table 8-3. *Optional Materials*

Quantity	Components
1	R1: 1K Ohm
1	D1: 1N4001 or 1N4004
1	Q1: 2N2222A or BC548
1	Relay

There are affordable shields with relays available in the market. Figure 8-15 shows an example of a shield equipped with two relays that operates up to 30 VDC and 10A and costs less than $4.00 on eBay.

Figure 8-15. *Example of an inexpensive shield relay*

The outdoor sprinklers in landscapes are equipped with solenoid valves responsible for activating water flow. Using the circuit shown in Figure 8-14, you can manage your sprinklers by directly replacing the sprinklers' timers. Just make sure you are using the relay and power supply compatible with your sprinklers.

Using Appropriate Wires

It's possible to find wires that are more appropriate for an outdoor application at any hardware store. The demo uses simple telephony wires, but it's better to use wires that withstand moisture and water, can handle high temperatures, and work underground in the soil. Usually, they are 16 AWG and are specified as burial wires.

Using a Commercial Sensor

You can replace the galvanized nails with commercial sensors. Many electrode sensors are very affordable and are more appropriate for this application. They are usually offered with tine *potentiometers*, which allow you to make fine adjustments to the analog port reading. They can be found on eBay for less than $5.00.

Figure 8-16 shows an example of a commercial sensor that can be used with this project.

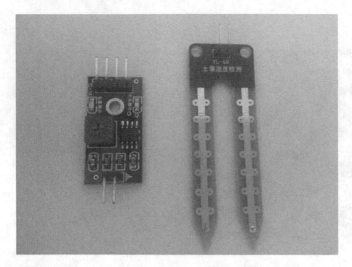

Figure 8-16. Commercial soil sensor with potentiometer

Tweeting

Tweeting is another way to improve this project. In the Chapter 6, you will learn how to tweet using Intel Galileo. I will talk again about this project and explain how to make the plants tweet in order to communicate when they need water.

Summary

This chapter explained how to build a project using parts that you can find in your garage, recycling, or in a construction store near you.

The next chapters offer resources that can be integrated into this project, like tweeting.

CHAPTER 9

■ ■ ■

Home Automation and Dynamic Web

This chapter discusses the implementation of a simple home automation system that transforms Intel Galileo into a web server with a dynamic web application. That application can be accessed using Internet browsers on personal computers and mobile phones, including Android and iPhone devices.

The system provides a web page that changes dynamically. It can show a temperature sensor reading, detect intruders with the PIR sensor, arm and disarm the system using a flexible keypad, and send commands to control devices in your home, like turning on and off lamps and TVs.

Each peripheral used in this chapter contains individual test code and schematics, so even if you are not interested in assembling the whole home automation system, you can use the four "micro-projects" that describe how to integrate a keypad, a temperature sensor, switch module relays, and PIR sensors individually.

Project Details

If you read Chapter 3, you will remember that SPI images are very small and do not contain all device drivers and software packages compared to SD card images. The sketches are not persisted.

The first requirement of this project is related to the firmware that you must add to the SD card image. This is because node.js is used to implement a web server running directly on Intel Galileo and the sketch must persist in the board.

A second requirement of this project is that you need to have Intel Galileo connected to some network using an Ethernet cable, with a WiFi module or LTE modem like the XMM7160. To reach Intel Galileo with your browser, you need to know its IP address as well, which means you need to have the serial cable open to the serial console.

The house in this case might be controlled using a web page that changes dynamically with new updates. This web page is dynamic because it will automatically be updated with sensor readings.

But why wasn't a desktop or mobile phone application created for this project? The dynamic application using a web page enables the program to run in most devices, including personal computers, tablets, laptops, and mobile phones.

The main component on this project is a web server that's implemented using node. js. If you do not know what node.js is, it is a very nice platform that provides a very simple way to quickly implement scalable applications like web servers. Node.js is based on the JavaScript language and doesn't require heavy software like Apache, which means it's good with Intel Galileo. For more details regarding node.js, visit nodejs.org.

This project controls two switch relays, receives events from a passive infrared (PIR) sensor responsible for motion detection, and monitors the temperature.

The Software Architecture

The architecture is simple and will help you understand the code. There are three components in this project: the web server, the web application, and the sketch.

The web server and the sketches run in Intel Galileo.

The web application runs in most browsers, including Chrome, Internet Explorer, Firefox, Safari, and others available on desktops, tables, phones, and laptops. Figure 9-1 shows this interaction.

Figure 9-1. *The interaction with the web server component*

The Web Server

In this project, the web server acts as an intermediary component that communicates with two elements: the sketches and the browsers. Keep in mind that the web application can send commands and control the house when the user interacts with the user interface in HTML and the web page can receive events from Intel Galileo that report the status of the sensors installed in the house dynamically and asynchronously.

In both cases, the web server converts the messages sent by the web page to Intel Galileo and vice versa and the channels for the message exchange are implemented using sockets.

Figure 9-2 illustrates how communication works across all the software components.

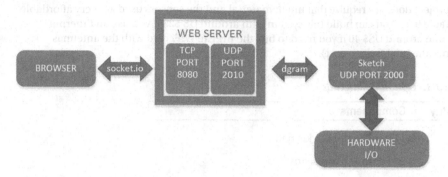

Figure 9-2. *Communication between the web server, browser, and skecthes*

The communication between Intel Galileo sketch and the web server is done using datagrams (UDP). For this function, the sketches keep a UDP server listening on port 2000 while the web server keeps a UDP server listening on port 2010. The communication between the web server and the browser uses socket.io, which essentially indicates a TCP connection.

Thus, when it is necessary to inform the sensors reading, UDP messages are sent by the sketch to port 2010 received by the web server. The web server is then responsible for transforming this message to an event transmitted to the browsers connected to the web server using port 8080. The browser receives the message through socket.io client pieces and the specific elements of the page are updated dynamically, thus avoiding having to refresh the whole page.

On the other hand, the user might send commands to control devices to turn on lamps, TVs, or any other AC device. In this case, the client socket.io in the web application sends a message to the web server using the socket.io function on port 8080 to the web server. The web server catches this message and converts it to a UDP message that is transmitted to port 2000. The UDP server running in the sketch and listening to port 2000 receives the message and interprets it by managing the Arduino's digital I/O headers in order to control devices through switch relays.

The web server and the sketch run in the same version of Intel Galileo, so you might wonder why you have to establish a connection using UDP instead of a simpler alternative, such as using signals or writing/reading operations in the file system. Remember that node.js is responsible for ensuring that the web server runs in a different instance than the sketch. That means the code is platform-dependent. If you decide to change the web server, the communication layer must be rewritten.

Regarding the communication with the web server and the browser, the choice regarding can be implemented with a few lines of code. As a result, you have a web page that changes dynamically and can avoid the annoyance of having to refresh the whole page like when you use <meta http-equiv="refresh" content="number of seconds" > in the HTML headers.

Materials List

This project does not require that much material and the sensors used are very affordable (see Table 9-1). You can build this system with around US $25 if you use an Ethernet cable and around US$ 40 if you need to buy the mPCIe WiFi card with the antennas (besides the Intel Galileo cost).

Table 9-1. *Optional Materials*

Quantity	Components
1	12-key membrane keypad
2	300 ohm 1/4 W resistor
1	LED green
1	LED red
1	HC-SR501 PIR sensor module
1	YwRobot module, two relays
1	TMP36 temperature sensor
1	0.1 uF ceramic
1	Intel Centrino Wireless-N 135 mPCIe or Ethernet
1	Breadboard (400 points are enough)
N (Several)	Dupont wires, female to male, and wire jumpers

In fact, you do not need to buy all the items if you do not want to have specific features like the movement detection provided by the PIR sensor.

Integrating the Components Individually

The home automation system contains software and hardware components and it is a good idea to test them individually in order to understand how each component works and how to write the code that interacts with each one. The next sections help you to test the keypad, the PIR sensor, the YwRobot relay module, and the TMP36 temperature sensor, all before you join all the pieces.

Testing the Keypad

The flexible membrane keypad used in this project has 12 keys, operates at 12V, is 76x60x0.8mm, and is very easy to integrate. However, you need only to know how the connector is mapped to the keys and have a simple way to write the code (see Figure 9-3).

Figure 9-3. *Top view (top) and lateral view (bottom) of the flexible membrane keypad*

If you cannot find this keypad easily, you can use any other type, but make sure you adapt the connections represented in the following sections.

The next sections describe the software functionality, the hardware connections, and the code that will be integrated with the system in general.

The Keypad Functionality

Before you learn about the connection and code, it is necessary to understand how the system will work.

Once you boot Intel Galileo, the system will be *locked*, which means if the PIR sensor detects movement, an alert will be sent. However, it's possible to unlock the system by entering the correct PIN. If the PIN entered matches the secret PIN, the system returns to the unlocked state and the PIR sensor doesn't send any alarms.

If the user enters the same PIN number again, the system is rearmed. In other words, the same PIN number is used to arm and disarm the system, locking and unlocking the system respectively.

There is a green LED that's on when the system is locked and off when the system is unlocked. It gives the user a visual indication as to whether the system is armed or not.

Every time the user press a key the LED blinks for a small period of time (the default is 500ms) to confirm the pressing event was recognized by the system. This is independent of whether the system is locked or not. In order words, the LED blinks even when it is already on (system is locked) or off (system is unlocked).

The keypad has a ENTER function that's used when the pound key (#) is pressed and the user must press this key every time he wants to confirm the PIN number. The star key (*)resets all the digits pressed and allows the user to re-enter the PIN if some wrong key was pressed.

The Keypad Connection

The rows 0 to 3 are related to the connector pins 1, 2, 3, and 4, respectively and columns 0 to 2 are related to the connector pins 5, 6, and 7, respectively. These pins must be connected to the Intel Galileo digital ports and are easily customizable using software. See Figure 9-4.

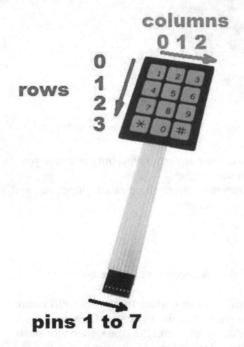

Figure 9-4. Keypad disposition of pins and identification of rows and columns

To test the keypad, an LED is being added. Figure 9-5 shows the keypad schematics.

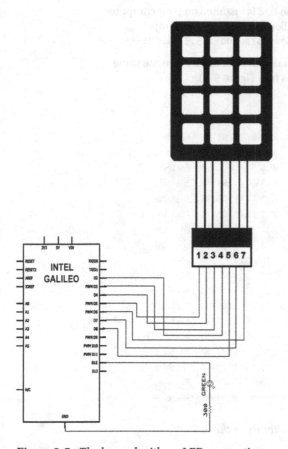

Figure 9-5. *The keypad with an LED connection*

Note for this project that the LED is being connected to the digital port 13, which means the LED is not really necessary because the built-in LED is also connected to pin 13. It is your choice to use an external LED or not.

Writing and Testing the Keypad Software

This section uses the code from Listing 9-1 (keypad_testcode.ino) contained in the code folder of this chapter. You also need to download the Keypad library from http://playground.arduino.cc/Code/Keypad.

Once the library is downloaded, integrate it with the Intel Galileo IDE as follows:

1. Locate where the Arduino IDE is installed on your computer and find the directory called libraries. For example, c:\arduino-1.5.3-windows\arduino-1.5.3\libraries.

2. Extract the ZIP file and make sure the library is in the same level as the other libraries (see Figure 9-6).

Name	Date modified	Type
Audio	2/15/2014 12:03 PM	File folder
DHT11	2/15/2014 12:03 PM	File folder
EEPROM	2/15/2014 12:03 PM	File folder
Esplora	2/15/2014 12:03 PM	File folder
Ethernet	2/15/2014 12:03 PM	File folder
Firmata	2/15/2014 12:03 PM	File folder
GSM	2/15/2014 12:03 PM	File folder
Keypad	2/15/2014 1:24 PM	File folder·
LiquidCrystal	2/15/2014 12:03 PM	File folder
Robot_Control	2/15/2014 12:03 PM	File folder
Robot_Motor	2/15/2014 12:03 PM	File folder
RobotIRremote	2/15/2014 12:03 PM	File folder
Scheduler	2/15/2014 12:03 PM	File folder
SD	2/15/2014 12:03 PM	File folder
Servo	2/15/2014 12:03 PM	File folder
SoftwareSerial	2/15/2014 12:03 PM	File folder
SPI	2/15/2014 12:03 PM	File folder
Stepper	2/15/2014 12:03 PM	File folder

Figure 9-6. *Installation of the keypad library in the IDE*

3. Open keypad_testcode.ino and run it. Press CTRL+SHIFT+M to open the serial console debugger. See Listing 9-1.

Listing 9-1. keypad_testcode.ino

```
#include <Keypad.h>

enum SYSTEM_STATUS{
  LOCKED,    // 0
  UNLOCKED,  // 1
};

static SYSTEM_STATUS currentStatus = LOCKED;
const String password = "1968";
String input;
```

```
const byte ledPin = 12;

const byte ROWS = 4; // four rows
const byte COLS = 3; // three columns
char keys[ROWS][COLS] = {
    {'1','2','3'},
    {'4','5','6'},
    {'7','8','9'},
    {'*','0','#'}
};

byte rowPins[ROWS] = {5, 4, 3, 2}; // pins on Intel Galielo I/O
byte colPins[COLS] = {8, 7, 6};    // pins on Intel Galielo I/O

Keypad keypad = Keypad( makeKeymap(keys), rowPins, colPins, ROWS, COLS );


void setup(){
    Serial.begin(115200);

    // in case there is an LED CONNECTED
    pinMode(ledPin, OUTPUT);
    digitalWrite(ledPin, HIGH);         // The default is system locked..
so, the LED must be HIGH
    keypad.addEventListener(handleKey); // this is the listener to handle
the keys
}

void loop(){

    // reading the keyboard
    char key = keypad.getKey();

    // if it's a valid key
    if (key) {

        if ((key != '#') && (key != '*'))
        {
            input += key;
        }
        Serial.print("key:");
        Serial.println(key);
    }
}
```

```
// this function is only called when the PIN code
// typed matches the secret PIN code and inverts
// the system logic. It means if the system was LOCKED
// it will be UNLOCKED and vice versa.
void updateLEDStatus() {
    if (currentStatus == LOCKED)
    {
        currentStatus = UNLOCKED;

        Serial.println("SYSTEM UNLOCKED");

        // turn OFF the LED
        digitalWrite(ledPin, LOW);
    }
    else
    {
        currentStatus = LOCKED;


        Serial.println("SYSTEM LOCKED");

        // turn ON the LED
        digitalWrite(ledPin, HIGH);
    }
}

// this function is responsible to handle
// the keypad events
void handleKey(KeypadEvent key){

    switch (keypad.getState())
    {
    case PRESSED:


        digitalWrite(ledPin, !digitalRead(ledPin));
        delay(500);
        digitalWrite(ledPin, !digitalRead(ledPin));

        // this is our ENTER
        if (key == '#') {
          Serial.println(input);
          if (input == password)
          {
                updateLEDStatus();
          }
```

```
    input = "";

}

break;

case RELEASED:

    // this is our CLEAR
    if (key == '*') {
        input = "";
    }
    break;
    }
}
```

Reviewing the Code

The original code sets the secret PIN to **1968**, which is the year Intel was founded. Feel free to change the PIN. To do this, change this line:

```
const String password = "1968";
```

The first line of the code calls the Keypad.h file responsible for having the function calls from the library. The next lines are related to an enumerator and they describe the two possible states of the system—LOCKED and UNLOCKED.

The next lines determine the keypad design and to which pins in the digital port I/O the keys must be connected.

```
const byte ROWS = 4; // four rows
const byte COLS = 3; // three columns
char keys[ROWS][COLS] = {
    {'1','2','3'},
    {'4','5','6'},
    {'7','8','9'},
    {'*','0','#'}
};

byte rowPins[ROWS] = {5, 4, 3, 2}; // pins on Intel Galielo I/O
byte colPins[COLS] = {8, 7, 6};    // pins on Intel Galielo I/O

Keypad keypad = Keypad( makeKeymap(keys), rowPins, colPins, ROWS, COLS );
```

Note the bidimensional array called keys. It describes the keypad design used in this project and the bytes' arrays called rowPins and colPins determine how the keypad is connected to the Intel Galileo digital port I/O.

If you are using a different keypad with different connections and designs, you need to change these lines accordingly.

The following line:

```
Keypad keypad = Keypad( makeKeymap(keys), rowPins, colPins, ROWS, COLS );
```

Is used only to "join the pieces" of the library. In other words, it is how the software informs the library of the keypad design and how the keypad's connector is connected to the Intel Galileo digital ports.

The setup() function contains a function callback that will be called when a key event like press, release, and hold is detected.

```
keypad.addEventListener(handleKey);
```

In this case, the callback function is named handleKey().

In the function loop(), the keys are read through the function getKey(), as follows.

```
char key = keypad.getKey();
```

And still in the function loop(), if the keys are valid and different from # and !, they are accumulated in the variable called input because the intention is only to store numeric keys types in this variable.

```
if (key) {

    if ((key != '#') && (key != '*'))
    {
        input += key;
    }
```

Finally, you use the callback function handleKey() when the PRESS and RELEASE events are detected and some actions are done. For the PRESS event, if the user types #, this key acts similarly to an ENTER event. The pin sequence accumulated in the variable input is checked to see if it matches the secret PIN number. If it matches, the system is UNLOCKED or LOCKED, according to the current state. Recall that the LED is on when the system is LOCKED and off when it's UNLOCKED.

```
switch (keypad.getState())
{
case PRESSED:
    // this is our ENTER
    if (key == '#') {
...
...
```

436

```
    if (input == password)
    {
        updateLEDStatus();
    }
...
...
```

For the RELEASE event, if the * key is pressed, the input variable is cleared and the user is allowed to re-enter the code.

```
case RELEASED:

    // this is our CLEAR
    if (key == '*') {
        input = "";
    }
...
...
```

Running the Keypad Code

Run the code and press CTRL+SHIFT+M to see the serial console debugger.

You will immediately see the LED on, which means the initial state of the system is LOCKED. Type some keys and you should see the LED blinking for small period.

If you press # and the PIN typed matches the secret PIN code, then the LED will turn off and the system will be UNLOCKED.

If you type the secret code again, the system will be rearmed and the LED will turn on.

If you type the key *, all input is cleared.

Figure 9-7 shows the keypad test.

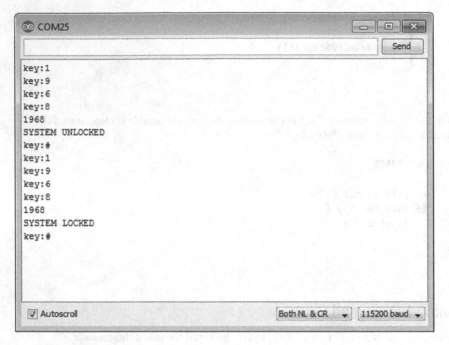

Figure 9-7. *Debugging the keypad functionality*

Testing the PIR Sensor

The human sensor passive infrared (PIR) module HC-SR501 is very simple to test. The purpose of this sensor is to detect movement in an environment. Figure 9-8 shows the PIR sensor used in this project.

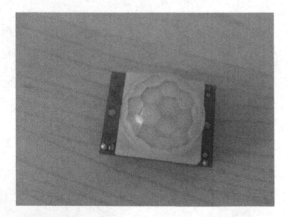

Figure 9-8. *PIR sensor*

The module requires some calibration according to your preferences or your needs. It's necessary to adjust the maximum distance the sensor must operate and to set how long the pulse indicating a detection must flash.

The module HC-SR501 does not have encapsulation and consequently it's not recommended for outdoor applications.

For more details about this module, check out http://www.mpja.com/ download/31227sc.pdf.

The PIR Sensor Functionality

The module has enough connections for three signals, as demonstrated in Figure 9-9.

Figure 9-9. PIR sensor headers

When a movement is detected, the OUT pin remains HIGH during an interval of 5 to 300 seconds according to the adjustments made in the micro-potentiometer Tx. The distance in the detection can be set between 2m (6.56ft) and 7m (22.9ft) using the micro-potentiometer Sx. See Figure 9-9 for details.

The PIR Sensor Connection

This PIR sensor can receive an input voltage between 5 and 20V. It means the sensor can use the +5V voltage supplied by Intel Galileo. If your intention is to create a demo or to understand how it all works, using the +5V provided by the Intel Galileo headers is more than enough. However, if you plan to use this sensor in your house and need to monitor a room quite far from Intel Galileo, it's better to use a 9V battery instead to pass wires all around your house and avoid the impedance provided by the wires interfere with the sensor functionality. According to the information related to this sensor, the quiescent current is lower than 50uA, and that's okay for a 9V battery.

If you want to connect the sensor directly to Intel Galileo, check out Figure 9-10.

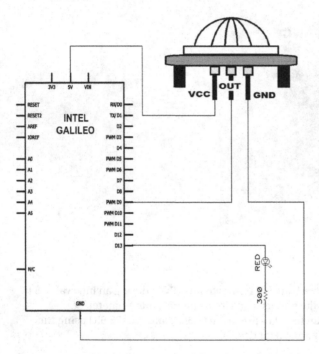

Figure 9-10. *PIR sensor connected directly to Intel Galileo*

Otherwise, if you want to use a 9V battery, check out the schematics represented in Figure 9-11.

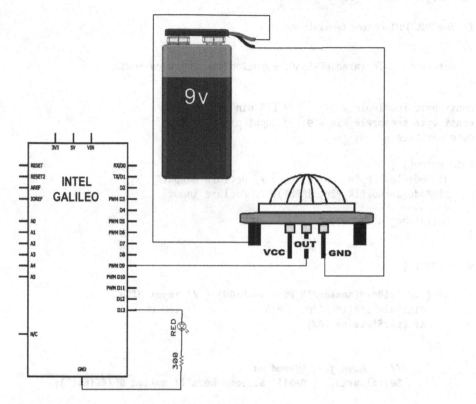

Figure 9-11. *PIR sensor using a 9V battery as the power supply*

Note the sensor is connected to the digital port number 9, which means if you were previously testing the keypad you can keep the keypad connected. Also, there is an LED connected to the pin 13, which means you can use the built-in LED to check the sensor functionality or you can connect an external LED, as used by the keypad test described earlier in this chapter.

Writing and Testing the PIR Sensor Software

For this, you'll use PIR_sensor_testcode.ino from Listing 9-2.

Listing 9-2. PIR_sensor_testcode.ino

```
//
// For testing Infrared HC-SR501 Pyroelectric Infrared Sensor
//

const byte ledPIRpin = 13;    // LED pin for the LED
const byte sensorPIR_Pin = 9; // input pin
byte pirState = LOW; //

void setup() {
    pinMode(ledPIRpin, OUTPUT);    // declare output
    pinMode(sensorPIR_Pin, INPUT); // declare input

    Serial.begin(115200);
}

void loop(){

    if (digitalRead(sensorPIR_Pin) == HIGH) { // input HIGH
        digitalWrite(ledPIRpin, HIGH);        // LED ON
        if (pirState == LOW)
        {

            // we have just turned on
            Serial.println("OPS!!! Someone here!!! motion DETECTED!");

            // We only want to print on the output change, not state
            pirState = HIGH;
        }
    }
    else
    {

        digitalWrite(ledPIRpin, LOW); // turn LED OFF
        if (pirState == HIGH){

        // we have just turned of
        Serial.println("Waiting for next moviment");

        // We only want to print on the output change, not state
        pirState = LOW;
        }
    }
}
```

The only thing the code does is detect the level changes in pin 9, which is connected to the sensor header OUT using the digital port. The sketch has a variable called pirState that starts LOW. When the sensor detects movement, the variable assumes the HIGH state. Then when the delay expires, the sensor header OUT goes to LOW and the pirState variable changes the state to LOW, thereby indicating there is no presence.

Run the sketch and press CTRL+SHIFT+M to see the serial debugger. The serial debugger will print messages when movement is detected.

This is the time to make adjustments! The potentiometers indicated in Figure 9-9 must be changed this way:

1. Distance Settings (Sx): Turn to the right and distance (sensitivity) increases; turn to the left and distance decreases.

2. Time Setting (Tx): Turn to the right and time delay increases; turn to the left and time reduces.

Remember the limitations: A distance between 2m (6.56ft) and 7m (22.9ft) and a delay between 5 and 300 seconds.

Testing the YwRobot Relay Module

The two-channel relay module YwRobot used in this chapter is one of the simplest components to test, but it is necessary to be aware of the limitation of the relays in terms of amperes and the maximum voltage that can operate when connected to lamps and other AC devices. Otherwise, your house may end up in flames.

This is the same relay that was mentioned in Chapter 5 as an improvement for the moisture sensor system to activate and deactivate electric valves.

The YwRobot Relay Module Functionality

In this chapter, the relay module YwRobot can support a maximum of 250V AC and 10A AC, or 30V DC with 10DC relay. This is enough to support simple lamps.

The input operation is 5V with a TTL level for relays. That means the Intel Arduino digital ports can be used to operate the module.

The module used in this project contains two relays, each of which is commanded according to the schematics shown in Figure 9-12.

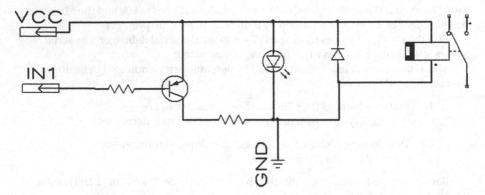

Figure 9-12. *Relay module command*

Each relay in this module contains a simple drive circuit with a PNP 8550 transistor that operates with 5V DC. When IN1 is LOW, the circuit is active and the relay is switched; otherwise, when IN1 is HIGH the circuit is off and the relay is inactive.

The module offers some LEDs that help debug because they indicate whether the module is powered on and indicate whether the relay is active or not, by setting LOW and HIGH respectively in the IN headers (see Figure 9-13).

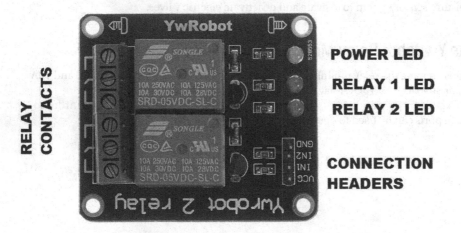

Figure 9-13. *YwModule LED and headers*

The YwRobot Relay Module Connection with Intel Galileo

The version used in this chapter contains two relays commanded by the header pins IN1 and IN2. You can buy modules with more relays and the only difference is the number of "INs" because the module contains unique VCC and GND (ground) headers, independent of the quantity of relays.

The VCC in the schematics is connected to Intel Galileo 5V. The GND is connected to the Intel Galileo ground and IN1 is connected to a digital port I/O of your preference. The driver circuit is active when the module input (IN) is set to LOW and inactive when it's set to HIGH.

For this project, the commands IN1 and IN2 are connected to Intel Galileo's ports 10 and 11, respectively. See Figure 9-14 as a reference.

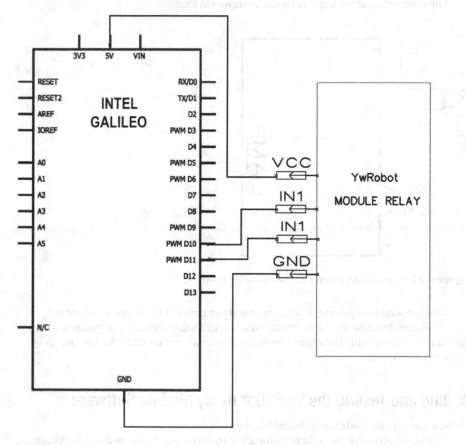

Figure 9-14. *Connecting the module relays to Intel Galileo*

The YwRobot Relay Module Connection with External Lamps

Warning   Before connecting your lamps to the AC with the module relay, it's important to note that 110 VAC, 127 VAC, and 220 VAC can cause severe personal injury, death, or substantial property damage.

Make sure the lamp or device you want to command with this project requires a current and voltage that fits the capability provided by the relay module's specification and that all the installation is completed using the proper wires.

The connection of the lamp or device is shown in Figure 9-15.

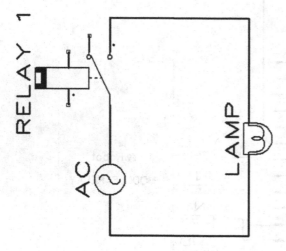

Figure 9-15. *Connecting a lamp to the one relay in AC*

When testing your system, it is not necessary to connect the lamps or any other AC component because the YwRobot module has LEDs that indicate connection, as explained in Figure 9-13. Therefore, you can consider this connection the last one to be made in your system.

Writing and Testing the YwRobot Relay Module Software

This section uses the code you can find listed as

Listing 9-3 provides the code for testing the module relay. relaymodule_testcode. ino is the simplest one in this chapter.

Listing 9-3. relaymodule_testcode.ino

```
//
// For testing YwRobot module relay
//

const byte relay1 = 10; // relay 1 command
const byte relay2 = 11; // relay 2 command

void setup() {
    pinMode(relay1, OUTPUT); // declare output
    pinMode(relay2, OUTPUT); // declare output

    Serial.begin(115200);
}

void loop(){

    digitalWrite(relay1, LOW);  // turn ON
    digitalWrite(relay2, HIGH); // turn OFF
    delay(5000);

    digitalWrite(relay1, HIGH); // turn OFF
    digitalWrite(relay2, LOW);  // turn ON
    delay(5000);
}
```

As you can see in the code, there is nothing special because the module relay input IN1 and IN2 are connected to the digital ports 10 and 11 on Intel Galileo.

The loop() function turns on and off the output of relay 1 controlled by IN1 and relay 2 controlled by IN2 in intervals of five seconds.

If you have the lamps connected to the relays, you will be able to see that when a lamp is on the other lamp is off and vice versa. If you do not have the lamps connected, you can see the LED in the YwRobot indicating which relay is active at the moment.

Testing the TMP36 Temperature Sensor

The TMP36 temperature sensor looks like a transistor. It doesn't require any calibration and provides an output voltage linearly proportional to the temperature in Celsius.

447

The TMP36 Temperature Sensor Functionality

The TMP36 has three pins, a VIN that must be between 2.7 and 5.5V DC, a GND, and a voltage output (VOUT).

There are different circuits with different precision described in the datasheet at http://www.analog.com/static/imported-files/data_sheets/TMP35_36_37.

The TMP36 Temperature Sensor Connection with Intel Galileo

Before you start to make a connection, it is very important to note, at the moment this book is being developed, that the datasheet revision G represents the TMP36 pin showing the *bottom* view instead the top.

Several developers claim that the sensor is extremely hot, but in fact it is because the sensor is connected inverted.

Figure 9-16 shows the bottom view of the sensor.

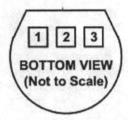

PIN 1, +V$_S$; PIN 2, V$_{OUT}$; PIN 3, GND

Figure 9-16. *TMP38, bottom view*

You need to connect the power to the sensor with 5V, connect the ground, and choose one of the analog ports to connect to the sensor VOUT. For this project, the analog port A0 is being used with VOUT and a capacitor with 0.1uF is used between the ground and the VCC (see Figure 9-17).

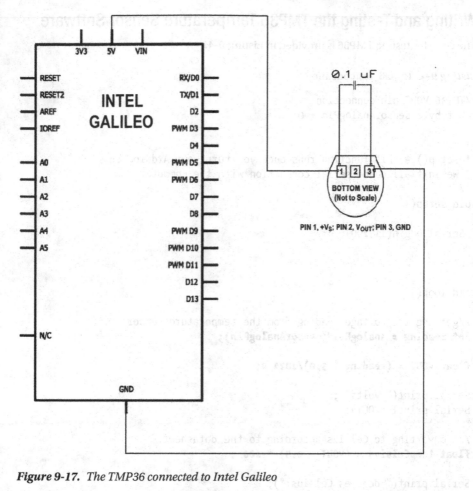

Figure 9-17. *The TMP36 connected to Intel Galileo*

For more details about this sensor, go to http://www.analog.com/static/imported-files/data_sheets/TMP35_36_37.pdf.

Writing and Testing the TMP36 Temperature Sensor Software

The code for testing TMP36 is provided in Listing 9-4.

Listing 9-4. tmp36_testcode.ino

```
//TMP36 VOUT pin connection
const byte sensorAnalogPin = 0;

/*
 * setup() - this function runs once you turn your Arduino on
 * We initialize the serial connection with the computer
 */
void setup()
{
  Serial.begin(115200);

}

void loop()
{
//getting the voltage reading from the temperature sensor
int reading = analogRead(sensorAnalogPin);

float VOUT = (reading * 5.0)/1024.0;

Serial.print(" volts");
Serial.println(VOUT);

// converting to Celsius according to the datasheet
float tempCelsius = (VOUT - 0.5) * 100 ;

Serial.print(" degrees Celsius:");
Serial.println(tempCelsius);

// converting to Fahrenheit
float tempF = (tempCelsius * 9.0 / 5.0) + 32.0;

Serial.print("degrees Fahrenheit:");
Serial.println(tempF);

delay(1000);
}
```

The code converts the real voltage in the output after reading the A0 port:

```
int reading = analogRead(sensorAnalogPin);

float VOUT = (reading * 5.0)/1024.0;
```

To convert to Celsius, use this formula:

```
Temperature Celsius = (VOUT - 0.5V)*100
```

The code to get the temperature in Celsius is as follows:

```
// converting to Celsius according the datasheet
float tempCelsius = (VOUT - 0.5) * 100 ;
```

Creating the Sketch

With all hardware components tested, it is time to create the sketch. The code will be only a junction of all the test code used to test the peripherals, including only the portion necessary to communicate with the web server using datagrams (UDP).

Intel Galileo does not require any special Arduino shield to get network connections and you can set the connection using an Ethernet cable or WiFi card with a mPCIe bus such as the Intel Centrino wireless N-135 or even using a modem card.

Considering that no shield is used, it is not necessary to use the libraries and write code for such a connection. This allows you to make the connection with a simple setting in Intel Galileo, as explained in the Chapter 5.

The sketch will need be able to send and receive datagrams. Linux libraries offer functions to do that, which means you don't have to use libraries created specifically for shields, which aren't used in this project.

Sending UDP Messages

The following code snippet represents a function responsible for sending the datagram. Note a socket descriptor socketfd is opened with the parameters SOCK_DGRAM and IPPROTO_UDP in order to specify the datagram and non-oriented connection.

The port the messages must be sent through is specified by WEBSERVER_UPD_PORT in the htons() function.

The IP address used to send the message is loopback 127.0.0.1 because the sketch and the web server run in Intel Galileo, which means the same device is sharing the same loopback port. You could use the IP provided by the element adapter when the connection is established but you should change the code all the time or implement some mechanism to pass this information parameterized.

To send the message, the function sendTo() is used.

```
#define WEBSERVER_UDP_PORT 2010 // this port is used to send message events
to Node.js

void sendUDPMessage(String protocol)
{
  struct sockaddr_in serv_addr;
  int sockfd, i, slen=sizeof(serv_addr);

  if ((sockfd = socket(AF_INET, SOCK_DGRAM, IPPROTO_UDP))==-1)
  {
    printError("socket");
    return;
  }

  bzero(&serv_addr, sizeof(serv_addr));
  serv_addr.sin_family = AF_INET;
  serv_addr.sin_port = htons(WEBSERVER_UDP_PORT);

  // considering the sketch and the web server run into Galileo
  // let's use the loopback address
  if (inet_aton("127.0.0.1", &serv_addr.sin_addr)==0)
  {
      printError("inet_aton() failed\n");
      close(sockfd);
      return;
  }

  char send_msg[BUFFERSIZE];  // more than enough
  memset((void *)send_msg, sizeof(send_msg), 0);
  protocol.toCharArray(send_msg, sizeof(send_msg), 0);

  if (sendto(sockfd, send_msg, strlen(send_msg), 0, (struct sockaddr
*)&serv_addr, sizeof(serv_addr))==-1)
      printError("sendto()");

  close(sockfd);

}
```

Receiving UDP Messages

To receive the datagrams, the socket descriptor is opened in the same way as when sending UDP messages. However, as soon as the socket is opened, the function bind() must be called. It specifies the port that will be used to receive messages from the web server, named SKETCH_UDP_PORT in this case.

```
#define SKETCH_UDP_PORT 2000      // this port is used to receive message
events from Node.js

int populateUDPServer(void)
{

    if ((sockfd = socket(AF_INET, SOCK_DGRAM, IPPROTO_UDP))==-1)
      printError("socket");
    else
      Serial.println("Server : Socket() successful\n");

    bzero(&my_addr, sizeof(my_addr));
    my_addr.sin_family = AF_INET;
    my_addr.sin_port = htons(SKETCH_UDP_PORT);
    my_addr.sin_addr.s_addr = htonl(INADDR_ANY);

    if (bind(sockfd, (struct sockaddr* ) &my_addr, sizeof(my_addr))==-1)
      printError("bind");
    else
      Serial.println("Server : bind() successful\n");

    memset(msg_buffer, 0, sizeof(msg_buffer));
}
```

Once the socket descriptor is opened and the bind() function is called, it is possible to receive the datagrams from the web server by calling the recvfrom() function periodically. The loop() function is perfect for this.

However, the recvfrom() function is used and is a *blocking* function. When the web server isn't sending messages, the function will block the execution of whole sketch, thus invalidating the project.

To resolve this issue, another function called select() must be used in conjunction with recvfrom() in order to implement a timeout in the blocking process. The recvfrom() function will respect the timeout and allow the program to be executed.

A flag is used to control this process and uses functions like FD_ZERO() for reset and FD_SET() for binding the flag with the socket descriptor. Such functions must be called before the select() function.

There is a detail when select() is called regarding the first parameter that must be the socket descriptor plus one, according to the documentation.

In the next code snippet, the timeout is set to 1,000 microseconds. If no message is received and the timeout occurs, the sensor's values are read and sent to the web server every second so that the web page is constantly updated.

If some message is received, the function FS_ISSET() will state it and the recvfrom() will be called and the data will be received.

```
void loop() {

    if (time0 == 0) time0 = millis();
...
...
...

    // clear the set ahead of time
    FD_ZERO(&readfds);
    FD_SET(sockfd, &readfds);

    // wait until either socket has data ready to be recvfrom()
        (timeout 1000 usecs)
    tv.tv_sec = 0;
    tv.tv_usec = 1000;

    rv = select(sockfd + 1, &readfds, NULL, NULL, &tv);

    if(rv==-1)
    {
        Serial.println("Error in Select!!!");
    }
    if(rv==0)
    {

        // TIMEOUT!!!!

        if ((millis()-time0) >= 1000)
        {
            // reached 1 seconds.. let's reads the sensor and
               send a message!!!
            time0 = millis();
...
...
...

            sendUDPMessage(protocol);

        }
    }
}
```

```
        // checking if the UDP server received some message from the web page
        if (FD_ISSET(sockfd, &readfds))
        {

            if (recvfrom(sockfd, msg_buffer, BUFFERSIZE, 0,
            (struct sockaddr*)&cli_addr, &slen)==-1)
                printError("recvfrom()");
...
...
...

            // let's clear the message buffer
            memset(msg_buffer, 0, sizeof(msg_buffer));

        }

}
```

Joining All Code in a Single Sketch

If you tested all the peripherals in this chapter, you should realize that the connection of the components to the Intel Galileo headers uses different ports. This allows you to keep all the peripherals connected and test them individually, thus making the hardware integration very easy.

Listing 9-5 is a simple join of all the test code. It integrates the UDP code for sending and receiving messages, but also reads the sensors and the system status after using the keypad to arm and disarm the system. Such readings are done every second. In other words, when you have the timeouts provided by select() and FD functions, as described.

The code also parses the commands received through the UDP server and changes the switch relays in the YwRobot module.

Listing 9-5. sketch_client.ino

```
#include <stdio.h>

// includes for the UDP connections
#include <arpa/inet.h>
#include <netinet/in.h>
#include <sys/types.h>
#include <sys/socket.h>
#include <unistd.h>
#include <stdlib.h>
#include <string.h>

// keypad
#include <Keypad.h>
```

```
// debugging
#define DEBUG 1                    // 1 to see the debug messages in the serial
                                   console, or 0 to disable

#define BUFFERSIZE 512             // UDP is limited and must be very
                                   short. 512 bytes is more than enough
#define SKETCH_UDP_PORT 2000       // this port is used to receive message
                                   events from Node.js
#define WEBSERVER_UDP_PORT 2010    // this port is used to send message events
                                   to Node.js
#define SENSOR_READ_INTERVAL 10    // number of seconds to read sensors and
                                   report to website

// for the UDP server
    struct sockaddr_in my_addr, cli_addr;
     int sockfd, i;
     socklen_t slen=sizeof(cli_addr);
     char msg_buffer[BUFFERSIZE];
     fd_set readfds;
     struct timeval tv;
     int rv,n;

// pin connections
const byte sensorAnalogPin = 0;

// Keypad
enum SYSTEM_STATUS{
  LOCKED,      // 0
  UNLOCKED,    // 1
};

static SYSTEM_STATUS currentStatus = LOCKED;
const String password = "1968";     // Intel foundation year..
String input;

const byte ledPin = 12;

const byte ROWS = 4; // four rows
const byte COLS = 3; // three columns
char keys[ROWS][COLS] = {
    {'1','2','3'},
    {'4','5','6'},
    {'7','8','9'},
    {'*','0','#'}
};

byte rowPins[ROWS] = {5, 4, 3, 2}; // pins on Intel Galielo I/O
byte colPins[COLS] = {8, 7, 6};    // pins on Intel Galielo I/O
```

```
Keypad keypad = Keypad( makeKeymap(keys), rowPins, colPins, ROWS, COLS );

// PIR sensor
const byte sensorPIR_Pin = 9; // input pin
byte pirState = LOW; //
const byte ledPIRpin = 13;

// Relays
const byte relay1 = 10; // relay 1 command
const byte relay2 = 11; // relay 2 command

// time control
unsigned long time0 = 0;

// this function is only called when some error happens
void printError(char *str)
{
    Serial.print("ERROR: ");
    Serial.println(str);
}

// this function is reponsible for sending UDP datagrams
void sendUDPMessage(String protocol)
{
  struct sockaddr_in serv_addr;
  int sockfd, i, slen=sizeof(serv_addr);

  if ((sockfd = socket(AF_INET, SOCK_DGRAM, IPPROTO_UDP))==-1)
  {
    printError("socket");
    return;
  }

  bzero(&serv_addr, sizeof(serv_addr));
  serv_addr.sin_family = AF_INET;
  serv_addr.sin_port = htons(WEBSERVER_UDP_PORT);

  // considering the sketch and the web server run into Galileo
  // let's use the loopback address
  if (inet_aton("127.0.0.1", &serv_addr.sin_addr)==0)
  {
      printError("inet_aton() failed\n");
      close(sockfd);
      return;
  }
```

```
   char send_msg[BUFFERSIZE];   // more than enough
   memset((void *)send_msg, sizeof(send_msg), 0);
   protocol.toCharArray(send_msg, sizeof(send_msg), 0);

  if (sendto(sockfd, send_msg, strlen(send_msg), 0, (struct sockaddr *)
&serv_addr, sizeof(serv_addr))==-1)
        printError("sendto()");

  close(sockfd);

}

// this function is responsible to init the UDP datagram server
int populateUDPServer(void)
{

    if ((sockfd = socket(AF_INET, SOCK_DGRAM, IPPROTO_UDP))==-1)
      printError("socket");
    else
      if (DEBUG) Serial.println("Server : Socket() successful\n");

    bzero(&my_addr, sizeof(my_addr));
    my_addr.sin_family = AF_INET;
    my_addr.sin_port = htons(SKETCH_UDP_PORT);
    my_addr.sin_addr.s_addr = htonl(INADDR_ANY);

    if (bind(sockfd, (struct sockaddr* ) &my_addr, sizeof(my_addr))==-1)
      printError("bind");
    else
      if (DEBUG) Serial.println("Server : bind() successful\n");

    memset(msg_buffer, 0, sizeof(msg_buffer));

}

// reading the temperature sensor in Celsius
float readTemperatureSensor()
{
  // getting the voltage reading from the temperature sensor
 int reading = analogRead(sensorAnalogPin);

 float VOUT = (reading * 5.0)/1024.0;

 if (DEBUG) {
     Serial.print(" volts");
     Serial.println(VOUT);
 }
```

```
// converting to Celsius according to the datasheet
float tempCelsius = (VOUT - 0.5) * 100 ;

if (DEBUG) {
    Serial.print(" degrees Celsius:");
    Serial.println(tempCelsius);
}

return tempCelsius;
}

// convert celsius to fahrenheit
float convertTempToF(int celsius) {
  // converting to Fahrenheit
 float tempF = (celsius * 9.0 / 5.0) + 32.0;

 if (DEBUG) {
    Serial.print("degrees Fahrenheit:");
    Serial.println(tempF);
 }

 return tempF;

}

// update the LED status when the system is armed or disarmed
void updateLEDStatus() {
      if (currentStatus == LOCKED)
      {
          currentStatus = UNLOCKED;

          if (DEBUG)
          {
              Serial.println("SYSTEM UNLOCKED");
          }

          //turn OFF the LED
          digitalWrite(ledPin, LOW);
      }
      else
      {
          currentStatus = LOCKED;

          if (DEBUG)
          {
              Serial.println("SYSTEM LOCKED");
          }
```

459

```
            // turn ON the LED
            digitalWrite(ledPin, HIGH);
        }
}

// this is the key handler for the PRESS, RELEASE, and HOLD event
void handleKey(KeypadEvent key){


    switch (keypad.getState())
    {
    case PRESSED: // this is our ENTER

        digitalWrite(ledPin, !digitalRead(ledPin));
        delay(500);
        digitalWrite(ledPin, !digitalRead(ledPin));

        if (key == '#') {
          if (DEBUG) Serial.println(input);
          if (input == password)
          {
              updateLEDStatus();
          }
          input = "";

        }

        break;

    case RELEASED: // this is our CLEAR
        if (key == '*') {
            input = "";
        }
        break;
    }
}

void setup() {

  Serial.begin(115200);

  delay(3000);

  // init variables for UDP server
  populateUDPServer();
```

```
  // keypad
  pinMode(ledPin, OUTPUT);
  pinMode(ledPIRpin, OUTPUT);

  digitalWrite(ledPin, HIGH);          // The default is system locked.. so,
the LED must be HIGH
  digitalWrite(ledPIRpin, LOW);        // Let's let the PIR sensor change the
LED state

  keypad.addEventListener(handleKey); // this is the listener to handle the
keys

  // relays
  pinMode(relay1, OUTPUT); // declare output
  pinMode(relay2, OUTPUT); // declare output

  digitalWrite(relay1, HIGH);
  digitalWrite(relay2, HIGH);

}

void loop() {

    if (time0 == 0) time0 = millis();

    // checking the keypad
    char key = keypad.getKey();

    if (key) {

        if ((key != '#') && (key != '*'))
        {
          input += key;
        }
        if (DEBUG)
        {
            Serial.print("key:");
            Serial.println(key);
        }
    }

    // PIR sensor
    if (digitalRead(sensorPIR_Pin) == HIGH) { // input HIGH
        digitalWrite(ledPIRpin, HIGH);            // LED ON
```

```
    if (pirState == LOW)
    {

        // we have just turned on
        Serial.println("OPS!!! Someone here!!! motion DETECTED!");

        // We only want to print on the output change, not state
        pirState = HIGH;
    }
}
else
{

    digitalWrite(ledPIRpin, LOW); // turn LED OFF
    if (pirState == HIGH){

    // we have just turned off
    if (DEBUG) Serial.println("Waiting for next moviment");

    // We only want to print on the output change, not state
    pirState = LOW;
    }
}

    // clear the set ahead of time
    FD_ZERO(&readfds);
    FD_SET(sockfd, &readfds);
    // wait until either socket has data ready to be recv()d
       (timeout 1000 usecs)
    tv.tv_sec = 0;
    tv.tv_usec = 1000;

    rv = select(sockfd + 1, &readfds, NULL, NULL, &tv);

    if(rv==-1)
    {
        if (DEBUG)
        {
            Serial.println("Error in Select!!!");
        }
    }
```

```
    if(rv==0)
    {

        // TIMEOUT!!!!

        if ((millis()-time0) >= 1000)
        {
            // reached 1 seconds  let's read the sensor and send a message!!!
            time0 = millis();

            String protocol = "";

            if (pirState == HIGH)
            {
                protocol += "*INTRUDER!!!*";
            }
            else
            {
                protocol += "*NO DETECTION*";
            }

                        // reading the temperature sensor
            int tempC = readTemperatureSensor();
            int tempF = convertTempToF(tempC);

            char msg[20];
            memset(msg, 0, sizeof(msg));
            sprintf(msg, "%dC - %dF", tempC, tempF);

            protocol += "*";
            protocol += msg;

            // checking the system status
            if (currentStatus == LOCKED)
            {
                protocol += "*ARMED*";
            }
            else
            {
                protocol += "*DISARMED*";
            }
            sendUDPMessage(protocol);

        }

    }
```

```
// checking if the UDP server received some message from the web page
if (FD_ISSET(sockfd, &readfds))
{

    if (recvfrom(sockfd, msg_buffer, BUFFERSIZE, 0,
        (struct sockaddr*)&cli_addr, &slen)==-1)
    {
        printError("recvfrom()");
        return; // let's abort the loop
    }
    if (DEBUG)
    {
        Serial.println("Received packet from %s:%d\nData:");
        Serial.println(inet_ntoa(cli_addr.sin_addr));
        Serial.println(msg_buffer);
    }

    String checkResp = msg_buffer;
    if (checkResp.lastIndexOf("L1ON", 0) < 0)
    {
        // There is no L1ON in the string.. let's switch off the relay
        digitalWrite(relay1, HIGH);

        if (DEBUG) Serial.println("The lamp 1 is OFF");

    }
    else
    {
        // Oops.. let's switch relay 1 to ON
        digitalWrite(relay1, LOW);

        if (DEBUG) Serial.println("The lamp 1 is ON");

    }

    if (checkResp.lastIndexOf("L2ON", 6) < 0)
    {
        // There is no L2ON in the string.. let's switch off the relay
        digitalWrite(relay2, HIGH);

        if (DEBUG) Serial.println("The lamp 2 is OFF");
    }
```

```
    else
    {
        // Oops.. let switch relay 2 to ON
        digitalWrite(relay2, LOW);

        if (DEBUG)Serial.println("The lamp 2 is ON");

    }

    // let's clear the message buffer
    memset(msg_buffer, 0, sizeof(msg_buffer));

    }
}
```

Creating Your Own Web Server with node.js

By now you should have tested all the hardware components with the small code snippets, so it is time to start writing and testing the main component—the web server.

This project uses node.js. As mentioned, node.js tried to simplify the development of the backend software. Maybe if you program in HTML before you should have played with JavaScript running in your web pages. If you need something very powerful, you should have implemented something using Python, Java, Perl scripts in a remote server, and so on. However, node.js brings the simplicity of JavaScript usage into the context of a web server in a light and easy implementation.

Updating node.js

Before writing and testing the code, make sure that the node.js is version equal or greater than 0.10.25. To check this, you can type the following in the terminal shell:

```
root@clanton:~# node --version
v0.10.25
```

or

```
root@clanton:~# node -v
v0.10.25
```

If you do not have the recommended version, you can update your system in three ways.

Option 1: Updating node.js with opkg (recommended)

Edit this file:

```
root@clanton:~# vi /etc/opkg/base-feeds.conf
```

And add the following lines:

```
src/gz all     http://repo.opkg.net/galileo/all
src/gz clanton http://repo.opkg.net/galileo/clanton
src/gz i586    http://repo.opkg.net/galileo/i586
```

The next step is to update opkg and node.js by typing:

```
root@clanton:~# opkg update
```

and then typing:

```
root@clanton:~# opkg upgrade nodejs --force-overwrite
```

Option 2: Updating node.js with the Source

It is possible to build node.js directly into Intel Galileo. Suppose you want to install version 0.10.25 (the minimum recommended), which is available at http://nodejs.org/dist/.

You need to add the following:

```
root@clanton:~# wget http://nodejs.org/dist/v0.10.25/node-v0.10.25.tar.gz
root@clanton:~# tar -zxvf node-v0.10.25.tar.gz
root@clanton:~# cd node*
root@clanton:~#./configure
root@clanton:~# make
root@clanton:~# make install
```

If the "make" command above fails, you need to install the build tools. For this, just update the /etc/opkg/base-feeds.conf as done in the "Option 1" and execute the command "opkg install packagegroup-core-buildessential --force-overwrite".

Option 3: Updating node.js in the Yocto Build

If you are building your own images and do not want to update node.js through the prompt shell, you can add a new recipe to your Yocto build and have node.js be automatically updated.

There is a thread on the Intel community that includes step-by-step instructions for this process. If you are interested, check out https://communities.intel.com/thread/48416.

About the npm

When you install node.js, it comes with some modules installed as dependences. For example, there is the dgram used for the UDP connection, the fs for file system operations, the http to provide HTTP server and client functionality, and others.

A module is necessary in a program when it's explicitly called by the require instruction, as shown:

```
var http = require("http").createServer(onRequest),
    fs = require('fs'),
    url = require('url'),
    cheerio = require('cheerio'),
    dgram = require('dgram'),
```

However, not all modules are pre-installed when you install node.js, because the community is constantly developing new packages to provide new modules. You can install them according your project's needs. Before you learn about the packages that will be used with this project, it is necessary to understand how to install them using the npm tool.

The node.js file has a package manager named npm that allows you to add and remove external packages and install modules created for node.js.

Most developers think that npm stands for "node package manager," but this is not exactly accurate. According to the author, npm is a recursive bacronymic abbreviation for "npm is not an acronym." William Shakespeare writes in *Romeo and Juliet* that "A rose by any other name would smell as sweet." Thus, you can call npm a node package manager if you want, because it works like one.

This project uses npm version 1.3.24. You can check your version with the following command:

```
root@clanton:~# npm -v
1.3.24
```

If you want to update npm, use this command:

```
root@clanton:~# npm update npm -g
```

To check the version installed in your system, you need to use the ls, list, or la arguments, followed by the package name. For example:

```
root@clanton:~# npm ls socket.io
/home/root
└── socket.io@0.9.16
```

If the package does not exist, the word empty will be displayed:

```
root@clanton:~# npm ls idonotknow
/home/root
└── (empty)
```

To list *all* packages and the dependences of each one installed on your system, use only the argument `list`:

```
root@clanton:~# npm list
/home/root
├─┬ cheerio@0.13.1
│ ├─┬ CSSselect@0.4.0
│ │ ├── CSSwhat@0.4.1
│ │ └─┬ domutils@1.3.0
│ │   └── domelementtype@1.1.1
│ ├── entities@0.3.0
│ ├─┬ htmlparser2@3.4.0
│ │ ├── domelementtype@1.1.1
│ │ ├── domhandler@2.2.0
│ │ ├── domutils@1.3.0
│ │ └─┬ readable-stream@1.1.10
│ │   ├── core-util-is@1.0.1
│ │   ├── debuglog@0.0.2
│ │   └── string_decoder@0.10.25
│ └── underscore@1.5.2
└─┬ socket.io@0.9.16
  ├── base64id@0.1.0
  ├── policyfile@0.0.4
  ├── redis@0.7.3
  ├─┬ socket.io-client@0.9.16
  │ ├─┬ active-x-obfuscator@0.0.1
  │ │ └── zeparser@0.0.5
  │ ├── uglify-js@1.2.5
  │ ├─┬ ws@0.4.31
  │ │ ├── commander@0.6.1
  │ │ ├── nan@0.3.2
  │ │ ├── options@0.0.5
  │ │ └── tinycolor@0.0.1
  │ └── xmlhttprequest@1.4.2
```

Before you install any package, first make sure the date and time of your Intel Galileo is properly set. You can use the command `date` and pass an argument formatted as MMDDhhmmYYYY (MM is the month, DD is the day, hh is the hour, mm is the minute, and YYYY is the year).

For example, the following command sets Intel Galileo to March 15, 2014 at 11:30AM.

```
root@clanton:~# date 031511302014
```

To install a package, use the argument install followed by the package name:

```
root@clanton:~# npm install socket.io
```

You can also install a specific version using install with <name>@<version>.
For example:

```
root@clanton:~# npm install sax@latest
```

More information regarding npm can be found at https://www.npmjs.org/doc/
misc/npm-faq.html.

Installing Cheerio

The package named cheerio is a light and fast solution that replaces the jsdom package
and allows you to parse and change HTML elements more easily.

To install cheerio, type the following command in the terminal shell:

```
root@clanton:~# npm install cheerio
```

Cheerio will be used to change the elements in the HTML page with the information
sent by sketch. More details regarding cheerio can be found at https://github.com/
MatthewMueller/cheerio.

This project uses the following cheerio version:

```
root@clanton:~# npm list cheerio
/home/root
└── cheerio@0.13.1
```

Installing socket.io

The package named socket.io is used in this project to receive data through sockets
between the web server and the web pages. Essentially the connection of socket.io is TCP.
The server implementation will be listening to the connections in the web server and the
client implementation is done in the web page. More details related to socket.io can be
found at https://www.npmjs.org/package/socket.io.

To install the socket.io package, use the following command line:

```
root@clanton:/# node install socket.io
```

This project uses the following socket.io version:

```
root@clanton:~# npm list socket.io
/home/root
└── socket.io@0.9.16
```

The Web Page

If node.js is used to write to the web server, this web server must be able to change dynamically. That means the web page must be defined first.

As mentioned, this web page will be able to control two switch relays (commands), receive information about the temperature and PIR sensors, and indicate whether the user armed or disarmed the system using the keypad.

The essential requirements for this page is illustrated in Figure 9-18.

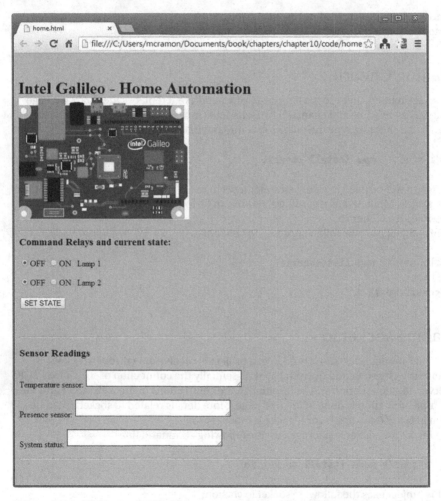

Figure 9-18. *Web page design for home automation*

The web page must be dynamic, which means the browser cannot refresh the page all the time because the sensors will send data every second and if the page is entirely refreshed the web application will be awful and will block the user interaction to send commands.

To avoid this problem, the page uses a socket connection to the web server that will be responsible for binding the socket channels.

This web page will receive information about the sensors and keypad in one message second by second in order to optimize the communication.

The message received will be very simple. Its fields are delimited by the * character, and will include the PIR sensor message, the temperatures, and whether the user armed or disarmed the system using the keypad. Something like the following:

"* INTRUDER * 32C - 89F * UNLOCKED *"

The web application must parse the string received through the socket's message and update each HTML element in the page properly.

The elements can be updated as is done with jQuery, accessing the elements using the $() function with the class name used by each element of web page. For example, you can check the textarea element:

```
<p>
Temperature sensor: <textarea class="txtsensor" id="temp" cols="1"
maxlength="10" name="txtsensor" readonly="readonly" style="margin: 2px;
width: 300px; height: 32px;"></textarea></p>
```

The textarea has a classname called txtsensor. To access this element using cheerio, you would use the following:

```
$('p .txtsensor').text('HELLO ADDING A TEXT HERE!!!');
```

To have all these functionalities, it is possible to create a web page using HTML, JavaScript, socket.io.js (the client in this case), and jQuery libraries. The HTML code is shown in Listing 9-6.

Listing 9-6. home.html

```html
<html>
<head>
        <script src="http://ajax.googleapis.com/ajax/libs/jquery/2.1.0/
jquery.min.js"></script>
        <script src="/socket.io/socket.io.js"></script>
        <script>
                var socket = io.connect();
                socket.on('server-event-info', function (data) {
                        console.log(data);


                        var rawPIRSensorText = new String();
                        var rawTempText = new String();
                        var rawKeypadText = new String();
                        var len = data.length;

                        // extracting the sensor frame
                        var i = data.indexOf("*",1);

                        // extracting the PIR sensor data
                        rawPIRSensorText = data.substring(1, i);


                        // extracting the temp sensor data
                        var i_old = i;
                        i = data.indexOf("*",i_old+1);
                        rawTempText = data.substring(i_old+1, i);


                        // extracting the keypad sensor data
                        var i_old = i;
                        i = data.indexOf("*",i_old+1);
                        rawKeypadText = data.substring(i_old+1, i);


                        console.log(rawPIRSensorText);
                        console.log(rawTempText);
                        console.log(rawKeypadText)

                        $('p .txtsensor').text(rawTempText);
                        $('p .presencesensor').text(rawPIRSensorText);
                        $('p .systemstatus').text(rawKeypadText);


                });
        </script>
```

```
</head>
<body bgcolor="#82CAFA">
        <form method="post" name="form1" target="_self">
                         
                        <h1>
                                        Intel Galileo - Home Automation
                                        <img class="img" src="galileo.jpg">
                                        </h1>
                        <h3>
                        <hr>
                                        Command Relays and current state:</h3>
                        <p>
                                        <input checked="checked"  class="l1"
name="l1" type="radio" value="0">OFF
                                        <input class="l1" name="l1"
type="radio" value="1">ON   Lamp 1</p>
                        <p>
                                        <input checked="checked" class="l2"
name="l2" type="radio" value="0">OFF
                                        <input class="l2" name="l2"
type="radio" value="1">ON   Lamp 2</p>
                        <p>
                                        <button name="commandButton"
type="submit" value="SET STATE">SET STATE</button></p>
                        <p>
                                         </p>
                        <hr>
                        <h3>
                                        Sensor Readings</h3>
                        <p>
                                        Temperature sensor: <textarea
class="txtsensor" id="temp" cols="1" maxlength="10" name="txtsensor"
readonly="readonly" style="margin: 2px; width: 300px; height: 32px;">
</textarea></p>
                        <p>
                                        Presence sensor: <textarea
class="presencesensor" cols="1" id="sensor" maxlength="10"
name="presencesensor" style="margin: 2px; width: 300px; height: 32px;">
</textarea></p>
                        <p>
                                        System status: <textarea
class="systemstatus" cols="1" id="systemstatus" maxlength="10"
name="systemstatus" style="margin: 2px; width: 300px; height: 32px;">
</textarea></p>
                        <div>
                                        <hr>
                        </div>
        </form>
</body>

</html>
```

473

Note that each HTML element defines a class ID that will be used for access, similar to the approach used with jQuery. The cheerios in the web server allow you to access and change such elements similarly.

The page uses the jQuery library version 2.1.0 and invokes socket.io to implement the client that will be connected to the web server.

```
<script src="http://ajax.googleapis.com/ajax/libs/jquery/2.1.0/jquery.min.js">
</script>
        <script src="/socket.io/socket.io.js"></script>
```

The JavaScript parses the string in the socket's message, separating the elements with the delimiter * and updating each element in the web page:

```
$('p .txtsensor').text(rawTempText);
$('p .presencesensor').text(rawPIRSensorText);
$('p .systemstatus').text(rawKeypadText);
```

Note that the relays can be managed through the radio buttons L1 and L2 and the web server will be notified. This is accomplished using a regular POST via a submit of the input button in an HTML form.

```
<form method="post" name="form1" target="_self">
...
...
...
<button name="commandButton" type="submit" value="SET STATE">SET
STATE</button></p>
```

The parameter target="_self" prevents a new page tab from being opened in your browser when the pages refreshes.

Writing the Web Server Code

Now that all the necessary packages are installed, you can write to the web server with a few lines of code.

For example if you want to develop a web server using node.js you just need the following lines of code. Suppose you created the file named mywebserver.js provided in this book:

```
var http = require('http');
http.createServer(function (req, res) {
  res.writeHead(200, {'Content-Type': 'text/plain'});
  res.end('Hello World.. my first web server running on GALILEO!!!!!!\n');
}).listen(8080);
console.log('Server running and listening port 8080');
```

To run the web server, you just need to call the node passing the file as an argument. For example:

```
root@clanton:~/livro# node mywebserver.js
Server running and listening port 8080
```

And if your Intel Galileo is connected to the Internet, you can see the web page in your favorite browser using Galileo's IP number. For example, type the web address <GALILEO IP>:8080 into your web browser.

See Figure 9-19 for an example using Chrome.

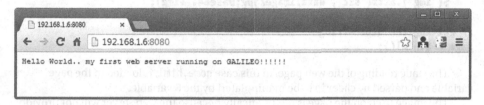

Figure 9-19. *Simple web server running node.js on Intel Galileo*

Defining the Ports

It is not the intention of this book to provide a detailed guide about how to use all the features of node.js needed to write a web server. However, the best way to understand how the web server works is to take a look at the code and discuss it.

```
var http = require("http").createServer(onRequest),
    fs = require('fs'),
    url = require('url'),
    cheerio = require('cheerio'),
    dgram = require('dgram'),

socketid = 0,
SKETCH_PORT=2000,
WEBSERVER_PORT=2010;
```

Note the definition of the port numbers to change datagrams between the sketch and the web server. The web server will listen for datagrams in the port WEBSERVER_PORT and will be able to send datagrams to the port SKETCH_PORT.

The next step is to read the page and the image used in the HTML page using cheerio and fs calls.

```
// reads the html page
var page = fs.readFileSync('home.html').toString()

// reads the image (static)
var img = fs.readFileSync('./galileo.jpg').toString("base64");

// using cheerio to transverse the page
var $ = cheerio.load(page);
    $('img').attr('src','data:image/jpg;base64,'+img);

// getting the html string
page = $.html();
```

The static reading of the web page, in this case home.html, is loaded in the page variable and parsed by cheerio to be manipulated by the $ variable.

The image used on the page is read statically because the web server will not provide methods specifically to load images when your browser asks for and changes the HTML at the same time. With node.js, it's easier to load statically and then change the properties of the img element in the HTML page to receive the image converted to base64 using cheerio, as follows:

```
"$('img').attr('src','data:image/jpg;base64,'+img)".
```

Creating the Sockets

It is necessary to create the UDP server using the dgram module and keep listening to the port defined by WEBSERVER_PORT in order to receive messages from sketch.

```
//
// UDP server
//

var server = dgram.createSocket("udp4");

// this 'message' event receives the sketch datagram
server.on("message", function (msg, rinfo) {

    udp_msg = msg.toString();
    console.log("from " +
                rinfo.address + " message:" + udp_msg);

    // just bypassing the message sent by the sketch
    io.emit("server-event-info", udp_msg);

});
```

```
// this is to bind the socket
server.on("listening", function () {
  var address = server.address();
  console.log("server listening " +
      address.address + ":" + address.port);
});
```

```
server.bind(WEBSERVER_PORT);
```

The UDP server, when it receives a message event from the sketch, simply bypasses this event to the web page using the socket.io call:

```
io.emit("server-event-info", udp_msg);
```

The web page will provide the scripts responsible for parsing the message and updating the element dynamically in the screen. The socketid is the identification number received. The web page that connects to the web server and the event that contains the message to be parsed by the scripts in the web page are called server-event-info.

At this point we have described the code in the web server that handles message exchanges using datagrams with the sketch and how the web server sends the messages to web pages using socket.io. However, the web server needs to keep listening and perform the bind with web page as well. The following code is responsible for this task:

```
// declaring the socket.io server using the "http"
var io = require('socket.io').listen(http);
```

```
// http will listen in port 8080
http.listen(8080);
```

```
// TCP socket
```

```
io.sockets.on('connection', function (socket) {

  socketid =  socket.id;

  socket.on('client-event', function (data) {
    console.log('just to debug the connection done, ' + data.name);
  });
});
```

Note that socket.io is managed by the variable io, which depends on the HTTP module provided by the variable http. That variable opens the channel to listen to port 8080. In other words, when the browsers request the pages, that request needs to be sent through port 8080.

When the connection is establish between the browser and the socket.io server, the socket.id is saved in the socketid variable in order to allow messages to be repassed using the emit method.

Creating the GET and POST Methods

The only thing missing are the GET and POST methods in the web server. The onRequest()
function is responsible for receiving the GET and POST requests.

GET doesn't do anything special because the web page was already loaded statically.
The GET method simply needs to provide the page, as shown in the following code:

```
function onRequest(request, response) {
  console.log("Request received.");

  var url_parts = url.parse(request.url,true);

//
// GET methods
//
  if (request.method == 'GET') {
      console.log('Request found with GET method');

      request.on('data',function(data)
        { response.end(' data event: '+data);
        });

      if(url_parts.pathname == '/')
          // when this message is displayed your browser
          // will be able to read the HTML page.
          console.log('Showing the home.html');
          response.end(page);
  }
/
//  POST methods
//
  else if (request.method == 'POST') {
...
...
...
}
```

However, POST is a little bit tricky in this case, because when the user presses the
commandButton on the web page, the form with the radio buttons that specify whether
lamp 1 and lamp 2 are set to on or off is received by the web server.

When this happens, the web server must transform this information from the
form into a message that's sent to the sketch, which will parse it and change the relays
according to the command sent.

The idea is to send a message with a simple string that indicates the status of each
lamp. "L1" is lamp 1 and "L2" is lamp 2, and "ON" and "OFF" indicate their statuses.
The message also uses the & delimiter character to create a single message.

For example, the message might be:

```
"L1ON &L2OFF"
"L1OFF&L2OFF"
"L1OFF&L2ON "
"L1ON &L2ON "
```

For simplicity in the algorithm, the space characters are used to keep the messages the same size and make the logic simpler.

The POST starts by saving the form as "chunks" and then the event data is received and is accumulated by the variable's body. The "chunks" are used because the page might not be received as a single data event.

```
else if (request.method == 'POST') {

        // the post we need to parse the L1 and L2
            // and assemble a nice message that will be received by
            // sketch UDP server
        console.log('Request found with POST method');

            // handling data received
        request.on('data', function (data) {
            body = "";
            body += data;
            console.log('got data:'+data);

        });

        request.on('end', function () {
...
...
...
}
```

When the form is received, the event named event is called with the data from the form. In this case, the states of lamps 1 and 2 are reported per their radio buttons.

The data received is a group element of the HTML element delimited by &. Each element is followed by the equals character (=).

It's necessary to extract element by element, observing the delimiter & and extract the values of each one by the =.

The easiest way do to this is to implement a utility function to parse the data received in the hash element, wherein the element name is the key and data of each element the value received.

```
hash4me = function(data){
    var firstSplits = data.split('&'),
        finalHash = [];
```

```
// scanning first list
for (i = 0; i < firstSplits.length; i++)
{
    var lastSplits = firstSplits[i].split('=');
    finalHash[lastSplits[0]] = lastSplits[1];
}
return finalHash;
}
```

Using the utility function to "hash" the data received and accumulated in the variable body, it's possible to identify the value of each element and assemble the message that will be sent to the sketch. This is being done with the variable message in the following snippet:

```
else if (request.method == 'POST') {
...
..
..

                var hash = hash4me(body);
        if (hash["l1"] == "0") {
...
...
...

            // command message
            message.write("L10FF&");
        } else if (hash["l1"] == "1") {
          console.log("LAMP 1 is ON");
...
...
...

            // command message
            message.write("L1ON &");
        }
```

The same is done with the l2 element until the message variable is ready to be sent to the sketch using the datagram, as shown in the following snippet:

```
        // informing sketch about the changes
    // this is the message sent from the web server to sketch
            server.send(message, 0, message.length, SKETCH_PORT,
"localhost", function(err, bytes) {
```

The Final Web Server Code

The final code with all details is shown in Listing 9-7.

Listing 9-7. server.js

```
var http = require("http").createServer(onRequest),
    fs = require('fs'),
    url = require('url'),
    cheerio = require('cheerio'),
    dgram = require('dgram'),
    page = "",
    body = "",
    udp_msg="",
        socketid = 0,
        SKETCH_PORT=2000,
        WEBSERVER_PORT=2010;

// reads the HTML page
var page = fs.readFileSync('home.html').toString()

// reads the image (static)
var img = fs.readFileSync('./galileo.jpg').toString("base64");

// using cheerio to transverse the page
var $ = cheerio.load(page);
    $('img').attr('src','data:image/jpg;base64,'+img);

// getting the html string
page = $.html();

//
// UDP server
//

var server = dgram.createSocket("udp4");

// this 'message' event receives the sketch datagram
server.on("message", function (msg, rinfo) {

    udp_msg = msg.toString();
    console.log("from " +
                rinfo.address + " message:" + udp_msg);

    // just bypassing the message sent by the sketch
    io.emit("server-event-info", udp_msg);

});
```

```
// this is to bind the socket
server.on("listening", function () {
  var address = server.address();
  console.log("server listening " +
      address.address + ":" + address.port);
});

server.bind(WEBSERVER_PORT);

//
// This function is to hash the response
//
hash4me = function(data){
    var firstSplits = data.split('&'),
        finalHash = [];

    // scanning first list
    for (i = 0; i < firstSplits.length; i++)
    {
        var lastSplits = firstSplits[i].split('=');
        finalHash[lastSplits[0]] = lastSplits[1];
    }
    return finalHash;
}


//
// Checking the GET and POST methods and
// respective responses
//

function onRequest(request, response) {
  console.log("Request received.");

  var url_parts = url.parse(request.url,true);

//
// GET methods
//
  if (request.method == 'GET') {
    console.log('Request found with GET method');

    request.on('data',function(data)
      { response.end(' data event: '+data);
      });
```

```
    if(url_parts.pathname == '/')
        // when this message is displayed your browser
        // will be able to read the HTML page.
        console.log('Showing the home.html');
        response.end(page);
}

//
//  POST methods
//
  else if (request.method == 'POST') {

        // the post we need to parse the L1 and L2
            // and assemble a nice message that will be received by
            // sketch UDP server
        console.log('Request found with POST method');

            // handling data received
        request.on('data', function (data) {
            body = "";
            body += data;
            console.log('got data:'+data);


        });


        request.on('end', function () {

            var message = new Buffer(20);

                    message.fill(0);

            if (body != '') {

                var command = "";

                // dividing the commands to understand the state of each one
                // note in the radio buttons L1 and L2 the parameter "checked"
                // must be removed. However, we are removing it twice
                    because there
                // is a bug. Some versions of node.js and cheerio even when you
                // remove the item checked="checked", sometimes the tag checked
                // remains in the HTML element and the browser becomes confused
                //
```

483

```
            // $(the element).attr("checked", null);
            // $(the element).removeAttr("checked");

                        var hash = hash4me(body);
                if (hash["l1"] == "0") {

                    console.log("LAMP 1 is OFF");
                                $('input[name="l1"][value="0"]').
attr("checked", "checked");
                                $('input[name="l1"][value="1"]').
attr("checked", null);
                                $('input[name="l1"][value="1"]').
removeAttr("checked");

                    // command message
                    message.write("L1OFF&");
                } else if (hash["l1"] == "1") {
                    console.log("LAMP 1 is ON");
                        $('input[name="l1"][value="0"]').attr("checked", null);
                        $('input[name="l1"][value="0"]').
removeAttr("checked");
                                $('input[name="l1"][value="1"]').
attr("checked", "checked");

                    // command message
                    message.write("L1ON &");
                }

                            console.log("len:" + message.toString().length);
                if (hash["l2"] == "0") {

                    console.log("LAMP 2 is OFF");
                                $('input[name="l2"][value="0"]').
attr("checked", "checked");
                                $('input[name="l2"][value="1"]').
attr("checked", null);
                    $('input[name="l2"][value="1"]').removeAttr("checked");

                    // command message
                    message.write("L2OFF", 6);

                } else if (hash["l2"] == "1") {
                    console.log("LAMP 2 is ON");
                                $('input[name="l2"][value="0"]').
attr("checked", null);
                                $('input[name="l2"][value="0"]').
removeAttr("checked");
                                $('input[name="l2"][value="1"]').
attr("checked", "checked");
```

484

```
                    // command message
                    message.write("L2ON ",  6);
            }

                            // informing sketch about the changes
                            // this is the message sent from web
server to sketch
                    server.send(message, 0, message.length, SKETCH_PORT,
"localhost", function(err, bytes) {

                                                            if (err) {
                                                                console.
log("Ops... some error sending UDP datagrams:"+err);
                                                                throw err;
                        }
                    });

                            body = "";
                }

                // update the page with the command
                response.writeHead(200);
            response.end($.html());
        });
    }
}

// declaring the socket.io server using the "http"
var io = require('socket.io').listen(http);

// http will listen in port 8080
http.listen(8080);

// TCP socket

io.sockets.on('connection', function (socket) {

  socketid =  socket.id;

  socket.on('client-event', function (data) {
    console.log('just to debug the connection done, ' + data.name);
  });
});

console.log("Home automation server running...");
```

Running the Home Automation System

If all the peripherals tested okay and are connected to the Intel Galileo headers, and the sketch and web server are ready, the system is ready for testing.

Open a terminal shell and transfer the three files—home.html, galileo.jpg, and server.js—to a subdirectory in the home directory. In my tests, I created a subfolder called auto.

Then transfer the files using ftp or ssh, as explained in Chapter 5.

Remember, this project requires that you have Intel Galileo connected to a network device like WiFi, Ethernet, or an LTE modem. This example uses WiFi with Intel Centrino N-135.

The first thing to do is check the IP number you set for your device. Using the terminal shell, type ifconfig eth0 if you are using Ethernet cables, ifconfig wlan0 if you are using WiFi, or ifconfig to see all adapters:

```
root@clanton:~/auto# ifconfig wlan0
wlan0     Link encap:Ethernet  HWaddr 0C:D2:92:58:F8:27
          inet addr:192.168.1.7  Bcast:192.168.1.255  Mask:255.255.255.0
          inet6 addr: fe80::ed2:92ff:fe58:f827/64 Scope:Link
          UP BROADCAST RUNNING MULTICAST  MTU:1500  Metric:1
          RX packets:845 errors:0 dropped:0 overruns:0 frame:0
          TX packets:13 errors:0 dropped:0 overruns:0 carrier:0
          collisions:0 txqueuelen:1000
          RX bytes:254690 (248.7 KiB)  TX bytes:1857 (1.8 KiB)
```

Test if the connection is working using a command like ping:

```
root@clanton:~/auto# ping www.intel.com
PING www.intel.com (63.80.4.74): 56 data bytes
64 bytes from 63.80.4.74: seq=0 ttl=60 time=30.617 ms
64 bytes from 63.80.4.74: seq=1 ttl=60 time=29.061 ms
64 bytes from 63.80.4.74: seq=2 ttl=60 time=28.823 ms
64 bytes from 63.80.4.74: seq=3 ttl=60 time=28.025 ms
```

With the IP number in hand and the Internet connection working, go to the directory where you transferred the three files mentioned previously and type node server.js, as follows:

```
root@clanton:~/auto# node server.js
   info  - socket.io started
Home automation server running...
server listening 0.0.0.0:2010
```

It takes a few seconds to see the message Home automation server running..., which means your web server is listening to the ports and can accept connection to the socket.io and the browser and UDP datagrams exchanges between the web server and the sketch.

Using a browser of your preference, type the following address in the address bar, including your IP address:

http://<YOUR **IP NUMBER>:8080**

In this case, you'd type:

http://192.168.1.7:8080

You can use the browser from your personal computer or mobile phone, including Android and iPhone versions. This project was tested using Chrome, Internet Explorer 10, Firefox, Android phones 4.4.1, and iPhones 4 and 5S.

The browser will take a few seconds to connect to this page because the socket.io is in the "binding process." Remember that there is static image used in the web page as well.

If you are under a proxy you might have to set up the proxy in Intel Galileo and make sure there is no firewall blocking its connection. For example, you can export HTTP connections using export http=<your proxy>:<your port>.

In few seconds you will be able to see the web page shown in Figure 9-20.

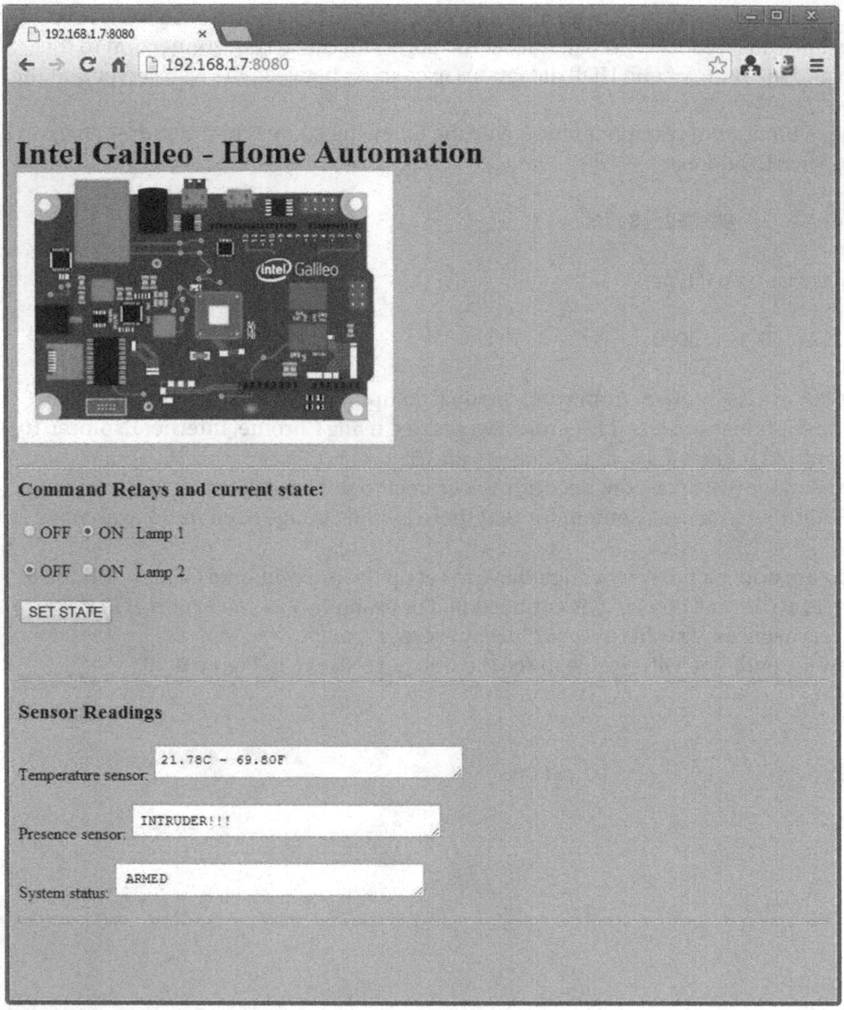

Figure 9-20. *Dynamic web page is working*

The PIR and temperature sensors must be working and they must integrate with your keypad and update the web page dynamically.

The relays must switch according to your command after you press the SET STATE button.

If you have reached this point in this book, congrats, your system is working!

Ideas for Improving the Project

The preceding material was developed to give the reader a very basic idea of how to begin building a sample project, but obviously there is much more you can do to extend the project in the direction of your particular needs. What follows are several possibilities to consider.

Power of Ethernet (PoE)

If you are building this project with Intel Galileo generation 2 and using Ethernet to connect the board to the Internet, be sure to check out Chapter 11. You want to use energy directly from the Ethernet cable, which is more reliable.

Using express and node.js

You can change the code to support the express web application framework instead of the regular HTML in the node.js.

If you are building a new web page with more images and more functionalities, it can be a little harder to implement things using only the regular modules available in the standard distribution of node.js.

Express has several advantages, including how to deal with static images and not having to reinvent the wheel.

According to the tests done in this chapter, Intel Galileo was not able to install the express modules using the node.js 0.8.0, so it's better to update to version 0.10.25 (as explained in the section called "Updating node.js" in this chapter).

To install express only, type the following in your terminal shell:

```
npm install express -g
```

The successful installation creates the following modules:

```
express@3.4.8 ../node_modules/express
├── methods@0.1.0
├── merge-descriptors@0.0.1
├── range-parser@0.0.4
├── cookie-signature@1.0.1
├── fresh@0.2.0
├── debug@0.7.4
├── buffer-crc32@0.2.1
├── cookie@0.1.0
├── mkdirp@0.3.5
├── commander@1.3.2 (keypress@0.1.0)
├── send@0.1.4 (mime@1.2.11)
```

For more information about express, check out the link https://www.npmjs.org/package/express.

Changing the Web Page and Web Server Without Experience with the Web

If you are not familiar with jQuery, JavaScript, or the other resources used in web development, you might have some questions about how to change the web page, add new elements, and make the cheerio parse the web page so it finds the elements to be changed or updated.

My recommendation is to install a tool called cheerio REPL available at https://github.com/kuhnza/cheerio-repl. This tool allow you to parse the web page while your web server is running and helps you understand how to change the code.

To install cheerio REPL, type the following on the command line:

```
npm install -g cheerio-repl
```

After you install cheerio, it should appear in /usr/bin/cheerio. If your web server is not running, start it manually as you did before but let it run in the background with & and send the debug messages to a null device so they don't bother your prompt shell.

```
root@clanton:~/auto# node server.js > /dev/null &
    info  - socket.io started
Home automation server running...
server listening 0.0.0.0:2010
```

Then call the cheerio-repl tool using your IP address or your loopback IP and the port number. Then you can reach the cheerio prompt as follows:

```
root@clanton:~/auto# cheerio http://127.0.0.1:8080
Request received.
{}
Request found with GET method
Showing the home.html
cheerio>
```

If you type $.html() in the prompt, you will see the HTML content of the page, as follows:

```
cheerio> $.html()
'<html>\n            <head>\n\t\t            <script src="http://ajax.googleapis.
com/ajax/libs/jquery/2.1.0/jquery.min.js"></script>\n                <script
src="/socket.io/socket.io.js"></script>\n\t\t\t\t\t<script>\n
var socket = io.connect();\n                    socket.on(\'server-event-
info\', function (data) {\n                    console.log(data);\
n\t\t\t\t\t\t \n\t\t\t\t\t\t   \n\t\t\t\t\t\t \tvar rawPIRSensorText =
new String();\n                    var rawTempText = new String(
);\n                var rawKeypadText = new String();\t\n\n\t
var len = data.length;\n\n                    // extracting the
sensor frame\n\t                var i = data.indexOf("*",1);\
n\n                 // extracting the PIR sensor data\
n\t             rawPIRSensorText = data.substring(1, i);\n
\n  \n                // extracting the temp sensor data\n\t
var i_old = i;\n                    i = data.indexOf("*",i_old+1);\
n\t             rawTempText = data.substring(i_old+1, i);\n
\n  \n                // extracting the keypad sensor data\
n\t             var i_old = i;\n                            i
= data.indexOf("*",i_old+1);\n\t                rawKeypadText =
data.substring(i_old+1, i);\n  \n  \n                    console.
log(rawPIRSensorText);\n                console.log(rawTe
mpText);\n                console.log(rawKeypadText)\n\t\
t\t\t\t\t \n\t\t\t\t\t\t     $(\'p .txtsensor\').text(rawTempText);\n\
t\t\t\t\t\t     $(\'p .presencesensor\').text(rawPIRSensorText);\n\t\t\
t\t\t\t     $(\'p .systemstatus\').text(rawKeypadText);\n\t\t\t\t\t\t
\n                });\n                </script>\n\n        </head>\n
<body bgcolor="#82CAFA">\n                <form method="post" name="form1"
target="_self">\n                 \n                      <
h1>\n                    Intel Galileo - Home
Automation \n\t\t\t\t\t\t\t\t\t<img class="img" src="data:image/
jpg;base64,/9j/4AAQSkZJRgABAQEAYABgAAD/2wBDAAIBAQIBAQICAgICAgICAwUDAwMDAwY
EBAMFBwYHBwcGBwcICQsJCAgKCAcHCgoKCgsMDAwMBwkODwODgsMDAz/2wBDAQICAgMDAwYDAwY
MCAcIDAwMDAwMDAwMDA
```

The cheerio REPL can parse the content provided by the web server, in this case the home.html page. For example, suppose you wanted to parse the element used to control lamp 1, which is named l1 in the HTML:

```
<p>
    <input checked="checked"  class="l1" name="l1" type="radio" value="0">OFF
    <input class="l1" name="l1" type="radio" value="1">ON   Lamp 1</p>
```

This radio button can assume two states. You need to type the following into the cheerio prompt:

```
cheerio> $('p .l1')
{ '0':
  { type: 'tag',
    name: 'input',
    attribs:
     { checked: 'checked',
       class: 'l1',
       name: 'l1',
       type: 'radio',
       value: '0' },
    children: [],
    prev:
     { data: '\n                                    ',
       type: 'text',
       parent: [Object],
       prev: null,
       next: [Circular] },
    next:
     { data: 'OFF\n                              ',
       type: 'text',
       parent: [Object],
       prev: [Circular],
       next: [Object] },
    parent:
     { type: 'tag',
       name: 'p',
       attribs: {},
       children: [Object],
       prev: [Object],
       next: [Object],
       parent: [Object] } },
  '1':
  { type: 'tag',
    name: 'input',
    attribs:
     { class: 'l1',
       name: 'l1',
       type: 'radio',
       value: '1' },
    children: [],
```

```
        prev:
         { data: 'OFF\n                            ',
           type: 'text',
           parent: [Object],
           prev: [Object],
           next: [Circular] },
        next:
         { data: 'ON   Lamp 1',
           type: 'text',
           parent: [Object],
           prev: [Circular],
           next: null },
        parent:
         { type: 'tag',
           name: 'p',
           attribs: {},
           children: [Object],
           prev: [Object],
           next: [Object],
           parent: [Object] } },
     length: 2 }
```

You can obtain the same result using the following:

```
cheerio> $('input[name="l1"]')
```

In this case, cheerio parsed the whole element given the attributes (attribs) of both states 0 and 1 as the child and parent object elements as well.

Suppose you want to check a specific attribute, such as checked:

```
cheerio> $('input[name="l1"][value="0"]').attr("checked")
'checked'
```

Then you want to remove this attribute:

```
cheerio> $('input[name="l1"][value="0"]').removeAttr("checked")
{ '0':
   { type: 'tag',
     name: 'input',
     attribs:
      { '0': 1,
        checked: false,
        class: 'l1',
        name: 'l1',
        type: 'radio',
        value: '0' },
     children: [],
```

```
    prev:
     { data: '\n                                          ',
       type: 'text',
       parent: [Object],
       prev: null,
       next: [Circular] },
    next:
     { data: 'OFF\n                                    ',
       type: 'text',
       parent: [Object],
       prev: [Circular],
       next: [Object] },
    parent:
     { type: 'tag',
       name: 'p',
       attribs: {},
       children: [Object],
       prev: [Object],
       next: [Object],
       parent: [Object] } },
  length: 1 }
```

The value checked was removed but the attribute checked=false is still there. To remove that property, you need to set it to null:

```
cheerio> $('input[name="l1"][value="1"]').attr("checked", null);
{ '0':
   { type: 'tag',
     name: 'input',
     attribs:
      { '0': 1,
        class: 'l1',
        name: 'l1',
        type: 'radio',
        value: '1' },
     children: [],
     prev:
      { data: 'OFF\n                                    ',
        type: 'text',
        parent: [Object],
        prev: [Object],
        next: [Circular] },
     next:
      { data: 'ON   Lamp 1',
        type: 'text',
        parent: [Object],
        prev: [Circular],
        next: null },
```

```
      parent:
       { type: 'tag',
         name: 'p',
         attribs: {},
         children: [Object],
         prev: [Object],
         next: [Object],
         parent:
```

Now check the HTML contents of this element specifically:

```
cheerio> $.html('p .l1')
'<input 0="1" checked class="l1" name="l1" type="radio" value="0"><input
0="1" class="l1" name="l1" type="radio" value="1">'
```

The command used to manipulate the HTML content using this tool is the same one you might use in your code. The difference is that it's much faster to check if the syntax is correct instead of starting and reloading the web server or JavaScript all the time.

Creating an Analogic Keypad and Having More I/Os Available

The keypad uses eight digital port I/Os, which is a lot compared to the 14 digital pins. If you want to connect more relay and more PIR sensors, the keypad might cause a problem.

One idea is to use an R-2R resistor ladder and one of the analog ports as the input to convert analog-to-digital signals when keys or switches are pressed.

The R-2R resistor ladder is a circuit that contains only two types of resistors. One type value is the double of the other, and they are arranged sequentially (see Figure 9-21).

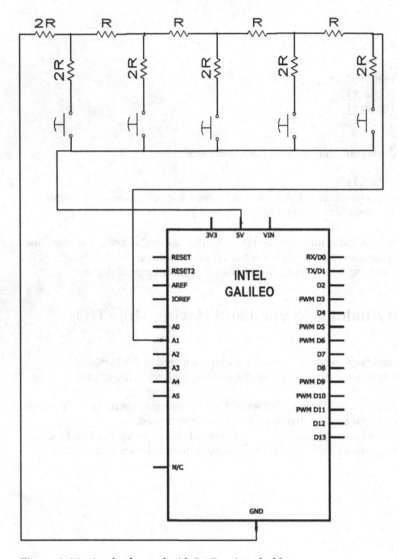

Figure 9-21. *Analog keypad with R-2R resistor ladder*

Each time a key is pressed a different voltage level is applied to input port A1. The value of resistor R is the double of resistor 2R. You can choose 10K ohm and 20k ohm, for example.

It's recommended that you use the resistor with the maximum precision possible, so try to get a resistor with a tolerance of 1% if you can.

You need to create a code in the sketch that can read the port A1, test the maximum and minimum reading of each key, and convert them to a correspondent event. You can reach such values experimentally pressing the keys and checking the maximum and minimum reading. You then add your code or resolve the Thevenins theorem for each condition, following the standard electronic theory.

Adding a Username and Password

The project hasn't incorporated a username or password, which means anyone could potentially access your system once they discover the IP.

There are several ways to implement this protection. Due to the simplicity of the code provided by the framework and the diversity in terms of methods for authenticating the user, I recommend that you read the passport found at https://github.com/jaredhanson/passport.

Using the DHT11 Sensor

In this project the TMP36 sensor was used to measure the temperature in the environment. However, if you are interested in monitoring the humidity instead, you can use the DHT11 sensor. For more details on how to use this sensor, read the section called "Project - DHT Sensor Library with Fast I/O APIs" in Chapter 4.

Summary

In this chapter you learned how Intel Galileo communicates with different sensors, including the integration of sketches with a keypad.

You also learned how to use Linux to create a web server using node.js, which is different from other Arduino boards based on microcontrollers. Thus, by using a web client, you can control and monitor the sensor connected to Intel Galileo. This enables you to control and monitor your house when you're away.

This project provides very basic functionality in terms of home automation, but it is a starting point from which you can expand the system and make it more sophisticated.

CHAPTER 10

■ ■ ■

Power over Ethernet (PoE)

The Intel Galileo Board Gen2 can be powered with an Ethernet cable, which means you don't need a separate power supply. It requires that you install the Power over Ethernet (PoE) module that complies with IEEE 802.3af, which you must purchase separately.

Once you install the PoE module on Intel Galileo Gen2, all you need to do to power the board is connect the Ethernet cable that's fed by the PoE injector.

Depending on the nature of your project, it might be necessary to install the Intel Galileo board in difficult-to-access environments, such as from a rooftop. Such access can mean it's difficult to install new cables and gain access to a power supply.

In other segments, such as with industrial automation, there are many protocols used on this environment—including Profibus, ModBus, and many others—that require specific and expensive equipment to be installed on the network. However, regular LAN devices are affordable and offer data speed that's good enough to attend to the industrial environment. This provides an affordable alternative in the automation control segment.

Other criteria to be considered are mobility and flexibility. It can be important to provide easier installation options by reducing the concern about cables in general. The idea is to connect a single cable that provides data and power to your device.

With these constraints and requirements in mind, the goal is to reduce the complexity of the installation process and increase the mobility of your device around the network. To meet these concerns, a new standard was created called IEEE 802.3af.

With the IEEE 802.3af PoE, devices can operate up to 15.4W with a minimum of 44VDC and 350mA. In the real world, however, it is possible to have devices operating at 36VDC.

The first devices to use this technology were IP cameras, VoIP phones, WLAN routers, and remote POS (point of sales) systems. You can count Intel Galileo Gen2 on that list as well.

There is no software-specific discussion in this chapter; it is exclusively for Intel Galileo Gen2 boards because this board has a physical space to install the PoE modules. If you have one of the first Intel Galileo board releases, this chapter is not applicable.

Following the instructions in this chapter, your Intel Galileo Gen2 will be powered over an Ethernet cable up to 328ft using a PoE module and will operate normally.

Project Details

In order to set up Intel Galileo Gen2 to be able to receive power over Ethernet, it is necessary to install a PoE module that does not come with the board. Not everybody will use the PoE feature, so it doesn't make sense to increase the cost just to provide this feature.

You might wonder, if the USB cables provide data and power, why you would have to use the PoE technology? The answer is very simple—the USB cables are designed for short distances. They operate at a maximum of 16ft, with only 2.5W, while the PoE module can reach 328ft.

Intel Galileo Gen2 does not come with the PoE module embedded in the board but provides an area where you can solder a PoE module if you want to use the board for this purpose.

The area reserved for the PoE module is one of the factors that contributes to Intel Galileo Gen2 being a little bit bigger than its first version. Other factors that make the Intel Galileo Gen2 bigger are explained in more detail in Chapter 1.

The estimated cost is US $38, excluding the cost of Intel Galileo Gen2 board.

Materials List

This project requires the PoE module recommended by Intel, as well as a PoE power injector, Ethernet cables, and common material for soldering. Table 10-1 list other materials you'll use.

Table 10-1. *Additional Materials*

Quantity	Components
1	PoE module IEEE 802.3af compliant with AG9120-S
1	PoE injector; recommended TP-LINK model TL-POE150S
1	Handle soldering iron
1	Ethernet CAT5 cable with connector RJ-45
N	0.6mm tin lead solder wires

The PoE injector TL-POE150S comes with CAT5 Ethernet cable, but it is generally too short (around 3ft) to be helpful.

It's very important that you use CAT5 Ethernet cables because they have four pairs of twisted cooper wires, which are needed to make the PoE work properly. You need 328ft of CAT5 cable.

Assembling the PoE Module

This project uses the module model AG9120-S, which is manufactured by Arduino and works with conventional twisted pair Ethernet cables (CAT5). It complies with the IEEE 802.3af standard.

The module has a DC/DC converter that operates between 36VDC and 57VDC and supports 15W to the port. It was initially designed to be used with the Arduino Ethernet shield, but the Intel Galileo Gen2 supports it regardless of any extra shield.

Figure 10-1 shows the front view of the AG9120-S module.

Figure 10-1. *Front view of the Power over Ethernet module AG9120-S*

If you flip the Intel Galileo Gen2 board over, you will see a grid of 10 holes, with four holes on the left and the other six on the right. They are indicated by the "Power Over Internet" label, as shown in Figure 10-2.

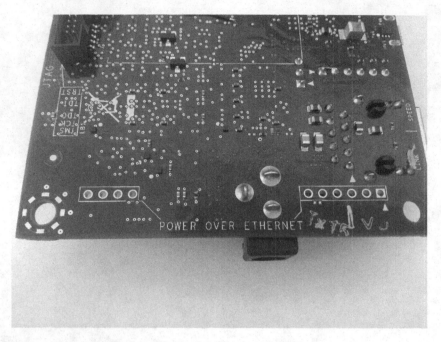

Figure 10-2. Bottom view of the Intel Galileo board and PoE space

These holes fit perfectly with the PoE AG9120-S module. All you need to do is place the AG9120-S module over the holes (see Figure 10-3) and solder the pins to the bottom of your board (see Figure 10-4).

Figure 10-3. *Inserting the PoE module*

Figure 10-4. *Upper view of the pins to be soldered to the PoE module*

Powering On with the PoE Injector

After you have soldered the PoE module to the Intel Galileo Gen2, you simply need to connect the PoE injector.

As mentioned in the Table 10-1, it is recommended for this project that you use the PoE injector TP-LINK model TL-POE150S, which is shown in Figure 10-5.

Figure 10-5. The PoE injector TP-LINK TL-POE150S

The PoE injector is powered by a 48VDC power supply and contains two Ethernet ports, called "LAN IN" (see Figure 10-6, left) and "POWER+DATA OUT" (see Figure 10-6, right).

Figure 10-6. The LAN IN (left) and POWER+DATA OUT (right) ports

The POWER+DATA OUT port connects the Ethernet cable to the Intel Galileo Gen2 board. If you are using the recommended PoE injector, it comes with an Ethernet CAT5 UTP cable; however, the cable is short (around 3ft), which means you will probably need to buy another one or assemble your own. Search the Internet for how to assemble such an Ethernet cable and you will find several tutorials. This chapter does not teach you how to assemble your own Ethernet cables.

The LAN IN port is where you connect your switcher or router that accesses the Internet or intranet. You can also use a regular Ethernet cable to make this connection.

Figure 10-7 shows how the system must be connected to the Intel Galileo Gen2 board.

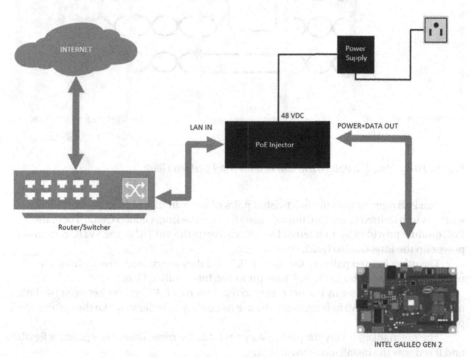

Figure 10-7. *Scheme for PoE connection*

How It Works

Figure 10-8 shows how the energy is provided by a single cable.

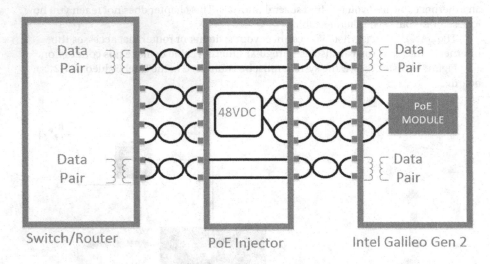

Figure 10-8. *How the PoE system works with Intel Galileo Gen2*

The PoE injector uses the two twisted pairs of wires in the cable to inject 48VDC, which is transmitted to the PoE module installed on the Intel Galileo Gen2. Then, the PoE module provided by an internal DC/DC converts the 48VDC to the 5VDC required to power up the Intel Galileo Gen2.

The other twisted pairs are the "data pair" and they are passed directly from the router or switcher through the PoE injector to the Intel Galileo Gen2.

Figure 10-8 shows why it is necessary to use Ethernet CAT5 cables between the PoE injector and Galileo. All four twisted pairs are necessary in order to make the system work perfectly.

The mechanism is very simple but very smart at the same time. The system is flexible and it reduces the installation cost and time.

Ideas for Improving the Project

If you do not like the idea of soldering the PoE module directly to your Intel Galileo Gen2 board, you can solder female stackable headers instead.

You need one 1x6 header (see Figure 10-9, left) and one 1x4 header (see Figure 10-9, right) to support the 10 pins. You then solder them the same way that's shown in Figure 10-4. Here, though, you solder these stackable headers instead of the module. Then you connect the module to the stackable headers.

Figure 10-9. *Female stackable headers—1x6 (left) and 1x4 (right)*

Summary

Power over Ethernet is a simple but very powerful technology that provides many advantages discussed in this chapter. Fortunately, Intel Galileo Gen2 is prepared for this technology.

There is no special software required. You just need to be able to solder the PoE module and the capacitor to the Intel Galileo Gen2 and then install it on your system.

■ ■ ■

## CHAPTER 11

Assembling and Controlling a Robotic Arm

In 1979, the Robot Institute of America (RIA) classified the robot as a reprogrammable, multifunctional manipulator designed to move material, parts, tools, and specialized devices through variable programmed motions for the performance of a variety of tasks.

Not including the word "reprogrammable" mentioned by RIA, the first introduction of the robot was in 1495 by Leonardo da Vinci, with his medieval robotic knight. This robot could wave, sit, and move its arms and neck. Of course it was totally mechanic. A representation of this robot is shown in Figure 11-1 (part of Wikimedia Commons under "Creative Commons Attribution/Share-Alike License").

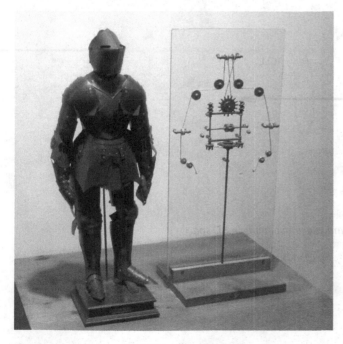

Figure 11-1. Leonardo da Vinci's robot

In 1920, the Czech novelist Karel Capek created a science fiction play called "Rosumovi Univerzální Roboti" ("Rossum's Universal Robots"), where humanoid robots were created to work for humans but then the robots decide to exterminate and extinguish the humans. The 1984 Arnold Schwarzenegger movie, *Terminator*, involves a similar story.

You will not build a full humanoid robot in this chapter but you will learn about robotic arm principles and design engineering. In the process, you'll learn how to build a simple robotic arm.

You will also build a six-channel controller that can be designed using inexpensive components. You can integrate the arm into the Intel Galileo boards or an Edison Arduino kit.

An introduction to Robotic Arm Theory

A robot arm has a mechanical structure that alters its form using a group of electric motors that behave like servo motors, pneumatic, or hydraulic actuators. They attempt to reproduce movement similar to a human arm.

A common term that's used when a robot arm is designed is the **DOF (degrees of freedom)**; it is related to roll, yaw, and pitch. Figure 11-2 shows a representation of these movements in 3D space.

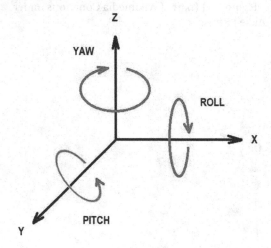

Figure 11-2. Roll, pitch, and yaw movements in 3D space

For example, using you own arm and following Figure 11-2, try to reproduce the following movements:

- **Shoulder pitch**
- **Shoulder roll**
- **Arm yaw**
- **Elbow pitch**
- **Wrist pitch**
- **Wrist yaw**
- **Wrist roll**

Your arm, as it turns out, has seven DOF; the wrist alone has an amazing three DOF.

There are several factors you must consider when constructing a robot arm, including the maximum load weight, the stall torques of each one of the servos, how much weight each servo must support related to its position in the arm, and the weight each frame that constitutes the arm.

In Chapter 4, you learned about servo motors, but not about stall torque, which is an important concept that you must understand. Stall torque helps determine which servos you need to use in your robotic arm.

When you order a servo motor, it comes with several items on its specification, including stall torque. Stall torque is usually measured in ounces per inch or kilograms per centimeter. To understand what this means, consider Figure 11-3.

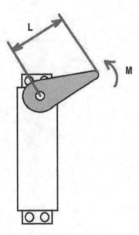

Figure 11-3. Units for measuring stall torque

511

In Figure 11-3, the length is represented by L and it's the measurement of center of the servo's shaft to the end of the arm. The letter M represents the quantity of mass (weight) attached to the end of the arm.

So, when you read that a servo supports a specific amount of Kg/cm or oz/inch, it means the servo hangs if you apply the weight mentioned in a 1-cm or 1-inch arm.

For example, suppose you have a servo with a stall torque of 100 oz/inch. That means when you use a 1-inch long arm, the servo will hang if you apply a weight equal to 100oz (M). In other words, the servo will not be able to rotate or it might rotate backwards.

Torque is force times length, but if you search for different servos on the Internet, you will realize that vendors only mention the mass, excluding the gravitational acceleration. A second point to be considered when the vendors provide such numbers is that the measurement is the worst-case scenario when the arm is holding weight in the horizontal position. This is explain further in a bit.

By definition, torque must consider the *perpendicular length*, as shown in Figure 11-4, and not the arm length as you see in the servo specification. This sometimes causes confusion.

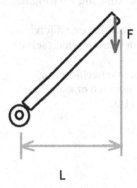

Figure 11-4. *The perpendicular length in determining torque*

The formula that defines torque can be expressed as follows:

$$T = F \times L$$
$$T = m \times g$$

So you can conclude:

$$T = F \times L = (m \times g) \times L$$

Where T means torque, L is the perpendicular length, m is the mass, and g is the gravitational acceleration. Of course, the force (F) in this case never changes since the mass is constant and subjected to the same gravitational acceleration.

With this torque formula in mind, note in Figure 11-5 that the worst-case scenario is when the arm is stretched out horizontally because the perpendicular length is bigger.

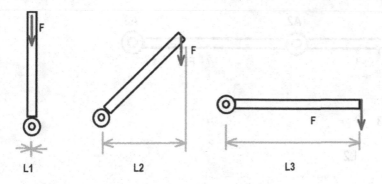

Figure 11-5. *The variation of perpendicular length*

Thus you can say the worst-case condition is:

$$T = F \times L3$$

Now imagine the arm with this perpendicular length and a load, as shown in Figure 11-6.

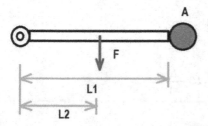

Figure 11-6. *Worst-case perpendicular length with a weight*

With a weight identified as A and located L1 from the servo, you can consider (approximately) that arm weight occupies the center of the mass of L2. The torque must take into account the two weights (A and F) and the two distances (L1 and L2). The torque in this scenario is as follows:

$$T = A \times L1 + F \times L2$$
$$T = A \times L1 + F \times (L1/2)$$

However, a robotic arm is a set of servos joined together to create one arm. Consider the robotic arm in Figure 11-7.

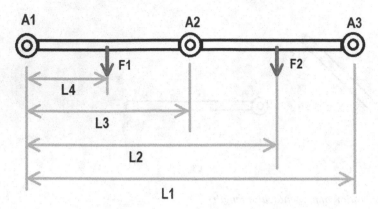

Figure 11-7. *Several actuators*

Suppose you need to evaluate the torque in servo A1. You will have:

$$T1 = A2 \times L3 \times A3 \times L1 + F1 \times L4 + F2 \times L1$$

If the weights F1 and F2 are located in the center of the mass, then you can conclude:

$$L4 = \frac{L3}{2}$$

$$L2 = L3 + \frac{\left(\frac{L1}{2}\right)}{2} = L3 + \frac{L1}{4}$$

Replacing the L4 and L2, you have:

$$T1 = A2 \times L3 \times A3 \times L1 + F1 \times \frac{L3}{2} + F2 \times \left(L3\frac{L1}{4}\right)$$

It means, if you know the weight of each servo and the length of each part of your arm, it's possible to evaluate the torque and determine which servos to use. In this example, you simply need to know L1, L3, and the weight of the servos and arm parts.

Note that each servo will have a different torque due to its location along the arm.

Another important point that you need to include in your calculation is the maximum load. For example, suppose the mechanical gripper of your arm is actuator A3 and you know its weight. You simply need to add the load weight to A3's weight and make the calculations.

Using an Online Tool to Calculate Your Servos

The web site robotshop.com offers a very nice online tool that helps you calculate the servos that must be used in your arm. To use this tool, visit http://www.robotshop.com/blog/en/robot-arm-torque-calculator-9712 and enter the arm and servo data. They use a different notation than presented on this chapter, where L is the arm's length, M is the weight in kg of each part of your arm, and A is the weight of your servos. Don't forget to include the load max in the gripper servo, as explained previously.

This tool is very simple to use and saves a lot of time and possible mistakes during your evaluation. Figure 11-8 shows a screenshot of this tool.

Robot Arm Torque Calculator

Posted on March 7, 2013 by RB1 & filed under Dynamic Tools.

The Robot Torque Arm Calculator is intended to help you choose the right motor for each joint of your robotic arm. The torque (T) required at each joint is calculated as a worst case scenario (lifting weight at 90 degrees). Ensure your units are consistent. Most common units are kg-cm and oz-in. Take a look at the Robot Arm Torque Tutorial for more information.

- L: length from pivot to pivot.
- M: link mass
- A: Actuator (servo or other) mass. Note: same units as for link masses.
- A1: can represent the load being lifted.

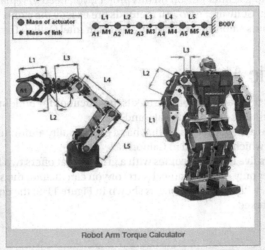

Robot Arm Torque Calculator

Use the image above to help you determine which torque corresponds to which joint. Note the numbering starts with the extremity of the arm, so the final torque is the one lifting the entire arm (start from A1 being the load you wish to carry at full reach.). The torque shown is the STALL TORQUE you can use for your search.

L: [cm]	M: [kg]	A: [kg]	T: [kg cm]
L1: 0	M1: 0	A1: 0	T1: 0
L2: 0	M2: 0	A2: 0	T2: 0
L3: 0	M3: 0	A3: 0	T3: 0
L4: 0	M4: 0	A4: 0	T4: 0
L5: 0	M5: 0	A5: 0	T5: 0
L6: 0	M6: 0	A6: 0	T6: 0

Tags: Arm Calculator tools

Figure 11-8. Web-based robot arm calculator provided by robotshop.com

Considerations About This Project

This project is recommended for Intel Galileo Gen 2. There are some issues when it's applied using Intel Galileo or Intel Edison Arduino Kit.

As explained in Chapter 4, Intel Galileo does not offer a sufficient PWM signal resolution in that the PWM signal does not offer a good resolution. That means your arm's movements might seem a little choppy due to the lack of precision in the PWM.

A similar issue occurs with the Intel Edison Arduino Kit. It offers only two PWM channels and this project requires six channels to run the robotic arm. However, if you own an Intel Edison with the Intel Edison Arduino toolkit, you can use the same sketches used in this chapter. Instead of using the Servo API you can use the SoftwareServo API. This API runs in the user space context and brings an emulation of PWM signal in the digital ports. The good thing is, you can use any digital port to connect your servos; however, considering it runs in the userspace context, small glitches in the servo might be observed because processes with higher priority run in the kernel context, which can impact the userspace performance.

If you decide to use Intel Edison on this project, you need to replace the objects called "Servo" with "SoftwareServo". All methods are exactly the same.

This project runs smoothly without any issues in Intel Galileo Gen 2.

The Robotic Arm

Internet sites offer thousands of robot arm kits, instructions for building your own robot out of wood, 3D printing, scrap materials, and more.

This book uses a low-cost arm kit that has a good quality aluminum form. This kit is sold by elabpeers, which is located in California.

The arm offers five DOF and comes with a gripper that offers two DOF, totaling seven DOF. You can order only the mechanical parts or you can include the servos as well.

The whole kit, with servos in place, is shown in Figure 11-9; the equivalent parts of a human arm are marked.

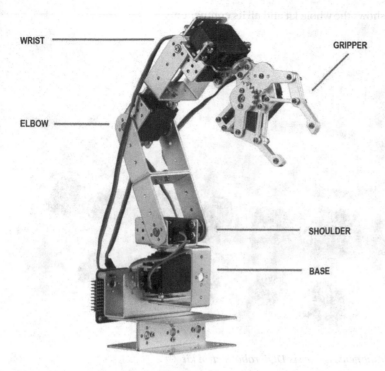

Figure 11-9. Parts of a robotic arm and gripper offering six DOF

The kit includes an arm with:

- Four U-shaped long brackets
- Three U-shaped brackets used for the base
- One mechanical gripper
- Six metallic servo wheels
- Four cup bearings
- Several screws and nuts (more than you need)

If you decide to get the whole kit, it includes:

- Four servos MG996R that provide a stall torque of 9.4kg/cm @ 4.8V and 12kg/cm @ 6V
- Two servos 5521MG with a stall torque of 17,25Kg/cm @ 4.8V and 20.32 Kg/cm @ 6V
- Three servo extension wire cables
- Servo accessories packages with rubber rings, horns, and fittings

Figure 11-10 shows the whole kit and all its components.

Figure 11-10. Components of the six DOF robotic arm kit

This configuration is enough to keep your servos running smoothly; however, if you have better servos you can order only the arm body with gripper for $68.

If your budget permits, I recommend replacing the MG996R servo with the HEXFLY servo.

The MG996R or MG995R servo are considered the worst available in the market. There are many clones of such servos in the market don't match the promised specification. Using these servos to work the base, wrists, and gripper is fine, but the elbow and shoulder need something better. These servos can't even handle the weight of the arm without a load in the gripper.

The other required components for building this arm are listed in Table 11-1.

Table 11-1. *Materials List for the Robotic Arm*

Quantity	Description
1	Robotic arm kit with servos (only if you do not have the servos recommended; otherwise, order the armor kit).
4	Servo extension wire cables.
1	Piece of wood around 7 x 12 x 0.5 inches (at least).
1	C-clamp if you are using the arm body in a table.
4	M6-30mm hex-head cap screw with nuts and flat washers or equivalent.
3	Dupont jumper cables, male-to-male, or pieces of 1/4 watt wires.
1	Five-inch nose plier.
1	Screwdrivers for M3 and M4 screws.

The piece of wood is used to create a base for the arm body. If you'll be using this arm over a table (mostly), it's best to use a c-clamp in order to hold the arm to the table. You can find c-clamps for $2.26.

The 1/4 x 2 inch screws with nuts are used to hold the arm body to the piece of wood and the flat washers are used to help the horizontal equalization of the arm body in relation to the wood.

■ **Note** The servos recommended in this chapter work in conjunction with the arm body. They are fast and strong enough to damage or scratch your table or any other surface, or even damage your Intel Galileo boards, your hand, or any other element in the reachable area of action. Make sure you and your Intel Galileo board are far from the robotic arm using the servo extensions. Use the c-clamp to hold the arm to the surface that sets the arm. If possible, protect your surface with cardboard, a rubber matt, or any other material.

The next section explains how to assemble the arm and put the servos in place.

Assembling the Robotic Arm

The assembly procedure of this arm takes around two hours when done without error. The kit has many screws divided in M3 8mm, M3 8mm flat, M3 10mm, and M4 10mm and it is very important to understand where each screw goes in order to guarantee the functionality of your arm body.

The usage of the screws is summarized as follows:

- The M3 10mm screws are used in the bearings to connect the servo that will manipulate the gripper and the wrist.

- The M4 10mm screws connect the servos with servo brackets, but if you are using the 5521MG servo then you need to use the M3 10mm screws. If you are using any other servo and M4 10mm is being difficult, try the M3 10mm screws.

- The M3 8mm flat screws connect the servo wheel to the servo only.

- The M3 8mm rounded screws connect the rest of arm parts—like the short U-shapes—to each other and the servo to the long U-shapes.

Figure 11-11 illustrates where the screws are placed. This is explained in more detail in the following pages.

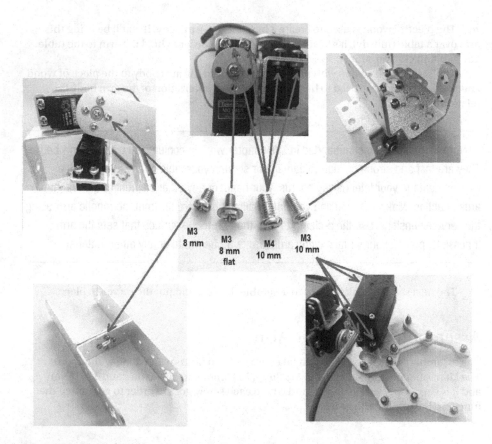

Figure 11-11. *Robot arm screws and where to place them*

Usually elabpeers sends more screws than necessary, so do not worry about the quantity of screws.

The following sections describe how to assemble the robotic arm.

Step 1: Preparing the Servos

You must first make sure all the servos are in place exactly 90 degrees. All you need to do is connect the servos according to Figure 4-2 (Chapter 4). Then run the program in Listing 11-1.

Listing 11-1. prepare_servos.ino

```
#include <Servo.h>

#define PIN 9

Servo prepareServo;
void setup() {

    // Attaching the servo to PIN
    prepareServo.attach(PIN);
}

void loop() {
    // moves the servo to 90 degrees
    prepareServo.write(90);
    delay(250);

}
```

The sketch is very simple and it defines an object called prepareServo as an instance of the Servo class and attaches to the pin 9 defined by PIN. In the loop, the servo then moves to 90 degrees. For more details regarding the Servo API, consult Chapter 4.

Using each of the six servos, connect to Intel Galileo and wait for all the servos to be moved to 90 degrees. This is the reference angle for assembling this arm body.

Connect the aluminum servo wheel to all the servos except the servo that will be used in the gripper. Try to make the servo wheel align to 90 degrees, as shown in Figure 11-12.

Figure 11-12. *Servo wheel placed at 90 degrees*

The next step is to assemble the base.

Step 2: Assembling the Base

Join the two U-shape bases using four M3 8mm screws and the respective nuts, as shown in Figure 11-13.

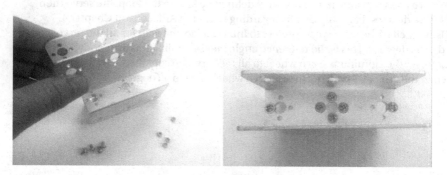

Figure 11-13. *Connecting two U-shapes for the base*

Fix a third u-shape perpendicular to the other two U-shapes, as shown in Figure 11-14. Use the M3 screws and nuts to do so.

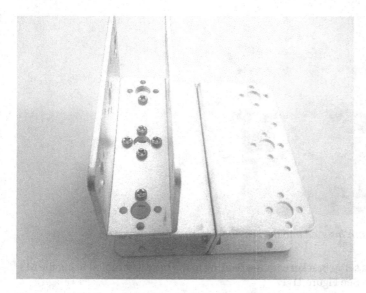

Figure 11-14. *Connecting the third U-shape to form the base*

Locate a bearing and a M3 10mm screw. Then insert the screw in the bearing, as shown in Figure 11-15.

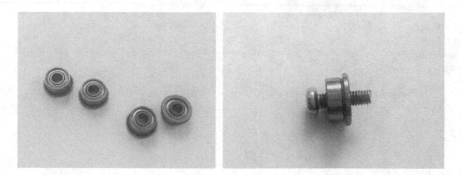

Figure 11-15. *Bearings (left); M3 10mm inserted in the bearing (right)*

Using a servo bracket shape, connect the bearing supported by the screw and fix it using the proper nut, as shown in Figure 11-16.

Figure 11-16. M3 10mm inserted into the bearing

Next, connect the servo bracket with the bearing to the base assembled using the M3 8mm screws and nuts. See Figure 11-17

Figure 11-17. Servo bracket with the bearing is connected to the base

The next step is to set the servo motor and the long U-shape. The long U-shape will be connected to the bearing and to the servo wheel. You need the parts shown in Figure 11-18 (left) to complete this step. The way the long U-shape must be connected is shown in Figure 11-18 (right). This figure is only illustrative so you can see how the connection is made; the servo must be fixed first.

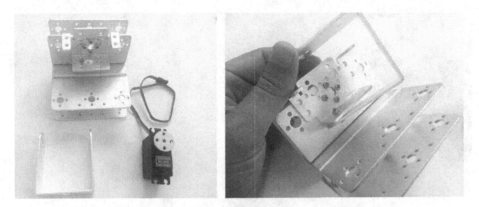

Figure 11-18. Long U-shape and servo (left) and connection example (right)

Connect the servo using the M4 8mm screws and connect the U-shape by first placing it in the bearing. Push it to the top of servo wheel, as shown in Figure 11-19.

Figure 11-19. Connecting the long U-shape to the base servo

Attach the servo wheel to the servo using a screen M3 8mm flat screw in the center of the wheel. Your base should be ready.

Assemble another servo bracket by connecting a new bearing with the corresponding screws, as shown in Figure 11-16. Figure 11-20 shows the elements being connected. Make sure the screws are not loose.

Figure 11-20. *Base mounted with final adjusts being done*

The next step is to assemble the shoulder.

Step 3: Assembling the Shoulder

To assemble the shoulder, you need two long U-shapes opposing each other, as shown in Figure 1-21 (left). Place both shapes as shown in Figure 11-21 (right) using M3 8mm screws and nuts.

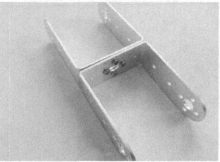

Figure 11-21. *Two long U-shapes (left) and arm with screws (right)*

Connect the servo you chose to be the shoulder to the servo bracket shown in Figure 11-20. Use M4 screws and place the two long shapes using M3 8mm screws and nuts, as shown in Figure 11-22.

Figure 11-22. *Connecting the shoulder servo and the U-shapes*

The shoulder servo and the arm will look similar to Figure 11-23 if you've placed them correctly.

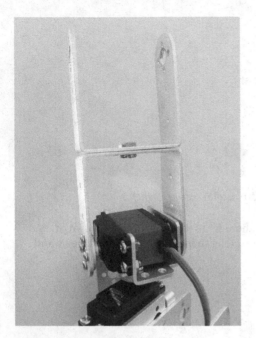

Figure 11-23. *Connecting the shoulder servo to the arm*

The next step is to assemble the elbow.

Step 4: Assembling the Elbow

To start, you need a servo bracket, a long U-shape, an L-shape, a bearing, one M3 10mm and four M3 8mm screws and nuts, as shown in Figure 11-24.

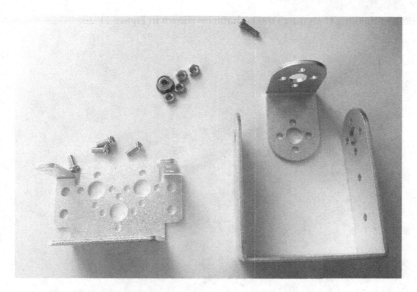

Figure 11-24. *Preparing the wrist servo for pitch movement*

Place the bearing using M3 10mm screws and the right nut and then connect the L-shape using the M3 8mm screws and nuts, as shown in Figure 11-25.

Figure 11-25. *Connecting the bearing and the L-shape to the servo bracket*

Then connect the long U-shape to the L-shape, as shown in Figure 11-26.

Figure 11-26. Long U-shape connected to L-shape

Next, connect the servo designated to be the elbow using M4 screws and nuts, as shown in Figure 11-27.

Figure 11-27. Connecting the elbow servo

Finally, connect the elbow to the arm you assembled in Step 3. Fix the servo with M3 8mm screws, as shown in Figure 11-28.

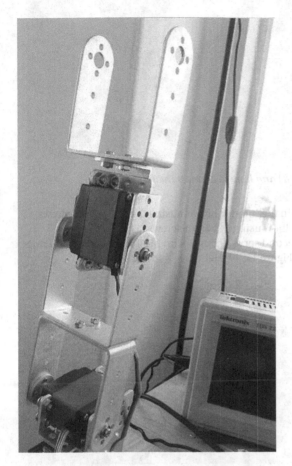

Figure 11-28. Elbow connected to the arm

The next step is to assemble the wrist.

Step 5: Assembling the Wrist

The wrist has two movements—pitch and rotate—and they require two servos and consequently two servo brackets, as shown in Figure 11-29 (left). To assemble the wrist, you also need a bearing connected using M3 10mm screws and nuts. Place both servo brackets using four M3 8mm nuts, as shown in Figure 11-29 (right).

Figure 11-29. Two servo brackets (left) and how to connect them (right)

Then connect one of the servos in the inferior bracket using the M4 10mm screws and nuts. Fix the servo wheel to the elbow using M3 8mm screws, as shown in Figure 11-30 (left). Finally, add the second servo, fixing it with M4 10mm screws and nuts in the superior bracket, as shown in Figure 11-30 (right).

Figure 11-30. Inferior wrist servo (left) and superior wrist servo (right)

Now let's assemble the gripper.

Step 6: Assembling the Mechanical Gripper

The gripper contains a very simple movement—it opens and closes—so only one servo is necessary. However, the assemble process is very laborious. First, you must connect the gripper to the wrist using two simple M3 8mm screws, as shown in Figure 11-31.

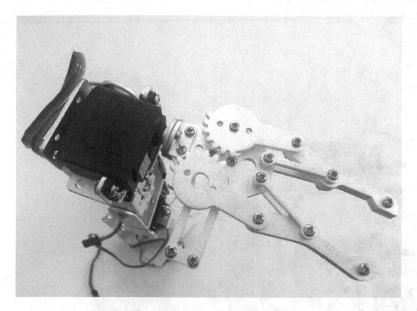

Figure 11-31. *Gripper connected to the wrist*

Then, using the servo accessories pack, pick four rubber rings as shown in Figure 11-32 (left) and place them in the holes of the servos, as shown in Figure 11-32 (right). Note that you don't connect the servo wheel to the servo this time.

Figure 11-32. *The rubber rings (left) being placed in the servo (right)*

Add the servo using the M4 screws to the bottom of the gripper, as shown in Figure 11-33.

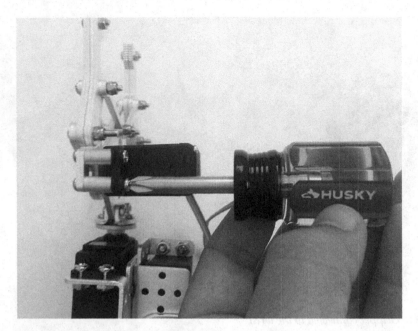

Figure 11-33. *Adding the servo to the gripper*

Fix a servo wheel to the bottom of the gripper gear, as shown in Figure 11-34 (left), using two M3 8mm screws, as shown in Figure 11-34 (right).

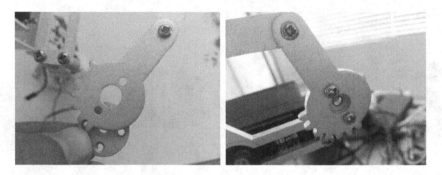

Figure 11-34. *Placing the servo wheel (left) and fixing it to the gripper (right)*

Finally, adjust the gripper gears by connecting them to each other. Keep the gripper opened around 0.8 inches (2 cm) and use the M3 8mm flat screw to place it in the center of the servo. Figure 11-35 shows the final gripper.

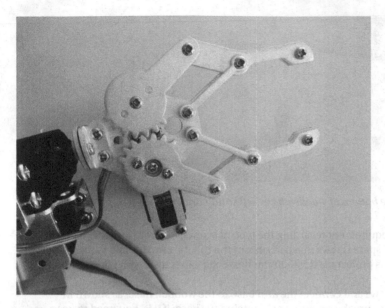

Figure 11-35. Final gripper assemlby

The robotic arm is ready at this point. Now you need to create a base to sustain the arm. That process is explained in Step 7.

Step 7: Assembling a Base

You need to set the robot arm in a base made of wood, acrylic, polycarbonate, metal, or any material you have available. This project used a small piece of wood. Using a pen or pencil, mark the center of the external holes in the aluminum base of the robot arm and use a 1/4 drill bit for the holes. It is also best to use a spade that's a bit bigger than the drill bit; for example, a ¾ one, as shown in Figure 11-36 (left). The function of the spade bit is to avoid any bounce caused by bumps that will fix the robotic arm, as shown in Figure 11-36 (right).

Figure 11-36. The bottom of wooden base (left) and hardware (right)

There is no requirement regarding the type of screws, nuts, or washers you have to use, so if you have spare screws that can sustain the robotic arm, it's fine to use what you have available. This project used M6-30mm hex-head cap screws with corresponding nuts and washers.

Insert the screws and connect the arm base to the wooden base, as shown in Figure 11-37. Make sure the screw is not bouncing the base; if it is, you need to use a smaller screw, add some washers, or cut your screws.

 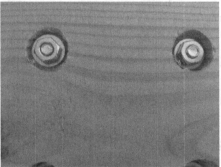

Figure 11-37. Top view of base with screws (left); bottom view with nuts (right)

Figure 11-38 shows the robotic arm in the wooden base.

If your base is small, the robotic arm will likely fall during its movement or when the gripper is holding something. To solve this problem, I fixed the base to my desk using a c-clamp, as shown in Figure 11-38 (right). Note that I had to use the spade bit to remove a little bit of the wood. This created a perfect socket for the c-clamp that basically penetrated the wood and formed a perfect join.

Figure 11-38. *The arm in the wooden base (left) and the c-clamp holding the base (right)*

You now just have to control the arm, which is explained in the next section.

Controlling the Robotic Arm

At this point you robot arm is ready to be controlled. To make this possible, you must be able to control the six servos. The board Intel Galileo Gen 2 contains exactly six PWM ports in the pins identified with a tilde (~), as explained in Chapter 3, Figure 3-10. Thus, there are enough PWM ports to control the robotic arm. It is possible to write simple software to make the robotic arm execute pre-programmed movements, but the project would not be so interesting.

Consider these relevant aspects:

- **Power supply:** During my tests I realized the servos can drain up to 2.2A for a load of 100 grams at 5V. That means Intel Galileo boards and Edison Arduino toolkit boards do not provide a current (source) that guarantees the functionality of all servos since the limit is 80mA.

- **Servos control:** The servos must be controlled somehow. You should have at least five potentiometers and a simple button to open and close the gripper. If you use joysticks or thumbsticks, each axis (x and y) could control two servo channels, so three of them would be enough to control the whole arm.

537

- **Quantity of wires:** Each servo requires three wires. including ground, power, and pulse. Considering there are six servos in the arm the quantity of wires goes to 18. Besides this, it is necessary to add wire expanders to guarantee the robotic arm will be far enough from Intel Galileo or Intel Edison and to avoid damaging your board. Considering you cannot use an Intel Galileo or Edison board to power the servos, as explained previously, you also need to consider more cables related to an external power supply. If you have a potentiometer or joysticks or thumbsticks to control the robotic arm, you need at least 15 wires. All these wires can lead to a considerable mess.

I decided to build a six-channel servo controller set on an universal soldering board to organize all my cables. I placed the thumbsticks and connector to receive the external power supply and 5V from Intel Galileo or Intel Edison boards designated to the thumbsticks. All for around $30.

And a specific API was created in order to use the thumbsticks in two different modes. This is explained further in subsequent sections.

Building a Servo Control Board

In order to build the servo's control boards, you can create a very simple board control and then create a new API, as explained in the next sections.

The Hardware

The servo board control is a very simple design, yet it can control six servos using three thumbsticks.

Table 11-2 lists the materials necessary to build this board.

Table 11-2. *Materials List for the Servo Board Controller*

Number	Description
3	Thumbsticks SKU 121340 from dealxtream.com or equivalent
3	1K Ohm 1/4W resistors
1	Single-sided prototyping board, 6x3 inches (universal board)
1	Three-pole terminal block
1	470uF electrolytic capacitor
1	Diode 5404 (or three 1N4007 or 1N4004 diodes)
2	40 header pins 2.54mm single row
6	Servo extension cables
1	Power supply 5 or 6 VDC with 3A (minimum)
12	M3 0.5 x 10mm screws with nuts
37	Dupont male-to-female cables
5	Hex or round M3 nylon spacers (standoff) with screws
1	Soldering iron with lead
Some	AWG23 0.5mm2 or breadboard cables with at least two different colors (30 inches is enough)
Some	18 AWG 1.5mm2 cables with at least two different colors (11 inches is enough)

It is important to understand the components that make up this board, and they are explained in the next sections.

The Thumbsticks

The main component in the material list that composes the servos control board is the thumbstick.

A thumbstick is an analogic stick that offers an analog variation through two internal potentiometers related to the central position of the stick. Each potentiometer refers to an axis, so two potentiometers give you x and y references. This kind of control stick offers much more precision in terms of movement when compared to the old joysticks from 80s, like the ones used on the Atari console system with simple contacts to right, left, up, and down only. Thumbsticks are used in stick controls like the ones in PlayStation and Xbox systems. They offer analogic readings that can be transformed into intensity and movement direction. The thumbstick chosen for this project has a button functionality if you press the thumbstick tower to down.

Interfacing with Intel Galileo or Edison is very simple and uses the analog headers to read the respective movements and a digital port to detect if the button was pressed. When you move the thumbstick, the corresponding potentiometer's value changes, the ADC on Intel Galileo or Edison reads the voltage of each potentiometer and converts it to digital. It is possible to identify in which direction and with what intensity the thumbstick is being moved.

There are different thumbsticks available in the market, including SainSmart, Arrela, Paralax, Xima, and many others with different prices.

The thumbstick chosen for this project is robust and very affordable, costing only $2.78 each when you order three on dealxtream (see http://www.dx.com/s/121340).

Figure 11-39 (left) shows a picture of the thumbstick and its terminals, and Figure 11-39 (right) shows its schematics.

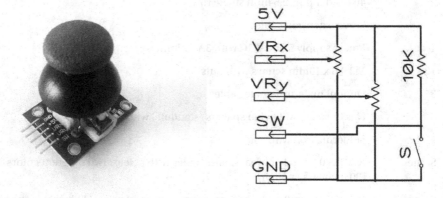

Figure 11-39. *The thumbstick (left) and its schematics (right)*

There are five terminals on this thumbstick—5V, GND, SW (a button click when you push the tower down), VRx (a variation on the x-axis), and VRy (a variation on the y-axis).

Then only problem with this thumbstick is a pull-up resistor of 10KOhms is required to enable the button functionality. It must be soldered manually, as shown in Figure 11-40, because this resistor is not part of the original stick. Some other vendors like SainSmart do not require this work, but are more expensive.

Figure 11-40. *Adding the 10KOhm pull-up resitor to the thumbstick*

The project works with any thumbstick and you are free to choose your favorite.

The thumbsticks are powered by 5V provided by 5V and GND headers provided by Intel boards. This separates them from any source of noise that could come from servos, even when it's filtered by the diode reducing wrong readings in the ADC.

When there is one thumbstick, the system is very easy and the APIs available on the Internet can handle it. However, when there are more than one, it is a little bit more complicated because each time you move one stick you also might affect the reading in the other stick. This is because the sticks share the same 5V, so the impedances of each thumbstick is impacted even if a single stick is moved. Figure 11-41 shows the circuit with three thumbsticks sharing the same power line and ground; imagine you move the first thumbstick to the left, thereby changing the reading VRx1. All the other VRxs readings will be affected because the equivalent impedance also changes for each VRxs and VRys and might cause "ghost" movements in the robot.

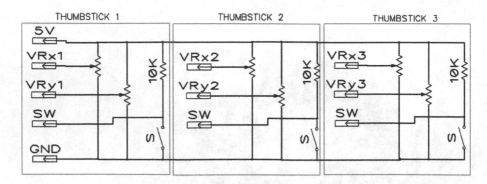

Figure 11-41. *The circuit formed by three thumbsticks sharing 5V*

In order to solve this problem, you need to separate the thumbsticks and not power them using a single 5V source as proposed in Figure 11-42. In this case, the idea is to power the thumbstick multiplexing the entries TS1, TS2, and TS3 with digital pin on Intel Galileo or Edison headers. Thus the software changes TS1 to HIGH state by powering on the thumbstick briefly with 5V, reads the VRx1, VRy1, and SW pins then changes TS1 to LOW state again by disabling the thumbstick. This process repeats with thumbstick 2, with thumbstick 3, and the returns to thumbstick 1 again. This process is very fast and you will be able to use all thumbsticks at same time without any interference or "ghost" movements in the arm. It is the implementation the simple idea of mux using digital headers.

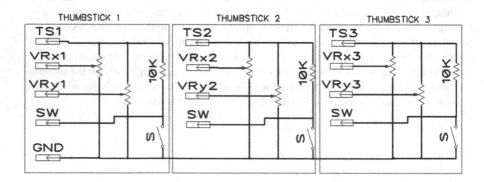

Figure 11-42. *The circuit formed by three independent thumbsticks*

The next discussion explains issues related to the external power supply.

External Power Supply

The servos used in this project can drain a good amount of current compared to the 80mA offered by the regular headers of Intel Galileo or Intel Edison boards, since they can drain up to 2.2A.

Thus an external power supply of 5V or 6V and 3A must be included.

Note the thumbsticks also use 5V but at a very low current and are read through analog ports. Thus to avoid interference from external power supply to the readings of these thumbsticks, the design selects the 5V provided by Intel Galileo or Intel Edison boards.

Also make sure the external power lines are filtered for any noises that might come from servo motors. 470uF was enough during the tests.

Circuit Protection

Considering a 5 VDC with a capacity of 3A is used, it is a good idea to protect the circuit to avoid catastrophic results if you were to invert the polarity.

For this purpose, a simple diode protects the external power line is best. The 1N5404 supports up to 3A. If you do not have a 5404 diode, but you have an 1N4004 or 1N4007 available, you can replace 1N5404 with three diodes in parallel, because each one supports up to 1A, as shown in Figure 11-43.

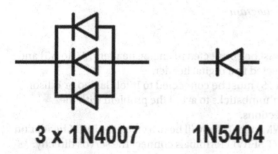

3 x 1N4007   1N5404

Figure 11-43. Replacing the 5404 diode with three 1N4004 or 1N4007 diodes

Assembling the Board

Based on the considerations discussed here, a simple idea for the board diagram is shown in Figure 11-44.

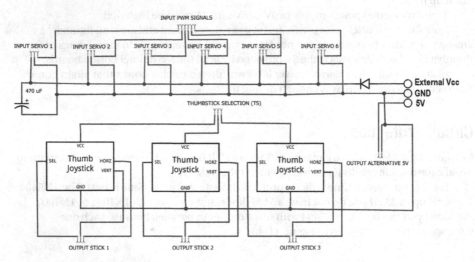

Figure 11-44. *Servos board controller diagram*

The OUTPUT STICK terminals must be connected to analog headers (A0 to A5) and the button of each stick must be connected to a digital header.

The THUMBSTICK SELECTION (TS) must be connected to Intel Galileo or Edison digital headers that will multiplex the thumbsticks to avoid the problem with the impedances mentioned in previous sections.

The INPUT PWM signal is the PWM signal that will be driven by the PWM header on Intel Galileo or Edison while the INPUT SERVO terminals connect the servos directly.

The OUTPUT ALTERNATIVE 5V can be used to connect an external peripheral. This chapter uses this terminal when the you learn about the ground coffee gripper later.

And finally, there is a three-pole terminal block that receives the external power supply, ground, and 5V provided by Intel Galileo or Edison.

To understand how the servos board controller works, it is also necessary to understand how this board connects to the external peripherals, in other words, how it connects with the servos and with Intel Galileo or Edison. Figure 11-45 shows such connections.

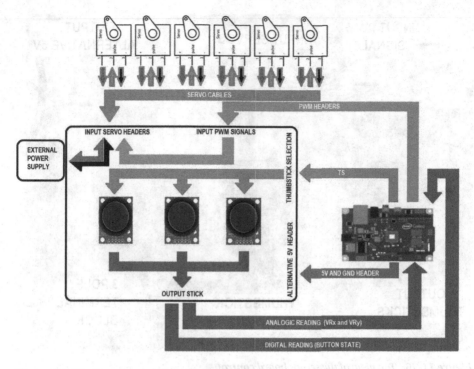

Figure 11-45. *How the servo board controller connects to the peripherals*

You can arrange the components in the prototyping board as shown in Figure 11-46 (top view) and Figure 11-47 (bottom view).

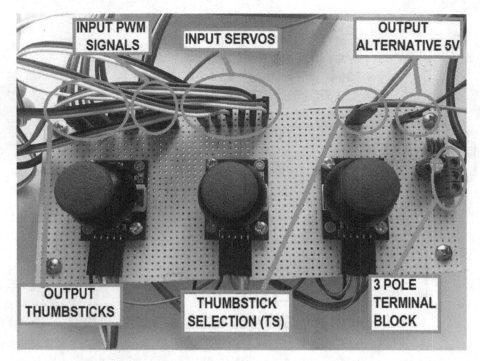

Figure 11-46. *Top view of the servos board control*

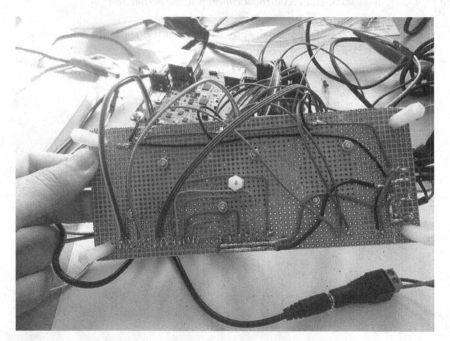

Figure 11-47. *Bottom view of the servos board control*

Before you start to build the board, consider these minor mechanical recommendations:

- The prototyping board is specified in the material list as 6x3 inches. If you use a small board (even if the thumbsticks fits), make sure the controllers will have space and the thumbsticks will not collide with each other when you move their towers. That's why there should be a gap of at least 1.2 inches between each thumbstick.

- Note in Figure 11-47 that five standoffs were used, four in the edges and one in the center. The reason for the central one is that, since you are using this board as a controller, you might rest your hands on the board. The central standoff will keep the board from warping given the weight of your hands. digikey.com sells different types of standoffs; the nylon ones are only around $0.23 each.

- Be wise when you arrange the terminals and avoid wires passing over the board. This can impact the thumbstick's usability.

Now that your hardware is ready to be tested, you must create the software and integrate it into a sketch, as explained in the next section.

The Software

Some APIs already provide thumbsticks that are available on the Internet. However, there are some challenges with these kinds of thumbsticks:

- There is more than one simple thumbstick to be controlled.

- The thumbsticks must be calibrated.

- The code should control the servo limits of each component in the robotic arm.

- Considering there are six servos to be controlled, the control must be easy for the user.

The first challenge was explained in the section entitled, "The Hardware," which discussed the digital header being used as a mux to select each thumbstick at a time. It's easy to implement in terms of software because every time a function is called to read the thumbstick state, you simply need to supply 5V to the respective stick, read the state, and then disable the thumbstick.

The second challenge is calibrating the thumbsticks. There is no guarantee that all the thumbsticks received will have the same impedance and the same mechanical adjustments to the center position. Therefore, it's necessary to make the software understand each thumbstick by identifying the value of the center position and the boundaries. This ensures proper conversion.

The third challenge is related to how the software programs each thumbstick so that it respects the mechanical limits that each servo must support. For example, it doesn't make sense for the servo that controls the gripper to rotate between 0 to 180 degrees because the gripper operates with an opening that limits the servo from 70 to 130 degrees. On the other hand, the servo in the base can work between 0 to 180 degrees without problems.

The final challenge is that the servo must be easily controlled and this is addressed further on this section.

The next step is to present the API and test it.

An API for Servos Board Control

The API provides a simple interface that allows you to read the state of each thumbstick by retrieving values that respect the angle limits of the servos controlled by the thumbstick.

Each thumbstick can control two servos, one in the x-axis and the other in the y-axis.

So, the API must convert the analog reading on the x- and y-axis to the limits that you specify.

In addition to the limit control, it is also necessary to determine how the analog headers (VRx and VRy) and button pin connect to Intel Galileo or Edison, and determine which digital header will select the thumbstick (TS).

It is also interesting to operate the thumbstick in two different modes:

- **Absolute position:** The servos will follow the thumbstick movement. So if you release the thumbstick, the servo will move to its initial position because the thumbstick automatically moves to the central position. You need to keep holding the sticks to move the servos that will follow the same movements.

- **Step in touch:** The servos do not follow the stick, but move in the direction you point the thumbsticks.

Listing 11-2 shows the header file of the API with the methods necessary to implement such functionalities.

Listing 11-2. Thumbstick.h

```
/*

    This file is part of Thumstick API.

    Thumstick API is free software: you can redistribute it and/or modify
    it under the terms of the GNU General Public License as published by
    the Free Software Foundation, either version 3 of the License, or
    (at your option) any later version.
```

```
        Thumstick API is distributed in the hope that it will be useful,
        but WITHOUT ANY WARRANTY; without even the implied warranty of
        MERCHANTABILITY or FITNESS FOR A PARTICULAR PURPOSE.  See the
        GNU General Public License for more details.

        You should have received a copy of the GNU General Public License
        along with Foobar.  If not, see <http://www.gnu.org/licenses/>.

        by Manoel Carlos Ramon (manoel.ramon@gm ail.com)
        Nov 2014
        version 1.0
*/
#ifndef _THUMBSTICK_API
#define _THUMBSTICK_API
#include <Arduino.h>

#define NOT_CALIBRATED     22
#define MAX_FLOATING       10
#define STEP_X             5
#define STEP_Y             5
#define NUMBER_OF_SAMPLES  25

#define DEBUG 1

class Thumbstick {

  private:

  int stick_step = 100;

  int lastButtonState = HIGH;
  long lastDebounceTime = 0;    // the last time the output pin was toggled
  long debounceDelay = 400;     // adjust this value if necessary to avoid
                                   flickering

  int X_max = NOT_CALIBRATED;  // max X retrieved during calibration
  int Y_max = NOT_CALIBRATED;  // max Y retrieved during calibration
  int X_min = NOT_CALIBRATED;  // min X retrieved during calibration
  int Y_min = NOT_CALIBRATED;  // min Y retrieved during calibration
  int centerX = 0;
  int centerY = 0;

  int pinAnalogX;
  int pinAnalogY;
  int pinButton;
  int pin_select;
```

549

```
bool centerCalibrated = false; // informs if the center was calibrated

// 0 and 180 are the default angles values
int servoX_MinAngle = 0;    // the minimum angle supported by servo
                               attached to axis X
int servoX_MaxAngle = 180;  // the maximum angle supported by servo
                               attached to axis X

int servoY_MinAngle = 0;    // the minimum angle supported by servo
                               attached to axis Y
int servoY_MaxAngle = 180;  // the maximum angle supported by servo
                               attached to axis Y

// number of samples to estabelish the center during the calibration
int samplesOfrCenterXCounter = NUMBER_OF_SAMPLES, samplesOfrCenterYCounter =
NUMBER_OF_SAMPLES;
int lastAngleX = -1, lastAngleY = -1;

// checks the button state considering the debounce
int checkButtonState();

public:

enum {
    ANALOG_RAW,            // Only brings the raw values... for testing only
    ABSOLUTE_POSITION,     // The servos will move according joystick position
    STEPS_IN_TOUCH,        // The servos moves increases and decreases its angles
    INVALID_MOVE           // Just to mark the invalid boundaries
} typedef MOVE_T;

MOVE_T move_type = ANALOG_RAW;  // initial mode

struct {
  int X;                  // the current X angle
  int Y;                  // the current Y angle
  int buttonPressed;      // True if thumbstick button is pressed
} typedef JOYSTICK_XY_T;

int  Xvalue;            // current X value read from analog port
int  Yvalue;            // current Y value read from analog port
int  Zvalue;            // current button state

// Contructor
//  _pin_select : which digital pin that selects the thumbstick during the
        multiplexation
//  pinX        : which analog port reads the variation of X axis
```

```
// pinY         : which analog port reads the variation of Y axis
// _pinButton   : which digital pin reads the button state
// minX         : the minimum servo angle on axis X (default is 0)
// maxX         : the maximum servo angle on axis X (default is 180)
// minY         : the minimum servo angle on axis Y (default is 0)
// maxY         : the maximum servo angle on axis Y (default is 180)

Thumbstick(int _pin_select, int pinX, int pinY, int _pinButton, int minX = 0,
int maxX = 180, int minY = 0, int maxY = 180);

// Destructor
~Thumbstick();

// init the pin mode (must be in setup() function)
void initPins();

// Performs the calibration
void calibrate();

// checks if the thumbstick was calibrated
// Returns: TRUE if calibrated or FALSE if it is not.
bool isCalibrated();

// only for debug purposes
void dumpCalibration();

// informs if center was calibrated
bool isCenterCalibrated() { return centerCalibrated; };

// reads the current status of thumbstick
// Parameter:
//     MOVE_T format - the mode of reading
// Returns:
//     JOYSTICK_XY_T - the coordinates and button state
JOYSTICK_XY_T read(MOVE_T format);
};
#endif
```

The implementation of each method is shown in Listing 11-3.

Listing 11-3. Thumbstick.cpp

```
/*
    This file is part of Thumstick API.

    Thumstick API is free software: you can redistribute it and/or modify
    it under the terms of the GNU General Public License as published by
    the Free Software Foundation, either version 3 of the License, or
    (at your option) any later version.

    Thumstick API is distributed in the hope that it will be useful,
    but WITHOUT ANY WARRANTY; without even the implied warranty of
    MERCHANTABILITY or FITNESS FOR A PARTICULAR PURPOSE.  See the
    GNU General Public License for more details.

    You should have received a copy of the GNU General Public License
    along with Foobar.  If not, see <http://www.gnu.org/licenses/>.

    by Manoel Carlos Ramon (manoel.ramon@gmail.com)
    Nov 2014
    version 1.0
*/

#include "Thumbstick.h"

  // Contructor
  // _pin_select : which digital pin that selects the thumbstick during the
  //     multiplexation
  // pinX        : which analog port reads the variation of X axis
  // pinY        : which analog port reads the variation of Y axis
  // _pinButton  : which digital pin reads the button state
  // minX        : the minimum servo angle on axis X (default is 0)
  // maxX        : the maximum servo angle on axis X (default is 180)
  // minY        : the minimum servo angle on axis Y (default is 0)
  // maxY        : the maximum servo angle on axis Y (default is 180)

  Thumbstick::Thumbstick(int _pin_select, int pinX, int pinY,
int _pinButton, int minX, int maxX, int minY, int maxY)
  {
      pinAnalogX = pinX;
      pinAnalogY = pinY;
      pinButton  = _pinButton;
      pin_select = _pin_select;

      servoX_MinAngle = minX;
      servoX_MaxAngle = maxX;
```

```
    servoY_MinAngle = minY;
    servoY_MaxAngle = maxY;

}

// Destructor
Thumbstick::~Thumbstick()
{
}

// init the pin mode (must be in setup() function)
void Thumbstick::initPins()
{
    pinMode(pinButton, INPUT);
    pinMode(pin_select, OUTPUT);

}

// Performs the calibration
void Thumbstick::calibrate()
{
    JOYSTICK_XY_T res = this->read(ANALOG_RAW);

    // the following logic tries to find the maximum and minimum
    // values for all axis. Such values will be used to identify
    // the limits of your thumbstick.
    if (res.X < X_min)
    {
        X_min = res.X;
    }

    if (res.X > X_max)
    {
        X_max = res.X;
    }

    if (res.Y < Y_min)
    {
        Y_min = res.Y;
    }

    if (res.Y > Y_max)
    {
        Y_max = res.Y;
    }

    // the center of each thumbstick must be found
    // considering the center is the first thing that calibration process
    search for
```

```
        // then some samples must be aquire until ADC turn stable.
        if ((centerX == 0) && (--samplesOfrCenterXCounter ==0))
        {

            centerX = res.X;
            Serial.print("centerX:");
            Serial.println(centerX);
        }

        if ((centerY == 0) && (--samplesOfrCenterYCounter == 0))
        {
            centerY = res.Y;
            Serial.print("centerY:");
            Serial.println(centerY);
        }

        // just to inform the centers were got
        if ((centerX !=0) && (centerY !=0))
        {
                centerCalibrated = true;
        }

        if ((lastAngleX == -1) && (centerX != 0) && (X_min != NOT_CALIBRATED)
&& (X_max != NOT_CALIBRATED) && (Y_max != NOT_CALIBRATED) &&
(Y_min != NOT_CALIBRATED))
            {
                lastAngleX = constrain(map(centerX , X_min , X_max ,
servoX_MinAngle, servoX_MaxAngle), servoX_MinAngle, servoX_MaxAngle);
                lastAngleY = constrain(map(centerY , Y_min , Y_max ,
servoY_MinAngle, servoY_MaxAngle), servoY_MinAngle, servoY_MaxAngle);
            }

    }

// checks if the thumbstick was calibrated
// Returns: TRUE if calibrated or FALSE if it is not.
bool Thumbstick::isCalibrated()
{
    bool result = false;
    if ((X_min != NOT_CALIBRATED) && (X_max != NOT_CALIBRATED) &&
        (Y_min != NOT_CALIBRATED) && (Y_max != NOT_CALIBRATED)) {
            result = true;
    }

    return result;
}
```

```
// only for debug purposes
void Thumbstick::dumpCalibration()
{
  if (DEBUG)
  {
      Serial.print("Xmax:");
      Serial.print(X_max);

      Serial.print(" Xmin:");
      Serial.print(X_min);

      Serial.print(" Ymax:");
      Serial.print(Y_max);

      Serial.print(" Ymin:");
      Serial.print(Y_min);

      Serial.print(" centerX:");
      Serial.print(centerX);

      Serial.print(" Angle centerX:");
      Serial.print(lastAngleX);

      Serial.print(" centerY:");
      Serial.print(centerY);

      Serial.print(" Angle centerY:");
      Serial.println(lastAngleY);
  }

}

// checks the button state considering the debounce
int Thumbstick::checkButtonState()
{

  // read the state of the switch into a local variable:
  int reading = digitalRead(this->pinButton);

  // check to see if you just pressed the button
  // (i.e. the input went from LOW to HIGH),  and you've waited
  // long enough since the last press to ignore any noise:

  // If the switch changed, due to noise or pressing:
  if (reading != lastButtonState) {
    // reset the debouncing timer
    lastDebounceTime = millis();
  }
```

```
    if ((millis() - lastDebounceTime) > debounceDelay) {
      // whatever the reading is at, it's been there for longer

      // if the button state has changed:
      if (reading != Zvalue) {
        Zvalue = reading;
      }
    }

    lastButtonState = reading;

    return lastButtonState;

}

// reads the current status of thumbstick
// Parameter:
//      MOVE_T format - the mode of reading
// Returns:
//      JOYSTICK_XY_T - the coordinates and button state
Thumbstick::JOYSTICK_XY_T Thumbstick::read(MOVE_T format)
{
    int stepX = 0, absoluteX, absoluteY, stepY = 0;
    Thumbstick::JOYSTICK_XY_T result = {0,0, false};

        // selecting the right thumbstick to provide 5V
    digitalWrite(pin_select, HIGH);
    delay(5);

    result.buttonPressed = false;
    if (checkButtonState() == LOW)
    {
        result.buttonPressed = true;
    }

    // reading the raw analog values
    Xvalue = analogRead(this->pinAnalogX);
    Yvalue = analogRead(this->pinAnalogY);

    switch (format)
    {
      case ANALOG_RAW:           // Only brings the raw values of the
                                 // joystick potentiometers
        result.X = Xvalue;
        result.Y = Yvalue;
      break;
```

```
      case ABSOLUTE_POSITION:   // The servo will move according joystick
                                   position
              result.X = constrain(map(Xvalue , X_min , X_max ,
  servoX_MinAngle, servoX_MaxAngle), servoX_MinAngle, servoX_MaxAngle);
              result.Y = constrain(map(Yvalue , Y_min , Y_max ,
  servoY_MinAngle, servoY_MaxAngle), servoY_MinAngle, servoY_MaxAngle);
          break;

      case STEPS_IN_TOUCH:        // The joystick moves increases and
                                     decreases servos coordinates

          int x;
          int centerx;

          x = map(Xvalue , X_min , X_max , 0, 255);
          centerx = map(centerX , X_min , X_max , 0, 255);

          // checking if the reading is floating
          if (abs(x - centerx) > MAX_FLOATING)
          {
              if (x > centerx) stepX = STEP_X;
              if (x < centerx) stepX = -STEP_X;
          }
          // reading the last angle and adding result.X

          int y;
          int centery;

          y = map(Yvalue , Y_min , Y_max , 0, 255);
          centery = map(centerY , Y_min , Y_max , 0, 255);

          // checking if the reading is floating
          if (abs(y - centery) > MAX_FLOATING)
          {
              if (y > centery) stepY = STEP_Y;
              if (y < centery) stepY = -STEP_Y;
          }

          if (lastAngleX >= 0)
          {
              lastAngleX += stepX;
              lastAngleX = constrain(lastAngleX, servoX_MinAngle,
                  servoX_MaxAngle);
              result.X = lastAngleX;
          }
```

```
lastAngleY >=0)
            {
                    lastAngleY += stepY;
                    lastAngleY = constrain(lastAngleY, servoY_MinAngle+1,
servoY_MaxAngle);
                    result.Y = lastAngleY;
            }
        break;

        default:
            if (DEBUG) Serial.println("Wrong mode chosen!");
        break;
    }

    // disable the thumbstick selection
    digitalWrite(pin_select, LOW);
    return result;
}
```

Reviewing the Thumbstick API

The API includes a class called Thumbstick that determines how the thumbstick is connected to Intel Galileo or Edison and the limits of each servo. In other words, how are the thumbstick's VRx and VRy terminals connected to the analog headers, how the button is connected to the digital ports, which pin on Intel Galileo or Edison will select the thumbstick (TS), and what the limits of the servos controlled by the x- and y-axis are.

A new type called MOVE_T defines the mode the thumbstick must work in; you can choose between ABSOLUTE_POSITION and STEPS_IN_TOUCH.

Another type called JOYSTICK_XY_T determines the position related to the X and Y axes and whether the button was pressed (buttonPressed). This type is specifically returned by the read() method, which receives MOVE_T as an input parameter and internally makes all the conversions to returns the angles in the correct mode.

Two other important public methods are calibrate(), which performs the calibration, and isCalibrate(), which checks if the thumbstick was calibrated properly.

The initPins() method must be added to the setup() function of the sketches to guarantee the digital and analog pins will be configured correctly.

Analyzing the **read()** method a little bit more, you will realize that the method selects the thumbstick in the beginning and disables it in the end of the method calling the digitalWrite() functions. Then it checks the button state by calling a private method called checkButtonState(), which checks the current button state using a debounce. It uses the same technique used in the project called "Moisture Sensor" described in Chapter 8. The rest of the code reads the analog values of x and y using analogRead() and, according to the mode passed through the variable format, makes the proper conversion. Remember that analogRead() converts the reading in a value between 0 to 23 (read Chapter 3 for more details), and the ABSOLUTE_POSITION or STEP_IN_TOUCH mode converts these values to the proper angles on each mode. Of course, the ADC is not perfect. Even with 12 bits and considering you built a decent prototyping board, a small amount of floating is expected; that tolerance is controlled by MAX_FLOATING.

```
Thumbstick::JOYSTICK_XY_T Thumbstick::read(MOVE_T format)
  {
    Thumbstick::JOYSTICK_XY_T result = {0,0, false};
...
...
...

      digitalWrite(pin_select, HIGH);
...

      if (checkButtonState() == LOW)
      {
          result.buttonPressed = true;
      }
...

      // reading the raw analog values
      Xvalue = analogRead(this->pinAnalogX);
      Yvalue = analogRead(this->pinAnalogY);


      switch (format)
      {
...
...
...

        case ABSOLUTE_POSITION:  // The servo will move according
joystick position

            result.X = constrain(map(Xvalue , X_min , X_max ,
servoX_MinAngle, servoX_MaxAngle), servoX_MinAngle, servoX_MaxAngle);
            result.Y = constrain(map(Yvalue , Y_min , Y_max ,
servoY_MinAngle, servoY_MaxAngle), servoY_MinAngle, servoY_MaxAngle);
          break;

        case STEPS_IN_TOUCH:     // The joystick moves increases and
                                 decreases servos coordinates

          int x;
          int centerx;

          x = map(Xvalue , X_min , X_max , 0, 255);
          centerx = map(centerX , X_min , X_max , 0, 255);
```

```
        // checking if the reading is floating
        if (abs(x - centerx) > MAX_FLOATING)
        {
                if (x > centerx) stepX = STEP_X;
                if (x < centerx) stepX = -STEP_X;
        }
        // reading the last angle and adding result.X

        int y;
        int centery;

        y = map(Yvalue , Y_min , Y_max , 0, 255);
        centery = map(centerY , Y_min , Y_max , 0, 255);


        // checking if the reading is floating
        if (abs(y - centery) > MAX_FLOATING)
        {
                if (y > centery) stepY = STEP_Y;
                if (y < centery) stepY = -STEP_Y;
        }
...
...
...

                lastAngleX += stepX;
                lastAngleX = constrain(lastAngleX, servoX_MinAngle,
                servoX_MaxAngle);
                result.X = lastAngleX;
...
...
...

                lastAngleY += stepY;
                lastAngleY = constrain(lastAngleY, servoY_MinAngle+1,
                servoY_MaxAngle);
                result.Y = lastAngleY;
...
...
...

        }

    // disable the thumbstick selection
    digitalWrite(pin_select, LOW);

    return result;
}
```

The calibration implemented in the calibrate() method reads the analog values when each thumbstick is on the central position during some samples controlled by the samplesOfrCenterXCounter and samplesOfrCenterYCounter variables. The user usually spins the thumbstick to check the maximum x and y values of each thumbstick. Such calibration is critical for getting the right result when the read() method is called. Note all values are initiated with the value defined by NOT_CALIBRATED, which is 22. The thumbsticks usually start in the center position and the analogic conversion varies between 0 and 1023. 22 is then too far from the center (average point) of 512 and mathematically you can conclude that the thumbsticks were not calibrated.

Installing the API

This library code is located in the code/Thumbstick folder and it must be installed in your IDE. The installation process is simple:

1. Close any running IDE instances.

2. Move the Thumbstick folder to the arduino-1.5.3/libraries directory of your IDE installation.

3. Open the IDE again and select Sketch ➤ Import Library from the menu. Check if it is listed as Thumbstick. If it is, open the RoboticArm.ino sketch in the examples folder of the library or select Files ➤ Examples ➤ Thumbstick ➤ RoboticArm. ino using the menu. If the library is not present, check if the library is properly installed. You can also learn more about libraries at http://arduino.cc/en/Guide/Libraries.

A Sketch to Control the Robotic Arm

With the API installed and the board built, it's time to create a sketch to control the arm.

Listing 11-4 shows the sketch for the Intel Galileo boards.

Listing 11-4. RoboticArm.ino

```
#include <Thumbstick.h>
#include <Servo.h>

#define PIN_SERVO_BASE      3
#define PIN_SERVO_SHOULDER  5
#define PIN_SERVO_ELBOW     6
#define PIN_SERVO_WRISTX    9
#define PIN_SERVO_WRISTY    11
#define PIN_SERVO_GRIPPER   10
```

```
// Defining the gripper angle limitations
#define GRIPPER_OPENED 90
#define GRIPPER_CLOSED 125

// Declaring the servos in the arm
Servo baseServo;
Servo shoulderServo;
Servo elbowServo;
Servo wristYServo;
Servo wristXServo;
Servo gripper;

// Declaring the sticks with
Thumbstick joystick1(8,  A0, A1, 0, 0, 180, 90, 180);
Thumbstick joystick2(12, A2, A3, 1, 0, 180, 0, 180);
Thumbstick joystick3(13, A4, A5, 2);

// Variables used to store the results
Thumbstick::JOYSTICK_XY_T res1;
Thumbstick::JOYSTICK_XY_T res2;
Thumbstick::JOYSTICK_XY_T res3;

void setup()
{

    // for debug purposes let's use the serial terminal
    Serial.begin(115200);

    // init the joystick pins
    joystick1.initPins();
    joystick2.initPins();
    joystick3.initPins();

    baseServo.attach(PIN_SERVO_BASE);          // joystick 1 - axis -> X
    shoulderServo.attach(PIN_SERVO_SHOULDER);  // joystick 1 - axis -> y
    elbowServo.attach(PIN_SERVO_ELBOW);        // jostick 2 - axis -> Y
    wristYServo.attach(PIN_SERVO_WRISTX);      // joystick 3 - axis -> X
    wristXServo.attach(PIN_SERVO_WRISTY);      // joystick 3 - axis -> Y
    gripper.attach(PIN_SERVO_GRIPPER);         // joystick 1, 2 OR 3 - button

    // initial position - all servos in 90 degrees and gripper opened
    baseServo.write(90);
    shoulderServo.write(90);
    elbowServo.write(90);
    wristYServo.write(90);
    wristXServo.write(90);
    gripper.write(GRIPPER_OPENED);
```

```
    // a small delay to allow the user to open the serial terminal
    delay(3000);

    Serial.println("*** Calibrating Joysticks **** ");
    Serial.println();
    Serial.println("Reading the CENTERS of each control stick");

    // let's run the calibration process for 15 seconds (15000 ms)
    boolean msgShown = false;
    long t = millis();
    while (millis()-t < 15000) {
        joystick1.calibrate();
        joystick2.calibrate();
        joystick3.calibrate();

        if (joystick1.isCenterCalibrated() &&
            joystick2.isCenterCalibrated() &&
            joystick3.isCenterCalibrated() &&
            msgShown == false)
        {
            msgShown = true; // only to show the message one single time
            Serial.println("Please, start spinning the thumbsticks !!!!");
        }
    }

    if (DEBUG)
    {
        joystick1.dumpCalibration();
        joystick2.dumpCalibration();
        joystick3.dumpCalibration();

    }

    Serial.println("*** Calibration process completed.");

}

void loop()
{

    static boolean isGripperOpened = true;

    // checking the joysticks calibration
    if (joystick1.isCalibrated() == false)
    {
        Serial.println("ERROR: Joystick 1 not calibrated");
    }
```

```
if (joystick2.isCalibrated() == false)
{
    Serial.println("ERROR: Joystick 2 not calibrated");
}

if (joystick3.isCalibrated() == false)
{
    Serial.println("ERROR: Joystick 3 not calibrated");
}

// In case some tumbstick is not calibrated the user must be informed
if ((joystick1.isCalibrated()   == false) ||
    (joystick2.isCalibrated()   == false) ||
    (joystick3.isCalibrated()   == false))
{

    // aborting
    Serial.println("You need to calibrate the joysticks !!! RESTART the
      sketch pressing RESET button!! ");
    delay(1000);
    return;
}

 Thumbstick::MOVE_T move_type = Thumbstick::STEPS_IN_TOUCH;
    //let's use this first
//Thumbstick::MOVE_T move_type = Thumbstick::ABSOLUTE_POSITION;
//Thumbstick::MOVE_T move_type = Thumbstick::ANALOG_RAW;

// making the reading of all 3 thumbsticks
res1 = joystick1.read(move_type);
res2 = joystick2.read(move_type);
res3 = joystick3.read(move_type);

if (DEBUG)
{
    Serial.print("Joystick1 -> X:");
    Serial.print(res1.X);

    Serial.print(" Y:");
    Serial.print(res1.Y);

    Serial.print(" Z:");
    Serial.print(res1.buttonPressed);

    Serial.print("   Joystick2 -> X:");
    Serial.print(res2.X);
```

```
    Serial.print(" Y:");
    Serial.print(res2.Y);

    Serial.print(" Z:");
    Serial.print(res2.buttonPressed);

    Serial.print("   Joystick3 -> X:");
    Serial.print(res3.X);

    Serial.print(" Y:");
    Serial.print(res3.Y);

    Serial.print(" Z:");
    Serial.print(res3.buttonPressed);

    Serial.print(" gripper:");
    Serial.println(gripper.read());

}

// moving the servos  according the responses of each thumbstick
baseServo.write(res1.X);
shoulderServo.write(res1.Y);
elbowServo.write(res2.Y);
wristYServo.write(res3.Y);
wristXServo.write(res3.X);

// in our example the button functionality of all button might be used
// to manipulate the gripper
if ((res1.buttonPressed) || (res2.buttonPressed) || (res3.buttonPressed))
{

    if (isGripperOpened)
    {
        gripper.write(GRIPPER_CLOSED);
        isGripperOpened = false;

    }
    else
    {
        isGripperOpened = true;
        gripper.write(GRIPPER_OPENED);
    }

    // this small delay is to allow the gripper complete
    // it is task before a new movement
    delay(600);
}
}
```

Before you run the code and try to control the robotic arm, it is essential that you read the code review in order to understand how the arm must be controlled.

Reviewing RoboticArm.ino

The code starts by defining the pins that each servo will be connected to, defining the mechanical limits of the gripper (90 to 125 degrees), and suggesting names for the servo objects according to their position in the arm.

```
#define PIN_SERVO_BASE        3
#define PIN_SERVO_SHOULDER    5
#define PIN_SERVO_ELBOW       6
#define PIN_SERVO_WRISTX      9
#define PIN_SERVO_WRISTY      11
#define PIN_SERVO_GRIPPER     10

// Defining the gripper angle limitations
#define GRIPPER_OPENED 90
#define GRIPPER_CLOSED 125

// Declaring the servos in the arm
Servo baseServo;
Servo shoulderServo;
Servo elbowServo;
Servo wristYServo;
Servo wristXServo;
Servo gripper;
```

Then the thumbsticks objects are created:

```
// Declaring the sticks with
Thumbstick joystick1(8,  A0, A1, 0, 0, 180, 90, 180);
Thumbstick joystick2(12, A2, A3, 1, 0, 180, 0, 180);
Thumbstick joystick3(13, A4, A5, 2);
```

Note that each object defines the pin that will select it, the analog ports the thumbstick is connected to, the pin that will receive the button press signals, and the minimum and maximum angles of servos on the X and Y axes, respectively. If the angles are not passed in as joystick3 the default values 0 and 180 degrees are used.

In the setup() function, the thumbsticks pins are initiated, the servos are attached to their respective pins, and the arm is placed at 90 degrees with the gripper opened. No calibration takes place.

```
// init the joystick pins
joystick1.initPins();
joystick2.initPins();
joystick3.initPins();

baseServo.attach(PIN_SERVO_BASE);            // joystick 1 - axis -> X
shoulderServo.attach(PIN_SERVO_SHOULDER);    // joystick 1 - axis -> y
elbowServo.attach(PIN_SERVO_ELBOW);          // jostick 2 - axis -> Y
wristYServo.attach(PIN_SERVO_WRISTX);        // joystick 3 - axis -> X
wristXServo.attach(PIN_SERVO_WRISTY);        // joystick 3 - axis -> Y
gripper.attach(PIN_SERVO_GRIPPER);           // joystick 1, 2 OR 3 - button

// initial position - all servos in 90 degrees and gripper opened
baseServo.write(90);
shoulderServo.write(90);
elbowServo.write(90);
wristYServo.write(90);
wristXServo.write(90);
gripper.write(GRIPPER_OPENED);
```

Still in the setup() function, the calibration is invoked in 15 seconds. It means you have 15 seconds to spin your thumbstick to calibrate them after the center of each thumbstick is detected.

```
while (millis()-t < 15000) {
    joystick1.calibrate();
    joystick2.calibrate();
    joystick3.calibrate();

    if (joystick1.isCenterCalibrated() &&
        joystick2.isCenterCalibrated() &&
        joystick3.isCenterCalibrated() &&
        msgShown == false)
    {
        msgShown = true; // only to show the message one single time
        Serial.println("Please, start spinning the thumbsticks !!!!");
    }
}
```

The rest of the code is concentrated in the loop() function and it is very simple. If the calibration was not made for any of thumbsticks, the program aborts and asks you to reset the sketch. Otherwise, the thumbsticks are read using "step in touch" mode, as explained previously.

```
Thumbstick::MOVE_T move_type = Thumbstick::STEPS_IN_TOUCH;
    //let's use this first
```

567

```
// making the reading of all 3 thumbsticks
res1 = joystick1.read(move_type);
res2 = joystick2.read(move_type);
res3 = joystick3.read(move_type);
```

The only thing to do is to "ask" the servos to move to the position returned by the thumbstick readings and check if the button was pressed to open or close the gripper.

```
// moving the servos  according the responses of each thumbstick
    baseServo.write(res1.X);
    shoulderServo.write(res1.Y);
    elbowServo.write(res2.Y);
    wristYServo.write(res3.Y);
    wristXServo.write(res3.X);

    // in our example the button functionality of all button might be used
    // to manipulate the gripper
    if ((res1.buttonPressed) || (res2.buttonPressed) || (res3.buttonPressed))
    {

        if (isGripperOpened)
        {
            gripper.write(GRIPPER_CLOSED);
            isGripperOpened = false;

        }
        else
        {
            isGripperOpened = true;
            gripper.write(GRIPPER_OPENED);
        }

        // this small delay is to allow the gripper complete
        // it is task before a new movement
        delay(600);
    }
```

Running RoboticArm.ino

Don't power the robotic arm. Instead, keep the external power supply disconnected. You can then test if your thumbsticks are properly connected to Intel Galileo or Edison, test the calibration, and check the debug messages on the serial monitor.

As soon as you download the sketch, open the serial console by choosing Tools ➤ Serial Monitor or pressing Ctrl+Shift+M.

You will see some messages regarding the calibration of the thumbsticks.

```
*** Calibrating Joysticks ****

Reading the CENTERS of each control stick
517
509
495
491
478
489
Please, start spinning the thumbsticks !!!!
```

At this point, spin each of the thumbsticks in all directions. Try to reach the maximum possible. Recall that you have 15 seconds to spin all the thumbsticks.

If your calibration attempt did not calibrate any of the thumbsticks, you will see error messages like these:

```
*** Calibration process completed.
ERROR: Joystick 1 not calibrated
ERROR: Joystick 2 not calibrated
ERROR: Joystick 3 not calibrated
You need to calibrate the joysticks !!! RESTART the sketch pressing RESET
button!!
```

In this case, download the sketch again or press Reset on Intel Galileo or Edison Arduino kit to restart the sketch.

If you calibrate successfully, information regarding each thumbstick is displayed in the serial console. It's time to check if the angle limits of each servo match the limits you programmed in when the thumbstick objects were created.

```
Joystick1 -> X:90 Y:177 Z:0    Joystick2 -> X:88 Y:88 Z:0    Joystick3
-> X:85 Y:88 Z:0 gripper:90
Joystick1 -> X:90 Y:177 Z:0    Joystick2 -> X:88 Y:88 Z:0    Joystick3
-> X:85 Y:88 Z:0 gripper:90
Joystick1 -> X:90 Y:177 Z:0    Joystick2 -> X:88 Y:88 Z:0    Joystick3
-> X:85 Y:88 Z:0 gripper:90
Joystick1 -> X:90 Y:177 Z:0    Joystick2 -> X:88 Y:88 Z:0    Joystick3
-> X:85 Y:88 Z:0 gripper:90
Joystick1 -> X:90 Y:177 Z:0    Joystick2 -> X:88 Y:88 Z:0    Joystick3
-> X:85 Y:88 Z:0 gripper:90
Joystick1 -> X:90 Y:177 Z:0    Joystick2 -> X:88 Y:88 Z:0    Joystick3
-> X:85 Y:88 Z:0 gripper:90
Joystick1 -> X:90 Y:177 Z:0    Joystick2 -> X:88 Y:88 Z:0    Joystick3
-> X:85 Y:88 Z:0 gripper:90
Joystick1 -> X:90 Y:177 Z:0    Joystick2 -> X:88 Y:88 Z:0    Joystick3
-> X:85 Y:88 Z:0 gripper:90
```

Play a little bit with the thumbsticks and check how far the angles change and if the buttons work. If everything is okay, you can power your robotic arm and play with it.

Note if you kept the robotic arm powered while you are calibrating, the arm stands in 90 degrees and then changes to another position when the calibration is successful.

In order to understand this process better, watch the video named calibrating_the_arm.mp4 in the video folder of this chapter. It shows the calibration process and the working arm.

A Gripper Based on Coffee and a Balloon

If you play with your arm, you will notice that some small objects, such as coins, small screwdrivers, and screws, are very difficult to catch using the mechanical gripper that comes with the kit. .

Fortunately for us, in 2010, a publication entitled "Universal Robotic Gripper Based on the Jamming of Granular Material" by Brown, E., Rodenberg, N., Amend, J., Mozeika, A., Steltz, E., Zakin, M., Lipson, H., and Jaeger, H., published in *Proceedings of the National Academy of Sciences (PNAS)*, Vol. 107, no. 44, pp.18809-18814, described a brilliant solution to this issue. It explains how to create a universal gripper using ground coffee, a balloon, and a vacuum pump that can crab small objects. If you are interested in reading the full publication, visit http://creativemachines.cornell.edu/sites/default/files/PNAS10_Amend.pdf.

Figure 11-48 shows how the process works. First the gripper approaches the object (1) and then forms over the object (2). The air pump then removes the air, forcing the ground coffee to hold the object (3). finally, the gripper holds the object (4).

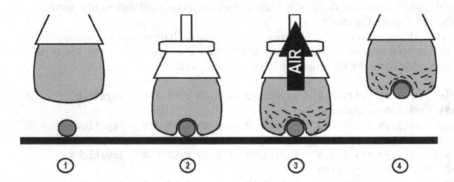

Figure 11-48. How the gripper with ground coffee works

In this chapter, you'll create a very simple version of this gripper using the materials in Table 11-3.

Table 11-3. *Materials List for Ground Coffee Gripper*

Number	Description
3	Vacuum pump, 12V 0-16" Hg
3	12V power supply 2A with switching power supply adapter
1	Relay module shield (one relay is enough)
1	Party balloon at least 24 inches wide
1	Funnel with 10mm or 8mm orifice
1	4 feet 3/8" (10mm) OD and 1/4" ID (8mm) clear vinyl house
1	Small piece (2x2 inch) of filter fabric socket (also called drain sleeve)
Some	Around 10 inches of 1/4w wires
Some	Around 10 inches of 1/2w wires of at least two different colors

Regarding the vacuum pump, it's best to order the ROB-10398 from sparkfun.com. Check out the product at https://www.sparkfun.com/products/10398.

The 12V power supply used in this project was ordered from Amazon (ASIN B006NTNGN0). You can check out the product at http://www.amazon.com/ JACKYLED-Switching-Power-Supply-Adapter/dp/B006NTNGN0. It comes with a switching power supply adapter that makes the connection to the air pump easier.

Make sure the filter can hold the balloon properly; if it's too big or too small it won't provide a good join.

The idea is illustrated in Figure 11-49.

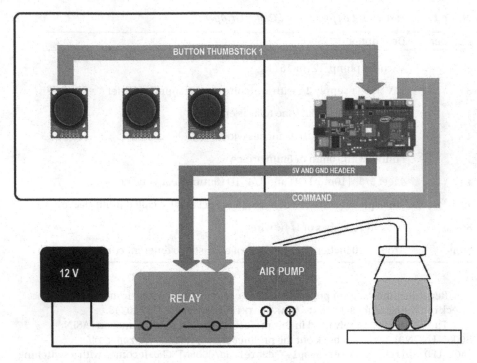

Figure 11-49. *How to control the gripper based in ground coffee*

The relay shield closes its contact, thereby allowing the 12V power supply to turn on the air pump. The air pump removes the air inside the gripper.

The relay shield needs 5V and you can use the terminal headers tagged as OUTPUT ALTERNATIVE 5V.

Figure 11-50 shows the air pump connected to the vinyl housing. The relay shield is already receiving 12V in one of its N.A. terminals. The vinyl house is connected to the right barb because it is the one that vacuums the air.

Figure 11-50. *Air pump connected to the relay and vinyl housing*

The relay shield used in this project has two relays, but you can use a shield with a single relay.

The next step is to create the gripper using the funnel, balloon, and coffee.

Preparing the Coffee Gripper

To prepare the gripper, you need to fill about 70% of the balloon with coffee. Use the funnel to insert the ground coffee, as shown in Figure 11-51.

Figure 11-51. *Filling the gripper with ground coffee*

Then insert the balloon in the funnel and pass its ribbon through the funnel, as shown in Figure 11-52 (left). You can use a screwdriver or some other object to help to pass the ribbon.

Put the little piece of filter fabric on the top of the ribbon and insert the vinyl housing, as shown in Figure 11-52 (right). This filter fabric socket will prevent the ground coffee from being sucked up by the pump.

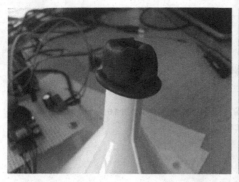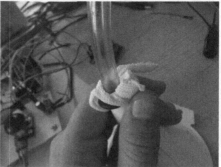

Figure 11-52. *The balloon ribbon (left) and the vinyl filter (right)*

If the vinyl housing is not tight enough, you can use a piece of tape to hold it in place.

A Sketch for the Coffee Gripper

Let's reuse RoboticArm.ino but make a small change to it. You'll use the first thumbstick declared as joystick1 to control the coffee gripper. The digital header pin 4 will command the relay. If you make these changes to Listing 11-3, you'll get the following:

```
void setup()
{
...
...
...

    pinMode(4, OUTPUT);
}
void loop()
{

    static boolean isGripperOpened = true, isCoffeeGripperActive = false;
...
...
...
  // in our example the button functionality of all button might be used
  // to manipulate the gripper
  if ((res2.buttonPressed) || (res3.buttonPressed))
  {

      if (isGripperOpened)
      {
          gripper.write(GRIPPER_CLOSED);
          isGripperOpened = false;
```

```
        }
        else
        {
            isGripperOpened = true;
            gripper.write(GRIPPER_OPENED);
        }

        // this small delay is to allow the gripper complete
        // it is task before a new movement
        delay(600);
    }

    if (res1.buttonPressed)
    {
        if (isCoffeeGripperActive == true)
        {
            isCoffeeGripperActive = false;
            digitalWrite(4, LOW);
        }
        else
        {
            isCoffeeGripperActive = true;
            digitalWrite(4, HIGH);
        }
    }
}
```

In the setup() function, the digital pin 4 was set to OUTPUT and it is used to command the relay shield. In the loop() function, a second static variable called isCoffeeGripperActive determines whether the air pump must be turned on. The second and third thumbsticks can control the mechanical gripper. On other hand, if the first thumbstick's button is pressed, the air pump is turned on due to the relay activation on pin 4. This means the coffee gripper is working.

In the code directory of this chapter, there is a sketch named **RoboticArmWithCoffeeGripper.ino** based on Listing 11-3 with these changes already made.

Running RoboticArmWithCoffeeGripper.ino

You might wonder why the code uses two grippers. If you created your "coffee gripper" based on the same material mentioned, it will weigh around 100g (0.22 pounds).

Considering the robotic arm was projected to raise objects around 200g (0.44 pounds) or less, it can hold the coffee gripper and catch small objects.

In other words, it is a gripper holding another gripper, which enables you to avoid new mechanical changes to the system.

Another important point—when you rest the coffee gripper over the object and turn on the air pump, wait at least four seconds before you move the arm because the air takes some time to leave the balloon and hold the object.

Figure 11-53 shows the mechanical gripper holding the coffee gripper. It's holding a mini screw driver.

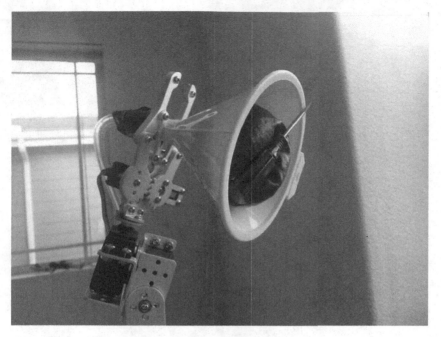

Figure 11-53. *The coffee gripper holding a mini screw driver*

Ideas for Improving this Project

There are many things you can do with your arm kit and one of them is create different manners to control the robotic arm. This chapter introduced a servo board controller, but you could use a different approach. For example, you could build an exoskeleton using wood and potentiometers in your joins (shoulder, elbow, and wrists). You could make the robotic arm reproduce your exact movements. A simple button in you palm could open and close the gripper.

You also can build your own robotic arm instead of ordering the kit, especially if you have a 3D printer or a laser cutter. There are several open projects on the Internet that will allow you to download the project and build the arm. Nothing prevents you from using the servo board controller to calculate which servos to use.

Summary

This chapter showed you how to create a robotic arm using several Arduino APIs.

You also learned a little bit about the robotic arm theory. You learned how to build your own robotic arm, evaluate which servos to use, determine the maximum load supported, and build a board that controls several servos. All this in order to create a simple human-machine interface.

Figure 25-15. ...

Ideas for Improving this Project

...

Summary

...

CHAPTER 12

■ ■ ■

Using an LTE Modem

Chapter 5 discussed how to use WiFi and Ethernet network adaptors to make Intel Galileo boards to connect to other devices and the Internet.

These adaptors are perfect if you need a stationary project like a board that controls your house or if you a building a mobile project that's limited to your WiFi coverage like a mini-robot that vacuums your floors.

What about building a drone that can fly long distances or a robot that walks around and monitors your neighborhood?

In these cases, Ethernet and WiFi adaptors are not applicable; you will need an efficient method to control your project remotely with a good coverage.

One possible solution is to use a modem that interfaces with Intel Galileo boards. Once the modem is properly configured to work with Intel Galileo and the connection between modem and carriers is established, the data exchange occurs like any other network adaptor.

Therefore, this chapter shows:

- How to physically connect an LTE modem to Intel Galileo.

- How to make Intel Galileo communicate with and configure the modem to camp in your preferable carrier provider.

- How to create a network adaptor in the Linux userspace context to make the data change possible.

This chapter contains the most expensive project of this book; LTE modems usually cost more than $100, but the same procedures used for the LTE modem can be used in 3G modems, which are more affordable (in the order of $65). If you have a 3G modem, the procedures mentioned in this chapter are applicable as well. The only difference is that you need to know the configuration required by your carrier, like the Access Point Names (APNs). You also need to have a data plan attributed to the SIM card that will be used in the modem tests.

This project teaches you how to create the network interface provided by the modem work and apply it to your project.

The LTE modem used in this chapter is module Intel XMM7160. You can also use Intel XMM7260 as well as any other LTE modem that is compliant with the 3GPP specifications. The 3GPP TS 27.007 V12.5.0 (2014-06) specifications are available from http://www.3gpp.org/DynaReport/27007.htm.

An Introduction to XMM7160 and XMM7260

The XMM 7160 and XMM 7260 modems were the first low-power consumption LTE modems with hardware and software entirely developed by Intel. Both modems are LTE (4G), and their differences are explained in Table 12-1.

Table 12-1. *Differences between the XMM 7160 and XMM 7260 Modems*

Feature	XMM 7160	XMM 7260
Launch year	2013	2014
LTE category	4	6
Peak downlink speed (downstream)	150 Mbits/s	300 Mbits/s
Supports 2G(GSM/Edge)	Yes	Yes
3G(HSPA+)	Yes	Yes
4G (LTE)	Yes	Yes
Bands supported	Quadband GSM/EDGE 8-band WCDMA 15-band LTE	Quadband GSM/EDGE 8-band WCDMA 21-band LTE

The modems are part of a capsulated module that provides mini-PCIe (mPCIe) or NGFF bus formats. If your laptop contains a 3G or 2G modem, there is a high probability of this modem being modular in one of the interfaces mentioned (mPCIe or NGFF) instead of built in, and you can replace your old 3G modem with a faster and great 4G modem like Intel XMM7160 or XMM7260. For this, you need to open your laptop as recommended by the service guide of your manufacturer and replace the modem manually. Once it's been replaced, you need to make sure you are using the right antennas and SIM card, and that the laptop has the Intel modem drivers properly installed. In this chapter, you learn how to integrate the modem with Intel Galileo boards.

The initial idea of XMM7160 and XMM7260 was to create a reference design modem that allows other manufacturers like Huawei and Foxconn to create their own modems based on Intel SoCs. However, there are laptops in the market using the XMM7160 or XMM7260 as end modems.

This chapter does not require you to use Intel modems; you can use any modem 2G/3G/4G that supports standards AT commands and can communicate using the cdc-acm interface, which will be explained later.

In summary, the Intel XMM modem was used in this chapter because it is a reference design and it works as a common model independently of a specific vendor. The AT commands discussed will work on any modem that uses Intel XMM as reference or on any modem that's compliant with 3GPP specifications.

Project Details

The interface used to communicate with modems is typically serial and AT commands are sent to the modem in order to set up the carrier configuration, search for a network signal, open the data channel, and establish the connection with other devices.

At the end of this configuration and connection process, the modem will provide a new interface to the Intel Galileo boards with an IP address, and all communication with the Internet and other devices is done through this new interface. In other words, the new IP behaves like any other adaptor, such as WiFi or Ethernet.

This project connects the modem to Intel Galileo using a USB OTG adaptor with a SIM card slot. The modem antennas are also selected in order to make sure it is possible to camp in the 4G network. Once the hardware configuration is ready, you must read the correct device driver in the Linux context in order to allow communication with the modem using a serial port.

With the modem device driver properly loaded and the serial port ready, a series of AT commands is sent to the modem in order to configure the modem with the correct APN, check the SIM card connection, and camp the modem in the network, thereby opening a data channel.

Finally, a PPP connection is established and an IP number that proves Internet access is provided.

Materials List

This project requires an LTE modem, a pair of antennas compatible with the modem and the LTE bands, a SIM card related to your carrier, and more, as listed in Table 12-2. Table 12-3 lists the optional materials.

Table 12-2. *Required Project Materials*

Quantity	Components
1	LTE modem card with mPCIe or NGFF bus. Intel XMM 7160 or Intel XMM 7260 is recommended.
1	USB OTG mPCIe or NGFF adaptor with SIM card slot (generic).
1	NGFF to mPCIe or mPCIe to NGFF adaptor (only if the OTG-USB adaptor contains an incompatible bus with the modem module used; read "The NGFF/mPCIe Adaptor").
2	LTE/UMTS antennas with SMA male connector (part number TG.30.8111) Apex Taoglas or GA-107 Taoglas (part number GA.107.201111).
1	Micro-SIM card with data plan already set (depends on your carrier/plan).
1	OTG-USB 2.0 adaptor with micro-USB male to USB A female, only if your board is Intel Galileo instead of Intel Galileo Gen 2. This is for physical connection only because OTG-USB is not supported in this case.
2	SMA bulkhead female/jack to IPEX MHF (part number 071113-04).
1	Serial debugger cable (FTDI if your board is Intel Galileo Gen2 or audio jack serial if it is Intel Galileo).

Table 12-3. Optional Materials for Incompatible Form Factors

Quantity	Components
1	NGFF to mPCIe or mPCIe to NGFF adaptor if your modem form factor does not match the connector type provided by the USB-OTG adaptor.
1	Ethernet cable or WiFi mPCIe if you want more than one terminal for debugging using an SSH connection.
1	Nano-to-micro-SIM card adaptor if your SIM card is not micro-SIM.
1	Scissors and tape or needle-nosed pliers (read "Connecting the Modem Card").

You might ask if Intel Galileo boards provide an mPCIe connector, why you simply do not connect the modem directly to Intel Galileo's mPCIe bus. Intel Galileo boards do not provide a built-in interface that allows you to read the SIM card and, without communication, the SIM card can't camp the modem in the LTE network.

Thus, the USB-OTG adaptor is necessary. It also must be able to provide a connector to your modem. Sometimes it is difficult to find this kind of adaptor that matches your modem. If your OTG-USB connection does not offer the same connection bus of your modem, you must include a second adaptor in the project in order to connect the modem to the OTG-USB adaptor.

The following conditions require extra materials:

- If your OTG USB adaptor with the SIM card slot contains an incompatible connector with your modem card. You will need a NGFF to mPCIe or mPCIe to NGFF adaptor.

- If your OTG USB adaptor contains a SIM card slot that's incompatible with your SIM card format. For example, if your OTG USB adaptor accepts micro-SIM cards, but your SIM card is nano, you will need a nano-SIM to micro-SIM adaptor.

- If you want to debug the modem with more than one shell, you might also need an Ethernet cable or a WiFi mPCIe card to open several shells using SSH.

Considerations Related to Antennas

There are several affordable antennas in the market; my preferable brand is Taoglas Limited. These antennas usually cost $10-20 and they are built in different form factors, including mounted in magnetic mountings that allow you to connect the antennas in any metallic structure, thereby avoiding holes, screws, or any other kind of apparatus.

This book recommends two LTE/UMTS antennas with an SMA male connector Apex Taoglas (part number TG.30.8111) or GA-107 Taoglas (part number GA.107.201111).

If you are using an LTE modem, the TG.30.8111 antenna is recommended. Note this antenna also offers GPS reception. That means if your modem supports a GPS sensor in the M2M module, you will be able to retrieve your location as well.

The XMM 7160 and XMM 7260 cards have a GPS module, but unfortunately, the AT commands are confidential and consequently I did not receive authorization to publish information about them in this book. If you are using a modem that is not LTE, I recommend the GA.107.201111 antenna, which includes magnetic mounting and reaches 3.5G camping in the best scenarios in 2.2GHz. It does not mean your LTE modem will not work with this antenna but the bands that you will camp will not provide the optimal download streaming.

The datasheets for both antennas are in the datasheet folder of this chapter. You also can find them at http://taoglas.com/images/product_images/original_images/ TG.30.8111.pdf and http://www.taoglas.com/images/product_images/original_ images/GA.107%20Magnetic%20Telematic%20Cellular%20Penta-band%20Antenna %20300410.pdf.

The cost of the recommended antennas is $12-16 each, plus shipping.

There are several other decent antennas with different form factors, but make sure the antennas can camp and get optimal performance.

Preparing the Hardware

This book uses the worst scenario as its example, in other words, it uses a XMM 7160 with an NGFF bus that's connected to an OTG-USB adaptor that accepts only mPCIe modems and a nano-SIM card that must be coupled to a micro-SIM card slot. Thus, a NGFF to mPCIe adaptor is included in this project and a nano-to-micro-SD card is used as well.

Of course, if your scenario is simpler, you don't need to follow all these steps.

Step 1: Preparing the SIM Card

The OTG-USB adaptor contains an mPCIe slot, as shown in Figure 12-1 and a micro-SIM card slot, as shown in Figure 12-2.

Figure 12-1. mPCIe to OTG-USB adaptor, top view

Figure 12-2. *mPCIe to OTG-USB adaptor, bottom view*

If your SIM card uses a micro-SIM form factor, simply insert your SIM in the bottom of the mPCIe-OTG adaptor. Otherwise, you need to use a SIM card adaptor to connect the SIM card to the mPCIe/OTG-USB adaptor. Figure 12-3 shows an example of a micro-SIM card adaptor used with a nano-SIM card.

Figure 12-3. *Nano-to-micro-SIM adaptor (1) and nano-SIM card (2)*

Just insert the nano-SIM and make sure the nano-SIM is completely tied and flat against the surface of the SIM adaptor. Then cut a piece of tape a little bit bigger than the SIM card adaptor and fasten it over the surface without contacts. Fold the tape into the borders. Figure 12-4 shows this procedure; note that the nano-SIM's contacts aren't covered by the tape.

Figure 12-4. *Inserting the nano-SIM and taping it to the adaptor*

Then insert the SIM adaptor to the mPCIe-OTG SIM card's slot, as shown in Figure 12-5.

Figure 12-5. *Connecting the SIM card*

You need to make sure the nano-SIM's contacts are properly touching the contacts of the SIM card slot. Otherwise, you will receive errors when trying to read the SIM card.

Step 2: The NGFF/mPCIe Adaptor

If your modem card's bus is compatible with your mPCIe to OTG-USB adaptor, move to Step 3. This step is unnecessary if you don't need to use adaptors. This chapter covers the worst-case scenario, so the equipment used is a modem card with NGFF format and an mPCIe to OTG/USB adaptor that forces you to use an NGFF to mPCIe adaptor, as shown in Figure 12-6.

Figure 12-6. *NGFF to mPCIe adaptor (left) and modem card (right)*

Connecting both devices, you will have the configuration shown in Figure 12-7.

Figure 12-7. *Modem card connected to the NGFF to mPCIe adaptor*

Step 3: Adapting the Modem Card

The modem card that's directly connected to the NGFF to mPCIe adaptor is connected to the mPCIe to OTG-USB adaptor, as shown in Figure 12-8. The red arrow on this figure shows the locker mechanism. If your modem is not using a NGFF to mPCIe adaptor, you will be able to lock the modem to this locker mechanism without any problem.

Figure 12-8. *Connecting the modem card to the mPCIe to OTG-USB adaptor*

However, if you are using the adaptor as described in the Step 2, there is a good chance that you will not be able to use the locker because the modem will not fit. In this case you have two options—remove the locker mechanism using needle-nose pliers and screw on the NGFF/mPCIe to the mPCIe/OTG-USB adaptor or simply tape the modem card, as shown in Figure 12-9.

Figure 12-9. *Taping the modem card to the mPCIe to USB-OTG adaptor*

Step 4: Connecting the Antennas

The modem card is provided by a mini RF connector, more precisely specified as I-Pex 20449-001E. You need to use the SMA bulkhead cables female/jack to IPEX MHF in order to connect the modem to the antennas.

Figure 12-10 shows the cables and gives you an idea how fragile they are.

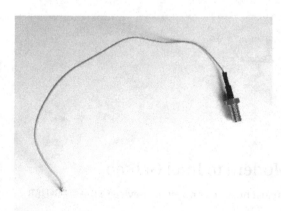

Figure 12-10. *SMA bulkhead female/jack to IPEX MHF*

Figure 12-11 shows the main antenna (MAIN) and the auxiliary (AUX) connected to the mini-RF connector.

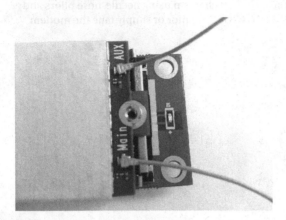

Figure 12-11. *Connecting the cable to the mini-RF connectors*

Using the SMA bulkhead cables female/jack IPEX MHF, you must connect to the antennas using its male SMA connectors, as shown in Figure 12-12.

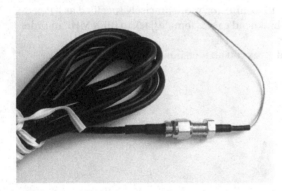

Figure 12-12. *Connecting the antennas*

Step 5: Connecting the Modem to Intel Galileo

If your board is Intel Galileo Gen 2, you just need to connect the device to the OTG-USB connector, as shown in Figure 12-13.

Figure 12-13. *Connecting the devices to Intel Galileo Gen 2*

However, if you are using Intel Galileo only, you need the OTG-USB 2.0 adaptor with micro-USB male to USB A female to connect the devices.

Power on your board. If you assembled everything as expected, you are ready to start!

The next section explains how to prepare the software and confirm that everything is working properly.

Preparing the Software

These next steps guide you through the process of checking if the hardware is working and setting up the modem.

Step 1: Checking the Modem

Connect the proper cable to debug the board, FTDI, or audio jack for Intel Galileo Gen 2 and Intel Galileo respectively, and open a Linux terminal shell as explained in Chapter 1.

Connect the modem as shown in Figure 12-13 and type the following command:

```
root@clanton:~# lsusb
Bus 002 Device 006: ID 1519:f214
Bus 001 Device 001: ID 1d6b:0001
Bus 002 Device 001: ID 1d6b:0002
```

The first device just after lsusb command is the modem and it means a new device was recognized in OTG-USB with the respective vendor and product IDs.

If you see only the last two devices, it means your mPCIe/OTG-USB adaptor is not working or you have a problem with your modem card.

Step 2: Loading the CDC-ACM Driver

Communication with modem is done using the CDC-ACM serial driver by sending and receiving responses of AT commands. By default the driver is not loaded during the board startup and you must therefore load the driver manually using the modprobe command.

Then type the following command:

```
root@clanton:~# modprobe cdc-acm
```

If your modem is connected as shown in Figure 12-13, you will see a series of messages saying the device is not a modem.

```
[  135.720822] cdc_acm 2-1:1.2: This device cannot do calls on its own.
It is not a modem.
[  135.738315] cdc_acm 2-1:1.2: ttyACM0: USB ACM device
[  135.748033] cdc_acm 2-1:1.4: This device cannot do calls on its own.
It is not a modem.
[  135.765753] cdc_acm 2-1:1.4: ttyACM1: USB ACM device
[  135.775111] cdc_acm 2-1:1.6: This device cannot do calls on its own.
It is not a modem.
[  135.792294] cdc_acm 2-1:1.6: ttyACM2: USB ACM device
[  135.801241] cdc_acm 2-1:1.8: This device cannot do calls on its own.
It is not a modem.
[  135.818946] cdc_acm 2-1:1.8: ttyACM3: USB ACM device
[  135.827775] cdc_acm 2-1:1.10: This device cannot do calls on its own.
It is not a modem.
[  135.845711] cdc_acm 2-1:1.10: ttyACM4: USB ACM device
[  135.860799] usbcore: registered new interface driver cdc_acm
[  135.866545] cdc_acm: USB Abstract Control Model driver for USB modems and
ISD N adapters
```

Do not worry! Your device is a modem and you will be able to use it as a USB modem without problems. You can just ignore these messages. If you want to get rid of such messages, you need to generate your own image after you change the .../linux/driverusb/class/cdc-acm.c driver code:

```
/*
 * USB driver structure.
 */

static const struct usb_device_id acm_ids[] = {
        /* quirky and broken devices */
        { USB_DEVICE(0x0870, 0x0001), /* Metricom GS Modem */
        .driver_info = NO_UNION_NORMAL, /* has no union descriptor */
        },
...
...
...
```

```
{ USB_DEVICE(YOUR_VENDOR_ID, YOUR_PRODUCT_ID) }, /* ADD YOUR MODEM
HERE !!!!!!*/

...
...
...

/* Motorola H24 HSPA module: */
{ USB_DEVICE(0x22b8, 0x2d91) }, /* modem                              */
{ USB_DEVICE(0x22b8, 0x2d92) }, /* modem              + diagnostics */
{ USB_DEVICE(0x22b8, 0x2d93) }, /* modem + AT port                   */
{ USB_DEVICE(0x22b8, 0x2d95) }, /* modem + AT port + diagnostics */

...
...
...
```

Once you've changed the code, recompile and flash your Intel Galileo or generate a new BSP SD card release, as explained in Chapter 2. Again, this is not mandatory. Do this only if you do not want to see these error messages.

At this point you should have at least one ttyACM device available. If it is the first time you have connected the modem and you did not block any ttyACM devices, the ttyACM0 should be available. You can check it with a simple ls command:

```
root@clanton:~# ls /dev/ttyACM0
/dev/ttyACM0
```

If the ttyACM0 is not found, you should see a message like this one:

```
root@clanton:~# ls /dev/ttyACM0
ls: /dev/ttyACM0: No such file or directory
```

The next step is to see if your modem card can respond to AT commands.

Step 3: Checking if the Modem Responds to AT Commands

At this point, the modem is connected, the driver is loaded, and the ttyACM device is available to receive the AT commands. Before you send the AT commands, you can program the ttyACM device to echo the commands and responses. In order to change the ttyACM setting, use the sty command as follows:

```
root@clanton:~# stty -F /dev/ttyACM0 -echo
```

The -F specifies the device to be changed, such as ttyACM0, and the -echo option enables the echo of input commands with their respective responses as well.

To visualize the behavior of the ttyACM device when an AT command is sent, you should keep watching the device's responses. You have two options at this point. If you have only one cable for debugging using serial, you can keep watching the ttyACM device in the background. For example:

```
root@clanton:~# cat /dev/ttyACM0 &
```

However, if you have an Ethernet cable or a WiFi card, you can open multiple Linux terminals using SSH, as explained in Chapter 5. This way, you can send the AT command in one shell and debug the ttyACM responses in the other. For the shell, you observe the ttyACM responses and do not need to run **cat** in background:

```
root@clanton:~# cat /dev/ttyACM0
```

Then send a simple AT command to the device using an **echo** command and check if you receive **OK** as a response:

```
root@clanton:~# echo "AT" > /dev/ttyACM0
root@clanton:~# AT

OK
```

As you can see, once the command is sent, the ttyACM0 replies. In this example, the modem successfully responded with OK, which means the system is operational and ready to be configured.

If you do not receive a response, check if you are sending the command to the right ttyACM device and re-check the hardware.

Step 4: Checking the SIM Card Connection

If you have a nano-SIM and you are using a nano-SIM to micro-SIM adaptor, you need to check if the nano-SIM is good enough to guarantee that the SIM card's contacts are properly contacting the pins of the SIM card slot.

To test if your SIM card responds to your AT commands, you need to send the following command:

```
root@clanton:~# AT+CPIN?
+CPIN: READY

OK
```

If you receive **+CPIN:READY** followed by **OK**, your SIM card is fine. If you receive **ERROR**, you need to re-check the SIM card; see the section entitled "Preparing the SIM Card" in this chapter.

Step 5: Configuring the APN and Attaching it to the Network

Every carrier has a gateway that allows the device to access the Internet. This gateway is called the Access Point Name (APN) and each carrier contains different APNs for different technologies, such as GPRS, 3G, and 4G.

Before you continue with this chapter, it is fundamental that you know the configuration that your SIM card needs. Thus, if you operator is AT&T, Verizon, Sprint, Claro, or any other, you need to find out how the APN must be set.

You have three options to discover the APN required by your card—search the Internet; call your provider and request support; or if your SIM card is the same one you used in your mobile device, you can simply check the configurations of your mobile device. Following the last option and assuming your device is Android, you would check the configuration as follows:

1. Go to the settings of your device.

2. Disable the WiFi and select More Networks. Then click on Mobile Networks, as shown in Figure 12-14.

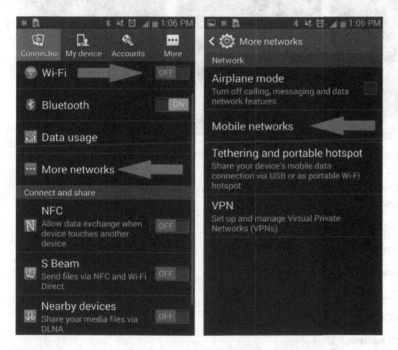

Figure 12-14. Disabling the WiFi and selecting mobile networks

You must disable here because some devices claim to be Android-compatible but aren't. In this case, the Google Play application is not available. When WiFi is ON, the devices camp in a very low band like 2G to reduce the battery consumption. If you check the APN in this case, an APN for 2G or 3G might be enabled instead of 4G because the network updates the configuration automatically and it's transparent to you. The next step is to select the APN of your carrier provider, check the APN name, provide a username and password if necessary, and then select the type of IP connection (IPv4 or IPv6) and the MCC and MNC numbers. For example, the red arrows in Figure 12-15 shows the AT&T APN settings in the United States.

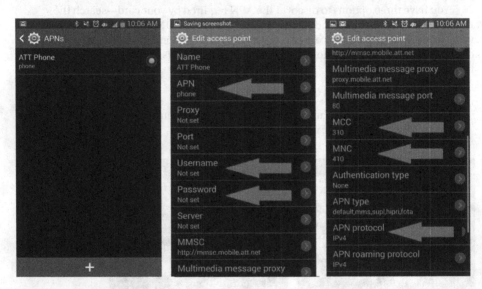

Figure 12-15. *Disabling the WiFi and selecting mobile networks*

As you can see in Figure 12-15, the AT&T 4G data connection requires the following settings:

- **APN:** Phone number

- **Username:** Not necessary

- **Password:** Not necessary

- **MCC:** 310

- **MNC:** 410

- **APN protocol:** IPv4

You can now configure your modem card. Before you program your modem, first check if the modem has some APN stored in it. You need to execute the echo AT+CGDCONT? command as follows:

```
root@clanton:~# echo "AT+CGDCONT?" > /dev/ttyACM0
+CGDCONT: 1,"IPV4V6","","",0,0
OK
```

The command returned says there is already an APN set in the modem card. It is empty. You can add a second one or you can replace this one.

To set the APN, you need to use the CGDCONT AT command, but send the APN name, the protocol type, and the APN number in the modem card list. Considering there is only one APN, if you want to include a second one, you just specify the number 2 in the command and include the second one. If you want to replace the APN already set, just use the number 1. This example includes a second APN so you can see how a modem card with several APNs is configured.

When strings are part of the arguments, the command's syntax can be a bit confusing. The strings must be between double quotes. For example, the command in this case will be:

AT+CGDCONT=2,"IP","phone"

Where 2 indicates that you are adding a second APN and preserving the first one, "IP" is because the protocol is IPv4, and "phone" is the APN name used by AT&T for 4G.

However, considering that you are sending the AT commands using echo in the Linux terminal, if you type echo without the double quotes, the modem will not understand the command. If the string requires double quotes, you must also differentiate between echo's double quotes and the string's double quotes. To do this, you need to use \".

With this in your mind, the previous command will be:

```
root@clanton:~# echo "AT+CGDCONT=2,\"IP\",\"phone\"" > /dev/ttyACM0
OK
```

The OK means the command was accepted and the APN was created. Recheck the list of APNs running using the **AT+CGDCONT?** command.

```
root@clanton:~# echo "AT+CGDCONT?" > /dev/ttyACM0
+CGDCONT: 1,"IPV4V6","","",0,0
+CGDCONT: 2,"IP","phone","0.0.0.0",0,0,0,0,0,0
OK
```

The APN was added successfully. The next step is to activate PDP in the network using the following command:

```
root@clanton:~# echo "AT+CGACT=1,2" > /dev/ttyACM0
OK
```

The number 1 means "**activate**" and 2 is the number of the profile index that you programmed with the AT+CGDCONT command. If you want to deactivate the PDP later, you can send the same command but use 0 instead of 1 as the first argument.

This command may take a few seconds, so don't expect an immediate response.

Once the network is activated, it is necessary to inform the MCC (Mobile Country Code) and MNC (Mobile Network Code), which together informs your network operator code using the AT+COPS command. The following example shows the AT&T network operator code in the United States:

```
root@clanton:~# echo "AT+COPS=1,2,\"310410\"" > /dev/ttyACM0
OK
```

The last AT command to be sent is AT+CGDATA and it's responsible for opening the data stream with the modem to establish a connection with the network. An LTE modem uses the M-RAW_IP mode; the 1 argument means "attach" as shown in the following example:

```
root@clanton:~# echo "AT+CGDATA=\"M-RAW_IP\",1" > /dev/ttyACM0
CONNECT
```

Step 6: Creating an IP Interface with pppd

At this point, your modem card is connected to the network provider and the data stream is open. It's time to establish an interface to the modem and acquire a local IP address. The IP will then be able to connect to the Internet, open sockets, create programs to exchange data with other devices, and other possibilities, such as the ones you learned about in Chapter 5.

The modem can have an IP in the network NAT but Intel Galileo must be able to have an IP that links to this connection. One of the solutions is to use the point-to-point Protocol (PPP) and create a link with the external IP to a local IP on Intel Galileo.

The SPI and BSP images created for Intel Galileo contain an application called pppd (Point to Point Protocol Daemon) that creates this local IP and establishes the link with the Internet.

You must first create a configuration file that will be used by pppd. This configuration file contains relevant information about how to communicate with the modem card. Transfer the configuration file in the code folder named **options-att** to your board in the **/etc/ppp/peers** directory. Listing 12-1 shows the contents of this file.

Listing 12-1. The options-att Configuration File

```
ttyACM0
115200
lock
crtscts
passive
novj
defaultroute
noipdefault
usepeerdns
```

```
noauth
hide-password
persist
holdoff 10
maxfail 5
debug
connect '/usr/sbin/chat -f /etc/ppp/isp_chat'
```

Each of these options is explained in the official documentation at
https://ppp.samba.org/pppd.html. They are adapted to Intel Galileo in the
following list:

- **ttyACM0:** Uses the serial port called ttyname to communicate
  with the peer.

- **115200:** A decimal number that's taken as the desired baud rate
  for the serial device. This is the maximum rate for the USB with
  Intel Galileo.

- **Lock:** Specifies that pppd should create a UUCP-style lock file for
  the serial device to ensure exclusive access to the device.

- **Crtscts:** Specifies that pppd should set the serial port to use
  hardware flow control using the RTS and CTS signals.

- **Passive:** Enables the passive option in the LCP (Link Control
  Protocol). With this option, pppd will attempt to initiate a
  connection. If no reply is received from the peer, pppd will wait
  passively for a valid LCP packet from the peer, instead of exiting,
  as it would without this option.

- **Novj:** Disables Van Jacobson-style TCP/IP header compression in
  both the transmit and the receive directions.

- **Defaultroute:** Adds a default route to the system routing
  tables, using the peer as the gateway, when IPCP negotiation
  is successfully completed. This entry is removed when the PPP
  connection is broken.

- **Noipdefault:** Disables the default behavior when no local IP
  address is specified, which is to determine (if possible) the local
  IP address from the hostname. With this option, the peer will have
  to supply the local IP address during IPCP negotiation (unless it
  specified explicitly on the command line or in an options file).

- **Usepeerdns:** Asks the peer for up to two DNS server addresses.
  The addresses supplied by the peer (if any) are passed to the
  /etc/ppp/ip-up script in the DNS1 and DNS2 environment
  variables, and the USEPEERDNS environment variable will be set
  to 1. In addition, pppd will create an /etc/ppp/resolv.conf file
  containing one or two nameserver lines with the address(es)
  supplied by the peer.

- **Noauth:** Does not require the peer to authenticate itself. This option is privileged.

- **hide-password:** When logging the contents of PAP packets, this option causes pppd to exclude the password string from the log. This is the default.

- **Persist:** Does not exit after a connection is terminated; instead tries to reopen the connection. The maxfail option still has an effect on persistent connections.

- **holdoff n:** Specifies how many seconds to wait before re-initiating the link after it terminates. This option has an effect only when the persist or demand options are used. The holdoff period is not applied if the link was terminated because it was idle.

- **maxfail n:** Terminates after n consecutive failed connection attempts. A value of 0 means no limit. The default value is 10 and you are using 5.

- **Debug:** Enables connection-debugging facilities. If this option is given, pppd will log the contents of all control packets sent or received in a readable form. The packets are logged through syslog with facility daemon and level debug. This information can be directed to a file by setting up /etc/syslog.conf appropriately.

- **connect "script":** Usually you need to do something to prepare the link before the PPP protocol can be started; for instance, with a dial-up modem, commands need to be sent to the modem to dial the appropriate phone number. This option specifies a command for pppd to execute (by passing it to a shell) before attempting to start PPP negotiation. The **chat** program is often useful here, as it provides a way to send arbitrary strings to a modem and respond to received characters.

In this example, the connect option is calling /usr/sbin/chat -f /etc/ppp/isp_chat. The isp_chat file is available in the code folder of this chapter and you need to copy this file into the /etc/ppp directory.

This option calls the program chat that receives and sends data through the userspace and the pppd daemon. The -f option specifies the script that the chat program must run before connecting.

Listing 12-2 shows the contents of the isp_chat script.

Listing 12-2. The isp_chat Script

```
''  ATD*99#
TIMEOUT 30
CONNECT
```

The chat script is a sequence of pairs of strings and expected strings. In general, it contains what is expected before something that must be sent.

If you use ' ' nothing is expected as a response and this is the case of the first line of the isp_chat script. The ' ' makes a pair with ATD*99## that represents the dial string to the modem.

In the second line, the script sets a TIMEOUT with the maximum of 30 seconds.

Finally the third line waits for the CONNECT and nothing is sent as a reply.

To get the local IP, it is necessary to run mknod and pppd commands.

```
root@clanton:~# mknod /dev/ppp c 108 0
```

The first mknod command is necessary only when you are using the regular Intel Galileo release and want to create a device that can open a file node to communicate with the modem using PPP. However, if you recompiled the kernel enabling all options to support PPP, your customized kernel will have the /dev/ppp device already available and ready to be used. In the c 108 0 option, the c stands for character file non-buffered, the and 108 and 0 refer to the major and minor numbers, respectively, used to identify the device. It's the same methodology used with any regular char driver. Then you call pppd as follows:

```
root@clanton:~# pppd call options-att debug nodetach
Script /usr/sbin/chat -t3 -f /etc/ppp/isp_chat finished (pid 1486), status
= 0x0
Serial connection established.
using channel 1
Using interface ppp0
Connect: ppp0 <--> /dev/ttyACM0
sent [LCP ConfReq id=0x1 <asyncmap 0x0> <magic 0xbcbf1398> <pcomp> <accomp>]
rcvd [LCP ConfReq id=0x1 <asyncmap 0x0> <magic 0x52181044> <pcomp> <accomp>]
sent [LCP ConfAck id=0x1 <asyncmap 0x0> <magic 0x52181044> <pcomp> <accomp>]
rcvd [LCP ConfAck id=0x1 <asyncmap 0x0> <magic 0xbcbf1398> <pcomp> <accomp>]
kernel does not support PPP filtering
[ 921.149938] PPP Deflate Compression module registered
sent [CCP ConfReq id=0x1 <deflate 15> <deflate(old#) 15>]
sent [IPCP ConfReq id=0x1 <addr 0.0.0.0> <ms-dns1 0.0.0.0> <ms-dns2
0.0.0.0>]
rcvd [LCP ProtRej id=0x2 80 fd 01 01 00 0c 1a 04 78 00 18 04]
Protocol-Reject for 'Compression Control Protocol' (0x80fd) received
sent [IPCP ConfReq id=0x1 <addr 0.0.0.0> <ms-dns1 0.0.0.0> <ms-dns2
0.0.0.0>]
rcvd [IPCP ConfReq id=0x1]
sent [IPCP ConfNak id=0x1 <addr 0.0.0.0>]
rcvd [IPCP ConfNak id=0x1 <addr 10.8.194.5> <ms-dns1 172.26.38.1> <ms-dns2
172.26.38.2>]
sent [IPCP ConfReq id=0x2 <addr 10.8.194.5> <ms-dns1 172.26.38.1> <ms-dns2
172.26.38.2>]
rcvd [IPCP ConfReq id=0x2 <addr 10.8.194.5>]
sent [IPCP ConfAck id=0x2 <addr 10.8.194.5>]
```

```
rcvd [IPCP ConfAck id=0x2 <addr 10.8.194.5> <ms-dns1 172.26.38.1> <ms-dns2
172.26.38.2>]
local IP address 10.8.194.5
remote IP address 10.8.194.5
primary DNS address 172.26.38.1
secondary DNS address 172.26.38.2
Script /etc/ppp/ip-up started (pid 1501)
Script /etc/ppp/ip-up finished (pid 1501), status = 0x0
```

This second pppd command will start the PPP daemon, calling an options-att file (do not worry, you will learn about this later) in debug mode. nodetach means the pppd will not detach until you or any other input device asks to kill it. For example, if you press Ctrl+C, you will kill the daemon.

After a few seconds, the Internet ppp0 will be available with a local IP.

Step 7: Testing the Internet Connection

Everything is in place at this moment—your pppd is running, you have a local IP, and the modem is camped with the data streaming opened. It's now time to test your Internet connection.

Try to ping a server to check if the interface works.

```
root@clanton:~# ping www.google.com
PING www.google.com (74.125.239.145): 56 data bytes
64 bytes from 74.125.239.145: seq=0 ttl=54 time=49.897 ms
64 bytes from 74.125.239.145: seq=1 ttl=54 time=78.188 ms
64 bytes from 74.125.239.145: seq=2 ttl=54 time=78.101 ms
```

The command shows that the Internet access is operational and the modem is ready to exchange data though the internet.

At this point, you are ready to communicate through your modem card. You are ready to send your robot, your quad-copter, or the mobile project to remote distances and control it.

You can also use this connection in the home-automation project explained in Chapter 9.

Testing the Internet Bandwidth

There are several mechanisms for testing your Internet bandwidth, and each mechanism has its proponents and detractors. It really depends on many variables.

To test bandwidth with Intel Galileo, use a Python script called speedtest-cli.py that you can download from https://pypi.python.org/pypi/speedtest-cli.

This scripts test your Internet bandwidth using the web site www.speedtest.net. Python must be available in your Intel Galileo image. In this case, if you are using BSP SD card images, the regular image contains Python packages.

Basically it tries to reach the best and optimal servers based on your IP location and executes the download and upload tests.

The procedure is very simple:

1. Make sure your modem is set and you have a local IP available according to the procedure described in the section entitled "Testing the Internet Connection" in this chapter.

2. Go to https://pypi.python.org/pypi/speedtest-cli and download the latest Python version.

3. Extract the contents of the package using tar -zxvf <package_file_name> if you are using Linux or OSX. Use Winzip or 7Zip if you are using Windows.

4. Among the files extracted, there is a file named speedtest_cli.py that must be transferred to your Intel Galileo. If you do not know how to transfer files, see Chapter 5 and choose the best alternative for you.

5. Simply execute the script using Python:

   root@clanton:~/speedtest# **python speedtest_cli.py**

6. As a result, this script will show the speed of downloading and uploading.

Why Aren't the Download/Upload Bandwidths Optimal?

In real LTE networks, will you never be able to reach the max of 100 Mbps because there are several factors that interfere with the performance. This includes latency issues, number of users occupying the data channel of different bands, the quality of the service provider, and many other variables.

If you are using AT&T in California with an LTE modem and the correct antenna, you might reach an average download speed of 7 to 12 Mbps and an upload speed of 4 to 7 Mbps.

Ideas for Improving the Project

The following sections discuss a couple of ways to improve this project.

Improving the Chat Script

The AT commands in this chapter are passed manually, and the main reason for this is to help you to check if your hardware is OK and if the settings allow you to connect to your carrier network for data connection.

It does not mean that all AT commands must be manually typed, because as you read in the section entitled, "Creating an IP Interface with pppd," the isp_chat listed in Listing 12-2 accepts AT commands.

Once your know all the AT commands with their specific arguments for making your modem work, you simply need to mode these AT commands to the script.

For example, the AT commands used to set up the AT&T APN in this chapter are as follows:

```
AT+CPIN?
+CPIN: READY
OK

AT+CGDCONT=2,"IP","phone"
OK

AT+CGACT=1,2
OK

AT+COPS=1,2,"310410"
OK

AT+CGDATA="M-RAW_IP",1
CONNECT
```

You simply include the respective AT command in the isp_chat script, as shown in Listing 12-3.

Listing 12-3. The isp_att_chat Script

```
OK  AT+CPIN?
OK  AT+CGDCONT=2,"IP","phone"
OK  AT+CGACT=1,2
OK  AT+COPS=1,2,"310410"
''  AT+CGDATA="M-RAW_IP",1
TIMEOUT 10
''  ATD*99#
TIMEOUT 30
CONNECT
```

Then change Listing 12-1 in order to call the isp_att_chat script.

```
ttyACM0
115200
lock
crtscts
passive
novj
defaultroute
```

```
noipdefault
usepeerdns
noauth
hide-password
persist
holdoff 10
maxfail 5
debug
connect '/usr/sbin/chat -f /etc/ppp/isp_att_chat'
```

Run the pppd command again:

```
root@clanton:~# pppd call options-att debug nodetach
```

This way, none of the AT commands have to be invoked from the terminal.

Loading the cdc-acm Driver Automatically

Instead of having to invoke the modprobe cdc-acm manually every time your board boots, you can load it automatically. The procedure is very simple if you are using BSP SD card images:

1. Connect your FDTI cable or serial jack cable and open the Linux terminal.

2. Enter the /etc/modules-load.quark directory by typing:

    ```
    root@clanton:~# cd /etc/modules-load.quark
    ```

3. If your board is Intel Galileo Gen 2, edit the galileo_gen2.conf file; otherwise, you need to edit galileo.conf if your board is Intel Galileo. You can edit directly in the Linux terminal using the vi editor or any other method. These files represent a configuration file with all the modules that must be loaded just after the boot.

4. Insert the cdc-acm line into the configuration file.

    ```
    pch-udc
    g-serial vendor=0x8086 product=0xBABE
    stmmac
    ehci_hcd
    ohci_hcd
    ehci-pci
    usb_storage
    gpio_sch
    intel_qrk_gip
    gpio-pca953x
    ```

```
pca9685
at24
i2c_dev
spidev
spi-pxa2xx-pci
spi-pxa2xx
industrialio
adc1x8s102
iwlwifi
btusb
usbhid
evdev
sdhci-pci
mmc-block
cdc-acm
```

5. Reboot the board by typing reboot and pressing Enter.

If you are using custom SPI images, the procedure is very similar but you need to change this in the yocto build. In this case the configuration files galileo.conf and galileo_gen2.conf are present in the directory .../meta-clanton_v1.0.3/meta-clanton-bsp/recipes-kernel/quark-init/files. Do the same changes mentioned in Step 4, rebuild your SPI image, and flash your Intel Galileo with your new custom SPI image.

After the boot, the cdc-acm drive must be loaded automatically. You can check it by typing lsmod into the Linux terminal shell.

Summary

This chapter explains a solution based in modem cards for applications that require large-scale mobility when WiFi coverage is not enough.

It also explains how to connect modem cards to Intel Galileo boards by using adaptors, how to use the SIM card, what to do when there's a form factor adaptation, and how to select and connect the antennas.

In terms of software, this chapter introduced the modem setup using AT commands, explained how to establish a local IP using the PPP protocol, and covered the scripts and utilities needed to connect to the Internet.

APPENDIX A

■ ■ ■

Intel Galileo I/O and Muxing

Table A-1 presents the I/O mappings for Intel Galileo. This table is the official port I/O mapping provided by Intel and also can be found accessing "https://communities.intel.com/docs/DOC-21920".

Table A-1. *Intel Galileo I/O Mappings*

Pin	Source	GPIO Pin	Linux	PWM Linux	Int	Dir	Muxed with
IO0	Cypr	GPORT4_BIT6_PWM2	50	N/A	-	BI	UART0_RXD
IO1	Cypr	GPORT4_BIT7_PWM0	51	N/A	-	BI	UART0_TXD
IO2	SoC (Cypr)	GPIO<6> (GPORT2_BIT0_PWM6_A3)	14 (32*)	-	0	BI	-
IO3	SoC (Cypr)	GPIO<7> (GPORT0_BIT2_PWM3)	15 (18*)	3	1	BI	(PWM)
IO4	Cypr	GPORT1_BIT4_PWM6	28		-	BI	-
IO5	Cypr	GPORT0_BIT1_PWM5	17	5	-	BI	(PWM)
IO6	Cypr	GPORT1_BIT0_PWM6	24	6	-	BI	(PWM)
IO7	Cypr	GPORT1_BIT3_PWM0	27		-	BI	-
IO8	Cypr	GPORT1_BIT2_PWM2	26		-	BI	-
IO9	Cypr	GPORT0_BIT3_PWM1	19	1	-	BI	(PWM)
IO10	Cypr	GPORT0_BIT0_PWM7	16	7	-	BI	(PWM) SPI1_SS_B
IO11	Cypr	GPORT1_BIT1_PWM4	25	4	-	BI	(PWM) SPI1_MOSI

IO12	Cypr	GPORT3_BIT2_PWM3	38	-	BI	SPI1_MISO
IO13	Cypr	GPORT3_BIT3_PWM1	39	-	BI	SPI1_SCK
IO14	Cypr	GPORT4_BIT0_PWM6	44	-	BI	AD7298:VIN0
IO15	Cypr	GPORT4_BIT1_PWM4	45	-	BI	AD7298:VIN1
IO16	Cypr	GPORT4_BIT2_PWM2	46	-	BI	AD7298:VIN2
IO17	Cypr	GPORT4_BIT3_PWM0	47	-	BI	AD7298:VIN3
IO18	Cypr	GPORT4_BIT4_PWM6	48	-	BI	AD7298:VIN4
IO19	Cypr	GPORT4_BIT5_PWM4	49	-	BI	AD7298:VIN5

Following are acronyms for Table A-1:

- **Cypr:** Crypress GPIO Expander
- **BI:** Bidirectional
- **I:** Input without pull-up off
- **Int:** Interruption pins
- **Dir:** Direction

Table A-2 presents the Mux Selectors for Intel Galileo.

Table A-2. *Intel Galileo Muxing*

Mux Selector		Cypress GPIO pin	Linux GPIO ID	Dir	Initial Setup
0	**1**				
UART0_RXD	IO0	GPORT3_BIT4_PWM7	40	O	U
UART0_TXD	IO1	GPORT3_BIT5_PWM5	41	O	U
SPI1_SS_B	IO10	GPORT3_BIT6_PWM3	42	O	U
SPI1_MOSI	IO11	GPORT3_BIT7_PWM1	43	O	U
SPI1_MISO	IO12	GPORT5_BIT2_PWM3	54	O	U
SPI1_SCK	IO13	GPORT5_BIT3_PWM1	55	O	U
AD7298:VIN0	IO14	GPORT3_BIT1_PWM5	37	O	LOW
AD7298:VIN1	IO15	GPORT3_BIT0_PWM7	36	O	LOW
AD7298:VIN2	IO16	GPORT0_BIT7_PWM1	23	O	LOW
AD7298:VIN3	IO17	GPORT0_BIT6_PWM3	22	O	LOW
AD7298:VIN4	IO18	GPORT0_BIT5_PWM5	21	O	LOW
AD7298:VIN5	IO19	GPORT0_BIT4_PWM7	20	O	LOW
IO2 via SoC GPIO<6>	IO2 via Cypress GPORT2_BIT0_PWM6	GPORT1_BIT7_PWM0	31	O	U
IO3 via SoC GPIO<7>	IO3 via Cypress GPORT0_BIT2_PWM3	GPORT1_BIT6_PWM2	30	O	U
I2C	(AD7298:VIN4 or IO18) and (AD7298:VIN5 or IO19)	GPORT1_BIT5_PWM4	29	O	HIGH

Following are acronyms for Table A-2:

- **O:** Output

- **Dir:** Direction

- **U:** Undefined

The following commands demonstrated some examples how to use the table using Linux terminal shell:

- Setting IO7 as GPIO output:

```
echo -n "27" > /sys/class/gpio/export
echo -n "out" > /sys/class/gpio/gpio27/direction
echo 0 > /sys/class/gpio/gpio27/value # will set OUTPUT as LOW
echo 1 > /sys/class/gpio/gpio27/value # will set OUTPUT as HIGH
```

- Setting IO7 as GPIO input:

```
echo -n "27" > /sys/class/gpio/export
echo -n "in" > /sys/class/gpio/gpio27/direction
cat /sys/class/gpio/gpio27/value
```

■ ■ ■

Intel Galileo Gen 2 I/O and Muxing

Table B-1 provides the I/O mappings and Muxing for Intel Galileo Gen 2. This table was created by Emutex, one of Intel's partners (see www.emutexlabs.com).

Table B-1. *Intel Galileo Gen 2 I/O Mappings and Muxing*

Shield pin	Function	Linux	Shifter GPIO	22K PullUp GPIO	Pin Mux 1 GPIO	Pin Mux 2 GPIO	Interrupt modes
IO0	UART0 RX	ttyS0	gpio32	gpio33	-	-	-
	GPIO	gpio11			-	-	L/H/R/F
IO1	UART0 TX	ttyS0	gpio28	gpio29	gpio45 (H)	-	-
	GPIO	gpio12			gpio45 (L)	-	L/H/R/F
IO2	UART1 RX	ttyS1	gpio34	gpio35	gpio77 (H)	-	-
	GPIO	gpio13			gpio77 (L)	-	L/H/R/F
	GPIO	gpio61	-		gpio77 (L)	-	R/F/B
IO3	UART1 TX	ttyS1	gpio16	gpio17	gpio76(H)	-	-
	GPIO	gpio14			gpio76(L)	gpio64(L)	L/H/R/F
	PWM	pwm1			gpio76(L)	gpio64(H)	-
	GPIO	gpio62	-		gpio76(L)	gpio64(L)	R/F/B
IO4	GPIO	gpio6	gpio36	gpio37	-	-	R/F/B
IO5	GPIO	gpio0	gpio18	gpio19	gpio66(L)	-	R/F/B
	PWM	pwm3			gpio66(H)	-	-

IO6	GPIO	gpio1	gpio20	gpio21	gpio68(L)	-	R/F/B
	PWM	pwm5	-	-	gpio68(H)	-	-
IO7	GPIO	gpio38	-	gpio39	-	-	-
IO8	GPIO	gpio40	-	gpio41	-	-	-
IO9	GPIO	gpio4	gpio22	gpio23	gpio70(L)	-	R/F/B
	PWM	pwm7	-	-	gpio70(L)	-	-
IO10	GPIO	gpio10	gpio26	gpio27	gpio74(L)	-	L/H/R/F
	PWM	pwm11	-	-	gpio74(H)	-	-
IO11	GPIO	gpio5	gpio24	gpio25	gpio44(L)	gpio72(L)	R/F/B
	SPI MOSI	spidev1.0	-	-	gpio44(H)	gpio72(L)	-
	PWM	pwm9	-	-	-	gpio72(H)	-
IO12	GPIO	gpio15	gpio42	gpio43	-	-	L/H/R/F
	SPI MISO	spidev1.0	-	-	-	-	-
IO13	GPIO	gpio7	gpio30	gpio31	gpio46(L)	-	R/F/B
	SPI SCK	spidev1.0	-	-	gpio46(H)	-	-

(continued)

Table B-1. (*continued*)

Shield pin	Function	Linux	Shifter GPIO	22K PullUp GPIO	Pin Mux 1 GPIO	Pin Mux 2 GPIO	Interrupt modes
IO14	GPIO	gpio48	-	gpio49	-	-	R/F/B
	ADC A0	in_voltage0_raw					-
IO15	GPIO	gpio50	-	gpio51	-	-	R/F/B
	ADC A1	in_voltage1_raw					-
IO16	GPIO	gpio52	-	gpio53	-	-	R/F/B
	ADC A2	in_voltage2_raw					-
IO17	GPIO	gpio54	-	gpio55	-	-	R/F/B
	ADC A3	in_voltage3_raw					-
IO18	GPIO	gpio56	-	gpio57	gpio60(H)	gpio78(H)	R/F/B
	ADC A4	in_voltage4_raw			gpio60(H)	gpio78(L)	-
	I2C SDA	i2c-0			gpio60(L)	-	-
IO19	GPIO	gpio58	-	gpio59	gpio60(H)	gpio79(H)	R/F/B
	ADC A4	in_voltage5_raw			gpio60(H)	gpio79(L)	-
	I2C SCL	i2c-0			gpio60(L)	-	-

The follow are acronyms listed in the column **"Pin Mux 1 GPIO"** and **"Pin Mux 2 GPIO"** of table B-1 means:

- L: GPIO configured as OUPUT and level LOW (0)
- H: GPIO configured as OUTPUT and level HIGH (1)

The following are acronyms listed in the column **"Interrupt Modes"** of Table B-1:

- L: low-level
- H: high-level
- R: rising-edge
- F: falling-edge
- B: both edges

The following commands demonstrated some examples how to use the table using Linux terminal shell:

- Setting IO1 as GPIO output:

```
echo -n "28" > /sys/class/gpio/export
echo -n "29" > /sys/class/gpio/export
echo -n "12" > /sys/class/gpio/export
echo 0 > /sys/class/gpio/gpio28/value
echo 0 > /sys/class/gpio/gpio29/value
echo out > /sys/class/gpio/gpio12/direction
echo 0 > /sys/class/gpio/gpio12/value # will set OUTPUT
as LOW
echo 1 > /sys/class/gpio/gpio12/value # will set OUTPUT
as HIGH
```

- Setting IO1 as GPIO input (no pull-up):

```
echo -n "28" > /sys/class/gpio/export
echo -n "29" > /sys/class/gpio/export
echo -n "12" > /sys/class/gpio/export
echo -n "45" > /sys/class/gpio/export
echo 0 > /sys/class/gpio/gpio45/value
echo 1 > /sys/class/gpio/gpio28/value
echo 0 > /sys/class/gpio/gpio29/value
echo 12 > /sys/class/gpio/export
echo in > /sys/class/gpio/gpio12/direction
cat /sys/class/gpio/gpio12/value
```

- Setting IO1 as GPIO input (with pull-up):

```
echo -n "29" > /sys/class/gpio/export
echo -n "12" > /sys/class/gpio/export
echo 1 > /sys/class/gpio/gpio29/value
cat /sys/class/gpio/gpio12/value
```

APPENDIX C

■ ■ ■

Video Capturing

Listing C-1 provides the complete code discussed in the "A Program for Capturing Video" section in Chapter 7. The parts required by webcam C270 are highlighted in bold.

Listing C-1. galileo_video_capture.c

```
/*
 *  V4L2 video capture example
 *
 *  This program can be used and distributed without restrictions.
 *
 *      This program is provided with the V4L2 API
 * see http://linuxtv.org/docs.php for more information
 */

#include <stdio.h>
#include <stdlib.h>
#include <string.h>
#include <assert.h>

#include <getopt.h>             /* getopt_long() */

#include <fcntl.h>              /* low-level i/o */
#include <unistd.h>
#include <errno.h>
#include <sys/stat.h>
#include <sys/types.h>
#include <sys/time.h>
#include <sys/mman.h>
#include <sys/ioctl.h>
```

```
#include <linux/videodev2.h>

#define CLEAR(x) memset(&(x), 0, sizeof(x))

enum io_method {
        IO_METHOD_READ,
        IO_METHOD_MMAP,
        IO_METHOD_USERPTR,
};

struct buffer {
        void    *start;
        size_t  length;
};

static char             *dev_name;
static enum io_method   io = IO_METHOD_MMAP;
static int              fd = -1;
struct buffer           *buffers;
static unsigned int     n_buffers;
static int              out_buf;
static int              force_format;
static int              frame_count = 70;

static void errno_exit(const char *s)
{
        fprintf(stderr, "%s error %d, %s\n", s, errno, strerror(errno));
        exit(EXIT_FAILURE);
}

static int xioctl(int fh, int request, void *arg)
{
        int r;

        do {
                r = ioctl(fh, request, arg);
        } while (-1 == r && EINTR == errno);

        return r;
}

static void process_image(const void *p, int size)
{

        // keep saving frame by frame
        if (out_buf)
                fwrite(p, size, 1, stdout);
```

```
        fflush(stderr);
        fprintf(stderr, ".");
        fflush(stdout);

}

static int read_frame(void)
{
        struct v4l2_buffer buf;
        unsigned int i;

        switch (io) {
        case IO_METHOD_READ:
          printf("IO_METHOD_READ\n");
                if (-1 == read(fd, buffers[0].start, buffers[0].length)) {
                        switch (errno) {
                        case EAGAIN:
                                return 0;

                        case EIO:
                                /* Could ignore EIO, see spec. */

                                /* fall through */

                        default:
                                errno_exit("read");
                        }
                }

                process_image(buffers[0].start, buffers[0].length);
                break;

        case IO_METHOD_MMAP:
          printf("IO_METHOD_MMAP\n");
                CLEAR(buf);

                buf.type = V4L2_BUF_TYPE_VIDEO_CAPTURE;
                buf.memory = V4L2_MEMORY_MMAP;

                if (-1 == xioctl(fd, VIDIOC_DQBUF, &buf)) {
                        switch (errno) {
                        case EAGAIN:
                          printf("EAGAIN\n");
                                return 0;
```

```
                                case EIO:
                                   printf("EIO\n");
                                           /* Could ignore EIO, see spec. */

                                           /* fall through */

                                default:
                                   printf("default\n");
                                           errno_exit("VIDIOC_DQBUF");
                                }
                        }

                assert(buf.index < n_buffers);

                process_image(buffers[buf.index].start, buf.bytesused);

                if (-1 == xioctl(fd, VIDIOC_QBUF, &buf))
                        errno_exit("VIDIOC_QBUF");
                break;

        case IO_METHOD_USERPTR:
                CLEAR(buf);

                buf.type = V4L2_BUF_TYPE_VIDEO_CAPTURE;
                buf.memory = V4L2_MEMORY_USERPTR;

                if (-1 == xioctl(fd, VIDIOC_DQBUF, &buf)) {
                        switch (errno) {
                        case EAGAIN:
                                return 0;

                        case EIO:
                                /* Could ignore EIO, see spec. */

                                /* fall through */

                        default:
                                errno_exit("VIDIOC_DQBUF");
                        }
                }

                for (i = 0; i < n_buffers; ++i)
                        if (buf.m.userptr == (unsigned long)buffers[i].start
                            && buf.length == buffers[i].length)
                                break;
```

```
                assert(i < n_buffers);

                process_image((void *)buf.m.userptr, buf.bytesused);

                if (-1 == xioctl(fd, VIDIOC_QBUF, &buf))
                        errno_exit("VIDIOC_QBUF");
                break;
        }

        return 1;
}

static void mainloop(void)
{
        unsigned int count;

        count = frame_count;

        while (count-- > 0) {
                for (;;) {
                        fd_set fds;
                        struct timeval tv;
                        int r;

                        FD_ZERO(&fds);
                        FD_SET(fd, &fds);

                        /* Timeout. */
                        tv.tv_sec = 2;
                        tv.tv_usec = 0;

                        r = select(fd + 1, &fds, NULL, NULL, &tv);

                        if (-1 == r) {
                                if (EINTR == errno)
                                        continue;
                                errno_exit("select");
                        }

                        if (0 == r) {
                                fprintf(stderr, "select timeout\n");
                                exit(EXIT_FAILURE);
                        }
```

```
                                if (read_frame())
                                        break;
                                /* EAGAIN - continue select loop. */
                        }
                }
        }

static void stop_capturing(void)
{
        enum v4l2_buf_type type;

        switch (io) {
        case IO_METHOD_READ:
                /* Nothing to do. */
                break;

        case IO_METHOD_MMAP:
        case IO_METHOD_USERPTR:
                type = V4L2_BUF_TYPE_VIDEO_CAPTURE;
                if (-1 == xioctl(fd, VIDIOC_STREAMOFF, &type))
                        errno_exit("VIDIOC_STREAMOFF");
                break;
        }
}

static void start_capturing(void)
{
        unsigned int i;
        enum v4l2_buf_type type;

        switch (io) {
        case IO_METHOD_READ:
                /* Nothing to do. */
                break;

        case IO_METHOD_MMAP:
                for (i = 0; i < n_buffers; ++i) {
                        struct v4l2_buffer buf;

                        CLEAR(buf);
                        buf.type = V4L2_BUF_TYPE_VIDEO_CAPTURE;
                        buf.memory = V4L2_MEMORY_MMAP;
                        buf.index = i;

                        if (-1 == xioctl(fd, VIDIOC_QBUF, &buf))
                                errno_exit("VIDIOC_QBUF");
                }
```

```
                        type = V4L2_BUF_TYPE_VIDEO_CAPTURE;
                        if (-1 == xioctl(fd, VIDIOC_STREAMON, &type))
                                errno_exit("VIDIOC_STREAMON");

                break;

        case IO_METHOD_USERPTR:
                for (i = 0; i < n_buffers; ++i) {
                        struct v4l2_buffer buf;

                        CLEAR(buf);
                        buf.type = V4L2_BUF_TYPE_VIDEO_CAPTURE;
                        buf.memory = V4L2_MEMORY_USERPTR;
                        buf.index = i;
                        buf.m.userptr = (unsigned long)buffers[i].start;
                        buf.length = buffers[i].length;

                        if (-1 == xioctl(fd, VIDIOC_QBUF, &buf))
                                errno_exit("VIDIOC_QBUF");
                }
                type = V4L2_BUF_TYPE_VIDEO_CAPTURE;
                if (-1 == xioctl(fd, VIDIOC_STREAMON, &type))
                        errno_exit("VIDIOC_STREAMON");
                break;
        }
}

static void uninit_device(void)
{
        unsigned int i;

        switch (io) {
        case IO_METHOD_READ:
                free(buffers[0].start);
                break;

        case IO_METHOD_MMAP:
                for (i = 0; i < n_buffers; ++i)
                        if (-1 == munmap(buffers[i].start,
                        buffers[i].length))
                                errno_exit("munmap");
                break;
```

```
        case IO_METHOD_USERPTR:
                for (i = 0; i < n_buffers; ++i)
                        free(buffers[i].start);
                break;
        }

        free(buffers);
}

static void init_read(unsigned int buffer_size)
{
        buffers = calloc(1, sizeof(*buffers));

        if (!buffers) {
                fprintf(stderr, "Out of memory\n");
                exit(EXIT_FAILURE);
        }

        buffers[0].length = buffer_size;
        buffers[0].start = malloc(buffer_size);

        if (!buffers[0].start) {
                fprintf(stderr, "Out of memory\n");
                exit(EXIT_FAILURE);
        }
}

static void init_mmap(void)
{
        struct v4l2_requestbuffers req;

        CLEAR(req);

        req.count = 5;
        req.type = V4L2_BUF_TYPE_VIDEO_CAPTURE;
        req.memory = V4L2_MEMORY_MMAP;

        if (-1 == xioctl(fd, VIDIOC_REQBUFS, &req)) {
                if (EINVAL == errno) {
                        fprintf(stderr, "%s does not support "
                                        "memory mapping\n", dev_name);
                        exit(EXIT_FAILURE);
                } else {
                        errno_exit("VIDIOC_REQBUFS");
                }
        }
```

```
        if (req.count < 2) {
                fprintf(stderr, "Insufficient buffer memory on %s\n",
                        dev_name);
                exit(EXIT_FAILURE);
        }

        buffers = calloc(req.count, sizeof(*buffers));

        if (!buffers) {
                fprintf(stderr, "Out of memory\n");
                exit(EXIT_FAILURE);
        }

        for (n_buffers = 0; n_buffers < req.count; ++n_buffers) {
                struct v4l2_buffer buf;

                CLEAR(buf);

                buf.type        = V4L2_BUF_TYPE_VIDEO_CAPTURE;
                buf.memory      = V4L2_MEMORY_MMAP;
                buf.index       = n_buffers;

                if (-1 == xioctl(fd, VIDIOC_QUERYBUF, &buf))
                        errno_exit("VIDIOC_QUERYBUF");

                buffers[n_buffers].length = buf.length;
                buffers[n_buffers].start =
                        mmap(NULL /* start anywhere */,
                                buf.length,
                                PROT_READ | PROT_WRITE /* required */,
                                MAP_SHARED /* recommended */,
                                fd, buf.m.offset);

                if (MAP_FAILED == buffers[n_buffers].start)
                        errno_exit("mmap");
        }
}

static void init_userp(unsigned int buffer_size)
{
        struct v4l2_requestbuffers req;

        CLEAR(req);

        req.count  = 4;
        req.type   = V4L2_BUF_TYPE_VIDEO_CAPTURE;
        req.memory = V4L2_MEMORY_USERPTR;
```

```
        if (-1 == xioctl(fd, VIDIOC_REQBUFS, &req)) {
                if (EINVAL == errno) {
                        fprintf(stderr, "%s does not support "
                                "user pointer i/o\n", dev_name);
                        exit(EXIT_FAILURE);
                } else {
                        errno_exit("VIDIOC_REQBUFS");
                }
        }

    buffers = calloc(4, sizeof(*buffers));

    if (!buffers) {
            fprintf(stderr, "Out of memory\n");
            exit(EXIT_FAILURE);
    }

    for (n_buffers = 0; n_buffers < 4; ++n_buffers) {
            buffers[n_buffers].length = buffer_size;
            buffers[n_buffers].start = malloc(buffer_size);

            if (!buffers[n_buffers].start) {
                    fprintf(stderr, "Out of memory\n");
                    exit(EXIT_FAILURE);
            }
    }
}

static void init_device(void)
{
    struct v4l2_capability cap;
    struct v4l2_cropcap cropcap;
    struct v4l2_crop crop;
    struct v4l2_format fmt;
    unsigned int min;

    if (-1 == xioctl(fd, VIDIOC_QUERYCAP, &cap)) {
            if (EINVAL == errno) {
                    fprintf(stderr, "%s is no V4L2 device\n",
                            dev_name);
                    exit(EXIT_FAILURE);
            } else {
                    errno_exit("VIDIOC_QUERYCAP");
            }
    }
```

```
if (!(cap.capabilities & V4L2_CAP_VIDEO_CAPTURE)) {
        fprintf(stderr, "%s is no video capture device\n",
                dev_name);
        exit(EXIT_FAILURE);
}

switch (io) {
case IO_METHOD_READ:
        if (!(cap.capabilities & V4L2_CAP_READWRITE)) {
                fprintf(stderr, "%s does not support read i/o\n",
                        dev_name);
                exit(EXIT_FAILURE);
        }
        break;

case IO_METHOD_MMAP:
case IO_METHOD_USERPTR:
        if (!(cap.capabilities & V4L2_CAP_STREAMING)) {
                fprintf(stderr, "%s does not support
                streaming i/o\n",
                        dev_name);
                exit(EXIT_FAILURE);
        }
        break;
}


/* Select video input, video standard and tune here. */


CLEAR(cropcap);

cropcap.type = V4L2_BUF_TYPE_VIDEO_CAPTURE;

if (0 == xioctl(fd, VIDIOC_CROPCAP, &cropcap)) {
        crop.type = V4L2_BUF_TYPE_VIDEO_CAPTURE;
        crop.c = cropcap.defrect; /* reset to default */

        if (-1 == xioctl(fd, VIDIOC_S_CROP, &crop)) {
                switch (errno) {
                case EINVAL:
                        /* Cropping not supported. */
                        break;
                default:
                        /* Errors ignored. */
                        break;
                }
        }
```

```
        } else {
                /* Errors ignored. */
        }

        CLEAR(fmt);

        fmt.type = V4L2_BUF_TYPE_VIDEO_CAPTURE;
        if (force_format) {
                fmt.fmt.pix.width        = 1280;
                fmt.fmt.pix.height       = 720;
                fmt.fmt.pix.pixelformat  = V4L2_PIX_FMT_MJPEG;
                fmt.fmt.pix.field        = V4L2_FIELD_NONE;

                if (-1 == xioctl(fd, VIDIOC_S_FMT, &fmt))
                        errno_exit("VIDIOC_S_FMT");

                /* Note VIDIOC_S_FMT may change width and height. */
        } else {
                /* Preserve original settings as set by v4l2-ctl
                   for example */
                if (-1 == xioctl(fd, VIDIOC_G_FMT, &fmt))
                        errno_exit("VIDIOC_G_FMT");
        }

        /* Buggy driver paranoia. */
        min = fmt.fmt.pix.width * 2;
        if (fmt.fmt.pix.bytesperline < min)
                fmt.fmt.pix.bytesperline = min;
        min = fmt.fmt.pix.bytesperline * fmt.fmt.pix.height;
        if (fmt.fmt.pix.sizeimage < min)
                fmt.fmt.pix.sizeimage = min;

        switch (io) {
        case IO_METHOD_READ:
                init_read(fmt.fmt.pix.sizeimage);
                break;

        case IO_METHOD_MMAP:
                init_mmap();
                break;

        case IO_METHOD_USERPTR:
                init_userp(fmt.fmt.pix.sizeimage);
                break;
        }
}
```

```
static void close_device(void)
{
        if (-1 == close(fd))
                errno_exit("close");

        fd = -1;
}

static void open_device(void)
{
        struct stat st;

        if (-1 == stat(dev_name, &st)) {
                fprintf(stderr, "Cannot identify '%s': %d, %s\n",
                        dev_name, errno, strerror(errno));
                exit(EXIT_FAILURE);
        }

        if (!S_ISCHR(st.st_mode)) {
                fprintf(stderr, "%s is no device\n", dev_name);
                exit(EXIT_FAILURE);
        }

        fd = open(dev_name, O_RDWR /* required */ | O_NONBLOCK, 0);

        if (-1 == fd) {
                fprintf(stderr, "Cannot open '%s': %d, %s\n",
                        dev_name, errno, strerror(errno));
                exit(EXIT_FAILURE);
        }
}

static void usage(FILE *fp, int argc, char **argv)
{
        fprintf(fp,
                "Usage: %s [options]\n\n"
                "Version 1.3\n"
                "Options:\n"
                "-d | --device name  Video device name [%s]\n"
                "-h | --help         Print this message\n"
                "-m | --mmap         Use memory mapped buffers [default]\n"
                "-r | --read         Use read() calls\n"
                "-u | --userp        Use application allocated buffers\n"
                "-o | --output       Outputs stream to stdout\n"
                "-f | --format       Force format to 640x480 YUYV\n"
                "-c | --count        Number of frames to grab [%i]\n"
                "",
                argv[0], dev_name, frame_count);
}
```

```c
static const char short_options[] = "d:hmruofc:";

static const struct option
long_options[] = {
        { "device", required_argument, NULL, 'd' },
        { "help",   no_argument,       NULL, 'h' },
        { "mmap",   no_argument,       NULL, 'm' },
        { "read",   no_argument,       NULL, 'r' },
        { "userp",  no_argument,       NULL, 'u' },
        { "output", no_argument,       NULL, 'o' },
        { "format", no_argument,       NULL, 'f' },
        { "count",  required_argument, NULL, 'c' },
        { 0, 0, 0, 0 }
};

int main(int argc, char **argv)
{
        dev_name = "/dev/video0";

        for (;;) {
                int idx;
                int c;

                c = getopt_long(argc, argv,
                                short_options, long_options, &idx);

                if (-1 == c)
                        break;

                switch (c) {
                case 0: /* getopt_long() flag */
                        break;

                case 'd':
                        dev_name = optarg;
                        break;

                case 'h':
                        usage(stdout, argc, argv);
                        exit(EXIT_SUCCESS);

                case 'm':
                        io = IO_METHOD_MMAP;
                        break;

                case 'r':
                        io = IO_METHOD_READ;
```

```
                        break;

            case 'u':
                    io = IO_METHOD_USERPTR;
                    break;

            case 'o':
                    out_buf++;
                    break;

            case 'f':
                    force_format++;
                    break;

            case 'c':
                    errno = 0;
                    frame_count = strtol(optarg, NULL, 0);
                    if (errno)
                            errno_exit(optarg);
                    break;

            default:
                    usage(stderr, argc, argv);
                    exit(EXIT_FAILURE);
            }
    }

    open_device();
    init_device();
    start_capturing();
    mainloop();
    stop_capturing();
    uninit_device();
    close_device();
    fprintf(stderr, "\n");
    return 0;
}
```

APPENDIX D

■■■

Picture Grabber

Listing D-1 provides the complete code discussed in the "A Program to Capture Images" section in Chapter 7. The parts required by webcam C270 are highlighted in bold.

Listing D-1. picture_grabber.c

```
/* V4L2 video picture grabber
   Copyright (C) 2009 Mauro Carvalho Chehab <mchehab@infradead.org>

   This program is free software; you can redistribute it and/or modify
   it under the terms of the GNU General Public License as published by
   the Free Software Foundation version 2 of the License.

   This program is distributed in the hope that it will be useful,
   but WITHOUT ANY WARRANTY; without even the implied warranty of
   MERCHANTABILITY or FITNESS FOR A PARTICULAR PURPOSE.  See the
   GNU General Public License for more details.

   Changed by Manoel Ramon:
    - added command line support see usage() function for details.
    - added YUYV or RGB pixel format support
    - added convertion function from yuyv_to_rgb24() function extracted
      from OpenCV, copied without any changes under Intel licenses from the
      file cvcap_v4l.cpp.
    For reference the whole file can be visualized on this link:
    https://code.ros.org/trac/opencv/browser/trunk/opencv/src/highgui/
    cvcap_v4l.cpp

 */


#include <stdio.h>
#include <stdlib.h>
#include <string.h>
#include <fcntl.h>
#include <errno.h>
#include <sys/ioctl.h>
```

```
#include <sys/types.h>
#include <sys/time.h>
#include <sys/mman.h>
#include <linux/videodev2.h>
#include <libv4l2.h>
#include <getopt.h>               /* getopt_long() */
#include <errno.h>
#include <unistd.h>

int images_count;

static const char short_options[] = "W:H:yc:d:h";

static const struct option
long_options[] = {
        { "width",  required_argument, NULL, 'W' },
        { "height", required_argument, NULL, 'H' },
        { "yuyv",   no_argument      , NULL, 'y' },
        { "count",  required_argument, NULL, 'c' },
        { "device", required_argument, NULL, 'd' },
        { "help",   no_argument,       NULL, 'h' },
        { 0, 0, 0, 0 }
};

#define CLEAR(x) memset(&(x), 0, sizeof(x))

static char *dev_name;

/* convert from 4:2:2 YUYV interlaced to RGB24 */
/* based on ccvt_yuyv_bgr32() from camstream */
#define SAT(c) \
   if (c & (~255)) { if (c < 0) c = 0; else c = 255; }

static void
yuyv_to_rgb24 (int width, int height, unsigned char *src, unsigned char *dst)
{
    unsigned char *s;
    unsigned char *d;
    int l, c;
    int r, g, b, cr, cg, cb, y1, y2;

    l = height;
    s = src;
    d = dst;
```

```
        while (l--) {
          c = width >> 1;
          while (c--) {
              y1 = *s++;
              cb = ((*s - 128) * 454) >> 8;
              cg = (*s++ - 128) * 88;
              y2 = *s++;
              cr = ((*s - 128) * 359) >> 8;
              cg = (cg + (*s++ - 128) * 183) >> 8;

              r = y1 + cr;
              b = y1 + cb;
              g = y1 - cg;
              SAT(r);
              SAT(g);
              SAT(b);

            *d++ = b;
            *d++ = g;
            *d++ = r;

              r = y2 + cr;
              b = y2 + cb;
              g = y2 - cg;
              SAT(r);
              SAT(g);
              SAT(b);

            *d++ = b;
            *d++ = g;
            *d++ = r;
          }
        }
}

struct buffer {
        void    *start;
        size_t length;
};

static void xioctl(int fh, int request, void *arg)
{
        int r;

        do {
                r = v4l2_ioctl(fh, request, arg);
        } while (r == -1 && ((errno == EINTR) || (errno == EAGAIN)));
```

```
        if (r == -1) {
                fprintf(stderr, "error %d, %s\n", errno, strerror(errno));
                exit(EXIT_FAILURE);
        }
}

static void usage(FILE *fp, int argc, char **argv)
{
        fprintf(fp,
                "Usage: %s [options]\n\n"
                "Version adapted to Intel Galileo\n"
                "Options:\n"
                "-d | --device name   Video device name\n"
                "-W | --width         Sets image width\n"
                "-H | --height        Sets image height\n"
                "-y | --yuyv          Sets YUYV encode, if not used the
                                      encode if RGB24\n"
                "-c | --count         Sets number of images to be
                                      captured\n"
                "-h | --help          Prints this help\n"
              "", argv[0]);
}

static void errno_exit(const char *s)
{
        fprintf(stderr, "%s error %d, %s\n", s, errno, strerror(errno));
        exit(EXIT_FAILURE);
}

int main(int argc, char **argv)
{
        struct v4l2_format          fmt;
        struct v4l2_buffer          buf;
        struct v4l2_requestbuffers  req;
        enum v4l2_buf_type          type;
        fd_set                      fds;
        struct timeval              tv;
        int                         r, fd = -1;
        unsigned int                i, n_buffers;
        char                        out_name[256];
        FILE                        *fout;
        struct buffer               *buffers;
        unsigned char               isYUYV = 0;
        int                         width = 1280;
        int                         height = 720;

        dev_name = "/dev/video0";
        images_count = 10;
```

```
for (;;) {
        int idx;
        int c;

        c = getopt_long(argc, argv,
                        short_options, long_options, &idx);

        if (-1 == c)
                break;

        switch (c) {
        case 0: /* getopt_long() flag */
                break;

        case 'W':
                errno = 0;
                width = strtol(optarg, NULL, 0);
                if (errno)
                        errno_exit(optarg);
                break;

        case 'H':
                errno = 0;
                height = strtol(optarg, NULL, 0);
                if (errno)
                        errno_exit(optarg);
                break;

        case 'y':
                isYUYV = 1;
                break;

        case 'c':
                errno = 0;
                images_count = strtol(optarg, NULL, 0);
                if (errno)
                        errno_exit(optarg);
                break;

        case 'd':
                dev_name = optarg;
                break;

        case 'h':
                usage(stdout, argc, argv);
                exit(EXIT_SUCCESS);
```

```
                default:
                        usage(stderr, argc, argv);
                        exit(EXIT_FAILURE);
                }
        }


        fd = v4l2_open(dev_name, O_RDWR | O_NONBLOCK, 0);
        if (fd < 0) {
                perror("Cannot open device");
                exit(EXIT_FAILURE);
        }

        CLEAR(fmt);
        fmt.type = V4L2_BUF_TYPE_VIDEO_CAPTURE;
        fmt.fmt.pix.width       = width;
        fmt.fmt.pix.height      = height;

        if (!isYUYV)
          {
            printf("Encode RGB24\n");
            fmt.fmt.pix.pixelformat = V4L2_PIX_FMT_RGB24;
          }
        else
          {
            printf("Encode YUYV\n");
            fmt.fmt.pix.pixelformat = V4L2_PIX_FMT_YUYV;
          }
        fmt.fmt.pix.field       = V4L2_FIELD_INTERLACED;
        xioctl(fd, VIDIOC_S_FMT, &fmt);
        if (fmt.fmt.pix.pixelformat != V4L2_PIX_FMT_RGB24 &&
            fmt.fmt.pix.pixelformat != V4L2_PIX_FMT_YUYV) {
                printf("Libv4l didn't accept RGB24 or YUYV format. Can't
                proceed.\n");
                exit(EXIT_FAILURE);
        }
        if ((fmt.fmt.pix.width != width) || (fmt.fmt.pix.height != height))
                printf("Warning: driver is sending image at %dx%d\n",
                        fmt.fmt.pix.width, fmt.fmt.pix.height);

        CLEAR(req);
        req.count = 5;
        req.type = V4L2_BUF_TYPE_VIDEO_CAPTURE;
        req.memory = V4L2_MEMORY_MMAP;
        xioctl(fd, VIDIOC_REQBUFS, &req);
```

```
buffers = calloc(req.count, sizeof(*buffers));
if (!buffers) {
        fprintf(stderr, "Out of memory\n");
        exit(EXIT_FAILURE);
}

for (n_buffers = 0; n_buffers < req.count; ++n_buffers) {
        CLEAR(buf);

        buf.type        = V4L2_BUF_TYPE_VIDEO_CAPTURE;
        buf.memory      = V4L2_MEMORY_MMAP;
        buf.index       = n_buffers;

        xioctl(fd, VIDIOC_QUERYBUF, &buf);

        buffers[n_buffers].length = buf.length;
        buffers[n_buffers].start = v4l2_mmap(NULL, buf.length,
                        PROT_READ | PROT_WRITE, MAP_SHARED,
                        fd, buf.m.offset);

        if (MAP_FAILED == buffers[n_buffers].start) {
                perror("mmap");
                exit(EXIT_FAILURE);
        }
}

for (i = 0; i < n_buffers; ++i) {
        CLEAR(buf);
        buf.type = V4L2_BUF_TYPE_VIDEO_CAPTURE;
        buf.memory = V4L2_MEMORY_MMAP;
        buf.index = i;
        xioctl(fd, VIDIOC_QBUF, &buf);
}
type = V4L2_BUF_TYPE_VIDEO_CAPTURE;

xioctl(fd, VIDIOC_STREAMON, &type);

for (i = 0; i < images_count; i++) {
        do {
                FD_ZERO(&fds);
                FD_SET(fd, &fds);

                // Timeout.
                tv.tv_sec = 2;
                tv.tv_usec = 0;
```

```
                r = select(fd + 1, &fds, NULL, NULL, &tv);
        } while ((r == -1 && (errno = EINTR)));
        if (r == -1) {
                perror("select");
                return errno;
        }

        CLEAR(buf);
        buf.type = V4L2_BUF_TYPE_VIDEO_CAPTURE;
        buf.memory = V4L2_MEMORY_MMAP;
        xioctl(fd, VIDIOC_DQBUF, &buf);

        sprintf(out_name, "out%03d.ppm", i);
        printf("Creating image: %s\n", out_name);
        fout = fopen(out_name, "w");
        if (!fout) {
                perror("Cannot open image");
                exit(EXIT_FAILURE);
        }
        fprintf(fout, "P6\n%d %d 255\n", fmt.fmt.pix.width, fmt.fmt.
        pix.height);

        if (isYUYV)
        {
            // each pixel 3 bytes in RGB 24
            int size = fmt.fmt.pix.width * fmt.fmt.pix.height *
            sizeof(char) * 3;
            unsigned char * data = (unsigned char *) malloc(size);

            yuyv_to_rgb24(fmt.fmt.pix.width,
                          fmt.fmt.pix.height,
                          (unsigned char*)(buffers[buf.index].start),
                          data);

            fwrite(data, size, 1, fout);

            free (data);
        }
        else
        {
            fwrite(buffers[buf.index].start, buf.bytesused, 1, fout);
        }
        fclose(fout);

        xioctl(fd, VIDIOC_QBUF, &buf);
    }
```

```
        type = V4L2_BUF_TYPE_VIDEO_CAPTURE;
        xioctl(fd, VIDIOC_STREAMOFF, &type);
        for (i = 0; i < n_buffers; ++i)
                v4l2_munmap(buffers[i].start, buffers[i].length);
        v4l2_close(fd);

        return 0;
}
```

Index

A

Access Point Name (APN)
  AT+CGDATA command, 596
  AT+CGDCONT? command, 595
  AT+COPS command, 596
  AT&T 4G data connection, 594
  CGDCONT AT command, 595
  configuration, 593
Analogic keypad, 495
Analog I/O
  analogWrite–PWM, 114
  int analogRead, 114
analogRead() function, 419
API
  Arduino reference (*see* Tone API)
  DHT sensor library
    bits[] array, 211
    bytes value, 197
    code implementation, 202
    data readings, 204
    debugging, 213
    definition, 195
    DHT_4_Galileo class, 212
    DHT11 and DHT.cpp file, 202
    fastGpioDigitalRead()
      method, 210
    fastGpioDigitalWrite()
      method, 210
    Intel Galileo's digital
      I/O headers, 197
    materials list, 195
    p_gate, 204
    pinMode() function, 197–198, 210
    p_read, 204
    "read" the sensor's values, 197
    read() method, 204

    sendCommand()
      method, 204, 210
    single-wire two-way, 195
    temperature and humidity, 196
    tri-state buffers
      (*see* Tri-state buffers)
  I/O speed
    digitalRead() function, 162, 164
    digitalWrite() function, 162, 164
    distribution, 165
    fastGpioDigitalRead()
      method, 173–175
    fastGpioDigitalRegSnapshot()
      method, 177, 179–180
    fastGpioDigitalRegWriteUnsafe
      method, 172, 177, 179–182
    fastGpioDigitalWrite()
      method, 171–172, 180
    fast I/O macros, 169
    INPUT_FAST, 166
    limitations, 163
    memory-mapped interface, 164
    north- and south-cluster pins, 182
    OUTPUT_FAST, 166
    pinMode() function, 162
    pinMode() method, 184
    port-mapped interface, 164
    setup() function, 162
  pulseIn API
    code implementation, 188
    digital I/O header, 189
    IDE serial console, 190
    implementation, 189
    limitations, 189
    material, 189
    pinMode(), 190
    PWM, 188

API (*cont.*)
   serial ports
      code implementation, 158
      limitation, 157
      materials list, 158
      println() method, 160–161
      schematic diagram, 158
      testing, 157
   servo motors (*see* Servo motors)
Arduino integrated development
      environment (Arduino IDE)
   board connection, 96
   board selection, 103
   button
      code, 120
      materials list, 119
      schematics, 119
      sketch, 122
   debounce
      code, 125
      materials list, 125
      schematics, 125
      sketch, 127
   driver installation
      Linux, 100
      MacOS, 101
      Windows, 99
   drivers troubleshooting, 130
      oracle virtual box, 136
      serial communication issues, 130
      64-bit Linux,
         warning messages, 135
      VMware problems, 135
   fade
      code, 118
      materials list, 117
      schematics, 117
      sketch, 118
   firmware update process, 127
   Getting Start Guide, 94
   graphical interface, 102
   history, 93
   installation process
      Linux 32/64 bits, 95
      Linux machines, 98
      MacOS, 99
      MacOSX, 95
      Windows, 95, 97
   language reference and APIs
      analog I/O (*see* Analog I/O)
      digital I/O (*see* Digital I/O)

      loop() function, 113
      setup() function, 113
      time duration, 115
   makers community, 94
   port selection, 104
   ReadAnalogVoltage
      code, 123
      materials list, 122
      schematics, 122
      sketch, 124
   serial console, debugging
      (*see* Serial communication)
   7-zip tools, 96
   Sketch (*see* Sketch)
   sudo apt-get install
      p7zip-full command, 96
Arduino reference page, 112
AT+CGDCONT command, 596
attach() method, 152
available() method, 160–161

B

Booting from SD card images
   card reader, 60
   copying files, 63
   Mac OSX, 61
   Ubuntu, 62
   USB adaptor, 60
   Windows, 61
Booting from SPI card images, 64

C

checkButtonState() function, 414, 419
Consumer key, 311
Consumer secret, 311
Cypress CY8C9540A datasheet, 150, 191

D

DC/DC converter, 500
DediProg SF100, 86
delay() function, 106
Digital I/O
   digitalWrite, 113
   int digitalRead, 113
   pinMode, 113
digitalRead() function, 119
digitalWrite() function, 106, 119, 419
drawMatrix() function, 414

■ E

Edge detection
   apertureSize argument, 363
   Canny function, 362
   cvtColor() function, 362
   opencv_capimage_
      canny.cpp, 361–363
emailCounter.py script, 138
Emotions classification
   database creation, 373
      CSV File, 380–382
      directory, 379–380
      image cropping, 374
      pixel coordinates, 374
   faceDetect() method, 391
   FaceRecognizer code, 383
   fisherface model, 383
   happy face detection, 398
   image cropping, 393–395, 397
   image extraction, 398
   main() function, 391
   opencv_emotion_
      classification.cpp, 383–388
   original code, 372
   prediction method, 392
   public algorithm, 392
   surprised face detection, 399
   testSample image, 392
   uvcvideo driver, 397
   void FaceRecognizer method, 392

■ F

Face and eyes detection
   CascadeClassifier() object, 364, 367
   code's sequence, 370–371
   components, 367
   detectMultiScale() method, 368–370
   haarcascade_eye.xml code, 364
   haarcascade_frontalface_
      alt.xml code, 364
   opencv_face_and_eyes_detection.
      cpp, 365–367, 372
   Point center object, 370
   rectangle() and circle() functions, 364
fastGpioDigitalRegSnapshot()
   method, 177
fastGpioDigitalRegWriteUnsafe()
   method, 177, 179

Flashing, capsule files
   with Firmware Update Tool, 81
   with Linux Terminal Shell, 78
   with the Intel Arduino IDE, 77
   with UEFI Shell, 79
Flower face test, 410, 415

■ G

GET and POST methods, 478
Graphics Processing Units (GPUs), 324
Ground coffee gripper
   air pump, 572
   assembling, 573
   control, 572
   materials, 571
   RoboticArm.ino, 575
   RoboticArmWith
      CoffeeGripper.ino, 576
   working principle, 570

■ H

Hacks
   library, 190
   PWM
      beginTransmission() method, 192
      clock source, 191
      custom_pwm.ino, 193
      duty cycle, 191
      endTransmisstion() method, 192
      frequency, 191
      implementation, 194
      minimum granularity, 192
      PLATFORM_NAME directive, 194
      register period, 191
      write() method, 192
Home automation system
   adding username
      and password, 497
   analogic keypad, 495
   cheerio REPL, 490
   DHT11 sensor, 497
   Ethernet cable, 425
   home.html page, 491
   LTE modem, 425
   materials list, 428
   PIR sensor
      connection, 440
      headers, 439

Home automation system (*cont.*)
    9V battery, 441
    software writing and testing, 442
PoE, 489
running, 486
SD card image, 425
sketch creation
    join all test code, 455
    network connections, 451
    receiving UDP messages, 452
    sending UDP messages, 451
software and hardware components
    code review, 435
    keypad code run, 437
    keypad connection, 430
    keypad functionality, 429
    keypad software, 431
    keypad testing, 428
software architecture
    communication, 427
    send commands, 427
    UDP server listening, 427
    web server, 426
TMP36 temperature sensor
    connection with Intel Galile, 448
    software writing and tresting, 450
    voltage output, 448
web server, 426
web server creation
    (*see* Web server creation)
WiFi module, 425
YwRobot relay module
    connection with
      External Lamps, 446
    connection with Intel Galileo, 445
    Intel Arduino digital ports, 443
    LED and headers, 444
    PNP 8550 transistor, 444
    software writing and testing, 446
    two-channel relay module, 443

■ I, J, K

IEEE 802.3af.standard, 499
Intel Galileo boards
    Arduino headers
      analog ports, 12
      analogReference() function, 12
      I2C/two-wire interface, 12
      input/output pins, 12
      power, 12–13
      source and sink currents, 13
    average costs, 5
    cables
      serial debugging, 24–26
      testing, 33
      types, 23–24
    components, 4, 9, 11
    DipTrace tool, 3
    Fritizing tool, 3
    guitar model, 1–2
    I2C address jumper, 15
    Intel Galileo Gen 2
      block diagram, 22
      components, 18
      Cypress GPIO expander, 18
      elements, 23
      FTDI terminals, 19
      GPIO mapping, 23
      issues, 22–23
      JTAG connector, 20–21
      jumpers and buttons, 21
      MAX 3232, 19
      power over ethernet, 19
      serial cables, 26–28
      user guide, 17
    Intel Quark SoC X1000
      code-named Clanton, 6
      core processor, 7
      Pentium opcode, 6
      peripheral support, 7
      security, 8
      software support, 8
      specifications, 7
    inventors, 1
    IOREF jumper, 14
    limitations, 8
    Maker Fair Rome, 2
    mini-PCIe connector, 11
    reboot button, 15
    requirements, 3
    reset button, 15
    schematics
      block diagram, 15
      Intel Quark support, 16
      multiplexers, 16
      serial debugging, 16
      voltage-level translator, 17
    sketches, 4
    VIN jumper, 14

Windows
    busybox software, 32
    COM port, 29
    configuration, 30
    hexadecimal sequence, 32
    Mac OSX, 31
    Ubuntu terminal, 30–31
    Yocto build system, 2
Intel Galileo images
    booting (*see* Booting from
        SD card images; Booting
        from SPI card images)
    capsule files
        compiling steps, 66
        compiling UEFI firmware, 65
        flashing
          (*see* Flashing, capsule files)
        preparing environment, 65
        preparing layout.conf, 70
        troubleshooting, 69
        using SPI tool, 77
    cross-compiler toolchain
        architectures, 52
        Hello World program, 57
        installation, 56
        Linux, 54
        OSX, 54
        output files, 56
        Windows, 55
    debugging, 59
    metafiles preparation, 47
    preparing computer, 44
    SPI Images Flash files
        (*see* SPI Images Flash files)
    SPI *vs.* SD card images, 46
    testing, 90

■ L

LAN IN port, 505
Leonardo da Vinci's robot, 509
linux-cdc-acm.inf, 100
Logitech webcam C270, 321
loop() function, 105, 142, 155
LTE modem
    antennas, 582
    hardware settings
        adapting modem card, 586
        antennas connection, 587
        Intel Galileo connection, 588

        NGFF/mPCIe adaptor, 585
        SIM card preparation, 583
    internet bandwidth, 600
    materials list, 581
    project details, 581
    project settings
        CDC-ACM DRIVER loading, 603
        Chat Script, 601
    software settings
        APN (*see* Access Point
          Name (APN))
        CDC-ACM driver, 590
        commands and responses, 591
        internet connection, 600
        IP Interface (*see* Point to Point
          Protocol Daemon (PPPD))
        modem checking, 589
        options-att configuration, 597–598
        SIM card connection, 592
    XMM 7160 and XMM 7260 modems,
        580

■ M

Memory mapped buffers
    (mmap) function, 333
Modem manager, 98
Motion JPEG encode, 330
myservo2.attach(3, true) method, 155

■ N

Networking and hacks
    Ethernet API
        DHCP connection, 247, 254
        Ethernet.begin() method, 253
        Ethernet class, 248
        EthernetClient, 247
        Ethernet objects removing, 271
        EthernetUDP, 247
        IPAddress and Server, 247
        mac[] array, 248
        NTP, 248
        Quark SoC, 247
        static IPs (*see* Static IPs)
        WiFiUdpNtpClient.ino review, 252
    sketch transfer
        clloader application, 277
        clupload_linux_
          and_osx_hacked.sh, 284

Networking and hacks (*cont.*)
    clupload_linux.sh, 281
    clupload_osx.sh, 281
    clupload_win_hacked.sh, 284
    clupload_win.sh, 281
    code/hacked_platforms_files, 282
    configuration, 278
    file transfer mechanism, 277
    hacked IDE running, 285
    platform file, 282
    platform.linux64.txt, 281
    platform.win.txt file, 280
    SCP protocol, 279
    script reviewing, 285
    TCP/IP, 277
    tools.izmirdl.cmd.path field, 281
    tools.izmirdl.upload.
      pattern field, 281
    ZMODEM protocol, 276
  transfer files
    ftp deamon, 272
    pscp.exe, 273
    scp tool, 273
    SD card, 273
    USB pen drive, 274
  WiFi API
    ConnectWithWEP.ino, 233
    ConnectWithWPA.ino, 230
    firmware version, 228
    IDE serial console, 236
    Linux terminal shell, 237
    listNetworks() function, 228
    network's key and key index, 236
    printEncryptionType(), 229
    printMacAddress(), 228
    ScanNetworks.ino, 225
    WiFi router, 237
    WiFi.begin(), 238
    WiFi.encryptionType(), 229
    WiFi.SSID(), WiFi.RSSI(), 229
    WL_NO_SHIELD, 228
  WiFi cards
    antennas connection, 220
    bracket connection, 219
    BSP SD card image, 221
    iwlwifi driver, 218
    Linux terminal shell, 222
    materials, 218
    micro SD card, 221
    mini-PCIe form factor, 218
    SD image, 218
    SD image upgradation, 223
    WiFi card and
      bracket connection, 220
  WiFi library
    begin() methods, 243, 245
    connection restart, 242
    getLocalIP(), 245, 247
    int WiFiClass, 245–246
    iwconfig command tool, 245
    WEP connection, 241
    wlan0, 239
    WPA connection, 240
    wpa_passphrase command, 245
Network Time Protocol (NTP), 248
Node package manager (npm), 467

■ O

OAuth secret, 311
OAuth token, 311
Open source Computer Vision (OpenCV)
  BSP image and toolchain
    build process, 325
    GPUs, 324
    rootfs size increment, 324
    Video4 Linux, eGlibc, 324
    Yocto project, 323
  command line, 353
  computer vision, definition, 319
  C++ *vs.* Python performance, 352
  development library package, 325
  device communication, 319
  fisherface model, 400
  image capture
    buffer allocation, 350
    file transfer, 351
    flowchart, 353–354
    fprintf() function, 349
    magic identifier, 349
    mmap() function, 333
    opencv_capimage.cpp, 355, 358
    pixel format selection, 348
    PPM file extension, 349
    read/write application, 333
    RGB24 and BGR24, 348
    RGB24 format,
      352x288 resolution, 351
    software, requirements, 347–348
    storage, JPEG file, 355

userspace pointers, 333
V4L2, 353
YUYV to RGB24 conversion, 350
yuyv_to_rgb24() function, 350
y/-yuyv argument, 352
image processing
    edge detection
        (see Edge detection)
    emotions
        (see Emotions classification)
    face and eye
        (see Face and eyes detection)
Intel Galileo, 320
libraries, 320
materials list, 321
Python
    opencv_capimage.py, 359
    performance analysis, 360
robotic head, 400
USB video class (UVC), 322
V4L2, 320
video capture
    buffer allocation, 337–338
    buffer dequeue, 339–340
    buffer enqueues, 338
    -c argument, 343
    device closed, 341
    device initiation, 335
    -f argument, 343
    ffmpeg installation, video
        conversion, 344
    force_format variable,
        resolution, 336
    free() function, 341
    image cropping, 336
    IOCTL calls, 333
    isOpened() method, 356
    Mat class, 357
    Mat object, 357
    mmap() function, 333
    MP4 file, 346
    munmap() function, 341
    -o argument, 343
    open the device, 335
    params argument, 358
    properties, 356
    querying process, 338
    read/write application, 333
    release() method, 357
    sequence flowchart, 334

simple argument, 343
streaming process, 339, 341
userspace pointers, 333
VideoCapture class, 356
VIDIOC_G_FMT, 336
webcam capabilities, v4l2-ctl
    camera properties, 329
    Logitech C270, 327–328
    pixel format and resolution, 330
    set/change properties, 327
webcam connection, 326

■ P, Q

pinMode() function, 116, 119, 166
PoE injector TP-LINK TL-POE150S, 504
PoE system, 506
Point to Point Protocol Daemon (PPPD)
    isp_chat script, 598
    mknod command, 599–600
    nodetach, 600
    options-att configuration, 596–597
    SPI and BSP images, 596
POWER+DATA OUT port, 505
Power of Ethernet (PoE), 489
Power over Ethernet (PoE)
    advantages, 499
    assembling, 500
    connection, 505
    goal, 499
    LAN IN port, 505
    materials, 500
    POWER+DATA OUT port, 505
    soldering, 506
    TP-LINK TL-POE150S injector, 504
pulseIn() method, 188
PythonP Code, 138

■ R

read() method, 160–161
Real time clock (RTC), 3
Robotic arm
    actuators, 514
    assembling
        connecting U-shaped base, 522
        elbow, 528
        gripper, 535
        preparing servos, 521
        screws, 520

Robotic arm (*cont.*)
  shoulder, 526
  wooden base, 535
  wrist, 532
  controlling (*see* Servo control board)
  degrees of freedom, 510
  materials, 519
  online torque calculator, 515
  parts and components, 516
  perpendicular length, 512–513
  stall torque units, 511–512

■ S

sendCommand() and
    read() methods, 204
Serial communication
  print messages, 109
  Serial.available() function, 109
  Serial.begin(int speed), 108
  serial monitor console, 110
  Serial.print(data) argument, 108
  Serial.read(), 109
  setup() function, 111
Servo control board
  assembling, 544
  circuit Protection, 543
  external Power Supply, 543
  hardware, 538
  power supply, 537
  quantity of wires, 538
  servos control, 537
  software, 547
  Thumbstick API
    challenges, 547
    header file, 548
    installation, 561
    modes, 548
    review, 558
    RoboticArm.ino, 561
  thumbsticks, 542
Servo motors
  code implementation, 148
  CY8C9540A, 150
  loop() function, 155
  materials list, 147
  MIN_PULSE_WIDTH and MAX_
      PULSE_WIDTH methods, 150
  myservo2.attach(3, true) method, 155
  schematic diagram, 147, 153

setup() function, 155
specifications, 155
testing, 154
theory, 145
uint8_t Servo::attach(int pin,
    int min, int max, bool
    force48hz = false), 152
uint8_t Servo::attach(int16_t pin,
    bool force48hz = false), 152
void Servo::set48hz(), 152
void Servo::set188hz(), 152
write() method, 149
writeMicroseconds() method, 150
setup() function, 105, 142
Sketch
  blink, 105
  code reviewing, 142
  code running, 141
  done compiling, 106
  "Done uploading" message, 106
  hardware components, 106
  LED connection, 107
  loop() function, 105
  persisted and not persisted, 107
  POSIX functions
    materials list, 137
    schematics, 138
  Serial.println(data) method, 108
  serialtest.ino, 109
  setup() function, 105
  "Transfer complete" message, 106
  verify concept, 106
  WiFi/Ethernet, 141
soil_moisture.ino., 416
Soil moisture sensor
  appropriate wires, 423
  automatic irrigation, 421
  calibration procedure
    boundary values, 417
    connections, 417
    flower face, 419
  commercial sensor, 423
  electrical assembly, 404
  electrodes, 401
  flower face connection, 406
  flower face test, 410, 415
  happy face, 402
  increasing sensors, 421
  materials, 402
  mechanical assembly, 403

review code
  checkButtonState() function, 414
  drawMatrix() function, 414
  loop() function, 414
  setup() function, 413
  tweeting, 424
SPI Images flash files
  binary file, 85
  Ethernet MAC address, 82
  flashing, 86
  sample-platform-data.ini, 83
Static IPs
  configuration, 268
  MacOSX 10.0
    DNS servers, 266
    Ethernet cable
      connection, 266–267
    internet connection
      sharing, 267–268
    IP configuration, 264–265
    Thunderbolt to gigabit
      Ethernet adapter, 264
  Ubuntu 12.04
    IPv4 properties, 262
    IPv4 settings, 261
    network connections, 260
    wired connection, 260
  Windows 7
    internet connection sharing, 258
    ipconfig command, 257
    IPv4 properties, 256–257
    local area connection
      properties, 255–256
    new IP, 260
    Wireless Lan Adapter, 258
  wireless adapter, 255
sudo apt-get install
    p7zip-full command, 96

■ T

Thumbstick API
  challenges, 547
  RoboticArm.ino
    review, 566
    running, 568
    sketch for Intel Galileo boards, 561
Tone API
  implementation, 184
  melody_pin0 and
    melody_pin1 arrays, 188

non-blocking calls
  code implementation, 187
  materials list, 185
  schematic diagram, 186
OUTPUT_FAST and INPUT_FAST, 184
void noTone, 185
void tone, 185
Tri-state buffers
  diode, 215
  logic states, 200
  low-enabled gate operation, 201
  NTE74HC125, 199
  74HC125 and pin-out disposition, 200
Twitter application
  access level, 300
  BATT terminal, 292
  coin battery, 293
  create my access token, 299
  create token and consumer keys, 301
  creating account, 294
  Linux shell script, 289
  POST methods
    bash code, 310
    cat command, 310
    curl command, 308
    debug messages, 315
    identify API, 301
    input data session, 304
    message header, 312
    mPCIe module, 310
    OAuth signing results, 305
    OAuth string codes, 314
    OAuth tool, 303, 311
    popen() function, 315
    post() function, 315
    request settings, 304
    should_post_today(), 315
    signature_key, 311
    soil_moisture_
      with_twitter.ino, 316
    system() function, 315
    terminal shell, 305
    tweet text messages, 311
    twitter.sh, 308
    twitter_sketch.ino, 312
  sha1 algorithm, 289
  signing application, 297
  system and hardware clock, 290
  temporary and
    dirty workaround, 293–294
  WiFi list, 290

■ U

USB-OTG adaptor, 582
uvcvideo module driver, 326

■ V

Video4Linux (V4L), 327
Video4Linux 2 (V4L2), 327
Virtual machine (VM), 101

■ W, X

Web page
    home automation, 470
    home.html, 472
    invokes socket, 474
    jQuery library version 2.1.0, 474
    socket connection, 471
    switch relays, 470
    temperature and PIR sensors, 470
    txtsensor, 471
Web server creation
    cheerio installation, 469
    code writing
        final code, 481
        GET and POST methods, 478

mywebserver.js, 474
    ports defining, 475
    running node.js, 475
    sockets creation, 476
node.js updating, 465
npm, 467
socket.io installation, 469
web page
    (*see* Web page)
WiFi mini-PCIe cards, 218
write() method, 148–149

■ Y

Yocto build system
    class file, 43
    code structure, 38
    configuration file, 42
    Poky, 36
        (*see also* Intel Galileo images)
    recipe file, 40
YUYV encode, 330

■ Z

ZMODEM protocol, 277

Printed in the United States
By Bookmasters

Printed in the United States
By Bookmasters